From Inquiry
to Argument

From Inquiry to Argument

Linda McMeniman

Rowan University

Allyn and Bacon

Boston ■ London ■ Toronto ■ Sydney ■ Tokyo ■ Singapore

Vice President: Eben W. Ludlow
Series Editorial Assistant: Linda M. D'Angelo
Executive Marketing Manager: Lisa Kimball
Composition Buyer: Linda Cox
Manufacturing Buyer: Suzanne Lareau
Cover Administrator: Linda Knowles
Production Administrator: Rosalie Briand
Editorial-Production Service: Trinity Publishers Services
Text Designer: Denise Hoffman
Electronic Composition: Omegatype Typography, Inc.

Copyright © 1999 by Allyn & Bacon
A Viacom Company
160 Gould Street
Needham Heights, Massachusetts 02494

Internet: www.abacon.com

Library of Congress Cataloging-in-Publication Data

McMeniman, Linda.
    From inquiry to argument / Linda McMeniman.
       p.   cm.
    Includes bibliographical references and index.
    ISBN 0-205-20041-9 (pbk.)
       1. English language—Rhetoric.   2. Research—Methodology.
  3. Persuasion (Rhetoric).   4. Report writing.   I. Title.
  PE1431.M46   1999
  808'.042—dc21   98-25702
                                       CIP

Printed in the United States of America

10 9 8 7 6 5 4 3 2 1   03 02 01 00 99 98

Credits begin on page 549, which constitutes a continuation of the copyright page.

Brief Contents

Contents

■ *Chapter 5*   Inquiring about Facts and Information   179

■ *Chapter 8*   **Writing to Refute, Inquire, and Moderate Opposing Ideas   301**

■ *Chapter 10*   **Examining Style in Argument   383**

Part III   **The Formal Research Paper   465**

■ *Chapter 12*   **Extended Inquiry and In-Depth Research   467**

Preface

Moving from inquiry to argument seems a logical progression. First you ask questions and discover information and ideas; then you analyze, evaluate, and draw conclusions; and finally you argue. So I like the phrase that became my title, "from inquiry to argument," even if it doesn't quite reflect the full complexity of the process. In fact, teaching writing for twenty years has shown me that the interplay between knowledge and argument, between questions and claims, is not linear. Rather, these elements interact in an ascending spiral in which skills and information, procedural choices, and sparks of ideas all have influence.

As a teacher, I have found that working on arguments before honing what I call inquiry skills doesn't yield good results. Students need to know how to find out about an issue, how to read closely and critically, and how to manipulate ideas and information: paraphrase, summarize, compare, contrast, and synthesize. They need to understand how information and ideas come to be by generating information and constructing ideas themselves. They need to expand outward, to locate and enter the many-stranded conversations about topical issues. I have found that no matter how much my students have been coached about argument's formal elements, if they argue in a vacuum, without the living breath of dialogue about an issue, the results can be hollow. But if the teacher begins with research skills, other awkwardnesses may develop—students may feel they are simply doing busywork or may feel swamped by waves of free-floating information.

Thus, a main goal for this textbook has been to teach argument and inquiry—meaning research and analytic skills—in tandem. I wanted to create a context in which students could confront and investigate issues and ideas using a growing stock of resources: analysis, critical thinking, writing, and research. I wanted to spark a dialogue between argument and inquiry, with the hope that having the skills with which to shape and interweave ideas would inspire research and that practicing research all along the way would improve the rigor and depth of ideas.

Also, the argumentation and research courses I teach are writing courses first and foremost; students must write from the start, without waiting to learn a body of knowledge about the subject. So this book provides a base for writing about ideas early on and ties in writing assignments of many types to each chapter. It contains extensive "how-to" sections, tips and guidelines for particular writing goals.

As a nod to practicing what I preach, I use formal references to my own sources, so that the book reflects the way many strands of thought can blend and, I hope, generate other voices and views. A Works Cited list follows each chapter.

Assignments tie in with each chapter's focus and provide many writing options; some specify informal or journal writing or require addressing a particular audience or performing a specific task, such as writing an op-ed, a synthesis, or a logic or style critique. Some suggest collaborative prewriting, research, or writing; others require a specific type of research, such as doing a survey, reading in reference material, searching on the Internet, or identifying opposing or allied commentaries. In addition to writing assignments, each chapter contains activities that offer practice of the skills or concepts discussed.

Professional readings at the ends of the chapters both model argumentation and contribute to the dialogue of ideas. Students are exposed to op-eds and commentaries, editorials, reflective essays, humorous or ironic arguments, and scholarly articles. Many of the readings have not appeared previously in college anthologies and include pieces by unknowns as well as by such writers as John Leo, George Will, Dr. Louis Sullivan, Ellen Goodman, Cathy Young, Luis Rodriguez, and Christopher Lasch. Articles cover many current issues and controversies, including such topics as "Turned Off by Politics," "The First-Year Student as Immigrant," "Growing Up in the Shadow of AIDS," "TV or Not TV?" and "How to Detect Propaganda." Each reading selection is followed by Questions for Inquiry and Questions for Argument, as well as writing assignments.

■ PLAN OF THE BOOK

Part I addresses analytic, critical, and investigatory skills and builds a base of understanding about argument and research. Chapter 1 introduces argument in the context of academic and civic discourse. Chapter 2 focuses on the nature of reading in relation to analysis and writing. Chapter 3 provides comprehensive guidelines for those skills needed to understand, extract, and use information from written sources—summary, paraphrase, and quotation—and introduces the issues that underlie academic honesty. Chapter 4 offers in-depth preparation for creating a dialogue between ideas—for comparing, contrasting, and synthesizing material from various sources. Chapter 5 explores the nature of evidence and sets the stage for student primary research. Then Chapter 6 places the reasoned analysis of and response to ideas in the context of an individual's personal make-up and values; a discussion of Toulmin logic stresses the role of assumptions in reasoning.

Intertwined with these topics are fundamentals of argumentation and introductions to library and online research. Specifically, explorations in periodical research follow the work in comparison, contrast, and synthesis (Chapter 4), so that students can begin analytic work on sources they themselves discover. The use of reference sources follows the material on primary research (Chapter 5), so that students can acquire general information as background to the collection of data. In these early explorations of sources, students take informal notes and use informal references to sources, waiting to practice formal research procedures and formal documentation until they write formal arguments and the research paper (Parts II and III).

Part II develops the elements of argument in conjunction with appropriate writing assignments. Chapter 7 covers argumentation in the form of the position paper. Chapter 8 focuses on approaches to handling opposing ideas: refutation, Rogerian strategies, and inquiry essays. Then three chapters provide work based on the appeals of argument. Chapter 9 elaborates the use and misuse of logic (*logos*) and sets the stage for a student critique of logic in a professional essay. Chapter 10 provides guidance in probing the effects of style on readers' responses (*pathos*) and provides for an assignment analyzing how language contributes to the persuasiveness of an argument. Chapter 11 focuses on *ethos* by offering detailed guidance in evaluating sources for level and ideological positioning.

Part III provides in-depth process work on the argumentative research paper. Chapter 12 covers choosing a topic, planning, identifying a preliminary claim or focusing question, creating a preliminary bibliography, and taking notes. It also provides guidance for writing a formal or informal research proposal and a progress report. Chapter 13 discusses the drafting of the research paper; formal documentation in MLA and APA formats; academic honesty; and revising, editing, and preparation of the final manuscript. All these matters are pulled together in the sample student research paper, "Should Public Broadcasting Survive?"

■ ACKNOWLEDGMENTS

So many people deserve my thanks and appreciation. At Rowan University, my thanks go to Mary Anne Palladino, David Cromie, Janice Rowan, Tom Kloskey, Dean Pearl Bartelt, and Dean Toni Libro, who have been supportive colleagues over many years; to Martin Itzkowitz and Roberta Zehner, who made specific, helpful suggestions on this manuscript; to the many other members of the College Writing Department at Rowan who have stimulated and influenced my teaching over the years. And to Judith Nadell and John Langan, I owe many thanks for their guidance in the complex world of textbook writing.

And I am grateful to my many students who have helped refine my approach and strengthen my presentation and whose questions and perspectives have lent depth to my own. I am especially indebted to those who were kind enough to permit their work to appear as examples.

I also appreciate the earnest comments of the reviewers who saw earlier versions of this manuscript: Kathleen Bell, University of Central Florida; Ben W. McClelland, University of Mississippi; Mary Anne Reiss, Elizabethtown Community College; and Stephen Wilhoit, University of Dayton. And I thank Eben Ludlow for the chance to turn my ideas into reality, and Linda D'Angelo, whose patience I must have tried more than once, and the production people who designed, copyedited, and prepared the final book, including Rosalie Briand, Pamela Fischer, and John and Evelyn Ward.

Especially, my deepest thanks go to my family: my husband, Larry Schwab, ever supportive and forbearing; my little girl, Laurel, whose joy and playfulness continually remind me of what's really important; and my two college kids, Emily and Jeremy, who probably know more than they ever wanted to about college writing.

Part I

 **From Inquiry . . .**

Chapter 1

Inquiry and Argument

■ Read the following selection carefully, then respond as indicated below:

> Imagine that you enter a parlor. You come late. When you arrive, others have long preceded you, and they are engaged in a heated discussion, a discussion too heated for them to pause and tell you exactly what it is about. In fact, the discussion had already begun long before any of them got there, so that no one present is qualified to retrace for you all the steps that had gone before. You listen for a while until you decide that you have caught the tenor of the argument; then you put in your oar. Someone answers; you answer him; another comes to your defense; another aligns himself against you. . . . However, the discussion is interminable. The hour grows late, you must depart. And you do depart, with the discussion still in progress.
>
> —Kenneth Burke, *The Philosophy of Literary Form*

Writer's Journal

In your notebook, write informally to explain the meaning of the passage. Then describe its effects on you and express any other responses you may have. Strive for an entry of at least 150 words.

■ FROM INQUIRY . . .

Let's begin with the term *inquiry,* a simple word, one we all know how to use. If you examine the following uses of *inquiry* (and its relative, *to inquire*), some may strike you as more appropriate than others:

1. Sal inquired about the penalty for late payment of his gas bill.
2. Judith made an inquiry as to the location of the restroom.
3. The House of Representatives began an inquiry into the states' enforcement of highway traffic laws.
4. The counterman inquired what flavor ice cream I wanted.

If you discuss your responses with classmates, you might discover you agree—that in sentences 1 and 3 *inquiry* works well, but that in 2 and 4 it seems artificial or awkward. In these sentences, you may prefer *asked* as less grand, less affected. Or perhaps you disagree because you can envision a scene or context for sentences 2 and 4 that calls for a special, more elevated word than *ask*. You can agree, however, that the word *inquiry* and the act of *inquiring* are not about asking just any question; an inquiry is more self-conscious, more intentional.

A look in the dictionary reveals that the word *inquiry* shares the same Latin root as *question*: *quaerere,* meaning "to seek." The prefix *in* serves as an intensifier, so we might say that inquire is built from its roots to mean "to seek intensely." In the actual definition, an inquiry is said to be a "question or query" or "a close examination of some matter in a quest for information or truth."

I like this last definition because the phrase "quest for information or truth" reflects the deepest purpose of academic life, the discovery of explanations that will endure—at least until the next inquiry. And "close examination" implies study and research, processes that flow beneath and animate all the teaching and talking, paper writing and e-mailing, reading and note taking that form the day-to-day activities in higher education.

But this definition doesn't tell us much about the context of inquiry or about its inspiration. Why bother to inquire? What creates the need to know?

The Motives for Inquiry

Consider a time when you made an intensive search for knowledge. Make a list of such times. Do these occasions have anything in common? What motivated your need to know?

Often, the search for information or "truth" results from a problem, an impending decision, a conflict between possible choices, or some other controversial situation. The need may be immediate and practical. Perhaps someone whose father has developed cataracts wants information about eye disease in order to understand possible treatments.

Or the need may be to plan for the future. A student may be about to make the life-altering decision to attend college and so collects and studies many college catalogues in order to make the most appropriate choice. A county might study traffic patterns over the course of the workday and workweek so that future road improvements can be planned.

Or the necessary information may be more abstract: solving a societal problem such as a rise in high school dropout rates requires analyzing and perhaps conducting numerous studies of adolescent behavior, the educational system, family dynamics, and so forth.

So an inquiry implies certain things: a problem, dilemma, or controversial issue, first of all, and a community that has a stake in resolving that problem.

The Context of Inquiry

Such a community can be official, such as a township, a civic or professional group, or a university. But many communities or groups of people linked by a common interest or situation are informal and unofficial. Cliques in a high school, recreational groups such as golfers or quilters, and fans of the ballet or progressive jazz are examples. Any group that uses discourse—that is, any form of written or spoken communication—to maintain itself, articulate and solve group problems, and otherwise assist its own cohesiveness and identity is called a **discourse community.** Members of discourse communities—and we are all members of several—base their interactions with each other on the discourse expectations of the group. The discourse community is an active collaborator in any member's use of language, providing a vocabulary and expected styles of discussing and handling issues of concern and even limiting or defining acceptable topics. Such a community has conventions for discussing, analyzing, and proving ideas and for addressing conflicts.

A high school clique may evolve a trademark vocabulary that reaffirms its identity and may develop customary ways of discussing academic work, friendships, romances, and other topics. Inside jokes can be cued with a few words, and greeting or parting may involve signature phrases or gestures. To a certain extent, any member's behavior and talk, both subject and style, will be based on the group's expectations.

■ *Activity 1*
Identifying Discourse
Communities, p. 17

A town-council meeting will also be characterized by a customary discourse. Some characteristics of its discourse will be common to town-council meetings throughout the United States, for local government officials and politically active citizens constitute an informal national discourse community. Most likely, the discussion will be sprinkled with technical terms or jargon derived from various professional domains: the law, real estate, health and public safety, and so on. The discourse will be generally polite and somewhat formal but probably will include informal segments in which humorous asides and little in-jokes lighten the mood. Discourse will follow an agenda, the shape of which may be mandated by law or determined by custom. Proceedings will follow parliamentary procedure to a greater or lesser extent. Decisions will be made by the head official or the council through voice vote, secret ballot, or consensus as local law requires or as is customary.

It is fair to say that any inquiry a person conducts occurs within the web of a discourse community, and it involves interaction with that community. Individual inquiries require dialogue, perhaps oral, perhaps written. How a problem is defined, how study and research are performed, and what counts as a result or solution are all determined by our linguistic and social environment. Discourse communities limit their members to the discourse formulations within them; but discourse communities also open pathways for members by providing conventions of wording and expression and patterns of thought out of which understanding is built.

■ *Activity 2*
Exploring Discourse
Communities, p. 17

■ *Activity 3*
Recognizing Discourse
Communities, p. 17

As Gregory Clark writes, "Using language is necessarily an act of collaboration through which we create the meaning we share, a socially constructed meaning that is inherently incomplete" (17).

The Civic and Academic Discourse Communities

Two broad discourse communities that encompass specialized and regional discourse communities are the academic and the civic discourse communities.

The Civic Discourse Community

The civic discourse community is the broad discourse community of U.S. public life and includes all of us who communicate with each other about the issues and topics of the day, either interpersonally or through reading newspapers and magazines, listening to radio or television news, and so on.

Strictly defined, *civic* means pertaining to citizenship, but in an expanded sense civic refers to everything affecting the community in which people live, including issues national, local, and international, and topics directly and indirectly governmental. The topics of the chitchat that hums around us—about the sensational murder trial, the latest crime statistics, shocking infant mortality rates, the search for effective treatments for AIDS and cancer—and the goings-on of our lawmakers in Congress all come under the banner of civic issues.

In a free society, discourse about issues is a part of the democratic process. As political science professor John Nelson writes, "The relationship of politics to rhetoric [effective language use] is especially intimate in the domestic policies of America and other representational democracies. . . . To ask about the legitimacy of governors, laws, and policies in a representational polity is largely to ask how well it communicates public opinions to public officials, how well the officials communicate public needs to citizens, and how well the citizens communicate among themselves about public problems" (210). In a sense, democracy comes down to communication. As a result, orienting people to take an interest in and function well in the national and local civic discourse communities is an important goal of education.

Civic discourse also encompasses the information and ideas flowing to us via the mass media. But the civic discourse community is not a creation of the mass media; there was a civic discourse community before there was CNN or television or the *New York Times*. Civic discourse has always been assisted by the media, whether printed one-page broadsides sold for a penny on the streets of colonial Philadelphia or presidential debates broadcast by national networks or extremist diatribes uploaded to an Internet forum. But civic discourse goes on among individuals and in public arenas, in meetings of town councils and parent-teacher organizations, student councils and boards of trustees. This discourse community, although broad in its inclusiveness, does foster conventional, accepted ways of thinking, discussing, analyzing, and ultimately approving or discrediting ideas that affect everyone within it.

Several reading selections at the end of this chapter draw from and comment on the civic discourse community. John Leo, whose column appears regularly in the national weekly newsmagazine *U.S. News and World Report,* comments on the failure of our discourse community—at least as it is represented by call-in and talk radio—to be sufficiently argumentative. Josie Mazzaferro, whose opinion piece was published on the *Philadelphia Inquirer*'s op-ed page, writes to defend the civic-mindedness of her twenty-something generation, which has often been discounted as "slackers." Complaining that the civic discourse community is too often short-circuited by a knee-jerk hopelessness, Chris Satullo, a *Philadelphia Inquirer* editor, shows how the tone of discussion in our discourse community can affect the solving of such civic problems as graffiti, school discipline, and television violence.

The Academic Discourse Community

The academic discourse community is sometimes called "academia"; others refer to it, not so approvingly, as "the ivory tower." Sarcasm aside, the academic discourse community is a national, even international, one that shares many characteristics with the civic. But, in addition to discussion and analysis, the academic discourse community mandates research and the active or conscious creation of new perspectives, new connections between ideas, and new ways of looking at the world—that is, new knowledge.

The local academic discourse community that you, your classmates, professors, and other college staff members belong to has its own specific characteristics, many of which are shared by people at other colleges and universities around the country and even around the world. Within any academic institution, there are smaller discourse communities, the academic disciplines. Like the academic discourse community as a whole, your college's academic departments are local sites of larger discourse communities of each discipline. Within each, there will be customary types of problems and controversies and expectations about how inquiry is conducted and what form the outcomes of inquiry will take.

For example, you can imagine how different the research conducted by an English major on the topic "symbolism in Stephen Crane's novels" would be from that of a psychology major assigned to write about recent research on infants' reactions to sweet, salt, and bitter tastes. An education major preparing a case study of a dyslexic child would conduct a different inquiry and write quite a different paper than a biology major assigned to do a laboratory experiment and write a lab report. If you at are the beginning of your college experience, you are a member-in-training of academia, and you may be somewhat unsure of the language expectations this community has. This book focuses on the expectations of the broad academic community rather than the requirements of specific disciplines.

■ *Activity 4*

Exploring Academic Discourse, p. 17

The academic discourse community has a somewhat stronger emphasis than the civic on the written word, in that texts in libraries have been the major medium of interaction among scholars within a field. Although today many researchers turn to the World Wide Web or the Internet for some of their research, the outcome is still printed text read privately. Oral and public discourse does occur in academia, of course, not only in the college lecture hall and discussion classroom but in disciplinary conferences, forums, public lectures, and, increasingly, online in electronic forums. Academia is and will likely remain a text-oriented culture in which writing is a fundamental aspect of issue discovery, problem solving, and knowledge creation. Understanding and using well the modes of inquiry and discussion common to the academic disciplines are necessary for success in college.

At the end of this chapter, Jay Chaskes's "The First-Year Student as Immigrant" models academic discourse: an analytic paper using sources to support independent thinking and documenting those sources in a list of references.

■   . . . TO ARGUMENT

Taken in its everyday sense, the word **argument** may imply a battle: my side versus your side, "us" against "them," often a fruitless banging of heads that can be ended only with an insult or a begrudging remark like "everyone's entitled to an opinion."

Our day-to-day experience with argument is often strongly oppositional and intensely frustrating.

Within the academic and civic discourse communities, argument refers to the building and presenting of a developed case in support of a position on an issue or controversy. When people analyze and evaluate the results of their quests for truth and knowledge—their inquiries—and formulate a position convincingly for presentation to others, they engage in argument. We often become interested in a controversy in midstream, like a person entering the parlor where Burke's unending conversation is going on. Arguments are already flowing, and so our inquiry must begin with understanding the arguments that have already been made.

Disputes over ideas raise new questions and inspire new inquiries, resulting in a landscape of understandings, possible truths, and perspectives. Arguments themselves weave in and out of the inquiry process and usually don't boil down to a simple pro and con or "us" against "them." In fact, the win-lose mind-set can cause people to overlook the range and complexity of viewpoints on an issue. Besides the form of argument that defends an opinion, our common discourse includes other argumentative forms in which negotiation or reconciliation between oppositional views is sought and in which inquiry and the posing of questions are prominent.

Consulting the dictionary on **argument** is informative. There we learn that the root of the word is *arg,* meaning "to shine, white, or the shining or white metal, silver." The Latin word *arguere* based on this root means "to make clear, or demonstrate" ("Arg-"). Knowing about these related roots helps me get a feel for the goal of argument: to come up in clear water after diving in deep, to achieve some clarity about important issues.

Arguments can open minds, encourage complexity of opinions, and advance the appreciation of evidence, but they don't always change minds. As we shall see, many factors underlie a person's choice of opinion, and not all of them are easily addressable in an argument. (Chapter 6 will address some of these factors.) If argument's goal is converting readers, then most arguments are failures. But when argument is seen as a mode of participation in our discourse community, as a vehicle for personal and intellectual growth, and as a means to encourage and validate new options, perspectives, and solutions, then argument can be a vital and exciting process.

With the discourse community in mind, we can put aside those images of raised voices and pounded tables and see argumentation in a more positive light: as a means of participation in the larger intellectual forum of our society. In addition, in its testing of our ideas, argument can provide personal growth and intellectual maturing that is lifelong and ever-complicating. Argument, then, is an honorable and productive activity that seasons our own perspective and makes a responsible contribution to our society.

■ *Activity 5*

Exploring Real-Life Arguments, p. 18

The Elements of Argument

Argument in the broadest sense is an ancient discipline—a form of discourse cultivated by the ancient Greeks and Romans and passed down through the centuries as a means of engaging and advancing ideas and activating support. The writings that have come down to us about argument, from Aristotle through Cicero and Quintilian, provide terminology and strategies about argumentation that are still in use today. This is so even though the ancient rhetoricians (that is, specialists in effective language use) concentrated on oral rather than written language because oratory was then the major component of civic discourse. The ancients associated argumentation with citizenship; it was considered a communal activity designed to promote good civic policy as well as a method for testing ideas, philosophical, ethical, political, or otherwise. As one scholar in the field puts it, the "Greeks and Romans invented and developed rhetoric . . . specifically for their politics" (Nelson 209).

Formal argumentation involves more than batting around ideas in a free-for-all. Rather, in argumentation, a person presents a position, also called a **claim, assertion,** or **proposition.** A claim can clarify facts, explain causes (of problems), promote a value, or advocate a solution, policy, or change. An argumentative claim asserts the most believable or best position to hold on an issue or policy. What is most believable or best will necessarily be determined by the standards of the discourse community in which the argument occurs—and even then a debate frequently occurs over which standards should hold sway. The argumentative writer's goal is to set out the claim in a manner most convincing to the members of the discourse community being addressed.

Argument today includes a broad field of methods, techniques, and perspectives on how meaning is attached to events and situations, how viewpoints are articulated, developed, and lent credence—that is, supportability. But many expectations about argumentative discourse hold true throughout academic and many civic discourse communities:

1. Ideas are valued on the basis of evidence.
2. Ideas build on the ideas and evidence of others, as acquired through research.
3. Arguers will be knowledgeable about the major relevant ideas on a subject of controversy.

Expectations about Evidence

In the civic and academic discourse communities, whether an idea has value or not is usually determined by whether it is supportable—that is, whether there is evidence for it. This may seem so obvious that it might go without saying, and it often does. But requiring ideas to be backed up in order to be valued is a basic assumption that is especially strong in the academic and, to some extent, the civic discourse communities.

In our culture, as a result of our Greek and Roman heritage, the test of whether a claim should be believed lies in the reasonableness of the analysis and evidence. Logic, explored in depth by the ancients, is one of the ways such credence is achieved. Factual information also comes into play in creating a reasonable claim. But there is no formula for reasonableness, no one definition or standard. Rather, reasonableness encompasses a broad spectrum of qualities, including logicality of ideas, depth and breadth of evidence, coherence with similar historical events or cases, practical concerns for fairness and effectiveness of consequences, and comprehensiveness. Philosopher Richard Rorty claims that reasonableness is a state of mind: "to be rational is simply to discuss any topic—religious, literary or scientific—in a way which [avoids] dogmatism, defensiveness and righteous indignation" (40).

The term *evidence* may remind you of a court of law, and to some extent this image is appropriate. Evidence for an argument must be weighed and evaluated, just as in a courtroom.

Not all evidence is "created equal." There are different types, and not all types work to support every claim or work well in different discourse communities. Some evidence, for example, is factual. Facts include the results of scientific research and experimentation; data acquired by taking surveys of people's opinions or living conditions; details gathered by observation; information about events, people, and so forth recorded in public records, documents, or news reports. Examples, which are individual factual cases, also weigh in as evidence.

But only some claims call for facts as evidence. Sometimes explanations and analyses are offered as support for belief in a claim. In an argument against zoos, for example, a person might explain how different the behavior of a wild gorilla is from that of a captive, leading to the assertion that the educational value of watching a gorilla in a zoo is negligible.

Analytic evidence might take the form of discussions of causes and effects; comparisons or contrasts with similar situations, events, or issues in history, politics, culture, or nature; processes or procedures. And whether evidence is logically applied remains another concern. (Evidence is discussed further in Chapter 5. Logic is covered in Chapter 9.)

People argue about what evidence should be acceptable to answer questions raised about civic and social issues. Should a dramatic or extraordinary example alter one's perspective? Does, for example, the televised trial of a scandalous murder case accurately inform us of the ways our justice system works most of the time? To what extent can statistics be relied on as a determinant of truth? If the SAT test scores of U.S. students have been declining since the 1960s, and television became almost universal in U.S. households in the 1950s, should television be blamed for the decline in student ability? Should SAT scores be accepted as a reliable measure or definition of how educated our students are?

As you can see from these questions, even the idea of what is reasonable is subject to inquiry and debate.

Expectations about Research

A second convention within both the civic and academic discourse communities is the expectation that ideas will build on other ideas. For most arguers of claims, supporting evidence comes through research in printed or multimedia sources and is borrowed from other analysts, experimenters, or researchers. The discourse community assumes that research will be done accurately and thoroughly, that it will be focused and analytic, and that other thinkers and writers who contribute to the understanding gained will be acknowledged.

In our culture generally, ideas are perceived as "owned." People who formally present ideas to the discourse community—in print or via a recordable medium—are held accountable for them. When anyone refers to, discusses, or incorporates the ideas or articulated knowledge of another, it is conventional to acknowledge the original source.

In civic discourse, such acknowledgment is usually informal, often just a mention of a commentator's or writer's name or an author's book title. In the academic discourse community, however, the procedures for acknowledgment of ideas are codified into formal documentation rules that members of each discipline are expected to follow.

When Al Gore appears on *Larry King Live* to talk about the environment, his discourse represents his distillation of everything he's read and heard about the subject; his book, *Earth in the Balance,* acknowledges his debts in notes. Gore's handling of sources reflects an academic seriousness and respect for others' ideas. When a student jots down Gore's televised words and quotes them in a paper, she will acknowledge her debt to Gore, but not to all the influences on his thinking.

Attributing ideas to their authors, either formally or informally, suggests ownership, but technically and in a legal sense ideas cannot be owned—that is, they cannot be copyrighted or registered with the federal government as the property of a particular person. Only the specific expression of ideas can be legally tied to a person through copyright. So a poem, a newspaper opinion piece, or a film review can be copyrighted. Reviewer Janet Maslin's opinion of the film *The English Patient* cannot be copyrighted, but her review—the actual words—can be. But the convention of acknowledgment is more inclusive than legal copyright. Any idea or information borrowed from someone who has formally presented ideas, either in published words or "for the record" on electronic media, must be acknowledged as originating in that source.

Expectations about Coverage

Both the academic and civic discourse communities expect that arguers will, to some extent, possess a command of pertinent evidence and other relevant arguments on all sides of the issue in question. The civic discourse community is more lenient on this requirement, but, still, in most contexts, an informed arguer is a more believable one. Depending on the context, it may be important to be knowledgeable about the most recent discussions and evidence on the issue or about the well-known, controversial, or classic arguments about the topic, and most likely to show awareness of positions opposed to your own.

In the academic discourse community, arguers are expected to present a complete view of the issue—that is, to review and engage the important ideas and viewpoints about the topic. Many academic disciplines expect their full members—graduate students and professors—to "review the literature"—that is, to identify all the relevant claims and evidence on the topic—before going on to build their own arguments. It is expected that new understandings and interpretations will build on previous arguments and defend against possible objections by providing disqualifying reasoning or evidence.

Academic writers strive for complete, encyclopedic coverage of a controversy, but expectations for undergraduate students are not so stringent. In responding to college assignments, students should determine what the expectations of coverage are and then limit coverage of the controversy or issue accordingly. Time, if nothing else, should force you to both read selectively and present a relevant sampling of other writers' positions.

Classical argumentation provides for the consideration of alternate viewpoints in the **refutation** stage of an argument. Refutation is a catchall for a variety of ways of dealing with opposing claims. A writer might simply acknowledge the existence of differing points of view; maintain the priority or special relevance of his or her own view; briefly discount other views; accept a qualified or partial version of an opposing view; or identify and thoroughly critique flaws in opposing arguments. Some writers even structure or develop their own presentation of evidence through the refutation of differing views. (Refutation is covered in depth in Chapter 8.)

Beyond refutation, there are other ways of interacting with different viewpoints. Striving for a **middle ground** or writing to establish common ground is one technique for using arguments to advance solutions to current societal problems. Writing to foster negotiation between differing views or adopting a "Rogerian," or noncombative, stance are other ways people work with multiple viewpoints. And using an **inquiry perspective,** in which questions are identified instead of answered, can also be a constructive approach to competing claims. Chapter 8 discusses these alternative argumentation processes.

The Subject of Argument

Not everything is fair game for argumentation. Statements or assertions of personal preferences and tastes, for example, are just that—personal. No one can argue with you about your love of Cherry Garcia ice cream or your enjoyment of *The X Files.* Such tastes are unarguable. However, the healthfulness of a Cherry Garcia–based diet or the artistic merits of a television series are suitable topics for argument because such arguments involve establishing a common standard of value or merit and comparing the specific choice—Cherry Garcia or *The X Files*—to these standards. Personal tastes become arguable when objective criteria can be established. Wine lovers, for example, have a system of taste analysis that removes the subjectivity from wine tasting and provides a standard for discussion and debate.

Assertions that proclaim accepted facts are usually deemed unsuitable for argument. Consider the following claims:

Automobile seatbelts save lives.

Vitamin C is a requirement for good health.

Dyslexia can seriously affect a student's ability to learn.

At one time, all these claims were hypothetical, but as research was conducted, these assertions have come to be considered facts.

Sometimes "facts" may turn out to be less than proven, or they may be alleged to be less than certain. Hence, although most people accept as a fact that smoking is unhealthful, some in the cigarette industry mounted the argument that smoking has nothing to do with cancer and heart attacks and is not addicting. Likewise, it's hard to argue with the facts that show the dangers of motorcycling bareheaded, yet motorcyclists have risen up to contest these facts and have mobilized to get helmet laws changed.

Legitimate and well-positioned arguments against "facts" sometimes do occur. After all, at one time, it was considered a fact that the sun revolved around the earth, and someone had to contest this idea to establish the reality. Within the discourse community of particular academic disciplines, for example, arguments do occur over facts. In history and science, new discoveries or reinterpretations of existing evidence may cause an argument over whether to revise a "fact," or something previously thought to be true. New discoveries of fossils and bones cause frequent revisions of the facts about when and where and how humans developed.

In many academic fields, there are areas where the facts are constantly uncertain or where debate rages over what the facts are. "Is there life elsewhere in the universe?" is a factual question that remains open to debate because science just has not accumulated enough evidence. More down-to-earth facts can also be uncertain. The authorship of a book sometimes attributed to Mikhail Bakhtin is uncertain, for it was published under the name of Bakhtin's less important colleague, V. N. Voloshinov, at a time when Bakhtin was in danger of imprisonment for his ideas. *Marxism* is either a collaboration between Bakhtin and Voloshinov, wholly by Bakhtin, or by Voloshinov under Bakhtin's influence, depending on which Bakhtin scholar you read.

Finally, it is difficult to argue over assertions of belief that are based on faith, tradition, or membership. The disciplines of philosophy and religious studies have developed modes of inquiry and debate about such matters as whether God, devils, angels, and so forth exist, but outside such specialized study assertions about religious matters are nearly unarguable.

■ *Activity 6*

Arguable and Inarguable Claims, p. 18

The Appeals of Argument

While reasonableness—in all its possible manifestations—is our discourse community's overall standard for strength of ideas, arguments are directed to readers, whose response to argument occurs on many levels, not just the analytic. Aristotle identified three types of appeals to the audience that arguments may make: the **appeal to logic** (*logos*), to **emotions** (*pathos*), and to **credibility** (*ethos*). Writers addressing readers in today's civic and academic discourse communities still make use of these classical strategies. An effective argument is one that balances the appeals of *logos*, *pathos*, and *ethos* in accordance with the intended audience's mind-set.

Appeals to Logic

The claims of argument should withstand the tests of reason. Aristotle identified *logos* as the rational component of argumentation. *Logos* comes from the same Greek root, meaning "word," that underlies the English words *logic* and *logo*. In achieving reasonableness, language use needs to be analytic, clear, specific, and logical, and the substance of the argument should predominate over emotional aspects. Evidence of all types, analyzed and related logically, can be most effective with audiences that value reasonableness and can restrain their personal biases.

Appeals to Emotions

Any issue of importance will generate heat as well as light. Aristotle identified as *pathos* the "heat" of argument, the component that appeals to our emotions. *Pathos* gives us the root of such English words as *pathetic* (which originally meant "overflowing with emotion") and *pathology* (the study of disease, once thought to result from imbalances in body fluids regulating both emotions and health). *Pathos* refers to the wringing of feelings, the wrenchings of the heart, that may occur when any matter crucial to human life, culture, institutions, or ethics is under scrutiny. Almost all arguments, inevitably, have an emotional dimension because we are most likely to argue about matters that are significant for us personally. Arguers design their arguments to have more or less emotional impact according to their judgment of how their audience will respond. Word choice and evidence type both play into the presence of *pathos.*

Even those who wish to remain rational must attend to the emotional dimension of argument because we can all be tossed about by feelings like tall trees in crosswinds. Our language constantly evokes feelings. In addition, our emotional responses tie into our values—that is, to principles and qualities that we hold dear and rank above all else.

Although our civic and academic discourse communities value reasonableness as a standard for ideas, many times in our culture an idea is valued because of some other quality, such as its cleverness, rather than its supportability. Slogans are a case in point. People like the sound of slogans; they're zippy and powerful: "guns don't kill, people do"; "it's not a choice, it's a child"; and "if you think education is expensive, try ignorance." The brevity, brightness, and bluntness of a slogan can lure people to get behind it without a careful examination of any evidence supporting its validity. Other language effects—the beauty of imagery, the poetry of a comparison, the symmetry of an idea's expression—can be equally seductive to some audiences.

Appeals to Credibility

In the marketplace of ideas, as people advocate for particular positions, the image of the arguers comes into play. Argument does not occur as a dialogue of minds but is instead the interplay of actual people with motivations and goals that may or may not be known. We might put this as, "Ideas don't argue; people do."

Aristotle therefore identified a third possible appeal of argument, *ethos,* the power that derives from the person doing the arguing. *Ethos* supplies the root of the English word *ethics,* and the known ethical reputation of an arguer is a part of what we mean by *ethos. Ethos,* or credibility, operates on several levels in a text. Establishing it may involve showing that the argument advances positive ends or derives from positive values, that the author is both knowledgeable and a person of goodwill, and that the assertions made in the argument are supported by those with expertise.

The emphasis on personal credibility results from argumentation's origins in Greek democracy, where argument was oral and the physical person advocating a position could not be ignored. In written text, too, the element of *ethos* comes into play with great force. Readers can sense whether an author is likable or abrasive, straightforward or devious, neutral or externally motivated, and this affects their response to an argument. (See Chapter 10 for more about language and style.)

When a writer calls on experts for data in support of a claim, *logos* is in play as well as *ethos*. But when an author cites experts who merely second the author's claim without additional evidence, the experts' worth as evidence depends on their reputations. There is a legitimate debate about how the opinions of experts with differing credentials should be weighted. In a reasonable discussion, should those who speak from the authority of tradition, position, expertise in sacred texts, or religious enlightenment be granted equal weight with scholars, researchers, and specialists? Does the opinion of someone with personal experience weigh equally with that of someone who has done extensive research? The answer to such questions depends on the discourse community involved. For example, some people who advocate the death penalty do so because they believe the Bible indicates that God supports it ("an eye for an eye . . ."). This argument will be effective among those who interpret the Bible that same way, but it may have limited force in the wider civic discourse community. Of course, many people who support the death penalty can supply evidence other than religious evidence—facts, reasons, and benefits—to defend it.

■ *Activity 7*
Recognizing Appeals, p. 18

There are no general rules about choosing experts; depending on the subject, the discourse community, and who is doing the arguing, different experts will be accepted or spurned. Some people believe that our mainstream culture accepts too uncritically the opinions offered by experts or pseudo-experts. Advertising is a case in point: actors playing doctors tell us certain medicines will cure our ills; baseball players urge us to drink milk.

Furthermore, in today's civic and academic discourse communities, those participating in argumentation need to evaluate the credibility not only of the individual writer but also of the media source. Most ideas and information these days are delivered by media—magazines, newspapers, books, or electronic media—which may themselves be more or less credible, reliable, and objective. Dealing with *ethos* at the turn of the twenty-first century means becoming media literate—that is, savvy about the reputation and credibility of media sources. Chapter 11 focuses on evaluating sources.

■ *Activity 8*
Evaluating Appeals to Authority, p. 19

Using the Appeals

Imagine that when you are skimming a magazine in the doctor's waiting room, you encounter an opinion piece advocating the reintroduction of the grizzly bear to the U.S. wilderness along the Canadian border. If you had to classify yourself, would you say you would be (a) an interested, supportive reader, (b) a decidedly opposed reader, or (c) a neutral, perhaps apathetic reader? However you classify yourself, which appeal or combination of appeals would affect you positively on this issue?

If you were a supporter of the grizzly's return, you wouldn't need much reasoning. Rather, an article that made you feel good about your support of the grizzly—that is, that made use of *pathos*—would be effective for you. An arguer who recognizes that an intended audience is allied writes to reinforce that position, disseminate new evidence, or spur readers to action by rousing strong emotions. If the opinion piece is to appear in an environmental magazine, for example, the writer recognizes that many readers will be positive on the issue.

If your reaction to the grizzly restoration were negative, however, a different kind of article might at least set you thinking if not change your mind. The writer's most effective approach to those opposed to more grizzlies would be even-toned, to bolster credibility, and *logos* would dominate. A writer producing this article for a logging-industry newsletter, for example, would provide relevant facts and stress the benefits of the restoration project.

If you were neutral or had a mixed opinion, you would first of all need motivation to read the article, and then you would need some rational convincing. Expecting this type of audience, the writer would balance the three appeals. An emotionally catchy introduction and evocative descriptions throughout might attract readers, a serious tone might impress them with the writer's believability, and pointing out benefits and providing evidence of the possibility of the success and safety of the restoration might make them look favorably on the grizzly project. This approach would be best for a writer placing the article in a newspaper or a general magazine where most readers would be uninterested or uncertain of their opinion.

This chart identifies the appropriate mix of appeals in each situation:

Audience	Appeals	Purpose
Supportive	Main: *pathos*	Reinforce support; inspire action
	Secondary: *logos*	Provide new evidence
Hostile	Main: *logos*	Tip weight of evidence in favor of claim
	Secondary: *ethos*	Present serious, rational, fair self-image
Mixed or neutral	Main: *logos*	Give evidence in favor of claim
	ethos	Present serious, rational, fair self-image
	pathos	Keep readers interested and involved through human-interest touches

The Writer's Discourse Community

Below are listed some conventional techniques and processes used in teaching and learning about college writing—that is, in the academic discourse community of college writers. Look through the list to identify any that are not familiar to you. Your instructor may wish you to discuss and investigate terms that are unfamiliar with others in your class. Or you may be asked to discover the meanings of unfamiliar terms by chatting about writing with other students on campus, your professors in other courses, computer or writing lab staff, tutoring staff, and so on. Activities and practices throughout this book will ask you to use these techniques in order to improve your writing ability.

Journal writing
Free writing

Brainstorming
Rough outlining
Drafting or composing
Collaboration
Peer discussion and review
Patterns or modes of analysis: illustration, division-classification, process analysis, cause-effect, comparison-contrast, definition

Activities

1   **Identifying Discourse Communities**

Make some notes in your notebook about the discourse communities to which you belong. Choose one and jot down a list of phrases and concepts that are natural to the members but would be strange or new to someone outside the discourse community. Also note any typical language interactions or styles typical to this community. Then, meet with a small group of your classmates and take turns reading items from your lists. How long does it take for other group members to guess your discourse community?

2   **Exploring Discourse Communities**

Attend a meeting of a discourse community you are not a member of and take notes about the characteristics of the discourse there. Try to notice not only vocabulary but also how issues, decisions, inquiry, and conflicts are handled.

3   **Recognizing Discourse Communities**

Which of the following are examples of discourse communities? Which may be? How can you tell?

Soap opera addicts
Shoppers at the Urban Guerrilla Clothing Store in Soho
Vendors at a gun show at a local convention center
Law school graduates sitting for a state bar exam
People eating at the lunch counter in Friendly's at the mall

With three or four other students, generate a mixed list of groups that are and are not discourse communities. Present your list to another group in the class so they may determine which groups are discourse communities.

4   **Exploring Academic Discourse**

Ask several professors in different fields to give you an example of a typical writing assignment in an upper-level course. (Most instructors have a handout for each assignment and can provide you with one with little trouble.) Remember to ask for writing assignments.

Form a group with other students, read the assignments through, and make notes about the expectations reflected in each assignment. What similarities do you notice? What differences?

5 Exploring Real-Life Arguments

Make a list of any recent or memorable arguments or disputes you have had. Then, identify the discourse community within which it occurred. What aspects of the argument or dispute seemed customary? (For example, a typical dispute with your younger sister might end with her stomping off or slamming her door when she doesn't get her way.) How do arguments or disputes typically end in this discourse community?

6 Arguable and Inarguable Claims

Work with several other students to compile lists of arguable and inarguable claims. Scramble the list, write instructions, and present it to another group of students as an activity for them to complete.

7 Recognizing Appeals

Which appeal, *logos, ethos,* or *pathos,* predominates in each of the arguments below?

[A] [Today, fascism] is recognizable by its determination to convert all public services to private entrepreneurship; all nonprofit organizations to profit-making ones—so that the narrow but protective chasm between governance and business disappears. It changes citizens into taxpayers—so individuals become angry at even the notion of the public good. It changes neighbors into consumers—so the measure of our value as humans is not our humanity or our compassion or our generosity but what we own. It changes parenting into panicking—so that we vote against the interests of our own children; against their health care, their education, their safety from weapons. And in effecting these changes it produces the perfect capitalist, one who is willing to kill a human being for a product—a pair of sneakers, a jacket, a car—or kill generations for control of products—oil, drugs, fruit, gold.

—Toni Morrison, speech at Howard University, March 2, 1997

[B] In addition to differences that existed prior to their arrival on campus, African American students knew far fewer other people on campus when they arrived. Over one-third (34%) of the African American students knew no one upon arrival, compared to 10% of the White students. . . .

The two groups did not differ in their involvement in campus organizations nor in their degree of participation in campus groups. However, their social worlds were notably distinct, at least as far as the racial composition of their social networks is concerned. African American students more often shared housing with other African American students than did White students. Specifically, 13% of African Americans reported having African American roommates, compared to 6% of Whites.

—Anthony R. D'Augelli and Scott L. Hershberger, "African American Undergraduates on a Predominantly White Campus: Academic Factors, Social Networks and Campus Climate"

[C] Last, industry leaders argue that the $2.6 billion-plus spent on cigarette ads . . . doesn't persuade anyone to smoke . . . [but] only influence[s] a small percentage of existing smokers to switch among brands.

Advertising experts agree that market expansion, especially for an industry that loses over 2 million consumers a year who die or quit, is an important objective of nearly all advertising. Emerson Foote, former chairman of McCann-Erickson, one of the world's largest advertising agencies, once remarked that "I am always amused by the suggestion that advertising, a function that has been shown to increase consumption of virtually every other product, somehow miraculously fails to work for tobacco products." Foote's view is seconded by advertising executive Charles Sharp, a former vice president of Ogilvy and Mather.

—Mark Green, "Luring Kids to Light Up"

[D]   Under the Truman Doctrine and the Marshall Plan, the world had become a system to be both protected and manipulated by the United States. Within the quasi-religious American mythos, no ideogical space remained for other conflicts. Truman's construction of the bilateral world in his 1947 speech presented Congress with a simple binary decision: democracy or Stalinist communism, freedom or slavery, good or evil.

—Paul N. Edward, *The Closed World*

8   Evaluating Appeals to Authority

Below are pairs of authorities on an issue and a description of communities in which the argument is held. For each discourse community, which expert do you believe would be considered the most credible?

Expert	Issue	Discourse Community
1. Violent crime victim 2. Expert on criminal behavior	Whether to forbid parole for repeat assailants	1. Readers of a national newsmagazine 2. Viewing audience of a popular television talk show 3. State lawmakers deciding on proposed law
1. Famous athlete 2. U.S. surgeon general	Discouraging young people from using tobacco	1. Watchers of a network sitcom 2. Readers of a serious political magazine

Assignments

INFORMAL WRITING

1. **Ideas Have Consequences**   Sketch out the meaning this passage conveys to you, and then relate it to your own experience of language or reasoning.

Ideas do have consequences, rhetoric is policy, and words are action.

—Ronald Reagan, speech, April 22, 1986.

2. **Truth and Ideas** React to the following quotation, and give any examples that occur to you that support or challenge the idea.

Truth happens to an idea. It becomes true, is made true by events.

—William James, "Pragmatism's Conception of Truth"

3. **The Unending Conversation** Look back at the passage from Kenneth Burke that begins this chapter. Read it again, and write in your notebook how you now interpret this image.

4. **Ideas in the Air** Spend a day trying to notice and even count the times when ideas or information float into your life accidentally or unbidden. As you watch or overhear media, scan print, encounter friends, or eavesdrop on strangers, notice when ideas drawn from others become part of your mental landscape. Report your experience in free writing in your journal.

5. **Outsiders in a Discourse Community** Brainstorm a list of discourse communities you belong to. Compare your list with those of others near you, and add or delete items as a result of your discussion. Individually, free-write about one specific discourse community. Focus on a time when an outsider appeared and didn't fit or on the moment when you realized you were an outsider in a discourse community new to you. If your instructor requires, rework your free writing into an essay narrating one personal experience, either positive or negative, with discourse communities.

6. **Discourse Communities Cause Disputes** Brainstorm a list of times that you can remember being in an argument. Examine your list to see whether, on closer inspection, you can now recognize that some part of the arguments had to do with the fact that you and your opponent were members of different discourse communities. For example, membership in conflicting discourse communities is often the root of disputes between members of different generations. Try to identify some of the characteristics of the conflicting discourse communities as you write a rough draft of an essay explaining the causes and results of a conflict. If your instructor requires, rework your rough draft into a formal essay.

7. **Exploring an Argument** Free-write about a recent argument or dispute you had with someone. As you write, or after you are through, try to identify the claim or claims you were battling over. Also consider these issues: Which person had evidence? Did you both remain reasonable? Did anyone introduce other appeals, such as the perspective of experts or rules or principles supplied by authorities? After free writing, sketch a rough outline of a formal essay in which you present your analysis of an argument that played out in either a reasonable or unreasonable fashion. If your instructor requires, use your outline as the basis for a formal analytic essay.

FORMAL WRITING

1. Brainstorm a list of arguable claims that you would like to write about or learn more about. Choose one or two to sketch out or free-write a starting argument (list of reasons for your belief in your claim).

2. Find others in your class who have one or more similar claims on their list. Meet with them to discuss your points of view and what you know and don't know

about one of these mutually interesting claims. Identify a preliminary claim for an argument and sketch out its development.

■ WORKS CITED

"Arg" in Indo-European Roots. *American Heritage Dictionary,* 3rd ed. 1996.

Clark, Gregory. *Dialogue, Dialectic, and Conversation: A Social Perspective on the Function of Writing.* Carbondale: S. Illinois UP, 1990.

Nelson, John S. "Stories of Science and Politics: Some Rhetorics of Political Research." In *The Rhetoric of the Human Sciences: Language and Argument in Scholarship and Public Affairs.* Ed. John S. Nelson, Allan Megill, and Donald N. McCloskey. Madison: U of Wisconsin P, 1987.

Rorty, Richard. "Science as Solidarity." In *The Rhetoric of Inquiry: Language and Argument in Scholarship and Public Affairs.* Ed. John S. Nelson, Allan Megill, and Donald N. McCloskey. Madison: U of Wisconsin P, 1987.

 *Readings*

The Unmaking of Civic Culture

JOHN LEO

One night last summer, I was the substitute host on one of the popular late-night radio talk shows in New York. For four hours, the switchboard lit up with listeners eager to talk about the two hot-button topics of the evening: domestic violence and Afrocentrism. Calls rolled in from feminists, antifeminist women, abused women, abused men, blacks and whites discussing the fine points of ancient Egypt and the treatment of blacks by white historians. With one exception (a man who calls in regularly to disparage blacks), the callers conducted a very serious, informed debate with great civility.   1

Why doesn't this happen more often? On most talk radio, 75 percent of the listeners seem to phone in to echo what has just been said. Most others seem to be patrolling for group slights or to point out that the guest is full of beans.   2

So far, the political discussions on the online computer services haven't seemed much better. Last week in the *U.S. News* forum on CompuServe, an exasperated woman named Julie tapped out the message that "Reading some of the threads online is like listening to my two teens arguing over anything and everything; 'Did not . . . Did too . . . Did not . . . Did too . . . MOM!!' "   3

Many social critics have tried to explain the low level of political discussion and debate. Some think the increasingly truculent and ideological tone of American politics makes debate seem too wearing and pointless: Each side knows what the other will say, so why bother going through it again and again?   4

5   In his last book, *The Revolt of the Elites and the Betrayal of Democracy*, the late Christopher Lasch blamed the rise of television debate (which puts a premium on appearance and unflappability rather than on the substance of argument) and the rise of "commercial persuasion" (an increasingly cynical electorate comes to feel manipulated by PR people, lobbyists and advertising campaigns).

Instant Plebiscite

6   Jean Bethke Elshtain, in her new book, *Democracy on Trial*, makes a related point. Technology, she says, has brought us to the brink of a politics based on instant plebiscite: With telepolling and interactive TV, politicians can respond to the majority's wishes (and whims) on any subject, "so there is no need for debate with one's fellow citizens on substantive questions. All that is required is a calculus of opinion."

7   This is a skewed form of democracy, that fits the current atomized state of American society. Politics can be based on the offhand views of mostly semi-informed individuals sitting alone in front of the TV, randomly pushing buttons. But as Elshtain says, "A compilation of opinions does not make a civic culture; such a culture emerges only from a deliberative process."

8   Lasch argued that a citizenry can't be informed unless it argues. He wrote that only an impassioned political argument makes the arguer look hard for evidence that will back up or tear down his position. Until we have to defend our opinions in public, he said, they remain half-formed convictions based on random impressions: "We come to know our own minds only by explaining ourselves to others."

9   Many critics argue that the rise of state bureaucracies, converting citizens into clients, has eliminated the local meetings that served as seedbeds of public political argument. So has the rise of politics based on litigation, which downgrades all political argument not conducted in front of a judge. This has gone hand in hand with the "rights" revolution. Once a desire is positioned as a right, by definition it can't be challenged. It's a trump card, beyond debate.

10   A great many of these offenses against ordinary democracy have been conducted by the left, but the right has been guilty too, chiefly of importing strongly held moral positions directly into politics as assertions rather than as matters of debate. A conviction may be personal or religious, but it has to be defended rationally against people with different principles, or there is no point in discussing it at all.

11   The hollowing out of our civic culture has many causes that help explain the decline of political debate. A crucial one is the rise of the therapeutic ethic. Starting in the 1960s, the nation's sense of itself has been deeply influenced by the rapid spread of therapies, encounter groups, self-help, the language of self-esteem and personal growth and an array of New Age notions, some of them quasi religions based on the primacy of the self.

12   This has created a vast Oprahized culture obsessed with feelings and subjective, private experiences. In some ways, this culture of therapy has positioned itself as the antidote for America's fragmentation and the decline of civic culture. It pushes young people into monitoring their own psyches and away from environments where they might learn civic and political skills. And it tends to kill any chance for political debate by framing values as mere matters of personal taste. You like vanilla. I like butter pecan.

13   It's important to reverse this process. We need a lot more emphasis on public discourse and common problems, and a lot less mooning about our individual psyches.

Questions for Inquiry

1. According to Leo, what is the problem that is "unmaking" our civic culture? What examples of this problem does he offer? According to him, what should be the goal of public discourse in a democracy?
2. What do the two authors, Lasch and Elshtain, contribute to Leo's analysis? What does the reference to these two authors suggest about the audience Leo expects for his column?
3. What causes for the of the "low level of political discussion and debate" does Leo identify?

Questions for Argument

1. **Group Work.** Today's technology has multiplied the opportunities people have for engaging in discussion with others. Yet Leo finds that productive discussion is rare. With your instructor's assistance, identify news groups, local or national call-in shows, and other participatory forums to which class members have access, and divide the class into several groups; each group should choose to monitor a specific public forum in order to confirm or refute Leo's assertion. Groups should meet briefly before the next class to consolidate their findings. In class, discuss your findings in response to this question: Are the debates on call-in talk shows and online forums repetitive and useless? Do they degrade our civic culture?
2. Leo warns that "importing" strong moral positions into political discussion can render debate useless (10). But he also asserts that treating "values as matters of mere personal taste" can also kill political debate (12). Do you see any contradiction in these criticisms? What should be the role of moral beliefs and values in our society?
3. Near the end of his argument, Leo attacks our society for its overvaluing of "subjective, private experiences," leading to a "culture of therapy" in which people are preoccupied with "monitoring their own psyches." Do you agree that the modern emphasis on self-understanding undercuts our ability to "learn civic and political skills"?

Writing Assignments

Informal

1. Consider the last time you discussed (or listened to your peers discuss) a political or civic controversy. In an in-depth journal entry, describe what you remember of the discussion. (You might jot down your memories in dialogue form.) Then mull over the discussion and comment on these questions: Was the discussion productive? Did the participants get trapped by the problems that Leo isolates: repetition, inflexibility, moralizing, or subjectivism?
2. Write in response to this quotation from Christopher Lasch: "we come to know our own minds only by explaining ourselves to others." You might write about whether you agree or disagree, about examples you have of knowing your own mind, or about any other issues this quotation prompts. (Lasch's article appears at the end of Chapter 7.)

Formal

3. After listening to talk radio or following an online debate (possibly in response to Question for Argument 1 above) or examining the letters to the editor on a specific topic in a local or regional newspaper, write a column in response to Leo's. Begin by invoking

what you heard or read in the participatory forum you studied. Then present your opinion about the quality of political discussion today and discuss evidence for it.

4. Leo ends with a plea for us to "reverse this process" of declining civic culture. Do you, in fact, agree that this "hollowing out of our civic culture" (11) can be reversed? Write an essay in which you explain your view and indicate what, if anything, a private individual can do to foster productive political discourse.

■ ■ ■

Turned Off by Politics

JOSIE MAZZAFERRO

Josie Mazzaferro is currently codirector of A Room of Our Own, a support center for gays and lesbians. This piece appeared in the *Philadelphia Inquirer* on October 22, 1997. (Reprinted by permission of the author.)

1   In the beginning there was a baby boomer with a lot of fancy degrees who looked out at the Americans born between 1961 and 1981 and saw high voter apathy. This person then waved his hand, and we all became forever after known as "Generation X."

2   Terms such as *apathetic, lazy, disinterested, disconnected* and *selfish* began to be used to describe us. He looked out over what he created, and he thought "This is good." Apparently Madison Avenue agreed, and we began to see commercials targeted to us that featured dudes on skateboards with flannel shirts and greasy hair.

3   The real "truth" about Generation X:

4   A sure way to turn me off from buying any product is to market it featuring dudes with skateboards, flannel shirts and greasy hair. In fact, I often wonder where these slackers live because as a 25-year-old who has always been quite involved with her community and her peers, I can tell you that I have not met many people in my generation who are at all like this image.

5   I'll be the first to admit that my generation has a poor track record when it comes to voting. In the 1996 election, less than a third of us went to the polls. The 1995 UCLA Freshmen Norms Poll found that only 29 percent of college freshmen thought it was important to keep up with politics and only 15 percent said they discussed the subject often, both all-time lows. The Harwood Group's study *College Students Talk Politics* observes that our generation "seems to be missing a context for even thinking about politics."

6   But disaffection with politics does not really equal apathy. A statistic from a 1996 Youth Voices study suggests, for example, that high voter apathy should not be taken at face value: 61 percent of 18- to 24-year-olds have participated in community service and volunteerism. So we are not disinterested in our communities; we just are turned off from politics. We grew up during Watergate, Abscam, Iran-Contra, Whitewatergate and campaign-finance scandals. How can we have faith in a system that generates so much controversy and corruption?

7   I am not saying that every politician is corrupt and that my generation should just walk away. I am saying just the opposite. As citizens living in a democratic society, if we see a problem, we have a responsibility to fix it. Leadership does not come from above; it comes from the masses. Look at the civil rights movement for an example of effective social action. Masses of African Americans participated and showed the leaders that they would not sit

back and be treated as second-class citizens anymore. It was this public participation that created change.

I am the executive director of a national nonprofit called the Foundation for Individual   8
Responsibility and Social Trust. FIRST works to amass that public participation from my generation and channel that energy into creative problem-solving not only for my generation's future, but for our country. We held our second annual Convention on National Issues for Young Adults (ages 18–36) last weekend in Philadelphia.

At this convention, we launched our Next Century Plan, an ambitious proposal to part-   9
ner with other nonprofits, social-action groups and colleges to hold deliberative discussions on national issues among young adults across the country. We will conduct these discussion groups for the next two years, using the results to form a Generational Action Plan. This Action Plan will be a strategic plan for the country, serving as a guide to the society in which we want to live and the actions and responsibilities we will take to create that society.

We've fallen from grace, but we are trying hard to get up—clear up the misconceptions,   10
that is—and get to work. The future of our country depends on all of us working together to overcome our obstacles creatively.

Questions for Inquiry

1. What is the stereotype of a typical Gen Xer, according to Mazzaferro? What does she find wrong with the stereotype? And what flaws does Mazzaferro admit are possessed by Generation X?
2. **Group Research.** According to Mazzaferro, how did Generation X get its name and its stereotypical image? Do you know how or when the term and stereotype of Generation X originated? What type of investigations could you conduct to find out about this term? Brainstorm some research possibilities and then form pairs or small groups and divide up the research tasks. For the next class meeting, come prepared to share what you have discovered about the origins and meanings of the label *Generation X*.

    For more information about how to conduct library and online research, see Chapters 5 and 6.
3. Mazzaferro relates the naming of Generation X to the creation in Genesis: "In the beginning . . . " What effect on the reader does this reference have? What is she referring to in her last paragraph, where she writes, "We've fallen from grace . . . "?

Questions for Argument

1. Do you agree that the polls and research Mazzaferro cites in paragraph 5 fairly describe today's young adults, those now aged eighteen to thirty-six? If not, how would you characterize this generation? Is it a generation that volunteers instead of votes, as Mazzaferro asserts in paragraph 6?
2. Mazzaferro is very upfront about the values that underlie her essay: she believes that "as citizens living in a democratic society, if we see a problem, we have a responsibility to fix it." Do your agree?
3. What is the reason that young adults are turned off by politics, according to the author? From your point of view, are there other factors affecting the political awareness and involvement of young adults in college and those who work? Do you think young people ignore politics for justifiable reasons? Or are they making excuses?

Writing Assignments

Informal

1. In your journal, write your version of the "truth about Generation X."
2. Mazzaferro points out that "the future of our country depends on all of us working together." Write about a time when you experienced or participated in a group "working together . . . creatively." Did you end up optimistic or pessimistic about group work?

Formal

3. Mazzaferro writes that "leadership does not come from above; it comes from the masses" (7). Do you believe that leadership from the masses is a positive or a negative? Write an essay in which you discuss where our nation's leaders should originate.
4. **Collaborative Writing.** Mazzaferro states that her organization, FIRST, is devising a "Generational Action Plan." Divide your class into several committees and charge each one with a focused area of civic responsibility that will be important in the future, such as the environment, the welfare of children, the infrastructure (roads, bridges, communications lines), education and employment for young people. Each committee should discuss and develop a statement of goals in its area and then write a paper explaining the goals and proposing their inclusion in the Generational Action Plan.

■ ■ ■

That's No Panacea

CHRIS SATULLO

Chris Satullo is deputy editorial-page editor of the *Philadelphia Inquirer,* where this piece appeared on March 19, 1996. (Copyright 1996 by the Philadelphia Inquirer. Reprinted by permission.)

1   When the behavior of the physical universe conforms to the laws cooked up by old Sir Isaac, it's comforting. The apple will go thud today, just as it did yesterday.

2   But, when the political universe follows Newtonian rules of action and reaction, it can be dismaying.

3   Just dare to suggest that neighborhoods flinching beneath a scrawled bombardment of graffiti might be helped by a ban on the sale of spray paint and, sure as gravity, someone will snort derisively:

4   *That's no panacea.*

5   Propose that televisions ought to include technology to help parents screen their children from the daily onslaught of gore, groping and leers, and you'll be told:

6   *That's no panacea.*

7   Suggest that, when schoolchildren are wounding each other over Starter jackets, it might make sense to give school uniforms a try, and skeptics will cry out:

8   *That's no panacea.*

9   It won't matter that you never claimed any of these steps *was* a panacea, a magical cure-all. It won't matter that you see them as one experiment in a many-pronged assault on a problem. You'll get the "P-word" thrown back in your face.

This bit of rhetoric has become the all-purpose defense of the intellectually bankrupt status quo.   10

Threatened by an adventurous idea? Then insist on judging it by an impossible standard: Will it cure the problem in one stunning stroke? Is it free of imaginable pitfalls? Does it involve no tradeoffs between competing ideals?   11

Since no human action in a fallen world can live up to such absolutes, you'll be free to yelp, "See, it's not perfect," and save yourself from the pain of having a new idea jostle your settled wisdom.   12

The ideas cited above—spray-paint bans, the V-chip and school uniforms—are similar in that each is a favorite of the still-amorphous civic virtue movement, which wonders how to reassert healthy community values in a landscape of moral breakdown, without trampling individual rights. And the defensive cries of "it's no panacea," come mostly from traditional liberals (who are appalled by heretics like me who seek to escape the deadends to which unalloyed rights rhetoric can lead).   13

I chose these examples because it's more honest to admit first where your own team has gone awry, before blasting the other side.   14

But permit me an observation: Government-bashing, free-market-loving conservatives are the grand masters of the panacea game, both at applying phony tests to the other guy's ideas, and in hyping their own as magical elixirs.   15

Consider that pet phrase of conservatives, "Throwing money at problems never solved anything." It's a powerful first cousin to "That's no panacea." Once you've sown doubt by shouting that the other side's idea won't fix everything, it's a short step to the claim that none of its ideas will ever fix anything.   16

It's too bad that liberals, cranky upon being roused from a decades-long critical torpor, are settling for the same sly debating tricks long used to torment them.   17

Look, for example, at spray-paint bans. Liberal critics of the idea—unable to shake the indulgent view of graffiti vandalism as the street art of the oppressed—point triumphantly to the irony of having a Philadelphia where you can't buy Krylon but can buy assault weapons. And they predict that "taggers" will still obtain spray cans. What they don't seem to recognize is how such gibes mimic the rhetoric of the gun crowd they despise.   18

As for the V-chip, media corporations who fear how it would complicate their sweet deal have worked the "no panacea" theme hard—and some liberals, picking up a false scent of censorship in this bid to empower consumers, bay in chorus.   19

So we get argument by folklore: The V-chip is useless because kids, who are all computer geniuses, will outwit their parents, who are all incompetent technoboobs. (Funny, I've been able to keep the PIN on my MAC card a secret from my kids.) And the "It'll never fly, Wilbur" argument: Somehow, even when vast riches await the person who builds a better V-chip, Yankee ingenuity will never find a way. And the blame-the-victim argument: The V-chip will never work because parents will be too irresponsible to use it properly.   20

As for school uniforms, we tend to judge the idea by flashback, by our feelings about the vice principal who sent us home for having hair too long or a skirt too short. But this idea is being pushed by some pragmatic educators who are not paramilitary nuts, who aren't part of the crowd that believes in magical, no-cost fixes for bad schools. No sensible person thinks school uniforms will end the need for better textbooks and teaching—but plenty of sensible people wonder whether uniforms might help stem a chaos that is fueled in part by consumer lusts.   21

Yes, the woods *are* full of quick-fix pushers who'd love to avoid the hard work that awaits us. And, in the face of their glibness, there's a role for "it's no panacea" rhetoric.   22

23   But such rhetoric is no (ahem) *substitute* for the honesty to admit failure, the courage to court change, the maturity to accept that, when the painful night won't turn instantly into a healing dawn, lighting even one candle is well worth it.

Questions for Inquiry

1. Identify Satullo's argumentative claim and explain his reasons for asserting it.
2. Before he introduces his claim, the author presents several examples. How does this delaying strategy help the reader understand the claim? Also, how does the reference to Newton's law of gravity and "rules of action and reaction" help clarify the claim?
3. What is Satullo's tone throughout the essay? What groups are the target of this tone? To which readers is Satullo making his appeal?

Questions for Argument

1. Satullo suggests that resistance to change comes about because people are threatened by "adventurous ideas" (11) and that they are too comfortable with the "status quo" (10) and their "settled wisdom" (12) about how the world works. Besides fear and stodginess, what other reasons might there be to resist change? Are all such reasons signs of weakness?
2. Satullo is arguing for a more mature and supportive response to helpful proposals. Do you see a contradiction between this main idea and his immoderate, some might even say hostile, expression of his views? Or is his tone a valid expression of the "courage to court change"?
3. Is change in search of solutions—"one experiment in a many-pronged assault on a problem" (9)—always a good thing? Might there be good reasons to hold back on some of the changes Satullo suggests?

Writing Assignments

Informal

1. Resisting change is a common human reaction. In your journal, write about your reactions and those of friends or family to a necessary or unavoidable change in your life.
2. Satullo says that people's resistance to new ideas is "sure as gravity" (3). In your experience, are there other annoying "sure as gravity" reactions?

Formal

3. **Collaborative Writing.** Satullo derides the predictability of people's responses to creative and positive suggestions: "That's no panacea." Brainstorm with your class to list other sayings that parents, teachers, bosses, friends, and group leaders use to discourage new ideas, different solutions, and changes in behavior. Divide into small groups, each one focusing on one type of interaction: parent-child, boss-employee, teacher-student, or organization leader–member. In your group, generate some typical examples of interactions that prompt naysaying and stonewalling. Then collaborate on an essay in which you make a case for openness to new solutions. You may choose to use a sarcastic style, like Satullo, or use a different approach, perhaps humorous, pleading, or serious, to your audience.

4. Satullo seems to be indicating that a partial solution to a problem is better than nothing, even if it's not a panacea. Taking a cue from Satullo, write an essay in praise of partial solutions or small steps to confront large problems. To develop support, think about social issues that never seem to get solved or about stubborn problems that are common among your peers, on campus, or at your workplace. Brainstorm to list small changes that might help improve or resolve the issue(s) and use these to build your case that partial solutions, or, as Satullo puts it, "lighting even one candle," can make a big difference.

■ ■ ■

The First-Year Student as Immigrant

JAY CHASKES

Jay Chaskes is professor of sociology at Rowan University and coordinator of the First-Year Seminar Program. This article was published in the *Journal of the Freshman Year Experience.* (Copyright 1996 by the University of South Carolina. Reprinted by permission.)

Abstract.   This paper offers a meaningful and unifying model for understanding the social and psychological dimensions of the student's transition from high school to college. This model rests on the analogy to the immigrant experience. The student's first-year experience is a process of resocialization to a new cultural environment very much like the process that immigrants experience upon their arrival in their new homeland. This resocialization process involves culture shock, "language" acquisition, and the internalization of academic, bureaucratic, and social norms as well as the values and expectations of the college milieu.

Although the academic community recognizes the transition of students from high school to college as problematic, it has failed to establish a single unifying frame of reference or a model to appreciate fully the social and psychological dimensions of this transition. Recently, some scholars have sought to review and evaluate a variety of developmental perspectives and the vast body of accumulating research regarding college as a transforming experience. In the past, some have sought to understand the student experience as analogous to a minority group experience (Farber, 1968; Horowitz, 1969). More recently both Horowitz (1987) and Moffatt (1989) have taken the ethnographic approach of the anthropologist. Others have sought to understand the student's environment from an ecological perspective (Banning, 1989). Bergquist (1992) has recently suggested that the academy may be understood as a complex of organizational cultures, but primarily from the perspective of the work environment of its employees.

This paper is an attempt to create a unifying model for viewing this transition. I propose that we understand the student's transition from from high school to college as if the student were an immigrant entering a country. Grinberg (1989), in his psychoanalytic exploration of immigration observes that, "Using migration as a metaphor, human development itself can be seen as a succession of migrations whereby one gradually moves further and further from his first objects" (p. 191). My purpose here is to create a meaningful and unifying model for those higher education professionals who interact regularly with first-year students or those responsible for formulating policy relevant to first-year students. My intention here is not to offer a comprehensive review of the most salient aspects of the first-year experience or to uncover some vital new element of it. Most recently, Erickson and Strommer (1991) have offered comprehensive and insightful observations about the first-year experience.

The Immigrant Analogy

3   Tinto's (1988) three stages in the process of institutional persistence—"separation, transition, and incorporation"—parallel the process of immigration and acculturation (p. 441). Oscar Handlin (1973), in his Pulitzer Prize-winning history of American immigration observed that,

> Emigration took these people out of traditional, accustomed environments and replanted them in strange ground, among strangers, where strange manners prevailed. The customary modes of behavior were no longer adequate, for the problems of life were different. With old ties snapped, men faced the enormous compulsion of working out new relationships, new meanings to their lives. (p. 5)

4   More recently, Pascarella and Terenzini (1991) in *How College Affects Students*, note in a parallel fashion that,

> One of the major transitions from high school to college involves the unlearning of past attitudes, values and behaviors and the learning of new ones. For students going away to college, it also means cutting loose from past social networks and established identities. In their place, new identities and interpersonal networks must be constructed, and new academic and social structures, attitudes, values, and behavior must be learned. This represents a major social and psychological transition and a time when students may be more ready to change than at any other point in their college career. (p. 650)

5   The immigrant analogy is apropos precisely because it contains so many of the same elements encountered by students when making the transition to college. Immigrants to a new land are not a random sample of the population from whence they come, but are more typically the younger, brighter, and more adventuresome of their native land (Gill, Glazer, & Themstrom, 1992). They migrate to a new land in the hope of improving their social and economic standing. Similarly, first-year students are often a select population of their age co-hort seeking to advance their economic and social position.

6   Just as immigrants often carry with them a set of myths about "the streets being paved with gold," so too do students bring with them a set of myths about what they will encounter in their "new homeland" (Gill et al., 1992, p. 317). Perhaps the most dangerous myth students bring with them is that their secondary school experience has prepared them for college life. Although we might not expect the students of parents who attended college to hold to this myth, undergraduate life of 25 or 30 years ago may prove to be an obsolete set of experiences.

7   Members of a host culture expect the immigrants to adopt their new culture, and so too do we expect first-year students to assimilate into the "campus culture." In addition, we ex-

pect these students to acculturate into their immediate local neighborhood (i.e., the particular college or university they are attending).

At the typical college or university, students do constitute a minority group in the sense that they are located in a socially and politically inferior position to the faculty, staff, and administration. Also, first-year students arrive as "green horns," who by virtue of having just arrived, are in a socially inferior position to students in their second year and beyond, themselves socially and politically inferior to faculty, staff, and administrators (Horowitz & Friedland, 1972).   8

Although the element of xenophobia is absent, students (particularly new students) do constitute a minority group in the sense that they occupy a socially and politically inferior position relative to faculty, staff, and administration. With regard to ability to create rules of conduct, set standards of performance, and participate in the process of institutional governance, students may be permitted to participate but are relatively powerless. Like the immigrant, students possess low social status within the community. Like immigrants who arrive with a lack of understanding about the structure and processes of government, first-year students view the governance structure as an amorphous and incomprehensible bureaucratic tangle of offices and titles. Their secondary school experience simply does not apply in higher education.   9

The Student as Immigrant

Culture Shock

Immigrants are often, upon arrival in their new homeland, simultaneously confronted with a number of new tasks that they find difficult to manage because the cultural experiences of their native land do not prepare them for these new tasks they face. They experience a form of "cultural shock" when all the old ways of accomplishing a variety of social and academic tasks are no longer useful. Research data suggest that both the academic and social aspects of self-concept experience a decline during the student's first year (Pascarella & Terenzini, 1991). Initially they revel in their new-found freedom, unencumbered by the constraints of close parental supervision. Culture shock may not overtake some students until well into the first semester (e.g., the "midterm slump").   10

Often by the middle of the first semester, it becomes apparent to the student that things are not as they should be. A vague sense of uneasiness begins to overtake the student as midterm exams are taken and as papers and other projects become due. Other students may already be experiencing the pangs of separation from their "homeland" and find themselves missing parents, siblings, friends, and the familiar environs of home. At the same time, they are coping with creating a *modus vivendi* with their roommate and with their "neighbors" in the residence halls. Creating and maintaining a social network with other new immigrants and with "natives" becomes an important part of adjusting to the new collegiate milieu. Few of them have had to work at it this assiduously before, and many may become too absorbed in the creation of a social network.   11

As with all newly-arrived immigrants, students must learn various skills and acquire certain knowledge bases before they can be recognized as citizens of their adopted country (i.e., they must successfully complete their first year of college). These skills and knowledge bases include communication skills, cultural rules and expectations, geography, performing as a "good citizen," and learning the community's services and structure.   12

Communication Skills

13   One of the most daunting tasks facing the immigrant is learning the language of the new country. Although first-year students are English-speaking, they do not understand nor can they speak "academese," the language of higher education. Students encounter titles of functionaries which they have never seen or heard before (e.g., "If you want a refund, you get the form from the *Registrar,* have it signed by the *Assistant Deputy Provost,* and then return it to the Office of the *Bursar.*"). Students are confronted with a bewildering set of initials symbolizing a variety of things (e.g., "You can use R.O.T.C. to pay for your B.S. in M.I.S. as long as it is listed on your F.A.F. and provided you are not enrolled in the College of L.A.S."). Terms, expressions, and abbreviations that simply roll off the professor's or counselor's tongue are often as strange as a foreign language to a new first-year student (e.g., "Only a matriculated undergraduate, who has completed all the distributive ed requirements including Soc ['Sock'] seven and Eco ['Echo'] three, but excluding any CLEP credits may enroll in an interdisciplinary Humanities or Soc Sci ['Sock Si'] Concentration.").

14   In addition to the jargon barrier, students are expected to have a reasonable facility with written and oral expression that is typically more demanding than what they have experienced or expect to experience. They have yet to learn and appreciate the linkages between writing and critical thinking which require a process of writing, rewriting, and editing. In this new "promised land," the student immigrants strongly hold to the myth that the natives (the faculty) produce books and articles by going from outline to printable text with no intermediate steps!

"Cultural" Rules and Expectations

15   The normative order that first-year students encounter in a collegiate environment appears to be much like the one they became so comfortable with in secondary school. However, students soon learn that they are "strangers in a strange land." It is a bit like an American's first trip to Great Britain. It is simultaneously very familiar and unsettlingly strange.

16   First-year students come to campus expecting a somewhat more sophisticated version of their secondary school experience. However, they quickly begin to encounter a new set of "rules of the game" which seem to be rather unfamiliar until the end of the semester nears and they have had time to experience their new cultural setting.

Professors and Academic Culture

17   Compared to their high school teachers, college professors may present a more aloof and distant demeanor. The student discovers that the rhythm of the professor's work day may limit when he or she might be seen. The comings and goings of the professoriate seem somewhat inscrutable. They do not seem to keep "school hours" (and in fact may not come to campus at all on certain days), some "vanish" for entire semesters while others seem to always be unavailable because they are attending a committee meeting somewhere on campus.

18   For students attending institutions with large lecture sections, the professor may seem very remote in a spatial as well as a social sense. The first-year student recognizes that the professor is very unlikely to ever learn the names of more than a few students in the class. In addition the student may encounter a new member of the community (i.e., the teaching assistant). The status of the teaching assistant (TA) is ambiguous to the student because the

TA is simultaneously a student and one who performs certain professorial tasks. In addition, the TA may function as a gatekeeper, controlling student access to the professor.

The student as immigrant begins to notice that professors make several assumptions   19
about the student's academic management skills. They assume that students can read and write at the level they are demanding, that they will use their study time wisely, and that they require few reminders of deadlines for assignments or the dates of examinations. The student encounters a bewildering variety of lecture styles among professors, ranging from the very formal and pedantic to the very Socratic and informal style of class discussion.

Some professors appear to be "word imperialists" who continually "oppress" the new   20
student with a vocabulary that is totally incomprehensible to the new immigrant. This perceived indignity is compounded by the professor's assumption that the burden of understanding (i.e., translating) rests with the student as immigrant. Some professors expect students to be active participants in the learning process while most students come to class with the expectation that the professor will tell them "what they need to know" in order to complete the class successfully (Karp & Yoels, 1991).

Professors may only offer the student two opportunities to be evaluated during the en-   21
tire semester. Quizzes, extra credit assignments, and unit exams are rarely encountered. The academic clock and calendar are much different from what they have previously experienced. Classes meet less frequently; marking periods are replaced by midterm and final exams; while semesters, trimesters, or quarters replace the school year. The workload increases at the same time that the pace at which the material is covered has quickened. Homeroom, late slips, hall passes, class period bells, and study hall become only memories. The rhythm of the school day, week, and year has been starkly altered. This lack of daily structure is erroneously identified by the immigrant as "free time." However, other areas of cultural rules and expectations also prove enigmatic to the student as immigrant.

Negotiating the Bureaucratic Maze

First-year students have accrued very little of the experience necessary for negotiating   22
the bureaucratic complexity of a college or university. Although subject to many bureaucratic rules and regulations, students previously negotiated any bureaucratic process under the supervision of parents or counselors. More importantly, students shared the responsibility and culpability for meeting their bureaucratic obligations with their parents.

College or university life presents a challenging bureaucratic environment for the first-   23
year student to manage. Like the immigrant who migrates from a rural community to an urban setting, the first-year student is thrust into a more formal, complex, and impersonal organizational environment than a secondary school milieu.

The student is expected to interpret established policy accurately and then successfully   24
participate in a wide variety of bureaucratic processes and procedures. The student is confronted with an imposing assortment of actual and potential interactions with a variety of persons in positions of authority. These may include four or five professors, the bursar, registrar, an entire assortment of residence hall staff, and department chairpersons to name only a few.

In addition, each organizational unit has its own set of rules and procedures that may   25
have no analogue anywhere else on campus. Thus the student must learn one set of rules regulating behavior in residence halls and another for Greek life or one set of procedures for financial aid and another set applying for on-campus work assignments. The same area of regulation may be subject to a variety of regulations depending upon the group affiliation

or bureaucratic unit. For example, the minimum grade point average as a threshold may vary for student participation in intercollegiate athletics, Greek life, academic honor societies, and an academic major with restricted enrollments.

26   First-year students often do not know what they need to know before attempting some process. For example, students do not learn how to withdraw from a course until they perceive their situation to be a crisis, and only then discover that they are beyond the deadline dates. They have yet to learn how to navigate through some of the more subtle roleplay within the bureaucracy such as the gatekeeper role of secretaries and the necessity of maintaining a file of transactions with the institution.

Non-Academic Life

27   As Moffatt (1989) asserts, most college students seem to define their college experience as composed of two approximately equally salient spheres of activity (i.e., the academic and the social). Moffatt (1989) notes that,

> Incoming freshmen usually had two goals for their first year in college: to do well in classes and to have fun (or to make friends, or to have a good social life). Older students looked back on college as either an even or a shifting mixture of work and fun. And students in college who were deviating from the ideal balance almost always knew that they were, and sounded defensive about it. (p. 33)

28   It would be erroneous to assume that this aspect of college life is considerably less alien or anxiety producing to the student than the changes the student is experiencing in the academic sphere of college life (Schwartz & Lever, 1976).

29   For many students, this is their first opportunity to exercise their eagerly anticipated autonomy fully. Along with its pleasures, first-year students find a bewildering array of social and personal tasks confronting them. These include doing one's own laundry, budgeting, and balancing a checkbook, establishing a *modus vivendi* with strangers now occupying the status of roommate and suitemates, and making friends and finding social activities from among virtual strangers.

30   For those first-year students who live more than a few hours from home by car, the first year may be riddled with bouts of homesickness. Without the frequent face-to-face social support of parents, siblings, household pets, friends of both genders, and the familiar sounds and aromas of home, assimilation for the student as immigrant is all the more discomforting.

Conclusions

31   I have argued that the transition of first-year students to the college experience is, in fact, a process of resocialization to a new cultural environment very much like the process of acculturation that immigrants experience in their new homeland. Unlike the immigrant, however, the first-year student is expecting the new cultural terrain to be very similar to the one the student has emigrated from. As the first semester or term begins, it becomes increasingly apparent to first-year students that they are "strangers in a strange land." They find themselves immersed in a rather complex cultural milieu that they must master in a relatively brief span of time.

32   Although orientation programs have a positive impact on ameliorating the difficulties of the first-year transition, extending these programs throughout the duration of the first

year has even greater benefits for the student (Pascarella & Terenzini, 1991, p. 651). I am suggesting that colleges should maximize the first-year student's opportunities to internalize the norms, values, and technology of their new academic, social, and bureaucratic cultural landscape. If the postmodernist thinkers, such as Gergen (1991) are correct, then "the relatively coherent and unified sense of self inherent in traditional culture" (p. 80) that we have so relied upon in the past will no longer easily respond to our traditional methods of orientation. Gergen's concept of "saturated self" suggests that identities are so bombarded with manifold relationships that the capacity of new college students to make a successful transition from high school is diminished.

It is a serious miscalculation to believe that students will assimilate to their new cultural surroundings in an efficacious and rewarding fashion without the programs, policies, and procedures that take specific aim at the resocialization process. For example, the traditional freshman orientation seminar must be integrated into one or more traditional academic programs in order for new college students to assimilate the values, expectations, and required skills. Residence life programs might do more to immerse students in the culture of higher education and its local campus version, its language, its values, and its expectations. We might do more to work with the parents of first-year commuting students to make them partners with their sons and daughters in the first-year experience process. We have, I believe, failed to appreciate fully the complex and multifaceted nature of the culture of the academic community and its implications for the first-year experience.

References

Banning, J. (1989). Impact of college environments on freshman students. In M. L. Upcraft & J. N. Gardner (Eds.), *The freshman year experience.* San Francisco: Jossey-Bass.

Bergquist, W. (1992). The *four cultures of the academy.* San Francisco: Jossey-Bass.

Erickson, B., & Strommer, D. (1991). *Teaching college freshmen.* San Francisco: Jossey-Bass.

Farber, J. (1968). The student as nigger. *This Magazine Is About Schools.*

Gergen, K. (1991). *The saturated self: Dilemmas of identity in contemporary life.* New York: Basic Books.

Gill, R., Glazer, N., & Thernstrom, S. (1992). *Our changing population.* Englewood Cliffs, NJ: Prentice-Hall.

Grinberg, L., & Grinberg, R. (1989). *Psychoanalytic perspectives on migration and exile.* New Haven: Yale University Press.

Handlin, O. (1973). *The uprooted.* Boston: Little, Brown & Co.

Horowitz, H. (1987). *Campus life: Undergraduate cultures from the eighteenth century to the present.* New York: Knopf.

Horowitz, I. L. (1969). The student as Jew. *Antioch Review* (Winter).

Horowitz, I. L., & Friedland, W. (1972). *The knowledge factory.* Carbondale, IL: Southern Illinois University Press.

Karp, D., & Yoels, W. (1991). The college classroom: Some observations on the meanings of student participation. In H. Robboy & C. Clark (Eds.), *Social interaction.* New York: St. Martin's Press.

Moffatt, M. (1989). *Coming of age in New Jersey: College and American culture.* New Brunswick: Rutgers University Press.

Pascarella, E., & Terenzini, P. (1991). *How college affects students.* San Francisco: Jossey-Bass.

Schwartz, P., & Lever, J. (1976). Fear and loathing at a college mixer. *Urban Life, 4,* 413–430.

Tinto, V. (1988). Stages of student departure. *Journal of Higher Education, 59*(4), 438–455.

Questions for Inquiry

1. What is Chaskes's claim? What does he indicate is his purpose in the essay? And what purposes does he disclaim?
2. What are the similarities between the situation of a first-year college student and an immigrant? What differences does Chaskes acknowledge?

3. What problems in language and communication do first-year students typically encounter? In the article itself, are there any places where the author's language or presentation style strike you as noticeably different from material you read for high school? Was his style a problem at times?
4. With the insight that first-year students are like immigrants, what kinds of programs should colleges and universities offer to help students make the transition to college life, according to Chaskes?
5. Who is Chaskes's intended audience? What characteristics of his text, its presentation and its style, indicate its audience?

Questions for Argument

1. Does the analogy of the first-year experience to the trials of an immigrant in a new land hold up for you? Are there any ways in which you think an immigrant has it harder than a first-year student? Or do you think there is more continuity between high school and college than Chaskes admits?
2. Do colleges do an adequate job of orienting students to their new culture? Do you feel that your college effectively helped you and other students resocialize to your new environment? Should this essay be a wake-up call for college officials to design comprehensive first-year student programming?
3. Are students "relatively powerless" on campus, compared with the permanent members of the college or university community, as Chaskes says (9)? If you think so, what examples are there on your campus of students being overpowered by faculty, administration, or staff? Does it matter to students that they are members of a fairly powerless group? Should it matter? What might change on your campus if students had equal power to faculty or administration?

Writing Assignments

Informal

1. What new aspects of college life were hardest for you to master? Write a journal entry in which you describe what ranked highest for you as an obstacle to feeling comfortable in your first months in college.
2. The author quotes one researcher who found that "students . . . who were deviating from the ideal balance [of work and fun] almost always knew that they were, and sounded defensive about it" (27). What is "the ideal balance" of the academic and the social parts of college life, in your opinion? Is the balance a personal matter, or is it much the same for everyone? Write an informal paper in which you present a definition and examples of the "ideal balance" in operation.

Formal

3. In a brief paragraph, the author points out that social life on campus can be just as "alien or anxiety producing" as any academic experiences (28). Write an essay in which you detail the ways in which campus socializing is "alien" to a student used to high school social life and comment on any "unlearning" you feel a student has to do to join in the college scene (4). You may want to frame your paper as a "warning" or as advice to the students a year behind you in high school Or you may want to direct the

paper at college officials, peer counselors, or residence fellows to awaken them to the fears, dilemmas, and pressures first-year students experience in their social lives.

4. **Collaborative Writing.** Brainstorm with a group of students to identify other analogies besides that of immigrant that would explain or express how it feels to be in a particular college situation—either positive or negative. For example, you might want to find analogies that express what it's like to live in a dorm, be an enforced pedestrian, pledge a Greek organization, exercise among huge college athletes and aging professors at the gym, or navigate a library several stories high. Or you may identify analogies that express the low social status of the first-year student, the distance between faculty and students, or the intimidation experienced by a novice trying to deal with college bureaucracy. Then, with your group, plan an essay in which you present some of these analogies; decide on a specific audience for your paper and develop it accordingly. For example, you may wish to design your paper as a warning or word of advice to the naive high school senior; or perhaps you will orient the essay as a humor piece to appear in a college publication. Assign each student or pair of students in your group to write an explanation of one of your chosen analogies in a paragraph-length section of the essay.

5. **Research Possibilities.** From this article, choose one quoted or paraphrased reference that interests you and trace it to its listing in the References. Then locate the source in your college library and read it (if it is an article) or skim and read it selectively (if it is a book). Choose a focused aspect of the article or book, take notes, and prepare a brief (ten-minute) presentation on the material to be given to your class.

■ ■ ■

Chapter 2

Reading as Inquiry

■ Consider the following excerpt, then respond as indicated below:

> What is everywhere passes unnoticed. Nothing is more commonplace than the experience of reading, and nothing is less well-known. Reading is taken for granted to such an extent that at first glance it seems nothing need be said about it.
>
> —Tzvetan Todorov, "Reading as Construction," *Genres in Discourse*

Writer's Journal

In your notebook, write informally to respond to this passage. Indicate your agreement or disagreement with Todorov's view, and write about your view of reading. What, in your opinion, do we do when we read?

> There can be no such thing as an innocent reading.
>
> —Louis Althusser, quoted by Warren Montag, "Reading Capital"

Writer's Journal

In your notebook, write informally to respond to this passage. What do you think Althusser means by this comment? Does he mean we read without innocence and therefore with "guilt"? Can you imagine a context in which an "innocent" reading takes place? Or a "noninnocent" (or "guilty" one)?

■ UNDERSTANDING READING

Our ideas have many sources—television, radio, the lunchroom, to give just a few examples. However, print media, ranging from newspapers to online computer databases to in-depth articles and scholarly books, are important resources for educated people. As a member of the academic discourse community, you will find that written sources of ideas matter most because, once written out, ideas and information hold still long enough to be examined, studied and recalled, evaluated, accepted, qualified, or refuted. Writing pins ideas down so readers can take a good long look at them.

Learning to be a college-level reader may involve some behaviors and skills unfamiliar to you. Most of the reading that goes on in our culture is not done at the college level and reflects less rigorous purposes. People read in order to learn to do something practical (grow a patio garden, interpret handwriting, improve memory) or to probe some behavior or phenomenon (understand dreams, comprehend the dynamics of addiction) or to escape (through romance novels, science fiction, or true-crime stories). Partially because these kinds of reading do not challenge our reading abilities, reading seems automatic to us. We don't experience our own reading so much as we look through it to gain entrance to a text. Reading seems like a transparent window.

Reading for ideas and complex information moves us away from the concrete goals of satisfying practical or emotional needs and challenges us to read at a higher level or, at the least, to read differently. Reading for specialized and expert knowledge in college and after involves skills beyond those you used to study in your high school courses. In college, you will encounter texts whose difficulty will "cloud" the window and reveal that reading is not just looking through glass. Rather, it is a transaction between the reader and the text and, ultimately, between reader and writer.

The Collaborating Reader

In any reading that you do, you seem to "take in" meanings, but actually you are using clues provided by the author to construct a meaning for yourself. You probably remember being taught that an imperative sentence, such as "Don't walk on the wet cement," has as its subject *you*, a word that is not actually in the sentence but that is "understood." Reading is always a case of "something understood," in the sense that there is much that is not written down on the page but that we understand to be there because we share the same discourse community as the writer. When we read works outside our discourse community, we may not be able to understand quite as well.

Reading as Inference

The process of understanding works through guessing or interpreting and inferring. In our daily lives, we use **inference** constantly when we look around at objects and events, make mental notes, and believe we know what is going on. We don't even notice the dozens of inferences we make each day. For example, when your neighbor shrieks "Here Kitty, Kitty, Kitty!" every few minutes, you infer that her cat has gone wandering. When a friend excludes you from a get-together, you infer that she is not really

■ *Activity 1*
Noticing Inferences, p. 61

your friend anymore. From the trivial to the significant, inferences are the foundation of our everyday life. Inference is the process of reasoning from the known to the unknown.

Likewise, when we read, we look at the text—mere spots of ink on a page or electrons shooting to a screen—and our mind registers meaning. We think thoughts that began in the mind of another, some of which we have never thought before. The act of collaborating with a writer to create meaning can pull us completely into the author's mind-set; this is why it can be easy to "believe everything you read."

Inferences are a delicate matter. You will likely discover that in a class discussion of an essay, many inferences made by different students will be coordinated; however, some inferences made by others will seem to go too far or to exaggerate or misinterpret a statement. Differences in personal experience, membership in different discourse communities, and different amounts of experience in reading arguments can prompt such variant interpretations. As longtime teacher of writing and literature Louise Rosenblatt puts it, "Each individual, whether speaker, listener, writer, or reader, brings to the [reader-writer] transaction a personal linguistic-experiential reservoir, the residue of past transactions in life and language" (381).

Group discussion benefits readers because it allows them to compare their constructions of meaning with others. Sometimes, such group discourse can lead to a general consensus about the meaning of a text; other times conversation reveals differences in interpretations that cannot be resolved.

Reading as Inference in Action

Read the following passage by Walter Ong. Then respond to the questions below.

> Many people like to believe that today reading is on the wane. We have all heard the complaint that television is ruining the reading habits of children. This is a contrastive judgment: "ruining" implies that all the time today's children spend before television sets yesterday's children spent with books. The implication appears at the very least naive (126–27).

Jot down your answers to these questions. If you are reading this text as homework, bring your responses to your next class for discussion.

- At what point in your reading did you begin to suspect that the author is distancing himself from the people he's describing?
- At what point could you tell that the author is criticizing an idea?
- What is the author's feeling about the idea he's critiquing? How can you tell?

In class, compare your responses to these questions with those of a group or your class, as your instructor chooses.

As you begin to construct the meaning of this passage, you might infer quite a few things on the basis of just the first clause, *Many people like to believe:* that the author may be pointing out these people because he's not among them; that the belief he's about to describe is more a whim than something proven (the word *like* suggests people hold the belief on the basis of personal preference), and, possibly, that a critique of the belief will follow. From the word *today,* you might infer that a comparison with the past is being constructed. The phrase *reading is on the wane* might strike you as a cliché, and a bit of a musty one at that, and reinforce the implication that this idea is a weak one. *We have all heard* implies you are on the author's side, for it joins you with him in the plural pronoun *we.* From the word *complaint* you might sense the charge is thin. And you immediately infer that television viewing is the culprit, not the television itself. From the rather vague phrase *ruining the reading habits of children,* you comprehend that a decrease in the amount of reading is meant.

So, even in two easy-to-read sentences, we use our powers of inference to gather clues as to the author's full message: his negative judgment about a common belief. Looked at this way, the text appears not to contain meaning but to provide hints so that you mentally fill in the gaps—make inferences—and create understanding. The informative or argumentative writer's job is to be in tune with the readers in the discourse community so that the reader doesn't notice this inferential process. This makes reading seem a transparent window. When a writer creates a text with too few gaps, a reader's mind has little to do, and the text may seem elementary. A text that provides too few clues to inference—that leaves many large gaps for the reader to fill—will seem difficult or obscure. When the text is accessible, the careful reader's job is to suspect the ease of reading, to inquire into and test the implied meaning of a text.

The Inquiring Reader

A good reader tries to become the reader that the writer wants to address: a reader "tries on" the role of audience to a writer. At least at the start, you need to enter willingly into the dialogue of ideas represented by the text. This can mean suspending your own point of view and balancing your preferences and biases with openness to divergent ideas. (Chapter 6 will examine the role of personal values in responding to texts.)

Reading complex material well involves more than just attentively reconstructing the text's meaning. Because the act of reading is involving and brings the reader in as cocreator of meaning, readers come to have a stake, as it were, in the text's meaning. Often, this means you will find it hard to challenge or question a text.

Being an inquiring reader means

- being prepared to enter the text's discourse
- uncovering assumptions, those beliefs that are "understood" or implicit in the text
- recognizing the writer's strategies

The Prepared Reader

Each reader is an individual who brings different abilities to reading a text. Some readers may know about the topic but be unaccustomed to reading a specialized text. Others might have less subject-related information but be used to reading specialized works in other fields. This reader might easily tolerate complex sentences and abstract language, even in an unfamiliar field.

■ *Activity 2*

Reading Difficult
Text, p. 61

Readers need to compensate for their own shortcomings in reading the text. For one text, this may be as basic as looking up new words in the dictionary. In other cases, a reader may have to seek some background knowledge in a reference work such as an encyclopedia. Or a reader may have to reread abstract language or slowly work through a difficult text.

In addition, a reader must have patience and read to understand the whole of a writer's ideas. You must beware of two "short-circuit" types of reading:

1. Don't assume that a writer whose ideas seem agreeable duplicates your opinion in every respect. Be careful not to "read in" your own point of view.
2. Beware of jumping to a negative conclusion and discounting the ideas of a writer you disagree with. Instead, suspend your evaluation until you fully comprehend the writer's point.

Uncovering Assumptions

A text's assumptions are ideas or values that a reader must believe in order to assent to the text's meaning. By bringing a reader's mind into the creative action of inferring its meaning, a text can sometimes make a reader feel that the assumptions are his or her own. By keeping its foundational beliefs unstated, a text can sometimes slide its assumptions into a reader's mind and into acceptance without the reader's being conscious that this is happening. Teasing out hidden assumptions that create validity for a reader is an important aspect of the analysis of logic developed by British philosopher Stephen Toulmin. Toulminian logic will be discussed in Chapter 6.

■ *Activity 3*

Reading for
Assumptions, p. 61

Look back at the short paragraph by Ong. In this passage, Ong is critiquing the commonplace belief he describes in the first two sentences. In his reading of this belief, he finds it to be based on a hidden assumption: that the children of yesteryear spent their leisure time with books. Ong is acting as an inquiring reader or interpreter of this commonplace idea. Once this assumption is exposed, the weakness of the argument becomes apparent.

Recognizing the Writer's Strategies

An inquiring reader also tries to identify the strategies of presentation that the writer of the text is using. How are ideas ranked? What is primary, and what is secondary? What reasoning and evidence appear in the text? What attitudes of the writer come through in the style of the text? The next section discusses argumentative strategies and shows how you can identify them in a text.

Reading Argumentative Writing

Argumentative writing includes a broad range of discussion about ideas and beliefs on a focused issue or subject. Such discussion may include writing that exposes, considers, evaluates, and advocates ideas. A reader should try to identify as soon as possible what argumentative goal the writer has. This goal might be any of the following:

- to argue for or demonstrate support for a position
- to critique or refute ideas

- to establish a middle ground between competing ideas
- to examine issues in order to locate questions that need to be answered

■ *Activity 4*

Recognizing Argumentation, Negotiation for a Middle Ground, Refutation, and Inquiry, p. 62

In this text, these various approaches to controversy—argumentation, refutation, middle ground, and inquiry—are covered in Chapters 7 and 8.

Argumentative writing requires that the writer devise a strategy to draw readers into the issue and convince them that the writer's perspective, whether critical or conciliatory, assertive or questioning, is the best one. Readers of argumentation need to examine the common elements in all these types of discourse:

- a focused position or claim about a controversial idea
- a strategy designed to affect the intended audience
- a pattern of development

Understanding the Claim of Argument

A reader of argumentative writing should be alert to recognize the claim about the issue in question. The **claim** is a statement of the author's position on the controversy or subject. Most arguable claims are refined—that is, they are stated to be true or accurate in a limited situation, a qualified period of time, or under a narrowed set of conditions. On any issue or topic, there is likely to be a range of possible positions, each qualified in a different way or oriented to a different result.

Here are some possible claims about the controversy over the phenomenon of young mothers who give birth secretly and abandon or kill their infants.

- Such young women are not a danger to the public and should receive intensive counseling.
- Such young women should receive harsh punishments, from stiff prison sentences for abandonment to the death penalty for murder.
- Such young women are not the only guilty parties; the father and the woman's parents or guardians should also be held partly responsible.
- Each such mother should be examined carefully and should receive counseling, be required to provide community service, or be imprisoned as appropriate.
- These cases are a sign that something is seriously wrong in our society; both health education and the instilling of values must be improved.

These variations show that claims do not exist in pairs of pro and con, for and against. There is often a range of possible positions on an issue because of variations in approach, differing values and assumptions, and so on.

The claim of an argument is often placed early in the text, but it doesn't necessarily have to be in the first few paragraphs. Sometimes, especially if a claim is unappealing to its prospective audience, the writer releases the claim in small bits or only hints at it later in the text. Sometimes the claim appears as a summative statement near the conclusion. Other times, writers imply their position; this strategy is common with ironic or satiric treatments and can also occur in arguments made through a narration of personal experience. Location is not a definite guide to identifying a claim. Rather, reading for meaning, to understand what is being argued, is the way to discover the claim.

Claims come in several flavors: there are claims of fact, claims of causation, claims of value, and claims of policy. Sometimes a claim is purely one type or another, but often showing the strength of one type of claim involves or depends on the validity of other claims of other types. Here is a brief discussion of the types of claims. (They are discussed in depth in Chapters 5, 6, and 7.)

Claims of fact aim to show that certain debatable facts are true or that a circumstance, situation, event, or idea should be labeled or defined a certain way. Whether cigarettes are addicting, whether children dominate the workforce in Chinese factories, whether officials of certain nations collaborate in the production and export of illegal drugs—all these are questions of fact.

Claims of causation express ideas about the origins, background, cause, or effects of some situation, event, belief, or change. Statements about whether the existence of welfare tempts people to become its clients, whether sex education has positive or negative or no effects on students, and whether part-time work decreases the academic achievement of high school students are all about causes and effects. Causal claims attempt to identify main causes or effects in the thick fabric of events and consequences in our lives and in the political, societal, and natural worlds. They are inherently complex.

Claims of value assert whether some thing, action, change, event, or situation is good or bad, right or wrong, foolish or impractical, beautiful or ugly. Assertions about the rightness of wetlands protection, the inappropriateness of the off-color humor in many television sitcoms, the excellence of Woody Allen's latest film all are claims of value.

Claims of policy propose actions, laws, changes in policies, and so forth in order to solve problems. Policy claims are complex because they are often based on a mixture of other claims of fact, causation, and value.

Return for a moment to the argument made by Ong in the passage above. What type of claim does he make? Is his claim explicit or implied?

Some discourses about controversies and societal problems raise questions or establish the need for inquiry rather than argue a position. When you are working with a publication that discusses alternatives, demonstrates the limits of our understanding or knowledge, or exposes the complexities and ambiguities of an issue, you will probably identify a question instead of a claim as the unifying force of the text. The inquiry can be explicit, as in this statement by Trudy Rubin, international columnist for the *Philadelphia Inquirer:*

> Will North Korea's current famine and its leaders' fear of national collapse drive its military to strike across the South Korean border where U.S. forces serve with South Koreans? Should America give North Korea tons of food aid to help the starving, and thus dissuade North Korea from resorting to violence? Or will that merely prolong the world's most repressive regime? . . . So what to do, when you are dealing with a regime whose behavior you can't fathom?

■ *Activity 5*

Recognizing Types of
Claims, p. 64

Or instead of actual questions, there may be implications about what we need to know, find out, or discover before we can get to work to resolve an issue. (Chapter 8 discusses the inquiry approach.)

Understanding the Intended Audience

A writer arguing a position has a special task—to maintain the reader's coopera-tion while yet pressing for acceptance of an idea. The reader must be led to think the writer's thoughts; the writer can't accomplish this feat without imagining the reader, gauging his or her attitudes, and strategizing accordingly. A writer who wishes, for ex-ample, to bring students to support a strike by campus cafeteria workers needs to think about what students might feel they have in common with the workers and what val-ues the two groups hold in common.

The arguing writer needs to take the reader's starting point in the discourse into account and build the argument from there. While readers use inference to construct a meaningful text in their own minds, an effective writer has also used inference—to imagine a typical reader—and has designed the text to be accessible and resonant to that reader, the "intended audience."

Inferring the intended audience is a good way to discover a writer's tack. A reader encountering argument should ask, who is supposed to be reading this argument? Does the writer expect an audience opposed to the claim? Or is the implied audience receptive, perhaps even already in favor? Or is the audience partial to some aspects of the argued position and not others? Is the audience mixed? confused? uncertain? or even apathetic?

As reader, you might be able to glean the writer's intended audience quite easily. Perhaps the introduction chides the audience for its ignorance or apathy. Or perhaps the writer begins by acknowledging the reader's likely negative attitudes to the writer's views. But other times, to determine the intended audience, you need to examine the tone and style, as discussed in Chapter 10.

Consider the passage above by Ong. What type of audience do you think he ex-pects? Are you, a student of college composition, a typical member of his intended au-dience? Would you say he uses *logos, ethos,* or *pathos* in this passage?

■ *Activity 6*

Recognizing Intended
Audiences, p. 64

Understanding Argument Development

Independent of which appeal is foremost, argumentative writing may be orga-nized in any number of ways. The classical writers on argumentation recommended one format, but there are many variations. In addition, in much argumentative dis-course, organization follows the internal logic of the author's angle on the subject or the development pattern the writer believes will best expose the strength of his or her position.

The ancient Greeks and Romans divided an argument into segments, each with its special purpose; much of today's writing still follows this organization or a variation of it, whether the writers are aware of the classical structure or not, because the classical pattern has a common sense logic to it. The five parts of the classic argument form are

1. the introduction, which leads the audience into the text and informs them of the author's position on the subject
2. the statement of facts, which provides information—such as the basic facts, what is currently known, or background information—necessary for under-standing the argument

3. the confirmation, which is the core of the argument, the demonstration or "proof" of the main point
4. the refutation, which disputes other opinions or views on the subject
5. the conclusion, which ends the discourse and may take one of several forms: summary, amplification of the idea, emotional inspiration, or a call to action, to name a few

There are many variations on the classical pattern. For example, the place in which the author discusses or deals with opposing ideas is extremely flexible. Sometimes writers decide to defuse opposing ideas before presenting positive evidence for the claim. Or the section presenting the background of the issue might incorporate a discussion of the opposition as well. Sometimes writers begin with refutation, using as an introduction a rebuttal of divergent views.

Two other variations of the classical format are the problem-solution format and the extended definition. In a problem-solution pattern, the description of the problem replaces the statement of facts, and the solution is presented as the "proof" of the situation. Opposing solutions can be rebutted before, during, or after the recommended solution is defended. In an extended definition, statement of facts may be replaced by a clear definition. The definition may then be developed through the use of additional strategies, such as description and narration of circumstances, environments, and events; illustration and examples; analysis of a process or system; analysis into classifications or segments; or analysis of cause and effect. These strategies are the same as those you may have studied in expository writing.

■ READING AND DISCUSSING

A Process for Reading Well

In *How to Read a Book,* writer and *Encyclopedia Britannica* editor Mortimer Adler explained not how to enjoy a book or escape in a book but how to understand a text by engaging in conversation with it—that is, by examining and responding to its ideas and presentation. "Reading, if it is active, is thinking, and thinking tends to express itself in words, spoken or written. The marked book is usually the thought-through book," he wrote in 1940 (304). When you are reading complex new material, you will want to use a reading process that helps you establish such an inner dialogue. The kind of reading recommended to you here is similar to that which Adler described.

Here are the recommended steps:

- preview
- skim
- clarify your goal
- read closely and annotate (or outline)
- analyze

- evaluate
- communicate

Preview the article or text by examining its title, its subtitle, blurbs, or teasers (if any), and any biographical note about the author. Then glance through the text to see how long it is and whether it is sectioned by headings or contains any visuals. These elements will often give clues to the article's focused subject, the central idea, or the writer's particular perspective. Through these clues, you can glean whether the writer's discourse community is congruent with your own and whether you share the same assumptions. For example, the biography of the writer of a newspaper opinion piece on Bosnia may tell you that she is an economics professor, and the title may signal that the article criticizes NATO policy. With these hints, you may be ready to focus in on job discrimination and other historic economic stresses between the Serbs and Bosnians—or you may decide not to read the article.

Skim to make reading efficient and improve your overall comprehension. In skimming, strive to cull sentences and phrases from the piece that indicate the writer's main idea. You might scan introductory paragraphs to identify the thesis statement, the writer's initial phrasing of the main idea to be developed by the text. You should definitely look at the end, to see whether there is a summative statement that represents the writer's idea in its wholeness. Or you might skim backward, searching near the end for a full thematic statement, and then skip forward, seeking stages or phases of the argument. Skimming helps you get the gist of a piece before diving all the way in.

Skimming should also give you a sense of the writer's intention and the kind of reading the writer expects. As Tzvetan Todorov has pointed out, "The text itself always contains an indication of the way it is to be read" (46). You should attend to clues that let you know whether the writer intends to shock you with a new approach, move you with a personal experience, take you into statistical depths, or whatever. In addition, when skimming, heed signs that imply a particular kind of reader, perhaps one with extensive knowledge of the subject or one with a sympathetic predisposition to the writer's ideas. You will need to put on that reader's hat, at least temporarily, to get the most out of the text.

Clarify your goal in reading the piece. After skimming, you may feel the essay offers crucial evidence on the subject or an innovative point of view. Or you may conclude that it is a rehash of ideas and information you have already encountered or that, despite its run-of-the-mill treatment of the issue, it includes statistical evidence you've not seen before. Or perhaps you realize it's an amusing piece that plays with the subject in a humorous way. At this point, come to a conscious decision about what you'll be looking for as you read.

Then, **read closely** and **annotate.** You will be reading to understand the author's ideas and taking notes on major points and questions you have. If you are reading with a purpose, you might safely skim much of the article and concentrate your annotating on sections that relate to your goal. For example, if you are hoping to pull out references to wrongly applied capital punishment or to locate arguments that challenge your views about freedom of speech as applied to flag burning, you will read with special radar on. You might bypass whole paragraphs in order to focus on those that contribute to your goal.

The activity of annotating while you read is likely to improve your attention to the text, as would any other physical activity. Note taking, reading aloud, pacing, or even rocking in your seat can keep you alert and your mind on its task, be it reading, studying, or memorizing material.

The annotation techniques you use depend on whether the text is your own, belongs to someone else, or is downloaded. Your own books, periodicals, or photocopies can be annotated right on the page. Annotations include underlining, bracketing, and highlighting and also making margin notes, jotting down queries, noting connections with other ideas in and outside the text, and reacting to and commenting on the ideas. Note that highlighting is only one facet of annotating a text. As much as you might like dabbing your texts with pink or green, highlighter pens don't allow you to write words.

If you are working with a borrowed or library text, you should, of course, avoid making any marks. So, for any text that is not yours, make a photocopy. Or jot your notes on a card or notebook page. Some people use stick-on notes placed so their edges are visible and later transfer them to a notebook.

If you are doing your research online, you will end up with articles filed on your hard drive or floppy disk. Most people prefer to print out downloaded files for careful reading and annotating. If you are reading in preparation for writing, don't trash your file after you print; if you wish to quote from the text, you can transfer the quotation directly from the article on-screen rather than retype it from your printed copy. Especially for long quotations, transferring text from one file to another saves your weary fingers, and it ensures accuracy.

Some people do take notes on-screen. They might highlight important ideas by using bold or underlining. They might use a different typeface (font) or enclose their own comments or questions in square brackets after paragraphs or sentences. (Square brackets are used to include comments in a text by someone other than the author, say an editor. They look like this: [ ].) If you alter a downloaded text, be careful to indicate clearly what comments are yours. Later, if you wish to quote from or refer to the article in your own essay, you should be able to identify your own comments. You don't want to quote yourself by mistake and attribute it to the source—or, vice versa, quote the source without attribution because you think the quotation is your own writing.

If you are going to be using a text for formal research, you should annotate or take notes in a special way. For example, you need to keep track of the page numbers from which you take notes and be clear in your own mind as to whether notes you have taken use your wording or that of the source. Taking notes for formal research is covered in detail in Chapter 12.

Once you have annotated the text, you then **analyze** it. During your close reading, you will have noticed textual features. Perhaps the way the writer has ordered ideas has become apparent; unusual comparisons may strike you, or some other matter of style, organization, or approach may catch your eye. Readers often read on more than one level at once and are attentive to many features of a text, even if they are concentrating for the moment on one aspect.

Such secondary impressions should be the starting place for analyzing to determine how the piece creates its argument. At this stage, you should notice where examples and evidence are offered, where exceptions or problems are mentioned, and whether opposing positions are discussed. If the article is complex, you should build an outline or create a map to reflect the structure of the text. Outlining is covered later in this chapter. (Examining a text for its approach will be covered in Chapter 10.)

Evaluation grows naturally from examining the writer's approach. You might answer such questions as: Is the text convincing, competent in its use of facts and evidence, coherent in its presentation of ideas? Does it contain unfounded assumptions and extreme interpretations, or does it focus and qualify its interpretations? In this stage you are evaluating the writer's interpretation of the evidence and forming a judgment about the piece as a whole. Techniques to use in annotating and analyzing a text are provided later in this chapter.

Communication about a text is the last step in the reading process. By framing our meaning so as to explain it to another, we come to terms with what we think. Communicating can take many forms. You may be able to discuss a text with others in a class or in an informal college setting. Or you may communicate your perceptions by free writing, journal writing, or other informal or personal writing. Or you may be assigned formal writing about some aspect of the text. Whatever type of communication you engage in, it will complete the reading process.

From Reading to Discussion

A discussion about a text is a collaboration. The participants put forward and compare their inferences and interpretations, their questions, their comments, and their evaluations. The goal is to supplement each other's understanding by using unique backgrounds and discourse experiences to create full interpretations of the text. Through this, blindered interpretations can be challenged and necessary further inquiries identified.

Effective group discussions have a few things in common:

- participants who have read the text
- a clear goal or "charge"
- a leader or facilitator
- active, pertinent contributions by participants
- active, focused listening by participants
- helpful coleadership by participants

Participants Who Have Read the Text

Group members must first privately engage the text. A discussion group member who forgot to do the reading, who never got beyond the skimming stage, or who read only the first few paragraphs has chips to put into the pot. (Of course, some people can discuss with seeming knowledge after reading two sentences, but most of us are not so skilled in the art of "blabbing shamelessly.") The nonreader cheats the group of his or her responses and loses out on the chance to relate his or her relevant experiences to the text.

A Clear Goal and a Leader

Unless they are very experienced in the discussion process, groups also need a definite task to accomplish. In a whole-class discussion, the instructor guides the discussion toward certain goals by prompting responses or suggesting questions. In a class broken into small groups, the instructor can set goals for each group. Another approach is for the group to brainstorm a list of key places or points in the text that invite inquiry. This list can serve as a discussion agenda, and one group member might serve as monitor to keep members moving through the list.

Active, Pertinent Contributions by Participants

Groups also need members who speak up, listen attentively, and cede the floor willingly to others. Individuals differ in their abilities to participate well in a group. Any group may have one or two of the following: over-talkers, butt-iners, and sideline-hangers, all types who need to modify their discussion-group personalities. But most participants will try to be calm, intelligent contributors and sensitive listeners.

Active, Focused Listening by Participants

Listening is a skill, many people are surprised to learn, and it's a skill that tends to lose out when students are given experiences in public speaking, panel membership, debating, and so on. Following this section there are some tips to improve your ability to listen in a group.

Helpful Coleadership by Participants

Group participants are entitled to guide the group process when it seems necessary. For instance, a member might call the group's attention back to to the main theme of the discussion after work on a minor point, a personal reaction, or someone's experience tie-in. Or one person might see the need to "push the hold button" and seek clarification (see the next section in this chapter). Or a member might have an insight about the discussion itself that can improve it; perhaps, for example, a disagreement is occurring because group members are using words differently. Members can and should assist the group process because the leader may not see the need or may be distracted, taking required notes, checking the agenda, or whatever. But members should resist taking over a role that has not been assigned or delegated to them.

Improving Listening and Responding

It can be hard to pay attention to someone else's ideas if your own mind is buzzing with things to contribute. We are all distracted by our inner streams of consciousness as well as by external factors: a noisy group nearby, music floating through an open window, and so on. And few of us have ever paid much attention to how we listen or whether we could be better at the task. Here are some tips for improving your listening:

- Take action against distractions. Close the window or the door; move your group further away from a noisy one; request a lowering of the volume if persons nearby are shouting or laughing loudly.

- Make sure you know the names of everyone in your group. It's hard to focus on content when the person isn't "real," doesn't have a name or identity. In an ongoing group, spend a few minutes at the first meeting introducing yourselves by name and interests, major, and so forth.
- Look at the person who is speaking as much as possible. Politely request a louder tone if you can't hear.
- Make a brief note, of just a word or phrase, to signal what point each person contributes.
- Use the "say-back" technique. If you aren't sure you understand or if the point is subtle or complex, say back what you think you heard so the speaker can agree you have it right or can correct you.
- Request that a person repeat an idea if you are sure you didn't get it. You may do this at the end or by politely interrupting the speaker. However, if you keep missing points because your attention is elsewhere, don't keep asking for repetitions. Signal that you'd like to take a look at your neighbor's notes, and try to pick up the discussion from there.
- Use encouraging and supportive body language. Lean forward as you listen. Nod, not necessarily in agreement, but to indicate you're in receiving mode.

▪ *Guidelines for Discussing Texts*

These are suggestions and are hardly carved in stone. Your instructor may have variations on these for you to follow.

1. Be prepared:
   - Privately, identify ideas, paragraphs, and so on that you think need discussing: these areas may prompt doubts or raise questions, may move you strongly or annoy you because of the presentation, may seem major, conclusive, or decisive.
   - Then prioritize these items so that you have your own "private agenda" as you go into the discussion.
   - Some of your items will be on others' lists as well. Be aware, however, that in the time allotted the group may not be able to cover every item on each member's list.

2. When you speak, keep focused on the text you are discussing. Make sure your comments are tied to some statement in the text.

3. When you speak, help everyone to "be on the same page" by referring to the specific statement, paragraph, or sentence you are going to comment about.

4. Reserve comments about other texts or information, discussions of the text's personal meaning for you, and broad evaluations for near the end of the discussion, unless these are part of the group's goal.

Responding to others can also be an art: you can do it constructively or crudely. Here are some pointers for responding:

- Wait for the end of a comment before adding your own remarks, moving on, disagreeing, or critiquing the ideas. If you're afraid you'll forget what you want to say, jot your idea down for reference. Politely squelch others' interruptions by saying, "Hold on, I don't think [name] is finished."
- Keep the environment "safe" by responding appropriately for the goals of the group. If your mission is to brainstorm, critiquing is usually out of order. If the goal is to open up possible interpretations and air questions, heavy criticisms might dampen the flow. In general, remember that most people are hurt by criticisms, so use a light touch.
- Disagree with ideas, not with people. Keep your disagreements analytic and specific. Make sure you understand the person's idea before you criticize it. Definitely stay away from broad swipes like "That's ridiculous!" and "You've got it completely backwards!"
- As an alternative to criticism or direct disagreement, consider a sideways move: propose alternate ideas or suggest another approach.

■ TECHNIQUES FOR INQUIRY INTO TEXTS

To come to terms fully with complex texts, you need a few special skills. Annotating, outlining, and mapping are discussed in the pages that follow. In Chapter 3, you will learn about paraphrasing and summarizing. After you have finished this section, use the reading selections by Louis Sullivan and Thomas Friedman at the end of the chapter to practice annotating, outlining, and mapping texts.

Annotating

Annotation is a kind of "anything goes" activity, you'll be glad to know. Pencil in hand, you can underline, circle, bracket, and draw arrows, and you can jot down your reactions, questions, comments, criticisms, and, well, anything else that helps you come to terms with what you are reading. People use words, punctuation marks, recognized symbols like the asterisk (*), check mark, and X, and sometimes private marks, made-up words, and terms used in a private way (zigzags or arrows, for example) to indicate their responses to their reading.

Responses might be emotional: "great!" "true," "I disagree," "yuck," and "ugh." And they can be questioning: "why?" "where's the proof?" "are figures available on this?" They might be interpretive: "shows different concepts of marriage." They might be evaluative: "fallacy here," "all generalizations," or "plays to reader's emotions."

Figure 2.1 reproduces student Sharla Gilroy's annotations to a passage from the essay "Television and the Shaping of Cognitive Skills" by Renée Hobbs (a reading selection at the end of this chapter). You can see that Sharla uses underlining to highlight important concepts. She uses arrows to point out unknown words and margin notes on the left to clarify definitions for herself. In some places, she notes important ideas in her own words or pulls out key concepts and places them in quotation marks ("edit

■ *Activity 7*
Annotation Practice, p. 65

early 1900s

fan ———

The relationship between television and attention is the area in which we have the best evidence for understanding television's influence. Writing in the early years of the twentieth century, Hugo Munsterberg was the first experimental psychologist recruited by William James at Harvard to begin the experimental laboratory. He was also an aficionado of film, which in the beginning of the twentieth century was exploding with creative new techniques and devices for manipulating the expressive potential of the medium. Munsterberg made some remarkable observations about the similarities he saw between editing conventions and attention. He viewed the close-up as an externalization of the process of paying attention, and in the same way, viewed the flashback as a technique for representing memory just as the flash-forward externalized the mental skills of imagining.[7]

It is absolutely remarkable to read a psychologist more than 70 years ago making these observations and, although the argument seems somewhat simplified in retrospect, it represents the first time psychologists looked at the relationship between the products that we use in creating film and video and the processes that we use inside our head.

from experience or experimentation ———→ We have more empirical evidence on the relationship between children's attention and editing conventions than about most other topics in the field of media studies. Researchers know that young children between the ages of two and five seem compelled to attend to editing conventions, and certain editing conventions draw the attention of children more than others.[8] Those editing conventions are ones that include high movement, rapid pacing, lots of edit points, and loud music. These editing conventions are intense in the use of movement that is perceptually salient, which compels attention. Researchers have discovered that

very noticeable ———→ young children are compelled to watch the screen when those editing conventions are used, but that over time, children are able to control their attentional behavior; that is, older children are not so compelled to watch the screen when those editing conventions are used. This bears a close relationship to what we know about the human perceptual system. Our eyes are designed to actively monitor change. It is built-in, hard-wired, as it were, into the perceptual system.[9] Younger children don't have very much control over using that perceptual system, and so they are compelled to watch the intense movement on the screen. And those of us who have seen children that age watching television can see the intensity with which their attention is drawn to the screen. Older children are better able to mediate their attentional skills and control that behavior.

Editing parallels attention
① close-up = paying attention
② flashback = memory
③ flash-forward = imagination

outer & inner processes similar

research on kids 2 to 5 drawn by movement
fast pacing, "edit points," loud music ⌐ *part of editing??*

"compelled to watch" older kids less compelled

eyes meant to monitor change little kids can't control eyes

FIGURE 2.1 Annotations

points"; "compelled to watch"). She inserts a question in square brackets and punctuates it with two question marks.

Outlining

Outlining is a formal technique for mapping out the internal logic of a text, either someone else's or your own (before or after you write). Most people are familiar with the structure of a formal outline—and most people have been overwhelmed with the tediousness of creating an outline. But outlining can pay off because it gives you a sense of mastery, not only over meaning but over the journey the author takes to expose, develop, and nail down that meaning for the reader.

Outlines move from big to small, from major to minor, in a series of waves or indentations. They result in a logical, down-the-page stretch of points from the start to the end of the outlined text:

    I.
      A.
        1.
          a.
          b.
        2.
          a.
          b.
      B.
        1.
          a.
          b.
        2.
          a.
          b.
    II.
      A.
        1.
          a.
          b.
        2.
          a.
          b.
      B.
        1.
          a.
          b.
        2.
          a.
          b.
   and so on

A complete outline is one that accounts for all the information and ideas in a text. Often, however, your need to understand a text is motivated by a research question or inquiry, and you will not need a complete outline; rather you will outline only the portions of the text that pertain to your inquiry.

An efficient process for generating a complete outline follows. It can be easily adapted to the task of outlining a portion of a text.

Process

Before you start, preview, skim, and read closely the text to be outlined (as described above). If you try to "outline as you go" while skimming, you will probably do both ineffectively. The most efficient method of outlining requires that you do a full careful reading first to get a strong sense of the meaning and the overall flow of development.

The outlining itself does not require that you read straight through the article again, meticulously entering each point, subpoint, and sub-subpoint (and so on) on your outline. Rather, it is more effective and more enlightening to search the article for points of a certain level. In other words, your first outlining step is to look through the article for points I, II, III, IV, and so on, finding the major points the author is making. This means that in a broad way you will outline the entire article in your first step. Then, go quickly through the article again, finding the next layer of points—A, B, C, and so on. You will have deepened the complete outline by one layer after this step. At this point, depending on the level of detail you want for your outline, you will return to point I. A in the article and search for details or subpoints that would fill out the 1, 2, and 3 level, and perhaps add details to fill the small letters, a, b, c. After finishing the outline for the I. A section, you will go on to complete the I. B section, and so on.

This method gives you quick control of the entire article's meaning and development. This can keep you from getting bogged down in the details of the early sections and running out of steam as you descend the outline. And it can help take the tediousness out of the outlining process.

Here's what the method looks like in brief:

- Preview, skim, and read closely.
- Make a top-level outline of the major sections of the text: points I, II, III, and so on.
- Fill in the next layer of points—A, B, C, and so on.
- Fill out the 1, 2, and 3 level of I. A, and fill the small letters, a, b, c, with details if possible.
- Continue for I. B; II. A and II. B; III. A and III. B; and so on.

Sample

Here is a possible outline for the article "Television and the Shaping of Cognitive Skills" by Renée Hobbs. Only the second section of this outline is done completely. It is important to realize that individuals outlining this article may use different wording.

Also, sometimes people differ in their interpretations of what is a major point and what is subsidiary because not all writers are strictly logical in their presentations; sometimes writers "go with the flow" of how their explanations work out in the drafting stage. This can mean, for example, that a major point is introduced in the middle of a paragraph rather than at the start or that a major point grows out of a minor one and seems both major in terms of content but secondary in terms of where it is presented. The placement of such a point on the outline is ambiguous, and different outliners might do it differently.

■ Make a top-level outline of the major sections of the text: points I, II, III, and so on:

  I. Introduction: Television's Influence
 II. Television and Attention (6 paragraphs)
III. Television and the Skills of Organization and Interpretation
IV. Television and the Skills of Prediction and Expectation

■ Fill in the next layer of points—A, B, C, and so on:

  I. Introduction: Television's Influence
    A. Influence by content much studied
    B. Influence by form also possible
    C. Specific techniques relate to mental processes
    D. Experiment to show television imitates natural mental actions
 II. Television and Attention (6 paragraphs)
    A. Best evidence for television's influence is in the area of television and attention
    B. Early understandings about attention and film techniques
    C. Much research exists on children's attention and television
    D. Television formats and attention
    E. Debate about television causing degeneration of attention
III. Television and the Skills of Organization and Interpretation
    A.
    B.
IV. Television and the Skills of Prediction and Expectation
    A.
    B.

■ Fill out the 1, 2, and 3 level of I. A, and fill the small letters, a, b, c, with details if possible (here, section II. A is shown; there are no subpoints for II. A in this article):

 II. Television and Attention
    A. Best evidence for television's influence is in area of television and attention.

- Fill out the 1, 2, and 3 level of I. B, and fill the small letters, a, b, c, with details (here section II. B and its subpoints are shown):

    B. Early understandings about attention and film techniques
       1. Hugo Munsterberg
          a. experimental psychologist at Harvard
          b. early twentieth century
       2. observed similarities between editing conventions and attention
          a. close-up is like paying attention
          b. flashback is like memory
          c. flash-forward is like imagining

- Continue for II. A and II. B; III. A and III. B; and so on (here continuing from II. C is shown):

    C. Much research exists on children's attention and television
       1. children two to five "compelled" to watch
       2. editing conventions that attract young children
          a. high movement
          b. rapid pacing
          c. many "edit points"
          d. loud music
       3. eyes built to monitor change
          a. young children can't control eyes
          b. older children and adults can control
    D. Television formats and attention
       1. predictability of types of shows
       2. allows audience to selectively pay attention or not
       3. multiple activities possible while viewing
    E. Debate about television causing degeneration of attention
       1. much discussed but not much evidence
       2. fragmented images and sounds paralleled in our attention
       3. viewers come to prefer fragmentation over continuous
       4. long attention spans become difficult

Differences in Outlining

The sample outline above identifies points as they are cued by the first sentences in paragraphs:

II. A—paragraph 9, sentence 1, on amount of research
II. B—paragraph 9, sentence 2, on early researchers
II. C—paragraph 11, sentence 1, on amount of research on children's attention
II. D—paragraph 13, sentence 1, on television formats
II. E—paragraph 14, sentence 1, on debate about attention degeneration

In this way, this outline is controlled by the writer's paragraphing. But another way of outlining this text would be to recognize that this section of Hobbs's article discusses three types of formal techniques that influence attention: editing conventions like rapid pacing and numerous edits (paragraphs 9–12); the predictability of formats (13); and fragmentation (14–15). Here's what this section would look like if analyzed this way:

> II. Television and Attention
>   A. Editing conventions like rapid pacing and numerous edits
>   B. Predictability of formats
>   C. Fragmentation

■ *Activity 8*

Outlining Practice, p. 66

This outline would not be incorrect, just different in emphasis from the sample outline.

Mapping

Mapping is a technique that allows you to draw a plan of a text by using phrases and connecting lines instead of outlining it. Some maps move down the page like a journey to a destination, as in Figure 2.2.

Another mapping technique, sometimes called bubbling, involves placing the main idea in a bubble in the center of the page. Secondary ideas are represented by spokes coming out from the main bubble, as in Figure 2.3.

Process

The first stage of mapping consists of writing the main idea in the starting position. Then the first point and its subpoints can be added in either branches or smaller bubbles flowing off the main one. When another important point is encountered, it is attached to the idea it flows from, and its branching subpoints flow from it. See Figures 2.2 and 2.3.

■ *Activity 9*

Mapping Practice, p. 66

Sample

Figure 2.4 is a map representing one reader's journey through the Hobbs article.

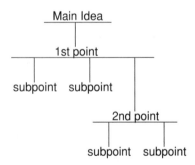

FIGURE 2.2   Mapping

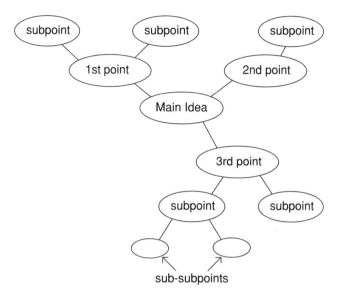

FIGURE 2.3 A Bubble Map

■ THE WRITING READER

In the world of the professions, writing and reading hold a larger place than many students realize. A survey of recent college graduates of seven academic departments conducted by a professor at Miami University in Ohio, as reported by Paul Anderson, indicated that 69 percent of respondents spent more than 10 percent of their work time writing. Thirty-eight percent indicated that writing took up more than 20 percent of their time, with 15 percent writing more than 40 percent, or two days' worth of time on the job per week. In addition, the alumni indicated that writing well at work was important. As Anderson notes, "Ninety-three percent said the ability to write well would be of at least 'some importance.' Fifty-seven percent stated that it would be of 'great' or 'critical importance' " (17–19).

In the community of learners on any college campus, reading is done not for its own sake but in order to participate in knowledge making and idea forging, the major activities of the academic discourse community. People read not just to understand but to use the ideas and information in creating their own formulations.

Readers choose how to read each text that comes their way in accordance with their particular goal. Sometimes a reader reads a text for its emotional wallop. Other times, a reader might seek to understand a writer's view or glean information and evidence. If a reader is reading extensively on a topic, the goal may be to compare different texts or writers' views or to pull material from disparate sources into one coherent statement. Sometimes, of course, writers have a combination of goals when they approach a text.

FIGURE 2.4 One Reader's Bubble Map of Renée Hobbs's Article

The rest of the chapters in this book present the many uses that readers have for texts and discuss the various writing responses that readers might have. The list below presents some possible reading goals, followed by the kind of writing such a reader would produce.

- emotional response (journal, sketchbook, or reaction piece)
- understanding meaning (paraphrase and summary)
- understanding structure, development, procedure of the writer (analysis)
- gaining information (note taking, paraphrase, targeted summary)
- comparison with another piece (comparison)
- combining ideas or information (synthesis, Rogerian argument)
- contrast with another piece (refutation)
- support a claim (argumentation)

Activities

1   Noticing Inferences

For a few hours, during an active part of your day, keep a small notebook handy and try to notice and write down inferences you make during this time.

2   Reading Difficult Text

Locate a few paragraphs of text that you find quite difficult to read. You may copy a page in an upperclass student's textbook or browse in the library for an advanced book in an unfamiliar field, for example. Read the passage several times, each time noticing what you do to try to comprehend it. Keep a record of the strategies you use, so that you have a record of your personal reading process for difficult texts. Bring your list of strategies to class for discussion.

3   Reading for Assumptions

A.   Examine this passage by Rush Limbaugh. What assumptions must you make to concur with Limbaugh's assessment that the media elite have become "more transparent"?

> Seeing themselves as sacrosanct, the self-important media elite have adopted a religious zeal toward the [media] business—which they actually consider a "mission." I pointed this out in my first book, but the situation has gotten both worse and more transparent. The Washington *Post*'s advertising campaign for new subscribers states it bluntly, "If you don't get it, you don't get it." Fortunately, most Americans don't get it.
>
> Meanwhile, the *New York Times Magazine* promotes itself as "What Sunday Was Created For," which might amuse the Creator, whom, I suspect, had something very different in mind when He did the creating. But that's just it. What you have here is the arrogance of power. And that is why so many people are looking elsewhere, and increasingly to me.
>
> —Rush Limbaugh, "Voice of America: Why Liberals Fear Me"

B.   What assumptions underlie this passage by columnist Molly Ivins?

> Whenever I hear particularly dippy public policy proposals or pronouncements on welfare reform or school vouchers, I make the same mistake. I keep wondering: "Don't these people know anyone on welfare? Don't they ever talk to poor folks? Haven't they ever spent any time in a ghetto, in an unemployment office, at a day-labor shape-up?" Well obviously, of course not. What a dumb question.
>
> Economic segregation is so marked in this country that we have almost no opportunities to get to know or even see people from different economic classes—no Army draft, very little public transportation, not much school integration, few public places. Middle-class Americans whiz from hither to yon in our subsidized automobiles, at most driving past "where the poor folks live" with the doors locked. Unless you have a rather unusual calling—social worker, cop, teacher in a ghetto school, or even newspaper reporter on assignment—you're unlikely to encounter people from other classes, much less get to know them.
>
> —Molly Ivins, "Life in the Other America"

C. What assumptions can you find in this passage?

> Your Senate has devised a simple way to "save" Medicare, the health program for America's retirees: Don't give it to them.
>
> With no analysis, no discussions and no debate, the Senate voted to raise the Medicare eligibility age to 67 from 65 over the next two decades. If this becomes law, workers now in their 40s and 50s who thought they would be covered by federal health insurance when they retire at 65 could now face up to two years during which they will have to obtain private health insurance. . . .
>
> How can the Senate be so callous? For one thing, the senators themselves are all covered by health insurance. For another, fewer than 20 of the 100 senators have ever worked in a normal employer-employee job—and even fewer have any experience of what it means to drive a truck or lay bricks at age 65.
>
> —Lars-Erik Nelson, "Medicare: The Unkindest Cut of All for Baby Boomers"

4   **Recognizing Argumentation, Negotiation for a Middle Ground, Refutation, and Inquiry**

Examine the following passages. Which argue or advocate for a position? Which strive to be convincing about a middle ground? Which refute an opposing idea? Which offer inquiry as the best approach to an issue?

[A]   Unions developed because teachers thought they needed them. Before unions, teachers were paid far less than other educated workers. Unions helped raise the pay scale to a decent level, though it is still far lower than the scales of other professionals like doctors or architects or accountants. Before unions, teachers were often compelled to punch a time clock and bring a written excuse from a doctor if they were sick. They were routinely ordered to give up lunch periods to monitor the cafeteria or the toilets. . . . Before unions, teachers could not take part in politics on their own time, and most places, they couldn't even have a beer in a pub.

—Albert Shanker, "Blaming Unions"

[B]   Why has civilization resulted in the most enormous augmentation of human violence since the human species first evolved from its primate forebears? I believe that that question can only be answered by taking into account the psychology of shame. Shame not only motivates destructive behavior, it also motivates constructive behavior. . . .

But—and this is the crux of the matter—this same emotion, shame, that motivates the ambition, activity, and need for achievement that is necessary for the creation of civilization also motivates violence. And when the enormous increase in technological power that civilization brings with it is joined to the enormous increase in violent impulses that shame brings with it, the stage is set for exactly the drama that the history (that is, the civilization) of the world shows us—namely, human social life as an almost uninterruptedly escalating series of mass slaughters, "total" and increasingly genocidal wars, and an unprecedented threat to the very continuation . . . of the human species for the sake of whose survival civilization was invented in the first place.

—James Gilligan, *Violence: Reflections on a National Epidemic*

[C]   Since 1981, American taxpayers have spent $23 billion on international drug control. Yet drug supplies have increased substantially both at home and abroad. Worldwide opium production has more than doubled in the past decade and now exceeds 3,400 tons per year, the equivalent of 340 tons of heroin. From 1984 to 1994, coca production almost doubled, although the United States provided more than $2 billion in narcotics-control assistance to Bolivia, Colombia, and Peru, the world's largest coca producers. Meanwhile, drug prices in the United States have fallen precipitously. . . . The administrator of the Drug Enforcement Administration (DEA), Thomas Constantine, testified before the House International Relations Subcommittee on the Western Hemisphere in March 1995 that "drug availability and purity of cocaine and heroin are at an all-time high."

—Mathea Falco, "U.S. Drug Policy: Addicted to Failure"

[D]   There is no escaping the need for American involvement in the events of the globe, just as there is no denying that the United States cannot be the world's policeman. Americans cannot and should not take on every cause. The United States alone cannot counter every threat to world peace. Moreover, it should hesitate to intervene militarily where victory is unlikely or where the price of victory cannot be justified by the most thoughtful and articulate U.S. leaders.

     Nevertheless, given the American interest in preserving and promoting its way of life and in making the world a better place, the promotion of world order and humanitarian values fairly deserves an important role in U.S. foreign policy.

—Robert I. Rotberg, "Clinton Was Right"

[E]   Alcohol use has repeatedly been found to be correlated with violent behavior; for example, more than 50 percent of the perpetrators or victims of murder and other serious violence (as well as of lethal automobile accidents) have alcohol in their bloodstreams at the time; diagnosed alcoholics commit violent crimes at a much higher rate than do their nonalcoholic peers; a large percentage of violent criminals are alcoholics.

     There is, however, no simple, one-to-one relationship between alcohol use and violent behavior. Studies . . . suggest that the relationship between the two is a complicated interaction among biological, psychological, and social and cultural factors. For example, there is some evidence that small amounts of alcohol taken quickly temporarily increase, and high doses temporarily decrease, aggressive behavior in many animal species, including primates and humans. Nevertheless, there is nothing inevitable about this in humans. . . . When an individual or a culture expects alcohol use to be followed by violence, it more often is. When violence is not the expectation, or when it is not accepted or approved of, it tends not to follow alcohol use."

—James Gilligan, *Violence: Reflections on a National Epidemic*

[F]   Being here now [walking through the welfare housing development where he lived as a child], I can sympathize with politicians' desire to do something about the ruin before me. However, I have a hard time understanding what dismantling welfare will accomplish. As best as I can tell, the deterioration of public housing has less to do with welfare than with the hemorrhage of manufacturing jobs that people without high-school diplomas could perform and rely upon for a viable income; less with food stamps or with meager monthly checks than with neglect by the authorities and the vanishing of middle-class hopes and values and decent role models. There was a time, after all, when the projects were actually a pretty diverse place, home to the unemployed and the working poor.

—Albert DiBartolomeo, "In Defense of Welfare: A Memoir"

[G]   Some people even blame the growth of teacher unions for the problems in our schools and the difficulty we are having in getting school reform. But if that were so, schools would be much better in states where there is no collective bargaining (like Mississippi or Texas) than in states where it exists (like California or Connecticut), and that plainly is not the case.

—Albert Shanker, "Blaming Unions"

[H]   Was the FBI complicitous in the killing of Martin Luther King, Jr.? Is it conceivable that America's greatest civil rights leader, whom we honor with a day of national recognition, was gunned down on the night of April 4, 1968, with the cooperation of government agents charged with protecting our freedoms?

Unfortunately, that question arises in light of recent ballistic tests of the gun allegedly used by convicted assassin James Earl Ray.

—Robert Scheer, "The FBI's Campaign to Destroy Dr. Martin Luther King, Jr."

5   Recognizing Types of Claims

Examine the following claims to determine whether they are claims of fact, value, policy, or causation.

1. Careful stewardship of the economy by the chair of the Federal Reserve has created fourteen months of prosperity and lowered unemployment.

2. Overreliance on public opinion polls means our elected representatives vote for what will bring them popularity and reelection, when they should instead study the issues, make informed judgments, and vote their consciences.

3. California's Proposition 209 conflicts with federal affirmative-action laws.

4. The media routinely portray poor people as black or minority, when in actuality a majority of the nation's poor are white.

5. The popularity of sports, soap operas, talk shows, and the rest of the artificial world on television means that most Americans need to "get a life."

6. Directing any advertising, not just cigarette or alcohol advertising, at children is unforgivable.

7. Confiscation of the vehicle should be used routinely in cases of flagrant speeding, drunken driving, or driving without a license.

8. The excessive precautions that average parents today routinely take to prevent their children from suffering molestation, kidnap, rape, and murder is a sign that our society has become seriously depraved.

6   Recognizing Intended Audiences

Examine the following beginnings to argumentative texts. What type of audience does the writer seem to expect for this text? Which appeal is predominant in each passage?

[A]   One day, at a nursing home in Connecticut, elderly residents were each given a choice of houseplants to care for and were asked to make a number of small decisions about their daily routines. A year and a half later, not only were these people more cheerful, active, and alert than a similar group in the same institution who were not given these choices and responsibilities, but many more of them were still alive.

—Ellen J. Langer, *Mindfulness*

[B]   Aw, gee. The Washington press corps thinks the campaign finance hearings are a bore. No bombshells. No sex. Bad story line. Chairman Fred Thompson may be an actor by profession, but he can't write dialogue worth squat. Call a script doctor.

—Molly Ivins, "Campaign Finance Is Real Source of Class Warfare"

[C]   In one of the founding texts of sociology, *The Rules of Sociological Method* (1895), Emile Durkheim set it down that "crime is normal." "It is," he wrote, "completely impossible for any society entirely free of it to exist." By defining what is deviant, we are enabled to know what is not, and hence to live by shared standards. This aperçu appears in the chapter entitled "Rules for the Distinction of the Normal from the Pathological."

—Daniel Patrick Moynihan, "Defining Deviancy Down"

[D]   The broadcast industry recently celebrated 50 Years of Television, and the half-century mark is accurate, given the medium's commercial inception in 1939. Accounting, however, for a decade of disruption in the flow of consumer products during World War II and Korea, the time span is closer to 40 years. One would think that nearly a half century of virtual saturation by this medium should be sufficient to assess its cultural effects. Strangely enough, this does not seem to be the case; the values and disvalues of the medium remain as evasive as ever.

—Alan M. Olson, Christopher Parr, and Debra Parr, *Video Icons & Values*

[E]   The text of the First Amendment is quite simple: "Congress shall make no law respecting an establishment of religion, or prohibiting the free exercise thereof; or abridging the freedom of speech, or of the press, or the right of the people peaceably to assemble, and to petition the government for a redress of grievances." These are not words that would lead the uninitiated to suspect that the law, both with regard to religion and with regard to speech, could be what the Supreme Court has made of it in the past few decades.

—Robert H. Bork, "What to Do about the First Amendment"

[F]   We experience the world by creating categories and making distinctions among them. "This is a Chinese, not a Japanese, vase." "No, he's only a freshman." "The white orchids are endangered." "She is his boss now." In this way, we make a picture of the world, and of ourselves. Without categories the world might seem to escape us.

—Ellen J. Langer, *Mindfulness*

[G]   The way they were carrying on like demented hyenas in the House of Representatives last week, you'd have thought they were debating the appropriation for the Louisiana Purchase, Lend-Lease, the Marshall Plan or the manned lunar landing.

Such was the general level of incivility attached to the debate on giving less than $100 million to the National Endowment for the Arts.

—Robert Reno, "The Beat Goes On . . ."

7   Annotation Practice

Divide the class into small groups and assign each group to a different section of Hobbs's article, "Television and the Shaping of Cognitive Skills." Group members should individually read and annotate the section assigned to their group and, then, when their annotations are complete, compare and discuss their margin notations and other marks.

8   Outlining Practice

Divide into small groups; each group should choose one unoutlined section of "Television and the Shaping of Cognitive Skills" by Renée Hobbs and devise an outline for it. Then each group should present its outline to the class.

9   Mapping Practice

Choose an article of interest to you from the op-ed page of a newspaper. Use mapping to describe how the text's ideas flow.

Assignments

INFORMAL WRITING: WRITER'S JOURNAL

1. **Picnic Time in the Library**   Read this brief excerpt, and then respond as described below:

> It has been said of Boehme that his books are like a picnic to which the author brings the words and the reader brings the meaning. The remark may have been intended as a sneer at Boehme, but it is an exact description of all works of literary art without exception.
>
> —Northrop Frye, *Fearful Symmetry: A Study of William Blake*; quoted in
> Wolfgang Iser, *The Act of Reading: A Theory of Aesthetic Response*

In this passage, literary critic Northrop Frye says that reading "literary art" is a "picnic." Does this image work for you as a description of your reading? Does the metaphor apply to nonliterary texts as well as literary texts? In your reading of the excerpt, does it matter if you don't know who Boehme is?

2. **Making Sense**   Read this excerpt, and then respond as described below:

> Sense is what we are supposed to make. Meaning is for us to manage, making mind out of all this "never matter." We ought always to have the gift of consciousness on our conscience. Who else can feel the warmth of someone's pleasure in a finger's touch? hear a voice rise like a slow bird from the meadow of the page?
>
> —William H. Gass, "Tribalism, Identity, and Ideology"

Read over Gass's passage two or three times. Identify the phrase or phrases that strike you most, and write about why the image speaks to you.

■   WORKS CITED

Adler, Mortimer. "How to Mark a Book." *Saturday Review* 6 July 1940. Rpt. in *The Macmillan Writer*. Judith Nadell, Linda McMeniman, and John Langan. 3rd ed. Boston: Allyn and Bacon, 1997.

Anderson, Paul V. "What Survey Research Tells Us About Writing at Work." *Writing in Nonacademic Settings*. Ed. Lee Odell and Dixie Goswami. New York: Guilford, 1985. 3–83.

Ong, Walter J., S. J. "Literacy and Orality in Our Times," *ADE Bulletin* 58 (1978): 1–7. Rpt in *Composition and Literature: Bridging the Gap.* Ed. Winifred Bryan Horner. Chicago: U of Chicago P, 1983. 126–140.

Rosenblatt, Louise M. "The Transactional Theory: Against Dualisms." *College English* (1993): 377–86.

Todorov, Tzvetan. "Reading as Construction." *Genres in Discourse.* Trans. Catherine Porter. New York: Cambridge UP. 39.

 *Readings*

Stop Peddling Tobacco to Kids

LOUIS W. SULLIVAN

Dr. Louis Sullivan is president of Morehouse College School of Medicine in Atlanta, Georgia. In 1990, when he wrote this opinion piece, he was U.S. secretary of the Department of Health and Human Services. The essay appeared in many regional newspapers across the nation. (Reprinted by permission of the author.)

Smoking is the chief preventable cause of mortality in America. It is implicated in one out of every six deaths in our country. It kills more Americans every year than died in all of World War II. It is addictive. It costs us some $52 billion a year.   1

If all this is familiar—even tiresomely familiar—then why do we look the other way when our young people, at a vulnerable and impressionable age, become hooked on a habit that will kill or disable so many of them?   2

The time has come to confront tobacco sales to young people. It is time for laws that work, laws that can be enforced, laws that will give more Americans more time and more maturity to deal with the fatal enticement of smoking.   3

We know that the younger a person is when he or she starts to smoke, the more likely that smoking will become a lifelong addiction and the more likely that it will cause disease. About 90 percent of adult smokers began their addiction as children and adolescents. So today's young smokers are likely to account for almost all of our future smokers.   4

Preventing youngsters from taking up smoking is far more cost-effective than treating addiction later, and far less expensive than treating the resulting diseases. Yet, as long as a significant proportion of teens view smoking as a desirable, adult pleasure and become addicted before they can make a mature judgment, we will never achieve a smoke-free society.   5

Earlier this year, I asked the inspector general of my department to assess the enforcement of state laws prohibiting the sale of cigarettes to minors. That report was released May 24, and its findings boil down to a simple and unacceptable fact: Our children can easily buy cigarettes, virtually anytime they want to, usually in violation of the law.   6

In all, 44 states and the District of Columbia have laws that make it an offense for retailers to sell cigarettes to minors. However, these laws are being blatantly ignored. Only a   7 handful of violations can be identified in states with laws prohibiting sales to minors. Yet we know that almost a billion packs of cigarettes are sold to youngsters each year.

8   Two-thirds of state public-health officials report that there is virtually no enforcement of their state laws prohibiting cigarette sales to minors, and most of the rest say enforcement is minimal. Also, because most youth-access laws are criminal statutes, only the police can enforce them.

9   But law enforcement officials confront many other enforcement priorities, and there is an understandable reluctance to take such cases into crowded court systems.

10   The bottom line is clear. Our laws are not enforced, and indeed they are flouted. Students and adults both agree with this assessment. In fact, so do most vendors.

11   It may be inevitable that young people will experiment with cigarettes. But it is not inevitable that those under the legal age to purchase cigarettes should be able to easily break the law and purchase tobacco products, in whatever quantity and however often they may wish.

12   This kind of easy access to tobacco puts youngsters at unnecessary risk for addiction and disease. And we are abdicating our responsibilities to our children and their health if we pretend we can do nothing.

13   In a few places, state and local officials have devised serious enforcement tools that are workable and effective. These laws can be successfully enforced, and they provide models that should be emulated.

14   I have recommended that every state adopt enforceable legislation to prevent cigarette sales to minors. Model legislation that my department has suggested would include:

- State or local licensing of tobacco vendors, with provisions for fines or even the revocation of licenses for violations. Licensing is the means already used by states to control the sale of alcoholic beverages. It is a sound model for protecting youngsters from unrestricted access to these products.
- The use of civil rather than criminal penalties for violators. My department's experience with civil money penalties has shown them to be more versatile and enforceable sanctions than criminal penalties. They can be applied successfully in this situation as well.
- Ban the use of vending machines to sell cigarettes. Beer is not dispensed from vending machines. Neither should cigarettes be sold in this way. Without such a provision, laws prohibiting cigarette sales to minors can have no real force. States could temper the economic impact by phasing in such a ban.

15   It is all too apparent that we—parents, educators, merchants, health-care officials and community leaders—have not taken seriously the problem of smoking by our children and adolescents. We need workable laws that will provide retail outlets the incentive and tools to obey the law and refuse to sell tobacco to minors.

Annotation, Outlining, and Mapping Activities

1. Annotate paragraphs 6–10.
2. Imagine you are reading "Stop Peddling Tobacco to Kids" as research for a paper about solving self-destructive behavior in our society by applying civil law and punishments rather than criminal law. Annotate the essay with this purpose in mind.
3. Outline the entire article to indicate points to the third level (1, 2, 3, and so forth).
4. Use mapping to set out the ideas of the entire essay.

Questions for Inquiry

1. Locate Sullivan's claim and identify whether it addresses facts, causes, policy, or values, or a combination of these.
2. What does Sullivan gain by admitting, in paragraph 2, that his topic is "familiar—even tiresomely familiar"? How does Sullivan, through his choice of evidence, tone, and point of view, counteract the reader's possible boredom with his topic?
3. Identify the places where Sullivan uses the first-person-plural pronoun, "we." What would you say is the effect of this pronoun on the reader and the reader's willingness to cooperate with the author's reasoning?

Questions for Argument

1. Sullivan writes, "It may be inevitable that young people will experiment with cigarettes" (11). Do you agree that as long as cigarettes exist, underage people will be attracted to them? What kinds of deterrents would prevent or lessen the attraction?
2. Sullivan assumes that we want "a smoke-free society" (5). Do you agree that this is the best goal for our society? Can you imagine other ways we might address the issues of the medical cost, deadliness, and addictiveness of tobacco?
3. Treating cigarettes more like alcohol is one aspect of Sullivan's proposed plan (see the first and third bullets under paragraph 14). Do you agree that alcohol laws are more successful than those that regulate underage smoking and that they should serve as a model for increased restriction of tobacco sales?

Writing Assignments

Informal

1. Teenagers are attracted to "desirable, adult pleasures," Sullivan notes (5). In your journal, write about the longing that teens feel for passage into the next stage of life.
2. So what about the adults? What should be done about adult smoking? What good effects might come from a nationwide decrease in the number of adults who smoke?

Formal

3. **Group Research.** "Smoking is the chief preventable cause of mortality in America," Sullivan writes, and "is implicated in one out of every six deaths in our country" (1). He does not supply any specifics, and, indeed, most of us assume we know how smoking kills and damages health. As a class, check this assumption by brainstorming a list of smoking-related diseases. Then divide into groups to use different resources of the library and the Internet and research the medical facts about the health consequences of smoking. Groups should report to the class about their discoveries. Then individually write an essay in which you discuss the attitudes of young people toward smoking and the extent of their knowledge or ignorance of the long-term effects of smoking.
4. Changing laws, increasing their enforcement, and upping penalties for violation are Sullivan's main recommendations. Do you agree that the youth-smoking problem is best addressed through laws and penalties? Are there other, perhaps more effective,

ways of discouraging young people from smoking? Write an essay, based on your knowledge of young people in college, in which you take another approach to deterring youthful use of tobacco.

■ ■ ■

My Fellow Immigrants

THOMAS L. FRIEDMAN

Thomas L. Friedman is foreign-affairs columnist for the *New York Times*. In the 1980s, he was chief correspondent for the *Times* in Lebanon and then in Israel and won two Pulitzer Prizes for his reporting on the Middle East. He is the author of *From Beirut to Jerusalem*, which won the National Book Award in 1989. This column appeared on September 10, 1995, during President Bill Clinton's campaign for reelection; his opponent was retired Senator Robert Dole. (Copyright 1995 by The New York Times. Reprinted by permission.)

1   Last week Senator Bob Dole told an American Legion convention that "ethnic separatism" was threatening American unity, and he called for making English our official language. These are valid issues. Unfortunately, Senator Dole has suddenly raised them not to unite the country but to divide it—to play on the patriotism of the American Legion and the fear of new immigrants. But give Mr. Dole credit. If he was looking for a hot-button issue to revive his campaign, he found it.

2   I discovered this for myself two years ago when I was asked to give a speech to a teachers' convention in Miami on what I had learned about multiculturalism from living in Beirut. I explained that watching Lebanon, a multiethnic society, unravel had instilled in me two very strong beliefs: one was the importance of the American public school system. In Lebanon, Christians, Sunnis and Shiites tended to go to their own schools, and it made their society that much easier to fracture when the strains came. It is the public school system in America that helps insure that out of many we remain one.

3   The other point was that in Lebanon education was in French, English or Arabic. There was no common language. I think that in America English should be the primary language and that students should only be taught in other languages as a bridge to English education. Permanent multilingual education is a road to ruin. We have enough trouble communicating in English.

4   What was striking was how many teachers said to me afterward that they felt the same way but that it was not "politically correct" for them to say so at their schools because multicultural extremists, pushing diversity as an end in itself, were the dominant trend.

5   This is sad. And what it produces are equally pernicious counter-reactions, like the Dole speech, which tries to use English as a club, or a code word, for stamping out diversity in education altogether.

6   The objective we should be working for is community. But how? Well, unless we give people of diverse ethnic backgrounds a sense of belonging, unless we give them a sense that their identity and heritage are valued threads in the tapestry of American society, real com-

munity is impossible. That is why it is important to bridge people into the community, if necessary with languages other than English, and to encourage people of different backgrounds to express their cultural identities as a way of enriching the community as a whole.

But we should oppose a notion of diversity that becomes an end in itself, a diversity that becomes a substitute for neighborhood and community, where Hispanics, blacks, Asians and Jews have their corners, separate but equal. Diversity without a spirit of community leads to tribalism. Community without a spirit of diversity leads to alienation for all minorities.   7

The goal should be a tension between the two. You won't feel the tension if you just live in your separate corner or walled community. And you won't feel the tension if the majority so overwhelms the minority that it is smothered into silence. You will only feel the tension when groups are rubbing against each other, trying to express their unique ethnic or linguistic identities, and at the same time trying to keep those identities enough in check to maintain the common bonds of community. That is the hard work of nation-building.   8

Unfortunately, that was not the hard work Senator Dole was engaged in. The giveaway was where he made his speech. It wasn't at Ellis Island. It wasn't at a language school where English was being taught to new immigrants. It wasn't somewhere where the tension between diversity and community was openly at play, and the Senator could talk about the right mix between the two.   9

No, it was at an American Legion convention, where Mr. Dole crudely assumed that people didn't want to feel the tension at all, and that was what he was selling them. He was selling community on the cheap—community without tension, community that is built from us against them and not us with them.   10

If Mr. Dole really wanted to wrestle with this issue, and not just exploit it, he would have begun his speech to the American Legion the same way F.D.R. once began a speech on this subject to the Daughters of the American Revolution: "My fellow immigrants . . . "   11

Annotating, Outlining, and Mapping Activities

1. Annotate paragraphs 1 and 2.
2. Imagine you are reading "My Fellow Americans" because you are writing a paper about the presidential election race between Dole and Clinton in 1996. Annotate the essay.
3. Outline the ideas of the entire essay to indicate points to the third (1, 2, and so forth) level.
4. Use mapping to set out the the ideas of the essay.

Questions for Inquiry

1. What is Friedman's claim? Is it a claim of fact, cause, values, or policy?
2. Making sense of Friedman's opening paragraphs depends to some extent on knowledge of U.S. politics, interest groups like the American Legion, and the long-running Mideast religious conflicts. How does Friedman keep you reading, even if you are not "up to speed" on these issues? In particular, what about Friedman's word choice, sentence style, and point of view in paragraphs 1–5 creates interest and involvement for the reader?
3. How, according to Friedman, should diversity be defined? What definitions of diversity would he oppose?

4. Friedman's discussion of community and diversity in paragraphs 6–8 is conducted almost entirely in the abstract—without examples or facts—yet it is clear and readable. What techniques does the author use to make his philosophy about community so accessible?

Questions for Argument

1. Friedman is harshly critical of Dole for playing on "the fear of new immigrants" among the American Legion members. Do you agree that support for making English the official language of the United States is a "code word" for fear of immigration and the stamping out of diversity (1, 5)? Or do you believe that there are valid reasons for supporting an official language?
2. Friedman seems, in paragraph 3, to agree with Dole that the United States should have one language. Yet later in the essay he seems to support allowing immigrants to use other languages (6). Is Friedman contradicting himself? Can our country do both these things? What might be the benefits of doing so?
3. Does Friedman's highly political approach—criticizing a presidential candidate's views on immigration and society—add to or detract from his argument, in your opinion? Or would the appeal of his argument be stronger without the political critique?

Writing Assignments

Informal

1. In your journal, write about aspects of your own ethnicity that you value and consider a significant "thread" in the "tapestry of American society."
2. Would thinking of your friends and neighbors and strangers on the street as "fellow immigrants" affect your behavior toward them? Write a journal entry in which you imagine a day in which you treat everyone you meet as a "fellow immigrant."

Formal

3. Friedman learned about multiculturalism, he says, from living in a multiethnic society in the Middle East (2). Write an essay in which you discuss what you have learned in the multiethnic society of the United States. Focus on one or two segments of your experience in which people from two or more ethnic groups interacted—perhaps at a club, church, school, or recreational activity. You may wish to make recommendations about how community can be improved or draw a conclusion about whether we should be optimistic or pessimistic about creating community from many different threads.
4. **Group Research.** Friedman calls "community on the cheap" a community built "from us against them and not us with them" (10). With classmates, brainstorm other areas of U.S. life and other contemporary problems—on your campus, in your neighborhood or town, or in the news—in which the battle seems to boil down to "us against them." Choose one of these situations and form a group with others interested in the same issue or problem. Devise a research plan so that you may become more informed about this problem. (You may wish to conduct primary research on a local issue, as described in Chapter 5, or do library and Internet research, as discussed in Chapters 4, 5, and 12, on a regional or national problem.) Then, after sharing your research results with your

group, write an essay in which you sort out some of the reasons for the "us against them" mentality or in which you make recommendations for instituting real community on this issue.

■ ■ ■

Television and the Shaping of Cognitive Skills

RENÉE HOBBS

Renée Hobbs teaches Communication at Babson College in Massachusetts. This article appeared in *Video Icons & Values,* an anthology by A. M. Olson, C. Parr, and D. Parr published in 1991. (Copyright 1991 by State University of New York Press. Reprinted by permission.)

Everyone knows that television has tremendous influence even though the word "influence" has been bandied about so much that it almost seems trivial. Nevertheless, for 30 or 40 years we've been hard-pressed to describe the nature of that influence. What is well documented is the way that people's behavior and attitudes are affected by the content of what they see on television. We have documentation on violence on television and its influence on behavior; on television's portrayal of sexuality; on consumer socialization; and how the content of advertising messages has influence.[1] However, if we think that only the content of television programming influences our society, we greatly underestimate the potency of the medium.

What I want to discuss are some of the social consequences resulting from the very form and structure of the medium; more specifically, I want to address the impact of format and editing conventions of television. My hypothesis is that two aspects of the structure of the medium, television format and television editing conventions, are both extremely powerful vehicles that reflect and shape the cognitive processes of attention, organization, interpretation, and prediction. Thus, in effect, I am proposing a mechanism for understanding *how* television influences culture and values, because although the content of television influences culture and values, so does its form, in highly specific and predictable ways.

We know that communication media, like language and television, are not simply vehicles for transmitting messages, not simply pipes through which we send messages. If they were, they wouldn't be so powerful. Communication media serve not only as vehicles for transmitting messages; they are used in creating and developing messages—that is, they are used in thought. We have internalized communications media, just as we have internalized language, so that these media can be used not only to transmit messages but as tools to think with.[2]

Early filmmakers surely exploited the new medium in ways that illustrate the relationship between media and mental processes. Consider the creative power of early filmmakers as they used celluloid to construct messages. Techniques like the close-up and the zoom are symbolic codes that are analogues of everyday patterns of visual attention. In some sense the zoom represents the actions we engage in when we pay attention, because when we pay attention, we move to focus on a single small part of the scene, and everything else blurs and disappears in the background. Filmmakers, either consciously or unconsciously, invented techniques of manipulating the distance between the camera and the subject which externalize this process of perception. Close-ups, long shots, and zooms are representations of a very complex mental skill—paying attention. A number of the editing conventions of television may be perceptual analogues of mental processes, which may explain why it is so easy to watch television. In fact, my colleagues and I developed the following experiment to get at this very issue.

5   The experiment was designed to test some assumptions regarding media literacy. For about 15 years now, we have been bombarded with the concept of media literacy. This concept is informed by the notion that the symbol systems of television, the editing conventions, are similar to print, in that viewers must learn how to decode them.[3] But do viewers need practice and experience with the medium to be able to decode editing conventions? Scholars have considerable evidence on how children understand television and know that some combination of age and experience is necessary to process television images accurately.[4] And of course, very young children don't decode television so well as adults.[5] With all the research evidence, however, it is unclear whether developmental factors regarding age or experience with the medium are essential prerequisites for understanding the editing conventions.

6   The question is, how do you find a population that has had no experience with television? Certainly none exists in this country! But in some remote areas of the world, there are some groups of people who have never seen films or television, although each year this population diminishes. Such a population could be used to help investigate whether editing conventions are comprehensible to adult viewers with no familiarity with film or television. The Pokot people of western Kenya are such a people. They have never seen televison, never seen film, never seen two-dimensional representations like photographs or maps. They live in an environment virtually as close to a tribal culture as exists in the twentieth century, the perfect group for a naturalistic experiment. We showed them two versions of a television program that we made using plausible occurrence in the village.[6] In one version, we turned the camera on, let the narrative event proceed in front of the camera as if it were a proscenium stage. When the narrative event was over, we the turned the camera off.

7   In the second version, we used only one editing convention: manipulated point-of-view. In other words, we changed the relationship between the camera and the subject using close-ups, medium shots, and long shots. In a three-minute narrative event, we used 13 edit points or "cuts." The content of both versions was otherwise identical. The length of the broadcast was identical. The only difference between these two broadcasts was that one had no editing at all, and the other had 13 edit points manipulating point-of-view, the distance between the camera and the subject.

8   What we found was rather surprising. We found that there were no differences in the ability of the tribal villagers to comprehend the message. The villagers who saw the edited version were just as competent at decoding as were the villagers who saw the unedited version. With no experience with the medium, these villagers were perfectly adept at decoding this mediaspecific symbol system, namely, point-of-view narration. Based on our research, we believe that some editing conventions are perceptual isomorphs of experience: You don't need experience with the medium to learn to decode them. This explains why television is so easy to watch, why it takes so little effort for us to decode, why it takes no mental effort to watch television. From this it follows that the representational codes of film and television can also help to develop or degenerate the cognitive skills of attention, comprehension, interpretation, and prediction.

Television and Attention

9   The relationship between television and attention is the area in which we have the best evidence for understanding television's influence. Writing in the early years of the twenti-

eth century, Hugo Munsterberg was the first experimental psychologist recruited by William James at Harvard to begin the experimental laboratory. He was also an aficionado of film, which in the beginning of the twentieth century was exploding with creative new techniques and devices for manipulating the expressive potential of the medium. Munsterberg made some remarkable observations about the similarities he saw between editing conventions and attention. He viewed the close-up as an externalization of the process of paying attention, and in the same way, viewed the flashback as a technique for representing memory just as the flash-forward externalized the mental skills of imagining.[7]

It is absolutely remarkable to read a psychologist more than 70 years ago making these observations and, although the argument seems somewhat simplified in retrospect, it represents the first time psychologists looked at the relationship between the products that we use in creating film and video and the processes that we use inside our head.   10

We have more empirical evidence on the relationship between children's attention and editing conventions than about most other topics in the field of media studies. Researchers know that young children between the ages of two and five seem compelled to attend to editing conventions, and certain editing conventions draw the attention of children more than others.[8] Those editing conventions are ones that include high movement, rapid pacing, lots of edit points, and loud music. These editing conventions are intense in the use of movement that is perceptually salient, which compels attention. Researchers have discovered that young children are compelled to watch the screen when those editing conventions are used, but that over time, children are able to control their attentional behavior; that is, older children are not so compelled to watch the screen when those editing conventions are used. This bears a close relationship to what we know about the human perceptual system. Our eyes are designed to actively monitor change. It is built-in, hard-wired, as it were, into the perceptual system.[9] Younger children don't have very much control over using that perceptual system, and so they are compelled to watch the intense movement on the screen. And those of us who have seen children that age watching television can see the intensity with which their attention is drawn to the screen. Older children are better able to mediate their attentional skills and control that behavior.   11

Although over time we gain control, even adults find this array of movement and visual changes on the TV screen compelling. Think of the time when you were in a conversation and the television was on in the room. Sometimes, no matter how interesting the conversation might happen to be, no matter how much you wanted to participate in the conversation, you found your eyes being drawn inexplicably to the screen. It is an attentional behavior that even adults find difficult to control. In this way, then, editing conventions shape attention patterns by capitalizing on our natural instinct to monitor changes in the visual display.   12

Television formats also interact with our attentional skills in a way that serves a useful function. After all, we watch television at home, in an environment with multiple distractions and multiple possible activities. Thus the predictability of certain kinds of formats, like the sitcom, the game show, the drama, even the commercial, permit us to allocate our attention very selectively. For example, young people will often walk out of the room when a program is on that they are supposed to be watching. If you ask them about it, they are very candid: "I don't have to watch now; I don't have to watch until after the commercial." Viewers engage in multiple activities while watching television because we have learned how to allocate our attention by our familiarity with program formats. The format of the medium simplifies the processes of paying attention, making it possible to watch television in conjunction with other activities of daily life.   13

14   Although generations of teachers and parents and physicians and psychologists have talked about the degeneration of our attention span owing to the influence of television, we have very little empirical evidence to support that belief. When you talk to teachers, especially older elementary school teachers who have been teaching in the schools for years, and who can compare the children of the 1950s and 1960s with the children of the 1970s and the 1980s, they will frequently comment on the decreased attention span of children and attribute these differences to the influence of television.

15   According to many media scholars, television presents a fragmented set of images and sounds, and that fragmentation becomes paralleled in our own attentional skills.[10] Because we are used to receiving fragmented information and information in discontinuous form, we come to prefer that form; and information, such as a formal lecture, that requires sustained attention over a long period of time, becomes more difficult because it is not habitually required in our culture. Consequently, it takes a great deal of effort and discipline to make the attentional adjustment to a formal lecture of 60 minutes or more, for it is an adjustment that runs against the grain of discontinuity.

Television and the Skills of Organization and Interpretation

16   Researchers can easily tell whether someone is paying attention or not. However, it is not so easy to examine the "black box" of the rest of the cognitive process. How are you encoding this information in memory? What meaning are you making of it? We have relatively little understanding of the way in which television affects the skills of organization and interpretation, primarily because those skills must be inferred. They are invisible to us except through indirect examination.

17   Nevertheless, I want to say more about how television affects how we store, organize, and interpret information by discussing television news. Researchers who examine viewers' ability to comprehend television almost always use television news programming because, given the manner in which the news is presented, it is easier to measure this mode of learning directly. The broadcast news on the major networks present us with isolated snippets of information: 45 seconds on upcoming elections, 100 seconds on business and economics, 35 seconds on health and science. Those snippets make it easy for viewers by permitting us to decide whether or not to encode that information. Clearly, the conventions and formats of television help us encode information from a television program in ways which are most profitable to the commercial medium.

18   For example, my understanding of economics is at such a rudimentary level that I don't bother to encode televised economic news in my memory, even though I may pay attention to it. Because my understanding of economics is not well developed enough for me to encode the information into my existing set of knowledge and beliefs, it simply slips by; and because this information is only on for a few seconds, it slips by easily. On the other hand, for science and health stories, politics or sports, I have a well-developed array of information. Thus, when I hear the cue for science and health or sports, I pay more attention and I actively encode this information into my existing knowledge.

19   In a sense then, isolated snippets are valuable: they help viewers retrieve information about which they already have well-developed schemas for understanding. On the other hand, television's isolated snippets do not help viewers encode information in memory if they don't have sufficient prior knowledge. The 45 seconds on economics or the 35 seconds on elections make it impossible to encode that information if viewers don't have an under-

standing of that topic to begin with.[11] In other words, a few seconds of information is not going to help develop the schemata viewers need to encode this information. Therefore, television's isolated news snippets do help to acquire information rapidly about topics already known. But conversely, the isolated snippets inhibit the ability to encode information on topics that viewers don't know very much about. Watching television news, then, really only helps viewers to reinforce what they already know; it does very little to make them more sophisticated in these topics other than to provide a few new bits of data.

Doris Graber comments on the obvious value implication of such behavior: 20

> When people fail to learn or create appropriate schemas for certain types of news, that news cannot be absorbed. The socialization of average Americans apparently leaves a number of gaps in schema structure. These gaps then make it difficult to focus public attention on some important problems. News about most foreign countries or news about science are examples. Even when such news is presented in simple ways, most of the audience fails to make the effort to absorb it because appropriate schemas did not form part of past socialization.[12]

Thus the simplicity of television news makes it possible for only a few viewers to extract meaningful information and excludes others who simply don't have a well-developed understanding of those current events. "What will happen," Graber asks, "to the quality of learning about public affairs if newspaper use continues to decline and electronic media capture an increasing share of the audience's attention?" 21

The answer seems obvious enough. Owing to the limitations imposed by the commercial format, television network news is unable to provide us with sufficient background and information to help us develop schemas for understanding complex events in places like the Middle East and Central America. Therefore, unless you already know something about these topics, unless you know, at the very least, where the Middle East and Central America are (and we've recently discovered that upwards of 50% of Americans do not know such elementary geographic facts) television news will be of no assistance in helping you develop your understanding in these areas. 22

The economic and commercial constraints on television as a medium of information are critical here, for television's failure to inform and to edify is not due to a limitation inherent in the medium itself. It is not inherent in the medium of television that a "cut" has to be made every three seconds, that the pacing and rhythm have to be what it presently is, causing viewers to change channels every 3.7 minutes.[13] In fact, the present shape, look, and feel of television are not due to the inherent capabilities of the medium, but are a result of the economic environment in which the medium was initially created and in which it, for the most part, continues. In other words, when we look at the format of television and when we think of the interpretive framework that television provides, we cannot overlook the economic forces that created these formats. 23

In the 1950s during the so-called "Golden Age of Television," there was a lot of experimentation and a diversity of social views were presented. "CBS Playhouse 90," Paddy Chayefsky's "Marty," and many other programs presented complex views of American social life. But such ambitious, socially relevant, and intellectually challenging programming has become obsolete, because of the influence of advertisers who looked for programs that provided a pleasant atmosphere in which to portray their product.[14] Do you want your soap advertisement shown next to a difficult and complex portrayal of social crises in America, or programming that generates ambiguity regarding the relationship between power and 24 the disenfranchised? Or do you want your product put in an environment that shows American middle-class people at their best, with healthy, white, smiling faces and beautiful teeth?

25   Decisions to minimize this kind of ambiguity were systematically made in the fifties and they have persisted to this day. In the 1980s programs emphasize affluence. Of course, "Dallas" and "Dynasty" are the first examples that come to mind. But think of programs that appear to us rather innocuous, like "The Cosby Show." The affluence which underlies this program is almost invisible. We don't even pay attention to it, yet it is part of the very fabric of the messages, the messages that represent the format, that represent the way advertisers and broadcasters want us to see ourselves and our society. In this sense, consider the broadcasting strategy called LOP ("least objectionable programming"), developed in the early 1960s. By the very economic nature of television, which has to appeal to the most number of viewers to be successful, the least objectionable programming strategy appeals to the largest number of viewers. Such a strategy has a very definite influence on the format of television, which in turn has a direct influence on messages communicated through television. By permitting this medium to evolve as it has, we have as a consequence reduced the diversity of media formats and messages, so that television formats reinforce mainstream social views.

26   Even with the increasing number of channels available with cable television, there is little diversity because it is still restricted by the prevailing formats. Michael Schudson comments: "These conventions help make culturally consonant messages readable and culturally dissonant messages unsayable. Their function is less to increase or decrease the truth value of the messages they convey than to shape or narrow the range of what kind of truths can be told."[15] Television formats reinforce certain assumptions about the political world, the social world, and the world of values as well.

Television and the Skills of Prediction and Expectation

27   When we pay attention, organize, encode, and interpret informal information, we are led to pay attention again and to make new choices. That is the cognitive skill of prediction and expectation, and in many ways it is television that has shaped our expectations about all elements of our culture, from politics to religion. And here I argue that repeated exposure to television format and editing conventions sets viewer expectations, directly shaping cultural and social values.

28   For example, I have found, over the years of teaching, that I have a difficult time trying to introduce video art to college students. My students sit patiently through video art pieces and after it is all over, say, "Huh? What is it? It's not a sitcom, it's not a game show, it's not a news program, it's not a documentary. What is it?" It's not good, because it doesn't fit their expectations about what television is. Now this is a very difficult objection to counteract, because they are telling me very explicitly that the conventions that exist on broadcast television are identical with television itself. Such conventions are good because students and the rest of us have been exposed to them over and over again. Many video artists combat this strategy by satirically playing on these conventions, manipulating and altering them. But that is still playing within the realm of our existing expectations.

29   Let us reflect on programs that do not use the editing conventions of network television with its rapid pacing, slickness, and visual intensity. Is it inherent in the medium that to be successful you have to use those conventions? Is it inherently bad television to portray, for example, a talking head? Is there something, as Murray-Brown (Chapter 2, this book) and

Postman suggest, basically boring about that? I don't think so. I think it has rather to do with our expectations, which develop over time. I do not think it is inherent to the medium that we have to prefer rapid pacing and ten-second sound bites to longer shots of people speaking in full sentences and paragraphs.

Viewers, however, through their repeated exposure to television, demand those conventions. Thus, for example, PBS, in order to be successful and to compete for viewers, has been forced to present educational and instructional programming with those techniques intact, using the conventions of commercial television to teach about culture, values, science, and all the rest.[16] And consider the multiple reasons why local access cable television programming failed to attract viewers, leading to its virtual demise. One reason is that people didn't watch it. Why didn't people watch it? It didn't look like "good" television. Viewers comment: "They only had two cameras; it was unprofessional; it didn't look good." Note here that reference to content is irrelevant; reference is rather to form and appearance. It didn't look like commercial television, and so it didn't attract viewers. Why fund such an endeavor? Through repeated exposure to a limited number of formats and a uniform pattern of editing conventions, our expectations have already been set as to what is good and what is bad on television. These expectations are not inherent to the medium, but are the result of repeated exposure to the conventions already familiar to us.

Obviously, the hegemony of commercial broadcasting formats has an influence on viewers' ability to accept new formats. In this regard, we have had an interesting naturalistic experiment in American television during the 1980s: the advent of music television, the first example of a dramatically new format in television in a long time. Music television, when it started in 1981, originally used a variety of formats, which are, however, hard to describe in words. Forget for a moment the arguments regarding the content of music television, the sexual and violent images and messages. The structure and the form of music television in 1981 was considerably more diverse then than it is now at the end of the decade. Only three or perhaps only two formats are commonly used on music television today: the narrative format, where a story is portrayed (like a little sitcom or soap compressed into three minutes), and the performance video (which has the musician displayed in all his or her splendor). Some would argue that the restriction of format in music television is probably a result of economic issues, so that record companies who are spending a lot of money don't take risks, and go with what's safe. While this argument has conventional feasibility, I would argue that the reduction in format is due rather to a sensitivity to what viewers like: a conventional format in music videos just as in everything else on television. Viewers like familiar formats. This is an empirical fact. They like narrative and performance videos, since narrative videos are easy to understand, are comfortable, and performance videos don't require much mental effort at all. Producers are responding to the interests of their audience; thus they deliberately reduce the diversity of formats.

Finally, it is clear that formats also influence our understanding and expectations regarding message content. As television becomes the dominant medium in our society, in our culture, we sense that it has influence far beyond itself and that it has a tremendous influence upon other media, especially print media. For example, the newspaper *USA TODAY* explicitly models its form on television; indeed, it is television-inspired. It is highly graphic, pictorial in nature, and brief and fragmented; one rarely has to jump to an inside page to finish reading anything in *USA TODAY*. Its fragmentation is its value because it doesn't take very long to read. You can't spend more than twenty minutes on *USA TODAY* even if you are among the slowest readers.

33   In other words, television format has determined public expectations regarding all formats, at least for the mass public, which itself influences the elite public more than we would like to admit. Television formats not only influence television but all other aspects of culture. It is precisely in this sense that formats and editing conventions have their greatest power.

34   Television's prominence in our society is neither good nor bad in terms of inherent value. But television's restrictions of formats and editing conventions can shape our expectations so that we are not exposed to a full range of information and ideas. Here is where the medium is potentially dangerous. It is here that specific value judgments intrude. By its ability to shape our interest in information, television editing conventions and formats encourage a value system that emphasizes fragmentation over continuity, repetition over diversity, and familiar messages over unfamiliar ones, all of it in 30-second bits instead of more sustained attentional patterns. It is this video legacy that has shaped modern American politics and business and religion and culture, not through the messages presented on television, but through specific utilizations of the form and structure of the medium itself.

Notes

1. David Pearl, Lorraine Bouthilet, and Joyce Lazar, eds., *Television and Behavior*, Vol. 1 (Rockville, Md.: National Institute of Mental Health, 1982).

2. David R. Olson, and Jerome Bruner, "Learning Through Experience and Learning Through Media," in *Media and Symbols: The Forms of Expression, Communication and Education*, David R. Olson, ed. (Chicago: National Society for the Study of Education, 1974), 125–150.

3. Patricia Marks Greenfield, *Mind and Media* (Cambridge: Harvard University Press, 1984).

4. W. Andrew Collins, "Schemata for Understanding Television," in *Viewing Children Through Television*, Hope Kelly and Howard Gardner, eds. (San Francisco: Jossey Bass, 1981), 31–46.

5. Gerald S. Lesser, *Children and Television* (New York: Vintage, 1974), and R. Liebert, J. M. Neale, and E. S. Davidson, *The Early Window: Effects of Television on Children and Youth* (New York: Pergamon Press, 1973).

6. Renée Hobbs, Richard Frost, and John Stauffer, "How First-Time Viewers Comprehend Editing Conventions," *Journal of Communication*, Autumn (1988): 50–60.

7. *The Photoplay: A Psychological Study.* (New York: Dover, 1970 [1916]).

8. Mabel Rice, Aletha Huston, and John C. Wright, "The Forms of Television: Effects on Children's Attention, Comprehension and Social Behavior," in *Children and the Formal Features of Television*, Manfred Meyer, ed. (New York: K G. Saur Munchen, 1982).

9. Julian Hochberg, "Motion Pictures and Mental Structures." Paper presented at the Eastern Psychological Association, Washington, D.C., 1978.

10. Neil Postman, *Amusing Ourselves to Death* (New York: Viking, 1985).

11. Renée Hobbs, "Visual Verbal Synchrony and Learning from Television News." Doctoral dissertation, Harvard University, 1985.

12. *Processing the News: How People Tame the Information Tide* (New York: Longman, 1984). This quotation and the one following are both from p. 206.

13. *Harper's*, Index, August 1988.

14. Christopher H. Sterling, and John M. Kittross, *Stay Tuned: A Concise History of American Broadcasting* (Belmont, Calif.: Wadsworth, 1978).

15. "The Politics of Narrative Form: The Emergence of News Conventions in Print and Television," *Daedalus* 3, Fall (1982): 97–112.

16. Gerald Lesser, *Television and Children* (New York: Viking Press, 1974).

Questions for Inquiry

1. Identify Hobbs's claim. What does she say is special about her approach to understanding television? What type of claim is she proposing? Also identify where Hobbs expresses the major segments or subpoints of her claim and examine how these subpoints affect her organization.

2. **Research Opportunity.** Examine Hobbs's account of the experiment she conducted (6–8) to identify the pattern of scientific experiment as it is used in the social sciences. If you are not familiar with the scientific method, use it as a key term to search reference works such as encyclopedias and dictionaries for its meaning.

   What was the goal of Hobbs's experiment? How did this goal affect the choice of subjects and the qualities of the films that were shown? Identify the conclusion she draws from this experiment.

3. **Research Opportunity.** Hobbs uses many terms unfamiliar to a lay reader—that is, someone not involved in the scholarship of communication studies. Although an outsider to this discipline, you may have been able to rely on context to glean the intended meanings of terms such as the following. If necessary, use standard dictionaries to determine the meanings of the terms below and any others that you found confusing. How does context constrain or limit the meaning of the words?

   consumer socialization (1)
   format and editing conventions (2)
   internalized communications media; internalized language (3)
   perceptual analogues (4)
   perceptual isomorphs of experience (8)
   schemata (singular: schema) (19)
   culturally consonant; culturally dissonant (26)
   local access cable (30)
   hegemony; commercial broadcasting formats (31)

4. How does discussing psychological observations about the parallel between film techniques and mental operations (paragraphs 9–10) help Hobbs identify the issue she wants to focus on? Identify other places where Hobbs incorporates statements by other scholars and the purpose of these quotations.

5. What evidence does Hobbs offer for her point that television's format fosters encoding of certain types of material and not others (17–22)? How does the commercial basis of television affect format and therefore viewers' mental abilities (22–26)? What evidence does the author present showing that television affects people's "cognitive skills of prediction and expectation" (27–30)?

Questions for Argument

1. Examine carefully the points developed in paragraphs 12 and 13. Do you see a contradiction between these ways in which, according to Hobbs, television affects adult viewers? Make sure you understand the lead-in to these points (paragraph 11) before you decide.

2. In paragraph 18, Hobbs uses her own experience viewing news to explain the mental process of learning new information. As she admits, "We have relatively little understanding of the way in which television affects the skills of organization and interpretation" (16). Do you accept her conclusion that televised information can be learned only by people with "sufficient prior knowledge" (19)? What assumptions lie behind her reasoning here? Do you agree that people can't learn about an unfamiliar topic through television news?

3. Do you agree that music television uses only two formats: the narrative ("like a little sitcom or soap") and the performance video (31)? If you have seen old videos from the beginning years of music television (the early eighties), do you agree that in format it

"was considerably more diverse then than it is now [in 1989]" (31)? If you disagree with her evaluation of music video, how does this affect your acceptance of the point she is making in paragraphs 27–33?

Writing Assignments

Informal

1. "Talking heads" are often considered a boring form of television (29). Write a journal essay about what person or persons you would enjoy seeing and hearing as a "talking head" on television. This person might be famous, someone you know of through friends or your reading, listening, or viewing, or someone you know personally. Explain what benefits viewers would get from exposure to this person's ideas.

2. Most college students have grown up with television. Think back to your childhood and the shows you watched. Do you think that your youthful television exposure has affected the way you watch, handle information, and even think? Write an informal paper in which you reflect on television and your intellectual growth.

Formal

3. Hobbs quotes scholar Michael Schudson's point that on television certain messages are "unsayable" (26). Is there a message you would like to see conveyed on television that, in the reality of today's television world, will always be "unsayable"? Or is today's television a world of "anything goes" in which all realities, situations, and messages are expressed? Write an essay in which you clarify a claim on this issue and support it with examples drawn from television.

4. **Group Research.** Hobbs refers to the strategy of LOP ("least objectionable programming") (25) adopted in the 1960s. Working with a group, identify some research paths that you might follow to learn more about LOP, and assign individual group members to these tasks. Share the results of your research. Then, individually, spend some time viewing particular sitcoms or dramatic television. Write an essay in which you express and defend your opinion about whether LOP is still a factor in television today.

5. **Individual Research.** Learn more about Hobbs's subject by doing follow-up reading in one of the sources she cites in her notes. Choose your source by your interest in the use Hobbs makes of it in her article, and investigate what other evidence and reasoning the source offers in support of Hobbs's ideas. Summarize what the source has to say about television and people's mental abilities in a report to your class. (Longer sources may be studied by a team of class members at the discretion of the instructor.) (See Chapter 3 for a discussion of summarizing.)

■ ■ ■

Chapter 3

The Writing Reader

Inquiring into Meaning through Paraphrase, Summary, and Quotation

■ Read the following quote carefully, then respond as indicated below:

> To keep the memory of . . . texts and authors, one has to cite them, to keep them encrypted in one's discourse so they can survive. . . . The desire to quote is therefore a desire to meet the other, to keep the other [author] as other, but also to recognize the other in oneself.
>
> —Claudette Sartiliot, *Citation and Modernity*

Writer's Journal

Consider Sartiliot's passage, and then think about quotations that have been meaningful for you—quotations that have represented or dramatized the ideas of another for you but that have also reflected back to you something of yourself. In your notebook, write informally to explain the impact a memorable quotation had on you. Strive for an entry of 150 words.

■ COMING TO TERMS WITH MEANING

Understanding a piece of writing—a text—means actively constructing the meaning on the basis of the words. You use what you already know of our language, our culture, and the subject to turn the written words into a meaning. Often, we speak of the meaning being "clear" when we understand. At the point of understanding, you seem to "see through" the "clear" words to a meaning you have built in your mind.

We sometimes speak of understanding a text as "coming to terms" with it. This expression, *coming to terms,* contains the interesting implication that we have "come to an agreement with" the text (Spears 62). The phrase reveals that understanding involves negotiating with the words of a text to create a new entity: the meaning as the reader sees it.

This agreement of understanding between the reader and the text is best explored and explained in writing. When you read a text and write down in your own words the meaning you reconstruct from it, you create a second text. This second text, your summary or paraphrase, allows others to have access to your understanding. Other readers may examine your restatement to discover whether it agrees with their own. It is likely that several readers with similar language and cultural backgrounds will restate the meaning of a text in about the same way. There will, however, always be some variation among paraphrases or summaries composed by different people.

Writing a paraphrase or summary also allows you, at a later date, to recover your understanding quickly. So this type of writing has value as a means of preserving your comprehension and providing you with a way to express your understanding of the text to others.

Writing for clear understanding can be useful in the academic world and beyond. To some extent, you already practice paraphrase and summary. For example, when you take notes in class, you may jot down in your own words what your instructor means. In annotating a text, you may write paraphrases of difficult passages in the margin. Or you may summarize a section of the text before going on to the next. In some courses, you may be asked explicitly to summarize assigned readings or independent reading required for the class. And when you pursue research, the ability to paraphrase and summarize will serve you well.

■ PARAPHRASE AND SUMMARY COMPARED

Paraphrase and summary are complementary; to paraphrase means to write down the precise meaning of a short excerpt in your own words. To summarize is to write down in brief the main meaning or most important points of a long section or entire article or essay. But producing both paraphrases and summaries requires use of some of the same skills, as we shall see. Here is a selection from the article "If Suicide Is Legally Sanctioned for the Terminally Ill, Why Not for the Rest of Society?" by Charles Krauthammer (a reading selection at the end of Chapter 4), followed by a paraphrase of its last paragraph and a summary of the whole passage.

ORIGINAL

In 1991 in the Dutch city of Assen, a perfectly healthy 50-year-old woman asked her doctor to help her die. Her two sons had died, one by suicide, one by cancer. She wanted to join them. After many hours of consultation, Dr. Boudewijn Chabot consented. He was at her side when she swallowed the lethal pills he prescribed for her death.

In Holland, physician-assisted suicide is for all practical purposes legal, but Dr. Chabot was tried anyway because this woman wasn't terminally ill. She wasn't even ill.

In fact, she wasn't even psychiatrically ill, a point that at trial Dr. Chabot made in his own defense. She was as lucid as she was inconsolable.

The three-judge court in Assen acquitted Dr. Chabot. So did an appeals court. Thus, notes Dr. Herbert Hendlin (in his study of euthanasia in Holland, "Seduced by Death: Doctors, Patients and the Dutch Cure"), has Holland "legally established mental suffering as a basis for euthanasia."

PARAPHRASE OF LAST PARAGRAPH

Dr. Chabot was acquitted by both the Assen judiciary and the appeals court. An expert on the Dutch use of euthanasia, Dr. Herbert Hendlin, believes that this case means assisted suicide to remedy mental pain is now legal in that country.

SUMMARY OF ENTIRE PASSAGE

In recent years, Holland has come to permit use of physician-assisted suicide beyond cases of the terminally ill. According to Charles Krauthammer, a Dutch woman despondent over the death of her sons but not herself near death was assisted in suicide by her physician. The doctor was tried and acquitted. This case can be interpreted to mean that, in Holland, assisting someone to commit suicide as a way out of despair is now legal.

Notice that the paraphrase retains most of the details of the original last paragraph but is written in quite different sentences: two instead of three, with different subjects or word order. The word choice is different also, although certain key terms are reused: *acquitted, appeals court, euthanasia,* and *mental.*

The summary omits many details found in the original but does include the essentials of the Dutch case. Its sentences, word order, and word choice are new, although, as with the paraphrase, some words from the original appear but in differently styled sentences: *physician-assisted suicide, terminally ill, tried, acquitted,* and *legal.*

This chart compares the characteristics of a successful paraphrase and summary:

Paraphrase	Summary
■ Length same or longer than the original text	■ Length shorter than original
■ Meaning is the same as the original	■ Meaning (re)states main idea of original
	■ States important secondary ideas
	■ May state main elements of support
■ Details are retained from original	■ Details are not included
■ Wording and style are your own	■ Wording and style are your own
■ "Translates" source meaning into your language style	■ "Condenses" the meaning of the original using your language style

As you can see, although these two skills differ in many ways, they also have some important commonalities. First, summary and paraphrase both require that you use clear signals to indicate that you are reporting the ideas and information supplied by a source. The use of such signals is discussed in the next section, on attribution. Second, writing summaries and paraphrases means explaining someone else's ideas in your own words—that is, using your own style. The process for accomplishing a translation of ideas into your own words is discussed in the section on paraphrase below.

■ ATTRIBUTION: SIGNALING THE USE OF PARAPHRASE AND SUMMARY

When you paraphrase or summarize in formal writing—in academic papers or perhaps in journalistic writing for college publications—you must let the reader know where your own ideas end and the paraphrase or summary begins. Otherwise, your reader will assume the information or ideas are yours. You can signal the start of a paraphrase or summary by providing an attribution—that is, mentioning the author's name in the first sentence of the paraphrase. Doing this is especially important when you refer to the ideas of several authors. Your reader must be able to tell the difference between your ideas and those of each of your sources throughout your entire paper.

Attributions may not be required in less formal uses of paraphrase or summary. For example, on a political science handout, you might write paraphrases of difficult sections without referring to the source because it is obvious. When you are summarizing informally to help yourself understand the meaning of your reading, you would probably write the author's name down once at the top of your page. When taking paraphrase notes on index cards, however, you would note the source's name on each card. You may be required to practice paraphrase or summary for this course or other courses. When your reader knows that your paraphrase or summary derives from an assigned source, you don't have to attribute the ideas unless your instructor requires you to.

Typically, the attribution will be part of a lead-in phrase to a longer sentence or sentences. Here are some examples of attributions leading in to a paraphrase or summary. (These examples and similar passages in the activities show the use of parenthetic documentation. In an actual paper, these references would be keyed to a formal Works Cited list.) Guidelines for informal source reference appear at the end of this chapter, and you can find out more about formal documentation in Chapter 13.

SPECIFIC ATTRIBUTION TO AUTHOR BY NAME
Michael Holquist explains that Mikhail Bakhtin believed people are both alone and linked inescapably to each other (20).

SPECIFIC ATTRIBUTION TO AUTHOR BY NAME AND QUALIFICATIONS
Michael Holquist, a scholar and translator of Bakhtin, explains that Bakhtin believed that humans are both alone and linked inescapably to each other (20).

SPECIFIC ATTRIBUTION TO AUTHOR BY QUALIFICATIONS
A scholar and translator of Bakhtin explains that the Russian theorist believed that humans are both alone and linked inescapably to each other (Holquist 20).

SPECIFIC ATTRIBUTION TO PUBLICATION
(WHEN AUTHOR IS ANONYMOUS OR UNIMPORTANT)
The *New York Times* recently reported that epidemics of serious infectious diseases threaten the new countries formed from the former Soviet Union (Specter 9).

Although it may be possible to place an attribution anywhere in a sentence, placing it at or near the start of the paraphrase or summary is important to signal where your restatement of the source begins. For example, in the following excerpt, the attribution is located at the end of the sentence. As a result, the reader cannot tell whether both sentences or only the second sentence contains a paraphrase:

INEFFECTIVE PLACEMENT OF ATTRIBUTION
The word *avant-garde* derives from military usage. This is appropriate, for modern art invades the future, using every new technological aid available, according to Susan Sontag (107).

Most of the time, avoid providing the attribution in a separate sentence. (Note that when you are quoting, the borrowed language is marked off from yours by the quotation marks, and the attribution may be placed anywhere in the sentence. See the complete discussion of quotation later in this chapter.)

Here are the expectations our civic and academic discourse communities have about how attributions appear. In the first reference to a source, identify the author fully and correctly with the name in the byline or on the title page. Don't abbreviate the author's name or drop middle initials unless the author does so. If the work is a collaboration, include all authors' names (up to four) in the order they are listed. For more than four authors, use the first-listed author's name and a phrase such as "and coauthors" to indicate the author named did not work alone.

Don't use "Mr.," "Ms.," "Dr.," or other personal or professional titles before the author's name, and avoid using first names only. Sometimes in the media, popular or infamous people are referred to familiarly by their first names: "Tonya and Nancy," for example, or "Sly," "Hillary." In most academic writing, stick to full names unless you are doing a piece in which discussing your subject familiarly adds to your tone and suits your purpose.

Use only last names in second or later references:

Holquist points out that Bakhtin viewed a human life as an event (27).

If you wish to put the *title* of the source in your attribution, you may shorten it by dropping some words off the end or by dropping a subtitle. Do use the first few key words of the title and shorten the title to a meaningful phrase. For example, *Fifty Key Contemporary Thinkers: From Structuralism to Postmodernity* might be shortened to *Fifty Key Contemporary Thinkers*. To use just *Contemporary Thinkers* would be to misrepresent the title, and to use just *Fifty Key Contemporary* would create confusion. (Note that when a title is needed in formal parenthetical citation, the shortened version

■ *Vary Verbs Used for Attributing*

Strive for variety when introducing paraphrases, summaries, and quotations. It is tempting to just use "Smith says" or "Jones writes," but there are many other possibilities. Here is a list of some verbs that work well in attributions:

notes	reveals	suggests	points out
claims	complains	shows	argues
proposes	reports	concludes	asks
adds	indicates	explains	questions

need not be meaningful; see Chapter 13.) When including a title in your attribution, use quotation marks to set off the titles of short works such as articles, essays, op-ed pieces, and the like. Use underlining (if typing) or italic print (if word processing) to indicate a book title. (See Chapter 13 for guidelines for handling titles.)

If relevant *biographical details* about the author are available, it is appropriate to include them briefly in the attribution. This is done by adding a short "tag" following the author's name:

Morton R. Carr, Harvard sociologist and author of numerous books about group behavior, . . .

Jeff Greenfield, nationally syndicated columnist, . . .

Dr. Louis W. Sullivan, U.S. Secretary of Health and Human Services under George Bush, . . .

■ PARAPHRASE

Paraphrase refers to writing the meaning of a phrase, sentence, or paragraph in your own words. Originally, paraphrase was used to mean a "loose translation" into English of ancient or religious texts in other languages. The word itself comes from a combination of Greek roots meaning "to show" (*phrazein*) and "alongside" (*para*), according to the *American Heritage Dictionary* ("Paraphrase"). Over time, the term *paraphrase* came to be applied to the method of writing out the meaning of any difficult text, including those in English, in clear words of one's own. "A translation or paraphrase tries to render the meaning in new terms" (Hirsch 136).

Today, paraphrase is used for two purposes: as a study technique to clarify meaning and as a means of presenting the ideas of other writers to your reader. Most likely, when you rephrase to improve your own learning, as in margin notes, you practice *literal,* or word-for-word, paraphrase. In your writing, when you wish to refer to, discuss, or otherwise make use of the ideas or information found in your reading, you should use *complete* paraphrase.

In performing a literal paraphrase to improve your understanding, all you need do is replace key terms with synonyms that are easier to understand. Literal paraphrase requires nothing more than word swapping. In your finance textbook, you might encounter a sentence like this:

> Because the issuance of new securities dilutes the proprietary strength of preexisting owners, most localities require the allocation of preemptive rights to current owners to purchase a proportionate share of a new stock issue.

While reading, you might underline the phrase *dilutes the proprietary strength of preexisting owners* and write a paraphrase nearby:

> Because the issuance of new securities <u>dilutes the proprietary strength of preexisting owners</u>, most localities require the allocation of preemptive rights to current owners to purchase a proportionate share of a new stock issue.

weakens ownership of old owners

This type of paraphrase, in which you replace hard-to-understand terms with easier ones, is sufficient for study purposes. But when you paraphrase to present a source's ideas to your reader, you must go further than just literal paraphrase. You must totally rewrite the passage from your source to produce a complete paraphrase—that is, one that conveys the source's ideas completely in your own language. Look back at the paraphrase of the Krauthammer passage to see how different it is in style (sentence order and type, as well as vocabulary) from the original. In other words, in borrowing ideas from a source, you can't "sort of" paraphrase or "mostly" paraphrase. A complete paraphrase involves thoroughly rewriting the source, not just tinkering with the wording. Rewording sometimes requires using two or three words where the source used only one; so paraphrases are sometimes longer than the original.

If you can't find suitable equivalents for some key words or unique phrases in the passage, you may express them as quotations. Some paraphrases thus contain a blend of quotation and paraphrase (blended paraphrase). If you do quote, you must carefully mark the boundaries between the source's wording and your own by using quotation marks. But if you do not paraphrase, you should quote; there is no middle ground between the two.

Paraphrases are usually performed on small pieces of text; you might paraphrase a sentence, a paragraph, or a short section. To paraphrase a long section or an entire essay would be extremely tedious.

Accuracy and Academic Honesty

Your main goal in writing a paraphrase is accuracy. In your studies, it may make a great deal of difference if you alter ideas as you take notes from your assigned reading. You need to paraphrase accurately in order to perform well in class or on examinations.

Mistaken paraphrases of your reading might also damage the logic or validity of a paper you are assigned to write. Be sure not to change the meaning as you reword.

However, using too many of the source's words in your paraphrase can also be a serious problem. In papers based on sources you have located yourself or even on sources read in common for classwork, the academic community expects that information will be quoted exactly or be completely reworded. Literal paraphrase is not sufficient. The concept of *academic honesty,* an accepted code in the academic world, requires that writers use complete paraphrase, paraphrase blended with accurate quotations, summary, or quotation when discussing ideas or information from sources.

To jumble the source's wording with your own and call it paraphrase is to leave yourself open to a charge of **plagiarism,** the serious error of passing off the work (ideas, information) of others as your own. Even if your faulty paraphrase is the result of haste, weak skills, or poor understanding, you have plagiarized, albeit inadvertently. In Chapter 12, you will find a full discussion of academic honesty.

■ *Activity 1*

Research
Opportunity, p. 112

Paraphrasing is a delicate balancing act. At first, it may seem easy to reword a few sentences in your own style, but in actuality a good paraphrase requires quite a bit of care.

You Must	But Avoid
use different words (reword)	changing the meaning
keep the same meaning	repeating source's phrasing
make the meaning clear(er)	oversimplifying meaning
say it your way (restyle)	adding your own slant to the idea
	drawing unwarranted inferences

Many misunderstandings about paraphrase roam today's classrooms. Sometimes students think that paraphrasing means keeping the significant words of a source and changing the unimportant words, as in changing "the" to "a" and "many" to "a lot." Other times, students have the idea that paraphrasing means changing the vocabulary a writer has used. Such students use a thesaurus to look up synonyms and pop them into the passage. But this results in only a literal paraphrase, sufficient only for studying or clarifying a text. Unfortunately, neither of these two common techniques produces paraphrase valid for use in a paper.

Paraphrase used to represent the ideas of a source to readers must be completely in your own style of language. Ideally, the paraphrase should reflect your own way of using words and not the source's. Here's a passage from a column by George Will, "Violence Is a Public Health Problem" (a reading selection at the end of this chapter), followed by two paraphrases, one literal and the other complete:

ORIGINAL

If the motor vehicle fatality rate of 1952 had been the same in 1989, 155,075 Americans would have died in vehicular accidents. But only 45,555 did, because the problem was treatable (with improved vehicle and highway design, licensing requirements, motorcycle helmet laws and other measures) (Will 00).

LITERAL PARAPHRASE

If the motor vehicle death rate from 1952 had continued to 1989, 155,075 people would have been killed in roadway accidents. However, only 45,555 did because the problem was curable (with better car and road design, different license standards, the requirement of motorcycle helmets, and other changes) (Will 00).

Note that even in this literal word-swapping paraphrase certain words resist translation: *motor vehicle, rate, accidents, problem,* and *motorcycle helmets.* In any attempt to paraphrase, it is likely that there will be some key terms that just cannot be replaced. In a literal translation used for study purposes, such carryovers are not a problem as long as you know what the terms mean. But the presence of such untranslated terms, along with the similarity of sentence structure, means that this literal paraphrase is too close to the original to be used in a paper. The writer might be accused of plagiarism because of the similarity in style and wording to Will's original passage. Instead, for use in a paper, you would create a complete paraphrase.

COMPLETE PARAPHRASE

George Will reports that 155,075 people would have died in traffic accidents in the United States in 1989 if the accident death rate from 1952 had continued. But because of improvements in the design of roads and cars, changes in license standards, the required use of motorcycle helmets, and other changes, only 45,555 Americans died on the roads in 1989, showing that the problem could be cured (00).

Here, some words still remain untranslated (*accidents, rate, license, motorcycle helmets,* and *problem*), but the passage no longer seems an echo of Will's writing. The freshness results from the altered sentence structure. Set in this new style, even the unchanged vocabulary does not cause the paraphrase to remind you of Will's writing. The paraphrase is also slightly longer than Will's original. Often, you will find you need more words to rephrase a passage than the author used. Note too that the numerical information is left as is, because "translating" numbers is usually impossible.

■ *Activity 2*
Evaluating
Paraphrases, p. 112

A Process for Writing Complete Paraphrases

Writing an accurate paraphrase is an extension of being a good reader. Your first step is to read the text well. Look up any difficult or new words to make sure you understand the meaning. Read the passage again, and then try expressing the overall meaning in your own words. Frankly, this is often easier said than done. Some people try to perform a literal paraphrase first, replacing each word with a synonym, and then try to change the style. Unfortunately, swapping words often locks in the author's style and makes it harder to state the meaning your own way.

A better way to start is to rearrange the parts of the sentence or move to a different type of sentence and then change the vocabulary to one more like your own. Here's
an example of this method of paraphrasing, using a passage about youth problems in
Los Angeles from a column by Roger E. Hernandez entitled "The Street Dictates How
Kids See Themselves." (Note that articles contained on one page do not require a page
number in the parenthetic citation. When the author's name is provided in an in-text
attribution, no parenthetic citation is necessary if the article is on one page.)

> On a recent weekend there were 21 murders, leading to concern that the truce between
> Crips and Bloods is dissolving, or that the hostility between black and Hispanic gangs is
> about to burst into warfare (Hernandez).

First, move the phrases around:

> leading to concern [by police in Los Angeles]
>
> the hostility between black and Hispanic gangs is about to burst into warfare
>
> the truce between Crips and Bloods is dissolving
>
> On a recent weekend there were twenty-one murders

Then substitute your own wording and provide an attribution:

> According to Roger E. Hernandez, there is some anxiety in Los Angeles that
> rivalry between ethnic gangs will soon explode into outright war. The peace
> between Crips and Bloods seems to be ending, and twenty-one killings
> occurred on one weekend.

Here the difference in sentence style announces that you have done your job of rephrasing. Note that although most words have been replaced by synonyms, two have been
retained because no synonym really worked: *weekend, gangs.* However, because the sentence flow is so different, no one would accuse this writer of laziness or dishonesty.

Cautions about Paraphrase Style

Most often, students err in not going far enough in their paraphrasing and end up
with a version that sounds a lot like the source (a too-literal paraphrase):

> Recently, according to Roger E. Hernandez, there were twenty-one murders,
> causing concern that the truce of Crips and Bloods is dissolving, and that
> hostility between black and Hispanic youths is about to burst into war.

Sometimes, however, the opposite problem appears. Students go too far in transforming the source into their own language:

Recently, according to Roger E. Hernandez, there were twenty-one wipeouts, making Angelenos worry that the truce between Crips and Bloods is just the calm before the storm, or that black and Hispanic toughs are gearing up for a rumble.

Other times, realizing that using everyday words in the paraphrase doesn't make it sound different enough, some students reach for a special vocabulary. Using the thesaurus might produce the following cumbersome paraphrase:

Lately, in one single weekend, twenty-one homicides were committed, elevating concern that the pacification between Crips and Bloods is evaporating, or that the belligerence between African American and Latino cliques is about to detonate into combat (Hernandez).

■ *Activity 3*
Paraphrasing Practice, p. 114

When to Choose Paraphrase

When the writing is discursive, the style undistinguished, the tone moderate or neutral, paraphrasing in an objective style is probably appropriate. Sometimes, however, you should hesitate before using paraphrase. If a source uses extreme language, imagery, or metaphors, the language may be too difficult to translate into your own phrasing. Or paraphrasing in a neutral style may do an injustice to the author because the author's passion or unique style is lost. In such cases, you should probably quote or summarize.

Blended Paraphrase

If a paraphrase is not completely in your own words, then it must be a blend of paraphrase and direct quotation. A direct quotation is a repetition of the exact words found in the source, placed between quotation marks. (Guidelines for the punctuation and use of quotations follow later in this chapter.)

Sometimes, a phrase difficult or impossible to translate occurs in the passage you are attempting to paraphrase. In that case, you may interrupt your paraphrase with a brief quotation, as short as one word, from your source. This is often done when the source uses or creates a key term that must be retained for the sake of clarity. Here are examples of complete paraphrases blended with quotations:

Today, untold numbers of children find school a respite from "the horrors of home" because, according to columnist Claude Lewis, they "live on a diet of fear, despair, and loneliness."

Roger E. Hernandez writes that people in Los Angeles are worried that rivalry between ethnic gangs "is about to burst into warfare." The peace between Crips and Bloods seems to be ending, and twenty-one killings occurred on one weekend.

■ *Tone, Style, and Diction: Barriers to Paraphrase?*

Suppose you have a source that provides an interesting viewpoint on a topic you are researching, but its language is extreme: it might be emotionally high pitched or connotative, or perhaps the source uses a great deal of slang or jargon.

Here is a paragraph from a syndicated newspaper column by Samuel Francis:

> Now if it's a crime bill you want, forget the Frankenstein monster that flopped about on Capitol Hill a couple of weeks ago. Look at the state legislation sponsored by Republican Gov. George Allen of Virginia. The Republicans on Capitol Hill get the Forrest Gump Man of the Year Award for their low-IQ selective opposition to President Clinton's bill, but Allen may turn out to be the Isaac Newton of crime control (Francis).

Examine the paraphrase of this paragraph below (a literal paraphrase is used here to make it easier to compare the original and the paraphrase). In what ways does it differ from the original? Would you consider it an acceptable literal paraphrase of Francis's ideas?

> Syndicated columnist Samuel Francis believes that if the American people are interested in legislation to solve the crime problem, they should ignore the crime bill that Congress recently considered. Instead, they should study the bill introduced in the Virginia state legislature by Gov. George Allen, a Republican. The Republicans in Congress acted incorrectly, according to Francis, by not strongly fighting against the President's anticrime legislation. However, Gov. Allen could be a genius in discovering how to lower the crime rate, Francis believes.

When you paraphrase a source that uses extreme language, do you think you should strive to "tone down" the wording so it is "academic" and neutral? Or is this a disservice to the source, in fact—a kind of misrepresentation? If you added a description of the source's style or point of view, would the paraphrase then be acceptable? Or should you try to maintain the tone, and seek a paraphrase style that matches that of the source? Or should you simply avoid paraphrasing in a case like this? (Additional considerations about whether to include sources with an obvious bias or extreme style will be discussed in Chapter 5.)

There are no prescribed answers to these questions. What you should do depends on the use you have for the paraphrase, the intent of the original writer, and so on. At times, in order to convey the information presented by a source, realigning the tone through a neutral word choice might be appropriate. But at other times the connotative language of a source might be crucial in creating a meaning or idea that would be lost if the source's tone were flattened out in the paraphrase. You might want to opt for quotation in such a case.

■ *Activity 4*
Connotations in
Paraphrase, p. 114

Just as in a complete paraphrase, the name of the author appears in the sentence when the source is quoted. The ideas are attributed to the source's author so that the reader understands where the quoted words come from. Each paraphrase is followed by the appropriate parenthetic citation. (The parenthetic citation for an article fully contained on one page does not include the page number, which can be found in the listing for the article on the Works Cited page.)

■ SUMMARY: WRITING YOUR UNDERSTANDING OF A SOURCE

A summary distills the main ideas from a source and expresses them in a new way. The ability to paraphrase—to reword ideas in your own style—is essential to summarizing. Summary is used as an academic exercise, to practice the skills of objectivity, of textual observation, of close reading, and of understanding, structuring, and restating ideas. These skills are building blocks in a student's ability to do academic research and to express ideas clearly in a research paper or in other academic writing. The skills involved in summary writing are useful and important throughout college and later academic work, as well as in problem solving, information acquisition, and clear communication in the professional world.

You can summarize an entire essay or article; you can also summarize a section, a few paragraphs, or just one paragraph, depending on your needs or purpose. If you are doing a research project, you will summarize entire articles and pieces of articles. In summarizing to take notes, your summaries will most likely be partial because you won't bother to summarize ideas or sections that don't pertain to the topic of your research. Accurate summarizing in your own words also prevents inadvertent plagiarism.

Types of Summaries

An **informal summary** is one you pull together to improve your studying or gather information for yourself. A **partial summary** is a summary in which you are selective about what you include because you are going to use the summary as support for a point you wish to make in a paper of your own. In it, you pull together the details that serve your purpose, being careful not to distort the source's overall meaning. A **summary note** is a research note in which you summarize data found in a source. (See Chapter 12 for information on partial summaries and note taking for research.) A **formal summary** is a paper whose purpose is to present the major ideas of an article, essay, or longer work.

An **abstract** is a very brief summary, often of a long work, that mentions only the major ideas. A **précis** or **synopsis** is, likewise, a concise summary. In specific discourse communities such as law, business, or publishing, these types of summaries may have particular requirements. In particular, a synopsis or abstract that appears at the start of a long report or study should follow the same organization as the work it summarizes.

A summary should not be confused with a description of a text. A description tells what an author does in a text rather than retelling the content. For example, here is a short description of Louis Sullivan's article (a selected reading at the end of Chapter 2):

> Dr. Sullivan questions the ease with which kids can buy cigarettes. He cites the statistics showing that the younger a beginning smoker is the stronger the addictive pull will be. Then he discusses his findings about how most states don't enforce their existing laws. He has three major suggestions about how to decrease young people's access to tobacco. In the end, he make a plea for all responsible adults to be more vigilant about this problem (00).

This description provides a "play-by-play" of Sullivan's writing. It never directly discusses content or explains his exact ideas.

The discussion of formal summary that follows elaborates the process and skills needed to do any type of summary.

A Process for Preparing a Formal Summary

The formal summary uses a neutral tone and strives to reproduce objectively, fairly, and completely the whole message given in a source. It avoids commentary, drops out supporting details, and focuses on representing the source author's ideas rather than elaborating or commenting on them.

As with doing a paraphrase, writing a summary begins with reading the article or essay with care. You then need to identify which ideas are central and which details can be dropped. And, of course, you must reword everything in your own style. To decide which ideas to retain, you need to thoroughly understand the article. Mark the original (or photocopy and mark it), or take notes. Especially, underline or bracket significant sections. Then skim through the article again, identifying and making notes about its main idea and numbering its supporting points as 1, 2, and so on. If the main idea is stated explicitly, summarize it using your own words. Sometimes you will need several words to convey the meaning of a complex term; don't be afraid to write longer sentences than in the original.

In order to plan your summary, you need to be aware of the expectations most readers have of a summary. You may find this outline of standard summary structure helpful.

Your **introductory paragraph** should, first, identify the author and article, preferably in the first sentence, through a lead-in attribution. Provide in this sentence also any significant background information on the author (*ethos*). Second, the introductory paragraph should summarize the main idea or claim of the article in your own words. Place quotation marks around any key words and phrases that you find impossible to restate in your own words. Usually, your summary of the claim statement should appear in the first or second sentence, often with the author-title identifier as a lead-in:

> In "Why Ducks Quack," Morton R. Carr, Harvard sociologist, maintains that peer pressure affects both ducks and people and causes people in groups to think and "quack" alike (262).

> Dr. Louis W. Sullivan, U.S. Secretary of Health and Human Services under
> George Bush, believes our nation should prevent children from buying tobacco
> products. In his article "Stop Peddling Tobacco to Kids," Sullivan argues that
> the state laws prohibiting tobacco sales to young people should be better
> enforced (00).

Optionally, in your introduction, you may wish to give an overview of the writer's
attitude or point of view. Sometimes, after you summarize the writer's main idea, it will
be appropriate to comment on the overall attitude or perhaps tone of the piece. This
is particularly true if a highly emotional tone dominates the article or if the writer has
a professional commitment to his perspective. Here are some examples of such
overview statements:

> Humorously comparing humans to a flock of ducks, Carr dramatizes the
> herdlike behavior of people to show how meaningless is much human
> "quacking" about current issues.

> In his role as overseer of health in the United States, Sullivan raises the alarm
> about how accessible cigarettes are to young people.

Alternatively, you may briefly describe the article's direction, structure, or development
in the introduction. If the article develops in a highly structured way, reporting this to
your readers might help them navigate the summary. For example, perhaps the article
gives numerous examples of a problem and then analyzes causes. Or an article may
show that a problem exists and then provide solutions. Here are some examples of how
a summarizer might indicate structure to the reader:

> After a long series of examples culled from experiments conducted at Harvard,
> Carr explains step by step how members of a group come to think alike.

> He [Sullivan] pulls together information about the extent of cigarette-induced
> disease, the economic costs of smoking, and the lax enforcement of tobacco-
> sale laws. Then he makes specific recommendations for solving the problem of
> smoking by young people.

Your **development paragraphs** should summarize the first main point and follow
with the other main points in order. Be careful to:

Use your own wording.
Drop out supporting details.
Arrange points in logical order, usually that of the source.
Give each main point equal weight; don't "peter out."
Refer to the author occasionally, using last name only.

Be aware that your summary does not have to present the content of each and
every paragraph in the source. Some paragraphs will not be important to the overall

meaning; some will contain only details. So your summary should not be a string of minisummaries of every paragraph.

Arrange your points in a logical order. Often, this will be the same order as in the source, but not necessarily. Some articles will be repetitious, redundant, or a bit disorganized.

Give each main point equal weight. Include the same type and amount of details for each point; as you move through the article, don't give more space and weight to earlier points, unless the author presented less detail about later points. Finally, refer to the author occasionally throughout the summary to remind the reader that you are discussing the ideas of that source.

Here is an example of a summary of Sullivan's article. Paragraph numbers are enclosed in brackets so you can trace this summary's ideas in the article. These would not normally be a part of a formal summary; you should include them in yours only if your instructor requires you to.

> An addictive habit, smoking causes one-sixth of the deaths in the United States, and each year $52 billion is spent to undo or combat its effects, Sullivan points out [1]. Statistics indicate that 90 percent of smokers started their habit when under age eighteen [4]. Sullivan cites a report that he commissioned [6] showing that even though forty-four states and the District of Columbia forbid cigarette sales to minors, these laws are rarely enforced [7]. As a result, each year about a billion packs of cigarettes are purchased by young people [7]. Enforcement lags because police are busy with more serious crimes and our court systems are already overburdened with other criminal cases [9].
>
> Rather than continue to ignore this situation and allow continual endangerment of the health of young people, our country should pass new laws, Sullivan argues, that would be enforceable [13–14]. First, those who sell tobacco products should be licensed, as alcohol vendors are [14a]. Second, punishment of violations should not fall to the criminal justice system. Rather, civil fines should be levied [14b]. Third, cigarette vending machines should be outlawed. (Sullivan notes that we do not have vending machines for beer.) [14c]

If you feel the article or essay you are summarizing is disorganized or repetitious, you may use an organization that is clearer or more succinct in your summary. Not all published material is highly polished or pruned down. But most summaries do flow along with the source's presentation of points.

The **conclusion** of your summary should state the author's last point and summarize the conclusion of the article. Here is an appropriate concluding sentence for the Sullivan summary:

> The author concludes with a plea that we take the issue of smoking by young people seriously and work toward preventing children from buying tobacco.

■ *Hints for Rewriting in Your Words*

- *Rethink* the main idea before trying to write it down.
- *Restyle* the idea in a new sentence structure. Join simple ideas, or split complex sentences into simpler ones. If you can, change the location of descriptive phrases, turn subsidiary phrases or clauses into independent parts, or reverse the way a sentence flows.
- *Reword* by replacing all key words and phrases with synonyms.

Optionally, you may wish to sum up by giving an overview of the writer's attitude or point of view, if not done before, or adding a point about another aspect of the piece. And if there is nothing notable to say about the writer's style or attitude, omit any discussion of them.

If appropriate, provide documentation for the article. If you are summarizing an article known to your readers (your classmates and your instructor), identification by title and author, such as you provided in your first sentence, is sufficient. If your audience is not familiar with the piece you are summarizing, you will probably want to provide complete bibliographic information. To do this, use accepted bibliographic format (see Chapter 13). Skip a line or two and place this information below your summary.

Hints and Tips

Use a neutral tone. No matter how opinionated the writer of the article is, your summary of the article should use neutral language. The article by Sullivan is extremely negative about how much tobacco is sold to and consumed by young people in the

■ *Checklist for Summary Writing*

After completing your summary, reread it to make sure:

- You have covered all major points of the article.
- You have clearly and accurately described each point.
- You have used the author's order of points or a more logical order of points.
- You have not added any new ideas or extended an idea beyond the author's presentation of it.
- You have not added emotionally suggestive or judgmental words.

■ *Activity 5*

Practice in Summarizing, p. 115

United States, but the summary itself uses neutral language. Here are two versions of a sentence from a summary of a different article:

FAULTY

Wilcox says that television has failed miserably as a substitute for real life; it only builds a stifling, impersonal cocoon around the individual so that the mind becomes polluted with false reality.

CORRECT

Wilcox says that television gives an impression of reality. This is a negative effect, in that it causes people to isolate themselves in their homes. They come to accept television's version of reality and so become separated from real life.

Don't add imagery or use clichés that don't appear in the source. They can change the tone and even create misimpressions. For example, the following would be inappropriate in summarizing Sullivan, whose approach is down to earth but hardly breezy:

Sullivan wonders why mere babes are smoking like chimneys, leading them to hang it up at a tragic young age.

Avoid asking questions instead of explaining ideas. Even if your source uses questions or rhetorical questions—that is, questions to which the answer is implied or obvious—you should state the author's ideas in declarative sentences. Below is an example of how to summarize an idea Sullivan expresses as a question in paragraph 2 of his article:

FAULTY

Why does our society ignore the use of deadly and habit-forming cigarettes by young people?

CORRECT

Sullivan wonders why our society ignores the use of deadly and habit-forming cigarettes by young people.

Use the present tense. Write about ideas in the present tense. Even though the article was written in the past by the author, you are reading, writing, and discussing the ideas at the present time. So, conventionally, we use present-tense verbs in writing about ideas.

FAULTY

Dr. Louis W. Sullivan's article stressed the importance of stopping children's consumption of cigarettes.

CORRECT

Dr. Louis W. Sullivan's article stresses the importance of stopping children's consumption of cigarettes.

The present tense is used even if the author of the article is dead.

Capitalize and punctuate titles correctly. Review the rules presented later in this chapter for capitalization of titles and for using quotation marks and underlining (italics) if you are unfamiliar with these conventions.

Punctuate quotations correctly. When you find you can't rephrase the original wording, use quotation marks to indicate the words of the source.

In punctuating quotations, remember that commas and periods go *inside* end-quotation marks:

FAULTY:	"the fatal enticement of smoking",
CORRECT:	"the fatal enticement of smoking,"

FAULTY:	"smoke-free society".
CORRECT:	"smoke-free society."

Note also the exceptions to the "punctuation inside" rule: colons and semicolons are placed outside the quotation marks unless part of the quotation:

FAULTY:	"Our laws are not enforced;" Sullivan wants them enforced.
CORRECT:	"Our laws are not enforced"; Sullivan wants them enforced.

FAULTY:	Sullivan suggests the following "model legislation:"
CORRECT:	Sullivan suggests the following "model legislation":

Likewise, exclamation marks and question marks go inside only when they are part of the quotation.

Use pronouns correctly. Leading into a summary by naming the author and title can sometimes create a pronoun reference problem. Remember the rule is that a pronoun must refer to a noun that is acting as a subject or object. A pronoun should not refer to a noun that is in the possessive form because then that noun is acting as an adjective.

FAULTY

In Dr. Sullivan's essay, he argues for the enforcement of tobacco-sales laws.

This version is incorrect because the pronoun *he* cannot correctly refer to a possessive form, *Sullivan's*. As the sentence is now written, *he* refers to the preceding noun, *essay*. This is truly nonsensical.

The solution is to take a small liberty with the rule that the referent of the pronoun must precede it.

CORRECT

In his essay, Dr. Louis W. Sullivan argues for the enforcement of tobacco-sales laws.

■ ADDITIONAL CONSIDERATIONS IN PARAPHRASE AND SUMMARY

A Source Written in the First Person

If you wish to paraphrase or summarize a source that includes substantial references to the author in the first person (*I, me, my, mine*), you will have to change the pronouns to the third person (*he, she, it; him, her, it;* and so on). Here is an example from an article against permissive gun laws by columnist Mary McGrory:

ORIGINAL

Giving someone like me a weapon would not equalize the situation. Someone who has never mastered the electric can opener would constitute a peril worse than a cluster bomb to herself and anyone in the vicinity.

PARAPHRASE

Mary McGrory humorously says that providing guns to unarmed people like her would not balance out the odds. As a person who is inept with machines, she would be a danger to herself and the public.

SUMMARY

Mary McGrory humorously rejects the option of giving every citizen a weapon because, in her own case, she is a klutz with machines.

Sometimes you can convert a phrase such as *I think, I believe, I realize,* and *I wonder* to an attribution:

ORIGINAL

I realize that the shock value of a concealed weapon is lost if the bearer is identified.

PARAPHRASE

Identifying carriers of hidden guns would take away the effect of surprise, McGrory realizes.

A Caution about Interpretation

In both paraphrase and summary, it can be hard to resist supplying ideas implied by the source. Often, drawing out the implications is part of making the sense of a passage clear to your readers. You need to be aware when you are doing this and make a conscious judgment about whether drawing the inference is necessary and whether your interpretation is accurate. If another writer might draw a different inference, you probably ought to hold off. For an example of an acceptable inference that extends but does not add new meaning, look again at the original sentence from the finance textbook:

> Because of the issuance of new securities dilutes the proprietary strength of preexisting owners, most localities require the allocation of preemptive rights to current owners to purchase a proportionate share of a new stock issue.

A literal paraphrase might be:

> Because the issuance of new securities weakens the ownership strength of old owners, most localities require that old stockholders be given a chance to buy a proportionate share of new stock.

If you were to extend the paraphrase of the final clause to draw out its implied meaning, it would say this:

> . . . old stockholders be given a chance to buy a proportionate share of new stock <u>to keep their percentage of ownership the same if they so desire.</u>

The underlined words represent meaning that is not actually stated in the original but that must be figured out if the sentence is to make any sense. It is an inference added by the paraphraser, and it seems warranted.

Here's an example of an inference added to a summary. In her mocking critique of Virginia's new law permitting concealed handguns in some types of businesses and on the streets, McGrory writes:

> What worries me is that Virginians can carry their firearms on the Metro—at least as far as the last stop before the train plunges across the Potomac to the first station in the gun-infested District of Columbia. Riders on the Orange Line have no way of knowing if the seated person with the . . . white buck shoes is armed—God forbid your foot might smudge his shoes; you'd find out with the help of hot lead.

You might infer from this paragraph that McGrory is concerned that Virginians might bring even more weapons into the District of Columbia, although she doesn't say it. In fact, she focuses the rest of the paragraph on a (humorous) potential conflict on the subway itself. Yet the implications of danger to the District of Columbia from this Virginia law are quite clear—a person with a concealed gun would probably not get off the train in Virginia—and few would quarrel with a summary that makes this interpretation.

Strictly, a paraphrase should avoid adding material that is not there. Likewise a summary. But if you are sure that your inference or interpretation is correct and that your reader would appreciate the clarity or the logical link that your inference supplies, it is usually acceptable to provide it.

A Source within a Source

Occasionally in writing paraphrases and summaries, you will encounter important ideas that do not belong to the author but to a person who is the subject of the article. This can easily happen, for example, if you are summarizing a news article about a speech made by an important official or paraphrasing an article about newly reported research. In such a case, you must be sure to attribute the ideas to the subject of the article, not to the author. The parenthetic citation (if any), however, would contain the author's name. In a news article, "Federal Judge Urges Legalization of Crack, Heroin, and Other Drugs" by Stephen Labaton that appeared in the *New York Times*, the important ideas are those of Judge Robert Sweet, not reporter Stephen Labaton.

In summarizing the article's ideas, you would need to attribute them to the judge:

> With almost twelve years of experience as a judge, Federal District Court Judge Robert W. Sweet has come to believe that drugs should be legal for adults. Legalization would put a stop to the futile sentencing of drug users and would end the flood of drug cases in the courts. He calls drug use a "social phenomenon" (Labaton).

■ QUOTATION SKILLS

Quotation can be the easiest way to borrow the ideas of others because you don't have to put yourself through the labor of rewording. But quotation requires other skills: the ability to choose quotations purposefully and to inset the chosen quotations coherently and smoothly, plus a knowledge of punctuation.

Choosing Quotations

Quoting shouldn't be your "default" method of referring to the ideas of others. Here are the positive reasons to choose quotation over paraphrase or summary:

- The source presents the idea eloquently, dramatically, powerfully, in a style that will add pizazz to your paper.
- The source's idea is complex or subtle, and you don't want to risk misrepresenting it.
- The author writes emotionally, ironically, or unconventionally, presenting major obstacles to accurate rewording.
- The source's idea is unusual, extreme, or eccentric, and you want to make sure your reader doesn't doubt your representation of it.
- You are going to refute the idea, and you want to make sure your reader has it "from the horse's mouth," so that your opposing points make sense.

Quotations should be special; they should add something substantial to the text, and there should not be too many of them. An average of one or two quotations per page of typed text is probably enough. Of course, there may be additional references to sources through paraphrasing and summary.

How Much to Quote

When choosing a quotation, you should pare it down so it is pointed and purposeful. Don't let the quotation become obscured by excess verbiage. Use the ellipsis when necessary to cut out wordiness and make a quotation effective. (See the section on the ellipsis below.)

Occasionally, you may discover a long passage containing explanations, definitions, or a system of categorizations, for example, that you feel is crucial to your discussion of a topic. If such material is longer than a few paragraphs or would run one-half to three-quarters of a page of your paper, you should summarize it. If you believe your reader should have a chance to inspect the original material, include it as an appendix at the end of your paper. (See Chapter 13 for more on using an appendix.)

Quoting Statistics, Charts, and Specifications

When you quote a passage that includes statistics, you will use quotation marks or, if the passage is long, block format. In these situations, the source of the statistics is clear. If, however, you incorporate statistics from a source in a paraphrase, you do not need to place quotation marks around the statistics. It will be assumed that you are giving exact figures when you put the statistics in your paraphrase. Here are examples:

QUOTATION

Researchers from the MacArthur Foundation's Working Poor Project "concluded that between now and 2005, an estimated 140,000 jobs will become available. Only about 25 percent of these will require a college degree" (Geoghegan).

PARAPHRASE

The MacArthur Foundation's Working Poor Project reports that college will be required for 25 percent, more or less, of the approximately 140,000 jobs that will arise between 1996 and 2005 (Geoghegan).

You may include a chart or other graphic in your text, with appropriate documentation. Even though you will reproduce it exactly, you do not need quotation marks. Unless you are producing a technical report where specifications and the like are expected in the text, you should summarize technical material running more than a half page or three-quarter page in length. You may then put the actual material at the end of your paper as an appendix. (See Chapter 13.)

Insetting Quotations in Your Own Text

Use Attributions

Like summary and paraphrase, quotations should be attributed in the text. Because quotations are delineated with quotation marks, a reader immediately recognizes that the words are not yours. The attribution can therefore be placed anywhere in relation to the quotation: before it, at a natural pause in the middle of it, or after it. (The various punctuation complications of these possibilities follow.) The conventions of attribution for summary and paraphrase discussed above apply to quotations also.

Build a Bridge to the Quotation

Quotations present problems different from summary and paraphrase. First, unlike them, quotations are not in your own words and may, in fact, use a markedly different style than yours. Second, you need to make sure that the reader sees what you see in the source's words. So before you insert a quotation, you need to build a bridge to it. Your bridge should briefly forecast or preview the concept, detail(s), or evidence that the quotation offers, so that the reader understands what the quotation is doing there. Sometimes you can build this bridge right into the attribution:

> Mary McGrory, a writer who works in Washington, D.C., has concerns that a law in Virginia might have effects on the capital. "What worries me," she writes, "is that Virginians can carry their firearms on the Metro—at least as far as the last stop before the train plunges across the Potomac to the . . . gun-infested District of Columbia."

Other times, you will need a sentence or two to explain the quotation. Here is an excerpt from a student paper:

> Once humans take the power of life and death into their own hands in one situation, it becomes hard to deny it in other situations. Assisted suicide would logically become legal in all cases. "If assisted suicide is a right for the terminally ill, there is no argument that can be made to deny it on grounds of mercy or autonomy or nondiscrimination to anyone else who might request it," concludes Charles Krauthammer.

■ *Activity 6*

Selecting and
Bridging to
Quotations, p. 117

Always avoid plopping a quotation into your text without a bridge. This can be jarring to a reader. Your paper will then seem like a patchwork of ideas and styles, instead of a flowing text that knits the discourse of various writers with your dominant voice and style.

The Mechanics of Including Quotations

How you present quotations has to do with the length of the quoted material. Short quotations are four lines or less in length. Long quotations run over four lines. Short and long quotations are presented differently.

Short Quotations

Short quotations consist of phrases, partial sentences, or full sentences. They become part of your text and may appear with a lead-in, interrupting, or follow-up attribution or be blended into your sentence. Here are examples:

> As Mary McGrory notes about a new law in Virginia, "What worries me is that Virginians can carry their firearms on the Metro."

> "What worries me," one resident of Washington, D.C., writes, "is that Virginians can carry their firearms on the Metro" (McGrory).

> "What worries me is that Virginians can carry their firearms on the Metro," writes columnist Mary McGrory about a new Virginia law.

Notice the commas that separate the student's text from the source quotation. The usual comma rules for an introductory dependent clause, an interrupting parenthetical clause, or concluding dependent clause apply to these attributions.

When quotations are blended into your own writing, you must tailor the quotation to fit your sentence. Here are examples:

> Columnist Mary McGrory is deeply concerned "that Virginians can carry their firearms on the Metro."

> Once the Supreme Court validates euthanasia for the terminally ill, Charles Krauthammer claims that "mercy or autonomy or nondiscrimination" will become the grounds for extending it to anyone.

Long Quotations

Quotations that run longer than four typed lines should be blocked rather than included in the flow of a paragraph. Even if a blocked quotation starts a paragraph in the original, do not indent it unless you are quoting more than one paragraph. The parenthetic reference comes after the period, not before. Here is a short section of a paper using a blocked quotation:

> Among Mary McGrory's concerns about the new Virginia law making concealed guns legal is the thought that Washington, D.C., will be affected:
>
> > What worries me is that Virginians can carry their firearms on the Metro—at least as far as the last stop before the train plunges across the Potomac to the first station in the gun-infested District of Columbia. Riders of the Orange Line have no way of knowing if [another] person . . . is armed.
>
> She anticipates that gun violence might erupt over small slights when some riders carry weapons.

Most blocked quotes are preceded by a lead-in using a colon. Occasionally, a comma is appropriate, especially when the lead-in is a simple attribution. Here is another piece of student writing that incorporates two source paragraphs into the text:

> Charles Krauthammer sees a tragic logic in the arguments for assisted suicide. He asks,
>
>> By what logical principle should the relief of death be granted only the terminally ill? After all, the terminally ill face only a brief period of suffering. The chronically ill, or the healthy but bereft—they face a lifetime of agony. Why deny them the relief of a humane exit?
>>
>> The litigants before the Supreme Court, however, claimed the right to assisted suicide on the grounds not of mercy but of liberty—the autonomy of individuals to determine when and how they will die.
>
> This argument means, for Krauthammer, that the courts will have to allow anyone to commit suicide. It will be everyone's individual right.

The first lines of the quoted paragraphs are indented an additional one-quarter inch or three typewriter spaces.

Punctuating Quotations

Long and short quotations are punctuated differently. The major difference is that only short quotations use quotation marks.

Short quotations—punctuating short quotations is complicated because there are so many variations. Short quotations can be set off with an attribution or be blended in to your style. Each variation requires some mix of quotation marks and a comma or end punctuation.

Here are the basic rules:

- All word-for-word material of less than four full lines should be enclosed in quotation marks.
- A comma follows a lead-in phrase or clause preceding a quotation and also follows the last word of a quotation that has an attribution or additional commentary after it.
- Commas enclose any parenthetic phrases or dependent clauses interrupting a quotation.
- A comma always goes before the closing quotation mark except when the quotation closes your sentence.
- The period goes before the closing quotation mark when the quotation closes your sentence.
- All other end punctuation (semicolon, question mark, exclamation mark) is placed outside the closing quotation mark, unless the mark is part of the quotation.

- When a parenthetic citation closes your sentence, there is no punctuation before it, and it is followed by the period or other end punctuation mark.
- Retain the capital letter at the start of a quoted sentence unless you are blending the sentence into your own style.

Here are examples of set-in quotations correctly punctuated.

Krauthammer writes, "She was as lucid as she was inconsolable" (21).

"She was as lucid as she was inconsolable," Krauthammer writes.

"She was as lucid," Krauthammer writes, "as she was inconsolable."

"As lucid as she was inconsolable," the woman was also perfectly healthy, Krauthammer reports.

Here is the same quotation blended in to the sentence:

Krauthammer writes that "she was as lucid as she was inconsolable."

Here is an example in which a short fragment is blended in:

According to Krauthammer, the suicide victim "wasn't even ill."

No comma is used after "victim" because there is no grammatical need for one between a subject ("victim") and a predicate ("wasn't").

Long quotations—passages running longer than four lines—should be blocked and should appear without quotation marks. *Blocking* means placing the quotation one double space below your text and setting the margin in one inch or five spaces on the left. Use double spacing throughout.

Blocked quotations usually require a stronger, more obvious lead-in, one that points to the upcoming block of text. Most of the time, this lead-in uses a colon, not a comma. Use initial capitalization for the quotation. Here is an example:

Once humans take the power of life and death into their own hands in one situation, it becomes hard to deny it in others. One critic of euthanasia concludes:

> If assisted suicide is a right for the terminally ill, there is no argument that can be made to deny it on grounds of mercy or autonomy or nondiscrimination to anyone else who might request it.
>
> That is why the Supreme Court decision will be so fateful.
>
> (Krauthammer)

Notice that the parenthetical reference appears after the final period of the quotation, not before it.

Internal quotations within a short quote, such as a quotation from someone else, the title of a short work, or a phrase used ironically or imprecisely, take single quotation marks (' '). Here are some examples:

> Vermulen sums up the sixties and seventies this way: "After the pill freed women from the fear of unwanted pregnancy, 'free love' and sexual exploration were condoned" (000).

> According to Mary McGrory, "Newt Gingrich . . . has an answer. He would 'break down the cult of macho behavior in prison.' "

> After a day of watching TV talk shows, Steenland humorously concludes, "I'd like to suggest a show topic—'I Had the Flu before I Tuned In but I'm Extremely Sick Now.' "

Because block quotations do not use quotation marks, any quoted material inside a blocked quotation takes double quotation marks.

Acceptable Changes to Quotations: Ellipses and Brackets

Quotations must be exact, but sometimes it is necessary to alter a quotation in order to make it clearer, more concise, or more to the point. The ellipsis and brackets are the two marks used to indicate omissions from and additions to a quotation. The guidelines here follow MLA format, appropriate for student essays and papers. (Book publishers frequently use other standards.)

Ellipsis

The ellipsis (. . .) is a series of three periods with spaces between them. It replaces words that have been removed in order to eliminate irrelevancies or wordiness from a quotation. The remaining quotation must be grammatical and read smoothly. It must also not distort the source's ideas. The examples above show the correct use of the ellipsis in MLA format. Here are some special considerations for using this punctuation:

- When words are deleted from the start of a quotation, the ellipsis is not needed.
- When a quotation is a fragment or phrase, the ellipsis is not needed because it is obvious that the quotation is not a full sentence.
- When an entire sentence or more is deleted from a quotation, insert the ellipsis after the period that ends the last quoted sentence. This results in four periods in all, with only the last three spaced out.
- When an omission requiring an ellipsis ends the quotation, place an additional period right after the last word of the quotation, and then use the ellipsis, resulting in four periods in all.
- When an ellipsis ends a sentence but is followed by a parenthetic reference, place the fourth period after the citation.

Brackets

These square parentheses, [ ], are used to indicate an addition to a quotation. This addition might replace a pronoun made vague by the quotation's removal from its context or might clarify some other term. For example, this quotation uses only the last names of two officials who have been previously mentioned in the source text.

> "What Barr and Allen are talking about is a quaint little concept that used to be known as 'justice'" (Francis).

The quotation is clearer if the identities of the two people are added in brackets:

> "What [former U.S. Attorney General William] Barr and [Virginia Governor George] Allen are talking about is a quaint little concept that used to be known as 'justice' " (Francis).

■ *Activity 7*

Practice in Punctuating Quotations, p. 117

■ GUIDELINES FOR INFORMAL SOURCE REFERENCE

In academic research, references to information and the ideas of other writers must be formally documented. There must be a bibliography or Works Cited list, and internal references to sources must be keyed to this list. But in other types of writing throughout the civic discourse community references to authors or works are informal. Journalists, essay writers, and other nonacademic authors acknowledge their sources simply, through attributions right in the text. The goal is to let readers know that ideas under discussion come from a reliable source.

There are no formal rules, obviously, for informal reference, but in the civic discourse community certain guidelines are tacitly agreed on. First, a source is referred to in the regular text. There is no parenthetic reference or Works Cited list.

Second, the author's name and, if the person is not famous, his or her claim to expertise are the major pieces of information provided. Here is columnist Barbara Ehrenreich introducing a paraphrase of a source:

> But Harvard economist Juliet Schor's research shows that women have been eliminating half an hour of housework for every hour they work outside the home—or up to twenty hours a week.

Ehrenreich does not expect her readers to look up Schor's work. If we do wish to know more, we will have to do some detective work in the library or on the Internet to discover the titles of Schor's books or articles.

Third, sometimes the title of the article or the name of the periodical it appeared in is provided instead of an author's name. This may be done because the article was anonymous. Here is another passage from Ehrenreich:

> Once food processing and garment manufacture moved out of the home and into the factories, middle-class homemakers found themselves staring uneasily into the

void. . . . "Too many women," editorialized the *Ladies' Home Journal* in 1911, "are dangerously idle."

Ehrenreich's source for this quote appears to be an unsigned editorial.

Other times, the author is not important (as in the case of routine newspaper reporting, for example), so the periodical name is provided instead:

> In a recent *New York Times* article, Federal District Court Judge Robert W. Sweet was described as supportive of drug decriminalization.

■ *Activity 8*

Practice in Using
Informal Reference,
p. 117

The writer whose byline appeared on the *Times* article, reporter Stephen Labaton, is not mentioned.

Activities

1   Research Opportunity

In a database or bibliography covering general periodicals or a major newspaper, look up one of these cases of scholarly or journalistic plagiarism:

> Stephen B. Oates, author of *With Malice toward None: The Life of Abraham Lincoln* (1977), accused of plagiarism in 1991
> Gary Owen Hughes, author of the Oxford University doctoral dissertation "The Redefinition of Pennsylvania Politics, 1740–90," accused of plagiarism in 1994
> Ruth Shalit, writer for the *New Republic,* accused of plagiarism in 1996
> Janet Daily, author of numerous romance novels, including *Notorious,* accused of plagiarism in 1997

Take notes about the controversy and be prepared to inform your classmates about it.

2   Evaluating Paraphrases

Read these original passages and compare them with the paraphrases. Identify whether the paraphrase is literal or complete. For those that are literal paraphrases, rewrite them as complete paraphrases.

[A]   It is a commonplace to note that we have little faith in our institutions, no faith in Congress, in the White House, little faith in what used to be called the establishment—big business, big media, the Church. But there's a sort of schizoid quality in this. We have contempt for the media, but we have respect for newscasters and columnists. When we meet them we're impressed and admiring.

> —Peggy Noonan, "You'd Cry Too"

Peggy Noonan says that, in the United States today, it is often noted that we don't have much trust in our government organizations, no trust in Congress, in the White House, little trust in what was once known as the establishment—major industries, the communications industry, and religious groups. We scorn the media, but honor news anchors and commentators. We act reverent and adoring when we encounter them.

[B]   Doctors note that in trials of new drugs, as many as 30% to 40% of the participants improve even if they have got nothing more than sugar water. This "placebo effect," says Dr. John M. Weiler, an immunologist at the University of Iowa medical school, suggests a very real link between the immune system and the brain, even if scientists don't fully understand it.

—Frederick Golden, "Now a Word from Our Doctors"

Time magazine writer Frederick Golden notes that "the placebo effect" causes 30 to 40 percent of people testing new drugs to get better, even when their medicine is only sugar water. One immunologist, Dr. John M. Weiler of the University of Iowa medical school, says that this shows that the mind and the immune system are connected, although researchers don't know how.

[C]   HIV/AIDS statistics are so rough because they are by necessity estimates: accurate data are simply not available in many parts of the world. Actual AIDS cases are especially difficult to count, since they tend to go both unrecognized and unreported in many developing nations. Even if doctors have the requisite training and equipment to make conclusive AIDS diagnoses, they may be unable to communicate their findings to record-keeping institutions.

—Aaron Sachs, "HIV/AIDS Cases Rising Steadily"

Aaron Sachs of the World Watch Institute claims that statistics on HIV and AIDS are approximate because they are of necessity guesses: correct statistics are not kept in many parts of the world. In particular, cases of full-blown AIDS are extremely hard to keep track of. When doctors can diagnose AIDS, they still may not be able to give their findings to health officials.

[D]   The role of a citizen in a democratic society is multifaceted. It goes beyond voting. Citizens are responsible for becoming informed, for assessing the individual and community implications of issues and then making judgments—choices—about those issues.

What distinguishes the individual from the citizen is that individuals make choices based on what is good for themselves or for a narrow group. But to be a "citizen" is to think more broadly.

—Harris Sokoloff, "Fixing Our 'Broken' Political Discourse"

According to Harris Sokoloff, of the University of Pennsylvania Graduate School of Education, citizens have a multifaceted role in democracies. Beside voting, they have to understand the issues and their effects on people and then choose what is best to do. He claims that a citizen is different from an individual because citizens think about the whole community when deciding issues, not just about themselves.

3 Paraphrasing Practice

Here are several passages that are suitable for any or all of the following activities:

1. Write a literal paraphrase of the selection.
2. Write a complete paraphrase of the selection.
3. Write a blended paraphrase of the selection—that is, a paraphrase that includes some carefully chosen quoted phrase(s).

[A] Women with college degrees contribute only 4 percent of white illegitimate babies, while women with a high-school education or less contribute 82 percent. Women with family incomes of $75,000 or more contribute 1 percent of white illegitimate babies; while women with family incomes under $20,000 contribute 69 percent.

—Charles Murray, "The Coming White Underclass"

[B] This idea—that there is content called "the news of the day"—was entirely created by the telegraph (and since amplified by newer media), which made it possible to move de-contextualized information over vast spaces at incredible speed. The news of the day is a figment of our technological imagination.

—Neil Postman, *Amusing Ourselves to Death*

[C] In technological terms, it's not at all hard to believe we live in a second Industrial Revolution. In what other lifetimes could you find technical advances such as the splitting of the atom, the development of the computer, and the decoding of the gene? Not even James Watt's time showed such a profusion of scientific breakthroughs. If Watt's steam engine was the popular epitome of the original Industrial Revolution, the epitome of the new one is William Shockley's transistor.

—Robert L. Bartley, "Time to Shake Our Hypochondria"

[D] But what is slavery nowadays anyhow? It is a question the United Nations has been wrestling with for decades by assigning experts to look at what are called "contemporary forms" of enslavement. There have been conventions signed and conferences held, and still the word is open to considerable interpretation.

—Barbara Crossette, "What Modern Slavery Is, and Isn't"

4 Connotations in Paraphrase

Below are selections from sources, each followed by a paraphrase. (Literal rather than complete paraphrases are used in this activity in order to make comparisons straight-forward.) Compare the original with its paraphrase and decide whether the paraphrase is acceptable. What problems are raised by the attempt to paraphrase these passages? Can you produce a better paraphrase, either literal or complete? Do you think paraphrase of these selections should be attempted at all?

[A] In an ambitiously strenuous polling project—done by double-dome statisticians from academia, not by political party hacks—the *Washington Post* (Jan. 28–Feb. 4 [1996]) has run a too-long series of non-stop, multiple page takeouts showing that 67 percent of the random sample of 1,514 people interviewed did not know the names of their Representative in Congress. Half did not know whether their Congress person was a Democrat or a Republican, 39 percent could not say which party now has a majority in the House and 46 percent did not know the name of the Speaker of the House. Only 24 percent of these folks bothered to vote in 1994.

No wonder, because here is the survey's bottom line: *58 percent said they got all or most of their non- or misinformation from television.*

—Ben A. Franklin, "Children Are Not the Only Victims of Television"

In a credible poll of American citizens, done by interviewing a random sample, it has been shown that Americans are politically ignorant. Large numbers of people didn't know their Representative's name or political party, what the majority party in the House is, or the Speaker's name. Fortunately, very few of these uninformed people voted. And where did they get their information, or should I say ignorance? From television, of course.

[B] Leadership [in the black community] cannot be handed by default to loudmouths with law degrees. It's time for those of us in positions of privilege, power, and authority to stop playing our cards so close to our chests. Start speaking from the heart and stop holding civil tongues out of gutless gratitude for honorary white status and fear of catching flak from the mau maus and mr. charlie. The time for piecemeal measures and mealymouthed apologias is over. Either we're about long-term organizational and political strategies that embrace the destinies of all of us regardless of pedigree, or we ain't about shit.

—Greg Tate, "Leadership Follies"

Writer and journalist Greg Tate believes that in the African American community pushy lawyers should not inherit leadership roles because no one else is willing to come forward. Middle- and upper-class blacks should act less grateful for their success and stop being afraid of being scolded by the less successful. They should speak out for the benefit of all African Americans. They should push beyond halfway measures and mumbled excuses. Either they should stand up for major long-reaching efforts to affect the future of all African Americans without regard to class status, or they are not serious about change.

5   Practice in Summarizing

Write a summary about one-quarter to one-third as long as each passage. Be sure to add appropriate attributions.

[A] Jazz, ragtime, and the blues all started up in different places at the same time—certainly all within a few years. How and why this happened so suddenly no one knows. A creative peak was reached at some point in the first half of the twentieth century. It's impossible to say exactly when that was—my guess is around World War II. But others say much earlier than that—perhaps in the first decade of the century. Unfortunately, no recordings were made at the time. We know as much about the origins of jazz and the blues as we do about the circumstances in which Shakespeare's plays were written; which is to say virtually nothing. The crucial early years, circa 1895–1915, are a blank. A few hazy photographs and hazier recollections are all that we have.

—Tom Bethell, "The Rise of Politics and the Decline of Black Culture"

[B]   I first started looking at population issues twenty-five years ago. One of the things I found when I did my research in Peru, in '64 and '69, was that the people I studied had the highest fertility of any human group. Their rate of population growth was almost 5% per year. But I also began looking at the environmental destruction that was going on in Latin America and other places that I visited. It was obviously quite serious. So in 1969 when I was studying for my Master of Public Health degree, I developed the idea that the human species is behaving very much like a malignant process on the planet. I was quite horrified by this idea and decided not to publish it because I thought it was too radical. I also didn't think I had the professional credentials to make it stick. In any case, I've thought about that for a long time. I'm quite sure it's true. I offer it as a hypothesis, not even a theory, because I think that it deserves to be examined critically by other people. I think it's a serious idea, but I think what it tells us is that this situation that we're confronting is population, and the way the human species relates to the rest of the environment is very critical at this point. The things that we're seeing in the newspapers and the scientific reports are very ominous signs that we need to take quite seriously and recognize that the situation is out of control. If we don't change the way we are behaving as species, the question becomes not whether we will become extinct, but how many other species we're going to take down with us. The most notable aspect of this is uncontrolled population growth. We can do anything we want about the environmental question, but unless we do something about population growth, we're sunk.

—Dr. Warren Hern, population activist, in an interview
published on the University of Colorado gopher site

[C]   Compare, too, the inaugural addresses of John F. Kennedy and Bill Clinton: where the one is assertive, the other is plaintive. In 1961, President Kennedy hailed "a new generation of Americans" who would gladly "bear the burden of a long twilight struggle" against tyranny, poverty, disease, and war, and who would support the use of American military power, where necessary, "to assure the survival and the success of liberty." In 1993, President Clinton, by contrast, identified "the urgent question of our time" as "whether we can make change our friend and not our enemy."

In short, the older liberalism was confident of progress; contemporary liberalism seeks merely to keep up with "change," and seems rather doubtful as to whether it can handle even that rather uninspiring task.

—William Kristol, "A Conservative Looks at Liberalism"

[D]   In 1987, however, Florida enacted a uniform concealed-carry law which mandates that county authorities issue a permit to anyone who satisfied certain objective criteria.

. . . Despite the fact that Miami and Dade County have severe problems with the drug trade, the homicide rate fell in Florida following enactment of this law [legalizing concealed weapons], as it did in Oregon following enactment of similar legislation there. There are, in addition, several documented cases of new permit holders successfully using their weapons to defend themselves. Information from the Florida Department of State shows that from the beginning of the program in 1987 through June 1993, 160,823 permits have been issued, and only 530, or about 0.33 percent of the applicants, have been denied a permit for failure to satisfy the criteria, indicating that the law is benefiting those whom it was intended to benefit—the law abiding. Only 16 permits, *less than 1/100th of 1 percent,* have been revoked due to the postissuance commission of a crime involving a firearm.

—Jeffrey B. Snyder, "A Nation of Cowards"

6 Selecting and Bridging to Quotations

Write a paragraph of your own in which you present a carefully chosen quotation from one of the passages in Activities 2–5, using an appropriate attribution and smoothing the transition to the quotation with an explanatory bridge.

7 Practice in Punctuating Quotations

In the following sentences, underlining indicates a quoted word, phrase, or sentence. Punctuate the quotations correctly,

1. Jefferson biographer Joseph J. Ellis maintains that the Declaration of Independence, with its emphasis on the individual as a sovereign unit, is a recipe for anarchy (23).

2. Life in Russia today is a welter of contradictions. The law forbids . . . the possession of foreign currency, notes David Remnick, but there are official exchange booths on every corner.

3. Wayne's innate qualities are not enough to explain so large a social fact [as his coming to stand for a political outlook]. He had to fill some need in his audience writes Garry Wills in his book *John Wayne's America: The Politics of Celebrity.*

4. About poetry, Marianne Moore said Complexity is not a crime but carry it to the point of murkiness/ and nothing is plain yet her own poems can be quite murky (Fenton 43).

5. If African art was not made by people who thought of themselves as Africans; if it was not made as art; if it reflects . . . no unitary African aesthetic vision; can we not still profit from [this] assemblage of remarkable objects . . . ? K. Anthony Appiah asks about the new collection at the Guggenheim.

6. Stun gun–type belts deliver 50,000-volt shocks to the left kidney, which fan out from there and can be administered by guards from a distance of 300 feet by pushing a button notes William F. Schulz.

7. The author makes a strong case that the sale of instruments which can potentially be used for torture or ill-treatment should be prohibited to any nation with a record of human-rights violations.

8. People should write the books they want to write; claims Noel Annan, and if they illuminate and entertain we should be thankful.

8 Practice in Using Informal Reference

Rewrite each of the following using informal reference.

1. Martin Feldman, tobacco analyst at Smith Barney, estimates that an additional tax today of $.50 a pack would curb cigarette sales by 8%.

—Daniel Kadlec, Wall Street columnist for *Time* magazine, May 12, 1997

2. A growing impetus behind welfare reform is the desire to answer middle-class complaints that the existing system creates dependency and wastes money.

—Kenneth Walsh, "Rival Suitors"

3. But now it has become apparent that our differentiation into Eskimos, Bushmen, Australians, Scandinavians and so on occurred only in the last 50,000 years, and that race is a short and superficial coda to the long song of evolution.

—Chris Stringer and Robin McKie, *New York Times*

4. There can be no vital political life, no viable institutions of government, no sense of mastery over our shared fate, no effective common endeavors of any kind without there being a foundation of public awareness and spirit.

—David Matthews, former cabinet officer, in *Public Administration Review,* March 1984.

5. Science, for example, can be seen as a mechanism for generating objective truth. . . . Or, science can be regarded as comprised of speech communities that are always linguistically adjudicating, among other things what will count as a fact.

—Manfred Stanley, of Syracuse University, "The Rhetoric of the Commons," in *The Rhetorical Turn*

6. The [gambling] industry has worked hard to shed its seedy reputation. It's not even called gambling anymore—it's now 'gaming.'

—Martin Koughan, "Easy Money," *Mother Jones* magazine, 1997

7. Sixty years ago, reporter and press critic George Seldes wrote in *Freedom of the Press* that advertisers, not government, are the principal news censors in the United States.

—Lawrence Soley, "The Power of the Press Has a Price"

8. Just as important to America's information infrastructure as fiber optics is cable TV. As a technology, cable is often underestimated.

—George Gilder, "America's Best Infrastructure Program"

■ WORKS CITED

Hirsch, E. D., Jr. *Validity in Interpretation.* New Haven: Yale UP, 1967.
Holquist, Michael. *Dialogism: Bakhtin and His World.* New York: Routledge, 1990.
"Paraphrase." *American Heritage Dictionary.* 3rd ed. 1996.
Spears, Richard A. *NTC's American Idioms.* Lincolnwood, IL: National Textbook Company, 1987. 62

 *Readings*

Violence Is a Public Health Problem

GEORGE F. WILL

George F. Will is a Pulitzer Prize–winning columnist whose commentaries are syndicated in newspapers around the country. His most recent collection of essays is *The Woven Figure.* This essay appeared in December

1992 in the *Washington Post.* Another essay by Will can be found at the
end of Chapter 8. (Copyright 1992 by the Washington Post Writer's
Group. Reprinted by permission.)

Atlanta—Few noticed, but in 1990, America passed a grim milestone. In at least two   1
states, Texas and Louisiana, the leading cause of death by injury was not motor vehicles
but guns.

Mark Rosenberg noticed. He is a doctor at the Centers for Disease Control and Preven-   2
tion, specializing in injury prevention, particularly the prevention of violence. Violence is
epidemic and epidemiologists' skills are relevant to rendering violence a treatable public
health problem.

Throughout history, the leading causes of premature death have been infectious dis-   3
eases and injuries. Control of infectious diseases began accelerating in 1796, when Edward Jenner developed the first vaccine, for smallpox. Since then, improved sanitation,
hygiene, housing, food handling, pesticides and education have joined the inventory of
disease controls.

The contrast with the failure to apply scientific intelligence to the preventing of   4
violence—self-inflicted (suicides) and assaultive—is marked. Violence is not a disease, but
neither is it something simply to be endured.

Consider two analogies. Smoking is not a disease, it is socially costly addictive behavior,   5
and it is demonstrably combatable. If the motor vehicle fatality rate of 1952 had been the
same in 1989, 155,075 Americans would have died in vehicular accidents. But only 45,555
did, because the problem was treatable (with improved vehicle and highway design, licensing requirements, motorcycle helmet laws and other measures).

About one-third of the 150,000 deaths per year from injuries are from suicide or as-   6
saultive violence. The U.S. homicide rate for black males 15–24 is 17 to 283 times greater
than the male homicide rates in 17 other industrial nations. Homicide is the second-leading
cause of death by injury among ages 1–19 and the leading cause of deaths for blacks, male
and female, 15–34. Furthermore, 2.2 million Americans suffer non-fatal injuries from violent and abusive behavior.

Epidemiology looks for patterns in large numbers. and for predictive and diagnostic im-   7
plications for at-risk individuals and groups, and for risky behavior. For example, Rosenberg
says, in 30 years the suicide rate in ages 15–24 has tripled. The prototypical suicide casualty is no longer an older, depressed male. The rate is rising most rapidly among younger
males (five times more numerous than female suicides) who are not usually depressed but
are angry, frustrated, resentful, often using drugs and unable to communicate their distress.

Another example: Many people think the way to avoid being a homicide victim is to   8
stay at home at night. But most homicides take place at home, among acquaintances, in
connection with drinking, in the context of an argument and in proximity to a gun.

The idea of government "treating" violence has occasionally aroused resistance on the   9
right, which fears the rise of a therapeutic state staffed by what C. S. Lewis called "official
straighteners," coercive utopians trying to make something straight from the crooked tim-
ber of humanity. On the left, the suspicion is that government's focus on violence masks an
attempt to control the disadvantaged by targeting racial and ethnic minorities, thereby diverting attention from social injustices.

The fiction that violence research is a racist plot was fueled recently by misguided pro-   10
posals for research on "genetic factors in crime." There is no behavior for which any single
gene has been identified as the cause. Granted, there are interesting avenues of research,

such as possible linkages between nutrition, brain chemistry and behavior. However, the CDC's objective, Rosenberg says, is not to find a pacifying drug or any other strategy of biological intervention. The objective is the empowerment of communities, so they will not be passive victims.

11   Practical measures against violence are many: conflict-resolution skills, for individuals and adolescents' gangs; improved public lighting; bulletproof barriers for cabdrivers; reduced alcohol and drug consumption; gun control; family life education; condemnation of entertainment that fosters acceptance of violence as a response to grievances; metal detectors to deter the one in 20 high school students who today carries a gun, and so on.

12   Clearly the criminal justice system is inadequate to the task of turning the tide of violence. So as a sound investment in improving the quality of American life, no federal funds are spent better than those for the CDC's research.

Summary, Paraphrase, and Quotation Activities

1. Use summary to express the point made in paragraphs 3 and 4.
2. Paraphrase the information about homicide rates in paragraph 6.
3. Paraphrase the description of the typical suicide in paragraph 7, and include in the paraphrase a brief partial paraphrase of an important or key term or phrase.
4. Summarize the objections some people have to the treatment of violence as a medical problem and include a quotation in the summary.
5. Write a one-paragraph summary of the entire article. Include two or three phrase-length quotations of important terms.
6. Write a three-paragraph summary of the article. Use at least one sentence-length quotation in the summary.
7. Imagine you are researching in order to write an essay on gun violence. Take notes from Will's article on this topic by writing paraphrases of the relevant material.

Questions for Inquiry

1. What is Will's claim? State it in your own words if he does not state it explicitly. What reasons does he offer in support of this claim?
2. What strategies does Will use to acquaint the reader with the nature, extent, and significance of the gun problem?
3. Identify where the author discusses the ideas of those opposed to his claim. How does he respond to these resistances?
4. What misunderstandings about violence does Will address?

Questions for Argument

1. The Centers for Disease Control and Prevention, a government agency, is the site of the studies and treatment of violence that Will discusses. However, as Will himself says, "Violence is not a disease" (4). Should the CDC be working in the area of violence if it is not a disease? What are the advantages and disadvantages of having a medical approach to violence?
2. Dr. Rosenberg indicates that the CDC's goal is not to find "a pacifying drug or any other strategy of biological intervention" for violence (10). If a drug or "biological intervention" for preventing a susceptible individual from acting violently could be invented, do

you think it would it be acceptable for society to require these people to be "treated"? Or would this overstep the bounds of a person's rights?

3. Examine the many practical measures against violence that Will lists in paragraph 11. Could these practical measures be easily adopted to improve the safety of Americans' lives? Could anyone possibly object to any of these measures when the benefits might be as momentous as the one-third cut in vehicular fatalities after new safety measures were put in place? What kinds of resistances might some of these measures encounter?

Writing Assignments

Informal

1. Do you and your friends feel safe from violence? What types of violence seem most common in your corner of the world? Write a journal entry about your feelings of relative safety or danger.

2. One assumption underlying Will's argument is that prevention is the best strategy in dealing with many problems, such as smoking, car accidents, and violence. Write an informal paper about a time when preventive measures could have or should have been taken but were not, leading to a serious problem.

Formal

3. Will deplores "the failure to apply scientific intelligence" to the problem of violence (4). Are there other societal problems that you feel could be best handled by the medical or scientific communities rather than by government or police? Write an essay in which you propose that nongovernmental experts, doctors, or scientists take over the management of a problem that government has not been able to solve.

4. Choose one of the "practical measures" Will suggests in paragraph 11, and develop an argument for or against its use as a means of decreasing violence in our society. If you oppose the measure, make sure your argument weighs the measure's high potential for saving lives against the disadvantages you envision. Write up your argument as a position paper on the measure directed to Dr. Rosenberg of the CDC.

■ ■ ■

Are American Schools Too Easy?

ALBERT SHANKER

Albert Shanker was president of the American Federation of Teachers (AFT), a national teachers' union, for 23 years until his death in 1997. As president, he wrote a weekly column on education that appeared in numerous papers nationwide in a paid advertisement sponsored by the AFT. This essay is one of those columns, and appeared in February 1993. (Copyright 1993 by American Federation of Teachers. Reprinted by permission.)

Recently I saw a TV interview with some Russian youngsters who now live in the U.S. After some standard questions, the interviewer asked them to compare their school experiences here with their experiences in Russia. Every one of these seventh and eighth graders had the same response: They'd already learned the material they were getting in our seventh- and eighth-grade classes when they were in third or fourth grade in Russia. They said that school in the U.S. was very easy.

2   There was nothing unusual about this exchange. Indeed, most people who have met foreign students from France or Germany or Japan have heard the same things. And if we question students like these a little further, we find that they are far ahead of their U.S. counterparts because they are assigned more work and more challenging work, and they work harder to get it all done. But why do they work harder? They have the same distractions as American kids. They have TV sets and pop culture.

3   One of the main reasons is that these other countries have national curriculums. They have decided what students need to know and be able to do by the time they graduate from secondary school. And they've worked back from these goals to figure out what children should learn by the time they are ages 14 and 9.

4   That's not true in the U.S. Our 50 state governments have developed curriculum materials, but they are very broadly defined. So each school or teacher can select from this broad array and develop what amounts to an individual curriculum.

5   This makes for plenty of variety but very little continuity. As a result, students who move from one school—or even one class—to another often find they are out of sync because they have not studied the math or history on which the coming year's work will be based. In countries where there is a national curriculum, fewer students are lost—and fewer teachers are lost because they know what the students who walk into their classroom have already studied.

6   A national curriculum gives everyone involved—students, parents and teachers—a different perspective on schoolwork. In the U.S., when a teacher piles on the work, students are likely to object. They say it's too hard and too much, and they complain that other teachers or other schools don't expect that kind of work. Often parents support these objections. So there is a process of negotiation about schoolwork in which students, and frequently parents, play a big role.

7   Sometimes teachers don't ask enough of students. They feel sorry for some youngsters because of their socioeconomic or racial or ethnic background and decide they won't be able to do real work. So they teach a watered-down curriculum and shortchange youngsters who could learn if they were given a chance.

8   In our system, how much work students do in a given class is up for grabs. Sometimes it's determined by the willingness or resistance of students and parents. Sometimes it's based on the teacher's expectations. In any case, the level and amount of work common in countries with national curriculums is practically never reached here. The choices our system allows inevitably lead to softer standards and less work just as the mandates in other countries lead to more work and much higher levels of achievement. If a student or a parent in one of these countries does complain, the teacher says, "All the other third-grade youngsters are doing this work, and you can, too." And the teacher probably reminds the parents and child that falling behind now can lead to serious consequences later—like not passing an important exam.

9   Learning to write well or be competent in math is a lot like preparing for the Olympics. Youngsters have to work hard and do more than they think they can. This can be unpleasant and even border on the painful, but it takes this kind of stretching to achieve high levels in any field. In the U.S., a teacher who pushes students to work hard is viewed as unreasonable or even mean. But where there are external standards, a teacher is more like a coach—someone who is helping prepare kids for the Olympics—than like someone who has odd, personal ideas about education.

With a national curriculum, everybody knows what is required. If there also are clear   10
and visible stakes—getting into university or an apprenticeship program—the pressure is on
to make sure youngsters meet the standards. Without national standards and a national
curriculum, there are no such pressures. That's why students in other countries work hard
and do so well—and why students in our "easy" and undemanding schools do not. Knowing that should lead us to act.

Summary, Paraphrase, and Quotation Activities

1. Use paraphrase to express the point made in paragraph 4.
2. Paraphrase the student objections to hard work in paragraph 6 (sentences 2–3). Then
   paraphrase the last sentence of the paragraph, including a brief partial quotation of an
   important or key term.
3. Summarize Shanker's reasons for instituting a national curriculum in a paragraph.
4. Summarize the ideas in paragraph 9, and include a quotation in the summary.
5. Write a one-paragraph summary of the entire article. Include two or three phrase-
   length quotations of significant terms.
6. Write a three-paragraph summary of the article. Use one sentence-length quotation
   and two or three phrase-length quotations.
7. Imagine you are doing research for an essay about students' poor attitudes toward education. What ideas from Shanker's article would you include through paraphrase and
   summary? What sentences or phrases would make good quotations?

Questions for Inquiry

1. What is Shanker's claim? At what point in the essay do you recognize what the claim
   is without his directly stating it?
2. Why, under our current system, do some teachers do less than a satisfactory job of
   teaching, according to Shanker?
3. Shanker develops his essay by comparison. What points of contrast are there between
   U.S. schools and students and their foreign counterparts? What point of comparison
   does he suggest between teachers and coaches under a system of external standards?
4. On the basis of Shanker's style and approach, what can you tell about the audience he
   expects?

Questions for Argument

1. Shanker bases his argument on the disparity between what foreign students report
   about their studies in their home countries and their studies in the United States. Do
   you agree that the reports of foreign students are a fair way to judge how the U.S. school
   system compares with those of Japan, France, Russia, and other modern nations? How
   should we judge our schools' success?
2. Under a national curriculum, how would quality be assured? How would we know
   whether states and schools were adhering to the curriculum? What other changes
   might go along with a national curriculum?
3. Shanker says external standards would make teachers more like coaches instead of
   people with "odd, personal ideas about education" (9). Do you feel this description of U.S.
   teachers is accurate or fair? Do you agree that teachers, for a wide assortment of reasons, do not ask students to work hard?

Writing Assignments

Informal

1. Shanker says that with a national curriculum, teachers would be more like coaches (9). Write an informal paper about a time when you experienced or witnessed "coaching," perhaps for a sport or for some other skill. Draw some conclusions about the benefits or drawbacks of having "coaching" go on in the academic classroom.

2. Imagine going to school in Japan or France, where national curricula are in place. How would your life as a child have been different, do you think, when your education was channeled according to external standards? Write a journal entry in which you describe your life as a foreign child studying under a national curriculum.

Formal

3. Who should decide the content of a national curriculum, Congress or the government? Or should it be left to teachers and educators? Should school boards, parent groups, citizen groups, or even students in high school and college be involved? Do you think the curriculum would be different, depending on who creates it? In an essay, examine the issue of who should design the national curriculum and draw some conclusions about the best way to go about it.

4. Is today's high school graduate truly educated in your opinion? Or does a person have to go to college to be truly educated? In an essay, define what you believe makes a person truly educated, and explain whether you think this ideal should be a goal of a high school education. If it should not be, explain why.

5. **Individual Research.** Shanker is not the first person to suggest a national curriculum. Using the library and the Internet, find out more about proposals for a national curriculum. Focus your research on one aspect of the issue—for example, you might target a particular field of learning, such as mathematics or writing; or the issue of who would design the curriculum, how it would be implemented (for example, would students have to use the same textbooks nationwide?), how standards could be enforced, or its economic costs. Then write an essay in which you summarize the problems or benefits a national curriculum might create in the area you researched. Come to a conclusion about whether a national curriculum would be a positive or negative development for the United States.

■ ■ ■

The Destruction of Childhood

LANGDON WINNER

Langdon Winner teaches science and technology at Rensselaer Polytechnic Institute. This article appeared in *Technology Review* in November–December 1996. (Copyright 1997 by MIT's Technology Review Magazine. Reprinted by permission.)

1   As free trade agreements forge new links to the rest of the world, we are implicitly endorsing brutal economic practices abroad that Western countries banned long ago.

As my sons devour their burgers and fries at the local fast food restaurant, I examine   2
the toy included with one of the "happy meals" and notice that it was made in faraway Asia.
Silently, I wonder: How happy was today's meal for the person who made this piece of
brightly colored plastic?

The interwoven, global economy connects us to countless people whose names and   3
faces we will never know. Seldom do we acknowledge these distant others or ponder our role
in their well being. Yet every time we buy a product manufactured in a developing country
or purchase shares in a global mutual fund, we implicitly endorse conditions of production
that affect how people live in other parts of the world.

Headlines of the past year have provided glimpses of the dark underside of the in-   4
ternational marketplace. An embarrassed Kathie Lee Gifford tearfully admitted that her
line of clothing was produced by sweatshops in Honduras. Michael Jordan smiled and
nodded, seemingly unperturbed by criticisms of the brutal Indonesian factories that
crank out the pricey sneakers bearing his name. Beyond these media bombshells, however,
is deeper, more troubling evidence about the plight of workers, especially children, in the
Third World.

A recent survey by the United Nations' International Labor Organization (ILO) revealed   5
that some 78 million children between the ages of 5 and 14 were substantially or fully engaged in labor in 1990—often toiling long hours in physically hazardous and socially abusive conditions. In farms, workshops, mines, and households, children accompany their
parents as unpaid laborers, enlisted in the family's struggle to rise from poverty. Given little
schooling and scant means for physical and intellectual growth, these young workers are
robbed of their childhood and face bleak prospects in their adult lives.

Such exploitation frequently involves the reintroduction of slavery, as children come to   6
be regarded as assets to be bought and sold. The world's economy now includes "tens of millions of child slaves," according to the ILO report. Sometimes adult workers sign contracts
that promise the availability of a child; sometimes a child is exchanged for a sum of money
that is described by the employer as an "advance on wages."

Extreme advocates of the free market sometimes argue that these practices will vanish   7
as developing societies achieve prosperity. Child labor, in that view, is a temporary problem,
one that will be overcome as families work, marshal their resources, and move up the economic ladder. According to one classic argument, children are the best capital families have
in their quest for upward mobility, because their "nimble fingers" make them superior to
adults for certain kinds of work—rug knotting and electronic assembly, for example.

But such arguments have no validity. What is true for our own children is true for the   8
world's poor as well: the way to improve one's lot in life is through education and the culti-
vation of higher skills. Varieties of labor that prevent this from happening are bound to per-
petuate poverty. Moreover, there is no scientific evidence showing children to be more
dexterous in production than their elders are—even if that mattered.

Most countries already have enacted laws that ban or strongly regulate child labor. Over   9
the years, however, governments and whole industries have chosen to look the other way as
new generations of youngsters are fed into the meat grinder. Thus the continuing exploitation and abuse of children in the workplace still festers in the shadows of "development."

For now, the most effective initiatives against child labor arise from consumer groups   10
who mobilize public opinion, pressuring governments and business firms to protect the
rights of children. A collection of church, labor, and consumer action groups known as the
Child Labor Coalition was galvanized by the rebellion and subsequent assassination last year

of 12-year-old Iqbal Masih, who had worked in Pakistan's rug factories since the age of 4. The coalition established the Rugmark label—a symbol attached to Asian carpets that the Rugmark Foundation certifies as being made without child labor. Similar efforts are under way to force the garment and sport-equipment industries to demonstrate that their goods, too, are produced under humane conditions. Public pressures of this kind may shame governments into taking steps to combat child labor.

11   We Americans like to believe that slavery ended with the Emancipation Proclamation and that child-labor abuses stopped with the laws and court decisions of the early twentieth century. Our woes about the global economy focus myopically on matters of national competitiveness and the rise or fall in our own standard of living. How small these concerns seem when confronted with evidence of the suffering of the world's children. We must be vigilant that our wealth and comfort do not rest on a secret inhumanity.

Summary, Paraphrase, and Quotation Activities

1. Use paraphrase to express the point made in the first two sentences of paragraph 3.
2. Paraphrase the comments about Kathy Lee Gifford and Michael Jordan in paragraph 4; then paraphrase the paragraph's last sentence and include in it a brief, partial quotation of a key term or important phrase.
3. Summarize the economic arguments for and against allowing child labor in a paragraph.
4. Write a one-paragraph summary of the entire article. Include in it two or three brief quotations of significant terms or phrases.
5. Write a three-paragraph summary of the article. Use one sentence-length quotation and two or three phrase-length quotations.
6. Imagine you are doing research for an essay about slavery. Take notes from Winner's article by paraphrasing relevant material,

Questions for Inquiry

1. How do children come to be employed as factory and farm laborers, according to Winner?
2. Why does Winner discount the argument that child labor is a stage in the oncoming prosperity of a developing country?
3. What language choices throughout the article show the strength of Winner's emotions regarding child labor?

Questions for Argument

1. Winner says that every time we buy a foreign product we "implicitly endorse conditions of production" in the lands in which these products are made (3). Do you agree that our purchases are "endorsements"? What is our responsibility for the ways in which products are made or developed?
2. One type of child labor, Winner says, occurs when parents require their children to assist "in the family's struggle to rise from poverty" (5). Do you consider this kind of child labor morally equivalent to the child slavery and other types of enforced labor that Winner discusses? Or is this use of children excusable because it occurs within the family?

Writing Assignments

Informal

1. "The interwoven, global economy connects us to countless people whose names and faces we will never know," Winner writes (3). In a creative journal entry, imagine two or three of these people. What are they like? How do they live? What do they want out of life?

2. As a child, were you required to do work in the home or in a family business? Or did you choose to do some kind of work, perhaps around your neighborhood, for pay? In an informal paper, write about your youthful work experiences in order to express your view of whether work bestows advantages or disadvantages on a child.

Formal

3. Winner buys his children "happy meals" that include toys possibly manufactured under cruel conditions. How should a parent handle such a situation? Should the parent deny his own children their small pleasures to protest international exploitation? Should a parent refuse to buy children's toys and clothing that may involve the "destruction of childhood" in other lands? Write an essay in which you take a stand on whether the childhood of U.S. children should be modified to improve the childhoods of foreign children. Be specific: use examples of products and items that children should or should not be forced to forgo.

4. **Collaborative Prewriting.** Winner concludes with a mention of actions that have been taken against child exploitation abroad. Brainstorm with class members to generate a list of specific actions that Americans could engage in to counteract the forced labor of children around the world. Select those you feel would be most powerful and then write an essay in which you propose an action plan that U.S. parents and others could adopt to publicize or exert pressure against child labor.

5. **Individual Research.** Winner says that child labor "involves the reintroduction of slavery" because children are considered "assets to be bought and sold" (6). "Tens of millions of child slaves" exist today, he reports. Using the resources of the library, investigate how international agencies define "slavery" today to determine whether some of the conditions that Winner describes—laboring on a family farm or in a family business (5); accompanying and assisting an adult laborer without pay (5 and 6); working while governments and industries "look the other way" (9)—are indeed slavery. Write an essay based on the definitions and information you discover. You may wish to argue that there is less or more slavery than Winner claims; or you may wish to argue for or against a specific definition of slavery; or you may wish to claim that the definition of slavery is irrelevant and that cruel and exploitive child labor, however defined, is wrong and should be regulated or protested.

6. **Research Writing.** Use library and Internet resources to learn more about one of the following: Iqbal Masih; the Rugmark imprint; the Child Labor Coalition; the outcome of publicity about Gifford's and Jordan's endorsed products; other products sold in the United States that have been shown to be produced by child labor. Summarize your findings and report them to the class orally or in a brief paper.

■ ■ ■

The Evidence Is Coming In: Dan Quayle Was Right

DAVID S. BRODER

> David S. Broder has been a writer for the *New York Times*, the *Washington Star*, and the *Washington Post*. His columns on current U.S. politics appear in many newspapers nationwide. This one is from 1997. (Copyright 1997 by the Washington Post Writers Group. Reprinted by permission.)

1   In a week when the future of Russia is hanging in the balance and the fate of President Clinton's first budget is being debated, it may seem frivolous to write about anything else. But believe me, the topic of this column is not frivolous.

2   It is the American family, whose condition, according to three reports that appeared within days of each other, is alarming.

3   William J. Bennett, the always provocative former secretary of education and drug czar, now working at the Hudson Institute, introduced an "Index of Leading Cultural Indicators" at a Heritage Foundation press conference. The 19 indicators, he said, show that "over the last three decades, we have experienced substantial social regression," particularly in matters related to families and children.

4   Since 1960, he reported, "there has been a 560 percent increase in violent crime; more than a 400 percent increase in illegitimate births; a quadrupling of divorce rates; a tripling of the percentage of children living in single-parent homes; more than a 200 percent increase in the teenage suicide rate; and a drop of almost 80 points in the SAT [pre-college Scholastic Aptitude Test] scores."

5   No sooner had that bleak message been absorbed than I picked up the latest issue of the Aspen Institute Quarterly, also devoted to children and families. David Gergen, the estimable editor-at-large of U.S. News & World Report, wrote the introductory essay for a volume based on papers prepared for an Aspen "domestic strategy group," co-chaired by conservative Bennett and liberal Sen. Bill Bradley (D., N.J.).

6   According to Gergen, an Aspen seminar last summer brought together a variety of experts, among them both strong advocates and sharp critics of past government welfare programs, and found "interesting convergences" of views; no unanimity, but "more common ground here than is often supposed."

7   The main points of agreement are that "our children are in worse shape than generally thought," and that they have been victimized by cultural trends (particularly the rise in divorce and illegitimacy), the abandonment of traditional values and the worsening economic conditions of many poor and middle-class parents.

8   Whatever their particular agenda, Gergen said, the participants agreed that "the best anti-poverty program for children is a stable, intact family." The person whose words Gergen is quoting is William A. Galston, a University of Maryland political analyst who has been brought onto the White House staff by President Clinton specifically to work on family policy.

9   In his essay, Galston acknowledges the relevance of both economic and cultural factors. He says that "the two most important forces affecting children for the worse in the past generation have been declining economic prospects for young, poorly educated male workers and the accelerated movement toward single-parent households."

Reflecting on what government can and cannot do, Galston says, "Returning to a   10
higher-wage, higher-productivity growth track is not just an issue for the American economy, but for America's children and families as well. Reversing the trends of the past generation toward non-marriage and divorce poses even more complex challenges, but I am
pessimistic that we can do more then scratch the surface of our social ills without real movement in that direction."

The policy debate is not new. Rival advocacy groups such as the liberal Children's De-   11
fense Fund and the conservative Family Research Council have been arguing for their favorite policies for years. But it is significant, I think, that conservatives now embrace some
government economic policies, like the earned income tax credit or higher personal exemp-
tions for dependents, while liberals now acknowledge the centrality of values like family stability, personal responsibility and work.

That is why the third of the week's reports is so significant. In last year's campaign,   12
what could have been an important debate on family policy took a disastrous turn when a
speech writer for Dan Quayle inserted into a serious and sensible speech on that subject a
paragraph criticizing television character Murphy Brown for her single motherhood.

The press went crazy, and thereafter, any real discussion was buried in hoo-haws over   13
Quayle and Murphy Brown.

Now, Atlantic magazine has taken almost half its April issue to bring the topic back into   14
serious public debate, in an article by Barbara Dafoe Whitehead summarizing much of the
current research on the topic. But the real value is its cover, which will be seen on newsstands
by millions of non-subscribers. In billboard size type, it says:

"DAN QUAYLE WAS RIGHT. After decades of public dispute about so-called family di-   15
versity, the evidence from social-science research is coming in: The dissolution of two-parent
families, though it may benefit the adults involved, is harmful to many children, and dramatically undermines our society."

That's the point.   16

Summary, Paraphrase, and Quotation Activities

1. Use paraphrase to express the point made in paragraph 6.
2. Paraphrase Broder's description of the Dan Quayle–Murphy Brown flap in paragraph
   12. Include in your paraphrase a quotation fragment of a significant or key term from
   the last sentence of the paragraph.
3. Summarize Galston's ideas in paragraphs 9–10 and include a quotation in the summary.
4. Write a one-paragraph summary of the entire article. Include two or three phrase-
   length quotations of significant terms.
5. Write a three-paragraph summary of the entire article. Use a sentence-length quotation and two or three phrase-length quotations of significant terms.
6. Imagine you are doing research for an essay on the effects of poverty on children.
   Use summary, paraphrase, and quotation to take notes about this topic from Broder's
   article.

Questions for Inquiry

1. Identify Broder's claim. What type of claim is it? How does former Vice President Dan
   Quayle tie in?

2. What types of authorities does Broder rely on? What kind of evidence do they contribute? How does the evidence relate to the point Broder is making?

3. Locate places where Broder uses summary to present the ideas of others. What role does quotation play in his references to sources?

4. What social problems does Broder connect to the breakdown of the family? In addition to problems in family structure, what other factors are mentioned as causes of some social problems?

Questions for Argument

1. On the basis of divorces you know of, do you agree that divorce and the lack of intact families cause today's social problems, such as lower SAT scores and poverty (4)? Do you think that children today are "in worse shape" than people realize (7)?

2. William Bennett believes that "substantial social regression" has occurred in the United States over the last thirty years (3). Do you think we have been moving backward in the way we conduct our lives? Does your family or those you know of personally show signs of "social regression"?

3. Broder never does much with his sources' comments about the economic roots of today's social problems. Has the author underplayed the effects of the economy, do you think, and perhaps overplayed the role of divorce? How important, in your experience, is economics to the strength of families and the successful rearing of children?

Writing Assignments

Informal

1. What references to recent historical events or uses of academic jargon in this article may create a problem for readers not in Broder's discourse community? In a journal entry, note material you found difficult to interpret. To what extent did context help you get the larger point? Were there passages that did not convey a meaning to you at all?

2. Broder quotes the *Atlantic Monthly*'s cover copy to the effect that "the dissolution of two-parent families, though it may benefit the adults involved, is harmful to many children" (15). Think about other events, changes, or behaviors of parents and children that could be considered beneficial to one part of the family but detrimental to others. Write an informal paper in which you discuss some of these mixed-result changes and advocate for a way to be fair when such changes must be decided on in a family.

Formal

3. According to Broder, "the abandonment of traditional values" (7) is a main negative factor in our society. Brainstorm with classmates or members of a small group to generate a list of what you think "traditional values" are. Based on this list and your group discussion, decide how you think "traditional values" should be defined. Write an essay in which you explain your definition and argue that such values are necessary or that moving away from traditional values represents a gain for society and individuals. You may want to focus on values in one or two areas of life: life-styles, child rearing, interpersonal or sexual relationships, parent-child relationships, work.

4. **Informal Primary Research.**   Consider the issue raised by William Bennett of "social regression" (3). Approach several people in the older generation—parents, faculty, administrators, neighbors, and so on—and ask them their opinion on this issue. Then discuss the issue with several people in the younger generation. (Rather than ask directly about "social regression," a term that might not be meaningful, ask whether they believe the United States has "regressed" or lost ground or moved backward in quality of life, morals, standards of behavior, and so on over the last thirty years.) Make notes about the answers you receive. Then write an essay in which you argue that "social regression" has or has not occurred, using your interviewees as references, much the way Broder used his print sources.

■ ■ ■

Chapter 4

Creating Dialogue between Sources

Comparing, Contrasting, and Synthesizing Arguments

■ Read the following excerpt and respond as indicated below:

> Democracy is precisely an institutional, cultural, habitual way of acknowledging the pervasiveness of conflict and the fact that our loyalties are not one; our wills are not single; our opinions are not uniform; our ideals are not cut from the same cloth.
>
> —Jan Bethke Elshtain, *Democracy on Trial*

Writer's Journal

In your notebook, write informally to explain the meaning of this passage. What does democracy have to do with "conflict," to your mind? Strive for an entry of about 150 words.

Up to now, we have been discussing ways of handling a single argumentation text. But when you are investigating an issue, you will read more than one article. Often you read quite a few. The articles and their differing or allied points of view begin to interact in your mind, begin to form a dialogue or "multilogue" of ideas and perspectives. Your active mental work on the contents of two or more sources creates a miniature discourse community right in your head, a place in which the competing voices of different sources interact. Your role in this interaction is to make sure you adequately and as accurately as possible understand the point of view of each argument and, in addition, understand its similarity to and differences from the other arguments you have read on the subject. Bringing two or more sources together in a dialogue involves moving beyond active reading to comparing and contrasting the arguments.

Comparison refers to examining texts to discover and then display the ways in which they are similar. **Contrast** refers to discovering and showing how source texts are different. Both these activities are pathways to help you enter the discourse about an issue and are vital when you need to pull ideas together to present a point of view on the issue.

In doing research, you may wish to discover a diversity of opinions on a topic so as to be comprehensive in your analysis. Understanding the range of ideas on the topic and the ways in which sources compare and contrast thus can become an important research task. Also, although you may sometimes be tempted to stop reading an article that presents a position you have already encountered, it's often valuable to explore sources that are similar. By reading carefully and looking beyond the common ground to discover differences, you can deepen your understanding of the issues.

Once you have come to terms with the ways two or more sources are similar or different, you might take your analysis and inquiry one step further: to decide which source makes the strongest case. This would be especially necessary if the articles differ greatly in their positions or the evidence they present. You would want to contrast and evaluate the articles.

Comparison and contrast are modes for analyzing how texts agree and disagree. Once you understand the ways two particular texts speak to each other, you may need to use the material in such texts by chaining or synthesizing. Drawing together material from two or more texts by stringing complete or partial summaries results in a chain of ideas or evidence. Such chained summaries can be a way of presenting a body of opinion or evidence as background or for discussion. In some academic fields, a review of the literature—essentially chained summaries of material on the same topic—is required before an issue is discussed or a position argued.

A **synthesis** is a way of unifying sources that are complementary, have a large area of common ground, or provide various supporting details about a topic. A synthesis combines paraphrases and summaries of the ideas and data of such related texts into a unified statement. Synthesis results in more than just a chain of summaries or paraphrases because it merges the ideas of the sources into a single statement. It is usually selective, in that you choose to synthesize only the portions of the sources that are compatible or the parts that tie into your approach to your topic.

Comparison, contrast, and synthesis can be part of the process of coming to terms with sources you are using as research for an argument paper, or you may write a comparison, contrast, or synthesis paper in response to a formal assignment. If you were working up material in support of an argument, informal notes comparing, contrasting, and evaluating the source texts would be sufficient. But your comparison and evaluation would be presented formally if your instructor required you to compare and contrast two or more sources.

In this chapter you will find out how to compare and contrast arguments and synthesize sources in preparation for writing formal assignments of these tasks and for use as support in your own arguments.

■ COMPARISON AND CONTRAST OF ARGUMENTS

When you are working with two or more sources, you will read them carefully and annotate, as you would in handling one text. But, in addition, you will probably take notes and make lists in order to clarify for yourself the similarities and differences between the sources. Writing about the ideas of your sources requires that you express their ideas in your own words, and so one important stage in comparing and contrasting is to paraphrase and summarize the ideas. (See Chapter 3 for details about paraphrase and summary.) The discussion below concerns comparing and contrasting two source texts, but it is possible to compare three or even several texts by expanding the process.

Process

Step 1: *Skim to get an overview and to determine whether the texts lend themselves more to comparison or to contrast.* Read quickly to locate the main idea of each article; check the introduction and the conclusion for clear statements of the writer's point of view.

Step 2: *Read each article for understanding using annotation, note taking, outlining, and summaries as necessary.* Identify the main idea and important supporting points, as you would in planning a summary of each article.

Step 3: *Write rough outlines or summarize each article in a paragraph or two.* This step will force you to discover the specific evidence and reasoning offered in each article and to begin to phrase them in your own words. Work on each article separately. On the basis of your annotations, list the important points of each text. Then cycle back and under each important point, jot down the evidence and reasoning that support the point. Keep in mind that authors do not always use a strict or straightforward outline in developing their arguments, and so your outline may have to account for digressions, repetitions, or jumps forward or backward in ideas. Also realize that it's not likely that two writers on an issue will follow similar organization plans or prioritize their points the same way. So you must avoid carrying assumptions from one article to another. (See Chapter 2 for a detailed discussion of outlining.)

Step 4: *Compare by listing ideas found in both articles, identifying each by paragraph location.* Once you have a clear sense of each writer's position, it's time to start comparing. At this point you need to make lists. Because you are comparing and contrasting articles on the same subject or issue, there is a basic **common ground,** and so your first list should cover the ways in which the authors' ideas are similar—that is, the ways in which the authors agree.

Try to make your list as complete and detailed as possible. Under each point of similarity, paraphrase each author's angle on the idea and note the paragraph in which it is found. You might begin each item in your list with the phrase "Both agree that. . . ." Make sure that you paraphrase or summarize the ideas you jot down or that you place quotation marks around each borrowed phrase. Your list of similarities might look something like this excerpt from a list of similar points in two essays about labor and minority involvement in the environmental movement:

1. Agree that "environmental justice" has become a concern as highly ranked as economic justice for many workers and minority groups
2. Agree that both workers and minorities have important environmental issues
    Frakes: Polluted air, lead, and toxic waste all affect workers' health as well as the communities, often minority, where they occur
    Kamener: Minority neighborhoods, especially black and Latino, have for decades been targeted for waste sites and polluting industries
3. Agree that environmental justice can link environmentalists, labor, and minority groups to benefit of all
    Frakes: Clean Air Act and Superfund were built by labor and environmentalists working together
    Kamener: Names numerous local victories in cleaning up landfills, resisting polluting industries or incinerators resulting from grass-roots action

Because writers rarely agree in every respect, once you have written your list of similarities, you will have already gathered some material for your list of differences.

Step 5: *Note differences between the sources in a second list.* Two sources might differ in some aspect separate from their similarities, or there might be differences in approach or emphasis within the points held in common. In the comparison list above, it is clear that the two writers agree with point one. In point two, the writers emphasize different realms of environmental action—one the national agenda, the other, local victories. You will often find that the common ground or agreement between two articles will be fertile for the sprouting of differences—differences in emphasis, as above, or differences in reasoning or evidence. Or the writers may be in great disagreement about some aspect of the issue. Whatever difference you discover should be entered on a second list, as here:

1. Disagree about mainstream environmentalists' reception of labor and minorities
    Frakes: Workers and environmentalists have seen themselves as enemies, and building coalitions is difficult
    Kamener: Environmentalists are surprised and joyous at energy and breadth of involvement by workers and minorities once issues are clear
2. Disagree about where "environmental justice" activists can be effective
    Frakes: National agenda can be influenced
    Kamener: Energy best spent locally on concrete problems

Step 6: *Sketch out a plan of your comparison or contrast.* Write a sentence that sums up the main way in which your sources compare or contrast. This will become the main idea or thesis of your formal paper. Then plan out the pattern of your analysis. See the Tips for Writing a Formal Comparison or Contrast Paper sidebar (p. 140) on possible ways of organizing comparison and contrast.

Step 7: *Write a draft of your comparison or contrast essay.* Begin with a sentence identifying the sources you are working with by title, author, and author's affiliation if known. Then state the main area of similarity or difference between the articles. Follow your outline to present each way in which your sources are similar or different. Make sure you substantiate your claim by referring to specifics about the similarities or differences in the articles.

Step 8: *Revise, edit, and proofread.*

Ways in Which Sources Can Agree or Differ

In analyzing similarities and differences between sources, most of the time you will concentrate on the content of the texts. This will include:

- claim
- reasoning and evidence offered
- interpretation of evidence
- underlying assumptions
- differing audience appeals
- style

Throughout your analysis, you should be aware that the common ground shared by two sources may be a sign of agreement or may be the foundation for disagreement. For example, two articles about recent insurgency in Mexico may fully agree as to the various causes and underlying problems. But within this major area of common ground, one source may emphasize poverty and landownership as primary motives for rebellion, while the second source may see political repression and corruption as major causes. These sources would lend themselves to a comparison in which the different emphases are mentioned. However, two sources discussing prospects for the U.S. economy may agree about the economic facts: current productivity, unemployment, inflation, the gross national product, and so forth, but interpret them in vastly different ways: one celebrating these facts and figures as an indication of stability, and the second interpreting them to be signs of stagnation and an underachieving economy. In this case, an emphasis on contrast would be appropriate.

A discussion of the components you should consider in examining a source for comparison and contrast follows.

Claim

The sources may make similar claims, or they may hold opposing positions on the common issue. Or their claims may be basically similar but different in emphasis or direction for the future. Here are some examples:

SIMILAR CLAIMS

Source 1:   Working, at whatever job and whatever salary, improves people's self-esteem and gives them a focus in their lives.

Source 2:   Workfare will provide the chronically poor with benefits they can't get from a welfare check: a sense of discipline, a feeling of contributing, and membership in a productive community.

Both these sources support workfare and have similar reasons for doing so. They lend themselves to a comparison.

OPPOSING CLAIMS

Source 3:   Workfare will impose unfair hardship and cruel separation on single mothers and their children.

Source 4:   Workfare will teach responsibility to chronically poor mothers and to the children who see their parents successfully begin to support them.

These claims differ in that one opposes workfare and the other supports it. These sources share a common concern for the children in workfare families but sense opposite outcomes of workfare programs. They would lend themselves to contrast.

SIMILAR CLAIMS WITH DIFFERENT EMPHASES

Source 5:   The advantage of workfare is that welfare recipients will participate in their own upkeep and repay society for its assistance.

Source 6:   Workfare will benefit the chronically poor by giving them a sense of discipline, a feeling of contributing, and membership in a productive community.

Both these sources believe workfare is beneficial to the poor, but the reasons given are different. These sources can be compared but with the reservation that they contrast in certain ways.

Reasoning and Evidence

Even when writers agree on a position, they rarely use the same evidence base or develop their support the same way. So the area of evidence is a place you will be likely to find differences in the type and selection of data. When writers are in agreement regarding their claims, as are sources 1 and 2 in the example above, any differences in reasoning or evidence are complementary—that is, they work together to build a complete case for the common claim.

In general, writers who disagree are using different bodies of evidence and develop their support in different ways. You may find that one source relies on testimony from academic authorities in the field and that an opposing source uses statistics generated by the federal government to support its position. In cases like these, you will find that trying to compare the evidence of the two sources is like comparing the proverbial "apples and oranges." For example, a source relying on U.S. government documents and the testimony of Environmental Protection Agency (EPA) personnel may demonstrate the many successes of the EPA. But a second source that relies on the experiences of local environmental groups may show a pattern of delays, lax enforcement of regulations, concessions to industries, and other weaknesses of the EPA. You would certainly want to point out this discrepancy in viewpoint and in the types of evidence. Later, if you go on to evaluate these sources, you will have to determine which body of evidence is more reliable. This will mean identifying any signs of bias in the sources and perhaps seeking additional sources that might confirm the view of one or the other.

Occasionally, you will find two sources that use the same type of evidence yet report conflicting results; for example, two sources might cite differing statistics about the same issue. This may occur because there is no one authoritative set of facts and figures on the issue. For example, the number of homeless people in the United States is often debated because it's hard to count people who don't have a permanent residence. There are several sets of statistics on the homeless, generated by the federal and various state and city governments, independent research organizations, homeless advocacy organizations, and so on. Likewise, the battle in Congress in 1996–1997 about whether to outlaw "partial birth abortions" was confused by different sets of statistics about how many such procedures occur in a year; reporting these procedures as such has not been required, and all the statistics were basically guesswork. Debates about world overpopulation, illegal immigration, children in poverty, underemployed workers, and so forth all require numbers about groups that are inherently difficult to count. Your comparison or contrast should carefully note any discrepancies in data. Depending on the type of project you are doing, you may want to make time to do additional research on the conflict in factual data to determine which set of facts is most likely accurate.

Interpretation of Evidence

Differences can also occur in how sources interpret evidence that is essentially the same. One source might cite a figure as alarmingly high; another might treat the same figure as normal and not at all alarming. The sources might place the figure in different contexts or consider its effects on different groups or apply it to different situations. For example, some in the business community and the government have considered a 5.6 percent national unemployment rate to be quite acceptable and about as low as unemployment can be expected to be. But, given this same figure, advocates for the unemployed and the "underemployed" (those in part-time jobs or positions for which they are overqualified) argue that at this unemployment rate too many willing workers are relegated to pickup work and chronic idleness.

Underlying Assumptions

In examining sources' claims and evidence, you may discover that they are based on different assumptions. In a comparison or contrast of sources you should try to understand how the writers' underlying beliefs produce their view of the topic. One writer, for example, may assume that the value of Congress's passing a proposed law lies in the benefits that the average household will gain, while another writer may support the law because it increases economic equality and is therefore the right thing to do. A third source may oppose the law because the writer assumes that people should succeed and prosper on their own initiative and that individual striving, not government assistance, deserves support.

Differing Audience Appeals

Likewise, in examining differing claims and ways that sources present their evidence, you may recognize that the sources assume different audiences and use different audience appeals. One writer's stand against legalized gambling may be directed at traditional middle Americans and appeal to family values and moral teachings (*pathos* and *ethos*). Another writer, also opposed, may assume an audience that values the general welfare and the protection of society's least secure members; such a writer may appeal to its reader's social conscience by demonstrating societal problems caused by gambling (*pathos* and *logos*). Finally, a writer who supports legalized gambling might assume a traditional audience somewhat hostile to gambling and thus use reasoning and research showing neutral effects of legalized gambling on community and family values and positive effects on unemployment and retail profits (*logos*).

Style

Distinctiveness of style may set your sources apart. Many argumentative texts use a neutral or analytic style, one that can persuade readers of its claim's validity by virtue of the *ethos* of reasonableness and objectivity that its tone conveys. But other times the word choice, sentence style, and other aspects of language can play a major role in building a text's meaning and effectiveness. For example, you may find that one source uses a straightforward explanatory style, while another incorporates imagery. Or one may use an objective, third-person point of view, while another may speak personally, using "I" and "you" and invoking personal experience. Or one source may stand out because of a harsh, negative, or joking tone, an exception to the usual moderate, reasonable tone chosen by most argumentative writers. All these stylistic differences may cause a text to be more or less convincing to an audience and deserve comment in your comparison or contrast of sources.

■ *Activity 1*

Analyzing for Comparison and Contrast, p. 159

Ways to Use Comparison and Contrast of Sources

Depending on your writing goal, the similarities and differences between sources may be of little or major significance for you. In a formal paper comparing or contrasting (or both) two or more articles, the amount of detail and the completeness of your description of similarities and differences will be determined by your assignment. You may be instructed to treat one important similarity or difference at length or to cover all major points of comparison or contrast. The length of the paper you are assigned will also be a factor in how detailed or complete your analysis is.

■ *Tips for Writing a Formal Comparison*
or Contrast Paper

When your subject is not just one text but two or more, your reader can find it difficult to keep the various authors and their ideas separate. Here are some steps you can take to make sure your reader can keep track of the different ideas you are describing.

1. For each point or observation you make about one source, make a parallel point or observation about the other. If, for example, you note that source A praises a bill passed in the Virginia legislature, you must indicate the stand taken by source B on this bill, or note that it is not discussed. This is a matter of meeting the expectations of your reader, who will assume that each point you make about one text will be matched by a point about the other text(s) you are discussing.

2. Use clear in-sentence attributions to signal which text you are discussing. See Chapter 3 for discussion of how to refer to authors within a text.

3. Use transitions and other signals to show how ideas relate. Transitions are terms that signal something important about the upcoming idea or point. A transition can clue the reader:

   ■ that an example is next ("for example" and "for instance")

   ■ that more discussion of the same is to follow ("and," "in addition," "also," and "likewise")

   ■ that a contrasting idea is upcoming ("however," "but," and "in contrast")

   ■ that points are being listed ("next," "first," "second," and so on)

If, however, you are informally comparing and contrasting sources to develop support for a researched argument of your own, the differences and similarities will be important or unimportant depending on your focused topic and claim. In such a situation, you will be selective and include only relevant comparisons and contrasts in your paper rather than including all such similarities and differences. If you were writing about the support that exists for continuing the United Nations, for example, you might include the contrasting reasons for supporting it from two sources. But if you were writing about the financial problems of the United Nations, you might not include the reasons for support but instead include the two sources' different ideas about United Nations funding.

Judging Sources

Many times, your comparison and contrast of sources will lead you to prefer one over the other because analyzing them has revealed that one source contains more and

■ that orientation in time or space is important ("now," "then," "before," "after"; "above," "below")

4. Choose an organization plan for your contrast. You have basically two choices: one side at a time or point by point. In one-side-at-a-time organization, you cover the points you wish to make about one source completely and then move on to the parallel points about the second source. This type of organization results in segmentation of your paper into two major sections, one about source A and one about source B, and works well if you do not have many points to make. "Point by point" organization refers to covering each point or observation you wish to make for each source in turn. Your paper thus weaves back and forth between the articles. Here is what these two outlines would look like:

One side at a time	Point by point
Introduction	Introduction
Source A, point 1	Point 1, source A
point 2	source B
point 3	Point 2, source A
Source B, point 1	source B
point 2	Point 3, source A
point 3	source B
Conclusion	Conclusion

5. Treat sources in the same order throughout your presentation, first *source A* then *source B*, for each point of comparison you make.

better evidence or stronger reasoning, makes fewer questionable assumptions, or remains more dispassionate and objective throughout the argument. If your assignment requests that you evaluate the sources you are comparing, then you need to look over your comparative lists one last time. Make notes about amounts and types of evidence, clarity and reasonableness of the argument, and so on. Remember, if you are asked to evaluate the sources, you must be able to build a case for the one you believe to be stronger.

STUDENT ASSIGNMENT

Honoré Duncan, "The *New York Times* and the *Economist* Oppose Internet Censorship"

Here is an example of a formal assignment to compare and contrast two texts with similar views. This assignment specifies comparison and asks the student to locate her own source texts. (More information on locating periodical articles can be found later in this chapter.)

> **ASSIGNMENT:**   Read two short (under 700 words) articles that take a similar viewpoint on a focused issue. Short pieces on current topics can be found on the op-ed pages of major newspapers or in news magazines.
>
> Write a formal comparison in which you clarify the similarities in the two sources' viewpoints. Once you have clarified the common ground of the two articles, then explain any differences between the sources in point of view, development of ideas, evidence, and so on.
>
> Be sure to paraphrase and summarize the ideas of the sources fairly and accurately, and use some direct quotations to support your comparison. Please attach copies of the articles to your assignment.

Honoré Duncan chose two short texts about Internet censorship, one an unsigned editorial in the *New York Times* and the other an unsigned source in the British weekly magazine the *Economist*. To begin (Step 1), Honoré skimmed the two articles to determine that both opposed government attempts to control Internet content. The two sources lent themselves to comparison.

Next (Step 2), she read and annotated each one carefully. Here are the sentences she identified as claims:

"Censorship on the Internet." Editorial. *New York Times* 22 June 1995, natl. ed.: A28.

Claim: the Communications Decency Act (CDA) is an "intolerably restrictive amendment" to a telecommunications bill and "deserves oblivion." "As a ban on obscenity, it is superfluous. As a ban on indecency, it is unconstitutional."

"Censorship in Cyberspace: A Bad Idea, Even If Pornographers Love the Internet." *Economist*, 8 Apr. 1995: 16–17.

Claim: "simply banning the 'transmission' of indecent material...is such a bad idea"; "it encroaches too far on freedom."

Then, for Step 3, Honoré wrote rough outlines of the two articles, and for Step 4, she jotted down a list of the points that the two articles have in common:

—*Problem is complicated (NYT); complex (Econ.); too many types of Internet communications (Econ.)*
—*Communications Decency Act (CDA) is superfluous (NYT); federal laws already exist about electronic transmission of porn (NYT); laws already exist (Econ.)*
—*Both point out adults have right to communicate about adult matters and have right to privacy*
—*Both suggest alternatives*

In Step 5, Honoré noted a few differences she discovered in the basically similar articles:

Economist suggests that existing laws may be ineffective; brings up international jurisdictional issue; cites different types of Internet communication and difficulty of effectively designing a law

Here is the formal comparison paper Honoré generated in response to the assignment:

Both the *New York Times* editorial, "Censorship on the Internet," published on June 22, 1995, and the article, "Censorship in Cyberspace: A Bad Idea, Even If Pornographers Love the Internet," in the April 8, 1995, issue of the *Economist,* argue that attempts to write laws specifically regulating pornography on the Internet are wrong-headed.

The issue of Internet pornography is not a simple one, both sources agree. Calling it a "complicated" problem, the *Times* quotes Newt Gingrich, who sees it as a balancing act between "the right of free speech for adults" and "protecting children." The *Economist* notes that "the issues . . . are complex, and not to be confused with a simple choice between free speech and censorship."

Laws already exist, though, that make current attempts at regulation "superfluous" (*Times*). U.S. federal laws ban the electronic transmission of pornography. The *Economist* gives examples: an e-mail threat to the president is a crime, and taking money but not delivering the goods is illegal when done through the Internet.

Both publications emphasize that adults have rights to privacy and freedom of communication. The *Times* cites the First Amendment rights of adults, and the *Economist* notes that broad attempts at control are likely to be restrictive of the rights of private communication between adults.

Beyond opposing simple legal solutions, both articles suggest other possibilities. The *Times* discusses Sen. Patrick Leahy's suggestion that Congress study how software might be used to solve the problem of children's unrestricted access to Internet material. The *Economist* suggests that Internet providers and suppliers warn users of sexual content.

Of the two, the *Economist* article goes more in-depth as to why laws may not work well in regulating Internet content: the Internet is international, and thus jurisdictions are hazy. The *Economist* cites several international attempts to regulate the Internet, those of the United States, New Zealand, and Singapore. The *Times* article focuses exclusively on the Communications Decency Act (CDA) and spells out its unconstitutionality.

Both articles take strong stands on the issue. The *Times* offers this maxim: "As a ban on obscenity, it [the CDA] is superfluous. As a ban on indecency, it is unconstitutional." And the *Economist* article ends, "Cyberspace is a microcosm of the ordinary world, with all the same mingled potential for good or bad. It cannot, and should not, be wished away by over-hasty legislation."

■ SYNTHESIS OF ARGUMENTS

In your reading about an issue, you are likely to encounter sources that cover common ground. Sources may agree in opinion, for example, but differ in how they develop and support the ideas. The evidence and reasoning in such sources often complement each other.

A **synthesis** that unifies complementary ideas and evidence from two or more texts into a single statement. Combining summaries, paraphrases, and quotations from each source, a synthesis creates a more complete statement on the issue than found in any of its sources. A well-done synthesis also permits a reader to keep track of each source text's contribution to the amalgam of ideas by providing clear attributions.

A synthesis is not the same as a comparison. In a comparison, you analyze two (or more) articles. In a synthesis, you blend the ideas to form a larger whole. Your synthesis is a result of your analysis, but does not itself analyze the articles for the reader.

Like a summary, a synthesis may be selective about the points included from each source. But the decision about inclusion depends on the commonality existing between or among the articles. In addition, the purpose to which a synthesis is being put can affect which information is included.

Types of Syntheses

There are many approaches to synthesis; the approach taken depends on the use the writer has for the statement of combined ideas. A **formal synthesis** attempts to be complete and to include all major parallel ideas in the source texts. An **informal synthesis** relates only the portions of the source texts relevant to the support or refutation of an idea. An informal synthesis can also be called a **partial** or **angled synthesis**, because it blends only portions of source texts, those portions that fit the angle of the synthesizing writer on the topic.

A formal synthesis can be of two types. A **full formal synthesis** blends similar ideas in the texts and includes supporting but often divergent details from either text. Thus, a full synthesis includes:

1. points of agreement and their expression in a unified paraphrased statement
2. evidence found in only one article but supporting the common ideas

A **brief formal synthesis** includes only the points that the articles have in common. Only the most significant pieces of support are included through summary.

For example, a full formal synthesis of two articles about the recurrence of previously controlled childhood diseases such as chicken pox and measles would include a statement of all ideas the articles had in common as well as the data from both articles that support these ideas. A brief synthesis of these same two articles would state only the ideas that occur in both articles.

But a student using these same articles for a research paper might create an angled synthesis that pulls together aspects of the articles that relate to her focused topic. If her paper is about flaws in the medical delivery system for the poor, she might synthesize from these articles a statement that the resurgence of childhood diseases is a consequence of flawed health care. She would ignore all other ideas in the articles, even if they parallel each other. Another student using the same articles but writing a paper on the upsurge of dangerous new viruses might synthesize from these sources a statement about the difficulty of totally eliminating viral diseases even when vaccinations are available.

Academic writing—as well as all writing that presents information—makes great use of synthesis, and the ability to construct a succinct and purposeful synthesis can serve you well. In academia, synthesis is necessary in the following situations:

- when reporting a body of viewpoints on a topic
- when presenting support for your own ideas culled from various sources
- when presenting opposition to your ideas in preparation for a refutation
- when pulling together the results of a survey, interviews, site visits, study of official records, or other primary research

Chaining together summaries of articles does not constitute a true synthesis. Rather, a series of concise summaries produce an overview or review of sources.

A Process for Writing a Full Formal Synthesis

Careful reading, accuracy, freshness of wording, and clear organization are crucial to creating a valid synthesis. As with most writing, there is no one way to synthesize. At the start, constructing a synthesis is like doing a formal comparison. You need to know in what ways the texts are similar and how they provide "variations on a theme." However, in the end, a synthesis blends the various supplementary details of the two texts into one unified statement. This section provides a process for writing a synthesis and an example of how a student handled an assignment to write a formal synthesis. Keep in mind that synthesizing ideas involves selection and judgment, and no two writers are going to do the task identically. There will always be some variation in how ideas are paraphrased, in what details are selected to support the similar ideas, and in how the synthesis is organized.

Step 1: *Read each article for understanding,* using annotation, note taking, outlining, or summarizing as necessary. *Identify the main idea and important supporting points,* as you would in planning a summary of each article.

Step 2: *Identify the most important point of agreement or similar idea* in the articles and locate by paragraph number. Then *summarize or paraphrase this idea.* This statement will become the basis for your synthesis.

Step 3: *Locate other points of similarity in the articles;* these may be similar secondary points or similar pieces of reasoning and evidence. *List these other similar points,* leaving room to insert under each relevant supporting details.

As you do this, also *identify the support for each of these parallel ideas.* Such support is not likely to be the same but different in each article and therefore supplementary. List such supporting items under the shared ideas, keeping track of the source of each piece of support. This step is difficult because you must identify both parallel ideas and the divergent support offered in the different articles. Depending on the difficulty of the articles and your experience with synthesis, you may wish to list the points of each article separately and then compare your lists. If you attempt to pull out the similar points mentally, without making notes, you may find yourself getting confused.

Step 4: *Sketch out the plan of your synthesis.* Begin by *revising your statement of the most important point of agreement so that it provides a solid overview of the articles.* Use this statement as your main idea and, usually, as the starting point for your synthesis. *Follow this main idea with statements of the secondary or less important areas of agreement in the articles.* The organization of these secondary points may seem obvious, or you may have to carefully consider how to arrange the secondary points. Draw up an outline or number your notes from the second step to show your decisions about organization. Then, after each statement of similarity, include the pertinent support—that is, the specifics drawn from one or the other of the source articles.

Step 5: *Write a draft of the synthesis.* Begin by identifying the articles' authors and titles and state the most important point of agreement. After that, provide important details as necessary from the articles to support the common idea. Then move on to your statements of the secondary areas of similarity and incorporate supplementary supporting details.

Step 6: *Reread and revise your draft.* Check your paper against your outline to assure yourself that any divergences from your plan are improvements. Examine your word choice and sentence style to make sure the paper says what you want it to clearly. Fix any errors. Also make sure you have paraphrased, summarized, and quoted ideas accurately and that your references to the sources are correct.

Step 7: *Edit for grammar, check spelling, and proofread your paper; then print the final version.*

STUDENT ASSIGNMENT

Seth Nobile, "Mandatory Sentences Cause Many Problems"

Seth Nobile was assigned to write a full formal synthesis using two articles about mandatory-sentencing laws for drug offenders, and then to revise this paper into a brief formal synthesis.

ASSIGNMENT: Write a full formal synthesis of the two articles listed below. Include all similar ideas that the articles have in common and also provide substantial support for these ideas culled from the two articles. Then after you have drafted your full synthesis, prepare a second, brief version of the synthesis.

■ *Tips for Writing a Formal Full Synthesis*

1. Be sure you understand the assignment before you begin. Does the assignment ask for a full formal synthesis? Or does it require a brief synthesis of only the ideas the articles have in common and not the support?

2. Remember to keep your paper focused on its subject—the issue or controversy discussed in your sources. Your purpose is to synthesize material in two agreeing articles, not to compare the articles with each other.

3. Select parallel ideas for inclusion rather than including every idea or detail of both articles.

4. Segment your synthesis so that the paragraphing separates the different points. Writing about only one source in each paragraph can sometimes improve clarity.

5. Organize your points in emphatic order or in some other logical way. For example, in synthesizing two articles about mistakes made in a congressional investigation, you might adopt a chronological pattern. Or, in combining various lines of reasoning in support of on-the-job-training for welfare recipients, you might first pull together the historical precedents and then go on to include statistics and expert testimony in favor of such programs.

6. Omit comments about differences between your sources, and avoid evaluative, judgmental, or comparative remarks. Or, if the assignment indicates that such commentary is appropriate, save it for the end.

7. Use an impersonal point of view and an objective, nonevaluative tone. Avoid references to yourself and your judgments about the sources.

8. Write about the ideas as belonging to the authors or experts who hold them, not as belonging to the article. Indicate clearly from whom each idea comes by leading in with or using an attribution to the source.

■ *Activity 2*
Synthesizing Brief
Passages, p. 160

Michael Brennan. "A Case for Discretion." *Newsweek* 13 Nov. 1995:18.
Anthony Lewis. "First, Do Less Harm." *New York Times* 1 Mar. 1996, late ed., sec. 4:13.

To begin (Step 1), Seth overviewed the articles, establishing in his own mind that they both took strong stands against mandatory sentences, currently a part of national drug policy. He noted that one was an opinion statement by a *New York Times* columnist, while the other was a personal piece submitted by a freelance writer to *Newsweek* magazine. He then reread carefully, making notes in the margins to identify the main ideas and information in each article. On his copy of the Brennan article, he starred a paragraph and underlined the phrase "oppose mandatory sentences." He also bracketed a series of questions and wrote "implies main ideas" in the margin. In the Lewis column, he underlined this sentence as its main idea: "The wasteful cruelty of mandatory minimum sentences cries out for reform."

In Step 2, Seth recognized that both articles took a similar strong stand on the issue. He summarized this idea this way:

Mandatory sentences for drug offenders often cause great injustices to those who receive them.

Then (for Step 3) he searched through the articles for other parallel ideas. Here are supporting ideas Seth located in the two articles:

Mandatory sentences are overly harsh
—dentist Dr. Ruder ignorantly invested in drug scheme; sentenced to 5 yrs. w/out parole (Lewis)
—innocent pregnant young black mother, Lomax, sentenced to life w/out parole for crack conspiracy (Brennan)

Mandatory sentences (definition)
—rigid minimums legislated by Congress, some states (Lewis; Brennan)
Problems of mandatory sentences
—result in high cost of prison to society
    father of criminal in Ruder case cited $25,000 per year (Lewis)
    3 women for 15-to-life in NY costs $1.35 million (Lewis)
    "average cost of housing a federal prisoner" is $20,804 (Brennan)
—result in cruel punishment; a "waste of their lives"
    Ruder; Lomax and 3 women (Lewis)
    Shoplifter given 25 yrs.; killed self (Brennan)
—Other negative consequences
    nonviolent drug offenders are 1/3 of drug prisoners (Lewis)
    violent offenders often freed for space for nonviolent drug offenders (Lewis)
    released "rapists, robbers and murderers" (Brennan)
    federal prisoners do life w/out parole for marijuana and rapists go free after 4 yrs. (Brennan)

Circumstances should affect sentences
—implies lack of dangerousness should be considered (Lewis)
—"youth, a previously clean record, or varying levels of culpability among codefendants" (Brennan)
Action advised
—change sentencing laws (Lewis)
—compassion; own example shows that people can change (Brennan)
Unique details
—important opposers of minimum sentences (Brennan)

As he drew up his list of parallel points and supplementary support, Seth decided certain details would not work in his synthesis. Lewis's discussion of former drug czar William Bennett and the medicinal uses of drugs and the details of Brennan's own case did not seem relevant to the shared focus of the articles. (Another student doing this same assignment might have found a way to work any of these in; the important thing to remember is that a synthesis results from analysis and selection, and individual writers will do these tasks somewhat differently.)

After this in-depth analysis of the two articles, Seth moved to Step 4. He looked again at his summary of the main idea of the two articles. He decided it needed some revision to make it more complete. He also knew he had to add identifiers for the two articles.

ORIGINAL

Mandatory sentences for drug offenders often cause great injustices to those who receive them.

REVISED

According to Anthony Lewis, a <u>New York Times</u> columnist, and Michael Brennan, an Oregon writer who is himself an ex-convict, mandatory sentences for drug offenders often cause great injustice to those who receive them and are extremely expensive as well.

Seth then looked over his list of points and support and recognized that some points needed combining and that the entire list needed reordering. He numbered his paraphrase of the main idea as "1" and then indicated the order in which he felt the rest of the points could flow. He still felt undecided about the placement of some material in the synthesis.

3	*mandatory sentences are overly harsh*
2	*mandatory sentences (definition)*
Then problems	
5a	*result in high cost of prison to society*
4a	*result in cruel punishment, a "waste of their lives"*
5b	*other negative consequences*
4b?	*circumstances should affect sentences [justice issue]*
6	*action advised*
?	*unique support: important opposers of minimum sentences*

Then, in Step 5, Seth produced a draft. As he wrote, he kept his copies of the articles nearby so he could make sure he was paraphrasing and so he could check his facts and details against the originals.

For Step 6, Seth reread and revised his synthesis paper. He double-checked references to ideas in each text to make sure he hadn't gotten any points confused. He refined some awkward wording and noticed he needed to split some overly long sentences into shorter units.

Finally, in Step 7, he edited his paper for grammatical errors, spell-checked it, and printed it. Here is his final version:

According to Anthony Lewis, a *New York Times* columnist, and Michael Brennan, an Oregon writer who is also an ex-convict, mandatory sentences for drug offenders often are unjust and extremely expensive as well.

Mandatory sentences are required minimums that judges must impose, since federal and some state laws passed since 1986, Brennan explains.

The problem with these sentences is that they are overly harsh. Lewis gives the example of a dentist, Dr. Fred Ruder, who invested in a company that turned out to be in the marijuana business. He was convicted and sentenced to five years without parole. Brennan provides another example, a young black mother and first-time offender convicted of conspiracy to sell crack and serving for life, also without parole.

Another case discussed by Brennan is a shoplifter who killed himself to avoid a 25-year sentence for this minor crime; while this man's crimes were not drug-related, his suicide shows the cruelty of mandatory sentences.

As Lewis notes, these extreme punishments result in a "waste of . . . lives." The dentist who can't practice and the young mother who cannot raise her child have lost everything because of one mistake. Lewis points to other examples profiled in a documentary on the Discovery channel: three women serving 15 years to life for drug convictions, yet who are clearly not dangerous.

Circumstances should be taken into account when criminals are sentenced; for example, the person might be young or a first offender (Brennan). Lewis clearly feels that a lack of dangerousness should be a consideration. About one-third of all drug prisoners are considered nonviolent, amounting to about 100,000 people, according to Lewis.

These mandatory sentences also present society with a high financial cost. Dr. Ruder's father estimates we are paying $25,000 per year for his son's jail time. The cost of the three women's sentences will be $1.35 million, according to Lewis. Brennan cites the "average cost of housing a fed prisoner" as $20,804.

There are other negative consequences as well. Sometimes violent offenders must be released to make room for nonviolent drug offenders with mandatory sentences; Brennan cites the Florida release of "rapists, robbers and murderers."

Lewis openly supports the change of mandatory sentencing rules, "so judges can . . . fit punishments to the facts before them." Brennan suggests that society should respond with compassion to the plight of individuals caught in this sentencing trap. His own example shows that people can change and improve if given the chance.

As he wrote, Seth moved a couple of points around; the reference to the shoplifter seemed to fit in earlier in his discussion of injustice, for example. He included the statistics about the number of nonviolent offenders after his discussion of offenders' individual circumstances rather than in the paragraph about negative consequences to society.

Here are some other points to note about the synthesis:

1. The student does not judge or evaluate the ideas in the articles. They are presented in a neutral tone.
2. The student gives brief informal citations for the holders of the ideas (since the instructor and the other students have also read the articles).
3. The various points of agreement are allotted different paragraphs.

Documentation

A synthesis written as an academic exercise does not require formal documentation as long as the instructor and student both know the articles being summarized. But each point should be attributed to its source either in the sentence or in a parenthetic reference. If not, in most cases, a list of articles referred to would be sufficient. A synthesis used in a research paper, however, would be formally documented.

Writing a Brief Formal Synthesis

The second part of this assignment required Seth to adapt his full synthesis into a brief synthesis. To do this, Seth basically followed the same organization pattern. He went through his paper, trying to express the points succinctly and substituting summary for most of the supporting details. He did decide to leave in certain telling details: the types of individual circumstances that should be considered in sentencing, the financial cost of prison, and the trade-off between keeping nonviolent and violent offenders in prison. He felt these details helped to show the seriousness and extremity of the problem. Here is his brief synthesis:

According to Anthony Lewis, a *New York Times* columnist, and Michael Brennan, an Oregon writer who is also an ex-convict, mandatory sentences for drug offenders are unjust and extremely expensive as well.

Mandatory sentences are required minimums that judges must impose, as a result of federal and some state laws passed since 1986, Brennan informs us.

The problem with these sentences is that they are overly harsh. Both Lewis and Brennan cite examples of basically good people who make one mistake and are cruelly punished. Also, nonviolent offenders are treated the same as dangerous criminals. Circumstances should be taken into account when criminals are sentenced, such as youth, a first offense (Brennan), or a lack of dangerousness (Lewis).

Mandatory sentences are also very costly, about $20,804 a year (Brennan). Other negatives include releasing violent criminals to make room for nonviolent drug offenders with mandatory sentences.

Lewis openly supports ending mandatory sentencing rules, "so judges can . . . fit punishments to the facts before them." Brennan suggests society should have compassion on individuals caught in this sentencing trap.

■ LOCATING PERIODICALS

Your instructor may provide you with or assign you readings from this text as the basis for your comparison and synthesis papers. Or you may be required to locate your own sources. You will thus find yourself looking for magazine, journal, or newspaper articles on your topic, and these will be found in the periodicals section of your library. This section comprises several different areas of document storage and encompasses everything issued "periodically," from daily newspapers to glossy monthly magazines to book-size academic journals issued quarterly or semiannually.

Since the early 1980s, libraries have undergone radical alterations because of computerization. This revolution has affected all areas of the library, especially the availability of and search methods for periodicals. Whereas at one time library periodicals could be divided into current issues and older issues kept in bound or microform formats, these days periodicals are available in other formats as well: on CD-ROM and installed databases and through online services of many types.

Nearly every library has the same set of printed resources for locating periodical sources. But in the electronic area there is a great variety of options available to libraries, and updates and upgrades keep flowing through the pipeline, so no one can predict exactly what array of computer resources a particular library will have. Not all systems are completely user friendly, unfortunately; most students will require some human help in using a college library that is new to them.

Process

Locating appropriate periodical sources involves several defined steps. Here's an outline of the process for locating periodical articles:

1. Use bibliographies and databases to identify articles (by author, title, journal name, and issue) on your topic.
2. Take bibliographic notes.
3. Discover whether your library provides access to these periodicals and where they are located.
4. Read or assess each article and take notes on (or copy, download, or print) each article you wish to take home

Step 1: Using Bibliographies or Databases

Bibliographies list articles published in periodicals and books. The contents of bibliographies are usually organized under three main identifiers: subjects, titles, and authors' names, all arranged alphabetically. Some bibliographies are broad and identify articles in numerous periodicals. Other bibliographies list articles in one particular periodical (the *New York Times Index,* for example). Other bibliographies are field-specific—that is, they contain information about periodicals, and sometimes also books, in a particular academic field. *Education Index, Historical Abstracts,* and *Engineering Index* are just of few of the many field-specific bibliographies. Some bibliographies, particularly those covering a limited number of topics, include brief descriptions of the articles and books listed; these resources are called abstracts instead of bibliographies.

Once upon a time, all bibliographies were published as books or pamphlets, but, of course, that is no longer the case. Today, there is a wealth of electronic sources of bibliographic information, some duplicating bibliographies available in print. To use your college library well, you need to be aware of all the potential print and electronic databases.

You can also find further readings on a topic by examining the reference lists in books and articles using formal citation.

Print Bibliographies.   All libraries carry certain standard general bibliographies, and many field-specific ones as well. Skill in using print bibliographies is useful when learning how to use electronic equivalences.

The basic, most general bibliography, one many people learn to use in in high school, is the *Reader's Guide to Periodical Literature.* It indexes mass-market periodicals that are too superficial, in many cases, for college-level work. The *Humanities Index* and the *Social Sciences Index* serve as broad periodical guides for the serious-to-scholarly research students do in college.

All these indexes use similar organization and formats, so if you learn to use one, you will be able to use any print index. At the start of the *Reader's Guide,* the *Humanities Index,* and the *Social Sciences Index,* you will find a list of all the publications each one indexes. Because so many periodicals are issued weekly, biweekly, and monthly, these bibliographies are published at intervals during the year in pamphlet form and then yearly as a bound book. The frontmatter also includes a guide to abbreviations used in the listings. In three separate volumes, there are subject, author, and title listings for all articles indexed. Subject headings are often followed by subheadings.

Most researchers begin by looking up the subject they wish to study. You might want to first brainstorm a list of synonyms for your topic, alternative terms in which it might be expressed, as well as some subtopics or narrow aspects of the topic. Look up each version of your topic so you can make sure you have uncovered all the sources on the subject in the bibliography you are using. If the bibliography suggests you turn to another topic ("See . . ." or "See also . . .") you should definitely check these other headings because they might offer additional useful sources.

Occasionally, your research will uncover a writer who has written extensively on the subject, and you may wish to look under this person's name for all of his or her articles. Or one source may refer to a related article by title and periodical without supplying issue and date; in this case, you might look up the title in a bibliography.

There are no rules for where libraries store periodical bibliographies. You need to become acquainted with your college library in order to discover the locations of these important resources. They may be stored near or in the library's reference department, with the current periodicals, or with the microform files and readers.

■ *Activity 3*
Discovering Print
Bibliographies, p. 162

Equivalent Electronic Databases.   Beyond printed bibliographies, you will probably have other research options. *Electronic* and *computerized* are general terms referring to any and all uses of these media for research. There are two basic ways bibliographic research material can come to you electronically: first, through a *fixed* or *installed* database that is located in your library, or, second, through a *live, online* connection.

Fixed or installed bibliographies may be accessible through your library's main computerized catalogue or through separate terminals that have CD-ROM databases installed. At the computerized-catalogue terminals, you may be able to choose whether to search for books, periodicals, or newspapers. Some main computerized catalogues have separate databases for business sources or other broad fields. Many campuses are wired so you can access and search your library databases (and sometimes download or print articles) through lab computers or your personal computer, whether you live on campus or off.

Supplied on CD-ROM, the electronic versions of specialized academic indexes may be available through separate terminals in the library. These indexes cover several years and are updated regularly. Like the print versions, these indexes are searchable by title, author, and subject. Some main-terminal or CD-ROM indexes are attached to printers so that you may print out listings, an abstract, or an entire article.

Online listings of periodical articles, as well as of many other types of sources, are available in some libraries and through computer labs or personal computers. Many libraries subscribe to online databases such as Nexis, a news and information source widely used by journalists, and Lexis, a law and government database. There is usually a fee for using or acquiring articles through these sources. These are also accessible via the Internet.

Those with private online connections to services such as Compuserve, for example, can access a magazine database that permits searching by subject, author, and title and through which articles can be downloaded for an additional fee. This online bibliography is equivalent to a library's general periodical database. Academic and scholarly sources are not indexed in general periodical databases however.

■ *Activity 4*
Discovering
Electronic
Bibliographic
Resources, p. 162

The Internet also offers many research opportunities, of which locating periodical articles is just one. A section on using the Internet and World Wide Web for research appears later in this chapter.

Step 2: Taking Bibliographic Notes

Bibliographic notes are your collection of potential useful sources on a topic. They consist of the information you need to locate a particular source and, if you are using formal citation, may include the details you need to document it. To locate a periodical source, you need the name of the periodical, the date of issuance or volume and number, plus the title, author, and page numbers of the particular article you wish to read. As you determine where your library keeps the periodical, you will add that information.

Recording Information.   If you are doing light research to locate a few articles on a topic, you might just take your notes on a blank page of your notebook. If you use this style, make sure to skip a few lines between each entry, so that you have room to add information about each source's location in the library, your success in locating it, and a comment about the article's content should you find and read it. When doing extensive research involving many sources, you can develop a working bibliography on 3 × 5 index cards. (See Chapter 12 for detailed information about bibliographic notes.) If you library permits you to print out search results, you will include these printouts in your working bibliography.

Choosing Sources.   Although bibliographic listings start with authors' names (and this is how you should take them down), at this stage you are interested in the titles because they are your only guide to the articles' content (unless you are using an abstract). Skim though all the titles to assess which might be useful to you. Don't just take down the first few titles that catch your eye. If timeliness is a factor, check the article dates as well. Record each source that seems to offer something about your topic. If you are working with a printout, skim through the titles and star those that relate to your focused topic; cross out those that seem irrelevant.

Number of Notes.   The number of bibliographic notes you take depends on your assignment. If you are looking for a variety of points of view about a subject, you may take down only a dozen titles and actually locate only a few. But if you are doing in-depth research on a topic for a lengthy research paper, you will have to collect numerous potential sources. Whatever your assignment, do note down more articles than you need because some of the sources may not be available in your library and others may turn out to be unhelpful.

Step 3: Accessing Articles

As you determine whether your library holds the periodicals you seek, note this information below your bibliographic information for each article.

There is no standardized way for libraries to inform users which periodicals are available. Libraries with a customized online periodical database often include a tag after each bibliography entry indicating whether the library holds the periodical. Some libraries have a separate card catalogue for periodicals or provide a list with periodicals arranged alphabetically according to title; these cards and lists include the dates of the library's holdings and the locations of issues in the library. Older issues are listed as bound, microformed, or perhaps archived on a CD-ROM; more recent issues may be in a current periodicals room or may be available through a computer terminal.

If you discover that your library does not subscribe to a periodical, you may have other options. You may have to travel to another college library to seek out the journal, or you may be able to access the periodical electronically. See the discussion above, in the section on equivalent electronic bibliographies, for some computerized options for locating periodical articles.

Step 4: Assessing and Taking Notes on or Copying Articles

For a comparison or synthesis project, you will need to have a copy of the articles you are going to work with. For a different type of research project, you may need only to take notes, although many researchers prefer to own a copy of every important article they will deal with in their final paper. (Formal note taking for lengthy and in-depth research projects is covered in Chapter 12.)

Before you start to photocopy or download everything you discover in your bibliographic search, take a few minutes to read or skim each article and assess its usefulness to you. Sometimes titles can be misleading. As you scan, you may want to jot down your assessment of or comments about the article. Do this on the page on which you've taken your bibliography notes, under the author-title information for the source.

Using the Internet for Research

Sources found through the Internet and World Wide Web (the "web" for short) are usually article-length, but they are not always periodical articles. The Internet contains a vast array of material: newspaper articles, congressional speeches, personal essays, institutional and individual web sites, and archives of various types.

What follows is a general guide to searching the World Wide Web and tips for locating periodical sources. Because the Internet changes on an hourly basis, the information here may unfortunately become outdated by the time you read it. The best way to learn about using the World Wide Web is to do it but also to read about it online, where numerous sites give instructions on how to maximize your time and energy in doing online research. Some informative sites are listed at the end of this chapter.

Doing bibliographic research on the World Wide Web can be a hit-and-miss endeavor, for you can turn up not just periodical articles but material of many types, from the archives of online conversations to material generated just for the web.

Some Useful Site Addresses

You can often guess the URL of a site if you are sure of its name. Commercial sites want to be found and usually have obvious addresses. By typing the standard web lead-in (http://www.) plus the name of the site and ".com" you may be able to go right to it. For example, HotBot, AltaVista, Magellan, and many other search tools and many major newspapers and periodicals are locatable by plugging the name into the basic address:

http://www.   .com

For example, Magellan is found at http://www.magellan.com. The *New York Times* site is at http://www.nytimes.com.

■ *Guidelines for Web Searches*

1. **Before you begin searching, define your search terms,** just as you would for a library bibliography search. You may have to try both narrow and broad ways of expressing your issue of interest in order to get results.

2. **Choose your search tool purposefully,** for it will determine the usefulness of the results. There are two major types of search tools, subject directories and search engines, and they work best for different types of searches. Search tools on the web are commercial products, for the most part, supported by ads and in competition with each other for users. A **subject directory** is most useful if you are searching for information about a subject. A **search engine** works well if you are looking up a key term specifying an event, incident, person, title, or very focused topic. Many search engines are now linked or sited together on the same page with an affiliated subject directory, and a search conducted in one will be optionally or automatically conducted in the other as well.

Subject directories, such as Yahoo!, Cybrarian, the Internet Public Library, and Lycos Sites by Subject, allow you to progressively narrow the kinds of sites to search, much as you would choose a shelf of books to browse in the library. If you read frequently in the field of political science, for example, you know you can go to that area of the library, within it locate the section containing U.S. political science, within that the shelves containing books about U.S. presidents, and within those the shelf or two containing books about Ronald Reagan. Once at that shelf you can sort through the specific offerings to find books that cover the issues in Reagan's presidency you wish to know about.

A subject directory allows you to select narrower and narrower topics from a series of menus until you get to the narrowest specification of your topic. Then the search will be conducted within that category only for your subject. For example, Cybrarian, the directory at Wired's HotBot site, allows you to choose from numerous categories: Reference, Technology, Current Affairs, Business, Recreation, Investing and Finance, Media, Culture, and Health and Science. With Current Affairs, you can choose News, Commentary, Cyber Rights, U.S. Government, or World Organizations. Choosing News gives you the option to search for a term in any of eighteen news sites, ranging from the obvious—the *New York Times,* CNN, and the *Los Angeles Times*—to the less well known: GINA (Global International News Agency), *BusinessWeek,* and *Synapse.*

Search engines comb through all the web sites in their particular catalogue for the search term or phrase you have specified. The narrower the search term, the better the results. A broad term like "Saddam Hussein" will result in thousands (4,577 on one try) of results. But a focused search for "Saddam Hussein" and "United Nations inspectors" produces a more manageable list of 141 entries. Alta Vista, Lycos, and HotBot are examples of search engines. There are also engines that search limited subjects: MapQuest finds maps of a designated

continued

■ *Guidelines for Web Searches (continued)*

place, for example, and MedWeb searches for medical topics. "Metasearch" engines comb through the catalogues of several search engines. Dogpile, Mamma, and Inference are examples of metasearch engines.

3. **Learn the correct way to formulate key terms and subjects** in the search tools you use. For example, Yahoo! will search for occurrences of each word you put in the search box. If you wish it to search for a phrase, you must put quotation marks around it. There is no uniform method of delimiting searches; you need to read the search tips linked to the main page of each search tool. Most methods are variations of Boolean logic. In Boolean, you use common words like "and," "or," "but not" to signal exactly the search term you want to use.

4. **Directly approach online periodical archives** to research contemporary issues and controversies. Major periodicals and newspapers have web sites through which you can read current articles, either whole or in summary. Most such sites also offer a link to an archive where some major stories from back issues of the periodical may be available. For example, one student researching drug legalization learned that *National Review* had devoted a whole issue to this topic and tried to track down the material through *National Review*'s web site. She was able to link to the issue, where excerpts from one article were archived. In the end, however, she had to go to the library to read the full set of articles in the print version. Some major periodical sites are listed at the end of this section.

5. **Bookmark liberally, download purposefully, and print selectively.** Bookmark any sites or finds that you think are interesting so you can return and take a closer look. Before downloading material, read enough of it to determine whether it will be of some use to you; at least skim it briefly. Otherwise you will wind up with a few dozen mysteriously named files in your download folder, files needing several hours to examine. Many computer labs limit the amount you can print, so you should take time to read files on-screen before printing.

6. **Keep track of site addresses.** Once you get the hang of it, research on the web can be deceptively easy. You might bookmark a dozen sites in a session, intending to go back and look through them later. You might discover, however, that the labels under which sites appear on your bookmark list are so cryptic or uninformative that you can't tell what a site is until you go there.

If you will be formally documenting your sources in a paper, you need to keep scrupulous records of site addresses, for you will have to supply them in the citation for any material you acquire from the web. Some browsers permit you to add the Uniform Resource Locator (URL) and date to a header on your printouts; computer labs may or may not have this preference preset. If not, you must manually record site addresses.

Some noncommercial sites use the end tag .org or .net; for example, Internet Public Library is located at ipl.org. And academic sites use .edu. Here are a few helpful sites:

NEWSPAPERS AND OTHER JOURNALISM SITES

latimes.com
washingtonpost.com
newsweek.com
Chicago Sun Times: suntimes.com
National Public Radio: npr.org
Time: pathfinder.com
Kennedy School of Government (Harvard) journalism site:
      http://ksgwww.harvard.edu/~ksgpress/journpg.htm
Internet Public Library periodicals links:
      ipl.org/reading/news   ipl.org/reading/serials

GUIDES TO USING THE INTERNET FOR RESEARCH

Tips and tricks for searching: tiac.net/users/hope/tips
Internet Public Library research help: ipl.org/ref/websearching.html

Activities

1   Analyzing for Comparison and Contrast

For each pair of passages, identify the common ground and decide whether the articles compare or contrast in claim, reasoning and evidence, interpretation, assumptions, audience appeals, and style.

[A]   Should schools teach morality and ethical decision-making to children? Do they really have a choice? After all, teachers play a major role in forming not only the intellects, but also the characters, of their students. Teachers teach morality, whether they intend to or not.

   After decades of attempting to create a value-neutral educational system, educators are today realizing that school not only can, but must, teach morality.

—John W. Cooper, "Should We Teach Values?"

As I sent my kids back to school this fall, I couldn't help wondering about the values they're soaking up for the tumultuous years ahead. They're both good kids—no complaints there—but they're also plunging into adolescence, and I know how volatile that is.

   I'm not alone in wondering. All across the country school leaders and parents are looking for ways to teach, or reinforce, qualities of character as well as academics. "Character education," as its usually called, is the buzz of education circles this fall, [the] latest approach in the battle to make schools work better and make kids better kids.

—Peter Landry, "Value Lessons"

[B]   Regaining civility is the pre-eminent challenge facing the country, social critics say. To make peace with diversity. To find a way to bind together atomizing forces in the interest of democracy, without sacrificing individual identity. "We may not share a common past, but we surely do share a common future," President Clinton declared in his recent [1997] State of the Union address. . . . Notes James Morris in a lively essay on civility in fall's *Wilson Quarterly:* To "imagine a past time of exquisite courtesy and refinement, if not 50 years ago, then 100, or 123, is to regret a world of bubbles."

—"Rudeness Awakening Going On in U.S.," *Los Angeles Times–Washington Post* News Service

According to Myron Magnet, most modern ills can be laid at the doors of the '60s—the counterculture's moral relativism, and permissiveness, the narcissist preoccupation with the self and the narrowness of movement politics. . . . How to re-engage citizens is a question without an easy answer. No one is arguing for rolling back the progress of the '60s, the permanent and positive achievements. . . . Indeed, many voices warn against nostalgia: The middle-class values of an earlier time often *were* stultifying; small-town America *was* bigoted in many instances; patriarchal institutions like the corporation and church *did* need to be questioned and shaken up a bit.

—Wray Herbert, "Our Identity Crisis"

[C]   One reason [for the defeat of referendums proposing legalized gambling] is that experience has shown the promise of state sponsored lotteries—that the proceeds would be used for more or better education—is a fraud. Money is fungible; when the state or city raises money "painlessly," from public or private gambling, some of that money is ostentatiously set aside for schools—but legislators soon treat that as a replacement for funds previously voted for education.

—William Safire, "Political Gambling"

Meanwhile, proponents of even more gambling are able to dismiss any social concerns as unfounded. They look at the gambling revenues and point to the beneficiaries: schools, the environment, economic development. Gambling, they say, is good for schools.

—Theodore Kulongoski and Peter Bragdon, "When Gambling Calls the Shots"

2 Synthesizing Brief Passages

For each set of passages below, prepare a brief synthesis.

[A]   Let me examine the first contention, that immigration plays a real, but minor, role in worsening the plight of the poor. It is said that other factors—economic globalization, technological change, the decline in unionization, the entry of women into the workforce—have played a far greater role than immigration in holding down the wages of the poor and in increasing income inequality. Even if this were true, immigration policy is the only one of these factors government can influence. Congress . . . *can* cut immigration.

—Mark Krikorian, "Our Nation's Immigration Policy Harms the Poor"

The large increase in low-skilled immigrant workers has added to the downward pressure on employment and wages in the low-skilled labor market. Of the 804,000 immigrants admitted to the U. S. in 1994, only 36 percent reported an occupation at the time of application. . . . Of the immigrants who were not students or under age 16, only 12 percent were in professional and technical occupations. The immigration of low-skilled workers has therefore had both a direct and an indirect effect on increasing income in-equality and poverty [in the United States].

—Barry Chiswick, "The Economic Consequences of Immigration"

[B]　Affirmative action is a tool to incorporate blacks as full citizens into American society. The cornerstone of the process of incorporation was the dismantling of segregation, but that is only the beginning. . . .

Without affirmative action, the recently created black middle class would shrink. It is also important to understand that the incorporation of blacks into the middle class has a ripple effect. Most middle-class blacks continue to have social connections with relatives and friends who are still among the ghetto poor.

Those who "make it" are thus potent role models for those in the inner city who have the option of striving for success either in mainstream society or on the street in the world of drug dealers and other, often armed, hustlers.

—Elijah Anderson, "The Reasons for Affirmative Action Still Stand"

A second false notion is that, as a result of such policies, blacks and other minorities are disproportionately represented in the professions.

False again.

According to the U.S. Bureau of Labor statistics for 1995 (the most recent year available), African Americans make up 10 percent of the workforce and 24 percent of the unemployed. That means that 1 out of every 10 employed Americans is black, while 1 out of 4 unemployed are black.

With the exception of education, there is not one profession in which black Americans make up 10 percent of the workforce. . . .

Blacks make up only 2.5 percent of architects, 4.7 percent of engineers and 7.2 percent of mathematicians and computer scientists. In the natural sciences, blacks make up only 3.9 percent of the total.

The concern over reverse discrimination ignores reality.

—Acel Moore, "The Numbers Unveil Myths about Affirmative Action"

[C]　When Hawaii becomes the first state to recognize gay and lesbian marriage this summer . . . the gay and lesbian marriages that some rabbis and ministers have been performing for the past decade or more will take on new meanings as the spiritual and the legal become connected as they are in heterosexual marriage.

As a lesbian and a rabbi, I have found myself on both sides of the bridal canopy in this matter. From a lesbian perspective, recognition of our relationships by civil authority is crucial to function as full members of society. We want and need the rights and privileges that marriage confers. We also want to affirm our connections to our religious heritage.

—Rebecca Alpert, "Same Sex Marriage Enhances the Social Good"

The two most sacred commitments in my life—my calling to the ministry and my same-gender marriage—are under attack because they are deemed threatening to a church and a society troubled by the lack of family cohesion, so-called "traditional family values." Our culture fails to see this as a largely heterosexual problem but instead scapegoats homosexuals, just as we who are gay and lesbian attempt to maintain relationships with our biological families and establish our own family units. Our birth families often come under attack for supporting us; our chosen families are refused recognition. Our families of faith treat us as society once treated illegitimate children. In the body politic, rights taken for granted by heterosexuals are called "special" when applied to us. . . .

Resistance to calling same-sex unions marriages is beyond my understanding. In no way does it lessen the sacred or civil nature of marriage. Indeed, its value is bolstered by the recognition that both homosexuals and heterosexuals wish to enter into such a covenant.

—Chris Glaser, "Marriage as We See It"

3 Discovering Print Bibliographies

Do research to locate broad and specialized bibliographies in your major (actual or likely) and in another favorite field or minor. For each index you discover, write the following information on 3 × 5 cards: full title, author, publisher, publication date, field(s) covered, time period covered, major sections of the bibliography, type of index(es) (subject, author, title), other features (abstracts, for example), call number, and location in your library.

4 Discovering Electronic Bibliographic Resources

Explore your college library to fine its electronic bibliographic resources in your major, favorite field, or minor. For each bibliographic resource you discover, fill out a 3 × 5 card with the following information: name of index, publisher or source, publication year, subjects covered, ways to search, and location in the library.

Assignments

All articles to be used for these assignments are selected readings at the end of this chapter.

COMPARISON

1. Write a comparison of these two articles:
   David R. Henderson, "The Case for Sweatshops"
   Cathy Young, "Sweatshops or a Shot at a Better Life?"
2. Compare or contrast (or both) these articles:
   Ellen Goodman, "The Ethical Gray Zone: Assisted Suicide"
   Charles Krauthammer, "If Suicide Is Legally Sanctioned for the Terminally Ill, Why Not for the Rest of Society?"

SYNTHESIS

3. Write a synthesis of these two articles:
   David R. Henderson, "The Case for Sweatshops"
   Cathy Young, "Sweatshops or a Shot at a Better Life?"

4. Write a synthesis of these two articles:

Myriam Miedzian, "How We Can Tune Out Children from Television Violence"

Marilyn Wheeler, "Young People Get an Eye-Opening Look at the Violence on TV"

 *Readings*

The Case for Sweatshops

DAVID R. HENDERSON

Picture this. Ten-year-old children get up before dawn every morning and go to work. They are paid by the piece, not by a guaranteed hourly wage. They get no benefits. And they work seven days a week, year-round, with no vacation unless they can find someone to take their place. 1

Aren't you glad you don't live in a country where children work under such harsh conditions? Actually, you do. In fact, some of you probably had this job while you were growing up. The country is the U.S.; the job is newspaper delivery. 2

Those of us who delivered papers when we were kids were glad we had the opportunity to make pocket change and would have been angry at anyone who tried to persuade our employers not to hire us. 3

Think how much angrier we would have been had we depended on those jobs, not for spending money, but for our very livelihood. That is how angry some people in Third World countries and in the U.S. have a right to be at Labor Secretary Robert Reich and at the National Labor Committee (NLC), an organization funded by U.S. labor unions that tries to intimidate American companies and consumers who wish to buy goods made with low-wage labor. The NLC hit the jackpot late this spring when it shamed talk-show host Kathie Lee Gifford for lending her name to clothing made in a Honduran "sweatshop," where some workers were paid 31 cents an hour. Gifford quickly joined the crusade, testifying before Congress and persuading other celebrities to withhold their names from product lines made by low-wage child laborers. 4

But neither Gifford nor Reich nor the NLC seems to have asked what happens to the children who lose their jobs. The answer, simply, is that they are worse off. This follows from the most important principle in economics: Exchange benefits both buyer and seller. Work, other than slave labor (which does persist in rare cases and is, of course, unequivocally evil), is an exchange. A worker chooses a particular job because she prefers it to her next-best alternative. To us, a low-paying job in Honduras or in Los Angeles's garment district seems horrible, but for many adults and children, it's the best choice they have. You don't make someone better off by taking away the best of her bad options. 5

Sure enough, workers in Honduras see the maquila (factory) as a good option. One apparel worker in Honduras told the New York Times: "This is an enormous advance, and I give 6 thanks to the maquila for it. My monthly income is seven times what I made in the countryside." Sweatshops, in short, are a path from poverty to greater wealth. Of course, it would be nice if a poor teenage Honduran's parents could afford to send her to school, but they can't, so those teenagers are doing the best they can by working. Take the 31 cents an hour some 13-year-old Honduran girls allegedly earn at 70-hour-a-week jobs. Assuming a 50-week year, that works out to over $1,000 a year. This sounds absurdly low to Americans, but not when you consider that Honduras's GDP per person in 1994 was the equivalent of about $600.

7   Should you feel guilty for buying clothing made in Honduras, Vietnam, or Bangladesh, remember this: You're helping the workers who made it—and who were unlucky enough to have been born in a poor country. The people who should feel guilty are Reich and the NLC, who push policies that hurt the very people they claim to care about.

Questions for Inquiry

1. What is Henderson's claim? Is it explicit or implicit?
2. How would you describe Henderson's approach to his reader? How does he build a connection with the reader?
3. Examine Henderson's introduction. What is the effect of the "picture" he presents? Is the "picture" he draws an accurate image of the life of a newspaper deliverer?

Questions for Argument

1. To your mind, how valid is the analogy between a U.S. child with a paper route and a foreign child working full-time in a factory? If you have a problem with the analogy, can you still accept Henderson's claim?
2. Should celebrities like Kathie Lee Gifford "lend their names" to products that they have nothing to do with and little knowledge of? Does such endorsing of products affect consumers that you know? Do such endorsements affect or complicate the economic "exchange" between buyer or seller so that the benefits are unequal?

Writing Assignments

Informal

1. Write a journal entry in which you discuss your feelings about the way products are sold through celebrity endorsements.
2. The author says that wrongheaded policy means "taking away the best of [foreign workers'] bad options"(5). Have you ever been in a situation in which you or someone you know (perhaps in the older generation) had to settle for the "best of bad options"? Write an informal paper in which you describe the impact of such a decision on the person, his or her family, and the person's future.

Formal

3. **Collaborative Writing—Argumentation.** As part of his argument, Henderson cites "the most important principle in economics" (5). Brainstorm with others to imagine examples of exchanges in which both parties benefit and examples in which one of

the parties, buyer or seller, does not benefit or even is disadvantaged. Then, with your group, outline a position paper in which you either support or dispute this "important principle." If your instructor makes time, present your argument orally in a classroom forum.

4. Henderson suggests that people wrongly feel guilty about buying products from certain nations because of the possibility of sweatshops. Should consumers use their purchasing choices to make a statement about a political or social issue? Should certain products or producing countries be boycotted? Or should people express concerns in some other way? Write an essay in which you discuss how consumers should act on their beliefs about products and production.

5. **Using Sources—Argumentation.** Read the next selection, "Sweatshops or a Shot at a Better Life?" by Cathy Young, and "The Destruction of Childhood" by Langdon Winner, a reading selection at the end of Chapter 3. Then write a paper in which you present a case for or against Americans contributing to the National Labor Committee or taking other actions to oppose sweatshops.

■ ■ ■

Sweatshops or a Shot at a Better Life?

CATHY YOUNG

Cathy Young is the author of *Beyond the Gender Wars,* published by the Free Press. This article appeared in several newspapers the first week of January 1997. (Reprinted by permission of author.)

The campaign against Third World sweatshops, and child labor in particular, has been gathering steam ever since the tots making clothes for Kathie Lee Gifford became the stuff of late-night monologues. 1

For the Christmas shopping season, newspapers advised consumers on making sure the gifts they bought were not made by underpaid or underage workers. Reebok has put a no-child-labor pledge on its soccer balls. Now, America's children are joining the crusade: writing letters to Congress and to offending companies, handing out fliers at shopping malls, raising money for the cause. 2

But is it a good cause? 3

Amid all the cries about the villainy of Nike and the evils of child labor, I have often asked myself if Third World workers would be better off without their jobs, however unenviable these jobs might seem to us. I have also wondered why, when we are shocked by reports of 50-cent-an-hour wages, we never think of those Save the Children ads reminding us that a contribution of $15 can feed and clothe a Third World child for a whole month. 4

Was it just my free-market knee jerking? As a matter of fact, it is not just economic conservatives who are beginning to understand that the sweatshop issue is about more than big bad corporations vs. downtrodden workers. 5

A few reporters who bothered to interview people in Indonesia and Central America have glimpsed the fact that often, the American union activist's horrible sweatshop is the Third World worker's chance at a better life. 6

7   A Honduran factory worker who had gone to work as a bus-fare collector at 13—14 hours a day with no days off, paid at the driver's whim—told the New York Times that he wished the much-maligned *maquiladora* plants had existed then: "The *maquila* represents progress."

8   *Maquila* wages may be low (about 40 cents an hour), but they have already driven up wages in Honduras, Mexico and other countries while improving conditions in other sectors, including agricultural and domestic work.

9   Already, due to pressure from the United States, most factories have stopped hiring workers under 16, and many have fired their underage employees. Where are those kids going? Mostly to other jobs—lower-paying, more arduous, more dangerous.

10   In Bangladesh in 1995, garment manufacturers threatened by a boycott agreed to end the employment of children under 14, on the condition that the children are placed in schools and get a $7-a-month stipend from aid agencies (about half of what they might have earned in a factory). Nevertheless, UNICEF found that a few months later, about 10 percent of the former garment workers had dropped out of school and, barred from factories because of their age, were working as newspaper vendors or housemaids.

11   Some children, left with no other means of earning a living, may even be forced into prostitution.

12   Certainly, some child workers are mistreated and some toil in virtual slavery. It is important to stop these abuses. But any effort to help these children must take into account the fact that in poor societies, a family cannot afford to support a child for 18 years. For virtually all of human history, most children worked—a condition that changed in the West with the advent of industrial civilization and prosperity.

13   No one expects American schoolchildren to understand this. "I thought kids our age should be out in school playing soccer, not working under horrible conditions" says one teenage activist. Yes, and they should all have CD players and color TVs. But what about adults like union activist Charles Kernaghan, who concedes that it's "tragic" when Third World kids are worse off after losing their factory jobs but says that he doesn't know how to resolve it, since he's "not an economist"? Talk about cultural imperialism.

14   Andrew Kaufman, a New York writer, suggests that American corporations doing business in the Third World might be required to give a small portion of their profits to local development programs—sanitation, health care, schools. It's a much better idea than closing the "sweatshops." But even without such contributions, the companies will make life better in the countries they are supposedly exploiting. That's how South Korea and Taiwan have gone from sweatshops to prosperous economies with a well-paid, well-educated workforce.

15   If multinationals were required to pay workers in underdeveloped countries at industrial world rates, they would have no incentive to go in there. Of course, American workers then wouldn't have to compete with Third World wages. But I don't think too many people would want to come out and say that they want to keep other countries poor to protect their own living standards.

16   Most people who attack the sweatshops have far nobler motives. Certainly, the idealism of the children working to end child labor is understandable and touching. What's less attractive is the self-righteous zealotry of adults, including teachers who encourage their students to get involved by giving them one-sided presentations of issues they are much too young to understand.

17   These adults might ponder an anecdote told by, of all people, Gloria Steinem. On a field trip in college, she saw a mud turtle by the roadside and carried it back to a stream at the

bottom of the hill—only to be told by her teacher that she had undone weeks of the turtle's efforts to get to the hilltop to lay eggs. Steinem claims that she learned a lesson from this, which she summed up as, "Ask the turtle."

Unlike turtles, Third World workers can speak; the least we can do is listen.   18

Questions for Inquiry

1. What is Young's claim? Is it explicit or implied?
2. What does Young mean by "a better life" (6)? According to her, what are the benefits of factory labor? What are the alternatives for Third World children?
3. What did Gloria Steinem mean by the maxim "Ask the turtle" (17)? To what extent is Young's argument based on "asking the turtle"?

Questions for Argument

1. What would be the consequences, for the United States and for poor nations, of paying wages in the Third World equal to U.S. wages?
2. U.S. children have been enlisted, Young says, to help fight foreign sweatshops (1–2, 13, 16). Whether you believe sweatshops should be eliminated or not, do you think that prompting or encouraging children to become activists for a political or social cause is a positive or negative for the children? For the cause?

Writing Assignments

Informal

1. "For virtually all of human history, most children worked," Young writes (12). Considering this fact, write a journal entry in which you put your life in perspective in relation to what life has been like for teenagers throughout "all of human history."
2. "Ask the turtle" is a suggestive rule of thumb. Free-write about what this phrase means to you and about any situations you have been in which you or someone else should have abided by it.

Formal

3. **Collaborative Writing.** Young admits that "most people who attack the sweatshops have . . . nobler motives" (16). Discuss with your class what the "noble" solution or solutions to the sweatshop dilemma would be. Group with students who feel similarly to you about what should be done, and brainstorm evidence and reasons in support of your concept. Assign each student in the group to generate one section of the support or the introduction to an essay. After you assemble the essay parts, polish and refine it, and brainstorm material for a conclusion. (You may wish to read the Henderson and Winner selections on this topic.)
4. Underlying Young's discussion is the assumption that how you judge the sweatshop situation depends on who you are and where you live. Prosperous U.S. workers, comfortable U.S. children, U.S. factory or garment workers whose jobs have been lost to overseas workers, and workers in Third World countries all see the sweatshops differently. Free-write about a situation, either personal or societal, in which perspective or

personal circumstances made a big difference in what beliefs people held. Then write an essay in which you explain how significantly one's income, profession, level of personal success, involvement in an activity or cause, and other personal characteristics play into people's opinions and viewpoints.

■ ■ ■

The Ethical Gray Zone: Assisted Suicide

ELLEN GOODMAN

Ellen Goodman is a writer for the *Boston Globe,* whose columns are syndicated nationally. This article appeared in April 1997. (Copyright 1997, by the Boston Globe Newspaper Co./Washington Post Writers Group. Reprinted by permission.)

1   Halfway through a recent conversation in Amsterdam with a Dutch medical school professor, he got up to consult his dictionary. Surely, he said, there must be an English equivalent for the Dutch word *gedogen.*

2   Gerrit van der Wal, who conducts research on doctor-assisted death in the Netherlands, flipped through the pages until he comes to the right place. *Gedogen,* he read slowly, tolerance. Then he shook his head and said, "No, that isn't quite right."

3   If the word is not easily translated, perhaps it is because the concept is so Dutch, so not-American. *Gedogon* describes a formal condition somewhere between forbidden and permitted. It is part of the Dutch dance of principle and pragmatism.

4   In the Netherlands, drugs are *gedogen.* They remain illegal, but soft drugs like marijuana are available in duly licensed coffee shops.

5   And euthanasia, too, is *gedogen.* The ending of a life by a doctor remains illegal, but doctors who follow careful guidelines may grant their patients' death wishes.

6   I came to Holland because our own Supreme Court has been asked to decide the question of physician-assisted suicide. Holland has grappled longer and more publicly with the end-of-life issues that we are only now beginning to confront seriously.

7   In a week of interviewing, people bristled at the notion that Americans think the Dutch are ridding themselves of the old and handicapped. In fact "euthanasia" is defined as the termination of life by a doctor at the express wish of a patient. Under the guidelines, the patient's suffering must be unbearable and without the possibility of improvement. The requests must be persistent and confirmed by a second physician.

8   Van der Wal, who warily led me through his most recent survey of doctors, pointed out that only 2.4 percent of deaths in Holland happen with a physician's assistance. Nine out of 10 requests are turned away. Most of those who had assisted suicide were not nursing home patients, but cancer patients in their 60s or 70s. They died in the last days or weeks of their illness, at home, treated by a family doctor they had known for an average of seven years.

9   The Dutch system is not fail-safe or without its own ethical dilemmas. Most euthanasia deaths are still not reported to the government, though failing to do so is illegal. The most troubling discovery is that between 900 and 1,000 patients a year die from what they call "nonvoluntary euthanasia."

As doctors here note, a bit defensively, this is not the result of Holland's euthanasia poli-   10
cies. It exists unseen and unreported in countries, even our own, where doctors deliver lethal
painkilling doses of medicine without consent.

In practice, half of those who were no longer physically able to give consent had ex-   11
pressed the wish for euthanasia earlier. Most were in the last stages of disease. But van der
Wal agreed, "It's a weak point in your system if you don't know what the patient really
wants. There is always the danger that you are ending life against the will of the patient."

It's a weak point as well that the Dutch laws don't make a distinction between mental   12
and physical suffering. Not long ago, a psychiatrist performed euthanasia on a physically
healthy woman who had lost her children and was in deep despair. He was acquitted in a
case that left public confidence rattled.

The policy of *gedogen* doesn't help the Dutch decide what to think of those who value   13
independence so much they want to control their own death. Nor does it help a doctor who
carries the burden and power of deciding when someone has suffered "enough."

What is notable is that 71 percent of the Dutch remain firm in their support of eu-   14
thanasia policies. There is a palpable pride in doing things "the Dutch way." Pride in a system in which the law evolves with public consensus.

Yet time and again, even the strongest supporters of euthanasia told me, as did a re-   15
tired family doctor, Herbert Cohen: "Euthanasia is not for export." The difference between
Holland and America, they say, is universal health care. No one here chooses to die to protect family finances.

Perhaps what is exportable, though, is the Dutch tolerance for ambiguity, for living in   16
the ethical gray zone.

If there is an American parallel to the Dutch way, it might be a state-by-state experi-   17
ment, a testing of different rules and experiences with assisted suicide. The truth is that we,
too, want to find a way of dying that is both merciful and careful.

Yet today, in the countryside of canals and *gedogen*, it's not always easy to find the right   18
words in an American dictionary.

Questions for Inquiry

1. What is Goodman's claim? Does she state it explicitly or imply it?
2. *Gedogen* is a Dutch word that has no English equivalent. How would you state its meaning? How does it apply to euthanasia?
3. What are the problems the Dutch see in their own system of assisted suicide? What
   guidelines do they have?
4. Why do the Dutch feel that their system of assisted suicide wouldn't work in the United
   States?

Questions for Argument

1. Goodman cites statistics on the Dutch use of assisted suicide: "nine out of 10 requests
   are turned away"; officially, only 2.4 percent of deaths involve assisted suicide (8). Do
   you think these figures reflect too few assisted suicides? Or too many?
2. Goodman suggests that perhaps the "tolerance for ambiguity" is exportable to the
   United States (16). Do you agree that the United States could become a place where
   "the gray zone" in ethics would be acceptable? Do you think this is a good idea?

Writing Assignments

Informal

1. Goodman refers to the "Dutch dance of principle and pragmatism" (3). Look up these terms if they are new to you. In your thinking about moral and ethical issues, would you say you tend more toward principle or toward pragmatism? Write a journal entry about where you fall in this opposition of perspectives.

2. What are your feelings about doctor-assisted suicide? In an informal paper, explain your position and whether you believe the United States should adopt it.

Formal

3. **Research.** "Soft" drugs, like marijuana, are available in licensed coffee shops in the Netherlands. Find out more about the Dutch experience with marijuana. Has it changed Dutch society? Is there a downside to the legalization? On the basis of your findings, write an essay in which you explain whether a *gedogen* approach to marijuana would be a good idea in the United States.

4. Goodman places assisted suicide in the ethical "gray zone." Can you think of other behaviors or acts that also belong in this zone? Choose one such behavior and brainstorm or free-write to explain why and in what way this behavior is ethically ambiguous. What aspects of it are "wrong"? What aspects make it right or at least "not wrong"? What is the legal status of the action? On the basis of your prewriting, develop a definition of what "in the ethical gray zone" means. Then write an essay in which you present your definition and explain this type of ethically "gray" behavior. Would you recommend that people commit acts in the "gray zone" or should they avoid them?

■ ■ ■

If Suicide Is Legally Sanctioned for the Terminally Ill, Why Not for the Rest of Society?

CHARLES KRAUTHAMMER

Charles Krauthammer, a physician by training, writes a nationally syndicated column. This article appeared in many newspapers in 1997. (Copyright 1997 by the Washington Post Writers Group. Reprinted by permission.)

1   In 1991 in the Dutch city of Assen, a perfectly healthy 50-year-old woman asked her doctor to help her die. Her two sons had died, one by suicide, one by cancer. She wanted to join them. After many hours of consultation, Dr. Boudewijn Chabot consented. He was at her side when she swallowed the lethal pills he prescribed for her death.

2   In Holland, physician-assisted suicide is for all practical purposes legal, but Dr. Chabot was tried anyway because this woman wasn't terminally ill. She wasn't even ill. In fact, she

wasn't even psychiatrically ill, a point that at trial Dr. Chabot made in his own defense. She was as lucid as she was inconsolable.

The three-judge court in Assen acquitted Dr. Chabot. So did an appeals court. So did the Dutch Supreme Court. Thus, notes Dr. Herbert Hendin (in his study of euthanasia in Holland, "Seduced by Death: Doctors, Patients and the Dutch Cure"), has Holland "legally established mental suffering as a basis for euthanasia."   3

Why is this important for Americans? Because last week the U. S. Supreme Court was asked to decide whether physician-assisted suicide should be legal in America. The two cases before the court both involve the terminally ill. But the deployment of these heartrending cases of terminal illness is part of the cunning of the euthanasia advocates. They are pulling heart strings to get us to open the door. And once the door opens, it opens to everyone, terminally ill or not.   4

How do we know? Justice David Souter asked that question in one form or another at least four times: Once you start by allowing euthanasia for the terminally ill, what evidence is there that abuses will follow?   5

The answer, in a word, is Holland. I'm not even talking here about the thousand cases a year of Dutch patients put to death by their doctors *without their consent.* I'm talking here about Dutch doctors helping the suicide of people not terminally ill, not chronically ill, not ill at all, but, like our lady of Assen, merely bereft.   6

Eugene Sutorius, the prominent Dutch attorney who defended Dr. Chabot, said after winning his case: "Euthanasia, which started with terminal illness, has moved to a different plane." And so it must. Why? Because the Dutch were being logical.   7

By what logical principle should the relief of death be granted only the terminally ill? After all, the terminally ill face only a brief period of suffering. The chronically ill, or the healthy but bereft—they face a lifetime of agony. Why deny them the relief of a humane exit?   8

The litigants before the Supreme Court, however, claimed the right to assisted suicide on the grounds not of mercy but of liberty—the autonomy of individuals to determine when and how they will die.   9

But on what logical grounds can this autonomy be reserved only for the terminally ill? The lawyers for the euthanasia side, Kathryn Tucker and Laurence Tribe, turned somersaults trying to answer the question. Tribe offered a riff on the stages of life: "Life, though it feels continuous to many of us, has certain critical thresholds: birth, marriage, child-bearing. I think death is one of these thresholds." It nearly got him laughed out of court when Justice Antonin Scalia cut him off with "this is lovely philosophy. Where is it in the Constitution?"   10

Tribe had no answer because there is no answer. If assisted suicide is a right for the terminally ill, there is no argument that can be made to deny it on grounds of mercy or autonomy or nondiscrimination to anyone else who might request it.   11

That is why the Supreme Court decision will be so fateful. It could be the beginning of something much larger: nothing less than historic legitimation—through the legal participation of the medical profession—of suicide.   12

In modern society, suicide is no longer punished, but it is still discouraged. When you see someone on a high ledge ready to jump, you are enjoined by every norm in our society to pull him back from the abyss. We are now being asked to become a society where, when the tormented soul on the ledge asks for our help, we oblige him with a push.   13

They do it in Assen.   14

Questions for Inquiry

1. What is Krauthammer's claim? Is it stated explicitly or is it implied?
2. In what way was the patient's lucidity and mental health a point for the defense of Dr. Chabot's assisting this suicide?
3. Why, according to Krauthammer, does the legalizing of assisted suicide for the terminally ill mean legalizing it for everyone?

Questions for Argument

1. Krauthammer says that U.S. euthanasia advocates are "pulling heart strings" in a "cunning" use of "heartrending cases of terminal illness" in order to advance their views (4). Later, he accuses the Dutch of being too "logical" in their application of assisted euthanasia to "mental suffering" (7, 10). Should the issue of assisted suicide be decided on the basis of "mercy" toward the suffering or on the basis of logic?
2. At the conclusion of the argument, Krauthammer says that legalizing assisted suicide means that we will actively "push" tormented and depressed people who threaten suicide. Do you agree that we will become a society of suicide "pushers" if suicide becomes legal?

Writing Assignments

Informal

1. The Supreme Court cases presented assisted suicide as a matter of "liberty—the autonomy of individuals to determine when and how they will die" (9). Do you believe that our Constitutional freedoms include this liberty? Is this a liberty we should have? Write a journal entry in which you consider these questions.
2. Consider the metaphor of "thresholds" in life used by lawyer Laurence Tribe. Do you feel you have passed through doorways and over thresholds in your life or experienced changes that disrupted the "continuous" feeling of life? Write an informal essay in which you discuss what the image of "thresholds" means to you in relation to your life so far.

Formal

3. **Collaboration.** Krauthammer claims that the events in Holland are proof that "abuses will follow" the legalization of euthanasia for the terminally ill (5–6). Are there laws or liberties that have "abuses" as an inevitable by-product? Brainstorm with your class or a group of classmates to identify good laws that have a downside or freedoms that sometimes cause problems. Then, individually or as a group, write an essay in which you discuss one (or a limited number) of such laws or freedoms and make recommendations as to how some of the abuses could be prevented.
4. **Dialogue.** Should Chabot have helped the bereft woman die? Discuss this question with other class members, and try to uncover additional arguments to those offered by Goodman and Krauthammer. Then, individually or in pairs, write a formal dialogue in which representatives of two different positions on the death of the "lady of Assen" have their say. You may create a dialogue between Krauthammer and Goodman, be-

tween yourself and one of the authors or one of the expert doctors and lawyers cited in the articles, or between two imaginary characters. Each speaker should begin with a firm point of view; let the unfolding debate between them determine who (or whether anyone) wins.

5. **Research.** Use the library and the Internet to learn what the Supreme Court decided in the 1997 cases that Krauthammer mentions and what changes occurred in our laws as a result. Then write an essay in which you compare or contrast Krauthammer's expectations with what really happened.

■ ■ ■

How We Can Tune Out Children from Television Violence

MYRIAM MIEDZIAN

Myriam Miedzian is author of *Boys Will Be Boys* and serves as director of the educational foundation, the Parenting Project. This article appeared in the *Philadelphia Inquirer* in 1992. (Reprinted by permission of author.)

By the age of 18, the average American child has seen about 26,000 murders on TV. Since the advent of TV in the mid-1940s, homicide rates have doubled in the United States.

Many Americans would scoff at the suggestion that there might be some link between these statistics. But the evidence is increasingly indicating that there is.

More than 235 studies have been carried out in the last 40 years on the effects of viewing violence on the screen, and an overwhelming majority indicate that viewing violence encourages violent behavior. Most recently, in an article in the Journal of the American Medical Association, psychiatrist Brandon S. Centerwall asserts that childhood exposure to TV violence is at the root of our 100 percent increase in violent crime.

He bases this on his study of homicide rates among white males in the United States and Canada, where TV was first introduced around 1945, and in South Africa where it was not introduced until 1975. In each country within 10 to 15 years after the advent of television, homicide rates had approximately doubled and then remained relatively stable.

Centerwall examined other possible causal factors such as urbanization and the availability of firearms, before drawing his conclusion. Even if his correlation between increased TV viewing and increased violent crime turns out to be too high, there is much other evidence that clearly shows that viewing violence puts children, especially boys, at higher risk for violent behavior.

Why isn't there an aggressive educational campaign making parents aware of this? For while they wouldn't dream of letting their young children see pornographic films, many parents think nothing of letting them watch graphic depictions of the vilest acts imaginable.

When I went to see the horror-slasher film, *Nightmare on Elm Street 5*, in which teenagers are dismembered, burned alive and drowned, I was shocked to find many children, some as young as 3 or 4, in the theater. These outings are in addition to a daily diet of TV mayhem and murder.

8   We cannot put the TV genie back into the bottle. But controlling the monster to protect our children is not an impossible task, especially in the era of renewed concern with family values.

9   In addition to a major education campaign, parents should be urged to acquire TV lock boxes which permit them to program their sets so that they can control what their children watch. Just like safety bolts and safety seats for children in cars, lock boxes should eventually become mandatory with the sale of every TV set.

10   To complement lock boxes, why not create a Children's Public Broadcasting System dedicated to top quality TV programming that is entertaining, pro-social and appeals to children of all social classes? This might seem like an impossible dream at a time when our national debt is in the trillions.

11   But we must begin to recognize that we are in the midst of a domestic national security crisis far more serious than any international crisis confronting us. More than 350,000 Americans have been murdered in the last 16 years alone. In all our wars since, and including, Vietnam, about 58,000 Americans have lost their lives.

12   While criminal violence has increased in all areas and among all social classes, our inner cities have been the hardest hit. They often resemble war zones in which citizens regularly take shelter from cross-fire and live in constant fear for themselves and their children.

13   Social science research indicates that the frequent absence of a father in the home leaves many inner-city boys especially vulnerable to the influence of endless violent male role models on the screen. Tragically, for this group, homicide is the major cause of death.

14   In light of this alarming data, doesn't it make sense to take approximately $500 million a year out of our $280 billion defense budget and spend it on two children's TV channels— one for younger and one for older children? The combination of parental education, lock boxes, and a CPBS would create a separate TV universe for children.

15   Besides being protected from violence, children would no longer be subjected to 350,000 commercials by the age of 18 (many of them promoting unhealthy foods), and often inappropriate sexual material. American kids watch more TV than the children of any other advanced industrialized country. They are also the least physically fit and the most likely to become single teenage mothers or irresponsible fathers.

16   We live in an unprecedented age of advanced technology. Our children spend more time being entertained by TV, films, videos, disks, tapes, Walkmen and videogames than they spend in school or with their parents.

17   If we are to have a healthy society, we must recognize that we cannot continue to allow a major part of the socialization of children to remain in the hands of the entertainment business whose primary goal is not necessarily the well-being of our children or our nation, but profit-maximization.

18   Our children deserve to be treated as a precious national resource rather than a commercial market to be exploited. Parents must be helped, not hindered, in the very difficult and demanding task of raising healthy, caring, responsible children.

Questions for Inquiry

1. What is Miedzian's claim? Is it explicit or implied?

2. What evidence is there that television causes violence? How does Miedzian support her claim that violence is a critical problem in the United States today?

3. What kinds of actions can Americans take against television-induced violence?

Questions for Argument

1. Miedzian imagines a "separate TV universe for children" (14). Would this be, in your opinion, a good idea? What might be the problems of having such a separate TV world for children?

2. Why don't parents take the exposure of their children to violent images as seriously as exposure to graphic sexuality? Should they be equally concerned about these images? Or is there a difference between violence and pornography that Miedzian is overlooking?

Writing Assignments

Informal

1. How violent were the shows or movies you watched as a child? Do you believe seeing such shows affected your behavior or that of other children you knew? Write informally about the conclusions you draw from your experience about television and film violence and violent behavior.

2. Miedzian writes that "we cannot put the TV genie back in the bottle" (8). Is the television genie "out of the bottle" in your life? Write a journal entry in which you describe and evaluate your own television-viewing habits, how they have changed over the years, and whether you think television will continue to have (or will ever have) a strong role in your life.

Formal

3. **Argumentation.**   Miedzian indicates that protection of children from televised violence should come through changes on the receiving end (parental education and lock boxes) and through chartering new public channels for children's TV. What do you think current network and cable broadcasters should be doing—if anything—to take responsibility for the effect violence seems to have on the public and especially on children? Write a position paper in which you state your claim as to whether broadcasters and television producers do have a responsibility in this matter and what actions could or should be taken to meet this responsibility.

4. **Collaborative Writing.**   Miedzian indicates that parents need to be educated about the need to protect children from violent imagery (6, 9), but she does not spell out what kind of "aggressive educational campaign" is called for. Meet with a group of other students to design a "campaign" or program to make parents aware of the connection between television and violence. Brainstorm to discover the specific message you would like to convey and some techniques or methods for bringing your message to parents. Then assign members of the group to write sections of an action plan in which you explain your message, identify its importance, and set out the ways in which you think your message should be delivered to the public.

■ ■ ■

Young People Get an Eye-Opening Look at the Violence on TV

MARILYN WHEELER

Marilyn Wheeler is a reporter for the Associated Press based in Fargo, N.D. This article went out on AP wires the week of August 10, 1992. (Copyright 1992 by the Associated Press. Reprinted by permission.)

1   Fargo, N. D.—A slap across the face is violent, but not life-threatening. Amy Hendrickson gives it an A.

2   Two men are shot. Deadly force gets C's.

3   Hendrickson is one of 120 Concordia College students who volunteered to rate violence on television during a week's worth of prime-time programming as part of a study for a U. S. senator.

4   It is a revealing exercise.

5   "I thought, 'How many violent acts probably occur in half an hour? Oh, probably one, when somebody gets blown away,'" said Hendrickson, 20.

6   She is tuned in to a CBS telemovie, *River of Rage.* The heroine, played by Victoria Principal, is on a rafting trip with her boyfriend.

7   At the 20-minute mark, the rafters are set upon by a pack of desperados. The boyfriend and river guide are shot to death. The heroine is abducted, slapped around, then stalked through the desert by a bowhunter.

8   That's C, C, B, A, C.

9   By the end of the hour, Hendrickson has counted 15 acts of violence. She puts down her pencil.

10   "I didn't realize how much I overlooked," she said.

11   Concordia, across the state line from Fargo in Moorhead, Minn., is conducting the study for U. S. Sen. Byron Dorgan (D., N. D.), sponsor of a bill that would require the Federal Communications Commission to issue a quarterly report card on TV violence.

12   Each volunteer rated a three-hour segment of programs taped between Sept. 28 and Oct. 4. They finished Tuesday: sample report cards are expected within two months.

13   "I hope this study will demonstrate that it can be done and that it should be done," Dorgan said.

14   At a Senate hearing Oct. 20, Attorney General Janet Reno warned that the government would intervene if the TV industry did not take steps to curb violence on television.

15   The Concordia study is part of a wave of national attention being paid to TV violence. For example, the Florida Parent-Teacher Association plans to monitor five days' of telecasts for violence in January and to issue a report to parents.

16   The study being done for Dorgan defines violence as the "deliberate and hostile use of overt force by one individual against another," a standard set by the National Coalition on Television Violence.

17   An A covers aggression that inflicts minor or momentary pain: pushing, grabbing, spanking, spitting, mild slapping.

18   A B is for stronger violence that still lacks deadly force.

19   A C is for acts in which a character clearly intends to kill, maim or incapacitate. Shooting, strangling, stabbing, poisoning, bombing, hanging, torture, and rape are covered.

Martin Franks, Washington vice president for CBS, said Dorgan's bill and all the other   20
anti-violence legislation pending before Congress have the same problem: They would require subjective judgements about what is violent.

"The feedback that's coming back from students was that they hadn't really watched   21
television with their eyes open," said psychology professor Mark Covey, coordinator of the
project.

He added: "On the one hand [the TV industry is] saying to sponsors, 'Buy time on this   22
show, because people will watch it.' They are trying to show television as an effective
medium for changing behavior, that is, getting people to buy products. On the other hand,
the industry is saying, 'There isn't that much effect to what we show.'"

Questions for Inquiry

1. Do you detect any elements of argumentation in this piece of reportage? Is there a
   claim? Is it explicit or implied?
2. What actions in the television movie rate a C? What actions rate a B or an A?
3. Why did Congressman Dorgan ask that the study be conducted? Why do the raters use
   a scale that parallels the grading system of A, B, and C?

Questions for Argument

1. The student who identifies five violent acts in twenty minutes of a television show comments, "I didn't realize how much I overlooked" (10). Why don't people notice violence
   in their normal watching of television? Would you say this indicates violence doesn't
   matter because so much of it goes "unnoticed" or is "overlooked"?
2. Examine the research being conducted by the Concordia students. How neutral is it?
   Do you agree or disagree with the CBS vice president who indicated that such studies
   are a problem because they "require subjective judgments" (20)? Can television (and
   movies) be rated for quantity of violence?

Writing Assignments

Informal

1. On television, Amy Hendrickson discovered, violence may occur fifteen times in one
   hour. How often does it occur in "real life," according to your experience? What is the
   reason for this discrepancy? Do you think television and movies should reflect the relative infrequency of violence that most people experience in their lives? Or are violence
   and other normally infrequent situations necessary to divert and entertain us? Write
   an informal paper in which you explain your position about the presence of "abnormal" events in television shows
2. The National Coalition on Television Violence defines violence as the "deliberate and
   hostile use of overt force by one individual against another"(16). Look the word *violence*
   up in a standard dictionary. What range of actions does the word cover?

Formal

3. **Argumentation.**   The brief sketch of *River of Rage* doesn't explain the motives for the
   violence or whether, in the end, the culprits were punished. Would the amount of vio-

lence be less of a concern if the couple on the raft were escaping murderers? Would the violence be more acceptable if the capture and punishment of the "desperados" climaxed the movie? Write a paper in which you describe and argue for "violence guidelines" that would indicate when and why violence might be acceptable in a television show and when and why it would not.

4. Prof. Mark Covey of Concordia points out a contradiction: that the TV industry assures advertisers that television influences behavior, while also assuring the public and the government that it does not (22). Is it possible that people might in fact be positively affected by ads but not moved to copy negative behavior displayed on television? Examine your own behavior and that of friends and family to determine whether and what kind of behavior change is prompted by television. Then write a paper in which you discuss your conclusions about television and its effect on the public.

5. **Research Opportunity.**   Using the library and the Internet, do research to discover what has been done about television violence since this news article appeared in 1992. Then write a paper in which you argue that progress on the issue of televised violence has been made or that much remains to be done.

■ ■ ■

Chapter 5

Inquiring about Facts and Information

■ Read the following excerpt, then respond as indicated below:

> A friend working one summer near Polar Bear Pass on Bathurst Island [in the Arctic] once spotted a wolf running off with a duck in its mouth. He saw the wolf bury the duck, and when the wolf left he made for the cache. He couldn't find it. It was open, uncomplicated country. He retraced his steps, again took his bearings, and tried a second time. A third time. He never found it. The wolf, he thought, must have a keener or at least a different way of holding that space in its mind and remembering the approach. The land then appeared to him more complicated. . . .
>
> One can only speculate about how animals organize land into meaningful expanses for themselves. The worlds they perceive, their Umwelten, are all different.* The discovery of an animal's Umwelt and its elucidation require great patience and experimental ingenuity, a free exchange of information among different observers, hours of direct observation, and a reluctance to summarize the animal. This, in my experience, is the Eskimo hunter's methodology. Under ideal circumstances it can also be the methodology of Western science.†
>
> —Barry Lopez, "The Country of the Mind," *Arctic Dreams*

Writer's Journal

Write a few paragraphs in response to the Lopez passage. Are you reminded of any experiences of your own? Have you ever been struck by the complete otherness of someone else's experience? Strive for an entry of about 150 words.

---

*The world we perceive around an animal is its environment: what it sees is its Umwelt, or self-world. A specific environment contains many Umwelten, no two of which are the same. The concept, developed by Jakob von Uexkull in 1934, assumes that the structure of the organs of sense perception, the emphasis each receives, the level of their sensitivity, and the ability of each to discriminate, are different in all animals.

†In practice, the two methodologies usually differ. The Eskimo's methods are less formal than those of the scientist, but not necessarily less rigorous. By comparison, Western scientists often fall far short on hours of observation; and they usually select only a few aspects of an animal's life to study closely. The Eskimo's ecological approach, however, his more broad-based consideration of an animal's interactions with many, some seemingly insignificant, aspects of its environment, is increasingly becoming a Western approach.

■ UNDERSTANDING FACTS AND INTERPRETATION

When we write to advocate for a position, just giving our opinion is not enough. Especially in the civic and academic communities, people want to know why: why what we say is true and why we believe as we do. In other words, we are expected to provide evidence for the ideas we write about. Facts—observations, descriptions, reports, and statistics that are accepted as true—and their interpretations and explanations make up the bulk of evidence. And most of the time our contact with these facts is very much secondhand: we deal in reports of facts, not personal knowledge, in much of our discourse. Much of our information comes to us via the media, and it is information that has been analyzed, shaped, and placed in context for our consumption. The process of acquiring information from media sources, be they books, television, or the Internet, is considered "secondary research." "Primary research" is investigation into events, opinions, or phenomena that produces new facts and new understandings.

Our civic and academic discourse communities have a particular way of processing information and constructing knowledge, but the passage from Barry Lopez shows that this way is not the only way. Our construction of knowledge emphasizes verifiable facts, and seeking facts constitutes much of the time spent in inquiry.

Facts, Just the Facts

In detective fiction, investigators claim to want "just the facts," but in real life determining what is a fact is not simple. At first, it may seem obvious what a fact is: a fact is a fact, the way "a rose is a rose." But, actually, facts are hard to define. David Crystal, the editor of a one-volume encyclopedia of information, *The Cambridge Factfinder,* notes that the definition of "fact" in the *Oxford English Dictionary* (OED) is one of the longest because so many complications come into play. As Crystal says, "There are facts about fictions . . . and fictions about facts. . . . There are situations where we cannot decide whether something is fiction or fact. . . . There are near-facts . . . , transient facts . . . , qualified facts . . . , arguable facts . . . , politically biased facts . . . , and contrived facts" (v).

Even some cut-and-dried facts turn out to have complications. In providing the flying times between major world cities, the *Factfinder* notes that "in order to travel between two points, it is [often] necessary to change aircraft. . . .Time between flights has not been included" (431). In other words, the flying times listed are ideal; if you are planning a trip, these facts may be misleading. In another case, the *Factfinder* lists the top twenty world languages, plus numbers of native speakers and total population numbers of countries where the languages are official. But a note explains that some languages are only one of several official ones, and therefore the official-language population figures are "over-estimations"—that is, they are not strictly true (448).

We want and expect our facts to be "truth[s] known by actual observation or authentic testimony," as the OED defines them (qtd. in Crystal: v). Nevertheless, facts sometimes collide with reality, as the examples above show. Crystal recommends that whoever uses facts should be informed about the complications. He writes, "A fact-book . . . must always remember to warn readers if 'there's something they should know' before swallowing a 'fact' whole" (v).

Establishing Facts as Factual

In the construction of facts from events, observations, and experiences, mere agreement is not enough to guarantee accuracy. All too often in human history, what people have agreed was factual was later shown to have been wildly untrue. You recognize the list: the world is flat; the sky is an inverted dome to which the stars are attached; the sun and moon revolve around the earth; diseases are caused by various body fluids being out of balance; leeches cure illness by sucking out excess blood; and many others. As time goes by, old "facts" are corrected and new facts are turned up—new planets and elemental particles discovered, medical techniques invented, and so on.

The last few years have seen numerous alterations or rejections of previously accepted facts. For example, the estimated age of the universe has been downsized from twenty billion to between fourteen and seven billion years, on the basis of sophisticated calculation methods. Two independent studies discovered the paradoxical "fact" that "the universe may be only about half as old as the oldest stars and galaxies it contains" (Hotz, "Universe").

Sometimes the commonplace "facts" of daily life turn out to be mere shadows. An article in the February 20, 1995, *Philadelphia Inquirer* reported that the concept of race has been found to be scientifically invalid. "Race is a social construct derived mainly from perceptions conditioned by events of recorded history, and it has no basic biological reality," according to C. Loring Brace, a biological anthropologist at the University of Michigan (Hotz, "Scientists").

Personal experience or witness makes strong claims to truth, but it is often not enough to ensure that a reported event is "true." Any number of factors can come into play to falsify or distort a person's observation or experience. Distractions, strong emotions, and physical positioning all can affect what a person reports as factual. You may have heard the story of the class interrupted by a gun-wielding thug, as the students later report; in actuality, the interruption was staged, and the intruder was holding a banana, yet the students perceived and reported a weapon was used because of their expectations.

"Fact insurance" comes in the form of the requirement that facts be verifiable. Observations and reports are needed from more than one person, from different and competing points of view, and over a period of time in order to ensure that something is a fact. Although many people over many decades have insisted they have seen the Loch Ness monster, the fact of its existence has not been verified from the competing vantage point of science: there are no unambiguous pictures or evidence of the feeding, breeding, nesting, or other activities of a huge creature in the lake.

The scientific method is an important way our culture ensures facts. Evidence derived from the scientific method has been tested by controlled observations or experiments. Such scientific method has proven the fact that water always boils at the same temperature, 212 degrees Fahrenheit or 100 degrees Centigrade, at the air pressure of earth at sea level.

The more variables affecting an event, the more difficult it is to establish the facts. In each academic discipline, the process developed to construct knowledge is often a variation of the scientific method.

The requirement that facts be verified means that we expect proof of what is factual in addition to expecting evidence in support of ideas. Lacking proof, we may agree that, in regard to certain facts, the "jury is out," that we do not know what the facts are. Or we may agree to accept certain facts as probable, although proof is inadequate.

In our discourse community, people expect others to be rational about their interpretations: thinkers should work from similar assumptions about how to construct and interpret facts. We expect, for example, that thinkers will assume that events have a cause or happen for a reason. We expect them to avoid certain other assumptions—for example, that outer-space aliens intervene in human affairs. In the case of severe flooding in which no one died, for instance, to assume that spiritual beings exist and that the people in the flooded area were saved by angels who bore them away to higher ground would be to rest one's interpretation on assumptions that are not generally credited in our culture today. Beyond basing interpretations on accepted assumptions, reasoners and thinkers are expected to use logic, cause-and-effect reasoning, and common natural laws.

■ *Activity 1*

Types of Facts, p. 205

■ THE CONSTRUCTION OF KNOWLEDGE

Inference

According to the OED, facts should be kept separate from "what is merely inferred" and "conjecture[d]" and from "the conclusions which may be based upon [them]" (qtd. in Crystal: v). In real life and in discussions about issues, such a separation is not so easily achieved. Many things that people report as facts are actually a result of inference. People naturally "read into" and interpret what they have experienced, just as they use inference in the act of reading.

Here's an example. Imagine you happen to be walking along a street staring at your feet, deep in thought, when a car crash occurs immediately in front of you. You glance up immediately and survey the scene. You catch the signal light for the traffic on your street just as it changes to red. You thus infer that the car traveling in your direction had the green light as it crossed the intersection and that the car from the side street was running an orange or red light. You may then report to the police that the car on the side street was speeding and going through a red light when it hit the other car. But this is not actually a fact, however accurate it might be. It is an inference you have made.

When people infer, they create meaning out of facts. This may involve constructing a cause, attributing a reason, imaging an effect, or connecting seemingly opposed or contradictory facts to make them coherent. The scientific method makes constant use of inference; when an event occurs over and over in an experimental situation, the scientist infers that it will always occur under the same conditions. So water boils at the same temperature (at sea level) in both the lab and your kitchen. When we do the inferring, we feel pretty certain of our interpretation. But we are often in the position of accepting that what is reported is actually a fact. Unless we can question an eyewitness, observer, or researcher, we have to go on secondhand knowledge.

With all due respect to the excellence of the *Cambridge Factfinder,* many of the fact sets in it are not "pure." For example, the list "Evolution of Early Humans" must contain knowledge created by inferences. Until someone invents a time machine, we have no way of verifying anything about the development of early human life. However, by studying the evidence we have (skeletal remains, early tools, primitive paintings, fossils and bones of early animals and plants, and so forth), numerous trained experts over many decades have inferred much about what these early people looked like, their time periods and range, and so on. In accepting this information as factual, we are accepting knowledge constructed by authorities we trust. New discoveries and new methods of analysis will constantly change the "facts" about human evolution.

Judgments

Facts and inferences based on them are further interpreted when writers apply values and make judgments and also present information in the context of their conclusions. Then, when we receive information, we interpret it for ourselves; we make additional inferences, view them through the perspective of our values, and draw additional conclusions from them.

Articles that we read in the newspaper or information that we hear about is often a mixture of fact, inference, and judgment. We hope, as we read reports of facts, that the writers have the pertinent experience, knowledge, rationality, and goodwill to infer causes, results, and relationships that are in line with reality.

When reading or using sources it's important to recognize and differentiate what is factual and what is interpretation, what is evidence that can be trusted, and what is judgment.

■ *Activity 2*

Inference, Facts, and Judgments, p. 205

To summarize:

Fact: verifiable event, occurrence
Inference: knowledge created by putting facts together
Judgment: a conclusion about facts and inferences created by applying values

Characteristics of Evidence

In order for evidence to be accepted as weighty, it must possess the following characteristics: it must be representative, relevant, sufficient, specific, and reliable.

Representative

Evidence should be <u>typical</u> and not exceptional. Relying on <u>unusual</u> examples or nonrepresentative situations can cause you to defend a <u>weak or shaky conclusion</u>. To maintain, for example, that severe childhood illnesses have the positive effect that their sufferers overachieve in athletics because ice skater Scott Hamilton suffered from a nutrition absorption deficiency syndrome as a child yet went on to win Olympic gold is to rely on an exceptional example. It would be more reasonable, in this case, to modify the claim and cite examples of more typical youths with childhood illnesses who grew up to lead healthy and normal lives.

Relevant

Evidence should <u>truly support</u> the point that is being made. A student who is discussing police brutality in a nearby city should provide facts and figures about instances of unwarranted force used during arrests. To describe the officers' tough-looking leather jackets, heavy clubs, and dangling handcuffs and assert that they strut around like thugs is to stray from the subject. The police force's uniforms and equipment have nothing to do with their treatment of suspects. The appearance and equipment are relevant only if, for example, you can cite a study that showed aggressively garbed and equipped police to be more abusive than police with sedate uniforms and hidden paraphernalia.

Sufficient

There should be several strong pieces of evidence, not just one. The more evidence, the better. If there is only one fact or example that supports a point, there is always the possibility that it is an exception. In addition to quantity, a sufficient amount of evidence usually includes a variety of types of evidence: some examples, reasoning, details, and so on. For example, to support the position that liberal arts degrees can lead to good jobs after graduation, you might include examples of friends' job-hunting success, comments from corporate personnel directors found in a newspaper report, and statistics from your college's placement office about last year's graduates. These provide a breadth of support from a variety of different angles for your point of view.

Specific

Evidence should "name names" and cite numbers whenever possible. Evidence needs to be concrete in order to be convincing. Stating that murders have declined in the United States recently is general and vague. But citing the latest statistics that show that homicide in New York City was down in 1996 compared with the previous year provides specific and convincing support.

Reliable

The quality of evidence should be high. Facts and information should be accurate, recent, and complete; reasoning should be logical. Authorities should be well credentialed in the appropriate field. If the support is the result of research, the sources should be acknowledged and should be acceptable to the audience. (See Chapter 11 for ways to evaluate sources.)

■ *Activity 3*
Characteristics of
Evidence, p. 206

■ GENERATING EVIDENCE THROUGH PRIMARY RESEARCH

Primary research is performed directly by a researcher and contributes new knowledge. It is different from secondary research, or library research in sources that describe, analyze, contest, or otherwise discuss evidence, both secondary and primary. We often conduct small amounts of primary research ourselves on an informal basis. Hearing about a study showing that teachers call on male students more often than on female students might prompt you to pay attention to the teacher-student transactions in your classes.

Traditionally, most research by students has been performed in a library. Certainly, as a way of acquiring a broad base of knowledge or in-depth understanding of a subject, secondary-source research is unsurpassed. However, engaging in some limited primary research has its benefits as well. You learn the importance of evidence in a personal way and experience some of the problems and difficulties an individual can encounter in trying to collect good information about a subject. In addition, doing primary research can be enjoyable, and it allows you to engage the topic of your research in a special way. Primary research can be gathered to support your academic writing if your instructors permit. Such information can come in many forms:

- eyewitness reports and personal experiences of events, incidents, or situations
- observations
- interviews or correspondence with experts or with observers
- surveys or polls of opinion or experiences
- collection of raw data or facts from files, internal reports, official records, and so forth
- experiments

No matter which method you choose, you should recognize that primary research, like that done in a library, is time-consuming and complex. You should expect to invest some time in planning the research before you start.

Note taking will also be important because you must keep track of your methods as well as your results. Library research is always documented, either formally or informally. Primary research is not documented; instead researchers must reveal the process and specifics of the research. Names and details of important research sites or experts must be recorded and provided to the reader (see guidelines below). For your own convenience, you should carefully keep track of names, affiliations, phone numbers, and so forth of contacts you make during your research so that you can check back or clarify data at a later stage.

Primary research requires quite different personal skills than library research. A reserved student might plunge willingly into weeks of library work but find it excruciating to telephone for an interview with a local expert on teen pregnancy. If you are upset by or reluctant to begin your primary research, consult with your instructor. Sometimes, working in teams or having a friend accompany you can ease the strain. Or your instructor can help you plan your calls or just be supportive while you begin your contacts on his or her office phone.

Following are specific guidelines for using each method of primary research.

Eyewitness Reports and Personal Experiences

We all have life experiences that may contribute to our understanding of a situation or issue. We may be in the right (or wrong, depending on circumstances) place at the right time and so witness an event personally. Although such personal knowledge is limited and therefore may not be sufficient to support a particular point of view, personal and eyewitness evidence can be powerful and dramatic.

Observations

You may make firsthand observations by going on a tour or making a visit to a place where a controversy exists. Your observing may be informal—through visits, for example, to a bar where underage drinking supposedly goes on or to the parking lots where skateboarders defy a new town ordinance. Or you may request a formal tour of a site. For example, a student researching automation in the food industry might take public tours of some local food-processing plants or request a tour if none are offered.

Observing can be done two ways: openly and as a participant-observer. Some situations are not altered by the presence of an observer who can stare and take notes freely. A visitor to a busy workplace might see things as they are every day. But in many other situations an observer is an outsider whose presence may alter the situation. If you were to visit a fraternity party and stand around making notes, you might be challenged or asked to leave; the behavior of the partyers might not be natural or "normal" until after you were gone. In such cases, observers usually choose to blend in, even though they then can't take notes. Some completeness and accuracy is lost in the trade-off of fitting into the scene. This mode of observation is often called being a participant-observer. Much anthropological and sociological research is conducted this way.

Guidelines for making observations:

- Go prepared; make a list of the information you would like to acquire from your on-site visit.
- Keep a record of the specifics: date, time, place (address), contact person, phone number.
- Take notes during or immediately after your visit; write down any surprising or unexpected points.
- On a formal tour get the name and number of the tour office or contact person in case you have questions later.

Interviewing

Interviews gather expert information from someone with scholarly, academic, or practical knowledge of your topic. A cafeteria worker, for example, might have quite a bit to say about the behavior and social attitudes of college students. The director of a job-training program might be able to provide invaluable commentary on what chronically unemployed people need to learn to become job-ready. Expert viewpoints and useful data can be collected though personal or telephone interviews or by submitting questions to a chosen and willing expert by mail or e-mail. People are often eager to help those who are learning and are flattered to be asked to share their expertise. So you need not feel embarrassed or intrusive when you request an informational interview.

■ *Guidelines for Informational Interviews*

- Choose the interview subject carefully: seek someone who has useful information on, professional or personal experience with, or insight about your topic. Find out what you can about your interviewee ahead of time if possible. Libraries contain reference works listing notables in many fields. Sometimes business and organization leaders are profiled in newspapers or the business press. If your background information on the interviewee is scant, ask him or her about education and relevant experience.

- Call or write to request the interview. Let the person know your reason for wanting it—provide a bit of detail about your research project. Request the amount of time you think you will need, up to a half hour; if you plan to tape the interview, ask permission or inform the person when you set up the interview. If you plan to bring someone to the interview, say so.

- Confirm the interview date and time by mail or phone. Thank the person for agreeing to speak to you at that day and hour; if the person has forgotten or there is a conflict, your note or call will set off alarms.

- Decide whether to tape. Taping can be intrusive but can ensure accuracy. Keep in mind that taping an interview requires a lot of listening time later. If you decide to tape, make sure you know how to work the equipment and that you have fresh batteries or a long-enough cord and a backup blank tape. If taping is new to you, try taping lunch with your friends to make sure you can start up smoothly, place the microphone effectively, flip the tape without fumbling, and so on.

- Show up on time, neatly dressed. (Students need not wear business clothes, but, for most interviews, they shouldn't be in jeans either.)

- Plan your questions, and if interviewing is new to you, make a readable, organized list or cue card for yourself. Don't ask everything under the sun; limit your interview to the special areas you need to know about. Try to find a good way to break the ice. Do stray from your list of questions to follow up on points made by the subject. Don't let your interviewee get off the topic however; steer the person back to your questions and away from irrelevancies.

- If you are nervous about conducting an interview, practice interviewing a friend or your instructor.

- Take notes (even if you tape). This is a must. You may handwrite or use a portable computer. (If you bring a laptop, make sure you have enough battery power and familiarity with the equipment.) Your notes will help you select which parts of the tape you want to listen to or transcribe. And they are your backup if you later discover your recorder wasn't working right.

continued

■ *Guidelines for Informational Interviews (continued)*

- Be accurate. Pause and read back to the interviewee any numerical information or any other important details. Ask the person to repeat complex ideas or statements that you feel are quotable.

- At the end, request permission to call the person to follow up or to clarify any points, especially if you only take notes.

- Send a note within a day thanking the person for his or her time and commenting on how the interview was helpful to your research.

Surveying

Like interviewing, surveying gathers information from those in the know, but it does so broadly and systematically. Surveying or polling is used to ask standardized questions of a target group. In exchange for a larger number of responses than one could ever get through interviews, pollsters sacrifice depth, individuality of response, and the ability to follow up.

Polls can solicit opinions:

What do you think is the major problem facing parents today?

Which mayoral candidate do you believe will best manage labor relations with city workers?

Or they can ask questions about experiences:

Have you ever been divorced?

Check off which states you have visited in the last five years.

List any problems you had with your XYZ automobile in the first year of ownership.

The basic assumption behind polling is that by obtaining information from a representative subgroup, you can know about the group as a whole. For example, if you ask 10 percent of the typical users of hardwood floor wax whether they prefer Zipshine liquid wax or Arbor paste wax and learn that 65 percent of these typical users prefer Zipshine, then you might generalize that about 65 percent of all who wax their hardwood floors will prefer Zipshine. In actuality, you have determined only that 65 percent of a 10 percent minority prefer Zipshine, or 6.5 percent, of typical users of hardwood floor wax.

It's important to know a bit about how survey research should be conducted if only because survey results are so prominent in political news today. It is difficult for a student or untrained pollster to duplicate the most scientific polling principles. There are entire courses, some at the graduate level, in the methods of polling. The guidelines here explain the rigorous standards for conducting surveys with the acknowledgment that in reality most surveying is informal and the results are less than scientific.

The Sample Should Be Typical, Sufficient, and Random

The characteristics of the group you wish to survey are called its **demographics;** they include such items as age, sex, educational level, and income level. You need to consider carefully which demographics are pertinent to your questions. For example, in a survey of how user-friendly campus registration and financial offices are, you might decide that respondents should be new students. In a survey to determine whether the campus radio station should start a jazz show, the target group may be listeners of the station, including both students and town residents, rather than only students.

Poorly designated demographics can spoil a survey's results. If the product survey team assumes that location doesn't affect choice of floor wax, they might survey only fellow Floridians. But if people in Minnesota find that paste wax protects floors better during long, centrally heated winters, then the survey results have been distorted by polling only the Floridians.

You also must make sure that the characteristics of your target group are distributed in about the same amounts in your subgroup of respondents. If your target group is 25 percent male and 75 percent female, then you have to ensure that your respondents break down about the same way by sex. If you are surveying first-year students, 30 percent of whom commute, then conducting your survey in the dorms prevents commuters from participating, and your results will not be valid about all first-year students. In other words, differences within the target group must be reflected in your subgroup for you to get representative information.

Surveys must also include a sufficiently large number of people to even out any oddities in responses. If you poll only three town-resident listeners to the campus station about jazz, you may get three negatives. But these may be atypical: perhaps one of the three listens because her niece is a deejay, and two others listen to keep up with modern rock. If you polled thirty residents who listen to the station, however, you might discover that ten of them like jazz and would tune into a jazz show. A definitive survey should involve a sample of at least 10 percent of the larger population. Informal surveys make do with fewer. Often, a small percent of the targeted sample will actually respond to a survey. People don't send back questionnaires; they hang up when pollsters call; they decline to answer questions when approached personally. To get an acceptable number of responses, you must approach a high number of possible respondents.

A survey should also give every member of the targeted group a chance to be a respondent. This is the official meaning of the term *random*. A poll of full-time students, for example, should be based on a printout of all names and addresses; the survey team should then choose respondents to contact according to a pattern, perhaps every fifth or tenth name. Standing outside the student center to gather opinion may sound like a reasonable way of approaching students randomly, but the students who don't use the student center would never have a chance to be polled, and thus the survey would not be truly random. Of course, your college will not give you a list of all enrolled students and their addresses, so any poll of students will have to be informal and less than scientific.

■ *Activity 4*

Designing a Survey, p. 206

Few surveys even begin to meet these sampling requirements. Surveys conducted by students often are limited by time and money. Results of informal surveys should be presented as such and not as definitive. Here is a list of some techniques that can be used to collect informal survey data:

- "Street-corner" survey. Passersby are approached and asked a question or are handed a clipboard with a short questionnaire to fill out and hand back. Visiting different locations over several days gives a wider range of respondents than doing such a survey only once.
- Mailing. Questionnaires are mailed or hand-delivered (in a dorm or apartment building). A collection box can be placed accessibly, or if funding is available, self-addressed, stamped envelopes are included.
- Handouts. Questionnaires can be distributed in classes, left on store checkouts or restaurant tables, or included in packets of information. Return is either by mail or through a collection box.
- Phoning. Targeted respondents are asked to answer a short list of questions over the phone.

Questions Should Be Neutral, Fair, and Appropriate

Questions should avoid bias and unfair assumptions, and choices should be worded neutrally. If asked, "Do you prefer to (a) apply polish conveniently with a mop or (b) get down on your knees and rub wax with a rag," most respondents will choose option a, because of a few words: "conveniently" biases responses toward option a, and "rub" against option b. The poll that appears with political satirist Ed Anger's article "Fry Death Row Creeps in Electric Bleachers!" (a reading selection at the end of Chapter 10) humorously demonstrates biased survey questions. The classic example of a biased yes-no question is "Have you stopped beating your wife?" All responses incriminate the responder.

Finally, questions should be written so that all respondents read them the same way. Ambiguous or value-laden questions can be misinterpreted and make survey results meaningless. To the question "Do you appreciate jazz?" one person may answer yes because he avidly listens to and buys jazz CDs. Another may answer yes because he knows jazz is important in music history, but he actually only listens to rock. In this type of situation, the two yes answers are far from equivalent and reveal little about jazz appreciation.

Behaviorally oriented questions like these often obtain precise information:

Do you listen to jazz? Y_____   N_____

If "yes," how much time do you spend listening to jazz per week?
    less than 1 hour _____
    1–3 hours _____   7–10 hours _____
    4–6 hours _____   more than 10 hours _____

Do you buy jazz CDs or cassette tapes? Y_____   N_____

If "yes," how many CDs/ tapes do you buy?
    fewer than 3 a year _____
    4 to 6 per year _____
    7 to 10 per year _____
    more than ten per year _____

Question Types

Like exam questions, survey questions can require either short or long answers. Short-answer questions are easier to tabulate but force respondents to simplify their answers. For example, if a survey asks you to respond either yes or no as to whether you enjoyed the food at restaurant X, you may have to "average out" your dining experience. If the salad was wilted and the soup watery but the steak absolutely perfect, you might answer yes. But another person with the same experience might say no. Long answers take time to read and force the survey tabulator, rather than the diner, in this case, to decide whether the meal was a success or not. Most surveys consist almost entirely of short-answer questions because the number of responses is considered more important than subtle shades of difference in people's responses. Here are the basic types of survey questions:

- Binary response: yes/no (as above); true/false; agree/disagree:

  Write an X to indicate your answer:

  Students should be discouraged from employment except in cases of need.
      True _____   False _____

  Students should strive to finish college in four years.
      Agree _____   Disagree_____

- Multiple choice:

  Circle your answer.

  Which type of news do you most depend on radio for:
  (a) current events   (b) sports   (c) weather
  (d) traffic   (e) art and entertainment

- Choice:

  Check off all ways you use a computer:

word processing _____	layout, design, graphics _____
data analysis _____	video _____
spreadsheet _____	access to network _____

- Ranking:

  Number the following types of popular music in your order of preference, using "1" to indicate your highest preference:

_____ oldies rock	_____ country
_____ classic rock	_____ acoustic / folk
_____ modern rock	_____ easy listening
_____ rap/ hip hop / club	

Answers to polls may be checked, marked with an X, circled, or written on a line. Try to have the same mode of response for all or most of your questions.

The Questionnaire Should Be User-Friendly

Aim for brevity and clarity in designing your questionnaire. Ask only the questions you need answered. In most situations, one page is enough.

- Use a pleasant, upbeat tone.
- Introduce the survey with a brief, neutral description of its goal: "To collect information on the potential audience for a jazz program on WZXX-FM," not "To show there is support for a jazz program among WZXX's listeners."
- Motivate the reader to answer the questionnaire by mentioning briefly some advantage or positive effect the survey might have. For example, you might indicate that your findings about the campus-radio audience will be given to the station's management for consideration.
- Provide brief instructions on how to answer the survey: "Check off all that apply." "Circle your best response to each question."
- Limit the types of questions you ask so that respondents don't have to change their mode of response for each question. Try to group questions by type of response if possible, so the yes-no questions form a group, and the ranking questions are together.
- At the end, explain how to return the questionnaire.
- Close by thanking the respondents for their time.

Collecting Raw Data or Facts

Sometimes you can acquire information by going to the source. The police station, the town hall, the college registrar's office, and other official sites keep records of information that may be useful for your project. Some will share information with the public, but some will refuse; government agencies are required by law to provide information on request. When you write for such information, pore through public records, or request data in person, you are doing primary research.

Use the phone first when you think pertinent records may be available; call to find out whether the information you wish is accessible, whether a written request is necessary, and so on. Information that you discover on the World Wide Web is considered secondary source material: it is "published" electronically and therefore is not primary data. If, however, you were to e-mail someone and receive unpublished data in return, you would consider that data as primary, acquired through consultation with an expert.

Experimenting

Sometimes researchers can conduct a trial run of a changed procedure or temporarily alter one aspect of a situation to gauge effects. For example, a business student assigned to write about a proposed solution to a organizational problem conducted an experiment at his job. He timed trucks using different loading procedures and routes to move materials between warehouse sites to see which was most efficient. Experiments may or may not be possible or relevant. But occasionally an informal experiment can yield interesting information.

■ INTERPRETING RESEARCH

Be careful how you generalize from your research findings. Your research may suggest a certain interpretation or may indicate a trend; it may contribute an original and intriguing perspective. But, as the work of a student with limited time and resources, your findings are not likely to be definitive. So, where relevant:

- acknowledge the limitations of your research
- qualify your conclusions, using such terms as "may," "might be," "could be," "shows the likelihood of," and so forth
- show your openness to new and possibly divergent information
- indicate that extensive research should be conducted

Don't drop out, ignore, or gloss over discoveries that "buck the trend" of your findings. A discovery that doesn't fit with your claim or your other results is a legitimate sign of your topic's complexity. You can discuss, comment on, or explain how disparate information affects the overall issue. Or if there are only minor discrepancies, you might indicate that the divergent research indicates the need for further study.

Finally, be aware that a researcher performing primary research is operating on the "honor system." The academic and civic discourse communities assume that participants will contribute honestly to the stock of common knowledge. Faking primary research by inventing survey results or pretending you personally gathered data that were posted on a web site is a species of dishonesty every bit as reprehensible as plagiarism or faking library research.

STUDENT ASSIGNMENT

Using Primary Research

Here is an example of an extensive use of primary research as the basis for an argumentative writing assignment.

ASSIGNMENT: By reading newspapers and magazines, locate an issue currently being debated in the civic discourse community that has a local angle or aspect. You may want to work with an editorial or opinion piece or with a news article. If necessary, do some background reading on this issue in the library. Identify two or more ways you can access some primary information about this issue. Use the research you acquire to help you decide your position on the issue and write an essay arguing your view.

For this assignment, John McLarron decided to work with an article about the increased safety of motorcycle riding because of mandatory helmet laws. John's reaction to the article was that motorcycle helmet laws have not been so widely successful; he believed he frequently saw young motorcyclists without helmets, even though his state has a mandatory helmet law. He was particularly sensitive to this issue because a friend had recently had an accident while riding a motorcycle and had been saved by his helmet from severe head injury.

John decided to keep track of motorcyclists on the road, and over a three-week period he discovered that fully half of the eleven motorcyclists he saw were bareheaded. After these observations, he decided his topic was workable and drew up a plan for the rest of his research. He realized he could talk to various experts: his friend's riding buddies who had personal experience with motorcycle laws and the emergency personnel who treated his friend after his accident. He also planned to see whether data about citations for helmet violations might be available through the county police. John wrote to the physician who handled his friend's case to request an interview about head injuries to motorcyclists. Then he called the county police station to determine what information he might collect there.

All of his research initiatives panned out. In informal chats, his friend's pals confirmed that not wearing a helmet had become a fad. The police desk sergeant invited him to stop by and examine printouts of the year's traffic citations; they showed a threefold increase in tickets issued to helmetless motorcyclists on the roads of the county. The sergeant also discussed the issue authoritatively, providing John with an interview he didn't expect to have. John's meeting with the doctor was also valuable, for he told of an increase in the number of motorcyclists suffering severe head trauma that he had personally seen.

Using the results of these investigations, John decided to write an essay in which he reported the apparent flouting of the motorcycle-helmet law, described the dangers of such behavior, and supported both increased police ticketing of helmet-law violators and a public-awareness campaign. (John's essay appears later in this chapter.)

■ WRITING BASED ON PRIMARY RESEARCH

When you write an essay based on primary research, you must move beyond inquiring, collecting information, and drawing conclusions. You need to synthesize, or combine, the separate strands of information into a new, unified statement. This is different from just reporting the results of your investigations. If you are writing a report, you probably organize the information you gathered from each of your inquiries in a separate section: one for observations, another for the personal experiences of participants, another for information supplied by an expert, and so on. When you are writing an essay, not a report—that is, when you are creating a coherent, well-knitted statement—you need to blend your interpretations and the supporting information rather than just report your findings as separate chunks of data. Below are some guidelines for synthesizing and attributing the results of primary research.

Synthesizing Primary-Research Results

There is no formula for synthesizing, as we learned in Chapter 4. Each essay will follow the internal logic of the issue at hand. The main principle in creating a synthesis of primary-research data is this: *group together information that supports the same subpoint, no matter where the information comes from.* Different sources might provide support for the same idea, so you must unite this information the same way you would link up related information from different print sources. It is also likely that, just as in library research, you will find you have too much material. Be selective in what you include in your argument. Do include information and material that directly supports your ideas. But don't feel you have to stuff into your essay everything you found out.

Attributing Primary-Research Results

Just as with print information, you should make sure your reader knows where each piece of primary research comes from as you incorporate it into your essay. The only type of primary research that needs to be formally documented is that acquired from experts through interviews or correspondence. Experts are considered to be "nonprint sources." The citation form for interviews or correspondence is provided in Chapter 13. Some instructors may not, at this point in the course, require formal documentation for experts. Like all information from sources, whether print or nonprint, primary or secondary, information received from experts should be presented with an in-text attribution (see Chapter 3).

Because there is no formal system of "documenting" other types of primary research, you should use informal attributions to indicate where a particular observation, experience, fact, or survey result originated. Here are some examples of how you might lead in to your research results:

> Over a period of one week, I observed students for a total of ten hours as they attempted to use the new electronic library catalogue. A total of ninety-two students' experiences were recorded.

Records kept by Streetwatch, a volunteer group in Brandon, Maryland, show that about ten homeless people a week are hospitalized for injuries, illness, or substance abuse.

An informal questionnaire returned by 103 first-year composition students here at West State revealed that about 50 percent felt "very experienced" with word processing.

In an interview, April Hampshire, executive director of Literacy Partners, explained how literacy volunteers are trained.

Ryan Litvak, head chemist for Scientific Metallurgy, Inc., indicated in correspondence with this writer that pollution safeguards are in place throughout his industry.

Specific details about observations, experiences, collected data, and experiments should be provided:

- method and extent of observations
- brief details of experiences
- survey type, demographics, and number of respondents
- type, purpose, and location (unless obvious) of organizations
- procedures for experimentation

For interviews and correspondence, specific details, such as the date of the contact, are necessary in the formal documentation.

Later references to these same primary sources may begin with shorter attributions:

The observations of electronic-catalogue users showed that. . . .

Streetwatch records show that summer is a peak time for injuries to the homeless.

The survey at West State indicated that about 25 percent of composition students feel inept when they attempt to write in the computer lab.

A college education is not required, according to April Hampshire, for a literacy tutor to be effective.

Few companies initiate pollution safeguards on their own, Litvak noted.

STUDENT ASSIGNMENT

John McLarron, "Helmet Laws Continue to Save Lives"

As John McLarron was concluding his primary research, he jotted down a likely plan for his paper. He knew he would begin his essay with a statement about the frequency of motorcycle riders going bareheaded. To support this opening, he planned to include:

- *my own observations*
- *comments of motorcyclist friends*
- *desk sergeant's info. about increase in local tickets for helmet-law violations*

His supporting paragraphs he expected to play out as follows:

proof of danger of going bareheaded:
- *Dr. Pernan's quotes*
- *Phil's survival of accident while wearing helmet*

As he generated his first draft, John determined which pieces of data deserved separate paragraphs and which could be blended with other information.

John's job of synthesis was facilitated by the fact that his various investigations led to similar results—all his observations and experts supported the same idea, that helmet laws save lives and should be followed consistently. If one source, the physician perhaps, had differed about the importance of helmets to motorcycle safety, John's job of synthesizing would have been more difficult. For example, if the physician stated that his experience indicated that it's not the lack of a helmet but poor riding skills and risk taking that cause deaths and injuries to motorcyclists, John would have needed to identify a place in his essay where he could mention and comment on this divergent view. He would have had to explain to his readers why this doctor's viewpoint didn't undermine the point he was making about motorcycle helmets.

Here is John's draft:

A recent article in the *Baltimore Sun* discussed the improvement in the injury rate of motorcyclists since the passage of the mandatory helmet law. But even though wearing a helmet is the law, many young motorcyclists don't bother when they are riding the back roads. There is a dangerous fad among motorcyclists: to "feel the wind in your hair" by leaving your helmet strapped to the back of your bike. If this fad continues, the injury rate is likely to go up again.

As I drive around the vicinity of Rockmore College, often taking the back country roads up to my family's home in Forest Heights, more and more often I see young men speeding around on their Hondas and Kawasakis without a helmet. Mark Leiber, a Rockmore senior who's been riding a motorcycle since he was seventeen, confirmed that it's become a fad to ride bareheaded. A lot of riders, Mark said, feel that "feeling the road under your wheels and the wind in your face" are major parts of the enjoyment of riding a bike, and they often ride in the country without their head gear. Even though going without a helmet will get you a ticket, a lot of riders will risk it. In fact, according to Robert Thacker, another motorcycling college senior, most guys "worry more about getting a ticket than getting into an accident" when they do have their helmets off.

Getting a ticket is a real possibility. Desk sergeant Michael Salina said that police will definitely stop a helmetless motorcyclist each and every time they see one. It's a "cut-and-dried violation," he said. Some police will issue a warning; others feel so strongly about it that they always ticket. Sgt. Salina told me there's been a definite increase in such tickets. He said motorcycling is becoming more popular, and the number of riders who are willing to flout the law is growing.

If more motorcyclists don't wear helmets, then more of them are going to be injured when accidents occur. Motorcyclist Mark Leiber said a lot of younger riders think they'll never have an accident, that they have the bike under total control. They don't realize, Leiber said, that it doesn't matter how good a rider you are. "You can still get hit by a car or slide out on a patch of gravel or slick pavement."

At Burdon Memorial Hospital, they see all the injured motorcyclists within a ten- or fifteen-mile radius. Dr. Laurence Pernan works as an emergency room specialist at BMH, and he reported that the difference in injury-levels of motorcyclists who do and don't wear helmets is dramatic. He personally has seen the two types of injuries, and he said, "On the basis of my personal experience, I would strongly recommend wearing a helmet if you want to live a full life after having an accident, heck, if you want to live, period."

Phil Chichester, a Rockmore junior, knows about surviving a serious motorcycle accident from personal experience. He was heading down College Avenue early one morning, when a car ran a stop sign and hit him broadside. He and his bike flew up and over the hood of the car before crashing to the paved shoulder of the road. He broke "too many bones to name," he says now, and had internal injuries as well. But he was wearing a helmet. "My skull would have been pulverized," he says, by the force with which he hit the ground. He skidded and rolled on the ground, and he says, '"I hate to think what my face and scalp would have looked like after that."

Helmet laws exist for a reason, for the protection of motorcycle riders. While wearing a helmet may make riding a bit less fun, it also makes motorcycling a lot safer.

■ *Guidelines for Writing Up Primary Research*

Overall

- Insert your primary research as support where it is relevant in the development of your argument.
- Don't dump all your findings into your paper in a large chunk.

- Be specific in presenting your findings. Use facts and figures and direct quotations if possible.
- Qualify your conclusions

Presenting Eyewitness reports and Personal Experiences

- Use such reports for drama and effect, often at the start or end of an argument.
- Use them sparingly because individual experiences can be exceptions.

Presenting Observations

- Briefly describe where and how the observations were made (a formal tour, an informal site visit, or whatever).
- Then present relevant details.

Presenting Experts' Opinions

- Identify experts by name, affiliation or background conferring expertise, and mode of communication (interview, correspondence, e-mail).
- In a documentation note, provide the type and date of your contact with the person (see Chapter 13).
- Summarize relevant comments by your expert(s).
- Quote if the person says something dramatic or striking.

Presenting Survey Results

- Briefly describe the methodology of the survey when you first mention it:
  formal or informal
  types of respondents sought
  written questionnaire, telephone, or "street-corner" personal approach
  percentage of return if relevant (and so on)
- Provide just the details that relate to the point you are making.
- Don't feel you have to include everything you found out in your survey.

Presenting Data or Facts

- Indicate how you collected the information (visiting the town hall, through correspondence or e-mail).
- Provide enough details about your source so that the reader theoretically could duplicate your research.
- Don't provide the name of the clerk or official who helped you unless only that person can access the information.

■ GETTING THE FACTS: USING REFERENCE SOURCES

Background information about a subject can be found in the reference section of the library, which contains books with historical, statistical, and biographical information on topics in all fields. It includes dictionaries and encyclopedias and many other types of references as well.

Reference works can provide information such as:

- undisputed facts; data about a topic commonly known within the field
- viewpoints considered universal—for example, "Shakespeare is the most important English dramatist"
- definitions; technical information on processes, measurements, specifications, and descriptions; statistical information; maps and charts
- sometimes, bibliographic information; additional sources or sources used in writing the entry may be listed at the end

Reference works usually do not provide an array of perspectives or points of view on an issue.

Locating Reference Works in the Library

Reference rooms of college libraries are organized according to the Library of Congress (LC) or Dewey Decimal book classification system, whichever is used in the rest of the library. (When a book is published, it is assigned both a Dewey and an LC number; if you have the call number of a book in one library, you have it for all libraries using that system.)

Knowing the basic classifications of the Dewey or LC system can be helpful, especially in looking for reference works. If you know that sociology is under H in the LC system, you might just browse the H section in the reference room when you are looking for statistics on families in the United States. Some, but not all, libraries provide a separate catalogue or list of the publications in the reference room. In others, you have to search the main library catalogue for the call letters of a reference book in the subject you are researching (books located in the reference section will have REF before the regular call number)—unless you know or can find out the relevant classification and browse that section.

Here are the main categories of the LC and Dewey classification systems:

DEWEY DECIMAL SYSTEM

000–099	General
100–199	Philosophy/Psychology
200–299	Religion

300–399	Sociology
400–499	Language
500–599	Pure science
600–699	Technology (applied science)
700–799	Arts
800–899	Literature
900–999	History

LIBRARY OF CONGRESS SYSTEM

A	General
B	Philosophy/Religion
C	History/Auxiliary sciences
D	History and Topography (except America)
E–F	America
G	Geography/Anthropology
H	Social sciences
J	Political science
K	Law
L	Education
M	Music
N	Fine arts
P	Language and literature
Q	Science
R	Medicine
S	Agriculture/Plant and animal industry
T	Technology
U	Military science
V	Naval science
Z	Bibliography/Library science

There is no "official" list of books considered "reference" books, although many books are typically located in the reference room. But it is possible that a book located in the reference room of your hometown library will be located in the stacks of your college library, and vice versa.

Types of Reference Works

Most of us are familiar with the obvious types of reference works: encyclopedias and dictionaries such as the *Encyclopedia Americana, Encyclopedia Britannica, American Heritage Dictionary,* and *Webster's Collegiate Dictionary.* But reference works can also be specialized in covering geography, biography, history, or other subjects. As a college student, you should seek out those reference works that are college-level, even though you may not have used them in the past. You can locate appropriate reference works in one of two ways. You can look in the computerized catalogue under the general subject of your inquiry and locate the titles of books with REF before the call number. Or you can go directly to the reference section of the library, locate the area where books on the appropriate subject are shelved, and browse for reference works that will meet your research needs.

■ *Activity 5*

Learning about
Reference Works in
Your Field, p. 207

Electronic Reference Sources

Most libraries offer print versions of reference sources. You may also have access to electronic versions of familiar reference works on CD-ROM, such as the *Encyclopedia Britannica,* or through online services or the Internet. Also, many new reference works have been written just for the electronic medium, such as the *Encarta Encyclopedia.* Finally, many people use the World Wide Web as a source of background and general information and turn first to their online hookup for reference reading.

■ *Guidelines for the Use of Computerized Reference Sources*

- Examine the introductory screens of an electronic version of a published source to determine whether you are getting a full-text or edited version of the work. Many CD-ROM and online versions of published print reference works contain shortened entries or fewer entries.

- Determine whether an electronic reference work has been created just for computers or whether it is based on a published print source. New reference works generated just for computer users may be "rush jobs" and not as accurate or as reliable as print reference works. However, because computer sources have been generated recently, they may contain more up-to-date information than a print source. It's always a good idea to have confirmation for any unusual or surprising information that you discover in any source.

- If you collect information from online sources such as World Wide Web sites, find out as much as you can about the sponsor of the web sites. This may mean following links until you can tell whether the information on the site comes to you from a neutral, reliable source or whether the web pages are designed as propaganda or advertising for an organization, point of view, or movement. (Chapter 4 covers Internet research and Chapter 10 covers evaluating sources in detail.)

Using the Reference Section Effectively

Bring the necessary tools to the library when you are planning to use the reference section. You will need a notebook page or 3 × 5 cards on which to keep track of the bibliographic details of reference works you use. (This chapter covers only background reading, bibliography, and note taking. See Chapters 12 and 13 for information about formal research, academic bibliography requirements, and formal note taking.) And you will need paper or 4 × 6 note cards for taking down content information, some spare change or dollar bills to use for photocopying, and paper clips or a ministapler to keep photocopied pages together.

Keeping Track of Reference Sources

Even though you may be skimming and reading around in several reference books before you happen on one that has information you need, you should keep track of sources you look at. Write down each source's name, its location or call number, and the title(s) and author(s) (if given) of the entries you read. Write a brief comment to yourself on the bibliography card about the source's usefulness. Then, if you have to do further research, you have a record of which sources you have consulted.

If you are doing formal research, write down the full bibliographic information for references sources from which you take notes and a comment about the usefulness of the book for your research. If you use an electronic version of a source, you must indicate that in formal documentation. (See Chapter 13 for full details about recording bibliographic information. In Modern Language Association citation style, different bibliographic items are required for reference sources than for other book sources.)

Getting Information from Reference Sources

If a reference source is new to you, take a moment to get an overview of its purpose, contents, and organization. Look at its frontmatter (preface, table of contents, and so forth) and especially notice if there are any guidelines for use. Then look up your subject.

Before reading the entry, skim it to determine its length and approach to the topic. If the entry isn't what you need, write a note to yourself on your bibliography card or list indicating that you located the source, examined it, and found it unhelpful. If the source seems on-target for what you want to know, read it carefully and take notes as needed.

If the subject is new to you, photocopying the entry to take home and study might be your best option. If you do make a copy of the article, make sure you clip pages together, note the source on the first page, and then read it promptly and annotate or take notes. Especially because reading in reference sources is primarily background to your research, you should gain a command of the information in such sources as soon as you can.

■ *Activity 6*

Reference Works New to You, p. 207

Using Reference Sources in Your Writing

When to Cite a Reference Work

The way you treat reference sources in your own text is determined by the level of research you are doing; whether you summarize, paraphrase, or quote from the reference source; and your instructor's requirements. If the point of your writing is to report some basic information about a subject, you might refer informally to your sources as appropriate in your text or list them at the end.

In an in-depth research project, your use of reference sources might be for your own benefit, to get yourself oriented to the generally known, commonly accepted basics of your topic. This information might be the general outline of historical events, biographical details, or the accepted scientific explanation of a process or discovery. If reading a reference work is a way of bringing yourself "up to speed" on your subject, then you do not need to mention or cite the sources.

But if you explicitly refer to, summarize, paraphrase, or quote a reference source in your final paper, then you do need to document it. Depending on your assignment, your documentation may be formal or informal. For example, in researching euthanasia, you might read in an encyclopedia about the derivation of the term (from the Greek roots for "good" and "death") and the difference between active and passive euthanasia. If your class were doing a unit on the euthanasia issue or you were taking a course on death and dying in sociology, these details would become common knowledge, and if you mentioned them in a paper you would probably not provide documentation. Otherwise, the decision as to whether to cite, either informally or formally, the source of this background information would depend on your instructor's wishes and the knowledge base of your classmates. If you summarize or paraphrase material that is not common knowledge, such as statistical data, or use a quotation from a reference work, you must formally document that source.

How to Cite a Reference Work

Be aware that the necessary bibliographic information for a reference work may be different from that for a book. You will be using only a titled entry within a reference work, not the entire work itself, so you must be sure you have the correct title of the selection and the name of the entry's author if given. (In some reference works, the author's initials are provided at the end of the entry; they are keyed to a list of the authors' names located at the beginning or end of the reference work.)

Provide the title of the reference work, but if the source is a well-known one, such as the *Encyclopedia Britannica,* you do not need to list its editors. In fact, for well-known, standard reference works, you do not need to list anything besides the title, edition number, and year of publication. The correct form for reference works can be found in Chapter 13.

If the reference work is specialized, discipline-specific, and relatively unknown, you should take down the name of the editor(s) and the usual publication data: place of publication, publisher, and year of publication, plus edition (if any). Include the number of volumes if the source is multivolume. Page numbers are not required. Electronic reference sources should be documented according to the appropriate form for the type of electronic medium, such as CD-ROM, online database, or web site.

Activities

1   Types of Facts

Form small committees to generate examples of two or three types of complex facts that *Cambridge Factfinder* editor David Crystal mentions:

> facts about fictions
> fictions about facts
> situations where we cannot decide whether something is fiction or fact
> near-facts
> transient facts
> qualified facts
> arguable facts
> politically biased facts
> contrived facts

You might want to try brainstorming examples together or adjourn so that you can individually skim through textbooks or periodicals to generate a list you can contribute to a second meeting.

Once you have collected a few examples of several types, you might want to consider the following questions. Do all members of your committee agree on how to categorize each example? Would you dispute whether the word *fact* applies to all the examples you have collected?

2   Inference, Facts, and Judgments

Examine the following fact-list items from the *Factfinder.* Do any seem to contain inferences as well as facts? Are any based on judgments?

> food additives categorized by purpose (sweetness, preservation, and so forth)
> length of pregnancy in various mammals
> tropical marine areas under threat
> recent notable environmental disasters
> deepest caves
> continental drift
> structure of earth from crust to core
> labeled drawing of terrain of far side of moon
> map of constellations
> British train lines
> Canadian newspapers by province
> development of computers
> film and television personalities
> Academy Awards

3 Characteristics of Evidence

Examine the following passages to determine which characteristics their evidence possesses; ask yourself whether it is representative, relevant, sufficient, reliable, and specific.

[A]   Throughout history, governments have taxed incomes when their citizenry is prosperous and holds cash (not just property) and when they are at war. When Great Britain was threatened in 1797 with insurgency sparked by French armies in Netherlands, Germany, and Italy; with an Irish rebellion; and with a mutiny of sailors at Spithead, William Pitt, prime minister, decided to tax incomes to support the necessary military actions. In the United States, it was the Civil War that sparked use of the income tax, in 1861.

And, historically, the end of war meant the repeal of the income tax. This is what Pitt did after the defeat of Napoleon in 1815. In this country, the tax was removed after the end of the Civil War. And late in the 1900s the income tax began to be used to improve government revenues when money was short.

[B]   New York has twice in history come close to an outbreak of bubonic plague. There were rats with the plague found in ship holds, but they never got on land. Similarly infected rats at the time did get ashore in California and caused some deaths in San Francisco. An epidemic is an out-of-control disease affecting a population. The process of searching for and destroying infected rats is laborious, but it needs to be followed in order for the country to be sure that rats from infected ports don't spread disease to our country.

[C]   The world is filled with places where a free press does not exist or where one is in constant peril. In those countries, journalists are heroes who risk their lives to spread the truth. In Colombia, for example, forty-three journalists have been murdered in the last ten years because they reported on the drug trade. Civil war is another cause of danger to writers because one or the other side wants them dead. In Russia, where the black market runs wild and government corruption is blatant, journalists who try to report on these things can be assassinated and no one will ever be charged. Turkey kills dozens of journalists for reporting about its repression of rebels. Americans and American journalists should just quit whining about freedom of the press in this country and be grateful about where they live.

[D]   Believing that there was no more room in landfills, Americans concluded that recycling was their only option. Their intentions were good and their conclusions seemed plausible. Recycling does sometimes make good sense—for some materials in some places at some times. But the simplest and cheapest option is usually to bury garbage in an environmentally safe landfill. And since there's no shortage of landfill space (the crisis of 1987 was a false alarm), there's no reason to make recycling a legal or moral imperative. Mandatory recycling programs aren't good for posterity. They offer mainly short-term benefits to a few groups . . . while diverting money from genuine social and environmental problems. Recycling may be the most wasteful activity in modern America: a waste of time and money, a waste of human and natural resources.

—John Tierney, "Recycling Is Garbage"

4 Designing a Survey

Choose one of the following issues and meet with a group of students to design a brief survey. Identify the goal of your survey and target your respondents. Also determine how you would reach an appropriate sample of this population. Then design the survey instrument itself by deciding what type(s) of questions you should ask? What demographics would you want to collect? Assign members of your group to write the introduction, topical questions, demographic questions, and conclusion. As your instructor requests, report to the class about your decisions.

> speed limits
> drinking age
> fast food in high school cafeterias
> explicit sexual lyrics in rock music
> land mines

5   Learning about Reference Works in Your Field

A. Identify the sections by specific call letters and numbers that pertain to your major and to a second field you are interested in.

B. Locate three reference works in each field and examine them carefully.

C. Write a description of each work, including the following information:

> number of pages
> how it is organized
> whether it includes a table of contents, index, glossary, maps, illustrations, pictures, or other information aids
> whether authors of articles are identified
> the goal or purpose of the book, according to its authors/editors
> the work's source, such as a professional, political, or academic organization
> its publisher

6   Reference Works New to You

A. Scan the reference-section shelves to locate three unusual reference works that you have never heard of before. These should be sources whose contents or focus surprises you or intrigues you.

B. Examine them and then write a paragraph about each, including the information asked for in Activity 5C.

Assignments

These assignments ask you to do primary research to discover additional evidence on the issues as preparation for writing your own opinion piece. Each assignment is set up for one type of primary research, but, with your instructor's permission, you may wish, in groups or individually, to do additional research of a different type.

1. Read "Kids and Guns," an editorial from the *Philadelphia Inquirer* (a reading selection at the end of this chapter). Make notes about your reaction to the *Inquirer's*

position and the evidence it cites as support, and then discuss your reactions with your class, either in small groups or as a whole. Working with a committee of classmates, identify a target group of teenagers and design a short questionnaire you could administer to find out what experience with and ideas regarding guns your target group has. Then proceed according to either A or B below.

Preparing a Survey

A. Get feedback from your instructor and class about your group's survey by duplicating it for class distribution, showing it on an overhead projector, or writing it on the chalkboard. After the feedback, revise the survey and administer it according to C or D below.

B. Or as a class, discuss which questions are most crucial for a short survey on teenagers and guns. Each group should contribute one question until a short composite questionnaire is generated. All students should take down the questions or a copy of the questionnaire should be distributed so that the class members can administer it according to C or D below.

Administering the Survey

C. Depending on the amount of time available for this project, the class working together may do a full survey of youth ages ten to nineteen in an attempt to duplicate the Harris poll. This means having the class design a strategy to distribute the survey to a large group of young people. An instructor or students with contacts in a local school system might be able to arrange such distribution.

D. Or the class may do a scaled-down, informal survey of young people. They may decide to focus on college teens and distribute the survey on campus, either in groups or working together as a class. Those with younger siblings may want to form a group to poll siblings and their friends. Asking each student to poll ten or fifteen other students means that when the class regroups, they will have collected a great deal of data.

Tabulating the Survey

E. Even if the class has worked in groups, the instructor might want to do a demonstration tabulation on the chalkboard. If the class has done one survey, then tabulation can be done at the board and the results discussed.

Writing Assignment

Reread the editorial on youth and guns, consider the data you acquired in your survey and the comments and personal experiences cited in your class discussions of the topic. Then brainstorm about the subject to define your point of view, and write an essay in which you argue your position. You may choose to agree or disagree with the editorial's conclusions, or you may wish to challenge the Harris poll evidence. If your instructor permits, pairs or small groups of students may collaborate on an essay.

2. Read "If It's (Black on White) Crime, Television Will Give It Time," by Kathleen Hall Jamieson and Dan Romer (a reading selection at the end of this chapter), and identify the conclusions they drew from their research. Write down your reactions to

this article and discuss the essay with your class. Then, as a class or in groups, plan a strategy to collect data about one aspect of how television news portrays crime, such as how frequently it does so or the race or ethnicity of victims, suspects, bystanders, and commentators. Different committees may be formed to examine different types of news shows: local news broadcasts, national news, cable news shows in your local market, or national cable news. Assign committee members to watch specified shows and keep track of the elements you are studying. Then write an essay in which you compare your class's or group's findings to Jamieson and Romer's or to data about crime frequency and ethnicity of victims and perpetrators, and draw conclusions about how and whether news shows "construct knowledge" about crime.

You might perform a similar analysis of violence on television by using the observation technique described in "Young People Get an Eye-Opening Look at the Violence on TV" by Marilyn Wheeler (a selected reading at the end of Chapter 4).

3. Reread the excerpt from E. D. Hirsch, Jr.'s *Cultural Literacy* (at the end of this chapter) to pull out a list of facts and information he believes young people today often do not know. Working in a group, use this material to design a "cultural-literacy test." Decide whether you wish to use the test to evaluate the knowledge of adults, "twenty-somethings," college students, or younger teenagers in high school. Polish your survey in relation to your target respondents and then administer it. After tabulating the results, write an essay (individually or as a group) in which you describe your research and what you discovered. Use your results to refute or agree with Hirsch's claim about fading cultural literacy. (One group may wish to design a "generational-literacy" test to discover how well over-30 adults are keeping up with new cultural developments.)

■ **WORKS CITED**

Crystal, David. "About This Book." *The Cambridge Factfinder.* New York: Cambridge UP, 1995.

Hotz, Robert Lee. "Scientists Say Race Has No Basis in Biology." *Philadelphia Inquirer* 20 Feb. 1995: A2.

---. "Universe Called Younger, Smaller." *Philadelphia Inquirer* 20 Sept. 1994: A28.

 *Readings*

If It's (Black on White) Crime, Television Will Give It Time

KATHLEEN HALL JAMIESON AND DAN ROMER

Kathleen Hall Jamieson is dean of the Annenberg School of Communications at the University of Pennsylvania, and Dan Romer is a research associate in the Annenberg School of Public Policy at the University of

Pennsylvania. This article appeared in the *Philadelphia Inquirer.*
(Reprinted by permission.)

1   In 1988, the National Security Political Action Committee made political history with an ad featuring the menacing mug shot of William Horton. The ad informed viewers that Horton had killed a boy, raped a woman, and assaulted her fiance. The spot showed that Horton was black; subsequent news reports filled in the rest of the story, showing that the victims were white.

2   Those who criticized the ad as racist did so in part because it implied that white audiences had reason to fear that they would fall victim to crimes by black men when, in fact, most violent crime was then and is now intra-racial not inter-racial.

3   Why were audiences so susceptible to the ad? Among the possible explanations is a pattern of news portrayal that implies that the atypical is typical; the unlikely, likely. From July 20 to Oct. 22 of last year, under a grant from the Ford Foundation, we coded 27 hours of 11 p.m. news broadcasts from Philadelphia's television stations WPVI (Channel 6), WCAU (Channel 10) and KYW (Channel 3). During that time the more than 600 stories about crime that we captured implied among other things that Philadelphia is an inhospitable place.

4   But is it? Philadelphia doesn't even fall within the list of the 50 cities with the highest per capita violent crime rate. In 1993, the FBI reports that you were less likely to fall victim to violence here than in such large cities as Miami, New York, Baltimore, or San Francisco or such smaller ones as Waco, Texas, or Albany, Ga. Nonetheless, the motto of our local stations appears to be: If it's crime, give it time.

5   The stories implied as well that ours is a city with a surfeit of white victims and nonwhite perpetrators. Yet in 1993 only 6 percent of the reported homicides in Philadelphia involved a black perpetrator and a white victim.

6   The cliche held true: If it bleeds it leads. But with a corollary: On all three stations, black and Hispanic persons were twice as likely to appear in crime stories as in other news. And when they appeared, they were much more likely to be identified as alleged perpetrators than victims.

7   By contrast, white persons not only dominated noncrime stories but were significantly more likely than African American or Hispanic persons to be shown as the victims of crime. Only one station (WCAU) was more likely to show nonwhite persons as bystanders or expert commentators in crime stories than it showed nonwhite persons in the rest of the news.

8   This pattern casts African Americans and Hispanics not as experts who explain crime, police who protect us from crime, bystanders who witness crime or citizens who are working to reduce crime—but as criminals. So for example, on WPVI, 87 percent of the perpetrators of violent crime were nonwhite compared to 57 percent of the victims, on WCAU 62 percent of the perpetrators were nonwhite compared to 40 percent of the victims, and on KYW 67 percent of the perpetrators were nonwhite compared to 44 percent of the victims.

9   To help explain these patterns, members of our research team met with representatives of the Philadelphia stations. We came away as puzzled as when we arrived.

10   A summary of their explanations will suggest why. First, when they are accused of crimes, white people may be more likely to elude the cameras. This might be accomplished by not appearing in court or refusing access to a photo.

11   We translate this to say that those responsible for news believe that Caucasians may be better at outwitting reporters. So, even if they cover a story about a white perpetrator, they will not have a picture of the person as often as when they cover a story of a black or Hispanic person.

Or, a second explanation, in defiance of the national trends, during that 14-week pe-   12
riod there may have been more black perpetrators and white victims in the Philadelphia
area. And we would add—during the periods in which other scholars have analyzed local
news in other cities. A study done by the Rocky Mountain Media Watch last Jan. 11 found
the same pattern across 50 local station broadcasts that aired on a single day.

For decades scholars have known about Heisenberg's Uncertainty Principle—in the act   13
of studying the phenomenon you may change its identity or behavior—but we had not before considered the possibility that the act of studying local news might change the patterns
of criminal behavior in local jurisdictions.

A third rationale suggested that since intra-racial crime is the norm and blacks more   14
likely than whites to be the victims of violence, black victims are not newsworthy. News focuses on the unusual—hence on black perpetrators whose victims are white and white victims regardless of the race of the perpetrator.

To this list we would add, patterns are often not evident to those assembling stories   15
under the pressure of deadlines.

Whatever the reality, to watch 3½ months of Philadelphia local news is to see a picture   16
of crime that raises serious questions about whether the news at 11 is showing the world as
it is or inadvertently and mistakenly constructing a violence filled city teeming with black
and Hispanic perpetrators and white victims.

Questions for Inquiry

1. What is the essay's claim? Is it stated or implied?
2. What are the distortions of reality that Jamieson and Romer detected in local news
   broadcasts?
3. What problems do Jamieson and Romer have with the explanations of the distorted
   news coverage given by station representatives? What reason do the authors suggest?
4. Why do the authors mention a law of physics, Heisenberg's Uncertainty Principle (13)?
5. Why do the authors use rhymes and slogans for the title and in paragraphs 4 and 6?
   What do these slogans suggest about the world of television news?

Questions for Argument

1. What is the reason white audiences were "so susceptible" to the ad featuring Willie
   Horton (3)? How does the distorted image of crime on local news explain the audience
   response to the Willie Horton ad? Do you agree that distorted news coverage such as
   that cited by Jamieson and Romer affects people's views of reality?
2. Should news focus on the "unusual" as the authors suggest in paragraph 14? Would
   you say the news is always going to show a distorted view of the community it reports
   on (3)?

Writing Assignments

Informal

1. What have been your assumptions about urban crime prior to reading this article? In
   a journal entry, note your previous assumptions about crime and indicate whether
   Jamieson and Romer's article corrected them.

2. Distortions of reality occur not only in the news. Have you ever discovered that your beliefs or ideas about a situation were distortions? Write an informal paper about a time in your life when distortions cluttered your decisions or about an issue on which, you later discovered, you held distorted ideas.

Formal

3. "If it's crime, give it time" seems to be the motto of local news broadcasters (4). If crime is not news, then what is? Establish a definition of what you think the news is, and apply it to specific types of events that might or might not fit the definition. Then write an essay in which you argue that occurrences of crime are or are not "news" that should be covered by local stations.

4. The authors conclude that local news may be "inadvertently and mistakenly constructing a violence filled city" instead of reporting life as it is. Are there other ways in which television news shows "construct" a reality that is then presented as actual and valid? Do other types of television shows also present inaccurate portrayals of life? Write an essay in which you compare the "reality" shown in a television show or series of ads with real life. Explain specifically how life would be different if it were patterned after the show or ad, and judge whether shows or ads of this type should be brought in line with reality.

5. **Research Opportunity.** Find out more about the Willie Horton ad and how it was used in the 1988 elections. Then look for statistics on the racial breakdown of violent criminals both nationally and in urban areas. Write a paper in which you discuss your findings and take a stand on whether the use of Willie Horton in an ad was ethical or unethical.

■ ■ ■

Kids and Guns

EDITORIAL, *Philadelphia Inquirer*

This editorial appeared in the *Philadelphia Inquirer* on July 24, 1993. (Reprinted by permission of the *Philadelphia Inquirer,* 1993.)

1   The results of a survey of American youths and the role guns play in their lives are ominous enough for us to urge an all-out effort to limit kids' access to firearms, particularly easily concealed handguns.

2   Pollster Louis Harris interviewed a cross section of 2,500 youths ages 10 to 19 about guns—whether they have them, use them and how they feel about them. Nearly one in 10 said he or she had fired a gun at another person. Even more startling, 59 percent said they could get a firearm if they wanted one, and 36 percent of those said they could do so in an hour or less.

3   Those findings aren't restricted to cities, where many have vainly tried to place all youth-with-gun problems. More than half—*58 percent*—of suburban students and *56 percent* of kids in rural areas say they, too, could get a gun if they wanted one.

4   So much for wistful, if racist, thinking that only certain kinds of kids know where to get weapons. The text accompanying the survey report emphasizes that point: "It is simply not accurate to characterize the gun problem among young people as one that is dominantly that of central cities, where more ethnic minorities are concentrated. Indeed, it is a pervasive problem that reaches into the suburbs in roughly equal numbers."

The results show such involvement with guns that many youths are anxious and pes-   5
simistic about their future: Almost 36 percent believe it is likely their lives will be cut short
by gunfire. And about 38 percent let the threat of violence determine where and how they
go out and with whom they are friendly.

Yes, some respondents, in a fit of youthful braggadocio, probably exaggerated their in-   6
volvement with guns, although Harris disputes that thesis. So what if they did? What if instead of nearly one in 10 youths claiming to have fired a gun, the number was one in 20? Is
this society so numb to violence that it could collectively dismiss that figure because "only"
about 5 percent of its future voters fired guns in what is allegedly a nation at peace?

Kids live what they learn. Many of this generation have learned that self-preservation   7
can be found only with a gun. And because many young people know where to get guns—
from family, friends or illegal dealers—75 percent of those surveyed feel the danger to all
young people has increased.

It's also clear from the rising numbers of young people who die by firearms—one in   8
every four deaths in 1990, the National Center for Health Statistics says—that this deadly
lesson is one our nation can no longer afford to dismiss.

Let's make the youthful victims of gun terror, those trapped in wheelchairs or hospital   9
beds for life, the media symbol of what guns mean to youths instead of some kiddie criminal draped in gold. Let's toughen penalties for all illegal gun-dealing, particularly to youths.
Let's get serious about restricting the growing stockpile of weapons—at least 200 million,
according to the feds—in American households. Let's stop making it easy for our kids to kill,
to maim and to die.

Questions for Inquiry

1. What is the editorial's claim? Why do you think it is located where it is?
2. What racist presumptions about gun availability does the poll contradict?
3. Where does the editorial refute a possible criticism of the statistics? Why does it maintain that even if the statistics are off, the point they make is still true?

Questions for Argument

1. The editorial reports a Harris poll finding that 10 percent of the children questioned indicated that they "had fired a gun at another person" (2). A few days later, an opinion
   piece appeared in which the author challenged this statistic, stating that if it is true, the
   children must be bad shots because few people are injured or killed each year by a child
   with a gun. What do you think of the 10 percent statistic? Is it realistic, in your view?
2. More than 50 percent of children reported that they could get a gun if they wanted to,
   presumably, in many cases, from their own homes. Is it a good idea to keep a gun in a
   home where there are children? Do you think the presence of guns in homes and businesses serves a legitimate purpose?

Writing Assignments

Informal

1. Write a journal entry in which you discuss your access to and awareness of guns in
   your childhood.

2. What should the role of adults or older youth be when fear of any kind becomes a frequent factor in the lives of young people? Write an informal paper in which you discuss how parents, older siblings, neighbors, and family friends should handle such a situation.

Formal

3. **Argumentation.** Some might question the results of this poll because the respondents were teenagers, who cannot be relied on to report accurately, without "braggadocio" or other distortions (6). Do you agree that young people make poor reporters about the reality around them because they may exaggerate or alter details? Should less credence be placed on young people's views than on those of adults (just as young people's judgment is considered less sound, leading to a high legal drinking age)? Write an essay in which you argue for or against society consulting children and young people more frequently, or less, on issues that concern them.

4. **Collaborative Writing.** Fear of violence, the editorial reports, leads many young people to alter their behavior: to change what they do, how they get there, and who they hang with. Brainstorm with others to generate other strategies young people might adopt when faced with a constant lack of safety or other neighborhood or societal problem. Work with a group of classmates to prepare a flyer or handout to be distributed to young people; the flyer should contain concrete recommendations for dealing with the fear of violence (or some other fear or anxiety). Include on the flyer a brief argument for why taking action is better than taking evasive action.

5. **Collaborative Research and Writing.** In the last paragraph, the editors support several changes to improve the gun situation in the United States. Form a group with others and choose one of these solutions. Individually or in pairs research the solution. What is or has been done along these lines? What proposals are there for implementing this change? (If little has been done in using this solution for gun control, has a variation of it been used to affect the illegal use of other materials? How successful was such use?) Then come together with your group to produce a background report describing the efforts to put this solution into play. At the end of your report, make a recommendation about whether this solution is a viable one for dealing with guns in society. (One group, depending on sentiment in the classroom, may instead wish to do research from the perspective that enough is already being done or that the problem of guns and youth is exaggerated.)

■ ■ ■

Cultural Literacy (excerpt)

E. D. HIRSCH, JR.

E. D. Hirsch, Jr., is William R. Kenan Professor of English at the University of Virginia. He is the author of numerous books and articles, including *Cultural Literacy,* from which this excerpt was taken. (Copyright 1987 by Houghton Mifflin Company. All rights reserved. Reprinted by permission.)

1   In order to put in perspective the importance of background knowledge in language, I want to connect the lack of it with our recent lack of success in teaching mature literacy to

all students. The most broadly based evidence about our teaching of literacy comes from the National Assessment of Educational Progress (NAEP). This nationwide measurement, mandated by Congress, shows that between 1970 and 1980 seventeen-year-olds declined in their ability to understand written materials, and the decline was especially striking in the top group, those able to read at an "advanced" level.[1] Although these scores have now begun to rise, they remain alarmingly low. Still more precise quantitative data have come from the scores of the verbal Scholastic Aptitude Test (SAT). According to John B. Carroll, a distinguished psychometrician, the verbal SAT is essentially a test of "advanced vocabulary knowledge," which makes it a fairly sensitive instrument for measuring levels of literacy.[2] It is well known that verbal SAT scores have declined dramatically in the past fifteen years, and though recent reports have shown them rising again, it is from a very low base. Moreover, performance on the verbal SAT has been slipping steadily *at the top.* Ever fewer numbers of our best and brightest students are making high scores on the test.

Before the College Board disclosed the full statistics in 1984, antialarmists could argue   2
that the fall in average verbal scores could be explained by the rise in the number of disadvantaged students taking the SATs. That argument can no longer be made. It's now clear that not only our disadvantaged but also our best educated and most talented young people are showing diminished verbal skills. To be precise, out of a constant pool of about a million test takers each year, 56 percent more students scored above 600 in 1972 than did so in 1984. More startling yet, the percentage drop was even greater for those scoring above 650—73 percent.[3]

In the mid 1980s American business leaders have become alarmed by the lack of com-   3
munication skills in the young people they employ. Recently, top executives of some large U.S. companies, including CBS and Exxon, met to discuss the fact that their younger middle-level executives could no longer communicate their ideas effectively in speech or writing. This group of companies has made a grant to the American Academy of Arts and Sciences to analyze the causes of this growing problem. They want to know why, despite breathtaking advances in the technology of communication, the effectiveness of business communication has been slipping, to the detriment of our competitiveness in the world. The figures from NAEP surveys and the scores on the verbal SAT are solid evidence that literacy has been declining in this country just when our need for effective literacy has been sharply rising.

I now want to juxtapose some evidence for another kind of educational decline, one   4
that is related to the drop in literacy. During the period 1970-1985, the amount of shared knowledge that we have been able to take for granted in communicating with our fellow citizens has also been declining. More and more of our young people don't know things we used to assume they knew.

A side effect of the diminution in shared information has been a noticeable increase in   5
the number of articles in such publications as *Newsweek* and the *Wall Street Journal* about the surprising ignorance of the young. My son John, who recently taught Latin in high school and eighth grade, often told me of experiences which indicate that these articles are not exaggerated. In one of his classes he mentioned to his students that Latin, the language they were studying, is a dead language that is no longer spoken. After his pupils had struggled for several weeks with Latin grammar and vocabulary, this news was hard for some of them to accept. One girl raised her hand to challenge my son's claim. "What do they speak in Latin America?" she demanded.

At least she had heard of Latin America. Another day my son asked his Latin class if   6
they knew the name of an epic poem by Homer. One pupil shot up his hand and eagerly said, "The Alamo!" Was it just a slip for *The Iliad?* No, he didn't know what the Alamo was, either.

To judge from other stories about information gaps in the young, many American school-children are less well informed than this pupil. The following, by Benjamin J. Stein, is an excerpt from one of the most evocative recent accounts of youthful ignorance.

> I spend a lot of time with teen agers. Besides employing three of them part-time, I frequently conduct focus groups at Los Angeles area high schools to learn about teen agers' attitudes towards movies or television shows or nuclear arms or politicians. . . .
>
> I have not yet found one single student in Los Angeles, in either college or high school, who could tell me the years when World War II was fought. Nor have I found one who could tell me the years when World War I was fought. Nor have I found one who knew when the American Civil War was fought. . . .
>
> A few have known how many U.S. senators California has, but none has known how many Nevada or Oregon has. ("Really? Even though they're so small?") . . . Only two could tell me where Chicago is, even in the vaguest terms. (My particular favorite geography lesson was the junior at the University of California at Los Angeles who thought that Toronto must be in Italy. My second-favorite geography lesson is the junior at USC, a pre-law student, who thought that Washington, D.C. was in Washington State.) . . .
>
> Only two could even approximately identify Thomas Jefferson. Only one could place the date of the Declaration of Independence. None could name even one of the first ten amendments to the Constitution or connect them with the Bill of Rights. . . .
>
> On and on it went. On and on it goes. I have mixed up episodes of ignorance of facts with ignorance of concepts because it seems to me that there is a connection. . . . The kids I saw (and there may be lots of others who are different) are not mentally prepared to continue the society because they basically do not understand the society well enough to value it.[4]

7   My son assures me that his pupils are not ignorant. They know a great deal. Like every other human group they share a tremendous amount of knowledge among themselves, much of it learned in school. The trouble is that, from the standpoint of their literacy and their ability to communicate with others in our culture, what they know is ephemeral and narrowly confined to their own generation. Many young people strikingly lack the information that writers of American books and newspapers have traditionally taken for granted among their readers from all generations. For reasons explained in this book, our children's lack of intergenerational information is a serious problem for the nation. The decline of literacy and the decline of shared knowledge are closely related, interdependent facts.

8   The evidence for the decline of shared knowledge is not just anecdotal. In 1978 NAEP issued a report which analyzed a large quantity of data showing that our children's knowledge of American civics had dropped significantly between 1969 and 1976.[5] The performance of thirteen-year-olds had dropped an alarming 11 percentage points. That the drop has continued since 1976 was confirmed by preliminary results from a NAEP study conducted in late 1985. It was undertaken both because of concern about declining knowledge and because of the growing evidence of a causal connection between the drop in shared information and in literacy. The Foundations of Literacy project is measuring some of the specific information about history and literature that American seventeen-year-olds possess.

9   Although the full report will not be published until 1987, the preliminary field tests are disturbing.[6] If these samplings hold up, and there is no reason to think they will not, then the results we will be reading in 1987 will show that two thirds of our seventeen-year-olds do not know that the Civil War occurred between 1850 and 1900. Three quarters do not know

what *reconstruction* means. Half do not know the meaning of *Brown decision* and cannot identify either Stalin or Churchill. Three quarters are unfamiliar with the names of standard American and British authors. Moreover, our seventeen-year-olds have little sense of geography or the relative chronology of major events. Reports of youthful ignorance can no longer be considered merely impressionistic.[7]

My encounter in the seventies with this widening knowledge gap first caused me to recognize the connection between specific background knowledge and mature literacy. The research I was doing on the reading and writing abilities of college students made me realize two things. First, we cannot assume that young people today know things that were known in the past by almost every literate person in the culture. For instance, in one experiment conducted in Richmond, Virginia, our seventeen- and eighteen-year-old subjects did not know who Grant and Lee were. Second, our results caused me to realize that we cannot treat reading and writing as empty skills, independent of specific knowledge. The reading skill of a person may vary greatly from task to task. The level of literacy exhibited in each task depends on the relevant background information that the person possesses.   10

The lack of wide-ranging background information among young men and women now in their twenties and thirties is an important cause of the illiteracy that large corporations are finding in their middle-level executives. In former days, when business people wrote and spoke to one another, they could be confident that they and their colleagues had studied many similar things in school. They could talk to one another with an efficiency similar to that of native Bostonians who speak to each other in the streets of Cambridge. But today's high school graduates do not reliably share much common information, even when they graduate from the same school. . . .   11

Cultural literacy is even more important in the social sphere. The aim of universal literacy has never been a socially neutral mission in our country. Our traditional social goals were unforgettably renewed for us by Martin Luther King, Jr., in his "I Have a Dream" speech. King envisioned a country where the children of former slaves sit down at the table of equality with the children of former slave owners, where men and women deal with each other as equals and judge each other on their characters and achievements rather than their origins. Like Thomas Jefferson, he had a dream of a society founded not on race or class but on personal merit.   12

In the present day, that dream depends on mature literacy. No modern society can hope to become a just society without a high level of universal literacy. Putting aside for the moment the practical arguments about the economic uses of literacy, we can contemplate the even more basic principle that underlies our national system of education in the first place—that people in a democracy can be entrusted to decide all important matters for themselves because they can deliberate and communicate with one another. Universal literacy is inseparable from democracy and is the canvas for Martin Luther King's picture as well as Thomas Jefferson's.   13

Both of these leaders understood that just having the right to vote is meaningless if a citizen is disenfranchised by illiteracy or semiliteracy. Illiterate and semiliterate Americans are condemned not only to poverty, but also to the powerlessness of incomprehension. Knowing that they do not understand the issues, and feeling prey to manipulative oversimplifications, they do not trust the system of which they are supposed to be the masters. They do not feel themselves to be active participants in our republic, and they often do not turn out to vote. The civic importance of cultural literacy lies in the fact that true enfranchisement depends upon knowledge, knowledge upon literacy, and literacy upon cultural literacy.   14

15   To be truly literate, citizens must be able to grasp the meaning of any piece of writing addressed to the general reader. All citizens should be able, for instance, to read newspapers of substance, about which Jefferson made the following famous remark:

> Were it left to me to decide whether we should have a government without newspapers, or newspapers without a government, I should not hesitate a moment to prefer the latter. But I should mean that every man should receive those papers and be capable of reading them.[8]

Jefferson's last comment is often omitted when the passage is quoted, but it's the crucial one.

16   Books and newspapers assume a "common reader," that is, a person who knows the things known by other-literate persons in the culture. Obviously, such assumptions are never identical from writer to writer, but they show a remarkable consistency. Those who write for a mass public are always making judgments about what their readers can be assumed to know, and the judgments are closely similar. Any reader who doesn't possess the knowledge assumed in a piece he or she reads will in fact be illiterate with respect to that particular piece of writing.

17   Here, for instance, is a rather typical excerpt from the *Washington Post* of December 29, 1983.

> A federal appeals panel today upheld an order barring foreclosure on a Missouri farm, saying that U.S. Agriculture Secretary John R. Block has reneged on his responsibilities to some debt ridden farmers. The appeals panel directed the USDA to create a system of processing loan deferments and of publicizing them as it said Congress had intended. The panel said that it is the responsibility of the agriculture secretary to carry out this intent "not as a private banker, but as a public broker."

18   Imagine that item being read by people who are well trained in phonics, word recognition, and other decoding skills but are culturally illiterate. They might know words like *foreclosure*, but they would not understand what the piece means. Who gave the order that the federal panel upheld? What is a federal appeals panel? Where is Missouri, and what about Missouri is relevant to the issue? Why are many farmers debt ridden? What is the USDA? What is a public broker? Even if culturally illiterate readers bothered to look up individual words, they would have little idea of the reality being referred to. The explicit words are just surface pointers to textural meaning in reading and writing. The comprehending reader must bring to the text appropriate background information that includes knowledge not only about the topic but also the shared attitudes and conventions that color a piece of writing.

19   Our children can learn this information only by being taught it. Shared literate information is deliberately sustained by national systems of education in many countries because they recognize the importance of giving their children a common basis for communication. Some decades ago a charming book called *1066 and All That* appeared in Britain.[9] It dealt with facts of British history that all educated Britons had been taught as children but remembered only dimly as adults. The book caricatured those recollections, purposely getting the "facts" just wrong enough to make them ridiculous on their face. Readers instantly recognized that the book was mistaken in its theory about what Ethelred-the-Unready was unready for, but, on the other hand, they couldn't say precisely what he *was* unready for. The book was hilarious to literate Britons as a satire of their own vague and confused memories. But even if the schoolchild knowledge had become vague with the

passage of time, it was still functional, because the information essential to literacy is rarely detailed or precise.

This haziness is a key characteristic of literacy and cultural literacy. To understand the *Washington Post* extract literate readers have to know only vaguely, in the backs of their minds, that the American legal system permits a court decision to be reversed by a higher court. They would need to know only that a judge is empowered to tell the executive branch what it can or cannot do to farmers and other citizens. (The secretary of agriculture was barred from foreclosing a Missouri farm.) Readers would need to know only vaguely what and where Missouri is, and how the department and the secretary of agriculture fit into the scheme of things. None of this knowledge would have to be precise. Readers wouldn't have to know whether an appeals panel is the final judicial level before the U.S. Supreme Court. Any practiced writer who feels it is important for a reader to know such details always provides them.

Much in verbal communication is necessarily vague, whether we are conversing or reading. What counts is our ability to grasp the general shape of what we are reading and to tie it to what we already know. If we need details, we rely on the writer or speaker to develop them. Or if we intend to ponder matters in detail for ourselves, we do so later, at our leisure. For instance, it is probably true that many people do not know what a beanball is in baseball. So in an article on the subject the author conveniently sets forth as much as the culturally literate reader must know.

> Described variously as the knockdown pitch, the beanball, the duster and the purpose pitch—the Pentagon would call it the peacekeeper—this delightful stratagem has graced the scene for most of the 109 years the major leagues have existed. It starts fights. It creates lingering grudges. It sends people to the hospital. . . . "You put my guy in the dirt, I put your guy in the dirt."[10]

To understand this text, we don't have to know much about the particular topic in advance, but we do require quite a lot of vague knowledge about baseball to give us a sense of the whole meaning, whether our knowledge happens to be vague or precise. . . .

Besides being limited in extent, cultural literacy has another trait that is important for educational policy—its national character. It's true that literate English is an international language, but only so long as the topics it deals with are international. The background knowledge of people from other English-speaking nations is often inadequate for complex and subtle communications within our nation. The knowledge required for national literacy differs from country to country, even when their national language is the same. It is no doubt true that one layer of cultural literacy is the same for all English-speaking nations. Australians, South Africans, Britons, and Americans share a lot of knowledge by virtue of their common language. But much of the knowledge required for literacy in, say, Australia is specific to that country, just as much of ours is specific to the United States.

For instance, a literate Australian can typically understand American newspaper articles on international events or the weather but not one on a federal appeals panel. The same holds true for Americans who read Australian newspapers. Many of us have heard "Waltzing Matilda," a song known to every Australian, but few Americans understand or need to understand what the words mean.

> Once a jolly swagman camped beside a billabong,
> Under the shade of a coolibah tree,
> And he sang as he sat and waited while his billy boiled,
> "You'll come a'waltzing Matilda, with me."

(Margin numbers: 20, 21, 22, 23)

Waltzing Matilda doesn't mean dancing with a girl; it means walking with a kind of knap-sack. A *swagman* is a hobo, a *billabong* is a pond, a *coolibah* is a eucalyptus, and a *billy* is a can for making tea.

24   The national character of the knowledge needed in reading and writing was strikingly revealed in an experiment conducted by Richard C. Anderson and others at the Center for the Study of Reading at the University of Illinois. They assembled two paired groups of read-ers, all highly similar in sexual balance, educational background, age, and social class.[11] The only difference between the groups was that one was in India, the other in the United States. Both were given the same two letters to read. The texts were similar in overall length, word-frequency distribution, sentence length and complexity, and number of explicit propo-sitions. Both letters were on the same topic, a wedding, but one described an Indian wedding, the other an American wedding. The reading performances of the two groups—their speed and accuracy of comprehension—split along national lines. The Indians performed well in reading about the Indian wedding but poorly in reading about the American one, and the Americans did the opposite. This experiment not only reconfirmed the dependence of read-ing skill on cultural literacy, it also demonstrated its national character.

25   Although nationalism may be regrettable in some of its worldwide political effects, a mastery of national culture is essential to mastery of the standard language in every mod-ern nation. This point is important for educational policy, because educators often stress the virtues of multicultural education. Such study is indeed valuable in itself; it inculcates tol-erance and provides a perspective on our own traditions and values. But however laudable it is, it should not be the primary focus of national education. It should not be allowed to supplant or interfere with our schools' responsibility to ensure our children's mastery of American literate culture. The acculturative responsibility of the schools is primary and fun-damental. To teach the ways of one's own community has always been and still remains the essence of the education of our children, who enter neither a narrow tribal culture nor a transcendent world culture but a national literate culture. For profound historical reasons, this is the way of the modern world. It will not change soon, and it will certainly not be changed by educational policy alone.

The Decline of Teaching Cultural Literacy

26   Why have our schools failed to fulfill their fundamental acculturative responsibility? In view of the immense importance of cultural literacy for speaking, listening, reading, and writing, why has the need for a definite, shared body of information been so rarely men-tioned in discussions of education? In the educational writings of the past decade, I find almost nothing on this topic, which is not arcane. People who are introduced to the sub-ject quickly understand why oral or written communication requires a lot of shared back-ground knowledge. It's not the difficulty or novelty of the idea that has caused it to receive so little attention.

27   Let me hazard a guess about one reason for our neglect of the subject. We have ignored cultural literacy in thinking about education—certainly I as a researcher also ignored it until recently—precisely because it was something we have been able to take for granted. We ignore the air we breathe until it is thin or foul. Cultural literacy is the oxygen of social in-tercourse. Only when we run into cultural illiteracy are we shocked into recognizing the im-portance of the information that we had unconsciously assumed.

28   To be sure, a minimal level of information is possessed by any normal person who lives in the United States and speaks elementary English. Almost everybody knows what is meant

by *dollar* and that cars must travel on the right-hand side of the road. But this elementary level of information is not sufficient for a modern democracy. It isn't sufficient to allow us to read newspapers (a sin against Jeffersonian democracy), and it isn't sufficient to achieve economic fairness and high productivity. Cultural literacy lies *above* the everyday levels of knowledge that everyone possesses and *below* the expert level known only to specialists. It is that middle ground of cultural knowledge possessed by the "common reader." It includes information that we have traditionally expected our children to receive in school, but which they no longer do.

During recent decades Americans have hesitated to make a decision about the specific knowledge that children need to learn in school. Our elementary schools are not only dominated by the content-neutral ideas of Rousseau and Dewey, they are also governed by approximately sixteen thousand independent school districts. We have viewed this dispersion of educational authority as an insurmountable obstacle to altering the fragmentation of the school curriculum even when we have questioned that fragmentation. We have permitted school policies that have shrunk the body of information that Americans share, and these policies have caused our national literacy to decline. 29

At the same time we have searched with some eagerness for causes such as television that lie outside the schools. But we should direct our attention undeviatingly toward what the schools teach rather than toward family structure, social class, or TV programming. No doubt, reforms outside the schools are important, but they are harder to accomplish. Moreover, we have accumulated a great deal of evidence that faulty policy in the schools is the chief cause of deficient literacy. Researchers who have studied the factors influencing educational outcomes have found that the school curriculum is the most important controllable influence on what our children know and don't know about our literate culture.[12] 30

It will not do to blame television for the state of our literacy. Television watching does reduce reading and often encroaches on homework. Much of it is admittedly the intellectual equivalent of junk food. But in some respects, such as its use of standard written English, television watching is acculturative.[13] Moreover, as Herbert Walberg points out, the schools themselves must be held partly responsible for excessive television watching, because they have not firmly insisted that students complete significant amounts of homework, an obvious way to increase time spent on reading and writing.[14] Nor should our schools be excused by an appeal to the effects of the decline of the family or the vicious circle of poverty, important as these factors are. Schools have, or should have, children for six or seven hours a day, five days a week, nine months a year, for thirteen years or more. To assert that they are powerless to make a significant impact on what their students learn would be to make a claim about American education that few parents, teachers, or students would find it easy to accept. 31

Just how fragmented the American public school curriculum has become is described in *The Shopping Mall High School*, a report on five years of firsthand study inside public and private secondary schools. The authors report that our high schools offer courses of so many kinds that "the word 'curriculum' does not do justice to this astonishing variety." The offerings include not only academic courses of great diversity, but also courses in sports and hobbies and a "services curriculum" addressing emotional or social problems. All these courses are deemed "educationally valid" and carry course credit. Moreover, among academic offerings are numerous versions of each subject, corresponding to different levels of student interest and ability. Needless to say, the material covered in these "content area" courses is highly varied.[15] 32

Cafeteria-style education, combined with the unwillingness of our schools to place demands on students, has resulted in a steady diminishment of commonly shared information 33 between generations and between young people themselves. Those who graduate from the same school have often studied different subjects, and those who graduate from different schools have often studied different material even when their courses have carried the same titles. The inevitable consequence of the shopping mall high school is a lack of shared knowledge across and within schools. It would be hard to invent a more effective recipe for cultural fragmentation.

34   The formalistic educational theory behind the shopping mall school (the theory that any suitable content will inculcate reading, writing, and thinking skills) has had certain political advantages for school administrators. It has allowed them to stay scrupulously neutral with regard to content.[16] Educational formalism enables them to regard the indiscriminate variety of school offerings as a positive virtue, on the grounds that such variety can accommodate the different interests and abilities of different students. Educational formalism has also conveniently allowed school administrators to meet objections to the traditional literate materials that used to be taught in the schools. Objectors have said that traditional materials are class-bound, white, Anglo-Saxon, and Protestant, not to mention racist, sexist, and excessively Western. Our schools have tried to offer enough diversity to meet these objections from liberals and enough Shakespeare to satisfy conservatives. Caught between ideological parties, the schools have been attracted irresistibly to a quantitative and formal approach to curriculum making rather than one based on sound judgments about what should be taught.

35   Some have objected that teaching the traditional literate culture means teaching conservative material. Orlando Patterson answered that objection when he pointed out that mainstream culture is not the province of any single social group and is constantly changing by assimilating new elements and expelling old ones.[17] Although mainstream culture is tied to the written word and may therefore seem more formal and elitist than other elements of culture, that is an illusion. Literate culture is the most democratic culture in our land: it excludes nobody; it cuts across generations and social groups and classes; it is not usually one's first culture, but it should be everyone's second, existing as it does beyond the narrow spheres of family, neighborhood, and region.

36   As the universal second culture, literate culture has become the common currency for social and economic exchange in our democracy, and the only available ticket to full citizenship. Getting one's membership card is not tied to class or race. Membership is automatic if one learns background information and the linguistic conventions that are needed to read, write, and speak effectively. Although everyone is literate in some local regional, or ethnic culture, the connection between mainstream culture and the national written language justifies calling mainstream culture *the* basic culture of the nation.

37   The claim that universal cultural literacy would have the effect of preserving the political and social status quo is paradoxical because in fact the traditional forms of literate culture are precisely the most effective instruments for political and social change. All political discourse at the national level must use the stable forms of the national language and its associated culture. Take the example of *The Black Panther*, a radical and revolutionary newspaper if ever this country had one. Yet the *Panther* was highly conservative in its language and cultural assumptions, as it had to be in order to communicate effectively. What could be more radical in sentiment but more conservative in language and assumed knowledge than the following passages from that paper?

> The present period reveals the criminal growth of bourgeois democracy since the betrayal of those who died that this nation might live "free and indivisible." It exposes through the trial of

the Chicago Seven, and its law and order edicts, its desperate turn toward the establishment of a police state. (January 17, 1970)

In this land of "milk and honey," the "almighty dollar" rules supreme and is being upheld by the faithful troops who move without question in the name of "law and order." Only in this garden of hypocrisy and inequality can a murderer not be considered a murderer—only here can innocent people be charged with a crime and be taken to court with the confessed criminal testifying against them. Incredible? (March 28, 1970)

In the United States, the world's most technologically advanced country, one million youths from 12 to 17 years of age are illiterate—unable to read as well as the average fourth grader, says a new government report. Why so much illiteracy in a land of so much knowledge? The answer is because there is racism. Blacks and other Nonwhites receive the worst education. (May 18, 1974)

The last item of the Black Panther Party platform, issued March 29, 1972, begins   38

10. We want land, bread, housing, education, clothing, justice, peace, and people's control of modern technology.
    When in the course of human events it becomes necessary for one people to dissolve the political bands which have connected them with another, and to assume among the powers of the earth the separate and equal station to which the laws of nature and nature's God entitle them, a decent respect to the opinions of mankind requires that they should declare the causes which impel them to the separation.

And so on for the first five hundred of Jefferson's words without the least hint, or need of one, that this is a verbatim repetition of an earlier revolutionary declaration. The writers for *The Black Panther* had clearly received a rigorous traditional education in American history, in the Declaration of Independence, the Pledge of Allegiance to the Flag, the Gettysburg Address, and the Bible, to mention only some of the direct quotations and allusions in these passages. They also received rigorous traditional instruction in reading, writing, and spelling. I have not found a single misspelled word in the many pages of radical sentiment I have examined in that newspaper. Radicalism in politics, but conservatism in literate knowledge and spelling: to be a conservative in the *means* of communication is the road to effectiveness in modern life, in whatever direction one wishes to be effective.

    To withhold traditional culture from the school curriculum, and therefore from students, in the name of progressive ideas is in fact an unprogressive action that helps preserve   39
the political and economic status quo. Middle-class children acquire mainstream literate culture by daily encounters with other literate persons. But less privileged children are denied consistent interchanges with literate persons and fail to receive this information in school. The most straightforward antidote to their deprivation is to make the essential information more readily available inside the schools. . . .

    I'm not suggesting that we teach our children exactly what our grandparents learned.   40
We should teach children current mainstream culture. It's obvious that the content of cultural literacy changes over the years. Today the term "Brown decision" belongs to cultural literacy, but in 1945 there hadn't been any Brown decision. The name Harold Ickes was current in 1945 but no longer is. Such mutability is the fate of most names and events of recent history. Other changes come through the contributions of various subnational cultures. Ethnic words (like *pizza*) and art forms (like *jazz*) are constantly entering and departing from

mainstream culture. Other subnational cultures, including those of science and technology, also cause changes in the mainstream culture. DNA and quarks, now part of cultural literacy, were unknown in 1945. In short, terms that literate people know in the 1980s are different from those they knew in 1945, and forty years hence the literate culture will again be different.

41   The flux in mainstream culture is obvious to all. But stability, not change, is the chief characteristic of cultural literacy. Although historical and technical terms may follow the ebb and flow of events, the more stable elements of our national vocabulary, like George Washington, the tooth fairy, the Gettysburg Address, Hamlet, and the Declaration of Independence, have persisted for a long time. These stable elements of the national vocabulary are at the core of cultural literacy, and for that reason are the most important contents of schooling. Although the terms that ebb and flow are tremendously important at a given time, they belong, from an educational standpoint, at the periphery of literate culture. The persistent, stable elements belong at the educational core.

42   Let me give some concrete examples of the kinds of core information I mean. American readers are assumed to have a general knowledge of the following people (I give just the beginning of a list): John Adams, Susan B. Anthony, Benedict Arnold, Daniel Boone, John Brown, Aaron Burr, John C. Calhoun, Henry Clay, James Fenimore Cooper, Lord Cornwallis, Davy Crockett, Emily Dickinson, Stephen A. Douglas, Frederick Douglass, Jonathan Edwards, Ralph Waldo Emerson, Benjamin Franklin, Robert Fulton, Ulysses S. Grant, Alexander Hamilton, and Nathaniel Hawthorne. Most of us know rather little about these people, but that little is of crucial importance, because it enables writers and speakers to assume a starting point from which they can treat in detail what they wish to focus on.

43   Here is another alphabetical list that no course in critical thinking skills, however masterful, could ever generate: Antarctic Ocean, Arctic Ocean, Atlantic Ocean, Baltic Sea, Black Sea, Caribbean Sea, Gulf of Mexico, North Sea, Pacific Ocean, Red Sea. It has a companion list: Alps, Appalachians, Himalayas, Matterhorn, Mount Everest, Mount Vesuvius, Rocky Mountains. Because literate people mention such names in passing, usually without explanation, children should acquire them as part of their intellectual equipment.

44   Children also need to understand elements of our literary and mythic heritage that are often alluded to without explanation, for example, Adam and Eve, Cain and Abel, Noah and the Flood, David and Goliath, the Twenty-third Psalm, Humpty Dumpty, Jack Sprat, Jack and Jill, Little Jack Horner, Cinderella, Jack and the Beanstalk, Mary had a little lamb, Peter Pan, and Pinocchio. Also Achilles, Adonis, Aeneas, Agamemnon, Antigone, and Apollo, as well as Robin Hood, Paul Bunyan, Satan, Sleeping Beauty, Sodom and Gomorrah, the Ten Commandments, and Tweedledum and Tweedledee.

45   Our current distaste for memorization is more pious than realistic. At an early age when their memories are most retentive, children have an almost instinctive urge to learn specific tribal traditions. At that age they seem to be fascinated by catalogues of information and are eager to master the materials that authenticate their membership in adult society. Observe for example how they memorize the rather complex materials of football, baseball, and basketball, even without benefit of formal avenues by which that information is inculcated.

46   The weight of human tradition across many cultures supports the view that basic acculturation should largely be completed by age thirteen. At that age Catholics are confirmed, Jews bar or bat mitzvahed, and tribal boys and girls undergo the rites of passage into the tribe. According to the anthropological record, all cultures whose educational methods have

been reported in the *Human Relations Area Files* (a standard source for anthropological data) have used early memorization to carry on their traditions.[18]

In Korea, "numerous books must be memorized including the five *Kyung*, and the four *Su*." In Tibet, "from eight to ten years of age, the boy spends most of his time reading aloud and memorizing the scriptures." In Chile, the Araucanian Indians use the memorization of songs as an educational technique to teach "the subtleties of the native tongue, and an insight into the customs and traditions of their tribe." In southern Africa, the children of the Kung bushmen listen for hours to discussions of which they understand very little until they "know the history of every object, every exchange between their families, before they are ten or twelve years old." In Indonesia, "memorization is the method commonly used." In Thailand, children "repeat their lessons until they know them by heart." In Arizona, the Papago Indians take children through the lengthy rituals "as many times as needed for the learner to say it all through, which may take a year."[19]

The new kind of teaching espoused by Rousseau and Dewey, which avoids rote learning and encourages the natural development of the child on analogy with the development of an acorn into an oak, has one virtue certainly: it encourages independence of mind. But the theory also has its drawbacks, one of which is that a child is not in fact like an acorn. Left to itself, a child will not grow into a thriving creature; Tarzan is pure fantasy. To thrive, a child needs to learn the traditions of the particular human society and culture it is born into.[20] Like children everywhere, American children need traditional information at a very early age.

47

48

Notes

1. National Assessment of Educational Progress, *Three National Assessments of Reading: Changes in Performance, 1970–1980* (Report 11-R-01) (Denver: Education Commission of the States, 1981). The percentage of students scoring at the "advanced" level (4.9 percent) has climbed back to the very low levels of 1970. See *The Reading Report Card: Progress Toward Excellence in Our Schools, Trends in Reading Over Four National Assessments, 1971–1984* (Princeton, N.J.: Educational Testing Service No. 15-R-01, 1986).

2. John B. Carroll, "Psychometric Approaches to the Study of Language Abilities," in C. J. Fillmore, D. Kempler, and S.-Y. Wang, eds., *Individual Differences in Language Abilities and Language Behavior* (New York: Academic Press, 1979), 29.

3. The College Board, *College-Bound Seniors: Eleven Years of National Data from the College Board's Admission Testing Program, 1973–83*(New York, 1984). The College Board has sent me further details from an unpublished report that shows the breakdown of scores over 600 between 1972 and 1984. The percentage of students who scored over 600 was 7.3 percent in 1984 and 11.4 percent in 1972. The percentage scoring over 650 was 3.0 percent in 1984 and 5.29 percent in 1972.

4. Benjamin J. Stein, "The Cheerful Ignorance of the Young in L.A.," *Washington Post*, October 3, 1983. Reprinted with the kind permission of the author.

5. *Changes in Political Knowledge and Attitudes, 1969–76: Selected Results from the Second National Assessments of Citizenship and Social Studies* (Denver: National Assessment of Educational Progress, 1978).

6. The Foundations of Literacy Project, under a grant from the National Endowment for the Humanities, has commissioned NAEP, now conducted by the Educational Testing Service of Princeton, to probe the literary and historical knowledge of American seventeen-year-olds.

7. I am breaking no confidences as a member of the NAEP panel in revealing these pretest figures. They were made public on October 8, 1985, in a press release by NEH Chairman John Agresto, which stated in part: "Preliminary findings indicate that two-thirds of the seventeen-year-old students tested could not place the Civil War in the correct half century; a third did not know that the Declaration of Independence was signed between 1750 and 1800; half could not locate the half century in which the First World War occurred; a third did not know that Columbus sailed for the New World 'before 1750'; three-fourths could not identify Walt Whitman or Thoreau or E. E. Cummings or Carl Sandburg. And one-half of our high school seniors did not recognize the names of Winston Churchill or Joseph Stalin."

8. Letter to Colonel Edward Carrington, January 16, 1787, taken from *The Life and Selected Writings of Thomas Jefferson*, ed. A. Koch and W. Peden (New York: Random House, 1944), 411–12.

9. W. C Sellar and R. J. Yeatman, *1066 and All That: A Memorable History of England, Comprising All the Parts You Can Remember, Including 103 Good Things, 5 Bad Kings, and 2 Genuine Dates* (London: Methuen, 1947).

10. Melvin Durslag, "To Ban the Beanball," *TV Guide*, June 8–14, 1985, 9.

11. See M. S. Steffensen, C. Joag-Des, and R. C. Anderson, "A Cross-Cultural Perspective on Reading Comprehension," *Reading Research Quarterly* 15, 1 (1979): 10–29.

12. See H. J. Walberg and T. Shanahan, "High School Effects on Individual Students," *Educational Researcher* 12 (August–September 1983): 4–9.

13. "Up to about ten hours a week, there is actually a slight positive relationship between the amount of time children spend watching TV and their school achievement, including reading achievement. Beyond this point, the relationship turns negative and, as the number of hours per week climbs, achievement declines sharply." R. C. Anderson et al., *Becoming a Nation of Readers: The Report of the Commission on Reading* (Washington, D.C.: National Institute of Education, 1985), 27.

14. Walberg and Shanahan, "High School Effects on Individual Students," 4–9.

15. Arthur G. Powell, Eleanor Farrar, and David K. Cohen, *The Shopping Mall High School: Winners and Losers in the Educational Marketplace* (Boston: Houghton Mifflin, 1985), 1–8.

16. The neutrality and avoidance of the schools are described in detail in *The Shopping Mall High School*.

17. Orlando Patterson, "Language, Ethnicity, and Change," in S. G. D'Elora, ed., *Toward a Literate Democracy: Proceedings of the First Shaughnessy Memorial Conference*, April 3, 1980, special number of *The Journal of Basic Writing III* (1980): 72–73.

18. *Human Relations Area Files*, microfiches (New Haven: Human Relations Area Files, 1899–1956).

19. Ibid. My examples are from more than two hundred entries, stretching from 1899 to 1949, under the topics "Educational Theories and Methods" and "Transmission of Beliefs."

20. L. A. Cremin, *The Transformation of the American School: Progressivism in American Education, 1876–1957* (New York: Knopf, 1964).

Questions for Inquiry

1. What is Hirsch's claim? Is it stated or implied?
2. How does Hirsch define "cultural literacy"? Why is it important? How is it related to the decline of literacy? What, in his opinion, does it mean to be "truly literate"?
3. What, according to the author, does background knowledge have to do with learning to read and write well?
4. What are some of the reasons that education in the United States has veered away from teaching the fundamentals necessary for cultural literacy? Why does he emphasize that changes must be made in education and not in other factors affecting children's learning, such as television, family well-being, poverty, and so on (31)?

Questions for Argument

1. Hirsch points out that young people do exchange much common knowledge but that this knowledge is "ephemeral and narrowly confined to their own generation" (7). Do you agree that young people lack "intergenerational" knowledge and that they dwell in a realm of disposable and trivial knowledge?
2. Hirsch acknowledges that some in education deemphasize the traditional literate culture because it is conservatively biased. On what grounds might one say that traditional American history, literature, and other subjects are "conservative"? How does Hirsch refute this idea? Do you agree that "literate culture is the most democratic culture in our land" (35)?

Writing Assignments

Informal

1. Have you ever thought about the educational level of your generation in relation to that of your parents or other adults? Do you think you are less well educated than they were at the same age? Write a journal entry in which you consider your parents' education and knowledge of the world.

2. Hirsch writes that "cultural literacy is the oxygen of social intercourse" (27). Sometimes people say it is common knowledge about sports that permits total strangers to chat with each other. Write an informal paper about the topics or issues that are the "oxygen" of conversation for your generation.

Formal

3. **Argumentation.** Examine the passage that Hirsch cites as an example of writing for the "common reader" (17) and the samples of writing from the *Black Panther* (37–38). What words or items in these passages are obscure or unknown to you? Would you say it is the passage of time that makes these items obscure? Write an essay in which you discuss these passages as "models" of civic discourse intended for the average person. Take a stand on this issue: Do today's newspaper writers need to write more comprehensibly, taking into account that today's readers know less about government and history? Or do we need to increase people's knowledge of civic matters?

4. Near the end of the extract, Hirsch likens cultural literacy to the "basic acculturation" accomplished by age thirteen in many cultures (46). He stresses the many tribal cultures that require memorization of important texts and traditions. Even though memorization may not be a current mode of learning, do you feel that U.S. youth are sufficiently knowledgeable about "traditional information"? Write an essay in which you defend today's young people against Hirsch's criticisms or, if you agree with him, in which you set out a plan through which our youth can be exposed to and "learn by heart" the important features of our culture.

■ ■ ■

Chapter 6

Inquiring into Values
Reactions and Opinions

■ Read the following selections carefully, then respond as indicated below:

> Freedom is perhaps the most resonant, deeply held American value. In some ways, it defines the good in both personal and political life. Yet freedom turns out to mean being left alone by others, not having other people's values, ideas, or styles of life forced upon one, being free of arbitrary authority in work, family and political life. . . . And if the entire social world is made up of individuals, each endowed with the right to be free of others' demands, it becomes hard to forge bonds of attachment to, or cooperation with, other people, since such bonds would imply obligations that necessarily impinge on one's freedom.
>
> —Robert N. Bellah, Richard Madsen, William M. Sullivan, Ann Swidler, and Stephen M. Tipton, *Habits of the Heart: Individualism and Commitment in American Life*

> Never was the human mind master of so many facts and sure of so few principles.
>
> —George Santayana, "Later Speculations," *Character and Opinion in the United States*

Writer's Journal

Choose one of the passages above and respond by explaining what the passage means to you. Strive for an entry of 150 words.

Most of us honestly admit that our response to things we read is a mix of emotional reactions, value judgments, and thoughts. We may be able to still our emotions long enough to examine and comprehend content, for example, when writing a summary, but our overall reaction to something we read will result from our feelings as much as from our thoughts.

Our emotional reaction may be caused by any number of features of a text, but the power of that reaction lies deep in our own personality, background, and culture. Both our rationality and our emotional makeup are the result of membership in a discourse community. We have been taught how to reason along certain lines. We have absorbed a way of looking at the world, and often we have been charged with automatic reactions to certain ideas and issues.

The academic community values reasoned judgment and evidenced opinions, as well as thematic, unified discourse. Other discourse communities, some within our own society, may have other values they hold higher than that of reasoning: the wisdom of an elder or religious leader, for example, or the teachings embodied in a religious document or the procedures and life choices handed down by tradition. In this book, the highest valuation is placed on reasoned analysis.

Values also come into play, however—values about which reasonable people will differ. This difference in values derives from the discourse communities in which each person has been raised and has been residing in as well as from the individual's reasoning about what it is good to believe.

So, beyond reasoning, we can work to comprehend the underlying values that cause us to react emotionally and to think along different lines from others. Only through such self-understanding can we grasp the differences in opinion that separate us from others. And, through examining the components of our own reactions, we can determine whether there are hidden contradictions in our values and whether we fully stand by these values.

■ *Activity 1*
Recognizing Values,
p. 243

■ WHAT ARE VALUES AND HOW DO THEY INFLUENCE OUR OPINIONS?

Values are beliefs about what is important in life, in our lives in particular but also in the lives of people as a community. Values endorse certain kinds of behavior. We are likely to share many broad values with those in our local, regional, and national community, and even internationally with all people around the world. The rights to survival and freedom are supported by most people and nations, at least in theory. These are values that are close to being universally sanctioned. Many such values have come to be formalized as principles, rules, or laws that provide guidance in many circumstances. In our culture, the Ten Commandments, the Declaration of Independence, the Bill of Rights, the Golden Rule, the judgments of the Supreme Court and appellate courts, and folk wisdom ("the apple doesn't fall far from the tree"; "no guts, no glory") are some of the sources for the principles we turn to for guidance in making judgments.

Although sometimes we deliberately inject our values into an argument or consciously refer to them as we read, our values often come into play as **assumptions**—that is, as ideas we believe and consciously or unconsciously apply as we respond to a text. If the text confirms our values, we are likely to approve it and enjoy reading it. A person who believes strongly in order may read an essay supporting the enlargement of the police force with approval. If a text affronts our values, however, we may feel rage or disgust. For example, someone who strongly values artistic creativity may be angered by an article advocating the elimination of federal funding for the arts.

Many texts fall between entrancing us and outraging us. Perhaps the value they engage is one we hold but not strongly, so our response is lukewarm. If we only mildly value exploration, an article arguing increased support for NASA might make little impression on us. When some of our values are supported while others are not, we may have a mixed reaction to what we read. Someone who disdains taxation and values the enterprising spirit may feel mixed about an article advocating the funding of small business start-ups through increased taxation.

In any single case, whether our response to a text is reasonable or not can be determined only through a careful examination of our own values. When we think an argument is extremely persuasive, we should try to determine where it meshes with values we already hold. Then we should go on to examine the argument itself to determine whether it is solid. For example, someone may initially find persuasive an article in support of laws permitting concealed weapons. On recognizing that the article plays into two of her highest values, individualism and personal freedom, she can realize that her acceptance of the argument is due not to its strength but to her personal value system. She needs to read the argument analytically to define whether it truly is logical and well supported.

■ *Activity 2*
Values and Opinions,
p. 243

■ THE HIERARCHY OF VALUES

Some values cover most everything we do in our lives; they are "global," or overarching. Other values are more local, or situational, and pertain only to one aspect of our lives. A mother may value consistency and fairness in parenting, and these values may come into play constantly in her daily life. Her childless sister may hold similar values but may enact them only when she babysits her nieces and nephews. Often, the weight you place on a particular value results from the situation you're in. You may barely realize how much you value privacy until you are stuffed in a dorm room for three. Your long-awaited first professional job may reveal to you just how much you value a flexible daily schedule and going outside four walls for some part of every day.

Although we hold some values unconditionally—that is, regardless of the situation—many other of our values are conditionally important. Simply, we all rank some values higher than others. For most people, survival is a higher value than pleasure, for example. For many parents, their children's survival is a higher value than their own survival. Most people in our culture would agree that honesty is a clear and obvious value that should always apply, but in some situations honesty would be outranked by survival. For example, few would consider it wrong to lie to a person holding a knife to your throat if the lie would defuse the threat to your safety. A text may appeal to some of your values and not others, or it may appeal to values you rank less highly than others; in each of these cases, your response may be mixed.

■ *Activity 3*
Recognizing Your
Own Values, p. 243

One way of categorizing values is to break them down into global, or overarching, values and situational values. Examples of **overarching values** are survival, truthfulness, integrity. Examples of places where **situational values** come into play are the workplace, college, social life, home, and place of worship.

Values Conflict

As you and your class constructed a lengthy list of values, you may have noticed that some of them contradict others. A valuation of tradition, for example, would be undermined by valuing the new or novelty. It is probably fair to say that, for many values you might hold, an equal and opposite value is held by somebody else. As Robert Bellah and his coauthors emphasize in their book *Habits of the Heart,* American life has a values conflict at its core: the values of cooperation and service, crucial to a functioning community, conflict with the dearly held values of individualism and freedom (23–25).

Conflicts about values occur in all of us. For example, the value of self-preservation may conflict with the value of adventure when a person decides to take up a dangerous sport. Or perhaps, in such a case, the value of self-preservation is outweighed because there are several opposing values—adventure, the value of having a daring reputation, and the value of excitement brought by indulging in risky behavior.

An amusing example of a personal value conflict occurred at a community protest of a nightclub featuring topless dancing. An observer noticed that one protester left the others to venture inside. The bar visitor later admitted he couldn't resist seeing what such a place was like. At first, taking action against what he considered to be obscene dancing in his town, the man ended up valuing curiosity more than solidarity with the protest. (He said he still opposed the topless dancing however.)

Psychological studies indicate that a typical inner value conflict of adolescence tends to be resolved differently depending on the person's sex. In a far-ranging landmark study of women's and men's attitudes about morality, Carol Gilligan identified two approaches to values: "The morality of rights is predicated on equality and centered on the understanding of fairness, while the ethic of responsibility relies on the concept of equity, the recognition of differences in need. While the ethic of rights [involves] . . . balancing the claims of other and self, the ethic of responsibility rests on . . . compassion and care" (164–65). Gilligan's study showed that in the transition to adulthood, men and women experience the same dilemma over whether "integrity" or "care" is the higher value. The upbringing (or, as we might say, the discourse communities) of the two sexes is significantly different however, so that for most men and women "this dilemma generates the recognition of opposite truths. Men's upbringing emphasizes separation and independence, resulting in an 'ethic of rights,' while the emphasis on relationships and attachment in women's upbringing supports their adoption of an 'ethic of care' " (164).

When you examine your values, you will probably discover that your situational values are different from those on your list of overarching values. You may also find that your situational values conflict somewhat. For example, you may decide that at work, being polite, reserved, and professional are significant for you. However, your behavior at a friend's party might be governed by different values: letting loose, being spontaneous, acting "natural." Or after looking over your various situational lists, you may decide that "fitting in with others" and "conforming to a situation" are two overarching values for you that you apply, with different effects, in your workplace and in your social life.

Values Change

The way a person ranks values may shift over time, along with the person's changing experiences, life situation, and psychological needs. Maturity and parenthood may cause someone to downgrade the value of competitiveness and upgrade good sportsmanship and teamwork, for example. William Perry, who researched the cognitive development of adolescents, discovered that maturity is characterized by the realization that "there is a diversity of opinion about what is good and what is right. . . . Truth is no longer conceived as absolute and singular but multiple and infinite" (qtd. in Belenky et al.: 62–63). Younger children tend to believe that values are rock solid. But adults may see values as relative to a situation because the "meaning of an event depends on the context in which that event occurs and on the framework that the knower uses to understand that event" (10).

Values Serve Needs

You've probably noticed that people believe what they want to believe or what helps them get through their lives with the least distress or most enjoyment. In other words, sometimes values serve our needs, and this makes them convenient to hold whether or not they are defensible in a rational manner. It is often most difficult to be objective about the values that "keep us going" in our daily lives.

Psychologist Abraham Maslow identified a hierarchy of needs, organized from most to least crucial. As a person's lower-level needs are satisfied, he or she moves on to address higher-level needs. In other words, those who can't pay the rent are not usually too consumed with actualizing their sculpting talents. Maslow wrote that, beyond the basic physical needs for water, food, shelter, and the like, people's needs are "for safety, belongingness and identification, for close love relationships, and for respect and prestige" (21). The highest need is for "self-actualization," the ability to put all one's talents to use. You may find this structured way of examining needs helpful as you sort out the sources of your own values.

■ *Activity 4*
Your Personal Needs Chart, p. 244

■ *Activity 5*
Maslow's Needs in Ad Pitches, p. 244

Students may be focused on self-esteem or self-actualization needs because their other needs are being met or their expectations (as for material comforts) are temporarily reduced or suspended. Some are preoccupied with their future needs for food and shelter, and sometimes students find themselves in dire straits, having to forage for food in friends' refrigerators or borrow couches and floors for sleeping because of changes in a marginal economic situation.

Sometimes what we may claim to be values verge closely on being **rationalizations.** These ideas serve as crutches to keep us going or as licenses that allow us to behave in a way not supportable by reason. If you are not familiar with the term *rationalization,* look it up, and also ask friends what they think it means. Don't confuse a "rationalization" with a "reason." While reasons are supposed to be clearly thought out and logical, rationalizations are merely wishful explanations. You can consider a rationalization an excuse for a reason—that is, a "decoy" meant to distract its owner from acknowledging the actual impulses that lie deeper down.

People sometimes spout values instead of admitting to failure or fear or to deny they care about an unpleasant consequence. This common habit of avoidance among humans appears to be the cause of many sayings:

"Practical knowledge is what counts."
"Smart as a whip but doesn't know to come in out of the rain."
"Don't be a stool pigeon."
"I'd rather be poor but happy."
"Everybody's doing it."
"I'm only a little bit bad."

You may recognize that many of these sayings are **clichés**—that is, stale phrases, timeworn, unimaginative, and easy to come by. They represent one of the worst aspects of a discourse community: the possibility that the language of the community will supply the thinking for the individuals within it. Some individuals prefer to think in formulas and to operate on impulse rather than on reason. They ache to follow the crowd (satisfying their need for belonging) rather than think things through for themselves. As the above list reveals, there is a cliché for every occasion, a formula to justify any and all beliefs and actions.

■ *Activity 6*
Discovering
Rationalizations,
p. 244

Almost any value can get out of hand and become a crutch supporting irrational needs or a license to perform antisocial or questionable behavior. For example, loyalty to and love of one's group can, if extreme, lead to provincialism, ethnocentrism, prejudice, stereotyping, superstition, overreliance on traditional practices, and resistance to change. A tragic example of extremism in loyalty was the mass suicide of the thirty-nine members of the Heaven's Gate cult during the visit of the Hale-Bopp comet in spring 1997 (Bruni 1).

■ VALUE ACTIVATORS

Our emotional reaction to a piece of writing may be prompted by any number of features of the text: the topic, the way the topic is treated, or the language effects created by the writer. Certain topics themselves affect all of us emotionally to a certain extent—child abuse, abortion, crime, international crises involving slaughter, bombings, starvation, and so on. Other times our personal histories sensitize us to particular issues. A person with a close gay friend may have a heightened awareness of discrimination against homosexuals.

A highly emotional response may also be sparked by the way a topic is treated. A satiric treatment of a person or institution that we respect may "get our goat." A blameful discussion of the poverty that can befall single mothers, for example, may enrage someone who has researched divorce and single motherhood or whose sister is an un-married mother. A negative or mocking appraisal of our favorite candidate's honesty may set us off long before we reach the middle of the article.

Writers who wish to play on readers' feelings can manipulate language to create effects. They use imagery, emotionally tinged words, repeated phrases, or language patterns that create drama and heighten feelings. In such texts, rhetoric is consciously employed to promote a claim. To be sure, all writers make use of rhetoric. How much a reader is affected depends on the extent to which the reader meshes with the writer's intended audience and how extreme the rhetoric is. When the language of a text is designed to provoke heavily emotional reactions, we speak of the text as *biased* or *slanted*. Such slanting usually goes beyond the style of language used; it often involves omitting evidence and information that might moderate or contradict the point of view taken in the text. Some writers deliberately adopt extreme styles in order to irritate mainstream readers. Being a gadfly or iconoclast is a time-honored role in Western culture: such writers take an adversarial or exaggerated stance just to touch off debate and inspire the flow of ideas.

■ ASSUMPTIONS AND VALUES IN REASONING: TOULMIN LOGIC

It's hard to get away from values and assumptions about them. Typically, values lie underneath arguments as unspoken assumptions. Although no one would maintain that you shouldn't argue with reference to values, it's a good idea to know what your assumptions are and also to take the assumptions of your intended audience into account.

British logician Stephen Toulmin showed how values (as well as beliefs) serve as assumptions that connect a **claim** to the evidence or **data** offered for it. Toulmin's term for such an assumption is **warrant**. A warrant is an assumption, often hidden, that "licenses" or permits us to use the facts of the situation as support for the claim. The assumption asserts a value or belief. For example, if you observe that your neighbor drives a British Sterling, you might reason that she is materialistic. Diagramed according to Toulmin logic, this bit of reasoning looks like this:

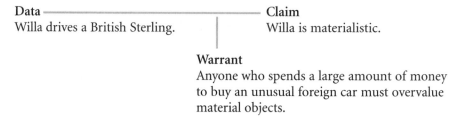

Data ————————————————— Claim
Willa drives a British Sterling.   Willa is materialistic.

Warrant
Anyone who spends a large amount of money
to buy an unusual foreign car must overvalue
material objects.

Here, the claim about Willa is based on your observation of the car she drives. But the idea that makes the claim possible is an assumption, a value judgment, that owning an expensive and unusual foreign car makes the owner materialistic. Without that assumption (or some other), Willa's car is just a car, and you can learn nothing about her from it.

For this bit of reasoning to work, both the audience and the arguer must agree on the truth of the assumption or warrant and its applicability to the claim. In presenting an argument, the writer must identify common ground shared with the audience. This common ground provides the assumptions or warrants that form the hinge of the argument. Most of the time, people within a discourse community hold similar values and make similar assumptions, but, within a large discourse community, there is lots of room for variety. Among college students, values are quite diverse, depending on background and length of exposure to the college environment. Students sometimes discover that beliefs shared by friends at home are not shared by those in their dormitory. A new college student might, for example, assume that using borrowed or faked identification to get into bars is a brazen violation of drinking laws, an outrageous, shabby, and even dangerous behavior. To her shock, she may learn that her dorm mates consider this action no big deal.

Widespread beliefs held by a cohesive community or group constitute what the social sciences call *mores.* Such values are not as formal or as consciously held as morals, but they nevertheless strongly govern the behavior of the group. The unspoken mores of a community work to produce *norms,* "a standard, model, or pattern [of behavior] regarded as typical" ("Norm"). Rules of politeness are norms. In the United States, for example, it used to be a norm for men to take off their hats when entering a building because of the belief that a man's wearing a hat inside was rude (women's hats, being decorative, were permitted indoors). This norm has disappeared among younger Americans, to the extent that many are surprised to learn it ever existed. Another norm that has changed is how people behave when they are victorious. Today, it is common for winners, from Olympic champions to schoolyard victors, to celebrate themselves by punching one or both fists in the air; in the past, such boastful, "I'm great" gestures were considered poor sportsmanship, especially when made by amateurs. Norms are more than just etiquette however. They cover all our interactions: how we behave in elevators, at parties, and in the cafeteria.

When your assumptions are not acceptable to your audience, you must provide **backing** for them. Toulmin makes the point that all warrants have backing—that is, material that supports the warrant, but the backing is not always out in the open. When your assumptions are not congruent with those of the audience, you need to be explicit about your backing. Otherwise, your claim is likely to be rejected. In the example above, the backing might include such statements as "a Sterling costs $45,000"; "only one in a thousand Americans owns a Sterling"; "it requires a large amount of money and effort to acquire an unusual foreign car"; "people who make such efforts are materialistic."

Toulmin acknowledged that even with backing, a claim is still only likely rather than definitely true, and so he added another element to the mix, the **qualifier.** The qualifier is a word, like "probably," that softens the claim. The **reservation** is a statement that, if true, invalidates the claim. In this example, a reservation might be "Willa's rich aunt asked her to use the car while she spends the year abroad." Or "Willa's company assists junior executives in the purchase of a high-status car." If the reservation is true, then the claim is false.

Diagramed completely according to Toulmin's structure, this argument looks as follows:

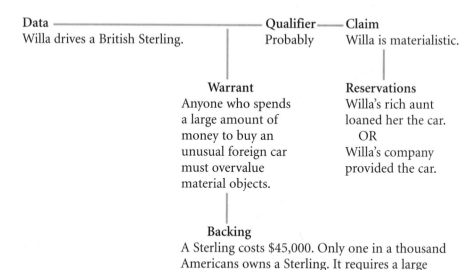

Data ——————————————————— Qualifier —— Claim
Willa drives a British Sterling.   Probably   Willa is materialistic.

Warrant
Anyone who spends
a large amount of
money to buy an
unusual foreign car
must overvalue
material objects.

Reservations
Willa's rich aunt
loaned her the car.
      OR
Willa's company
provided the car.

Backing
A Sterling costs $45,000. Only one in a thousand
Americans owns a Sterling. It requires a large
amount of money and effort to acquire an unusual
foreign car. People who make such efforts are
materialistic.

■ *Activity 7*
Exploring
Assumptions, p. 244

■ EXPRESSING AND RESPONDING TO VALUES

Often, an argument over facts, causes or effects, policies or choices is a dispute about values. And at times arguments are about values themselves: which value is best to live by or which value among several should be the highest in a particular context. Conflicts over values are about whether some thing or action is right or wrong, good or bad, constructive or destructive, useful or useless, artistically powerful or worthless. All these are value judgments. Such judgments are different from matters of personal taste—judgments about whether Chinese food is better than Mexican, whether acoustic guitar is superior to electric, whether abstract expressionist art is more valid than realistic portraiture, whether the mountains or the seashore makes a better summer vacation spot—which cannot be argued. (See the discussion about the subject of argument in Chapter 1.) In this section, several types of writing about values are discussed: the reaction piece, the personal opinion piece or op-ed article, and the review. The reading selections at the end of this chapter focus on values.

Writing a Reaction Piece

Writing about your responses to a text that strikes you powerfully can help you key into your most closely held values. In a personal reaction piece, done either as a formal essay or a private journal entry, you describe the ways you are affected by specific ideas, statements, or stylistic touches in a text, and then you trace the sources of your reactions. These sources may be in your values, upbringing, personal and educational history, or other influences your various discourse communities have had on you. The goal of such writing is to inquire into how your reactions to ideas may satisfy inner needs and to discover some of the sources of personal bias that all of us possess and that may come into play when we judge viewpoints that differ from our own.

Such personal reaction writing is hard to pin down just because it is so individual. As with most inquiry writing, such fundamental components as organization and tone grow out of the writer's core meaning. There aren't too many rules for how such writing should come out; but we can suggest a procedure for generating a reaction-and-analysis text.

- Read and annotate the article carefully.
- By summarizing, outlining, or discussing the article with others, make sure that you understand the article's ideas and that you are not misinterpreting because of emotional reactions.
- Jot down your main reactions and indicate the statements or items in the article that prompt particularly strong responses.
- Brainstorm about why you react as you do to the ideas in the article. What values are coming into play? Where did you get these values? Can they be rationally defended, or are they values that satisfy some of your important needs (or both)? What in your life history, your immersion in various discourse communities, your influences have produced your allegiance to these values?
- Look over your notes and group related points. Perhaps some of your reactions to statements in various places in the article result from one particular value. Or perhaps one important life event or your participation in one particular discourse community feeds your reactions. Some of your reactions may result from an unfair bias, but others may result from values you stand by.
- Choose the largest group of related points as the subject for your reaction paper. Or if you have several smaller groups of points, choose two or three for analysis in your paper.
- Write a statement that succinctly expresses what you have discovered about your reactions and the values that underlie these reactions. This will be the main point or thesis of your analytic reaction piece.
- Organization will most likely be a challenge because your paper has two goals: to indicate to the reader your major reactions to specific ideas in the text and to trace the origins of those reactions in your values, your past influences, and so on. You need to make two decisions: The first is the overall order in which to present your reactions. This might be in order from most to least important, emphatic order building to the most important, or some other order. The second decision is where to discuss the personal reasons for your reactions. You can discuss them either when you describe the reaction or later in your paper, in a section reserved for tracing your values to their origins.
- Write your first draft. Make sure you provide quotations or paraphrases of the specific ideas and statements in the article that triggered strong responses from you. Supply paragraph numbers if your readers have a copy of the article.

Writing a Personal Opinion Piece:
The Op-Ed Commentary

Setting out your views on a topic close to your experience in a personal opinion or op-ed piece can be a constructive use of the energy with which you respond to situations around you. In the civic discourse community at large, the terms *opinion piece* and *op-ed article* are catchalls for any essays that express a viewpoint about a contemporary issue of concern. Op-ed, in fact, is a newspaper term for the type of essays that appear "opposite the editorial page" (and doesn't mean "opinion/editorial," as many readers assume). For the purposes of this assignment, the opinion piece will be an informal argument for a viewpoint you have arrived at by living, looking around you, and understanding how current issues figure in your daily life.

Such personal takes on community or national issues are commonly found both on newspaper op-ed pages and in magazines; for many years, *Newsweek,* for example, has published columns written by readers under the heading "My Turn." In an article inviting readers to set down their views, *Philadelphia Inquirer* editor Mike Leary writes:

> A Dobbins High School student who thinks requiring kids to wear uniforms is un-American. . . . A retired nature photographer rhapsodizing about his formative years frolicking in Fairmount Park. . . . A meat-eating mother marveling at her vegetarian kids.
>
>   Every one of them had their say in Commentary Page pieces published in the last few weeks. And the only thing they had in common was a compelling point to make and the ability to make it eloquently.

In being chosen for publication, Leary says, "a piece that draws on personal experience or expertise has an edge." And that's the type of piece you'll design for this assignment.

To get a sense of the personal opinion piece, read the two articles by college students included at the end of this chapter. Karla Vermeulen, whose article was published in the *New York Times,* discusses the effects of "safe sex" on her generation as she compares her generation with those who came of age in the days of the sexual revolution. And John Viet's op-ed in the *Philadelphia Inquirer* clues readers in on the different treatment received by white suburban students who party and experiment with drugs and inner-city minority kids who do the same. Both these pieces make use of examples and narrative to create interest and credibility.

In writing this informal argument, your inspiration will not be a written text; instead, you will draw your ideas and your evidence from the "text" of your life. You will "read" and interpret some slice of your experience so as to show its meaning and relevance for a larger audience: that of your classmates, your peers at college, and, just maybe, the readers of your local newspaper if you choose to submit your op-ed for consideration.

Because you are presenting your position as it has evolved from your experience in life, one characteristic you assume about your audience is that their experience is different. They do not know what you know; if they did, you wouldn't be writing about that particular topic for them. To hook them, you have to convey the power of the problem and the special light your own experience casts on it.

■ *Writing an Op-Ed Commentary*

The op-ed is a personal piece, and it derives its substance, personality, and flow from the writer's unique situation. Few procedures or rules can be offered to assist the writer. You might begin by brainstorming a list of events in your life or in the lives of those near to you that connect to issues of public importance. Assume that your audience will be newspaper readers of all ages and that you are going to write about some aspect of life on which you have some expertise. Dating, working, major illnesses or physical restrictions, changes of all kinds may be some of the life events that could spur an opinion piece.

Discuss a few of your strongest possibilities with classmates or friends, and choose one to work on. Then, use brainstorming, mapping, or free-writing to get yourself going. You may explore particular events or incidents in your life or create a typical event on the basis of your experiences. Once you have amassed some material in either notes or a free-writing draft, consider showing it to classmates or other readers.

Here are a few guidelines for your finished op-ed:

- Write an introduction that will attract a reader's attention. Dramatize the issue by using a quotation, a surprising fact, or the description of an unusual scene, for example.
- Use explanation or summary to set out the issue that you wish to address. This may take a sentence or it may take a paragraph or even two.
- Describe personal examples, experiences, and so forth, or reasoning based in your experiences.
- Don't try to cover too much and don't go off into autobiography; focus on your main issue.
- Write a wrap-up that clearly states your position and any recommendations you have.

As to what your commentary should be like when it's done, here's Leary again: "The optimum length is 400 to 700 words. That said, there are no hard-and-fast rules on style, length or subject—well, no poetry."

STUDENT ASSIGNMENT

Gina Kirtow, "A View from the Crossroads"

ASSIGNMENT: Using experiences you have had—either ordinary ones from your day-to-day life or experiences that were unique in some way—write an opinion piece directed at the readers of a local or regional newspaper. Through describing and analyzing your experience, offer an interpretation of some aspect of life that is different from the usual or that reveals an unexpected view. You may wish to re-frame reality in some way, or you may wish to recommend that changes be made in some aspect of life.

In response to this assignment, Gina Kirtow wrote the following op-ed piece.

A liquor store is like a crossroads, where all sorts of people pass through. You see every type: guys buying a few six packs to take fishing with them; ladies stocking their bar for a party, buying one of every kind of liquor; and people my age, early twenties, buying a keg for a weekend bash.

I know, because I clerked at a liquor store the summer before my senior year in college. At first, I didn't know much about "the product," but pretty soon I could direct a customer to Smirnoff or Schlitz. At first, I didn't know the customers apart, either, but pretty soon I could tell the types.

We had regulars, men in the older generation who called me "honey." They'd ask me for a date, half joking, half hopeful. They were old guys, though, with paunches and loose flaps of skin on their jaws and necks. And there was another problem:

They exhaled beer. It was so strong sometimes I'd lean back to keep out of breath-range. They'd come in nearly every day. I quickly realized that I was not the attraction. It was really a date with booze that they wanted.

I soon became aware of another type of regular, ones who just went to the vodka or whiskey, picked the cheapest bottle, and came to pay. Their hands would tremble as they took the change. Their nails were dirty and cracked. I realized their distinctive odor was sweat and grime and alcohol in a toxic body-odor cocktail.

No matter that they came in four times a week; they treated me like a stranger, almost as if there were something wrong with our transaction. And grad-ually, I realized there *was*. These people were addicted. Their lives were stunted, their personalities drained. They were alcoholic zombies. And I was their source.

I began to view my other customers differently. The energetic young guys with their kegs, excited like kids with a toy: future booze hounds? The station wagon ladies with their gallons of Johnny Walker Red: secret lushes? The weekend fishermen swilling can after can: recreational drunks?

I began to view my boss differently too. His business wouldn't survive if people only had a beer on the weekend or drank wine with Sunday dinner. The regulars fed his family. And those who bought occasionally? Maybe it was a matter of time until they too couldn't live without a trip to the package store every few days.

You hear about drinking problems among the young. When you are at a college you hear of off-campus drunken parties spilling on to lawns and about Residence

Advisors confiscating half-empty beer cans from dorm rooms. But during my summer at the crossroads of liquor, I realized our alcohol problem is among the adults. Their world is swimming in booze of all kinds, and a lot of them are drowning.

Writing about Artistic Values: The Review

When you make a value judgment (not a statement of taste) about a creative work, you are passing an artistic verdict, one that can be argued just like other claims of value. To make your argument about an artistic work effective, you need to do the same basic things as in any argument: estimate your audience's knowledge and appreciation of the artistic work at issue, use a clear and defensible standard of value, and clearly and convincingly show that the work in question does or does not meet the standards.

A **review** is a short (usually) essay evaluating one specific work or group of works, written at the time of the first appearance or presentation of the work. A review may be about a new novel, short-story collection, or book of poems; a new exhibition of the works of a painter, sculptor, or craftsperson; a new film, play, ballet or dance performance, comedy show, or other theater piece; a new album or a performance by a rock group, pop singer, chamber quartet, orchestra, or other music group. Reviews appear in all kinds of media, from newspapers and magazines to specialized periodicals like *Film Comment* and *Art in America* to scholarly journals, where reviews tend to be lengthy and, well, scholarly. Not all reviews are arguments; some strive to be descriptive or entertaining.

The review you might write for this course should make a claim of value—that is, an evaluative claim—and should be geared to a college or mainstream audience. You should remember that reviews are not the same as reactions. In a review, you seek to explain your reactions and make a reasoned value judgment about the work at issue. Most often, reviews cue the values appropriate to the work of art under evaluation and then state how the work measures up. Sometimes reviewers are explicit about their standards, and sometimes they only imply them. Often, the intended audience for a review is assumed to share the writer's artistic values, which may be left unstated.

Examining reviews from widely different sources shows that powerful reviewing results when specifics are brought in to support the author's reactions. In reviewing Don DeLillo's novel *Underworld for Vanity Fair,* David Kamp intermingles brief tip-offs to his literary standards with appreciations of DeLillo's achievement. And he is careful to supply examples of every compliment he bestows.

> While it would be unwarrantedly gushy to say that DeLillo has evolved into a higher form of being, it's fair to say that he uses exponentially more brain than most of us. This would explain how, in his books, he is able to pile on sentence after sentence of note-perfect description, such as his appraisal of a home videotape as having "the jostled sort of noneventness that marks the family product." This would explain why he seems to be playing with the pinochle deck of words, "sough," "hawser," "riverine," inchmeal." This would explain how he is able to sustain an 832-page novel that hasn't so much a plot as an aggregation of recurring, chronologically shuffled mini-plots about subjects as disparate as garbage, infidelity, heroin, the Cold War, urban blight, Lenny Bruce, graffiti, the

art market, and the World Wide Web—all somehow refracted through the most famous baseball playoff in history, the '51 Dodger-Giants game in which Bobby Thomson hit his pennant-clinching homer, the Shot Heard 'Round the World. (202)

Kamp's own style emulates the literary. The repeated sentence opener, "This would explain how [or why] he . . . " stabilizes the "gush" of praise. The paragraph's last sentence is engorged with imagery yet gracefully and clearly itemizes the complexities of DeLillo's novel.

To look at another example, in a review of the film *Gridlock'd* in *Rolling Stone,* Peter Travers focuses on the career of its star, arguing that Tupac Shakur was a talented actor who got little credit. He briefly synopsizes Shakur's previous movies, all "gritty urban dramas," in which the actor was dismissed as just a rude guy "playing himself." Travers then argues:

> Never mind that Shakur began acting at age 13 (onstage in *A Raisin in the Sun*), that he received training in his craft at the Baltimore School for the Arts and that he could be astonishingly inventive at characterization. Most audiences thought his films were documentaries. (53)

He supports his claim by citing specifics from Shakur's other films.

> It's revision time. A closer look at Shakur onscreen reveals an actor of subtlety and substance. In Ernest Dickerson's *Juice* he went gonzo with a handgun, but not before he tried to mend some dangerously frayed ties. His first line in *Juice* is "Good morning, grandma." . . . In John Singleton's flawed but ambitious *Poetic Justice,* he delivers mail . . . to earn enough money to rescue his daughter from her freebasing mother. What people remember is the way he dissed Janet Jackson as a "crazy black feminist bitch." It's the stereotypes that stick. (53–54)

Then he focuses on the film under review, describing the actor's achievements.

> *Gridlock'd* encourages fresh thinking. . . . Though *Gridlock'd* is fiercely funny and sometimes just as fiercely violent, [director Vondie] Curtis-Hall permits Shakur to play a grownup instead of a boy in the hood. . . . The sly team of Shakur and [Tim] Roth give the material a sharp comic edge even when they're on the clichéd run from drug dealers and cops. (54)

Quite obviously, these reviewers know their subjects and have not come cold to the task of evaluating a work of art. And, obviously, a review can reveal a lot about the reviewer as well as about the reviewed.

Here are some general tips for writing a review:

- Do give appropriate (appropriate to the audience and to the work) background about the artist or art style, about the artist's previous works, or about the particular item under review.
- Don't dwell on the background. Keep it in balance.

- Don't give a plot outline, retell the story, or describe the lyrics blow by blow.
- Imply or state outright the standards you look for in such works.
- Don't gush, unless you can supply examples for each raving comment.
- Don't trash, unless you can cite specific items of garbage.
- Supply specific examples of each important characteristic you mention.
- Don't give your emotional reactions, but instead present your specific and insightful analysis of the work.

■ *Activity 8*

Understanding
Reviews, p. 245

Activities

1   Recognizing Values

Below is a list of eight commonly held values. Take ten minutes to brainstorm other examples of values, not necessarily your own, in order to expand the list by twenty or more items.

achievement	newness
comfort	popularity
flexibility	privacy
independence	unity

2   Values and Opinions

Examine each claim below to decide whether it sparks your approval or disapproval. Then make some notes about which of your values the claim has tapped.

1. Because discrimination and inequality are still widespread, affirmative action must continue.

2. A young man from Chester, Pennsylvania, robs a store and wounds the owner. Sentence: five to ten years. A young woman from England slams a baby in the head so hard it enters a coma and dies after five days. Sentence: nine months of time served. These are only two examples of our racist and class-biased justice system at work.

3. Presidents should be required to tape all meetings, phone conversations, informal consultations, and so on both in the interests of history and to make sure the business of government is performed ethically and honestly.

4. Even if some countries refuse to sign it, the international ban on land mines is a step forward for humanity.

5. Forcing children to recite the Pledge of Allegiance is a violation of their right to privacy.

6. Prostitution should be legalized.

3   Recognizing Your Own Values

Brainstorm a list of your own values. Decide what your main, general, overriding values are, those you apply every moment of your waking life, and write them down at the top of the page. Then make a heading for each context or situation of your life: your being at college, at work, at home, at a social gathering, in a store as a shopper, and so on. For each situation you are commonly in, write down what values affect your behavior and reactions. If you have trouble thinking of what your values might be, try imagining the qualities you'd like to instill in your children. Remember that values may be explained, accounted for, or defended in any number of ways; this chart asks you only to list values, not defend them.

4   Your Personal Needs Chart

List Maslow's needs down a page and then write for yourself how each of these needs is currently being met or not being met in your life. Where do you place yourself on the needs chart?

5   Maslow's Needs in Ad Pitches

Look through magazines or watch television to collect examples of ads that pitch to a need of a specific audience. (Photocopy ads in library magazines; tear out ads from friends' copies with their permission; jot down a description of ads on television.) Work with classmates to make a chart of the needs hierarchy and five or six different ads aimed at each need level.

6   Discovering Rationalizations

Listen hard over the next few days, and keep a list of rationalizations and clichés that you hear people using to assert their values or defend their behavior. Bring in your list for discussion.

7   Exploring Assumptions

Examine the reasoning expressed in the statements below. For each, try to determine the assumptions that allow the stated conclusion to be drawn. Then, decide whether you feel that assumption warrants the conclusion. Finally, diagram the statements according to Toulmin format.

1. I see that girl walking three dogs in the park every day. She must really love dogs.
2. The president held three press conferences this summer. I guess his popularity is increasing.
3. More and more people seem to be fishing from Cauman Bridge every time I pass it. It must be a good fishing spot.
4. The Food and Drug Administration forced a recall of twenty-five million pounds of beef. The FDA is sure doing a good job of watching out for the health of Americans.
5. Seven men were arrested on charges of conspiring to kill an organized crime kingpin so they could take over his illegal drug business. It's a crime that our government is letting these mob activities go on, only stepping in when murder is threatened.

8   Understanding Reviews

A. Read this excerpt from Geoffrey O'Brien's "The Ghost at the Feast," an extended review and commentary on film versions of Shakespeare's plays for the *New York Review of Books*, February 6, 1997. What is O'Brien looking for in a good film of a Shakespeare play, and where does he indicate what his evaluative standards are? Do you feel he is explicit about his standards? What assumptions does he make about films based on Shakespeare? How does the particular film he mentions measure up?

If Shakespeare movies are to be worth making at all, they can hardly duck the language. It isn't simply that the language cannot be handled gingerly or parceled out in acceptably telegraphic excerpts; the words must be entered, explored, reveled in. Syntax must be part of screen space. . . .

Disregard this problem of language and the upshot can be something like Baz Luhrmann's high-speed, high-concept "William Shakespeare's Romeo and Juliet." There is no real reason why Luhrmann's updating could not have worked; the whole mix, complete with automatic weapons, hip-hop cadences, religious kitsch, and teen sex, could have added up to the kaleidoscopic excitement obviously intended. As it is, the compulsive cleverness of the postmodernization—Friar Lawrence sending his message to Romeo by Federal Express, members of the Capulet and Montague gangs sporting CAP and MON license plates—keeps undercutting the teen pathos to the point of parodying it. . . .

It's the skittish handling of the language, though, that reduces Luhrmann's film to little more than a stunt. While he gets a bit of mileage from the accidental intersection of Elizabethan with contemporary usage (as when his gang members call each other "coz" or "man") any speech longer than a few lines just gets in the way, and the effect all too often is of sitting in on the tryouts at a high school drama club. The Shakespearean text begins to seem like an embarrassment that everybody is trying to avoid facing up to; . . . There are many ways to get Shakespeare's language across, but trying to slip it past the audience as if it might pass for something else isn't one of them.

B. Examine this excerpt from Marina Budhos's review of *The Color of Water: A Black Man's Tribute to His White Mother* by James McBride. What do we learn from this passage about Budhos's standards and expectations for a memoir?

Told with humor and clear-eyed grace, McBride's memoir is not only a terrific story, it's a subtle contribution to the current debates on race and identity. . . . Recent memoirs by black and ethnic authors have expressed two impulses: to tell of the journey of the assimilated self, and to pay homage to one's roots. What McBride offers is a moving example of how the self is formed by a subtle combination of these influences. It's that subtlety of consciousness that makes him so alert to the complexities of race that permeate our everyday lives. (33)

Budhos begins and ends her review with references to her own childhood. Why might she have decided that this overt commentary on her life was appropriate to this review?

James McBride grew up about a mile from where I did, in Queens, a borough of racially and ethnically separate communities. In the sixties, those of us who came from mixed families felt the racial fault lines start to crack. . . .

Reading this book I recalled my own West Indian dad trying to teach algebra at a St. Albans high school to students who wanted to join the revolution. . . . Not far away, an extraordinary woman was bravely raising her family as she knew best. I laughed and thrilled to her brood of twelve kids, whooping it up during times that confused us all. I wish I'd known them. I'm glad James McBride wrote it all down so I can. (33)

Assignments

1. Choose an essay from this text, and write a personal reaction piece in about three hundred words. Point to specific statements or ideas in the essay that create your reaction. Then analyze your reaction to show the underlying values that prompted your reaction. Name those values, trace their origins, and indicate whether you rationally support the value or whether it resides in you as a result of tradition, parental or peer influence, or for some other reason.

2. Over a period of several days, read the newspaper and listen to news programs. Make a list of news items that tie in or relate to experiences you have had. Then choose one topic and free-write to express your opinions and values about the issue. Use your own experiences and specifics drawn from your life or the lives of those you know to back up your point of view.

3. With your instructor's guidance choose a new film, book, television show, art show, dance, theater or other performance, or recording of music as the subject for a review. Before you see, listen, or read, make a list of your artistic standards relating to your choice. What qualities do you value in works of the type you are reviewing? Then, with notepad in hand, focus on the work you are reviewing. Consider seeing, reading, or listening to the work more than once so that you can become an expert on it. Using your notes and your list of valued artistic qualities, free-write to evaluate the item. Then revise and polish your writing to produce a final draft of your review.

■ WORKS CITED

Belenky, Mary Field, Blythe McVicker Clinchy, Nancy Rule Goldberger, and Jill Matuck Tarule. *Women's Ways of Knowing: The Development of Self, Voice, and Mind.* New York: Basic, 1986.

Bellah, Robert, N., Richard Madsen, William M. Sullivan, Ann Swidler, and Stephen M. Tipton. *Habits of the Heart: Individualism and Commitment in American Life.* New York: Harper, 1985.

Bruni, Frank. "A Cult's Two-Decade Odyssey of Regimentation." *New York Times,* 29 Mar. 1997, 1, 8.

Gilligan, Carol. *In a Different Voice: Psychological Theory and Women's Development.* Cambridge: Harvard UP, 1982.

Leary, Mike. "How to Get Your Opinions in Print." *Philadelphia Inquirer,* 7 Apr. 1996, E5.

Maslow, Abraham H. *Towards a Psychology of Being.* New York: Van Nostrand, 1968.

"Norm." *American Heritage Dictionary.* 3rd ed. 1996.

Readings

Turning Youth Gangs Around

LUIS J. RODRIGUEZ

Luis J. Rodriguez is director of Tia Chucha Press in Chicago and author of
Always Running: La Vida Loca, Gang Days in L. A., about his own youth.
This article appeared in the *Nation* on November 21, 1994. (Copyright
1994 by the Nation. Reprinted by permission.)

Pedro* is a thoughtful, articulate and charismatic young man; he listens, absorbs and 1
responds. His movements are quick, well-developed during his years surviving in the streets
of Chicago. Pedro is a 20-year-old gang leader. For most of his life, he has lived off and on
between his welfare mother and an uncle. He has been kicked out of schools and has served
time in youth detention facilities. He is also a great human being.

For four months in 1993, the courts designated me as his guardian under a house ar- 2
rest sentence. He was respectful and polite. He meticulously answered all my messages. He
was loved by my 6-year-old son. His best friend happens to be my 19-year-old son Ramiro.

During his stay, I gave Pedro books, including political books to help him become more 3
cognizant of the world. One of these was *Palante,* a photo-text about the Young Lords Party
of the 1970s. Pedro, whose family is from Puerto Rico, began to open up to an important
slice of history that, until then, he'd never known about. Pedro read *Palante* from cover to
cover—as he did other books, for the first time ever.

When Pedro was released from house arrest, he moved out of the neighborhood with 4
his girlfriend and her small boy. He found a job. He remained leader of the gang, but was now
talking about struggle, about social change, about going somewhere.

Last November, Pedro was shot three times with a .44. He was hit in his back, leg and 5
hand. Ramiro and I visited him at the Cook County Hospital. He lived, but he was not the same
after that. One day during Pedro's hospital stay, the same gang that had shot him ambushed
and killed Angel, a friend of Ramiro and Pedro. Angel, an honor student at one of the best
schools in the city, was on his way to school; a news account the next day failed to mention
this, reporting only that he was a suspected gang member, as if this fact justified his death.

I tried to persuade Pedro to get his boys to chill. I knew that Ramiro and the others were 6
all sitting ducks. Pedro went through some internal turmoil, but he decided to forbid retali-
ation. This was hard for him, but he did it.

Unfortunately, the story doesn't end there. Earlier this year, Pedro allegedly shot and 7
killed one of the guys believed to be behind Angel's murder and his own shooting. Pedro is
now a fugitive.

I tell you this to convey the complexity of working with youths like Pedro, youths most 8
people would rather write off, but who are also intelligent, creative and even quite decent.
The tragedy is that it is mostly young people like these who are being killed and who are
doing the killing. I've seen them in youth prisons, hospitals and courts throughout the land:

*Some of the names in this article were changed.

young people who in other circumstances might have been college graduates, officeholders or social activists. Unfortunately, many find themselves in situations they feel unable to pull out of until it's too late.

9   I've long recognized that most youths like Pedro aren't in gangs to be criminals, killers or prison inmates. For many, a gang embraces who they are, gives them the initiatory community they seek and the incipient authority they need to eventually control their own lives. These are things other institutions, including schools and families, often fail to provide. Yet without the proper guidance, support and means to contribute positively to society, gang involvement can be disastrous.

10   This August, a media storm was created when 11-year-old Robert Sandifer of Chicago, known as "Yummy" because he liked to eat cookies, allegedly shot into a crowd and killed a 14-year-old girl. A suspected member of a Southside gang, Yummy disappeared; days later he was found shot in the head. Two teenage members of Yummy's gang are being held in his death. Hours before his murder, a neighbor saw Yummy, who told her, "Say a prayer for me."

11   This is a tragedy, but without a clear understanding of the social, economic and psychological dynamics that would drive an 11-year-old to kill, we can only throw up our hands. Yet it isn't hard to figure out the motive forces behind much of this violence.

12   Sandifer, for example, was a child of the Reagan years, of substantial cuts in community programs, of the worst job loss since the Great Depression, of more police and prisons and of fewer options for recreation, education or work. Here was a boy who had been physically abused, shuttled from one foster home to another, one juvenile justice facility after another. At every stage of Robert's young life since birth, he was blocked from becoming all he could be. But there was nothing to stop him from getting a gun. From using it. And from dying from one.

13   No "three strikes, you're out," no trying children as adults, no increased prison spending will address what has created the Pedros and Yummys of this world. Such proposals deal only with the end results of a process that will continue to produce its own fuel, like a giant breeder reactor. This is not a solution.

14   Gangs are not new in America. The first gangs in the early 1800s were made up of Irish immigrant youths. They lived as second-class citizens. Their parents worked in the lowest-paid, most menial jobs. These youths organized to protect themselves within a society that had no place for them. Other immigrants followed identical patterns. Today the majority of gang members are African-American and Latino, and they face the same general predicaments those early immigrants did. But today something deeper is also happening. Within the present class relations of modern technology-driven capitalism, many youths, urban and rural, are being denied the chance to earn a "legitimate" living. An increasing number are white, mostly sons and daughters of coal miners, factory workers or farmers.

15   Los Angeles, which has more gang violence than any other city, experienced the greatest incidence of gang-related acts during the 1980s and early 1990s, when 300,000 manufacturing jobs were lost in California. According to the Gang Violence Bridging Project of the Edmund G. "Pat" Brown Institute of Public Affairs at California State University, Los Angeles, the areas with the greatest impoverishment and gang growth were those directly linked to industrial flight.

16   At the same time, the state of California suffered deep cuts in social programs—most of them coming as a result of the passage in 1978 of Proposition 13, which decreased state funding for schools after a slash in property taxes. Since 1980, while California's population has jumped by 35 percent, spending for education has steadily declined. Yet there has been

a 14 percent annual increase in state prison spending during the past decade; the state legislature has allocated $21 billion over the next ten years to build twenty new prisons.

Almost all areas in the United States where manufacturing has died or moved away are now reporting ganglike activity. There are seventy-two large cities and thirty-eight smaller ones that claim to have a "gang problem," according to a 1992 survey of police departments by the National Institute of Justice. Chicago, also hard hit by industrial flight, has many large multigenerational gangs like those in L.A.   17

What has been the official response? In Chicago "mob action" arrests have been stepped up (when three or more young people gather in certain proscribed areas, it is considered "mob action"), as have police sweeps of housing projects and "gang infested" communities. Recently there have been calls to deploy the National Guard against gangs, which is like bringing in a larger gang with more firepower against the local ones. This, too, is not a solution.   18

I agree that the situation is intolerable. I believe most people—from the Chicago-based Mothers Against Gangs to teachers who are forced to be police officers in their classrooms to people in the community caught in the crossfire—are scared. They are bone-tired of the violence. They are seeking ways out. First we must recognize that our battle is with a society that fails to do all it can for young people—then lays the blame on them.   19

It's time the voices for viable and lasting solutions be heard. The public debate is now limited to those who demonize youth, want to put them away, and use repression to curb their natural instincts to re-create the world.   20

I have other proposals. First, that we realign societal resources in accordance with the following premises: that every child has value and every child can succeed. That schools teach by engaging the intelligence and creativity of all students. That institutions of public maintenance—whether police or social services—respect the basic humanity of all people. That we rapidly and thoroughly integrate young people into the future, into the new technology. And finally, that we root out the basis for the injustice and inequities that engender most of the violence we see today.   21

Sound farfetched? Too idealistic? Fine. But anything short on imagination will result in "pragmatic," fear-driven, expediency-oriented measures that won't solve anything but will only play with people's lives.   22

Actually, the structural/economic foundation for such proposals as I've roughly outlined is already laid. The computer chip has brought about revolutionary shifts in the social order. The only thing that isn't in place is the non-exploitative, non-oppressive relations between people required to complete this transition.   23

I know what some people are thinking. What about being tough on crime? Let me be clear: I hate crime. I hate drugs. I hate children murdering children. But I know from experience that it doesn't take guts to put money into inhumane, punishment-driven institutions. In fact, such policies make our communities even less safe. It's tougher to walk these streets, to listen to young people, to respect them and help fight for their well-being. It's tougher to care.   24

For the past two years, I've talked to young people, parents, teachers and concerned officials in cities as far-flung as Hartford, Brooklyn, Phoenix, Seattle, Lansing, Denver, Boston, El Paso, Washington, Oakland, San Antonio and Compton. I've seen them grope with similar crises, similar pains, similar confusions.   25

Sometimes I feel the immensity of what we're facing—talking to Teens on Target in Los Angeles, a group made up of youths who have been shot, some in wheelchairs; or to teenage   26 mothers in Tucson, one child caring for another; or to incarcerated young men at the maximum security Illinois Youth Center at Joliet. I felt it when a couple of young women cried in Holyoke, Massachusetts, after I read a poem about a friend who had been murdered by the police, and when I addressed a gym full of students at Jefferson High School in Fort Worth and several young people lined up to hug me, as if they had never been hugged before.

27   Because I have to deal with people like Yummy and Pedro every day, I decided this summer to do something more than just talk. With the help of Patricia Zamora from the Casa Aztlán Community Center in Chicago's Mexican community of Pilsen, I worked with a core of young people, gang and nongang, toward finding their own solutions, their own organizations, their own empowerment.

28   In the backyard of my Chicago home, some thirty people, mostly from the predominantly Puerto Rican area of Humboldt Park (my son's friends, and Pedro's homeys) and Pilsen, were present. They agreed to reach out to other youths and hold retreats, weekly meetings and a major conference. All summer they worked, without money, without resources, but with a lot of enthusiasm and energy. They hooked up with the National Organizing Committee, founded in 1993 by revolutionary fighters including gang members, welfare recipients, trade unionists, teachers and parents from throughout the United States. The N.O.C. offered them technical and educational assistance.

29   The young people's efforts culminated in the Youth '94 Struggling for Survival Conference, held in August at the University of Illinois, Chicago. More than a hundred young people from the city and surrounding communities attended. They held workshops on police brutality, jobs and education, and peace in the neighborhoods. A few gang members set aside deadly rivalries to attend this gathering.

30   Although there were a number of mishaps, including a power failure, the youths voted to keep meeting. They held their workshops in the dark, raising issues, voicing concerns, coming up with ideas. I was the only adult they let address their meeting. The others, including parents, teachers, counselors, resource people and a video crew from the Center for New Television, were there to help with what the young people had organized.

31   Then the building personnel told us we had to leave because it was unsafe to be in a building without power. We got Casa Aztlán to agree to let us move to several of their rooms to continue the workshops; I felt we would probably lose about half the young people in the fifteen-minute ride between sites. Not only did we hang on to most of the youths, we picked up a few more along the way. In a flooded basement with crumbling walls in Casa Aztlán we held the final plenary session. The youths set up a roundtable, at which it was agreed that only proposed solutions would be entertained. A few read poetry. It was a success, but then the young people wouldn't let it be anything else.

32   Youth Struggling for Survival is but one example of young people tackling the issues head-on. There are hundreds more across America. In the weeks before the November 8 elections in California, thousands of junior high and high school students, mostly Latino, walked out of schools in the Los Angeles area. Their target: Proposition 187, intended to deny undocumented immigrants access to education, social services and non-emergency health care.

33   These young people need guidance and support; they don't need adults to tell them what to do and how to do it; to corral, crush or dissuade their efforts. We must reverse their sense of helplessness. The first step is to invest them with more authority to run their own lives, their communities, even their schools. The aim is to help them stop being instruments of their own death and to choose a revolutionary service to life.

We don't need a country in which the National Guard walks our children to school,   34
or pizza-delivery people carry sidearms, or prisons outnumber colleges. We can be more
enlightened. More inclusive. More imaginative.

And, I'm convinced, this is how we can be more safe.   35

Questions for Inquiry

1. What is Rodriguez's claim? Is it explicit or implied?
2. Why does Rodriguez single out Pedro as an example with which to begin the essay?
    What effect does this introduction have on the reader?
3. What characteristics do the gang members that Rodriguez discusses possess? What
    causes them to join a gang? Why have there always been gangs in the United States?
4. What is the remedy for youth gangs, according to the author? What kinds of things will
    not work?

Questions for Argument

1. Rodriguez's list of how society should "realign" its priorities is, he admits, "idealistic"
    (21–22)? But is it "too idealistic," or can we bring about the changes he suggests?
    Should we?
2. Rodriguez is emphatic that getting tough on crime is the wrong approach (22). What
    are his reasons? Do you agree that punishment is counterproductive?

Writing Assignments

Informal

1. Reread the passages about Pedro and "Yummy" Sandifer and write your responses in a
    journal entry.
2. "We can be more enlightened. More inclusive. More imaginative," Rodriguez writes
    (34). Free-write about ways you feel we could be more enlightened, inclusive, and
    imaginative in our solution to some human or societal problem.

Formal

3. **Collaboration.** Rodriguez speaks about youths' "natural instincts to re-create the
    world" (20). Meet with several students in your class to discuss or brainstorm individ-
    ually ways in which you would like to "re-create the world." Focus on one significant
    way, and then, as a group or individually, develop a paper that explains the need for this
    change and proposes how the change might be made.
4. Society "fails to do all it can for young people," the author writes (19). Brainstorm a list
    of ways you feel society either does or does not do all it can or all it should for young
    people. Consider what your values are on this issue. Then write a paper to be delivered
    to a group of adults and parents in which you discuss what society's role should be in
    helping young people and in which you strive to engender the appropriate values in
    your audience.

■ ■ ■

Another Kind of Sex Ed

SHARON A. SHEEHAN

Sharon A. Sheehan is a writer who lives in California. This essay appeared in *Newsweek* as a "My Turn" column in 1992. (Copyright 1992
by Newsweek, Inc. All rights reserved. Reprinted by permission.)

1   Our local newspaper ran an essay recently by the president of the Youth Council. It explained its vote favoring condom machines in high schools. He said that students should be
able to get the prophylactics in the school bathroom because they fear personal embarrassment at the checkout counter of the local drugstore.

2   Could it be that many teenagers would rather take their chances with AIDS than run
the risk of embarrassment? And what about the risk of pregnancy?

3   Family-planning workers have observed that many teenage girls cannot bring themselves to march into a clinic and declare that they are planning to lose their virginity. It's too
embarrassing. Running the risk of pregnancy is preferable.

4   After earning a graduate degree in public health, I was employed by the State of California to help solve the problem of teenage pregnancy by educating teenagers about birth
control. The fundamental origin of the problem—the premarital sexual activity of
teenagers—was accepted as a given. The Planned Parenthood professional assigned to train
me pointed out that the real solution to this problem was to eradicate the sense of shame associated with premarital sex.

5   I was stunned. But the logic was obvious: teenage pregnancy is a problem. Birth control is the solution. Shame is the barrier to applying the solution. Therefore eliminate shame
in order to solve the problem. But taking a young person's sense of modesty and giving back
a pill or a condom wasn't what anyone would call a fair trade.

6   Nonetheless, for the next several months I proceeded to talk to hundreds of teenagers
about various methods of birth control. But I was never convinced that I was genuinely helping them.

Cruel Shame

7   Professionally, I succumbed to the obligatory gag rule: don't say anything that could
arouse the sense of shame. In practice, then, I was compelled to imply that all sexual choices
were morally neutral. Thus everything that I had learned from my parents' marriage and my
own marriage was off-limits. Everything I believed about how human beings form meaningful and lasting relationships was not only irrelevant but counterproductive.

8   The new sexual ideology protected teenagers from shame by saying, "If you feel like you
are ready, then it's OK." Ready for what? Ready to build a life together? Ready for conquest?
Ready to feel like a slut? Ready to bring a new life into the world? Shame is a powerful word
that explodes in many directions. There is a cruel, destructive side to shame. Controlling people by shaming them into self-loathing or compliance, for example. But shame also protects
us. It prevents us from treating others in a despicable fashion. And it protects "the sanctity
of our unfinished or unready selves."

9   In his book, "The Meaning of Persons," Paul Tournier reflects on a young person's innate sense of modesty: "The appearance of this sense of shame is, in fact, the sign of the

birth of a person. And later the supreme affirmation of the person, the great engagement of life, will be marked by the handing over of the secret, the gift of the self, the disappearance of shame."

Recently, I returned to the high-school campus to talk with students about how they see themselves and what they hope for. Many were offended by the adult assumption that most teens are sexually active. One girl was so uncomfortable that she went to her teacher in Living Skills class to explain that she was not sleeping with her boyfriend. "It's like the adult world invading our world," another girl commented.   10

Yet they are embarrassed to ask the questions they care about most. "What should I look for in a guy?" "How do I know if it's morally right?" "How will I feel afterward?"   11

Behind their "correct," value-free façade lurks a deep sense of lose. They lament the lack of guidelines and moral structure. One girl described it this way: "It used to be that people got married and then they had sex. Then when the baby came there was a place all prepared for it. Now technology has taken away the worry of having children. That leaves sex to float around in everyone's life when there's no guy who's going to stick around."   12

"It used to be that kids wouldn't want to disappoint themselves or each other," a boy remarked. "I think it's really lonely," said another. "It's sad."   13

It's as if the gap between sex and marriage had opened up a huge empty hole in which there were "no real sure thing." A loving relationship that lasts. Hasn't that always been the goal and bottom line? Isn't the real C word for sex education commitment, not condoms?   14

It's time to give the thousands of couples in this country who have been happily married 20, 30, 40, 50 years equal access to sex-education classrooms. One boy told me, "I'd like to hear more stories . . . how they met . . . how they kept the love alive." If you have built a marriage and family the "old-fashioned" way, go to a classroom and tell your story. Share the wisdom gained by keeping the promises of your youth. Let them ask the questions they care about the most.   15

In coming face to face with other human beings, how much do we value the self that we glimpse through their eyes, that flutters past in a gesture or a smile? Sex education is about nothing less than how and when we hand over this astonishing gift of the self. The goal is that we can love and trust and believe enough to commit our whole self and our whole future.   16

Questions for Inquiry

1. Why does Sheehan argue that shame is both a positive and a negative feeling? Examine the reasons she offers for this claim.
2. Sheehan reports feeling that the logic of the sex-ed professional who trained her was "obvious" (5), yet she argues against the birth-control-for-teenagers position. What evidence does she supply to oppose this "logic"?
3. What aspects of the essay's tone and of Sheehan's self-presentation lend her credibility in the reader's eyes? Are there places where she takes advantage of this credibility to slant the evidence or language toward her argument?

Questions for Argument

1. Sheehan indicates that, to her mind, readiness for sex means either readiness for marriage and family ("Ready to build a life together? . . . Ready to bring a new life into the world?") or readiness for exploitive premarital sex ("Ready for conquest? Ready to feel

like a slut?" (8)). Do you agree that teen sex—or any sex—has to be one or the other of these types?

2. Sheehan writes that "shame . . . protects us" (8). Would the world be a better place if there were more shame (of all kinds)? Or should there be less?

3. The many quotations from students in paragraphs 10–13 suggest young people are confused and despairing about relationships. Does this correspond to your sense of the younger generation's outlook? Are most young people in need of or open to the "wisdom" of those who have lived life the "old-fashioned" way (15)?

Writing Assignments

Informal

1. Examine the quotation from Paul Tournier in paragraph 9, and, in your journal, write your reactions to his poetic connection of shame to a person's essential humanity.

2. Write about whether you think it is beneficial for schools to offer sex education or some other course in personal ethics, health, or sexuality. Refer to your own experiences with such courses in high school or in other contexts.

Formal

3. Sheehan writes that the important "C word" is commitment, not condom (14). Look through her essay to determine what she seems to mean by "commitment," and then think about the relationships you and your friends have had. On the basis of your and your friends' experiences, write an essay in which you discuss your definition of commitment and explain what levels of commitment you think high school and college-age young people are ready for. Use specifics to back up your points.

4. **Research.** The focus of Sheehan's essay is values and the behaviors that result from them; the author makes no reference to the success or failure of programs designed to encourage birth control and discourage out-of-wedlock births. Search in the library or on the Internet to find out about the effectiveness of programs such as the one Sheehan worked in. Then write an essay in which you take a stand on whether the effectiveness and availability of birth control or values should determine the content of classes about sexuality.

■ ■ ■

In a War, All Should Suffer

WILLIAM D. EHRHART

William D. Ehrhart won numerous medals including the Purple Heart in the war in Vietnam. He wrote this op-ed piece for the *Philadelphia Inquirer* on February 10, 1991 during the Persian Gulf War. (Reprinted by permission of the author.)

1   While the New York Giants and the Buffalo Bills battled it out in a close and hard-fought game in Super Bowl XXV, our brave men and women in the Middle East were waging a real battle. But our troops were never far from our thoughts, right? The players had U.S. flag de-

cals on their helmets. The halftime show was a rousing patriotic extravaganza of children and music and red, white and blue. Television viewers were even treated to videotape of U.S. soldiers enthusiastically watching the game in Saudi Arabia.

But it seems to me that, for all our heartfelt thoughts and gestures of support for the troops, this war isn't really costing most of us very much. We got to see our football game. We'll all get up tomorrow and go to work or school or whatever. We'll talk about what we did over the weekend, and maybe talk a bit in quiet tones about the latest news from the war zone, and then we'll go home and do it all again the next day. And the day after that.   2

Aren't we supposed to be at war? Don't 87 percent of the American people support this war? Talk's cheap. It's easy to support a war that doesn't cost you anything. It's easy to tie a yellow ribbon to the front lamppost and say you are behind the troops all the way. But if this is war, we ought to behave as if it is. All of us should be making sacrifices. I have a few suggestions.   3

- Cancel all sporting events for the duration of the war. In spite of the stirring halftime footage, most of our troops in the Persian Gulf didn't get to watch the Super Bowl. We shouldn't have either. In fact, we should cancel all television programming except news. Every time we turn on the TV, we'll be reminded of the sacrifices our brave young men and women are making for us. Life should not be comfortable in wartime.
- Shut down all colleges and universities for the duration or the war. What good are future literature majors and chemists and doctors if we lose this war to a man our own President has described as worse than Hitler? Moreover, all otherwise eligible students from schools of higher learning should be drafted into the military. Why should only those too disadvantaged or too poor to go to college bear the entire responsibility for defending all of us? And besides, if a half-million soldiers are sufficient to defeat the Iraqi army, surely 2.5 million soldiers would virtually overwhelm them.
- Outlaw all nonessential travel for the duration of the war. Our brave men and women in the Middle East can't hop in the car and drive over to the Smiths to play bridge or take a ride to the Poconos to go skiing. Why should we? Essential travel should be regulated through a voucher system and it should be enforced by military police officers. Our troops are dying for the oil we need. We ought to be willing to need less of it.
- Shut down all nonessential industries and businesses for the duration of the war. We don't need party hats and video games and bubblegum during wartime. People need jobs, of course, but we're going to need a lot of military police officers to enforce travel restrictions.
- Reduce all Americans' pay to the level of the military pay scale for the duration of the war. Chief executive officers, for instance, could be given generals' pay. Supervisors would get sergeants' pay. New employees would receive privates' pay.

What we would have received in excess of our new military pay could be donated to the federal government to eliminate the national debt. What better way to show our support for the troops than to unmortgage their futures even as they fight and die to defend ours?   4

Maybe you think I'm kidding about all of this, but I'm not. Super Bowl I was played while I was fighting in Vietnam. I was lonely and frightened, living like an animal. I doubt that the patriotic halftime show would have made me feel any better about it. But I didn't see the halftime show. I didn't see the game. You could have tied up all of Manhattan Island with a huge yellow ribbon, and I wouldn't have cared. I just wanted to come home fast and in one piece. War is a miserable place to grow up.   5

6   We have been told by our government that the only way to peace in the Middle East is through this war. OK, let's go to war then. All of us. Every last one of us. Let's start making some sacrifices around here. If we all pitch in, we might end this war that much sooner. If the rest of us have to pay even a fraction of the price being paid by the young men and women of our armed forces, the war might be over by tomorrow.

Questions for Inquiry

1. What is Ehrhart's claim? Is it explicit or implied? What value assumptions underlie his claim?
2. Through most of the essay, Ehrhart speaks of "we" and "our." Why does he turn and address the reader at the start of paragraph 5: "Maybe you think I'm kidding . . . "? What effect does this have on the reader?
3. Ehrhart uses mottolike pronouncements: the cliché "talk's cheap" (3); a variation on the familiar axiom "war is hell"—"war is a miserable place to grow up" (5); and some maxims of his own creation: "If this is war, we ought to behave as if it is" (3). "Life should not be comfortable in wartime" (3). "Our troops are dying for the oil we need. We ought to be willing to need less of it" (3). "We have been told by our government that the only way to peace . . . is through this war" (6). What assumptions must you make to accept these statements? What values do these ideas call into play?

Questions for Argument

1. Do you agree that sacrifices are a better way to show support for a war abroad than some of the other things mentioned, such as tying a yellow ribbon outdoors or displaying a flag decal?
2. Ehrhart touches on a question of policy that played a large role in the protests against the Vietnam War: the draft. He proposes reinstituting it so that the army would include students in addition to disadvantaged young people who enlist because of a lack of other opportunities (3). Do you think he has a point? In times of crisis, should our country be defended by people from all walks of life or just by those whose life circumstances lead them to join the military? Is a draft or mandatory military-service requirement a good idea?

Writing Assignments

Informal

1. Few of us talk much these days about sacrifice. Do you think there is any inherent value in making sacrifices? For example, does sacrificing improve a person in some way? Write about your beliefs about sacrifice in a journal entry.
2. Re-read Ehrhart's suggestions for life during wartime and imagine living under these restrictions. Write an informal paper in which you describe how different your and your family's life would be if these suggestions became reality.

Formal

3. **Collaborative Writing.** During this 1991 war, the author wanted our country to turn into a unified, focused, and purposive community. Would our country benefit if we

could act more as a community in dealing with some of the other problems that beset us nationally and locally? Brainstorm with others to identify some current issues class members feel cry out for unified and deliberate action. Then join with one or two other people with views similar to yours to generate evidence and an organization plan for an essay that describes our present weak attempts to deal with a problem and that sets out definite recommendations, perhaps requiring some major changes in how we conduct our lives. Then collaborate on writing the essay. You might wish to assign each member to write, revise, and polish different sections, or you might wish to sit together at a computer to write it.

4. **Research and Argumentation.** Use the library and the Internet to find out more about the Persian Gulf War: its causes, its battles, its outcome, and public opinion about it. As Ehrhart notes, this war was an extremely "popular" one, with few critics or protesters in the United States. If this war occurred now, would you protest it or support it? Write an essay in which you take a stand on whether the war was necessary and urge other students to join in activities expressing this point of view.

■ ■ ■

■ TWO OPINION PIECES BY COLLEGE STUDENTS

These two essays were published when the writers were in college. John Veit attended the University of Oregon; his essay appeared in the *Philadelphia Inquirer* in 1993. Karla Vermeulen was a senior at the School of Hotel Administration at Cornell University when her essay was published in the *New York Times* in 1990. (Reprinted by permission of the authors.)

Futures So Bright in White Suburbia

JOHN VEIT

Their futures are so bright they have to wear shades, these nice kids from the suburbs. 1
They're well-off, spoiled and privileged, golden boys and girls, soon to become the cream of university campuses. They've been shepherded to fancy pre-schools, prepped for the SATs since age 10, processed, homogenized and groomed for success.

I know of what I speak—I'm a recent graduate of Radnor High School in the heart of 2
Philadelphia's Main Line. But I know that there are other scenes, too, tough, hard, urban scenes where surviving often beats out college-prep on the list of priorities.

Yet the token charities that bring the young suburban crowd in contact with the city 3
don't give them the full picture. I have seen what most of the members of student government and even Trevor's Campaign do in their moments of freedom. What they do, to use a verb that melts my mind with its grotesqueness, is *party*. Let me take you to one now . . .

Biff and Andy are fighting on the lawn. The winner will swerve home, his SADD key 4
ring clanging. The loser will ride in the back of Molly's GTI, a bloody mess. The fight started over a spilled beer that went on one of the gladiator's legs and on to the couch.

5   Tunes from the 1960s—do lots of dope and have all the sex you can get—play over the sounds of gurgling bongs and giggles. Police are at the door. People scurry into the back yards, back rooms, into expensive cars that are parked down the street. The police joke with Bryan, whose parents are in Sweden enjoying the slopes. They leave, telling him to keep it down.

6   What amazed me while attending a school where 85 percent of the students typically go off to college was how many of these future execs were able to keep their bad habits secret from their parents, the concerned, proper models of suburban parenthood.

7   But what *bothers* me is that the golden boys and girls can get high and drunk dreaming of a bright, shining future; but when inner-city kids do the same, it's often to stop thinking about the bleak prospects awaiting them.

8   What seems even more unfair is that students from poor neighborhoods may have to devote themselves more vehemently to their educations in high school to achieve paltrier results. And their punishment for goofing off is—at best—a job at McDonald's. The suburban goof-off, on the other hand, may be "punished" by having to forgo one of the Ivies for a state university or community college.

9   In a country where wealthy elites control the levers of power, the needs of poorer minority communities will continue to be forgotten as 5 o'clock permits the suburban commuter to flee the city. What these fathers and mothers of suburban youth choose to ignore —and what their sons and daughters may never really understand—is that, without the filthy cities, the laborers who clean up the train stations and so forth, their lives of simplicity could not exist.

10   I have a case to make for both acknowledgment of the disparity and improving opportunities for inner-city kids. It is a case for higher taxes from commuters whose flight helped create the squalor that they now complain about.

11   It is a case for busing pristine little boys and girls from Villanova to West Philadelphia's schools. It is a case for equally distributing educational resources on a statewide basis. And, finally, it is a case for the colleges and universities of America to consider not the advantages an applicant might have enjoyed in high school—but the disadvantages that he or she had to overcome just to learn to even *read*.

Growing Up in the Shadow of AIDS

KARLA VERMEULEN

1   I was 12 years old when AIDS was first identified, and my entire generation came of age under its shadow. It existed during our first kisses, first dates and first relationships, bringing to an end a decade or two of sexual freedom. AIDS put my generation in a position closer to that of our parents than our older siblings and forced us to become responsible for our actions before we really wanted to.

2   Of course, everyone, gay or straight, is in the same situation now. But most people have experienced a time when sex did not mean risk. AIDS changed their behavior; it formed mine.

3   The years between the pill and AIDS were a time of freedom and casual relationships, when pregnancy was not an issue, when most things you could catch from a partner could be fixed with penicillin.

Those days are over, at least among the responsible and informed. So my generation missed out on the entire period of sexual freedom. The idea of casual sex is as inaccessible to me as it was to my mother when she she was my age—but with a difference. It probably never occurred to her, while for me it is a lost possibility.   4

In the 25 years between her youth and mine, the world changed twice. After the pill freed women from the fear of unwanted pregnancy, "free love" and sexual exploration were condoned. The next 15 or 20 years seem to have been a period when women were intent on making up for the experiences they had long been denied by society and biology, and men were happy to oblige them.   5

Promiscuity was socially acceptable, even encouraged. Then along came the plague, and the world has reversed itself again—but with a new twist: men are also at risk. Suddenly, they are as willing to make commitments as women traditionally have been, and monogamy is back in style.   6

I have heard this described as a "return to morality." A return to fear would be more accurate.   7

This is the world my peers and I entered when we became adults. My mother married my father at exactly the point of life I'm at now. My life, however, appears very different from hers, for I have lived with my boyfriend for two years while she moved directly from her parents' house to her husband's.   8

But in a sense I am as restrained as she was. Obviously, moral values have not returned to what they were in my mother's youth, so I don't need to worry about getting a reputation as a "bad girl," as she would have. But the fear of pregnancy no doubt reinforced her decision to commit herself to my father at an early age, just as the fear of AIDS has strengthened my commitment to my boyfriend.   9

I'm sure my mother observed the sexual revolution blossoming around her, and thought I would have opportunities and experiences never available to her.   10

On the contrary, I am even more controlled by sex than she was, since she faced a bad reputation or unwanted pregnancy while I face death. Perhaps it is because of AIDS that my parents accepted my early commitment to my boyfriend. It was better to see me living with someone at 18 than risking my life with multiple partners.   11

I am a member of the first generation to mature under the shadow of AIDS. Perhaps I shouldn't complain about how AIDS has affected my life, having lost few friends to it. But its existence has shaped my life, controlled my behavior and locked me into a situation I might not have been in otherwise.   12

My boyfriend, who is several years older than I, assures me that the promiscuity and wild times were not as exciting or fun as they may appear to have been. Still, he admits he finds it hard to imagine spending his entire life having known only one partner.   13

I do not regret my early commitment to my boyfriend, as my mother did not regret her marriage to my father. But I live with the knowledge that AIDS has cheated my generation of the freedom recently known by men and women.   14

■ ■ ■

Part II

 **. . . to Argument**

Chapter 7

Preparing an Argumentative Position Paper

■ Consider the following passage and respond as indicated below:

> You have noted . . . that when two opponents have been arguing, though the initial difference in their position may have been slight, they tend under the "dialectical pressure" of their drama to become eventually at odds in everything.
>
> —Kenneth Burke, "Semantic and Poetic Meaning"

Writer's Journal

Consider Burke's observation and write informally about what patterns or tendencies you have noted in arguments. You may wish to analyze a specific argument. Strive for an entry of at least 150 words.

Any topical issue in our society is like the subject of a conversation in the Burkean parlor—as you begin your involvement, you realize others are already deep inside the issue. Yet you will not begin with an empty head; rather, from the start you will be full of impressions and perspectives that you have gleaned from the tide of conversations that flow around you in everyday life. This has always been true, but never more than today, in the "information age." The issues we argue about are dialogues ongoing among people, in the media, and in our own heads.

Argumentation is, in one way, an offshoot of inquiry, in that the various ways of exploring sources discussed in Part I can lead to producing a formal position paper on an issue. Argumentation can also be seen to represent a different phase of inquiry, the phase in which ideas are formally presented and tested. In this chapter we will explore the elements of and the process for writing an argumentative position paper, one that

advocates for a position but is not yet full argumentation because it does not specifically address opposition viewpoints.

■ IDENTIFYING AN ISSUE

Although most writing does assert a position—even a poem attempts to convince
you of a certain way of seeing things—argumentation focuses on issues of concern to
a discourse community. Real-world problems intertwine and interact, so that it can be
hard at first to isolate a narrow slice of an issue to investigate. For example, if you
wanted to explore the issue of children's health care in the United States, you might
find yourself examining welfare laws, insurance regulations, parenting styles, single
motherhood, and other aspects of children's lives that pertain to the adequacy of their
health care. Your narrowing of the issue would be affected by the context of your discussion. Writing within the larger discourse community, you might focus on how current health-insurance policy affects the availability of health care for children. In
writing to parents or educators, you might concentrate on the need to educate parents
about some aspects of children's health.

All writing occurs within a discourse context, and how a topic is framed results
from the context. As British philosopher Stephen Toulmin put it:

> Certainly language as we know it consists, not of timeless propositions, but of utterances
> dependent in all sorts of ways on the context or occasion on which they are uttered.
> Statements are made in particular situations, and the interpretation to be put upon them
> is bound up with their relation to these situations: they are in this respect like fireworks,
> signals or Very lights. ("Uses" 180)

Look for a Controversial Subject

Controversy is a relative designation, in that what is controversial varies with the
context—with the discourse community. An exploration of whether the Smithtown Ice
Skating Club should become a nonprofit corporation might be controversial among
members. Outside this discourse community, however, the issue would be trivial. The
larger civic discourse community might, however, be concerned about what types of
institutions our society should designate as nonprofit and, therefore, tax-exempt. Some
states have held referenda on the question of whether to retain the tax-exempt status
of churches and religious institutions, for example.

Explore the Conversations about the Subject

If you are choosing your topic in response to an article or selection of opinions on
a topic, then you have a start in exploring the conversation. Some of your preliminary
reading is taken care of, but you may wish to do some further inquiry.

If you are coming to your topic "cold," you will certainly have to do some preliminary reading and research. You need to make sure your sense of an issue is accurate,

that the facts you may have casually acquired are verifiable, that your impressions are not illusions about the issue but a basis for extended thought.

You may wish to examine your topic in reference works; or you may feel that reading about current events related to your topic in periodicals is more appropriate. (Refer to Chapter 5 for information on the reference section of the library. See Chapter 4 for information on using periodicals.)

Whatever your position is going to be, it is going to fall within the context of the various other positions on the topic. Select a few articles or arguments representing the range of opinions on the topic to use as reference points as you move into developing your own argumentative position. These arguments should focus, for the most part, on one aspect of the topic, and thus they can help you narrow your exploration. They will also give you a jumping-off place for your own statement. For example, a student writing about Internet privacy might identify and focus on several articles about recent technological developments. These article might discuss

- attempts by major web-browser companies to prevent government regulation by adding newly developed privacy functions to their browsers
- proposed legislation to limit online acquisition and use of private information
- technical limitations on any attempt to control the information flow online
- the international perspective
- the concerns of the World Wide Web administrators' group about privacy

Once you have chosen a few representative articles, you may wish to summarize or to take notes on these sources so that you are sure you understand them.

Work within the Context of Your Assignment

Are the readings you are to use assigned? Or are you to discover arguments independently? If you are working independently, can you identify the discourse community within which your argument is vital? Ask yourself other questions about the requirements of your assignment. Are you to use informal documentation, perhaps because the articles you are going to use as reference are also being used by all your classmates? Or does your instructor prefer you to use formal citation? (See Chapter 13 for formal citation.) And make sure you understand the expectations about content. To what extent should the paper deal with the opposing viewpoints or engage in refutation? Are there other specifications about the argument?

Here is an example of an assignment that would answer these questions:

Choose a topic that concerns your campus or campuses nationwide, one that is of personal interest to you and other college students. Locate at least three articles on this issue and use them to prompt your thinking and generate your own informed viewpoint. Then write a position paper in which you present and argue a claim about this issue. Use informal citation to bring in material from your sources that supports your viewpoint and attach copies of your sources to your paper.

■ EXPLORING AND ANALYZING THE ISSUE

Controversial issues are unique, and so it's difficult to prescribe a process for entering the discourse, formulating a position, and drafting a position paper. Nevertheless, as you work on an argumentative topic, in addition to seeking input and information through the use of sources and discussion, you will need to take these three steps (which are described in detail below):

1. Identify any terms that are key, understand their range of meanings, and decide which **definitions** of such terms are fairest or most appropriate for use in your own treatment of the issue.
2. Identify **causes** and **effects** related to your topic. Seeking the solution to a problem may require analysis of causes, for example, or proposing a change may lead you to analyze effects.
3. Establishing your **specific claim.** Although you may enter the argument with a strong sense of what your position is going to be, it is quite likely that working with other positions on the issue will cause your own viewpoint to shift, become focused, or become qualified.

Use Definition to Identify and Examine the Terms of the Argument

At an early point in the analysis of your issue, you should consider the terms of the argument—that is, what key words mean and whether such key words can mean more than one thing. Some arguments ultimately boil down to questions of **definition.** Make sure you identify the abstract or general terms—such as *happiness, liberty, family, rights*—important to the issue. Also notice terms that **evaluate,** such as those used to praise or critique people's behavior or artistic achievements. A writer who criticizes a congressperson for "inconsistent" or "ineffectual" behavior needs to let a reader know what standard is being applied. If a critic uses the term *improvisational* in evaluating a film, she needs to let the reader know exactly what characteristics she is referring to and whether this is a flaw or an ideal.

Some arguments openly concern the way a term or issue is defined. For example, there have been challenges to the way our society defines alcoholism, violence, and drug addiction. Major breakthroughs occurred in the way alcoholism was handled in our society when it was redefined as a medical problem rather than a moral failing.

In some controversies, the choice of words determines the conclusion of the argument. Especially in controversies having to do with abortion and euthanasia, such terms as *life, beginning of life, fetus, brain death, murder, vegetative state* set up a chain of reasoning in which certain conclusions are inevitable.

In any argument, you need to examine the terminology and decide whether issues of definition come into play. You also need to think about your audience and their likely understanding of your topic. If you are writing for a general audience, whose values are mixed and varied, you probably have to define your terms in some depth. If your audience is likely to agree on the way you use your terms, then less definition is necessary. If you were arguing against the regulation of handgun sales before an audience of sportsmen, you would probably not have to do much defining. But if you were presenting an argument for such regulation, you would certainly have to define in depth what you mean by "regulation" and perhaps what you mean by "handgun."

■ *Activity 1*

Recognizing Needed Definitions, p. 287

Fitting Definitions to an Argument

Defining terms is not as easy as it may seem at first. Toulmin wrote that "definitions are like belts. The shorter they are, the more elastic they need to be. A short belt reveals nothing about its wearer: by stretching, it can be made to fit almost anybody. And a short definition, applied to a heterogeneous set of examples, has to be expanded and contracted, qualified, and reinterpreted, before it will fit every case" ("Foresight" 18). Definitions need to fit, and they need to contain enough detail to be useful in the discussion of your issue.

It may surprise you to learn that the dictionary, while helpful, may not supply a complete, useful definition—one that is large enough or complex enough to fit a complicated reality. Dictionaries can prompt our thinking and help us refine our sense of a word, but usually more than a dictionary check is needed to generate a definition for a key term in an argument. In fact, while many of us think of the dictionary as the rule book for word use, in actuality a dictionary provides a guide as to how words have been used. Definitions are not established by a dictionary but instead are compiled—that is, gathered from actual use—for reference. As S. I. Hayakawa put it in his well-known text, *Language in Thought and Action:*

> The writer of a dictionary is a historian, not a lawgiver. . . . We can be guided by the historical record afforded us by the dictionary, but we cannot be bound by it, because new situations, new experiences, new inventions, new feelings, are always compelling us to give new uses to old words. . . . Looking under a "hood," we should ordinarily have found, five hundred years ago, a monk; today we find a motorcar engine. (55–56)

The ways a word has been used within the context of an ongoing controversy will contribute to how you use the word as much as any dictionary definition will. So, while the dictionary may be a starting place, it has limitations. First, many words have more than one definition listed in the dictionary. Second, dictionary definitions are often too specific or too general for clarifying how a term is used in a controversy. If you do consult a dictionary, make sure it is a standard one.

Actually, most key terms in argument are ones that your readers know and that are in common use. What is needed is a definition that relates the meaning more completely to the issue than the dictionary can and specifies the values, positive or negative, that are implied by the word.

You have the freedom to define a term in a way that works in your argument. However, readers expect definitions to be congruent with actual usage in the discourse community. So, when Nicholas von Hoffman (in a reading selection at the end of

Chapter 9) defines abortion as a way of safeguarding society from the next generation of muggers and rapists, many readers are outraged. This is not the perspective they normally take regarding the word *abortion*. Unless, like von Hoffman, you want to raise the ire of your readers, your definition must be perceived as appropriate and acceptable within your discourse community.

Writing a Definition

Much of the time, it is not so much the definition of a word that is crucial to an argument but how the word is applied. The meaning of *family* is clear to all of us; none of us has to look it up. But how we apply this word may differ. You may agree that a grandmother rearing her two grandchildren constitutes a family and that an eldest sister supporting her younger siblings also constitutes a family. Some may disagree, however, that an unmarried couple raising their children is a true family, or that a man with his children and a gay lover constitute a family.

The classical method of defining is a two-step process. In addition, numerous other techniques can help you define a term.

Classical Definition.   In this technique, you first identify the larger classification into which the word fits. For example, to define a horse, you would classify it as a mammal. Then, to complete the definition, you specify how the word is different from all the members of its classification: "a horse is a large, grass-eating, domesticated mammal with solid hooves on four legs, used for riding or pulling vehicles."

Although it isn't too likely that the word *horse* will be the key term in an argument, consider a term that might come up in a controversy over whether it is cruel to use horses to pull tourists in antique carriages around the streets of modern Philadelphia. Here, the outcome of the argument hinges on how you define *cruelty to animals*. Using classification and differentiation, position holders can generate a definition for cruelty to animals that fits with their positions. An extreme animal-rights proponent might generate this definition: "animal cruelty is the use of an animal [classification] for any task or human purpose for which other resources exist [differentiation]." A proponent with a more moderate viewpoint might use this definition: "animal cruelty is the use or treatment of an animal [classification] with disregard for the health, safety, or pain experienced by the animal [differentiation]."

■ *Activity 2*
Generating Classical
Definitions, p. 287

Other Definition Techniques.   Classical definition is not the only way to define important terms. You can also:

- explain the meaning directly
- tell what the word or concept is like or similar to
- explain the history of the word
- provide examples
- describe a process of origin or continuance
- tell what the term is not
- cite an authority's definition
- provide a technical definition

To explain the meaning, you can directly tell readers how you are using the term by providing synonyms and by writing out some specifics of what the word covers. For example, in an article about the Internet, Associated Press reporter Elizabeth Weise explains the concept of "cookies": they are "nuggets of information" that are planted "into a user's PC" that "can track which web sites are visited, what pages are looked at."

To tell what the word or concept is like or similar to, you can use comparison, analogy, or metaphor. For example, in *Being Digital,* Nicholas Negroponte wants to clarify what "bits" are. He writes,

> Many people . . . think of bandwidth like plumbing. Thinking of bits like atoms leads to big pipes and little pipes, faucets and hydrants. A commonly used comparison is that using fiber [optic cable] is like drinking from a fire hose. The analogy is constructive but misleading. . . . A ski lift might be a better analogy. The lift is moving at a constant speed, while more or fewer people get on and off. (35)

Explaining the history of the word can add solidity or weight to your definition. You might rely on a dictionary that provides etymologies—the history of a word's use—or you might find information about the word's use in some other source. For example, arguers in favor of euthanasia often cite the word's Greek roots, which mean good death. In writing about an early and influential on-line chat room, Katie Hafner points out that the word *cyberspace* was first applied to the realm of online communication by an individual who "took science fiction writer William Gibson's term and applied it to the present" (124).

Providing examples—applying the term to concrete events, situations, items, or people—can clarify the word for your readers. The examples may be real or hypothetical. For instance, an argument for establishing a new, required course at a college, a "first-year seminar," might include examples of appropriate subjects: "courses that might be suitable for conversion to the 'first-year seminar' format include Calculus I, Biology I, Child Development, Introduction to Sociology, American Government, and Living Theater."

To describe a process of origin or continuance, tell your reader how the term came about or how it works or explain a process the reader can use to understand the term. If you need to define family therapy in a paper about responses to adolescent drug abuse, you might explain how sessions are conducted. If you are developing an opinion piece about the need to regulate the adoption of foreign-born children, you might define *regulation* by explaining how it would work in the adoption process.

To tell what the term is not is called giving a *negative definition* or defining by negation. Usually, a negative definition is complemented with further definition through direct statement or some other technique. In Negroponte's example cited above, the author provides a negative as well as a positive analogy, pointing out that using the plumbing image to explain digital communication "is constructive but misleading." In defining what scholastic excellence is, you might point out that it is not high grades, not high SAT scores, and not a high profile in class as an active contributor. Then you might go on to state directly what your definition of the term is.

By citing an authority's definition, you may impress your audience by showing that an expert or authority in the field concurs with your usage of a term. In support of the idea that rhetoric is used in situations concerning uncertainty of belief, scholar

Carolyn Miller quotes Aristotle: "Rhetoric, Aristotle tell us, has to do with 'things about which we deliberate but for which we have no systematic rules. . . . We only deliberate about things which seem to admit of issuing in two ways; as for those things which cannot in the past, present, or future be otherwise no one deliberates about them . . . for nothing would be gained by it' "(162).

Providing a technical definition is appropriate when a word has a severely restricted or specific use in a technical situation. Technical definitions must be accurate, and, depending on the audience, can be produced using any or several of the techniques above. In *Being Digital*, Negroponte has to clarify quite a few technical terms for a general audience. Here is his definition of a bit:

> A bit has no color, size, or weight, and it can travel at the speed of light. It is the smallest atomic element in the DNA of information. It is a state of being: on or off, true or false, up or down, in or out, black or white. For practical purposes we consider a bit to be a 1 or a 0. The meaning of the 1 or the 0 is a separate matter. In the early days of computing, a string of bits most commonly represented numerical information.
>
> Try counting, but skip all the numbers that have anything other than a 1 and a 0 in them. You end up with the following: 1, 10, 11, 100, 101, 110, 111, etc. Those are the respective binary representations for the numbers 1, 2, 3, 4, 5, 6, 7, etc. (14)

■ *Activity 3*

Locating and
Exploring Definitions,
p. 288

■ *Activity 4*

Generating
Definitions, p. 288

As you can see, a technical definition may partake of many other definition methods. Which can you identify here?

Analyze for Cause and Effect

In addition to establishing necessary definitions, you should explore any causes of the problem and any effects that changes or alterations could make. People in general have a drive to understand why. Physician James Gilligan notes in his book about the causes of violence that "before there were statistics, there were myths" (49) designed to explain the world in ancient times. In developing your argument, you may feel it is appropriate to trace causes and effects related to your issue, so you should sort these out as you analyze your material.

The Role of Causation in Argument

Sometimes examining causes can deepen your understanding of an issue. The sources of today's debate over abortion, for example, include twentieth-century medical advances that make abortion a safe medical option. Understanding that the legality of abortion has one root in medical history can help you keep the issue in perspective, and may play a part in your final position.

Other times, you need to explore cause because it is essential to presenting your argument. Claims that obscene or pornographic material affects behavior and causes crime, abuse, or deviance are used to support the censorship and regulation of such materials, for example. Assertions that certain processes or behaviors pollute or otherwise damage the environment underlie arguments for high-mileage cars, recycling, population control, regulation of land use, and so forth.

Sometimes your causal analysis will lead you to form a **claim of causation**—that is, to draw a conclusion that a significant causal relationship exists and must be taken into account. Or you might form a **claim of prediction**—that is, a claim asserting that particular actions will cause a particular effect in the future.

Claims of causation attempt to trace the origins or causes of an event, situation, or problem:

> Gasoline-powered lawn mowers and other landscape equipment create significant noise and air pollution in suburban areas.

> Overdevelopment of natural areas along rivers limits water absorption and is a major cause of devastating floods.

The process of cause and effect pertains not only to discrete situations in which why or how something came about is at issue. Sometimes, we want to understand a gradual process of change. We may be noticing a tendency or trend away from previous conditions, situations, or behavior. In such cases, you need to document or establish the reality of the trend before you account for why it is happening. For example, if you want to explain the reasons for a trend toward environmentalism, political cynicism, or a return to 1970s-style counterculture rebellion among today's college students, you need to provide evidence that student attitudes do show such a trend before you analyze possible causes of it.

Causal explanations also come into play when you predict the future or the result of events. When you make a **claim of prediction,** you are asserting that known causes will have particular effects, for better or worse; often your goal is to recommend or warn against actions that will bring about this result. In general, an assertion about effects that will soon occur is easier to defend than a claim of far-reaching or distant effects. That a major volcanic eruption will affect weather and air quality for a year or two throughout one hemisphere seems defensible, while the assertion that such an eruption is likely to affect weather, ocean levels, the polar ice caps, and animal extinctions for the next fifty years may be harder to support.

Characteristics of Cause-Effect Sequences

Causal explanations, if complete and accurate, are almost always complex. Few events have only one cause. Likewise, most events or situations that cause something to occur actually are the cause of multiple occurrences. Even if, for example, you might want to focus on new building regulations as the cause of the survival of a city's buildings after a large earthquake, these same regulations may be the cause of a number of other situations and events, including higher rents and purchase costs for new buildings, higher prices in the shops in new buildings, prosperity among companies marketing earthquake-protection materials, and a leveling off of insurance rates for buildings incorporating the new regulations. In an argument defending the regulations you would not need to discuss all the effects. Some of them, however, might be the source of opposition to your idea. The complexity of causation makes casual analysis difficult because you need to isolate the causes that are relevant to your argument without oversimplifying or distorting the situation.

Observers may vary in their reports of causes because of their vantage points or their partisanship. Politicians may blame teachers, schools of education, and teachers' unions for problems in education, but teachers, with their closer vantage point to the problem and their resistance to criticism, may point to parents, poverty, athletics, antieducation bias in popular culture, student jobs, and so forth as the causes of weakened education.

■ *Activity 5*
Determining Causes, p. 288

Sometimes a diagram such as Figure 7.1 is used to show the relation of cause and effect. In fact, causes usually have many effects and effects are likely to have many causes, as Figure 7.2 shows.

■ *Activity 6*
Determining Effects, p. 288

Another complication in the welter of causes and effects is that an effect produced by a cause may itself become a cause of later effects. The result is a sequence or **chain of causes,** as shown in Figure 7.3.

Types of Causes

Causes form an array in relation to any effect that is produced. Some causes are obvious, often because they immediately precede the effect. Such **immediate** or **precipitating causes** are like the spark that starts a fire: dramatic, perhaps, but not necessarily a full explanation of the event. So, in addition to understanding the precipitating or immediate cause, we need to examine **proximate** or nearby causes (such as the presence of dry underbrush and fallen trees in the wood and a recent drought), and even **remote causes** (weather systems over the Arctic region), events that may not be close in time but that may be important in bringing other events about. **Ultimate causes** are

$$C \longrightarrow E$$

FIGURE 7.1   A Cause Gives Rise to an Effect

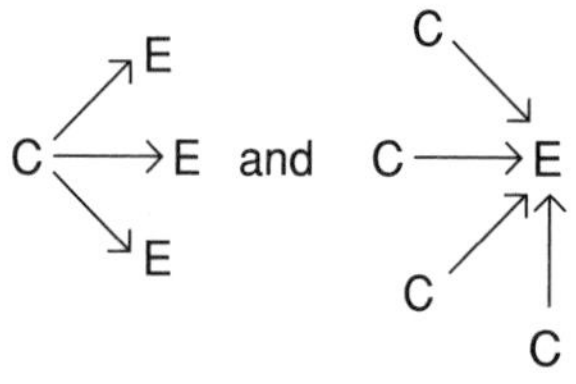

FIGURE 7.2   Multiple Effects and Multiple Causes

$$C \longrightarrow E = C \longrightarrow E = C \longrightarrow E \text{ and so on}$$

FIGURE 7.3   A Causal Sequence

the deepest causes. For example, a misunderstanding between a man and a woman interested in each other might be precipitated by her acting cold to him one day. But the ultimate cause might be factors in her personality—a tendency to play it too cool or to freeze up when emotions get too strong, a failure to handle conflicting feelings—or factors in his personality: insecurity, excessive pride, an unforgiving nature.

When there are multiple causes, one may be **necessary** to create the effect, but other causes may need to be present as well. In another situation, one cause may be **sufficient**. A necessary cause is one that "makes or breaks" the effect. For example, an off-ramp leading from one interstate to another was the site of several tragic tractor-trailer crashes. Many in the city complained that the ramp was improperly designed; the highway engineers and the department of transportation maintained that there was nothing wrong with the road's design and that driver error was the cause. When the highway department erected signs warning truck drivers to slow down on the accident-prone ramp, no more crashes occurred. Clearly, speed was a necessary condition for the accidents to occur, but not a sufficient one, since, obviously, truck drivers were accustomed to speeding around similar ramps without crashing. The ramp's design was also a likely factor in the crashes, but not a sufficient cause because most vehicles used the ramp successfully.

A sufficient cause is one that in itself is enough to generate a particular effect. In life, it is fair to say that sufficient causes are relatively rare. Complexity engulfs us. In his analysis of the excessive violence in U.S. society, Gilligan stresses that there is no one cause of a violent personality:

> Not all violent adults were subjected to violent child abuse. Nor do all who were subjected to violent child abuse grow up to commit deadly violence. Child abuse is neither a necessary nor a sufficient condition for adult violence, anymore than smoking is a necessary or sufficient cause for the development of lung cancer. There are, however, plenty of statistical studies showing that acts of actual and extreme physical violence, such as beatings and attempted murders, are regular experiences in the childhoods of those who grow up to become violent, just as we know that smoking is a major, and preventable, cause of lung cancer. (49)

■ *Activity 7*
Identifying Types of Causes, p. 288

Conditions of Causation

Cause and effect require proximity in space and time. In order for one event to be the cause of another, there must be contact between the events. The toxic chemicals buried at Love Canal, New York, cannot be said to cause your Aunt Ida's cancer in Omaha, unless she previously lived at Love Canal. However, proximity alone is not enough to prove causation occurred.

Time sequence is another condition for causation—the effect must follow the cause. But not everything in sequence occurs because of causation. When a foghorn blows in the harbor and Uncle Smitty has a heart attack, the sequence itself does not mean that the foghorn caused his coronary. Mistaking sequence for cause is a kind of logical fallacy called *post hoc* for the Latin phrase *post hoc, ergo propter hoc,* meaning "after this, therefore because of it." (See Chapter 9 for more about fallacies.)

Finally, causation is a specific and special kind of connection between events. Just any old connection will not do. Two events that occur close in time may seem related by cause and effect when in fact, they are correlated rather than causally related. **Correlation** means that the two events do depend on each other in some way but not through causation. Often, events that are related and that change together are not cause and effect but are the results of some other event. For example, if a researcher discovers that sales of ice-cream cones increase in July and August and that hospital admissions for heat prostration also increase at that same time, should he claim that the Good Humor man is spreading heat prostration? Of course, these two events are caused by something else, the summer's high temperature and humidity; eating ice cream and fainting from the heat are correlated, not causally related.

Although this example seems silly, there are many serious issues in our society in which there is a debate over correlation versus causation. The watching of television and the decline in SAT scores that occurred after television became commonplace in U.S. homes; a rise in youth drug use during the first administration of President Clinton, the only president who admitted trying marijuana; the rise in out-of-wedlock births after the invention of effective birth control—these events certainly correlate, but proving a causal relation is more difficult. Mathematician John Allen Paulos gives the example of a newspaper headline that suggests causation when only correlation is in play:

> Consider a headline that invites us to infer a causal connection: "Bottled Water Linked to Healthier Babies." Without further evidence, this invitation should be refused, since affluent parents are more likely both to drink bottled water and to have healthy children; they have the stability and wherewithal to offer good food, clothing, shelter, and amenities. Families that own cappuccino makers are more likely to have healthy babies for the same reason. (137)

Supporting Causal Links and Predictions of Effects

So how do you present an analysis of causation in a way that readers will accept? In our discourse community, causation is widely and wildly asserted but rarely proven, yet many assertions of cause are accepted. The extent of proof or support needed for a claim of causation depends on your audience. How familiar are they with the situation? To what extent will they consider your assertion of causation to be realistic and reasonable? How predisposed are they to accept your claim of causation? Are they likely to practice what Paulos calls "good statistical hygiene" and question correlation "when reading about 'links' between this practice and that condition" (137). Even such seemingly obvious causal relations as that between smoking and cancer have been disputed—primarily by the tobacco industry, which of course has a bias against accepting data suggesting cause. A news report in the *New York Times* explains the loophole that has allowed this dispute. "While many scientists have long been convinced by statistical studies and animal experiments that tobacco causes cancer, a statistical association was not in itself absolute proof. This shortfall has allowed defenders of smoking to deny that cigarettes cause cancer" (Stout A1).

In any causal analysis, the strongest assertion of causation is one that specifies how the effect is brought about by the cause. In the case of smoking, this level of analysis has only recently been possible technologically. "The findings, published . . . in the journal *Science,* report the first evidence from the cell biology level linking smoking to lung cancer. The scientists say a chemical found in cigarette smoke has been found to cause genetic damage in lung cells that is identical to the damage observed in many malignant tumors of the lung" (Stout A1).

The *statistical association* of cancer and smoking is what shows up when data are gathered about whether individuals who suffer from lung cancer were smokers; although in any one individual smoking may correlate with cancer, when this correlation occurs over and over, in thousands of cases, the likelihood of a causal connection increases. Animal *experiments* offer proof by *comparison:* if cigarette smoke induces cancer in animals, then it is considered likely to also cause cancer in humans. Both these methods can add reasonableness to a claim of causation.

In addition to statistical analysis, experimentation, and comparison, *tracing the process* by which an event is caused and using a *process of elimination* can bolster a causal claim. When an event or result occurs only when a certain agent or event precedes it and not in other circumstances, causation by that certain agent or event seems likely. For example, if you break out in hives after some visits to your grandmother's house, you might keep track of the foods she serves. If you discover that a case of hives always follows her serving turnips at dinner, you have probably located the cause of your allergic reaction. Making changes in a situation to eliminate possible causal factors can also reveal a causal link. For example, if my upgrade of a CD-ROM map program crashes when loaded, I can turn off and on various system extensions to see which one makes a difference. Gradually, by a process of elimination, I can determine what software conflict is the cause.

As you work your way toward establishing causation, make sure you consider the possibility of other factors' entering in. Don't grab for the first cause that you come across.

You should also be aware that people in our discourse community expect causes to accord with what we know about nature and human behavior. When identifying a person as a cause, we expect a motive, a repeated pattern of action, or a documentable mental problem to explain behavior. When natural or societal forces are asserted as causes, we find them believable only when they fit with the usual course of events. If we argue that the president's wife practices witchcraft and caused the stock market to sink to record lows or that flight 100 exploded because of an alien ray gun shot from a million light years away, we are not likely to be able to make our case.

Finally, because causation of social, cultural, and political events (and sometimes natural events) is difficult to determine, assertions of causation should often be qualified or limited. Even though the introduction of a strict dress code in your high school may seem to have solved certain problems, you should be careful of making a blanket assertion that dress codes are the solution to what ails U.S. education.

■ *Methods of Supporting Causal Links and Predictions of Effects*

Causation is usually inferred rather than scientifically proven. For that reason, it is best to have more than one type of support for a causal claim. Here are some ways of supporting a claim of causation or prediction:

- Statistical association: Over a sustained period of time statistics indicate that a change in one factor parallels a change in another.
- Experimentation: In a controlled situation, a particular process or event produces the same result over and over.
- Comparison: Two situations are similar in the extreme, leading to the conclusion that what causes a change in one is also the cause of a change in the other.
- Tracing the process: Show step by step how certain actions, behaviors, or interventions create particular changes.
- Process of elimination: Show the unlikelihood of all but one of the possible causes to create the inference that the one remaining possibility is the cause.

■ DECIDE ON A CLAIM

The claim of an argument is a statement of the position you are taking on the issue. Argumentative claims grow out of the process of reasoning about and sifting through the varied materials derived from research on an issue. They emerge from our inner dialogue with the ideas of others as presented in research and from discussing the issue with others around us. They will inevitably be tempered by our assumptions and values as we have accepted them from our discourse community or determined them for ourselves.

Your position might be a claim of **fact**—that is, a claim that a situation, condition, or event exists or existed or that a definition is valid. Or your position might be a claim of **causation**, as discussed above, or a claim of **value**, a statement that evaluates an action, event, situation, or aesthetic work. A final type of claim is the claim of **policy**, which asserts an action should or should not be taken. Sometimes argumentative claims are **mixed** in type, in that the support for the main assertion will involve several claims of different types, such as causation, fact, and value.

Claims of Fact

Claims of fact are those that assert a definition, a description, or a comparison. A factual claim may propose a new, controversial, or unproven point about the essential nature of something:

Violence in today's society is a national health problem, not a crime-control problem.

Or it may assert new or unproven qualities of something:

> Violence in today's society encompasses not only domestic abuse and criminal assault but also suicide and accidental injury and death from weapons.

A factual claim may compare in order to clarify its main idea:

> Like bicycle and automobile safety and alcoholism, violence in today's society is a concern to be addressed by the medical establishment.

Finally, claims can assert new facts—facts that have just been uncovered and must be proven. "Signs of water molecules have been identified on Mars," "cold fusion is possible," and "violent crime has declined in the past few years in major cities" are all factual claims that were announced in the press. "Cold fusion" turned out to be a misinterpretation of laboratory results and was not a fact after all. As you can see, many factual claims are technical in nature.

Claims of Value

People can argue directly about values by asserting claims of value:

> People should not violate small rules and minor laws.
>
> The poetry of Theodore Roethke is powerful, moving, and of enduring artistic value.
>
> For most people, using an accounting software program to monitor their personal budgets is time-consuming and impractical.

In these claims, the issue is a matter of right or wrong, of high or low artistic value, of negative or positive outcomes, of usefulness or uselessness. All of these are value judgments. A case can be made for these points because they are more than just matters of personal preference.

Providing support for values claims is complex because there are many variables. The value underlying the claim may be explicitly stated, or it may implied; the value may need justification or explanation, or it may be a near-universal assumption; more than one value may come into play in relation to an action or situation. As a result, support for a claim of value may involve several layers of reasoning, including:

- citing the value that is the foundation of the claim
- showing that the action or issue is the type referred to by the value
- giving reasons or support for how the value shows the action or issue to be right or wrong, good or bad, practical or impractical, beautiful or ugly, and so on

Sometimes writers deal only implicitly with the first two of these layers because their audience can be expected to agree, and the bulk of the discussion is focused on the last layer.

Consider this value claim pertaining to the Heaven's Gate suicides that occurred in 1997:

> As a matter of religious freedom, the Heaven's Gate cult members cannot be criticized for taking their own lives to satisfy their religious beliefs.

In this claim, the value appealed to is made clear at the start of the statement: "As a matter of religious freedom . . ." The writer must, however, show that the suicides were indeed due to religious belief and not to depression, mental illness or psychosis, constraint, or psychological control by some person. Then the writer needs to show the importance of religious freedom in judging this event and to convince readers that it is the supreme value to apply, more important than values about the preciousness of life and the wrongness of suicide. Finally, the writer must discuss the particular suicides in the light of this value.

Which aspect of a value claim will need the most support and whether that support should be explicit depend on the audience and whether it shares the values invoked by the writer. If the audience basically agrees with the value, the writer may not need to defend it or even spell it out. In the example above, most audiences would need much persuasion about whether religious freedom cancels out the preciousness of life. If a writer chose a different perspective on these cult suicides, however, the audience might be more likely to agree:

> The Heaven's Gate cult members were wrong to commit suicide because life is precious.

The decision about which support might be effective also depends on the expected readership. Some common methods of support for value claims include:

- drawing in authorities and experts
- citing the authority of tradition
- showing consequences, problems, outcomes, advantages, or disadvantages
- defining an important term so as to include or exclude the action in question
- comparing, contrasting, or creating analogies

Statistics, historical examples, and other hard evidence also come into play when writers argue about values. Showing the importance of an issue or problem may involve citing statistical reports or describing specific occurrences. Often, consequences and outcomes can be best demonstrated by reference to similar or previous situations culled from history. Providing comparisons or making a point through contrasts also means having factual details at your command. And examples may be useful in many places in an argument to support a claim of value.

Claims of Policy

Assertions about what should be done or what should be changed are claims of policy. These claims typically have "should," "must," or "ought" as part of the verb:

Buttonville should budget extra funds each of the next five years for the repair and installation of sidewalks throughout downtown.

The United States must pay its dues, including overdue funds from past years, to the United Nations.

Congress ought to pass a bill requiring that all children receive at least a year of half-day preschool to prepare them for entering the regular school system.

Policy claims are often based on causal analysis—that is, an analysis of which causes will prompt which effects—and they frequently rely on the application of values leading to the preference for certain results over others. For example, a claim asserting that gasoline-powered automobiles should be banned to cut polluting emissions might be based in an analysis of pollution's causes. This solution, while scientifically based, would be impractical because of the high value we place on travel, mobility, and efficient use of time. Acceptance of a policy claim supporting strict pollution controls on vehicles may also come down to values; if increased standards might reduce vehicle pollution 10 percent but might raise the cost of vehicles, maintenance, and testing by 16 percent, people who value low prices more than lowered pollution will oppose the standards. Many societal controversies about policies boil down to arguments not so much over data as over values. Policy arguments are therefore extra-complicated: you may have to support some causal (and perhaps definitional) assertions and justify the values behind your choice in order to fully support a policy claim.

■ *Activity 8*
Identifying Types of Claims, p. 289

Focusing and Moderating Claims

Claims for argumentation need to be realistic—that is, they need to be tempered by awareness of real life. For this reason, global or universal claims create problems. A global claim is one that makes a statement about a broad aspect of life. It is a claim that is held to apply "across the board" in all situations, at all times, in all places. For example, these are global claims:

Television destroys young people's minds.

Taking a life is murder and is always wrong.

Gambling should be legalized.

Most of us would regard all these statements as extreme because we can think of exceptions. Quite obviously, most of our youth watch television and are functional, thinking people. The effects of television, whatever they may be, are less drastic than this claim asserts. And, although most people would agree with the definition "taking a life is murder," most would also admit that there are times when killing is acceptable—for example, during wartime or in self-defense. Finally, the statement that "gambling should be legalized" states little about the realities of such a policy. Is all gambling, from the lottery to betting on sports, card games, and cockfighting, to be legal? And would it be regulated, licensed, government-operated, or completely privatized and unmonitored?

As you can see, broad assertions can be challenged easily and effectively. A first line of attack is to point out the confusions and even contradictions that flow from such extreme assertions. If all life taking is wrong, then isn't it wrong to kill and eat animals? how about plants? Is ending life support for a brain-dead person killing and therefore wrong? If you are being threatened with death by a criminal and have the opportunity to grab a gun and kill him but don't because killing is wrong, aren't you "committing suicide," in that you are permitting him to kill you? And so on. Make sure your claim is reasonable rather than broad, and make sure it is a claim you can defend in a paper of the required length.

■ WRITING SUPPORT FOR A CLAIM

A paper in support of a position is likely to be complex, and so you should outline carefully before you jump into a draft. And your organization plan should take into account both the material you have gathered to support your point of view and the kind of readers you expect. How you begin, where you state your claim, the location of refutation, the placement of defense against possible critiques, and the overall unfolding of your argument all depend on what will be most helpful in convincing your readers. Sometimes, you may gradually lead your reader to your claim; other times, you may wish to be upfront, brusquely announcing your position early in your paper. The basic organization pattern of argumentation is the same as that of expository writing: a claim (or thesis) is expressed and followed by support plus refutation where appropriate. In the position paper covered in this chapter, there is no or little refutation.

Assess Audience Values and Choose Support

We speak about the civic and academic discourse communities as if they are unified, but both are diverse and full of divergent opinions, approaches, and values. Any time you plan to present an argument for a claim, whether it be a claim of fact, causation, policy, or value, you need to imagine the values a typical reader will possess. Sometimes this is easy; when your classmates are your audience and you know them well through numerous discussions on many topics, you can spell out for yourself their probable values on your topic. Most times, however, writers are somewhat at sea as to their audience and its views. Occasionally, they know they want to address a particular segment of a potential audience, perhaps those who severely misunderstand some aspect of the issue or perhaps those who are sympathetic toward but inactive in furthering a cause.

The profile of your expected or desired reader will affect many of your choices, ranging from tone and style to the selection and amount of support, the organization, and introductory and conclusion strategies. In making a claim of value or a claim that assumes certain values, for example, you will be most convincing if you pitch your argument to show that it matches a value your audience already holds or agrees with. Many times, you can rely on widely accepted values about such things as life's preciousness, the importance of order in society, and the centrality of family to a person.

From analyzing your own values, you are aware how often human needs, as described by Abraham Maslow, come into play. (Maslow is discussed in Chapter 6.) Maslow's analysis has been used to great advantage by advertisers, who have based sales pitches on the perceived needs of the audience, often needs that have little to do with the product being sold. As James Twitchell writes in his book *Adcult USA,* "From the early sociological speculations of scholars like . . . Abraham Maslow, who posited a five-tier stair of 'needs growth,' the advertising industry has embraced the concept of positioning as a way to take advantage of the indwelling styles and aspirations of consumers" (125). To apply the hierarchy of needs when you are building an argument, you must estimate where on the "stairs" your audience stands and find a way to link your position to the satisfaction of those needs.

The audience you expect can determine your choice of support. Here is a chart of some possible audiences for a writer using the claim "Members of the Heaven's Gate cult were wrong to commit suicide because life is precious."

Audience	Reasoning/Support	Type of Support
Mainstream American: some education, average income and life-style	Life's preciousness as the highest value in our nation's Judeo-Christian tradition	1. Tradition 2. Experts (religious and lifestyle historical scholars)
Religiously minded	1. God opposes suicide. 2. "Religions" that support suicide are false religions or cults.	1. Expert testimony (Bible, religious scholars, priests) 2. Definition of a religion
Highly educated	1. Psychological explanation of cult membership 2. Societal problems in law and medicine if suicides are condoned	1. Process analysis and definition of brainwashing 2. Consequences
All readers	Compare religiously motivated suicide to suicide motivated by depression or tragic life situations to show they are similar and should all be prohibited	Comparison and contrast

As when arguing any claim, the writer should anticipate counterarguments that might occur to the reader and try to defuse them. This might be done by showing their irrelevance or by developing a full-blown refutation. (See Chapter 8 for refutation strategies.)

Organize for Emphasis of Main Idea

Your most important point, reasons, examples, and so forth should stand out so the reader can recognize and remember them. Transitions are one way to underline ideas. You might lead in with "most important . . . " or directly announce that "the crucial factor in this matter is . . . " or "the best solution to this problem is. . . ."

Organization can also create emphasis. The most important positions in a document are near the beginning and near the end. Skimmers always look in these two places for important points. Readers remember the way a piece starts because they are coming fresh to the argument, and they remember the last thing they read. The conclusion is considered the most emphatic position because at this point the reader has experienced the flow of your argument and is most primed to accept your final word on the matter. When you design the organization of your paper in support of a claim, place your important points where the reader will be most alert and accepting—that is, near the end. Your paper should build to a climax, moving from your initial points of development through the core of your support to a "high point," where you develop the most significant reasoning for your claim.

In addition to its location within your argument, the length and complexity of a point's development also convey its importance. Ideally, the most important point will be the longest and weightiest. You should be especially careful not to "peter out" toward the end of your argument, giving only short shrift to what should be developed in depth.

Generate an Overall Plan of Development

Your overall organization will be a function of your ideas and will be completely unique in that way. In a complex paper, several development patterns may be at work; these patterns may alternate, or some paragraphs within a section of a pattern may use a different pattern. Within an essay that asserts the value of weight-bearing exercise, for example, there might be comparisons between various sports. Within these comparisons, there might be examples or classifications of activities according to health benefits. Organization can sometimes seem like a series of boxes within boxes, as a pattern of development includes miniature versions of other patterns.

Organization may be developed in time order or in a conceptual pattern. Using time order means following the steps or stages of events or a process as they occur in real life. **Narrative, process analysis,** and **causation** are three organization patterns that use time order. For example, if you were to argue that federal disaster relief needs to be streamlined and delivered to victims promptly, you might discuss the step-by-step process currently used and the revisions you suggest. If there are specific factors in the process that hinder the delivery of aid, you would use a causal analysis of what events prompted which results. And, to help your reader visualize the pain of disaster victims, you might present a narrative about a typical victim and her problems acquiring aid.

Conceptual patterns of organization are those ordered according to an idea, such as the concepts of **comparison-contrast, cause-effect, classification, illustration,** or **problem-solution.** In writing about academic dishonesty on campus, for example, you might use classification, saying that there are several different types of cheating. And you might use illustration by giving examples.

In using the problem-solution pattern, you would first establish the existence, extent, and seriousness of the problem. Then, you might refute or disqualify current or oft-suggested solutions before presenting your defense of your own solution. For instance, in discussing the problems an extensive prison system presents to society, one student gave examples and provided statistics about the danger of violence to the public from escapes and the drain on government budgets that results from having to maintain a large number of correctional institutions. He offered his solution, that alternative sentencing techniques should be widely used, and gave examples and details about how they could be effectively employed.

■ REVISING AND EDITING

For most writers, revising is a major endeavor. A first draft is just that, a "sketch" of your ideas; it takes much going over to turn this sketch into a colorful, detailed, fully realized "portrait" of your argument. This analogy breaks down because the "original" of your argument is not sitting in your head waiting to be portrayed; you create the argument during and because of the process of creating it on paper.

In writing the draft, you are likely to be preoccupied with matters of content—formulating the ideas in a comprehensible way, pulling in the evidence where appropriate, working out the organization, and so on—and your writing will be rough. Your phrasing may be imprecise, you may repeat yourself as you struggle to get an idea down, you may shift your tone, and so forth, all because you are attending primarily to the flow of your reasoning. The revision stage allows you to examine your text comprehensively, going over it several times, to check all its features in light of your purpose.

In revising, writers usually begin with the major issues of tone and content, then move to localized issues, such as logicality of points, sentence style, and flow. These aspects interconnect; changes you make when considering tone will affect style, and so forth.

Approaches to Revising

You can try several different techniques to give yourself an edge when revising. Revision literally means "re-seeing," or having a "new view" of your work. You can sometimes attain this new view by physically shifting the way you see your text. Here are some techniques for seeing anew:

- Print out your text and revise on the hard copy instead of scrolling down through the document on-screen.
- Print out the text according to your goal for revising. If you are working to improve content or tighten it, you might want to print out your text single-spaced and in a smaller font size so you can see large sections of the text massed on each page and thus identify where it seems slack or disorganized. If you are

revising for style, you might want to print the text out triple-spaced or with extra-wide margins, so you can concentrate on words and phrases and have lots of room to rewrite.

- Read your text out loud to yourself (or to another person). Hearing your text can reveal where it is awkward, choppy, unclear, repetitious, or flawed in some other way.
- Ask someone else to read your paper out loud to you.
- Request reactions and comments from a few readers.

Revise Substance with Readers in Mind

One standard with which to measure your text in the revision stage is your reader's perspective. That reader wants things to be clear and accessible. And the reader wants to cooperate with you. Interacting with a text is most worthwhile if the reader comes away satisfied:

- knowing something new and relevant
- understanding something more deeply
- agreeing with well-said, eloquent thoughts
- solidifying hazy beliefs or opinions
- seeing new light thrown on an issue
- being aroused by a challenging point of view
- enjoying a dramatic, humorous, or ironic slant on the topic

When you re-read your argument wearing your reader's "hat," consider the substance of your argument from an outsider's point of view. Specifically, here are things to look at as you begin to revise:

What are my assumptions about this topic?

What am I assuming about my audience?

What values do I expect my audience to share?

Are there values or beliefs underlying my claim that I must support for this audience?

How do I want my readers to react to my argument? What emotions would I like to come into play?

Is my claim clearly stated?

Is the claim an adequate statement of the problem or the issue it pertains to?

Is my claim sufficiently restricted, limited, or qualified for my expected audience and in relation to the amount and quality of evidence?

Is the evidence appropriate and relevant to the claim? Is it sufficient to support the claim? Is the evidence varied in type?

Are all aspects of my claim discussed in the argument?

Does the organization flow logically?

Do I repeat myself unnecessarily?

Are there gaps or places where I need to explain more?

Revise Language and Style to Suit Your Purpose and Reader

As you work on changes in the substance of your argument, you will undoubtedly notice elements of the style that don't work well. Most writers try to mark such places and return to revise them later. When you are ready to deal with issues of language, here are some questions to ask yourself.

Is the diction level (informal, colloquial, formal) consistent throughout the paper?
Does the diction level work to promote your credibility and the solidity of your
    support to the audience you expect?
Does the tone create the appropriate rapport with the audience?
Do words have connotations appropriate to the tone and claim?
Are there clear and smooth transitions between segments of your argument?

STUDENT ASSIGNMENT

Robyn C. Nichols, "Down with Fraternities"

ASSIGNMENT: Within the broad subject of college life, choose a topic that has been prominent on this campus recently or that has been discussed in the national civic discourse community. Brainstorm to determine your focus, and support your claim with personal experience and information drawn from at least three sources.

Robyn at first intended to write on hazing, but as she got into her subject, she decided that the solution to hazing was abolition of the organizations that covertly used it, and so she broadened her topic. Her research focused on the hazing aspect of her topic; for the rest of the support she used personal experience and analysis to build her argument. Here is the result:

Fraternity hazing and its related activities—forced binge drinking, stupid stunts, comas, and death by alcohol poisoning—have recently been in the news. And these headline-attracting situations are not unusual. An article in the *New York Times* exposes how secret and dangerous initiation rites dominate college fraternities. "Behind those closed doors [of the campus justice systems at most colleges], thousands of criminal offenses virtually disappear each academic year" (Bernstein A1). In fact, the *Times*'s in-depth study indicates that in the 1990s, one-fourth of the liability claims against fraternities involved death, paralysis, or other serious injury (Bernstein B8).

Unfortunately, banning hazing or making it a criminal offense is not really dealing with the situation. Hazing is already illegal in 36 states (Bernstein B8). As long as fraternities and sororities exist, there will be hazing, because the nature of these groups demands it. Some psychologists say that the rituals of hazing "create a sense of belonging and loyalty" (Wagner). For many, going through hazing means "the group must [be] worth it"—the new member elevates the group because of the pain of hazing (Eastman qtd. in Wagner). Without hazing to bind the members together and create the group delusion of self-importance, these Greek organizations would probably cease to exist. Fraternities and sororities foster excess partying; they have no worthwhile purpose and should not be part of college life

Most of us can remember a time as kids when we became enamored of the idea of a club. We clustered in some secret place (mine was in a "cave" under the branches of a huge, spreading bush) and swore to be "blood sisters." We then teased other kids for not being members. But this in-group, out-group stuff was a stage which we outgrew. In adult life, clubs are formed around a recreation or common interest; there are golf clubs, bridge clubs, quilting clubs, and clubs based around religious beliefs, like the Knights of Columbus, and ethnic origins, like the Polish-American society. People do use these groups for socializing, but the clubs have a broader purpose than just plain clubbiness.

But fraternities and sororities are clubs that have no purpose other than to make the club insiders feel superior to outsiders and to provide members with an instant bunch of "friends." While the Greek organizations will tell you they are "service oriented," "service" is hardly the reason that the members join. After all, there are tons of on- and off-campus organizations for serving others. Students can work with Habitat for Humanity, or help a church bring meals to the housebound, or be a peer counselor for the crisis hotline, or volunteer for any of the worthy causes posted in the student center.

It is safe to say that students pledging fraternities or sororities don't have service on the top of their minds. Just like my grade-school friends, they are clustering under a bush to convince each other that they are special. Then, they go out into the world as a unit, proclaim their wonderfulness, and judge everyone else: who is cool enough to join and who is too dorky.

Most students would agree that the obvious main purpose of sororities and fraternities is the party life. The other reasons that Greeks give for joining are suspect. Joining a frat so you will have a place to live? Come on. Lots of students rent houses together and enjoy community living without being Greek. And "the chance to be a leader"? On this campus, there are 43 campus student organizations plus numerous academic clubs in which students can experience leadership.

The Greek culture drains away people who could contribute to campus life. And Greeks themselves suffer hangovers and other consequences of heavy partying, including weak grades or worse: actual physical harm.

In an article opposing hazing, the Dean of Students at Northern Arizona University writes that "power over others and the psychological pressure to maintain secrets" occur in abusive situations. "Our human need to be included with others is so great that we allow ourselves to be humiliated in order to be part of a special affiliation," Dean Brandel continues. Unfortunately, affiliation with a fraternity or sorority is not worth it and may stunt your growth, or even kill you. Colleges should begin the process of disbanding the Greek culture now.

Works Cited

Bernstein, Nina. "Behind Some Fraternity Walls, Brothers in Crime." *New York Times* 6 May 1996, nat'l ed: A1+.

Brandel, Rick. "Hazing Traditions Need to Stop." *The Lumberjack* 14 Feb. 1996. Online. Internet. Available: http://www.thelumberjack.nau.edu/021496/Per2.html. 23 July 1997.

Wagner, Betty. "Hazing's Uses and Abuses." *U.S. News and World Report 27* Jan. 1997: 16.

What values underlie Robyn's point of view? Is she explicit about her values? Do you find any statements in her argument that should have been supported but were instead left as assumptions? Overall Robyn's organization is clear, but there are places where her movement from one point to another is choppy. In particular, the sixth, seventh, and eighth paragraphs could use better transitions.

The reading selections at the end of this chapter are other examples of argumentative position papers.

Activities

1 Recognizing Needed Definitions

Consider each of the broad topics below and brainstorm with other class members about terms within each topic that might need definition.

> gun control
> curfews for youth
> illegal immigration
> legalization of drugs
> liquor advertising on television

2 Generating Classical Definitions

Work with a group to generate classical definitions of the terms below. First attempt to write a neutral definition. Then generate a definition that implies a position about the word. For example, a neutral definition of censorship might be "the limitation by a governmental or other supervisory group of what may be published." But an interpretive definition might be "the control of sexual or violent films and literature so as to prevent access by minors" or "restriction of free speech according to the values imposed by a dominant societal group."

        capital punishment
        unfair taxes
        excessive consumption of material goods
        free speech on campus
        sexual harassment

3   Locating and Exploring Definitions

Definition safari: Look through informative or persuasive reading material—your textbooks, newspapers, magazines, whatever is at hand—to locate instances of definition. Make a copy of definitions and the section of the text in which they were offered (their context) and bring them to class for discussion.

4   Generating Definitions

Choose one of the following terms and work with a group of classmates to generate definitions using as many of the definition techniques as possible.

        success in college
        success in life
        a good relationship
        a good boss/supervisor
        a true friend

5   Determining Causes

For each effect below, work with a group to analyze possible causes.

        an increase in underage drinking
        the popularity of a particular TV sitcom
        the popularity of extreme sports
        a decrease in homicide across the United States

6   Determining Effects

For each action below, work with a group to identify possible effects.

        raising the price of beer through taxation
        increasing the police presence in urban residential neighborhoods
        raising the speed limit to 65 mph
        permitting citizens to carry concealed, licensed weapons

7   Identifying Types of Causes

Work with the lists of causes you generated in Activity 5. Identify each cause as to type: immediate, proximate, remote, ultimate, sufficient, or necessary.

8   Identifying Types of Claims

Identify the following claims as a claim of fact, claim of value, claim of causation, claim of policy, or mixed.

1. Extremists have become more active in our society since the Internet has given them new, inexpensive ways to communicate.

2. The orchestral symphony is the height of musical expression.

3. Schools must teach the basic values on which society operates, and the desire to work hard and to produce good work will follow.

4. Humans consume half the planet's available water, most of it for agriculture.

5. More resources should be spent in providing both high school and college students with the opportunity to spend a semester abroad.

6. A preoccupation with people's looks and with appearances in general has created a society of shallow, status-conscious bores.

7. If development in the southwestern United States is not voluntarily curtailed, there will be extreme water shortages in that region.

8. Living together before marriage is not insurance against divorce; in fact, if they marry cohabiters are more likely to divorce.

Assignments

1. Choose an issue that has been recently in the news, and focus on a narrow aspect of it. Formulate a claim about the issue. Identify the type of claim and determine an audience to which to direct your argument. Then analyze your audience's values and brainstorm to generate support appropriate for this audience. Write an argumentative position paper in which you use specific evidence arranged in emphatic order.

2. When complete agreement could not otherwise be reached, a general massacre of all who have not thought in a certain way has proved a very effective means of settling opinion in a country.

> —Charles Sanders Peirce

With your class, discuss whether "complete agreement" is necessary or desirable in a country or an organization and the other options that are available when "complete agreement" on an issue cannot be reached. You might want to discuss this topic further with a variety of people outside your class to find out how disagreements are resolved in their professional and recreational organizations. Or you may choose to investigate such topics as consensus, conflict resolution, and decision science by doing formal research. Then use your notes and free writing to generate material for an essay in which you discuss Peirce's statement and take an informed stand on how groups should best make decisions and resolve conflicts.

■ WORKS CITED

Gilligan, James. *Violence: Reflections on a National Epidemic.* New York: Random, 1996.

Hayakawa, S. I. *Language in Thought and Action.* 2nd ed. New York: Harcourt, 1964.

Miller, Carolyn R. "The Rhetoric of Decision Science, or Herbert Simon Says." In *The Rhetorical Turn: Invention and Persuasion in the Conduct of Inquiry,* ed. Herbert W. Simons. Chicago: U of Chicago P, 1990.

Negroponte, Nicholas. *Being Digital.* New York: Vintage, 1995.

Paulos, John Allen. *A Mathematician Reads the Newspaper.* New York: Basic, 1995.

Stout, David. "Direct Link Found between Smoking and Lung Cancer." *New York Times* 18 Oct. 1996, nat'l. ed: A1+.

Toulmin, Stephen. *Foresight and Understanding: An Enquiry into the Aims of Science.* New York: Harper, 1961.

———. *The Uses of Argument.* New York: Cambridge UP, 1958.

Twitchell, James B. *Adcult USA: The Triumph of Advertising in American Culture.* New York: Columbia UP, 1996.

 *Readings*

Education to Learn and Not for Money

R. RICHARD BANKS

R. Richard Banks graduated from Harvard Law School and is currently clerking for a judge on the federal bench. He has contributed frequently to the *Los Angeles Times* and other newspapers and is the author of a recent law journal article. This piece appeared in newspapers in 1990. (Reprinted by permission of the author.)

1   The drug menace and declining international economic competitiveness stand as our nation's two gravest problems.

2   Drug addiction and the drug trade have ravaged many urban areas, with startling numbers of babies born addicted to cocaine and with equally startling numbers of people killed in drug related clashes. Our nation's once unquestioned economic pre-eminence has been toppled by foreign competitors, who make products cheaper, faster and better than we do.

3   To bolster the country's economic competitiveness, business leaders have championed efforts to increase the supply of skilled workers through the reformation of the American educational system.

4   Unfortunately, the emphasis on creating a more rigorous educational system to improve the nation's economic efficiency only compounds the drug epidemic. The same mentality that prompts business leaders to call for improved education as a means of enhancing the nation's economic competitiveness also promotes the illicit drug trade.

5   In hailing education as a means of creating the skilled workers necessary to make America once again the world's pre-eminent economic power, we put forth the notion that education's value is in what it leads to: money, economic productivity and efficiency. We tell youth to study hard so they can get good jobs and make lots of money.

We exhort youth to choose education but give them no reason to do so. The stated goal of education (economic productivity for the nation, money for the individual) can be obtained much more directly, quickly and easily through the illegal routes.

The standard artillery in the battle against drugs—just say no, the expansion of educational and employment opportunities, education about the evils of drug usage—are impotent in the face of the overwhelming economic incentives to sell drugs. Education and work will never provide greater *economic* rewards than the drug trade.

The new generation of drug merchants is chasing the American dream (as we all are) in the best way that they know how. Drug sellers are the newest entrepreneurs in an entrepreneurship-obsessed nation. The drug market is fiercely competitive and the costs of failure are high.

These entrepreneurs strive not in opposition to society, although it ostensibly seems so. Rather, they are heeding society's message: The goal is money. As Boesky, Milken and Keating shamelessly disregard the law in pursuit of wealth, so do drug dealers. They all embody in extreme form the values which are expressed more subtly throughout society. The ostentation of drug dealers' fancy cars and fat gold chains cannot match that of Trump Plaza.

The only way to lure kids away from the drug culture is to embrace the value of education in and of itself, not as a means to something else.

We have not always pursued education as a means to material wealth. In the early days of our nation, education was centrally important and vigorously pursued, and not to enable one to buy a Mercedes or a mansion. People learned to read in order to read the Bible, to expand their knowledge of the Word of God.

During slavery, black Americans, many of whom are now ravaged by the addiction and violence of the drug menace, risked death to learn to read. They knew that in knowledge was freedom, and that reading would open to them the world white Americans sought to deny them. Slaves struggled to grasp the written word, not in quest of riches or material success, but because of the much more intangible, and infinitely more valuable, sense of self and respect that knowledge bestows.

Who can doubt it, education makes one a better person; it broadens perspective, sharpens sensibilities and spurs curiosity. Education leads to a richer life, culturally, socially, emotionally and intellectually. Youth must be convinced of this fact.

If, as a nation, we value and pursue education for its own sake, we will no longer have to worry about our international economic competitiveness. Our nation will spawn scientists and engineers who expand the boundaries of knowledge and create products of lasting value, securing our position as an economic leader.

Until then, in our efforts to solve one problem we will surely exacerbate another.

Questions for Inquiry

1. What is Banks's claim? Is it explicit or implied? Is it a claim of fact, causation, values, or policy?
2. What, according to Banks, are the two "gravest problems" (1) affecting our country? What is the connection between them?
3. Why is the "just say no" approach to drugs useless, according to the author? Why? What is the best way to defeat drugs?
4. For what purposes have people valued education other than to use their learning to make money?

Questions for Argument

1. Do you agree that if money is the goal, it can be "obtained much more directly, quickly and easily through the illegal routes" (6)? If so, why aren't more people criminals? Are those who do not enter the world of crime actually rejecting our nation's most prominent value?

2. Banks sees drug dealers and the effects of their crimes—wasted lives and street violence—as by-products of U.S. "international economic competitiveness," which has "championed" career-oriented education (1, 14, 3). Do you agree that crime is the dark underside of our national economic success?

3. Besides "education and [hard] work" (7), what other components enter into a person's success in a career or vocation? Do you think some of these other factors play a role in a person's choosing crime over a legitimate job?

Writing Assignments

Informal

1. In your journal, write about whether your education has increased your sense of self and improved your self-respect, what Banks calls the "infinitely more valuable" benefits of education (12). If you feel education has not improved your self-concept, identify what aspects of it were detrimental.

2. The author notes that "we all are" chasing the American dream (8). Write an informal paper in which you describe your personal version of "the American dream" and what you are doing to make it your reality.

Formal

3. **Argumentation.** "Education and work will never provide greater economic rewards than the drug trade," Banks writes (7). Using examples of people you know and your own experience, write a paper in which you argue that the true rewards of work are also intangible. In preparation for writing, you may want to engage reflective people from various walks of life in conversations about this issue to gather perspectives besides your own.

4. **Collaboration.** Banks writes that youth must be convinced that the true wealth bestowed by education is a life "culturally, socially, emotionally and intellectually" rich (13). Brainstorm with others to identify specific ways young people get the message that the "quest of riches or material success"(12) is all-important and then define ways to convey the contradictory message, that education is its own reward and not "a means to something else" (10). Then write a paper as a group or individually in which you propose several programs that could be started to help students view education as personal enrichment rather than as a ladder to a career.

5. **Research Opportunity.** We are "an entrepreneurship-obsessed nation," Banks says (8). Use the library and the Internet to research the hows and whys of entrepreneurship in the United States. For example, determine the extent of Americans' interest in starting a business or "being their own boss" and the success rates for entrepreneurs. Then write a paper in which you argue that in the United States the opportunity to be an entrepreneur is overvalued, overestimated, or underused. Or, use your research to for-

mulate another argumentative claim about entrepreneurship, and write a paper explaining and defending it.

■ ■ ■

Pay Organ Donors to Increase the Supply

ED CARSON

Ed Carson writes for *Reason* magazine. This essay appeared in newspapers across the country in 1997. (Copyright 1997 by the Reason Foundation. Reprinted by permission.)

The federal government recently concluded a contentious three-day hearing on proposed changes to the way that livers are allocated for transplants. 1

In November, the organization responsible for setting scarce organ allocation policies, the United Network for Organ Sharing, decided that people with chronic liver disease will no longer be first in line for donated livers. 2

The organization believes that patients with acute liver diseases—those who face death unless they receive an immediate transplant—have a slightly higher chance of surviving. Many physicians voiced their opposition to the change, saying that hundreds of chronic liver patients will die as a result. 3

But Anthony D'Alessandro, a transplant surgeon at the University of Wisconsin at Madison and a supporter of the proposed changes, said the numbers of deaths would not be affected. "Changes in allocations at this time only change the address where a patient dies." 4

In other words, there are simply not enough livers to go around. And the problem is getting worse. In 1995, 20,006 organs were donated, but the waiting list was 44,057 at the end of the year. 5

The tragic result: 3,448 Americans died in 1995 while waiting for a transplant. The actual number of deaths caused by the organ shortage is probably far higher because transplant centers have set stringent standards for those who wish to get on a waiting list. 6

Rather than focusing time and energy on the allocation of organs, increasing the supply should be the priority. And the best way to increase the supply is to pay potential donors. But the National Organ Transplant Act of 1984 explicitly prohibits the purchase or sale of human organs. 7

People might find the thought of buying and selling organs extremely distasteful. But why shouldn't donors or their families be compensated for organs that save lives? 8

After all, we control our own bodies. Organ transplants are big business for doctors and hospitals that perform them. No one suggests that they work for free. 9

Several people at the government hearing suggested that the current dispute over liver allocation is in part a fight among transplant centers over the market share for organ transplants. 10

Relatively small compensation could encourage people to become organ donors. And it doesn't have to be a cash-for-organs swap. 11

A person could will his organs like any other possession. After his death, serviceable organs could be harvested, and his estate or beneficiary would receive a death benefit much like a life-insurance policy. 12

13   Some suggest that the hospital or organ bank pay the donor's funeral expenses. Others suggest that a person who agrees to donate organs be given preference if he or she requires a transplant.

14   Opponents of an organ market say it could backfire by offending potential donors and families who want to provide a gift of life. This is a serious point.

15   However, a market for organs would supplement the current system of charitable donations, not replace it—just as some blood donors are paid while others volunteer.

16   Many critics also contend that only the rich would be able to afford organs. But the Mickey Mantles of the world are already able to get organs, while the poor have difficulty getting on waiting lists.

17   And next to the cost of the operation—a liver transplant and the first year of anti-rejection drugs goes for $300,000—procuring organs would be a minor expense.

18   Another argument against an organ market is that the poor would become organ banks for the rich. This paternalistic way of thinking assumes that poor people are unable to make rational decisions.

19   A person might be better off after selling one kidney. And the sale of organs after death precludes concerns of preying on the living poor. We should continue to honor the sacrifice of altruistic donors, but at the same time we should recognize that there is nothing unethical about a legal organ market.

20   It is, on the other hand, unethical to continue to allow thousands of people to die because the solution offends the aesthetic sensibilities of some.

Questions for Inquiry

1. What is Carson's claim? Is it explicit or implicit? What is the effect of his placement of the claim so far into the essay?
2. What values underlie Carson's claim? What opposing values is he aware of? Where does Carson make the strongest statement of his values?
3. What type of audience does Carson seem to expect for his argument? What strategies does he use to approach this audience?

Questions for Argument

1. Given the short supply of organs, how should they be apportioned? Should those with the greatest likelihood of survival be given priority? Or should there be some other standard?
2. What are the dangers of an organ marketplace? Do you think there would be abuses if organs could be sold?
3. Carson writes that "relatively small compensation could encourage people to become organ donors" (11). Do you agree that money should be the compensation? What amount would induce you to donate an organ?

Writing Assignments

Informal

1. Becoming an organ donor is a personal decision. Write a journal entry in which you express your feelings about whether you or members of your family would donate your organs after death.

2. Carson says people might find the selling of organs "distasteful" (8). In an informal paper, describe the ways people might go about putting organs on sale. What would the "organ marketplace" be like?

Formal

3. **Argumentation.** Assume that the National Organ Transplant Act of 1984 continues in force but that there is agreement that increasing the numbers of organ donors is crucial. Brainstorm to generate arguments that could encourage members of the general public to become organ donors and develop examples and cases that you can use as support (you may use hypothetical or composite cases). Then write an argumentative paper in which you try to convince average Americans to sign organ-donor cards.

4. **Collaboration.** Consider steps that could be taken to confront the public with the problems surrounding organ donation and the need for change. With a group of classmates, brainstorm to discover creative ways that the United Network for Organ Sharing could use to inform people of the organ shortage and its consequences. Then, as a group, design a public information program including several components, and prepare a proposal describing it. Begin your proposal with a brief section,"Statement of the Problem." Then, in a "Goals" section briefly explain what your proposed program would accomplish. In a third, extended section, "Details of the Plan," summarize your program in one paragraph and then lay out its components with a paragraph devoted to each. End with a "Conclusion" section in which you state the benefits of putting your program into action.

■ ■ ■

The Lost Art of Political Argument

CHRISTOPHER LASCH

Christopher Lasch, who died in 1994, taught history at the University of Rochester and authored numerous books about modern U.S. society and culture. This article was printed in *Harper's Magazine* in September 1990. (Copyright 1990 by Harper's Magazine. All rights reserved. Reprinted by permission.)

Let us begin with a simple proposition: What democracy requires is public debate, not information. Of course it needs information too, but the kind of information it needs can be generated only by vigorous popular debate. We do not know what we need to know until we ask the right questions, and we can identify the right questions only by subjecting our own ideas about the world to the test of public controversy. Information, usually seen as the precondition of debate, is better understood as its by-product. When we get into arguments that focus and fully engage our attention, we become avid seekers of relevant information. Otherwise, we take in information passively—if we take it in at all.

From these considerations it follows that the job of the press is to encourage debate, not to supply the public with information. But as things now stand the press generates information in abundance, and nobody pays any attention. It is no secret that the public knows less about public affairs than it used to know. Millions of Americans cannot begin to tell you what is in the Bill of Rights, what Congress does, what the Constitution says about the powers of the presidency, how the party system emerged or how it operates. Ignorance of public affairs is commonly attributed to the failure of the public schools, and only secondarily to the failure of the press to inform. But since the public no longer participates in debates on national issues, it has no reason to be better informed. When debate becomes a lost art, information makes no impression.

3   Let us ask why debate has become a lost art. The answer may surprise: Debate began to decline around the turn of the century, when the press became more "responsible," more professional, more conscious of its civic obligations. In the early nineteenth century the press was fiercely partisan. Until the middle of the century papers were often financed by political parties. Even when they became more independent of parties they did not embrace the ideal of objectivity or neutrality. In 1841 Horace Greeley launched his *New York Tribune* with the announcement that it would be a "journal removed alike from servile partisanship on the one hand and from gagged, mincing neutrality on the other." Strong-minded editors like Greeley, James Gordon Bennett, E. L. Godkin, and Samuel Bowles did not attempt to conceal their own views or to impose a strict separation of news and editorial content. Their papers were journals of opinion in which the reader expected to find a definite point of view, together with unrelenting criticism of opposing points of view.

4   It is no accident that journalism of this kind flourished during the period from 1830 to 1900, when popular participation in politics was at its height. Eighty percent of the eligible voters typically went to the polls in presidential elections. (After 1900 the percentage began to decline sharply.) Torchlight parades, mass rallies, and gladiatorial contests of oratory made nineteenth-century politics an object of consuming popular interest.

5   In the midst of such politics, nineteenth-century journalism served as an extension of the town meeting. It created a public forum in which the issues of the day were hotly debated. Newspapers not only reported political controversies but participated in them, drawing in their readers as well. And print culture rested on the remnants of an oral tradition: Printed language was still shaped by the rhythms and requirements of the spoken word, in particular by the conventions of verbal argumentation. Print served to create a larger forum for the spoken word, not yet to displace or reshape it.

6   The "best men," as they liked to think of themselves, were never altogether happy with this state of affairs, and by the 1870s and 1880s their low opinion of politics had come to be widely shared by the educated classes. The scandals of the Gilded Age gave party politics a bad name. Genteel reformers—"mugwumps," to their enemies—demanded a professionalization of politics, designed to free the civil service from party control and to replace political appointees with trained experts.

7   The drive to clean up politics gained momentum in the Progressive era. Under the leadership of Theodore Roosevelt, Woodrow Wilson, Robert La Follette, and William Jennings Bryan, the Progressives preached efficiency, "good government," "bipartisanship," and the "scientific management" of public affairs, and declared war on "bossism." These reformers had little use for public debate. Most political questions were too complex, in their view, to be submitted to popular judgment. They liked to contrast the scientific expert with the orator—the latter a useless windbag whose rantings only confused the public mind.

8   Professionalism in politics meant professionalism in journalism. The connection between the two was spelled out by Walter Lippmann in the Twenties, in a series of books that

provided a founding charter for modern journalism—an elaborate rationale for a journalism guided by the new idea of professional objectivity. Lippmann held up standards by which the press is still judged.

In Lippmann's view, democracy did not require that people literally govern themselves.   9
Questions of substance should be decided by knowledgeable administrators whose access to reliable information immunized them against the emotional "symbols" and "stereotypes" that dominated public debate. The public, according to Lippmann, was incompetent to govern itself and did not even care to do so.

At one time this may not have been the case, but now, in the "wide and unpredictable   10
environment" of the modern world, the old ideal of citizenship was obsolete. A complex industrial society required a government carried on by officials who would necessarily be guided—since any form of direct democracy was now impossible—by either public opinion or expert knowledge. Public opinion was unreliable because it could be united only by an appeal to slogans and "symbolic pictures." Lippmann's distrust of public opinion rested on the epistemological distinction between truth and mere opinion. Truth, as he conceived it, grew out of disinterested scientific inquiry; everything else was ideology. Public debate was at best a disagreeable necessity. Ideally, it would not take place at all; decisions would be based on scientific "standards of measurement" alone.

The role of the press, as Lippmann saw it, was to circulate information, not to encourage argument. The relationship between information and argument was antagonistic,   11
not complementary. He did not take the position that argumentation was a necessary outcome of reliable information; on the contrary, his point was that information precluded argument, made argument unnecessary. Arguments were what took place in the absence of reliable information.

Lippmann had forgotten what he learned (or should have learned) from William James   12
and John Dewey, that our search for reliable information is itself guided by the questions that arise during arguments about a given course of action. It is only by subjecting our preferences and projects to the test of debate that we come to understand what we know and what we still need to learn. Until we have to defend our opinions in public, they remain opinions in Lippmann's pejorative sense—half-formed convictions based on random impressions and unexamined assumptions. It is the act of articulating and defending our views that lifts them out of the category of "opinions," gives them shape and definition, and makes it possible for others to recognize them as a description of their own experience as well. In short, we come to know our own minds only by explaining ourselves to others.

The attempt to bring others around to our own point of view carries the risk, of course,   13
that we may adopt their point of view instead. We have to enter imaginatively into our opponents' arguments, if only for the purpose of refuting them, and we may end up being persuaded by those we sought to persuade. Argument is risky and unpredictable—and therefore educational. Most of us tend to think of it (as Lippmann thought of it) as a clash of rival dogmas, a shouting match in which neither side gives any ground. But arguments are not won by shouting down opponents. They are won by changing opponents' minds.

If we insist on argument as the essence of education, we will defend democracy not as   14
the most efficient but as the most educational form of government—one that extends the circle of debate as widely as possible and thus forces all citizens to articulate their views, to put their views at risk, and to cultivate the virtues of eloquence, clarity of thought and expression, and sound judgment. From this point of view, the press has the potential to serve as the equivalent of the town meeting.

15   This is what Dewey argued, in effect—though not, unfortunately, very clearly—in *The Public and Its Problems* (1927), a book written in reply to Lippmann's disparaging studies of public opinion. Lippmann's distinction between truth and information rested on a "spectator theory of knowledge," as James W. Carey explains in his recently published book, *Communication as Culture.* As Lippmann understood these matters, knowledge is what we get when an observer, preferably a scientifically trained observer, provides us with a copy of reality that we can all recognize. Dewey, on the other hand, knew that even scientists argue among themselves. He held that the knowledge needed by any community—whether it is a community of scientific inquirers or a political community—emerges only from "dialogue" and "direct give and take."

16   It is significant, as Carey points out, that Dewey's analysis of communication stressed the ear rather than the eye. "Conversation," Dewey wrote, "has a vital import lacking in the fixed and frozen words of written speech. . . . The connections of the ear with vital and outgoing thought and emotion are immensely closer and more varied than those of the eye. Vision is spectator; hearing is a participator."

17   The proper role of the press is to extend the scope of debate by supplementing the spoken word with the written word. The written word is indeed a poor substitute for the spoken word; nevertheless, it can serve as an acceptable substitute as long as written speech takes spoken speech (and not, say, mathematics) as its model. According to Lippman, the press was unreliable because it could never give us accurate representations of reality, only "symbolic pictures" and stereotypes. Dewey's analysis implied a more penetrating line of criticism. As Carey puts it, "The press, by seeing its role as that of informing the public, abandons its role as an agency for carrying on the conversation of our culture." Having embraced Lippman's ideal of objectivity, the press no longer serves to cultivate "certain vital habits" in the community—"the ability to follow an argument, grasp the point of view of another, expand the boundaries of understanding, debate the alternative purposes that might be pursued."

18   The rise of the advertising and public-relations industries, side by side, helps to explain why the press abdicated its most important function—enlarging the public forum—at the same time that it became more "responsible." A responsible press, as opposed to a partisan or opinionated one, attracted the kind of readers advertisers were eager to reach: well-heeled readers, most of whom probably thought of themselves as independent voters. These readers wanted to be assured that they were reading all the news that was fit to print, not an editor's idiosyncratic and no doubt biased view of things. Responsibility came to be equated with the avoidance of controversy because advertisers were willing to pay for it. Some advertisers were also willing to pay for sensationalism, though on the whole they preferred a respectable readership to sheer numbers. What they clearly did not prefer was "opinion"— not because they were impressed with Lippmann's philosophical arguments but because opinionated reporting did not guarantee the right audience. No doubt they also hoped that an aura of objectivity, the hallmark of responsible journalism, would rub off on the advertisements that surrounded increasingly slender columns of print.

19   In a curious historical twist, advertising, publicity, and other forms of commercial persuasion themselves came to be disguised as information and, eventually, to substitute for open debate. "Hidden persuaders" (as Vance Packard called them) replaced the old-time editors, essayists, and orators who made no secret of their partisanship. And information and publicity became increasingly indistinguishable. Today, most of the "news" in our newspapers consists of items churned out by press agencies and public-relations offices and then regurgitated intact by the "objective" organs of journalism.

The decline of the partisan press and the rise of a new type of journalism professing   20
rigorous standards of objectivity do not assure a steady supply of usable information. Unless
information is generated by sustained public debate, most of it will be irrelevant at best, misleading and manipulative at worst. Increasingly, information is generated by those who wish
to promote something or someone—a product, a cause, a political candidate or office-
holder—without either arguing their case on its merits or explicitly advertising it as self-
interested material. Much of the press, in its eagerness to inform the public, has become a
conduit for the equivalent of junk mail. When words are used merely as instruments of publicity or propaganda, they lose their power to persuade. Soon they cease to mean anything
at all. People lose the capacity to use language precisely and expressively, or even to distinguish one word from another. The spoken word models itself on the written word instead of
the other way around, and ordinary speech begins to sound like the clotted jargon we see in
print. Ordinary speech begins to sound like "information"—a disaster from which the English language may never recover.

Questions for Inquiry

1. What is Lasch's claim? Is it stated or implied? Would you say it is predominantly a claim
   of fact, causation, value, policy, or mixed?
2. What does Lasch mean by "professionalism" in journalism (8)? Why does he consider
   it a problem rather than a virtue?
3. Why is democracy the most educational form of government (14)? What, according to
   the author, should be the role of the press in a democracy?
4. What are the advantages of spoken debate over written?
5. How did advertising encourage the move away from a press that expressed opinions
   and took sides on issues?

Questions for Argument

1. According to Lasch, the major influence on modern journalism, Walter Lippmann, believed that a government of experts was better than a government guided by public
   opinion. Do you agree that the U.S. public is "incompetent to govern itself" and is, in
   fact, disinterested in doing so (9)? Should we have experts making our societal decisions
   for us?
2. Lasch sees today's professionally neutral journalism as actually full of "hidden persuaders" (19) and the promotion of products, ideas, and candidates "without . . . arguing their case on its merits" (20). To what extent do you believe our news today is
   distorted? How far can we trust the press? Would it be better if papers returned to "old-
   time editors, essayists, and orators who made no secret of their partisanship" (19)?

Writing Assignments

Informal

1. "We come to know our own minds only by explaining ourselves to others," according
   to Lasch. In your journal, write about a time when you exposed your opinions in debate with another person or a group. Explore whether the exchange of ideas helped you

clarify and define your ideas or revealed that your opinions were full of "random impressions and unexamined assumptions"(12).

2. Much of today's press "has become a conduit for the equivalent of junk mail," the author notes (20). Do you find yourself an interested reader of the news, or do you pretty much treat the paper as "junk mail" or "junk news"? Write an informal paper in which you describe your attitude (and those of friends or peers) to the news and to public affairs. Explain why you have the attitude you do, attributing it perhaps to life-style, upbringing, or, as Lasch does, to the emptiness and fraudulent nature of the "news" today.

Formal

3. **Argumentation.** Walter Lippmann believed that "arguments were what took place in the absence of reliable information," Lasch writes (11). Do you agree that information is the cure for arguments? Think about arguments you have been exposed to recently, both personal and societal, and free-write about them to discover whether information or something else was needed. Then write a paper in which you argue a claim about the role of or necessity for information in resolving or dissolving certain kinds of arguments. Use the analysis of specific arguments as support for your claim.

4. **Collaboration.** In 1990, Lasch argued that opinion journalism, necessary for true democracy, died early in the twentieth century. But today, at the end of the century, have other journalistic media taken over the role of "carrying on the conversation of our culture" (17)? As a class, brainstorm to identify some television or radio shows or other media outlets that encourage and enable active debate about public affairs. Then, with a group of students or individually, choose one show or other outlet and study it as a possible exception to "the lost art of political argument" by reading, watching, or listening to it several times. You might also want to research it to discover whether anyone has written about the significance of the dialogues on this show or outlet. Then write a paper explaining that other media today are, or are not, providing the necessary opportunities for citizens to enter political debate.

5. In paragraph 19, Lasch suggests that the information we do get from the press today is not worth much: it is, he says, "churned out by press agencies" and "regurgitated intact" as news. Take some time to study some news stories in a major newspaper. Keep track of the number of times that information is provided by "spokespersons," government officials, official news agencies, press agents, or "personal representatives" such as lawyers, and compare those instance with instances when information is acquired by interviewing witnesses or participants or through direct observation. Then write a paper in which you report your findings about the quality and origin of news in this particular paper and evaluate the paper as a source of information and ideas. Relate your comments back to Lasch's opinion of the press today.

■ ■ ■

Chapter 8

Writing to Refute, Inquire, and Moderate Opposing Ideas

■ Consider the following excerpt, then respond as indicated below:

> How would practical rhetoric look if we assumed that writer and reader were not adversaries but partners in a common community-based enterprise? . . . How would it look if we no longer assumed that people write to persuade or distinguish themselves and their point of view and to enhance their own individuality by gaining the acceptance of other individuals? How would it look if we assumed instead that people write for the very opposite reason: that people write in order to be accepted, to join, to be regarded as another member of the culture or community that constitutes the writer's audience?
>
> —Kenneth Brufee, "Collaborative Learning and the 'Conversation of Mankind' "

Writer's Journal

Write a journal entry about Brufee's questions. What reasons move you to write—or to express yourself in another medium? Would you say you strive to "distinguish yourself" or to become part of an expressive community? Strive for an entry of 150 words.

You may find yourself contesting someone's opinion at the lunch table or perhaps at a family gathering where your obnoxious relatives spout what seem to you poorly thought-out opinions. This is a "me against him" (or her) situation. In your reading about a topic, you might discover sources that disagree, and you might seek to determine which one is wrong, and which is right.

Most of us grow up assuming that two opposing forces represent the natural structure of argumentation. Humans seem to like to think in dichotomies: they see things as black and white. Disagreements among several nations or parties in a nation often become battles between two sets of forces. Alliances may occur among conflicting groups until the many factions congeal into two, "us" and "them." Or the holders of alternate positions may be ignored or swept away by the ravages of the two major opposed forces.

In the United States, the long persistence of a two-party political system, despite its not being written in any legal statutes, speaks to the powerful draw of arguments between "us" and "them." Some European nations, however, operate with many political parties, suggesting that some civil discourse communities are not so attuned as ours to the opposing-forces idea of disputation.

The *refutation* strategy of argumentation operates by presenting and critiquing ideas that differ from those asserted. But refutation is only one method of handling disagreement between ideas. When argumentation is conceived as a process in which ideas are questioned, evaluated, and reformed, it becomes apparent there are many sides to an issue, and constraining argumentation into an opposing-forces model can limit the growth of ideas instead of furthering them.

Beyond the clash of pro and con, then, there are other strategies for dealing with differences of opinion. Instead of "beating down the opponent," for example, you might want to underscore the complexities of an issue and elaborate a position that is an alternative to both the pro and the con. You might want to seek the **middle ground** or a compromise position, a position that chooses pieces from both sides, or even a position that forges a whole new path in thinking about the issue. This mode of handling controversy has come to be called **Rogerian**, after psychologist Carl Rogers, who in the 1950s developed a method of moderating conflicts in interpersonal relations. His method emphasizes dialogue and commonality in a world dominated by conflict and strife.

Finally, a third way of handling differences, especially differences in evidence or statistics, is to stay in an **inquiry** mode. Inquiry writing discusses the disparate evidence from two or more sources, locates both common ground and conflicts in evidence, and then identifies the questions that need answering and the evidence that needs to be acquired before a solid position can evolve. This type of essay may explore possible solutions to a problem and demonstrate that uncertainty and nonresolution are sometimes the best position.

■ REFUTATION

The tendency to treat disagreements about ideas as a battle between two opposing forces results from what has been called the *agonistic* mentality. Agonistic is a term derived from the Greek word for contestant. In the media, the opposition of two ideas is exploited because battles have entertainment value. So *Sixty Minutes* has long featured a pro-and-con debate at the end of the show; *Crossfire* features "left" and "right" authorities discussing current events, with stinging remarks and clever put-downs encouraged. Even in the arts, the agonistic format is used; critics Gene Siskel and Roger Ebert argue sarcastically and wittily over movies. And debate format, of course, uses a pro-and-con structure.

Refutation is an umbrella term for a range of ways of handling opposing views. Strictly speaking, to refute is to argue against by revealing the flaws in the opposing argument. Added to your presentation of evidence for your side, refutation can clinch an argument for your readers. Typically, in supporting a position, the writer imagines objections that the reader might have or identifies opposition views and then counters them someplace in the argument. This results in a pattern of summary (of the opposition) followed by refutation—true rebuttal. Sometimes writers don't so much argue against a position as label it irrelevant, trivial, or off the mark. Other times, a writer might counter just one of several objections and ignore the rest.

Ignoring objections on the grounds that if the writer doesn't call attention to them the reader won't think of them is usually considered a poor strategy. Unfortunately, readers do resist the ideas of writers. This can happen when the reader does not match the writer's implied reader and when the reader is not a member of the discourse community the writer intends to address. Readers may believe that a writer who ignores obvious or common objections to a viewpoint is not thorough or not well informed or is pretending that there are no objections. So the recommendation has generally been to respect the cleverness of your readers and the possibility that they reside in a different discourse community. If there are likely objections to the position you are supporting, you should deal with them.

Because arguing against something puts you in the position of being a naysayer, you will probably wish to emphasize any **common ground**. You might, for example, briefly summarize and then grant the opposing view to some extent. If your ideas can coexist with some parts of the opponents' position, then acknowledging that the opposition is somewhat correct disarms negative readers and gives them some space to consider your points. If you do allow that the opposition is in some part correct, you may then go on to show why your position is more meritorious, practical, relevant, workable, all-encompassing, or fair.

When you refute ideas as a way of indirectly supporting your own, you will cite and discuss only those portions of an opposing argument that are relevant. You will section off a bit of the opponent's reasoning to summarize, paraphrase, or quote. Then you will discuss or critique this material and ignore the rest of an opposing position.

Techniques

There are too many ways of disagreeing to list them all. This is just a sampling. You can:

- point out an internal contradiction or logical flaw
- show that the facts are in error
- reveal that the reasoning is flawed, that the conclusions drawn from the situation don't follow
- give expert or "on-the-scene" examples
- change the grounds of the discussion, apply different values, challenge assumptions

In the first example here the author draws different conclusions from the facts. After several terrorist bombings of hotels and other public places in Cuba, some analysts began to think that Castro was on the way out. Reporter and commentator Gwynne Dyer took issue with this opinion:

> So speculation erupts: Is this the beginning of the end for Castro? Alvaro Prendes, a Cuban air force colonel who defected three years ago, believes that only people in the Cuban armed forces could have set the bombs. "Things in Cuba will get worse before they get better," he says. "Bloodshed is inevitable."
>
> The truth is probably quite the opposite. Castro has weathered the worst of the crises that followed the collapse of the Soviet bloc in 1989–91, and the bombers are trying to sabotage the Cuban tourist industry precisely because it is a major element in Cuba's economic improvement.
>
> *Recovery* is perhaps too positive a word for what has happened in Cuba. . . . Nevertheless, the recovery is real.

As a way of summarizing the opposition, Dyer uses a quotation from a prominent person; then he offers a countering explanation for the bombing and goes on to cite details of Cuban life and examples of Castro's resourcefulness in manipulating his people's attitudes. He comes across as close to his subject, well informed historically, and a credible commentator.

The letters-to-the-editor pages of many newspapers and magazines are filled with examples of refutation, as readers write in to express disapproval of published articles. In our second example, the writer takes issue with an article in *Policy Review* in which the author, William Craig Rice, suggested that federal funding for the arts should cease and the art world should compete for money in the private market. The director of a philanthropic foundation, Sanford Hirsch, wrote in reply:

> Rice's assumption that money is out there and should be found in sufficient quantities to make the NEA [National Endowment for the Arts] unnecessary is true enough. But this proposed solution—to increase admission costs and develop more effective marketing strategies—serves to make the arts more remote and less accessible to those who may derive the most benefit from it.
>
> The real question, I believe, is not whether the government has an obligation to fund the arts, nor whether there is a sufficient amount of private cash to support art venues and projects. It is whether we have the collective will to live up to the standards we claim for ourselves.
>
> The value of art is that it is not just for children, or the privileged, or the elite, but that it seriously engages adults from all walks of life as it allows them to interact positively, and to broaden the scope of their knowledge and associations. . . . The minuscule cost we're talking about—President Clinton's committee recommends $2 per taxpayer— is certainly warranted if we value informed, sophisticated, and independent citizens.
>
> On the other hand, if we want to send the message that we only value that which pays we can do so by further cutting arts funding.

Note Hirsch's strategy here: he first grants the truth of a point ("Rice's assumption . . . is true enough") and then goes on to change the grounds of the discussion. While admitting the economics of the situation are as Rice portrays them, Hirsch sees federal funding of the arts as a way of "send[ing] the message" about what the nation believes. In the same issue of *Policy Review,* author Rice replied to Hirsch:

> Sanford Hirsch . . . rightly caution[s] against a Panglossian view of the future of the arts absent the NEA. But there is good reason to believe that increased voluntary support for the arts will follow the end of mandatory (tax-based) support, as it has in other areas of charitable and nonprofit activity. People give where they see a need—but give less when they can ask, "Isn't the government taking care of that?" I agree with Hirsch that the government should encourage the cultivation of "informed, sophisticated, and independent citizens" through involvement in the arts. But this must be done indirectly and blindly— through tax code changes, for example—and not by centralizing aesthetic and cultural authority in a federal agency that gets to pick winners and losers.

Note that Rice's pattern of refutation is similar to Hirsch's. First he summarizes and grants a point made by his critics, and then he goes on to provide additional support for his own position.

In the third example, letter writer James Kavanaugh takes issue not with a specific article about the strike of United Parcel Service (UPS) workers in 1997 but with an opinion he feels is widespread:

> There is a suspicion that the UPS strike is only about greed. But the greed lies not with the work force but with the management and owners of UPS.
>
> It is important to realize that the share being offered by management is an extremely small portion of the growth in profits generated by the quality of the labor at UPS. If the workers were as undeserving as the managers and owners imply, how would there have been any growth in profits—let alone the record growth of the last few years?
>
> While the Teamsters union may not be the most reputable, it is the bargaining agent for the UPS work force. . . . It is well past the time when a moral management gave them what they earned.

Kavanaugh quickly summarizes the view he is critiquing and then goes on to use reasoning to expose an internal contradiction in the UPS attitude that workers don't deserve a deep share of profits. In the last paragraph, Kavanaugh dismisses the issue of the Teamsters union's reputation and instead makes a plea for just treatment: giving the UPS workers "what they earned."

■ *Activity 1*

Discovering Refutation, p. 320

■ *Activity 2*

Discussing and Analyzing Refutation: Refutation Workshop, p. 320

Writing a Formal Refutation Argument

A formal refutation is a paper that shows there is a serious flaw or flaws in the evidence or reasoning for an argument. This flaw may lie in the way statistics are applied. Or the evidence offered may be flawed—perhaps not relevant, current, or sufficient. There may be logical problems or fallacies in the reasoning. The way a significant term is used may be questionable or debatable. The reasons used as support may be weak.

Your first step is to identify an erroneous viewpoint on a controversial issue and brainstorm the reasoning that would support your view. Then read up on the issue,

■ *Dealing with Conflicting Data*

In some cases you will locate sources that use conflicting data, and in order to work toward your own position you need to figure out which source is the most correct. Here are some ways to handle statistics or other types of information that disagree.

1. Examine each article to determine the statistic's "pedigree." How old is it? How was it arrived at if the source generated it? If the source did not generate the statistic through primary research, where does it come from? In this examination, give points to a source that provides clear indications of the age and origins of information. Then you must recognize that older data may no longer be accurate. And information generated by a reliable source rates highly. (See Chapter 11 for discussion of source reliability.)

2. Examine how the data are interpreted or used. Are the conclusions drawn from the information reasonable? Do the facts add up the way the writers say they do? Can you think of other interpretations or explanations for what the facts mean? Can you think of exceptions or situations that show the information does not apply in all cases?

3. Continue researching to discover other writers who use or comment on the information you are questioning. Often, you will uncover the same data over and over as you go in depth on a topic. For example, in arguments about gun control, the number of gun deaths each year, as counted by the government, is often cited.

making sure you examine material for the viewpoint you wish to refute as well as that in support of your own view.

Once you are informed about the issue, write out an accurate statement of the position you are refuting. Then state your main criticism of this position. This statement will act as the claim of your argument. Then zero in on the specific criticisms you have of the position. Spell out the reasons you find the target position flawed. Use your research to provide facts, statistics, and quotations from authorities to show that your analysis is correct. Then make an outline of how you will present your refutation. Most often, an emphatic order, moving from least important to most important point, works best for structuring a refutation.

Here are guidelines for drafting a refutation argument:

■ Briefly summarize the main idea you wish to refute. You may explain subpoints now or wait until you move into your refutation. Make sure your presentation of the view is accurate and that your tone is objective.

■ Present your main statement of refutation, a statement criticizing the target viewpoint. Provide a general reason for your disagreement.

- Provide necessary background, definitions, or other information to set the stage for your analysis of the viewpoint.
- Develop your refutation by explaining and refuting subpoints of the target viewpoint.
- Arrange your points of refutation in a logical way: use emphatic order or some other pattern that will be clear to your reader.
- Conclude with a strong summary statement of the flaws in the viewpoint and possibly affirm your own viewpoint.
- As your instructor requires, use either informal reference or formal parenthetic documentation.

STUDENT ASSIGNMENT

Tim Anglen, "Marijuana as Medicine"

ASSIGNMENT: On a narrowed controversial topic, identify a viewpoint with which you disagree. On the basis of your research on this viewpoint, write an argument in which you refute the main reasons supporting it. Develop your refutation using specific examples, statistics, and reasoning.

Tim identified as his refutation target a focused aspect of the debate on the legalization of drugs: "marijuana should not be legalized for medical uses." Tim was aware that in some states the legalization of marijuana for medicinal purposes had recently been on the ballot.

In his brainstorming, Tim zeroed in on the idea that medical-legalization opponents feared gradual overall legalization of drugs. He wrote this preliminary claim: "opponents of the medical use of marijuana are incorrect in believing that such legalization will cause the legalization of all drugs for recreational use." But in his research Tim discovered that there were additional reasons for opposition to medical use. He thus broadened his claim: "federal drug-enforcement officials and the justice department maintain that marijuana is both useless and dangerous, but this is not the case." As he developed his draft, he decided to provide some background about the categories used to classify drugs before his refutation of individual points.

Here is his essay:

How many of us would deny pain relief to someone who is suffering or even dying? Very few. And most of us know that were we in the bed of suffering, we would want pain relief. Yet, our country's policy right now is to prevent doctors from prescribing a drug that has been proven to dramatically reduce pain and other symptoms in numerous diseases: marijuana.

Federal drug enforcement officials say that marijuana is both useless and dangerous. The drug has been classified as "Schedule I," a category for drugs that have no medical uses but can be abused. Moving the drug to "Schedule II" would mean that it or its active ingredient, delta-9-THC, would be available for physicians to prescribe and its use would no longer be prosecuted by the DEA.

Opponents of medical legalization believe there is no evidence that marijuana helps patients. However, this is just not the case. There have been small studies and much physician success with marijuana's pain-relieving abilities. Testifying in Congress in 1980, numerous prominent cancer physicians maintained that marijuana and derivatives are effective medically (Fine 52–53).

One reason the debate about marijuana's usefulness continues is that the Federal Drug Administration (FDA) has refused to allow clinical drug trials and has confined research to its negative effects (Fine 54). Proposed studies have been stopped by the government's refusal to permit patients access to marijuana. For example, to test the comparative effectiveness of smoked marijuana and Marinol (synthetic THC pills), Dr. Donald Abrahms of the University of California in San Francisco applied for permission and was refused (Pollan 40; Fine 54). As a result, many doctors rely on their positive experiences administering the drug to their patients in defending their recommendation of it (Pollan 40).

The diseases for which marijuana seems to be effective keep growing. Originally it was used by cancer patients to overcome pain and nausea of chemotherapy AIDS patients use it to increase appetite and combat wasting syndrome. In researching a *New York Times* article, Michael Pollan discovered supporters who used marijuana for a broad range of illnesses: "paraplegia; multiple sclerosis; insomnia; post-traumatic stress disorder; anorexia; anxiety; psoriasis, and even drug addiction" (27).

Aside from the question of medical effectiveness, government officials maintain that prescribing marijuana is dangerous. There exists no evidence to support this. Obviously, since marijuana is smoked, there are potential carcinogens in its smoke—about 400 compounds whose effects on the body are not understood (Pollan 29). But in the medical use of this drug, it is smoked briefly several times a day when needed, rather than several times an hour as is true for many cigarette smokers. In terms of its general use and abuse, marijuana is quite safe. As William Buckley, the editor of *National Review,* noted in testifying on this subject to the American Bar Association, "nobody has ever been found dead from marijuana." Instead, as Buckley asserts, the war on drugs has a huge casualty list of drug dealers and robbery victims. An oncologist in San Francisco, Dr. Seebasiah Tripathy, also confirms marijuana's safety as a medical drug: "Marijuana is far less toxic than many of the medicines I prescribe to my cancer patients" (Pollan 29).

Most seriously, government officials believe that medical use of marijuana will cause illegal use to skyrocket. They also insist that activists supporting medical use are really after broad decriminalization of drugs for personal use. The head of the

White House Office of National Drug Control Policy, Gen. Barry McCaffrey, is said to have called the medical marijuana movement "a stalking horse for legalization." He and others in the government believe that legal medical use will give the "wrong message" to children (Pollan 26).

But drugs similar to marijuana, morphine and codeine, have been legal to prescribe for decades. They are tightly regulated, and their legality for medical use "[has] done nothing to undermine the war against heroin," points out AIDS patient and San Francisco District Attorney Kenneth Vines (Pollan 27). Author David Fine notes that cocaine, a Schedule II drug that is prescribable, has actually dramatically decreased in use over the period of 1985 to 1994 (56). Finally, it is a fact of today's politics that, although many Americans approve of the legal medical use of marijuana (Fine 54), "there are almost no politicians who will even discuss [recreational] legalization," according to Bob Kolasky, assistant editor of the online journal *Intellectual Capital.* According to a Gallup poll, 85% of Americans oppose the general legalization of now-illegal substances (Wren).

The recent passage of referenda in California and Arizona shows that citizens as a whole do endorse the right of doctors to prescribe marijuana. Yet the federal government is contesting the new laws in these states and threatening to prosecute doctors who do recommend this drug. In light of the many benefits this simple remedy provides to patients of devastating diseases, this policy of prosecution is simply cruel.

Works Cited

Buckley, William F. "The War on Drugs Is Lost." *National Review* 12 Feb. 1996. Online. Available: http://www.nationalreview.com/nationalreview/ 12feb96/drug.html. 1 Jan. 1997.

Fine, David M. "Grassroots Medicine." *The American Prospect* Sept.–Oct. 1997: 51–56.

Kolasky, Bob. "Issue of the Week: Drug Legalization." *Intellectual Capital* 13 Feb. 1997. Online. Available: http://www.intellectual capital.com/issues/97/ 0213/icissues.html. 22 July 1997.

Pollan, Michael. "Medical Marijuana." *New York Times Magazine* 20 July 1997: 23+.

Wren, Christopher S. "Votes on Marijuana Are Stirring Debate." *New York Times* 17 Nov. 1996, nat. ed.: 16.

Writing an Argument with Refutation

A position paper becomes a true argument if you tackle the opposition; any of the techniques discussed in this chapter can work within an essay as well as when writing a formal refutation paper. But writing an argument with refutation poses some special problems: you need to determine whether countering possible objections to your position or critiquing the position of the opposition is the best way to go. You also need to decide on the extent of the refutation and where to place it in your argument.

You can go about supporting your claim in any combination of these three ways:

- directly by providing evidence for your claim
- indirectly by defending against possible criticisms of your claim
- indirectly by refuting opposite claims

In the direct approach, you provide specific evidence for your claim and for any assumptions that underlie it. This is the tactic used in the position paper discussed in Chapter 6. You may also indirectly support your claim by anticipating and countering specific criticisms of your claim or by showing the errors in the opposing position (refutation).

The readings by George Will and David Cole at the end of this chapter provide examples of refutation.

Decide on the Role and Placement of Refutation and Defense

As you plan, you need to think about your approach to conflicting views. Will a response to opposing points or potential criticisms be central to developing your view? Or will the focus of your development be direct evidence for your claim?

There are no rules as to where to position refutational or defensive material. Here are some possibilities:

- Begin with refutation as an introductory device.
- Disqualify opposing views at the start of the body of the argument before directly presenting evidence.
- Place refutation after the completion of the main argument.
- Use opposing points and your refutation as the backbone of the entire argument.

In the process of generating your outline, you might set up your own direct argument first, and then go back and place refutation where it works best. A challenge to a viewpoint that contradicts your own may form a strong lead-in to your own ideas. So you might begin your argument by invoking a position you find flawed and segueing from that into your own claim.

Or, after asserting your claim, you could pause to discuss contradictions that might occur to your reader and thereby disarm threats to your position. Another approach is to inject your refutation or defensive material where appropriate along the way as you present your own evidence.

Sometimes it works best to use opposing views as a scaffold for your own argument. You might, for example, go through an opposing position point by point, each time showing why your view is more solid. Your entire argument, in other words, might be a response to an opposing view, and in this way you can completely integrate the refutation with your own argument.

Decide How to Develop the Argument

In deciding how to support your claim, you should consider the possibilities from two perspectives. From the point of view of content and logic, you need to choose the direct evidence, refutation, and defense that most effectively show the merit of your claim. In this sense, your development will be content-oriented.

From another perspective, what will constitute the most effective support depends on the audience you intend to reach with your argument. As you select the reasoning, you should have in mind your readers' background, awareness of the topic, and potential biases. You need to evaluate your audience's needs and motivations. For example, if you suspect your readers will prefer the status quo instead of your recommendation, you will make sure to refute the merits of doing nothing and underscore the importance of taking action. Or, to soothe a readership likely to be agitated by your opinions, you might first point out areas of agreement and pointedly approve of any shared ideas.

Decide How to Establish Credibility

As you work on your paper, you need to take into account your readers' reactions to both what you say and how you say it. You want to be perceived as believable, for readers pay attention to the messenger as well as to the message.

Credibility derives from the image the readers receive of a writer based on the language of the text as well as from the content—that is, the information and reasoning in the argument. To be perceived as fair, reasonable, and informed, you need to demonstrate these characteristics. A neutral tone, a language style free of excessive emotionality, and the use of qualifications or moderating terms where appropriate are all helpful in achieving credibility.

Summarizing opposing views fairly and accurately and showing sensitivity to your reader's mind-set can help you gain trust. For example, if you are writing to decry attempts to pass legislation regarding victims' rights, you should take into consideration whether your audience might include crime victims or their relatives. Your representation of their point of view must recognize their situation. You might address their bias directly or perhaps show through your wording, choice of evidence, and so forth that you see their side.

Sometimes writers fall into a habit of "arguing by questions." Their paragraphs are full of questions—not genuine inquiry questions, but "rhetorical" ones, questions whose answers are so "obvious" the reader can supply them, whether in agreement or not. These questions can amount to indirect assertions. The very activity of reading the questions and providing the writer's answers makes the answers seem like the reader's own; it sneaks the ideas into the reader's mind. But sometimes chains of questions can amount to the fallacy of "begging the question" (see Chapter 9). So it's better to use a pattern of assertion plus support rather than strings of questions to build your argument.

■ EXPLORING THE MIDDLE GROUND: A ROGERIAN APPROACH TO ARGUMENTATION

In the 1960s, C. Rap Brown, a leader of the radical Black Panthers, wrote, "If you're not part of the solution, you're part of the problem." Catchy? Certainly. But also simplistic. In regard to racial discrimination, as with other societal issues, there have always been many people who are not helping to solve the problem but who also are not doing anything to worsen it. There are lots of people in the middle.

When only opposing views are allowed, people's views can become polarized. Problems and their solutions can become oversimplified. Complicated evidence and reasoning are sometimes ignored or denied. And, finally, if there can be only two sides, then resolution can come only when one side is vanquished, proven worthless and totally wrong. Few among us like to be vanquished. Many historical disputes cast as battles go on and on; the success of one party is only temporary, as the vanquished rises again to resume the struggle. The futility of two opposed sides battling it out is told throughout the world: in Northern Ireland, Bosnia, the Middle East, and many other places.

Besides leading to extremism and oversimplification, the opposing-forces style of disagreement may deny reality. In most battles, many people remain on the sidelines and refuse to participate because they think both sides are wrong. They see another way, a third way. An honest look at a controversy uncovers a range of viewpoints, not just two. In examining two opposing sources, you may feel this way—that neither view is completely accurate or represents your view. You may be able to identify a third possible position or even a fourth and fifth.

Peace or resolution of conflict tends to come through negotiation of a middle ground rather than through a victory in which one side devastates the other. Refutation is a piece of argumentation conceived as dispute between opposing forces. It can be used, obviously, to decimate an opposing argument so as to elevate one's own. But the thoughtful critiquing of others' arguments can be a step in building a composite position that takes the best from all sides.

You will often realize that there is some common ground between the two: in other words, there is an area of agreement as well as disagreement, although the area of agreement may not be obvious. An early theorist of conflict negotiation pointed out that repetitively arguing a position prevents people from seeing connections between their views and others'; they come to suffer from a "blindness of involvement" (Anatol Rapoport, quoted in Lewicki et al. 196).

Discovering the Middle Ground

If you want to explore the middle ground between extreme positions, there are several techniques you can adopt. All the techniques rely, however, on your having an accurate and open-minded understanding of the opposing positions. For Rogers, achieving this in interpersonal conflict meant both sides had to learn "active listening," a technique that involves listening carefully and repeating back the meaning of the communication. Active listening is a method of checking that one's understanding is accurate without resorting to questioning, which can cause defensiveness.

In dealing with sources, reading carefully for meaning first and then using annotation and paraphrase serve the same purpose as active listening: to "better understand the nature of the opponent's' position, [and] the factors and information that support it" so that we can determine a compromise or negotiated position (Lewicki et al. 196). Once you are sure you are clear about the opposing position(s), you can use several strategies to explore and multiply perspectives. You might try individual or group brainstorming to generate possible positions. Or you might use qualification techniques to moderate the extreme positions. Finally, you might use Rogerian strategies adapted to writing.

Brainstorming

Here's an example of a brainstormed list on a controversy with many possible positions: gun control. In a pro-or-con sense, there are two positions: one, that everyone should be allowed to own guns, and the other, that guns should be prohibited. In between are a multitude of viewpoints:

- Handgun ownership by private citizens should be banned.
- Handgun permits should be issued only to merchants who can prove a need for protection against robberies.
- Handguns should be limited to one per household or business.
- Handgun ownership by people who have been convicted of a felony or who have a history of mental illness should not be permitted.
- Handgun ownership by those who have committed any domestic violence or child abuse should be prohibited.
- Handgun purchase should be permitted only after a waiting period of some days and a background check to eliminate the mentally unstable and the violence-prone.
- Federal and state governments should aggressively lower the number of handguns in our nation by sponsoring "gun buybacks," in which people can turn in guns and receive a small payment or reward.
- Gun shows, where many guns of all kinds change ownership without any regard for regulations, should be closely monitored by the states.
- Handgun owners should be required to keep their guns unloaded and under lock and key at all times, on penalty of fines or of imprisonment if someone is injured with their gun.
- Handgun ownership should be unlimited, but every American from fifth grade up should receive education, comparable to sex education, in how to respect and handle a gun.

There are twelve positions on handgun control (and perhaps you and your classmates can think of others), and we haven't even touched possible positions on hunting guns or assault weapons!

As you can see from this list, some knowledge of a controversy is required before you can start to generate possible opinions. Background reading can be essential to "prime the pump" for brainstorming.

Qualification Techniques

In qualifying, you begin with the opposing positions on a topic and then try to qualify or modify them. Here are some suggestions for qualifying extreme views. First, break the issue or topic into subtopics and deal with only one; focusing in can help you see ways of locating middle ground. It's easier, for example, to think of moderate viewpoints about gun control if you work with a small part of the issue, such as how to make gun ownership safe for legal owners and their families. You might take the position, for example, that registered owners of guns who have families must have trigger locks. If you focus on control of illegal gun ownership, you might generate a different set of possible approaches.

Second, imagine exceptions or situations that would make the extreme pro-or-con view unworkable. For example, a common qualification of the antiabortion view is that abortions should be allowed in the case of rape, incest, or danger to the health of the mother. A common qualification of the pro-gun-ownership position is the concession that convicted felons and the mentally ill should not have access to firearms.

Third, use qualifying or moderating transitional phrases to direct you toward alternatives: "some," "few," "many," "sometimes," and "often." For example, the assertion that "Americans have the right to own guns" implies "all," but you might be able to moderate this assertion by adding a qualifier such as "sometimes." This might lead you to think about those for whom gun ownership is not advisable: children, those with impaired vision or unsteady limbs, and the mentally handicapped, among others.

Fourth, move from a values-heavy point of view to a policy orientation. Sometimes pro-and-con positions reflect ideals, and changing perspectives to look at real situations and the consequences of applying an ideal can inspire a multitude of alternatives.

Rogerian Techniques Applied to Argumentation

Another view of argumentation that strives to move away from the oppositional is Rogerian argumentation, a way in which interpersonal communication can move toward compromise rather than opposition. Rhetoricians in the 1970s adapted Rogers's method to written communication. Rogers believed effective listening fostered resolution between opposed parties. To demonstrate good listening, he advised opponents to restate the opposite position in a way the other side would agree was accurate. Such restatement requires genuinely searching for the meaning of others' statements and toning down one's own emotional reactions. Using this technique, people come to appreciate the other side's position, and polarization is decreased. People's views shift through such empathy, and they sometimes can find an acceptable middle position.

Such interpersonal exploration of beliefs creates empathy because it can lead to discussion of the experiences that make a person prefer a certain point of view. Many opinions are tightly tied to one's life-style or the culture in which one has been raised, as we learned in Chapter 6. Someone who was raised on a western ranch might have been given guns and taught to use them properly from a young age, and this person's anti-gun-control stance might be closely tied to a love for the way of life on the western range. An arguer might miss this piece of information about the westerner's support of legal gun ownership.

■ *Activity 3*
Finding a Middle Ground: Qualifying Extreme Statements, p. 322

■ *Activity 4*
Finding a Middle Ground: Rogerian Listening, p. 322

■ *Activity 5*
Finding a Middle Ground: Devising Many Positions on a Topic, p. 322

A person with a Rogerian bent—one who tries to listen carefully and completely to the other side and who aims to show that understanding by neutral restatements—may discover the personal background that underlies the westerner's support of gun ownership. Such understanding might help the discussion move toward a proposal that both agree is fair. Similarly, you may discover that a gun-control advocate is also a witness to or even a survivor of a crime in which a gun was used. By hearing about this experience, you may become more sympathetic toward the reasoning of those who advocate strict gun laws.

But a caution must be mentioned. Rogerian technique must be used by all involved. If only one person or some people in a discussion try to be understanding of the others' views, then those who strive to "win the argument" will have an advantage. Rogerian style will likely cause those who use it to be flexible and open to a change of position, and so it will be easy for those who aim to win to come out on top. In other words, Rogerian technique, or any negotiation style of interaction, can be manipulated to place those who use it in a weak position. If your class practices Rogerian argumentation in its brainstorming sessions, you may find that some class members have a problem being nonjudgmental and intellectually open.

Outside the classroom setting, Rogerians must be prepared to teach the goals and process to others and to advocate insistently for its use, or they will place themselves at a disadvantage. It has become something of a cliché, but it is still worth mentioning that women have typically been raised to seek peace and to strive for negotiation, while men have been raised to feel comfortable in combative situations. Of course, there are many exceptions to this tendency. Knowing about this aspect of men's and women's upbringing can help you find ways to support the search for moderate views and the middle ground.

Writing with a Rogerian Approach

Rogerian techniques can come into play in the writing process not only in group brainstorming to discover the rightness of other points of view but also in doing research and developing an argument in the final draft of an argumentative essay.

In doing research, you should go beyond collecting information and evidence that supports the position you prefer. You should also:

- Explore other points of view to comprehend why some people find those positions congenial.
- Read about the experiences of people who hold opposing views to increase your respect for other viewpoints.
- Read about a situation in depth to understand the history behind the range of positions; often, only through understanding the history of a problem can you propose a solution that is truly workable.

For example, a person choosing a position on workfare—that is, welfare programs that require clients to work—would do well to explore the history of such programs. By discovering that workfare has been tried in some states and has led to some success but also disasters in shifting people from welfare to jobs or homelessness, a writer might forge a complex and qualified position that supports workfare only if certain exclusions and qualifications are written into the laws.

To decide whether to use a Rogerian approach, you should examine your rhetorical situation. If your readership is going to be hostile to your point of view, it can be a good idea to employ a flexible or Rogerian stance, one in which you validate as much as you can of positions different from your own. By indicating empathy with and flexibility toward your readers, you will encourage them to view you favorably as a fair person and to regard your ideas with some openness.

The reading selections by Alysia Bennett and Suzanne Pharr at the end of this chapter provide examples of exploring the middle ground.

■ THE INQUIRY ESSAY: RAISING QUESTIONS

At times your research may get bogged down in contradictions as you read well-supported and strongly evidenced opinions that range across the opinion spectrum on your topic. Other times you may find general agreement about some aspect of your topic but feel that important issues remain unaddressed or that questions remain unanswered. For example, your sources might treat the subject abstractly, without providing statistical or other evidence that you feel is necessary.

The inquiry essay argues for openness on a topic and points out information that is needed or issues that need exploration before a firm position can be justified. It may seem like a contradiction to argue for openness, but often taking an inquiry stance on a controversial issue means refuting the positions of all sides, to some extent, and showing why there is an open question or questions about some aspect of the topic. The inquiry essay is not an essay written before you learn anything about your topic; it is the result of reading and investigating to a point where you know quite a bit about the context and pertinent data. It is not written off the top of your head but instead emerges out of the depths of your knowledge.

The inquiry essay is also not a critique of the sources you read. Understanding weaknesses in the material you read may be a necessary stage in formulating your questions about an issue, but the job of an inquiry essay does not include wholesale critiquing of sources. Neither does it mean dismissing your sources or ignoring them. Rather, your reading should become the ground of your inquiry, and it should be in sight all the time as you discuss the topic.

The reading selections by Jane Eisner and Richard Shweder at the end of this chapter are inquiry essays.

You may be directly assigned to write an essay of inquiry, an essay that argues that certain issues need addressing or certain questions need answering. Or, as you write an assigned argumentation essay, you may decide that you see more questions than answers, that your best "main idea" about the subject is a question (or questions), not an assertion. Here are some guidelines for preparing an inquiry essay.

- Perform your research carefully, annotating, taking notes, and making lists of comparable or conflicting points, values, emphases.
- Evaluate your sources as to seriousness and objectivity (see Chapter 11).

- Use informal writing, brainstorming, discussion to help you identify issues that seem open-ended, that need more research, that society needs to look at more closely.
- Use your sources to pinpoint the questions that are open. Your questions should be based on these sources and grow out of them. So as you plan your essay, you will search back through your reading for reference points for the issues you raise and the questions you pose.
- Identify your main question or open issue on the topic. This will form the basis for your inquiry claim.
- Plan your essay by listing your questions about the topic. Weave in references to the sources where they are relevant.
- Write your draft.
- Use informal or formal reference documentation, as instructed by your teacher.

STUDENT ASSIGNMENT

Sarah Carlyle, "How Poor Is Really Poor?"

After reading two assigned essays about whether the government fairly determines the numbers of U.S. "poor" and "working poor," Sarah Carlyle was assigned to write an argument about the controversy. Both essays contained many statistics, and she felt that together they raised more questions than they answered. The result was an inquiry essay.

To begin, Sarah read and annotated the two articles to make sure she understood them. She underlined the claims, took some notes, and wrote a summary of one or two sentences for each article. She felt the opposition opinion expressed in the articles resulted from the economic calculations each presented, so she then listed the details of how the numbers of poor people are determined. On the instruction of her teacher, she wrote a journal entry about her reaction to the essays.

Here is Sarah's first journal entry:

When you see an old guy lying on a grate on a city street, you know they're poor. I mean I've always known what poor is, or I thought so. Street people, people living in crowded slums, 10 in a tiny apt., that sort of thing. But these articles aren't about them, but a different kind of poorness. Some people who look "normal" are poor in the sense they can't pay normal bills. These are people I guess I thought were just lower class. Are they poor? Are lower class people poor? Is that what the statistics mean? Do they need help? Or are a lot of people mistakenly labeled poor by the government and then given unneeded aid? I hope we don't give food stamps to a guy who's got a million dollar business. Or do we? Is our government that dumb? Would a guy that rich even apply for aid?

After discussing the articles with a small group in class, Sarah wrote this follow-up journal entry:

Some people are in love with stats. I hated figuring out how these poverty numbers fit together. It's a revelation to me that the government has to do all this calculating to figure out who is poor. Really, to define poor. That's what Jeremy said, "We as a nation have to define poor." To him, <u>lower</u> <u>class</u> is not <u>poor</u>, and the statistic that 38% of Americans are poor is ridiculous. He said he bets they all have TVs and VCRs, and that's why they can't pay bills. Eva blew up. She said people work and save up to buy a TV or other luxury, but then when they lose a job or get sick and fall behind in payments, people criticize. Or their car breaks, and they have to fix it instead of paying some bills. I see that being poor is really complicated. The government has to get more information on who's poor. More information is needed about each possibly poor person, but how much info can you deal with? Maybe we need to look at our attitudes. I mean, if someone is suffering, we should do something about it.

A full class discussion was then held. Sarah took some notes from this discussion and then returned to planning her essay, writing a draft, and shaping it into an essay she could share.

Working poor is a term that's new to a lot of people. But there are many people who work at such a low wage or have so many dependents that they can't afford basic necessities. Determining who these people are and how many of them there are is a problem that must be solved even before our society can offer aid to the poor.

The number of poor is determined by how the counting is done, that is, by the income level set up as the poverty line. The articles by Schwartz and Volgy and by Schiller both attack the issue of how the government counts the poor, with one claiming the government undercounts, and the other that the government over-counts. Reading these two articles raises the question as to which perspective on American poverty is correct: is it over- or underestimated? How incorrect is the Census Bureau, and in which direction? How can we count the poor so that the people who need help receive it, and those who do not need it are not counted? Low-income or "lower class" shouldn't be equivalent to "poor," but we need some way to make the difference clear.

The Census Bureau counts the poor in a way that allows non-poor people to be listed as poor even though they're not. Some part-time-employed college students, business owners with temporary losses, and people with new babies often fit the government's definition. Economics professor Bradley R. Schiller gives examples of these types of people. But his examples raise the question of whether all the people who fit the government's definition of poor try to get aid. Do students with part-time jobs become welfare or Medicaid recipients or take up places in job-readiness programs? Do company owners suffering business losses apply for these types of aid? It wouldn't seem likely, and if they don't, then the overcounting is not such a problem. We need to find out whether these types of people get assistance.

How to draw the line between those who are low-income and those who are poor needs more thought. Schwartz and Volgy say that up to 38% of Americans should be considered poor in terms of the cost of buying the basic necessities. This number seems extremely high. If that many people were in financial trouble, I think it would be obvious to everybody in our society.

It is probably true, as Schwartz and Volgy claim, that life today is more expensive than the government's Consumer Price Index. Our class calculations indicate that an income of $19,300, an amount above the government's poverty line for four family members, is probably not enough for them to have the basic necessities. Rent alone could cost $9,600 and food $6,000 a year. This example raises the question of how the government can identify families that can't make it on what they earn and those that can. How can poverty be calculated to admit people whose life is a struggle and whose children are suffering into the ranks of the poor, without listing 38% of Americans as poor?

Both articles define the working poor as full-time workers, as does the government. But this should be rethought. Some part-time workers want to work full-time but can't find a job, and so can be classified as needy. Some have health or transportation problems, and also need various kinds of assistance. The inclusion of certain types of part-time workers in the definition of "working poor" should be considered.

After sharing her draft and receiving feedback, Sarah made some changes in her essay. She rewrote the last sentence of her first paragraph so it stated her claim of inquiry more clearly:

Our society needs to discover a better way to identify such people in order to ensure that they receive assistance.

She also moved her last paragraph up between the fourth and fifth paragraph because it was really a body paragraph, not a conclusion. Then she reread her journal entries and brainstorming, and devised a better conclusion:

We need to get past the quibbles about how the calculations are done. We need to ask ourselves whether counting the poor and arguing over the total are worthwhile ways to use our energy. More importantly, we need to find out how to identify poor people in the most efficient way. The question is, who should the government help? Then we can get on to the next question: How?

Sarah used informal reference in her essay because her classmates and instructor had also read the articles. Here are the sources she used:

Schiller, Bradley R. "All of Clinton's Working Poor Aren't What He Says They Are." *Philadelphia Inquirer* 21 July 1994: A19.

Schwartz, John E., and Thomas J. Volgy. "Above the Poverty Line—But Poor." *The Nation* 15 Feb. 1993: 191–92.

Activities

1 Discovering Refutation

Look carefully at letters to the editor in newspapers and magazines to discover examples of refutation. Bring these to class. When the class convenes, small groups of students should read each other's examples and nominate one as the most interesting. These will be read aloud to the whole class for discussion.

2 Discussing and Analyzing Refutation: Refutation Workshop

Here are a number of examples of refutation taken from op-ed articles and letters to the editor. Examine each to determine:

1. how the writer presents, summarizes, or evokes the viewpoint(s) he or she is refuting
2. the technique(s) used to refute the opposition
3. the writer's tone
4. the effectiveness of the refutation

A. The safety of estrogen pills was the subject of the article critiqued in the following letter to the editor of *Extra!* magazine (July–Aug. 1997):

> [Author Barbara] Seaman quotes the "current edition" of Goodman and Gilman's *Pharmacological Basis of Therapeutics* as stating that "The routine prophylactic use of estrogen is difficult to justify."
>
> Having consulted the actual current edition of that work (which is the ninth, published in 1996), I must report that Cynthia Williams and George Stancel, who wrote the chapter on estrogen and progestins, state the reverse on page 1423: "Hormone replacement therapy is now recommended for most post-menopausal women. . . . The discussion of "Untoward Responses" in the chapter (pages 1420–21) explains that current doses are much lower than those used in the past.
>
> —Morton H. Frank, Ph.D.

B. Author Barbara Seaman's response to her critic:

> Dr. Frank is correct that my quotes are not from the "current" edition of Goodman and Gilman's. They are from the eighth edition, published in 1990. I was not aware that a ninth edition had recently appeared. I wonder if the chapter in the new edition was written before publication of the disturbing new findings on the persistence—even in lower doses—of both endometrial pathology and thromboembolic disease. Rest assured that in the future I will refer to the specific edition—by number and year—of any reference work I may quote.

C. In a syndicated op-ed column, economist Walter E. Williams sketched out his view that greed is a social good. Here is an excerpt from his column plus a reader's response.

> High school and college students are routinely fed leftist propaganda about businessmen's greed. Quite often, the lesson begins with one of the "robber barons" such as John

D. Rockefeller. But Rockefeller should be celebrated, at least by the farthest left of the left, the animal rights wackos. Here's the story. . . .

When whaling finally stopped at the turn of the 20th century, [only] an estimated 50,000 whales were left. Surely, if an average annual kill of 15,000 whales a year had continued, whales would long since have become extinct.

What saved the whales? Was it a triumph by Greenpeace or early animal rights fanatics? If you say yes, then put on the dunce cap.

Whales were saved by the self-interested motives of much maligned J. D. Rockefeller. . . .

Rockefeller set up a network of kerosene distilleries that would later become known as Standard Oil.

As kerosene became cheaper and available throughout the nation, our whaling fleet fell from 735 in 1846 to 39 in 1876. The last American whaling ship left port in 1924. . . .

In other words, most good done in the world is done by people pursuing their own narrow, selfish interests. Ironically, most world evil is done in the name of good.

—"By Promoting Self-Interest, Robber Baron Benefits All"

A reader's response was as follows:

It seems reasonable enough to conclude that actions of self-interest can have wide beneficial effects even when such effects are unintended. It does not follow, however, that most good comes from acting in economic self-interest and that most evil comes from trying to promote good.

One can find many examples of actions of self-interest having broad and detrimental effects. Bank robbers, burglars, embezzlers, slumlords and drug dealers act in self-interest as did those responsible for Love Canal and the Exxon Valdez oil spill. . . .

In short, the relationships between self-interest, good intentions and a larger good are not simple. It is absurd to claim that the most good will result if we all do away with trying to do good and just pursue our "own narrow, selfish interests."

—Robert Goldschmidt, Letter, *Philadelphia Inquirer*

D. In an op-ed column, historian Tom Chaffe takes issue with the common opinion that terrorism is a rarity in U.S. history. Here is an excerpt from Chaffe's article:

"I think terrorism has come to America," Martin Medhurst, a presidential scholar at Texas A&M University, said recently. "It has been going on in Europe for two decades or more. . . . This just the beginning. . . ."

There is, in fact, a strong case for arguing that recent terrorist acts in the United States are but a continuation of a long-standing tradition. . . .

Missing-in-action is a kind of shadow history of ideological violence in America—a tradition of political and religious violence that has attended the United States from its infancy. From Bacon's Rebellion in colonial Virginia to today's militia bombings, we are a nation that, beyond its laws and "official" wars, also knows well the paramilitary, the clandestine, the extralegal. [Details of terrorism throughout U.S history follow.]

—"America the Violent"

E. Here are a few paragraphs from an op-ed piece about Puerto Rico by a resident:

Americans stateside assume Puerto Ricans would love to become the 51st state if only they didn't have to pay taxes as the price. At present, Puerto Rican residents can't vote in federal elections. In consolation, they pay no federal income tax.

But anti-statehood sentiment on the islands is not founded on dread of the IRS. A distinct national identity prevails despite the moribund independence movement. Puerto Ricans regard the island as their motherland, instinctually referring to it as *nuestra patria*—our native country. And, as in Northern Ireland, Quebec, and Palestine, the intensity of such nationalism is inversely proportional to the territory's size.

Declared in countless impassioned songs, on any given day, at any given hour, by independence, commonwealth and statehood supporters gathered at a bar, a concert or a street corner—or blaring from the radio—it's that reverberant nationalism, betraying a defiantly Latin American mindset, that makes statehood such a difficult proposition. Sure, the lyrics could be shrugged off as benign romanticism. But there are no statehood songs.

—William Santiago, "Puerto Rico, Where Self-Determination, Statehood Don't Mix"

3   Finding a Middle Ground: Qualifying Extreme Statements

For each one of the assertions below, try to devise as many qualified versions as you can, either individually or in groups.

1. Physical education requirements should be eliminated.
2. Fad and junk foods should be removed from all school cafeterias.
3. Fashion magazines present unrealistic images of women and should be boycotted.
4. Cloning and similar genetic engineering should be banned.

4   Finding a Middle Ground: Rogerian Listening

Jot down a few topics that you feel strongly about for personal reasons. Then, with your instructor's help, meet with a student who holds an opposite or different opinion on the same issue. One student should discuss his or her viewpoint, explaining in depth why this position makes so much sense. The listener should listen in silence until prompted by the instructor to repeat back to the speaker the ideas that have been discussed.

If the speaker agrees with the repeated ideas, then he or she can resume discussing the topic. If the speaker disagrees, then he or she must reexplain the area of confusion. After about ten or twelve minutes, the listener and speaker should switch and repeat the activity with roles reversed. When both students have had a chance as listener and speaker, the class should take a few minutes to write journal entries about the exercise and then should discuss it as a whole.

5   Finding a Middle Ground: Devising Many Positions on a Topic

Think of a current controversy. It may be local, such as whether your town should continue its expensive recycling program, or national, such as drug use among teenagers; it may be political, such as whether presidents should be limited to one six-year term, or social, such as whether there should be national tests for high school subjects. Brainstorm a list of as many positions on the subject as you can. Remember that moving beyond pro and con often requires going into some depth and detail about policies or solutions. You may work with another student or in a group, as your instructor permits.

Assignments

1. The paradox is irresoluble: the less one culture communicates with another, the less likely they are to be corrupted, one by the other; but on the other hand, the less likely it is, in such conditions, that the respective emissaries of these cultures will be able to seize the richness and significance of their diversity.

—Claude Lévi-Strauss, *Triste Tropiques*

If you think of opposing viewpoints as different "cultures," then what is the paradox that Lévi-Strauss, an anthropologist, warns of? Is it better for viewpoints to be isolated from each other, or is it better to risk being "corrupted" by other views? Write a journal entry about whether you believe exposure to opposing or diverse ideas on a subject "near and dear to your heart" is desirable or to be avoided.

2. Read the letters to the editor section of a major newspaper to locate a letter or letters in a "conversation" on a controversial issue that interests you. Trace back to locate the original article, editorial, or opinion piece that inspired the letter(s) and read recent news articles about the topic so that you feel well versed. Then plan and generate an essay in which you refute one side or one debatable point in the conversation about this issue. You may choose to join the letter writer(s) in critiquing the original article, or you may refute the opinion(s) of the letter writer(s). Make sure your refutation is focused on a limited aspect of the topic so that you can cover it thoroughly in your paper.

3. Identify a pro-and-con debate on a recent controversial issue. Some newspapers regularly run opposing opinion pieces; or you may watch a television show such as *Crossfire*. Or skim through this book to identify articles that treat similar issues. Brainstorm alone or with a partner to discover a way of bridging the gap between the positions. Then write an essay in which you sketch out an alternative view of the controversy that contains elements drawn from each side and shows why this view is preferable.

4. Read the coverage of a current issue in several different magazines and newspapers with an eye toward identifying unanswered questions and needs for further evidence. (Keep in mind that not all issues lend themselves to the discovery of questions.) Write an essay in which you use the evidence and analysis of your source articles to show that the issue is currently not resolvable or that the current evidence raises rather than answers questions.

■ **WORKS CITED**

Dyer, Gwynne. "Picking the Right Enemies for Cuba." *Philadelphia Inquirer* 19 Aug. 1997: A11.
Hirsch, Sanford. Letter. *Policy Review* July–Aug 1997: 4.
Kavanaugh, James M. Letter. *Philadelphia Inquirer* 19 Aug: A10.
Lewicki, Roy J., et al. *Negotiation.* 2nd ed. Boston: Irwin, 1994.
Rice, William Craig. Reply to Letters. *Policy Review* July–Aug. 1997: 5.

 *Readings*

Healthy Inequality

GEORGE F. WILL

George F. Will is a Pulitzer Prize–winning columnist whose commentaries are syndicated in newspapers around the United States. "Healthy Inequality" appeared in *Newsweek* in 1996. Another article by Will appears at the end of Chapter 3. (Reprinted by permission of the author.)

1   Economists today perform the stern duty formerly done by dour Calvinist divines, that of telling many complainers that nothing can be done about their complaints and, besides, the suffering is good for them. Now pastors Jeremy Greenwood and Mehmet Yorukoglu argue convincingly that something currently decried as a social dysfunction and injustice—the combination of slowing productivity growth and widening income inequality—is actually a recurring and benign phenomenon.

2   Greenwood and Yorukoglu, economists at the universities of Rochester and Chicago respectively, date the onset of current discontents about both productivity and inequality from 1974, when two lines on a graph began moving in ways which, taken together, looked peculiar. One line charted labor productivity. It had been ascending steeply since the mid-1950s. In 1974 the line began a modest decline. The other line charted investment in information technology. What had been an irregular and modest ascent since the mid-1950s began a dramatically steep ascent that continues to this day. It did so because of what a third graph line records—a steep decline in the price of information technology.

3   These three developments seemed counterintuitive. Should not rapid investment in new technology both explain, and be explained by, the increased productivity of labor equipped with the technology? Quite the contrary, say Greenwood and Yorukoglu. They say that often one consequence of new technology is an initial decline in productivity associated with the cost of learning to use the new machines. And the learning process puts a premium on quick learners, meaning skilled labor. This widens the gap between the incomes of the skilled and the unskilled.

4   So 1974 in America resembled 1770 in Britain, and 1840 in America. At those times, new technologies began appearing, machines that would eventually enhance the productivity of labor, but not before a period of costly learning. Information technologies are causing economic turbulence—discomforting but creative turbulence—much as steam and, later, electricity did.

5   When around 1770 Watt's engine brought steam power to British manufacturing, the mechanization of manufacturing spread rapidly, as did complementary inventions, such as new machines for spinning cotton. And the price of spun cotton fell two thirds by 1841. New methods of producing wrought iron caused production to increase 500 percent between 1788 and 1815 and prices to fall 36 percent between 1801 and 1815, although the general price level rose 50 percent between 1770 and 1815.

6   Then industrialism came to America. Between 1774 and 1815 the per capita stock of equipment grew just 0.7 percent per year. But between 1815 and 1860 annual growth

quadrupled to 2.8 percent, and it soared to 4.5 percent between 1860 and 1900. In 1830 there were just 30 miles of railroad tracks. By 1840 there were 2,808. In 1860 there were 30,000. The aggregate capacity of steam engines quadrupled between 1840 and 1860. All of which put a premium on the skills of engineers, machinists, boilermakers, carpenters and joiners, whose wages grew relative to those of common laborers.

Was this inequality a bad thing? No, it was an incentive for people to invest in self-improvement. And it advanced the nation's economic sophistication. (The increased industrial sophistication was concentrated primarily in the North. Was that inequality a bad thing? Not after Fort Sumter.)   7

At the dawn of this century, industrial applications of electricity were slowed by the existence of large stocks of equipment and structures for water and steam power. So at first electricity was used primarily in rapidly expanding industries that were designing new plants adapted to electricity. So the rapid-growers grew still more rapidly. More inequalities. And more social benefits.   8

By one estimate, since the Second World War 60 percent of U.S. economic growth has derived from the introduction of increasingly efficient equipment, the most important of which have been information machines. Around 1950 computers entered the economy, essentially as calculating devices, and the cost of crunching numbers plummeted. Between 1950 and 1980 the cost of a MIP (million instructions per second) fell between 27 and 50 percent *annually*. In the 1960s computers became labor-saving devices for storing, sorting and retrieving data, the cost of which probably fell at an annual rate of 25 to 30 percent between 1960 and 1985. But the labor-saving applications were job-creating: by 1980 there were 1.13 times as many information workers as production workers, up from 0.22 in 1900.   9

Now computers have become communication devices, producing myriad streamlinings in business organizations, and other economic efficiencies. Information technologies also are producing additional inequality, as those people who are talented at using information technologies reap rewards that are, in turn, incentives for other people to invest time and money in increasing their inventories of talents. Thus does society progress to higher levels of sophistication. Such progress is, as usual, accompanied by a chorus of laments from sentimentalists who consider it a cosmic injustice that progress has a price. And the laments are loudest from those who make a fetish of equality.   10

Equality—other than equality before the law—is a problematic, and often pernicious, social value. The celebration of equality of condition often is merely envy tarted up in the clothing of compassion. Furthermore, when equality of outcomes, rather than equal opportunity, is regarded as a matter of moral urgency, this often disposes society to a surly resentment of virtues and talents that, for good reasons, receive high rewards.   11

A society that chafes against stratifications derived from disparities of talents will be a society that discourages individual excellence. Such a society also will resent the excellence it cannot discourage, and hence such a society will have a curdled spirit. As a character in Mary McCarthy's novel "Birds of America" says, "I've decided that may be why the Parisians are so sullen and why they drink. They thought of equality first."   12

Questions for Inquiry

1. What is Will's claim? At what point in the essay does Will reveal it clearly? Why does he position the claim where he does? What might he expect a typical reader's response to it to be?

2. What is "counterintuitive" about the economic developments plotted by the graphs described in paragraph 2? How do Will's experts explain these seemingly contradictory facts?
3. What is the point of Will's "history lesson" in paragraphs 4 through 8? Why does he need to go into historical details to make this point effectively?

Questions for Argument

1. At the start of the essay, Will likens today's economists to old-fashioned "divines" who offered no hope for this world's troubles and then reminded us that "suffering is good" for you (1). He even calls his economist experts "pastors." Would you agree that, today, economists serve to explain the workings of life to us and that their role is "priestly"?
2. Will states that "equality—other than equality before the law—is a[n] . . . often pernicious, social value" (11). Do you agree that " equality of condition" is not a worthwhile goal? Or is it something that our country should be striving for?

Writing Assignments

Informal

1. Will suggests that before new technologies begin to improve the economy, there is "a period of costly learning" (4). Perhaps you (or someone close to you) have experienced a time when learning something slowed you down and seemed to impede your progress for a while. Write in your journal about the meanings the phrase "a period of costly learning" has for you.
2. According to Will, only "sentimentalists" bemoan the fact that "progress has a price" (10). What do you think of progress, especially the technological kind that Will bases his thinking on? Write an informal paper in which you express your appreciation for, or dread of, "progress."

Formal

3. **Argumentation.** Progress produces inequality, Will maintains, because talented people improve themselves in order to fill the needs created by new technologies. They thus reap the rewards they deserve and do better than the rest. Do you agree that progress bestows its riches on the deserving? Or is this a Pollyanna view of economic changes? Discuss this issue and brainstorm with classmates to generate examples of success through merit or luck. You may also wish to research the causes of income disparity and today's widening income gap. Then write an essay in which you either agree with or refute Will's endorsement of merit as the cause of economic inequality.
4. Will believes that economic inequality is the inspiration for "individual excellence" (12). Do you agree that economic conditions set the stage for excellence or are there other reasons why people improve their minds and develop their talents? Free-write about the causes of personal improvement based on people you know and know of, and then write an essay in which you argue for or against the economic motivation for excellence.

■ ■ ■

Five Myths about Immigration

DAVID COLE

David Cole is a professor at Georgetown University Law School and a volunteer staff attorney for the Center for Constitutional Rights. This article was first published in *The Nation* in 1994. (Copyright 1994 by the Nation. Reprinted by permission.)

For a brief period in the mid-nineteenth century, a new political movement captured the passions of the American public. Fittingly labeled the "Know-Nothings," their unifying theme was nativism. They liked to call themselves "Native Americans," although they had no sympathy for people we call Native Americans today. And they pinned every problem in American society on immigrants. As one Know-Nothing wrote in 1856: "Four-fifths of the beggary and three-fifths of the crime spring from our foreign population; more than half the public charities, more than half the prisons and almshouses, more than half the police and the cost of administering criminal justice are for foreigners."   1

At the time, the greatest influx of immigrants was from Ireland, where the potato famine had struck, and Germany, which was in political and economic turmoil. Anti-alien and anti-Catholic sentiments were the order of the day, especially in New York and Massachusetts, which received the brunt of the wave of immigrants, many of whom were dirt-poor and uneducated. Politicians were quick to exploit the sentiment: There's nothing like a scapegoat to forge an alliance.   2

I am especially sensitive to this history: My forebears were among those dirt-poor Irish Catholics who arrived in the 1860s. Fortunately for them, and me, the Know-Nothing movement fizzled within fifteen years. But its pilot light kept burning, and is turned up whenever the American public begins to feel vulnerable and in need of an enemy.   3

Although they go by different names today, the Know-Nothings have returned. As in the 1850s, the movement is strongest where immigrants are most concentrated: California and Florida. The objects of prejudice are of course no longer Irish Catholics and Germans; 140 years later, "they" have become "us." The new "they"—because it seems "we" must always have a "they"—are Latin Americans (most recently, Cubans), Haitians and Arab-Americans, among others.   4

But just as in the 1850s, passion, misinformation and short-sighted fear often substitute for reason, fairness and human dignity in today's immigration debates. In the interest of advancing beyond know-nothingism, let's look at five current myths that distort public debate and government policy relating to immigrants.   5

§ *America is being overrun with immigrants.* In one sense, of course, this is true, but in that sense it has been true since Christopher Columbus arrived. Except for the real Native Americans, we are a nation of immigrants.   6

It is not true, however, that the first-generation immigrant share of our population is growing. As of 1990, foreign-born people made up only 8 percent of the population, as compared with a figure of about 15 percent from 1870 to 1920. Between 70 and 80 percent of those who immigrate every year are refugees or immediate relatives of U.S. citizens.   7

Much of the anti-immigrant fervor is directed against the undocumented, but they make up only 13 percent of all immigrants residing in the United States, and only 1 percent   8 of the American population. Contrary to popular belief, most such aliens do not cross the border illegally but enter legally and remain after their student or visitor visa expires. Thus, building a wall at the border, no matter how high, will not solve the problem.

9   § *Immigrants take jobs from U.S. citizens.* There is virtually no evidence to support this view, probably the most widespread misunderstanding about immigrants. As documented by a 1994 A.C.L.U. Immigrants' Rights Project report, numerous studies have found that immigrants actually *create* more jobs than they fill. The jobs immigrants take are of course easier to see, but immigrants are often highly productive, run their own businesses and employ both immigrants and citizens. One study found that Mexican immigration to Los Angeles County between 1970 and 1980 was responsible for 78,000 new jobs. Governor Mario Cuomo reports that immigrants own more than 40,000 companies in New York, which provide thousands of jobs and $3.5 billion to the state's economy every year.

10   § *Immigrants are a drain on society's resources.* This claim fuels many of the recent efforts to cut off government benefits to immigrants. However, most studies have found that immigrants are a net benefit to the economy because, as a 1994 Urban Institute report concludes, "immigrants generate significantly more in taxes paid than they cost in services received." The Council of Economic Advisers similarly found in 1986 that "immigrants have a favorable effect on the overall standard of living."

11   Anti-immigrant advocates often cite studies purportedly showing the contrary, but these generally focus only on taxes and services at the local or state level. What they fail to explain is that because most taxes go to the federal government, such studies would also show a net loss when applied to U.S. citizens. At most, such figures suggest that some redistribution of federal and state monies may be appropriate; they say nothing unique about the costs of immigrants.

12   Some subgroups of immigrants plainly impose a net cost in the short run, principally those who have most recently arrived and have not yet "made it." California, for example, bears substantial costs for its disproportionately large undocumented population, largely because it has on average the poorest and least educated immigrants. But that has been true of every wave of immigrants that has ever reached our shores; it was as true of the Irish in the 1850s, for example, as it is of Salvadorans today. From a long-term perspective, the economic advantages of immigration are undeniable.

13   Some have suggested that we might save money and diminish incentives to immigrate illegally if we denied undocumented aliens public services. In fact, undocumented immigrants are already ineligible for most social programs, with the exception of education for schoolchildren, which is constitutionally required, and benefits directly related to health and safety, such as emergency medical care and nutritional assistance to poor women, infants and children. To deny such basic care to people in need, apart from being inhumanly callous, would probably cost us more in the long run by exacerbating health problems that we would eventually have to address.

14   § *Aliens refuse to assimilate, and are depriving us of our cultural and political unity.* This claim has been made about every new group of immigrants to arrive on U.S. shores. Supreme Court Justice Stephen Field wrote in 1884 that the Chinese "have remained among us a separate people, retaining their original peculiarities of dress, manners, habits, and modes of living, which are as marked as their complexion and language." Five years later, he upheld the racially based exclusion of Chinese immigrants. Similar claims have been made over different periods of our history about Catholics, Jews, Italians, Eastern Europeans and Latin Americans.

In most instances, such claims are simply not true; "American culture" has been cre-   15
ated, defined and revised by persons who for the most part are descended from immigrants
once seen as anti-assimilationist. Descendants of the Irish Catholics, for example, a group
once decried as separatist and alien, have become Presidents, senators and representatives
(and all of these in one family, in the case of the Kennedys). Our society exerts tremendous
pressure to conform, and cultural separatism rarely survives a generation. But more important, even if this claim were true, is this a legitimate rationale for limiting immigration in a
society built on the values of pluralism and tolerance?

    § *Noncitizen immigrants are not entitled to constitutional rights.* Our government has long   16
declined to treat immigrants as full human beings, and nowhere is that more clear than in
the realm of constitutional rights. Although the Constitution literally extends the fundamental protections in the Bill of Rights to all people, limiting to citizens only the right to vote
and run for federal office, the federal government acts as if this were not the case.

    In 1893 the executive branch successfully defended a statute that required Chinese la-   17
borers to establish their prior residence here by the testimony of "at least one credible white
witness." The Supreme Court ruled that this law was constitutional because it was reasonable for Congress to presume that nonwhite witnesses could not be trusted.

    The federal government is not much more enlightened today. In a pending case I'm   18
handling in the Court of Appeals for the Ninth Circuit, the Clinton Administration has argued that permanent resident aliens lawfully living here should be extended no more First
Amendment rights than aliens applying for first-time admission from abroad—that is, none.
Under this view, students at a public university who are citizens may express themselves
freely, but students who are not citizens can be deported for saying exactly what their classmates are constitutionally entitled to say.

    Growing up, I was always taught that we will be judged by how we treat others. If we   19
are collectively judged by how we have treated immigrants—those who appear today to be
"other" but will in a generation be "us"—we are not in very good shape.

Questions for Inquiry

1. What is Cole's claim? Is it explicit or implied?
2. Why does the author begin with a discussion about the Know-Nothings of the nineteenth century? What are the similarities between the immigration debates of the
   1850s and those today?
3. Examine Cole's treatment of the five myths. In which ones does he grant some points
   of the opposition? For which ones does he provide an explanation of why the myth is a
   popular belief? And which myths does he actively refute?
4. What types of people does Cole expect to read his article? In particular, what does his
   use of the terms "us" and "them" suggest about his implied audience?

Questions for Argument

1. Cole attributes the current immigration debates to the public's needing an enemy (3)
   and to "passion, misinformation and short-sighted fear" (5). Do you agree that concern
   about the extent and effects of immigration results from purely negative emotions?

Knowing what you now know on the basis of Cole's essay, do you feel immigration into the United States is a problem?

2. It is a myth, Cole indicates, that our Constitution bestows rights only on citizens (16). But our government has frequently behaved as if this myth were true. Should there be a distinction between the rights of citizens and immigrants—for example, noncitizen resident aliens? Should noncitizen residents have freedom of speech, assembly, religion, and so forth? And should noncitizen residents be entitled to such programs as unemployment insurance, social security, welfare, or health-assistance programs?

Writing Assignments

Informal

1. Cole points out that illegal immigrants usually are people who have overstayed a legitimate visa and that building walls, "no matter how high," is not a solution (8). In your journal, write about whether you think "building walls" against people, places, and ideas we dislike or fear is a good thing to do.

2. At the end of his essay, the author points out that, in a generation, those whom we are treating as "other" will have become "us," the mainstream Americans (19). In an informal paper, discuss the qualities and attitudes typical of those whom Cole calls "us" and indicate whether you think these qualities and attitudes are likely to change as those who are currently "outsiders"—the immigrants—become assimilated.

Formal

3. The feared immigrants of the past have now "become 'us' "—they are part of the mainstream from which other groups, "they," are excluded. Cole writes that "it seems 'we' must always have a 'they' " (4). Brainstorm with class members to identify other areas of U.S. life besides immigration in which the unofficial opposition of "us" and "them" often dominates attitudes, discussion, and behavior. Then choose one of these areas and free-write or conduct research to discover specific examples of the us-them dichotomy at work. Write an essay in which you analyze these examples to show the positive or negative effects caused by the opposition of "us" and "them."

4. Cole writes of the fourth myth that even if immigrants did refuse to assimilate, that fact would not be a reason to limit immigration because our society is "built on the values of pluralism and tolerance" (15). Free-write about the issue of assimilation, tolerance of differences, and the need to "blend in" as a response to what Cole calls the "tremendous pressure to conform" exerted by our society. Then write an essay in which you define how important blending in should be and describe how much—or how little—people should change or alter their life-style in order to fit in. You may want to discuss this as a cultural issue having to do with how much of their cultural background immigrants should give up to become "American." Or you may wish to focus on the struggle between one's personal style and behavior and the conformist pressures in our society.

5. **Research Opportunity.** Choose one of Cole's five myths and do research to uncover additional statistics and recent information about it. Then write a paper in which you defend or challenge Cole's denial of the myth.

■ ■ ■

It's Not All Heroes and Demons

ALYSIA BENNETT

Alysia Bennett is on the staff of the *Washington Post,* where this appeared
in 1997. She served in the U.S. Army from 1987 to 1991. (Copyright
1997 by the Washington Post. Reprinted by permission.)

Nine years ago, when I tried on my Army uniform for the first time, I had a lot of help 1
from my drill sergeant. Unconvinced that it fit properly, he inserted his hand in my pants and
slowly began to move his hand back and forth to demonstrate the point. His eyes not meeting mine, and his hand lingering, he asked: "Bennett, when are you going to do something
with your hair?" When his eyes finally rolled up to meet my nervous stare, he smiled in
amusement.

I was 17, a private just a few weeks into my enlistment, and distinctly uncomfortable. 2
But by the time I graduated basic training, that incident was less vivid in my mind than others involving my drill sergeant: his concern when I lost my appetite; his cheering when I
earned my sharpshooter badges.

All of which is a way of saying that the Army that I've read about in recent news cov- 3
erage about the problems with sexual harassment and rape at Aberdeen Proving Ground
and other bases is both familiar and foreign to me. Yes, my experience was wrought with imperfection, but the story doesn't end there.

Despite the difficulties, awkward moments and occasional misuses of power, I look 4
back on my enlistment with pride and—strange as it may sound—on my sometime tor-
mentors with appreciation. While at times they embarrassed me with inappropriate gestures, their faith in me as a soldier and as a person never wavered. And so my feelings toward
them are as complicated, and conflicted, as were their actions.

During basic training at Fort Jackson, in South Carolina, I shared the barracks with a 5
platoon of young women not unlike myself. For the most part, we had left home because
either we didn't have much, or we were too young to appreciate what we did have.

Our education began with the discipline of quiet submission. We learned how to say 6
"yes, drill sergeant" and "no, drill sergeant," and how to avert our eyes from theirs. With fa-
tigued muscles, we endured ruck marches, long runs and obstacle courses. We low-crawled
in sawdust pits and did sit-ups in the mud. We beat our bodies into subjection. "It's mind over
matter, privates," my drill sergeants quipped. "If you don't mind, it don't matter." That became my mantra.

Barely out of my prom dress, I had become one of America's finest, tossing hand 7
grenades, setting up land mines and firing my M-16. I was tougher and stronger than I ever
imagined I could be, and I owed that to the Army. But my newly developed confidence and
self-assurance had yet to be tested. My exam arrived the day my drill sergeant put his hand
in my pants.

At that moment, I locked eyes with the man who had encouraged me to "kill that com- 8
mie" during bayonet training. But to him, I replied with timidity and restraint. "I think they
fit, drill sergeant."

I walked away smiling, perhaps less amused by my embarrassment than his ability to 9
elicit it.

10   Looking back on the incident, I wish that I had been tougher, or at least wittier. But that would have been almost impossible. I had already been broken. I merely submitted to those in authority; I never questioned them. I was just bad enough to kill for my country, but not so tough that I would ever offend or disobey. That mentality makes for a great soldier, but it opens the door for a lot of misconduct.

11   The recognition that the quality of our lives during basic training rested with the drill sergeant prompted a few women to use flirtation for personal gain. With just the right word, glance or smile, they played the game just like he did. He was nicer to and more tolerant of them, but on some occasions the whole platoon benefited as well. Pizza parties and movies are practically unheard of in basic training—a place my drill sergeant characterized as no place for joy or happiness—but our platoon had both. As long as he was happy, we were happy.

12   For the most part, though, what I remember is my drill sergeant's encouragement to stand tall, even when I didn't believe I could.

13   In September 1991, my unit was deployed to the Persian Gulf for Operation Desert Shield and eventually Desert Storm. I was the only female in my squad.

14   I spent more than eight months in the desert, often in the isolated company of male soldiers. If ever the opportunity for harassment and abuse of power existed, that was it. Instead, they all looked out for me. The only enemy I knew was faceless and somewhere outside our perimeter

15   I was determined not to play the helpless female role during the gulf crisis, so I made every effort to be self-sufficient. I was successful until old neck and back injuries resurfaced. Simple tasks like filling sandbags or carrying water to the shower area were suddenly difficult. Once, I was struggling to carry a five-gallon container of water to the shower. Throbbing pain forced me to stop every few feet. Seeing the problem, my platoon sergeant finally insisted on carrying it. When we arrived, he waited in line with me, then climbed to the top of the stall and filled the outdoor container with water. He climbed down and left without his usual unsavory monologue.

16   My days in the Persian Gulf were filled with incidents like that one. So was my entire enlistment. Often these acts of kindness came from the same men who had grossly failed to exercise judgment on previous occasions. I don't make excuses for them. They don't deserve any. But in a world that only leaves room for heroes and demons, so much of the story is left untold.

Questions for Inquiry

1. What is Bennett's claim? Is it explicit or implied?
2. What, according to Bennett, are recruits trying to get out of their army experiences? What are their motives for joining?
3. What is the goal of basic training? What role does submission play?

Questions for Argument

1. Re-read the anecdote with which Bennett begins the essay. Even after granting that her drill sergeant was helpful throughout her basic training and that life's experiences, including a stint in the army, are "wrought with imperfection," do you agree with the way she handled the sergeant's hand in her pants? Should she have reacted differently? Would you say she reacted with or in spite of her "newly developed confidence and self-assurance" (7)?

2. Should women participate equally in all areas of the military? Should they be assigned to war zones or to potential war zones? Are there jobs in the military they should not take on? Or do you believe women should have all the opportunities and the risks that men in the services have?

Writing Assignments

Informal

1. Have you ever had in your life a person who presented you with a severely mixed experience, with some very positive interactions and some very negative ones, like Bennett's drill sergeant? Write a journal entry in which you describe this person.
2. What would make you join the military? Write an informal paper in which you explain the conditions that would have to exist for you to enlist—or why nothing could induce you to be in the military.

Formal

3. Bennett believes that "in a world that only leaves room for heroes and demons," a lot of reality gets left out (16). Think of another issue or area of life in which a heroes-and-demons approach fails to take complexity into account. This may be a controversy in the civic discourse community, such as abortion, policy toward land mines, or the treatment of animals in research. Or it may be an issue that grows out of a personal experience you have had, such as Bennett's experience in the military; this might be a perspective on educational standards, on regulations governing adoptions or foster care, or on care of the elderly. Then write an essay in which you argue that a good-and-bad or pro-and-con attitude toward this issue fails to deal with some crucial aspects of it.
4. **Dialogue.** Assume that Bennett has had a change of heart and now believes she should have taken actions against the sergeant for his behavior during her uniform outfitting. Join with another student and write a dialogue between Bennett and her sergeant in which she confronts him for his behavior and in which, at least at the start, he is defensive. Let the dialogue evolve as it will to see where the two arguers end up.
5. **Research Opportunity.** Using the library and the Internet, do research to learn more about the role of women in the military and the problems that have occurred in recent years. Narrow down to one controversy within the topic: sexual harassment, relationships between enlisted personnel, the prohibition against women on the battlefield, or some other issue. Then write a paper in which you establish a claim of policy about how the issue should be handled and use your research to support the claim.

■ ■ ■

A Match Made in Heaven

SUZANNE PHARR

Suzanne Pharr is a writer who also directs the Women's Project, a social-justice organization, located in Arkansas. This article appeared in the *Progressive* in 1996. (Reprinted by permission of the author.)

1   In February, as I boarded a plane to Portland, Oregon, I overheard a man say to a woman, "We're almost all Promise Keepers on this flight. We are returning from an Atlanta meeting of 43,000 pastors."

2   "Forty-three thousand pastors," I thought. "That's like 43,000 organizers because they have influence over their congregations." I entered the plane thinking, "We're sunk."

3   For the last couple of years I have been watching the growth of the Promise Keepers with fascination and fear. As a Southern lesbian-feminist and anti-racist worker, I am keenly interested in any group of white men organizing around issues related to women and people of color.

4   As a long-time community organizer, I have to admire the brilliance of the Promise Keepers' organizing strategy. How smart it is to recognize not only the anger and confusion that men have about this changing society, but also their desire for connection and purpose. How smart to bring them into sports stadiums around the country to sing, touch, do the wave, and bond through physical and emotional contact they rarely allow themselves.

5   I believe the Promise Keepers are the ground troops in an authoritarian movement that seeks to merge church and state. It does not matter that a rightwing agenda is not overt in the formative stages of this movement; when the leaders are ready to move their men in response to their agenda, they will have thousands disciplined to obey and command.

6   The plane was full of men dressed in casual clothes, many sporting new Promise Keepers shirts. During the flight, they stood in the aisles, talking excitedly. The scene reminded me of the 1987 March on Washington, which I attended along with thousands of lesbians and gay men. For the first time in our lives, we were the majority in airplanes, subways, buses, restaurants, and the streets The experience was exhilarating. The Promise Keepers on the plane seemed to be having a similar experience, as though they had found each other for the first time.

7   After trying to escape through reading, I finally gave up and began chatting with the man next to me, dressed in a blue work shirt and jeans and reading a Tom Clancy novel. He reminded me very much of my brothers from rural Georgia. I asked if he was returning from Atlanta. "Yes," he replied. "I've just been to the Promise Keepers meeting, and I'm returning to my small town in Oregon."

8   I told him that I was a feminist, a civil-rights worker, and a lesbian, that I have very mixed feelings about the Promise Keepers, and that I wanted him to tell me about them.

9   He told me that he was pastor at a Baptist church, married, father of a teenage son, and that he would enjoy talking about his experience with the Promise Keepers. "You are the second homosexual I've ever met," he said, adding with a grin, "I think." With that introduction, we launched into an hour-and-a-half-long conversation.

10   The pastor told me that the first thing the Promise Keepers make clear is that men are responsible for all that's wrong with the family; they are not victims.

11   I told him that was going a little too far for this feminist—I think women might have some responsibility for the negative side of the ledger, too.

12   He said the Promise Keepers were not to dominate their wives but to lead them. When I asked what this meant, he said, "Man's role is laid out in the Bible—'As God is to man, man is to the family'—and it is to take charge of his family. This means listening to their needs and wishes, then deciding what is best for them."

13   I said, "As a feminist, I am deeply concerned about shared decision-making, about equality."

14   "We share the conversations, but I make the decisions," he said. "My job is to lead."

This talk about leadership made me feel that I was in a time warp in which the women's movement had never occurred. I thought about the current status of women struggling with families, jobs, and intimate relationships. I thought about stories I have read that mention how pleased some Promise Keepers' wives are to have their husbands taking a dominant role in the family. With some sadness I considered how damning this is of many male-female relationships: that men are often so absent emotionally that women would be willing to give up autonomy in order to gain their husbands' presence. 15

I suggested the Promise Keepers could make an enormous contribution to women if they added an additional promise to their credo: that they would not lift their hand against women, and that they would stop other men from committing violence against women and children. 16

The Promise Keepers are against harming women, he said. They want to protect them. But adding an eighth promise would have to be up to the leadership. 17

Of everything that happened to this pastor at the meeting, the most life-changing, he said, was racial reconciliation. He said he had never thought about himself as someone prejudiced or discriminatory, and he came to recognize it in himself: "I'm not an emotional man, but I cried along with the audience when the men of color were called to the stage and they could not get there because they were intercepted by white pastors hugging them, shaking their hands, pounding them on the back." 18

The pastors were sent home, he said, to work to bring about racial reconciliation in their churches. 19

Since my conversation with the pastor on the airplane, Ralph Reed has been calling for racial reconciliation in the wake of the recent rash of black church burnings in the South. At a meeting with black pastors, Reed admitted that the Christian Coalition has a history of being on the "wrong side" when it comes to race. Now it wants to be on the right side, he says. But why? Calls from the Christian Coalition and the Promise Keepers for racial reconciliation do not include any effort to end institutional racism, or to stop coded attacks on "welfare mothers" or immigrants or affirmative action. Rather, moving into black churches gives the religious right a foothold in the black community. In this way, the call for racial reconciliation is one of the most insidious aspects of the Promise Keepers and their allies on the Christian right. Just as the right is hungry for people of color who are willing to denounce affirmative action and the civil-rights struggles that have traditionally benefited their communities, the Promise Keepers' recruitment of black church leaders looks like a way to persuade the black community to act against its own best interests. 20

I asked the pastor about the Promise Keepers' attitudes toward lesbians and gays. 21

The pastor said it was not for a Promise Keeper to judge homosexuals ("That is God's job") but that they believe homosexuality is immoral because the Bible says it is. 22

"This is not judging?" I thought. 23

He said that he was sure there were many of us who were fine people but that we suffered from being identified with our "fringe" people who marched in those San Francisco parades. 24

I asked him if Jesus today would not be thought of as gay—an unmarried thirty-three-year-old who spent almost all of his time with twelve close male friends, one of whom in particular was "beloved." 25

He said, "No doubt if Jesus returned today, he might not be accepted in many churches." 26

We then talked about how few were the references in the Bible to same-sex relationships and how many were the references to sharing wealth, caring for those who have less, 27 and opening one's home and heart to others. Why, then, did fundamentalists not have a strong economic agenda for the redistribution of wealth?

28   It's true, he said. This is a contradiction.

29   In the end, I thought we had communicated honestly with each other and that on some points, we had moved toward one another in understanding. It seemed to me that a great difference between us was his belief in the literal truth of the Bible, and my belief that it is a historical document with great spiritual content. I told him I thought that almost all of Christendom falls somewhere between those two positions. He agreed.

30   I wondered, can people who have very different beliefs and cultural practices live in peace with one another?

31   My final question to him was: Can you and I live in homes side by side, borrow sugar from one another, and encourage our children to play together? He said yes.

32   This conversation led me to think more deeply about the difference between the right's leaders (those engaged in an organizing strategy that threatens democracy) and its follow-ers (those searching for solutions to social and economic instability, whose heartfelt beliefs make them easy targets for manipulation). Many progressives write off the latter, discarding them as ignorant or mean.

33   Our conversation stayed on my mind for weeks afterwards, and I thought of this one Promise Keeper with respect and continued interest. Then one day he phoned me long dis-tance from his small town, saying he was just calling to keep in touch and to say what a pro-found effect our conversation had had on him.

34   "It eliminated whole areas of ignorance for me," he said.

35   "Me too," I replied.

36   My conversations with this Promise Keeper made me understand that progressive peo-ple must rethink their relation to the American right.

37   How do we point out the differences between the generals of this army and their recruits?

38   How do we talk to people who are different from ourselves?

39   How do we hold different beliefs and still live in harmony?

40   Is there any hope for preventing the merger of church and state if we do not hold au-thentic conversations with those who believe fervently in the inerrancy of the Bible?

41   How do we get closer to people's real needs and their values in our organizing for change?

42   Finally, how do we carry on this conversation and organize as progressives committed to equal rights for everyone—nothing more, nothing less?

Questions for Inquiry

1. What is Pharr's claim? Is it explicit or implied?
2. What is Pharr's opinion of the Promise Keepers? What about her political, occupa-tional, and personal conflicts with the values of the Promise Keepers?
3. What commonality does Pharr discover between her experiences and those of the Promise Keepers?
4. Identify the specific topics Pharr and the minister discuss. On which ones does she argue with him about his ideas? On which ones does she seem to "pass" instead of con-fronting him? What issues does she raise? Why might she have handled these particu-lar issues in these ways?

Questions for Argument

1. "This talk about leadership made me feel that I was in a time warp in which the women's movement had never occurred," Pharr writes (15). Does a return to solid family values and responsibility on the part of men mean that they must be in charge and women must be secondary? Can "family values" exist in an egalitarian relationship?

2. To what extent do you think Pharr (and the minister) were affected by this conversation with a person of opposite life-style and beliefs? Are there any indications that either person's ideas on the issues they discussed changed or shifted? What, then, was notable about the discussion?

Writing Assignments

Informal

1. Pharr recognizes that the Promise Keepers are having an exhilarating experience, similar to one she had at a gay march on Washington—as if "they had found each other for the first time" (6). In your journal, write about any times you have had in which you experienced closeness and validation through participation in a large gathering or group.

2. Both Pharr and the minister agree in a later phone conversation that their meeting "eliminated whole areas of ignorance" (34). Write an informal paper in which you reflect on what you learned from reading this article about either or both sides of these extremes of the civic discourse community.

Formal

3. Pharr indicates that she believes the Promise Keepers do not behave in accordance with their beliefs in the areas of familial violence (16), race (20), and economic justice (27). Do you agree that a religious organization such as the Promise Keepers should include social-justice action on its agenda or should it limit itself to spiritual and personal matters? What about individuals? Should they hold their beliefs privately, or should they commit themselves to social action, as Pharr apparently does? Write a paper in which you argue as to how politically and societally active a person should be in order to uphold his or her beliefs.

4. At the end of her article, Pharr recognizes that individual believers (the "recruits") are not the same as the official movement (the "generals") and questions how we can "talk to people who are different from ourselves" and how we can "hold different beliefs and still live in harmony" (37–39). Yet she herself has modeled a successful heart-to-heart talk with a political, religious, and life-style opponent. Work with your class through group discussion and individual free writing to identify the qualities of Pharr's conversation with the pastor that could account for the success of their interaction. Then, in small groups or individually, write an essay in which you set out guidelines for success (as you define it) in talking to the opposition.

5. **Primary-Research Opportunity.** In introducing herself to her seat mate, Pharr is quite frank about how her life-style and attitudes diverge from his (8). Think of an issue on which you hold fairly solid attitudes, and then brainstorm ways in which you could locate and chat with a person who holds an opposite, informed opinion. Your class might want to discuss possibilities for these informational interviews to help members identify

appropriate persons. Then, using the guidelines for interviews provided in Chapter 5, conduct a focused conversation about the issue with your person. Take notes, and then, using Pharr's essay as a model, write a description of your chat and an evaluation of such "meetings of minds" between holders of opposing views.

■ ■ ■

Do Condoms in the Classrooms
Encourage Sex, or Safe Sex?

JANE R. EISNER

Jane R. Eisner is editorial-page editor for the *Philadelphia Inquirer,* where this opinion piece was published in 1995. (Copyright 1995 by the Philadelphia Inquirer. Reprinted by permission.)

1   When I was growing up, not *that* long ago, sex was never discussed at home or in the classroom. The one semester of a health class required by my public high school was taught by a basketball coach who didn't seem to know a fallopian tube from a foul shot, and worse yet, didn't seem to care.

2   Even when I entered college, the formerly-all-male university I attended had not caught up with the medical needs of newly arriving female students. The contraception clinic would open in the spring, we were told, "when young men's fancies turn to romance."

3   I'm still captivated by that phrase, its quaintness seeming all the more ill-fitting today, like placing a Jane Austen character in a Stephen King thriller. For the times they have a'changed.

4   My fifth grader already has received sex education in school; we have conversations about subjects I've still never discussed with my own mother. And in contrast to the restraint foisted upon us that first autumn of college, girls and boys in 10 public high schools in Philadelphia can receive condoms, five days a week, free of charge.

5   The program so passionately debated in 1991 has proceeded quietly, rather carefully, but inconclusively. Even though the actual number of teen pregnancies reported among all Philadelphia school children—public and nonpublic—has declined for four consecutive years, those in charge of the school district's health services are reluctant to attribute the decrease to the contraceptive program.

6   "I'd love to claim credit for that," says Herb Hazan, director of school health services, "but it's difficult and problematical to attribute changes to any one program—especially one limited to 10 schools. A lot of these things are cyclical."

7   As the national debate over teen pregnancy intensifies, there remains a troubling absence of conclusive data on how to prevent a trend that President Clinton has called one of "our most serious social problems." Should condoms and full and frank sexual education be made even more available? Or knowing that the best form of contraception is abstinence, are we preaching a confusing and potentially dangerous mixed message to youngsters?

For not only are the messages about sex more pervasive than when I was young, the consequences of sex are far more serious. Over the span of a single generation, we've gone from a society in which Mary Tyler Moore and Dick Van Dyke did not share a bed in their televised marital life, to one in which explicit sexual scenes appear on network TV before a pre-schooler's bedtime . . . and one in which unprotected, indiscriminate sex can mean death.   8

Certainly, the spread of the AIDS virus has heightened educators' interest in sexual education and contraception. Condoms are available in Philadelphia public schools not just for pregnancy prevention, but to guard against sexually transmitted disease and HIV/AIDS. Even Molly Kelly, the engaging Philadelphia mother of eight who travels the country preaching teenage chastity, says that concern about AIDS has opened doors for her message of abstinence.   9

Hers is a straightforward theory: The only way to avoid AIDS, pregnancy, sexually transmitted disease, emotional havoc and moral decline is to postpone sex until marriage. Doing so enhances a teenager's self-image and strength—"The better you know yourself," she says, "the easier it is to say no."   10

There's a powerful attraction to this argument, and to its corollary: that school-based programs offering contraception deliver a potent dose of hypocrisy, telling teens to stay away from sex, but if they *do* indulge, use a condom. Is it reasonable to expect a teenager to remember to properly use a condom when he can't remember to take out the garbage?   11

But is that same teenager—the one who lives for the moment, who believes in his own infallibility—going to exercise ultimate restraint? Is he encouraged to have sex knowing that he can stroll into the school clinic, and as long as his parents did not previously object, receive a lecture and a batch of condoms? Or does the availability of contraception encourage not sex, but *safe* sex?   12

If only the answers were as simple to decipher as the blue line on a home-pregnancy test. At first blush, Philadelphia's experience could be instructive; there were 2,210 new pregnancies reported in the city's public and non-public schools in 1990–91, before the condom program began. Last school year, there were 1,314.   13

But there are so many caveats constraining those numbers that it would be irresponsible to believe that teen pregnancy would disappear if condoms were available in every classroom. The good in this experiment may indeed outweigh the bad, but by hardly an amount worth applauding.   14

Around the nation are examples of contraceptive programs aimed at students that do seem to work, because they are part of a comprehensive, consistent attempt to confront the many reasons teens have sex—and the many reasons they ought not to. Such programs must be carefully evaluated and, if effective, adopted.   15

Along with any scientific evaluation must come a lot of listening. That is why the Editorial Board chose the topic of teenage pregnancy for its next student essay project.   16

We know the world has changed since we were young, but we need to understand how and why.   17

Questions for Inquiry

1. What is Eisner's claim? Is it explicit or implied?
2. What is the purpose of the comparison between sex education in Eisner's youth and sex ed today in paragraphs 1–4 and 8?

3. Why is the marked decline in teen pregnancy throughout Philadelphia an inconclusive indicator of the success of the condom-distribution program?
4. How does Eisner handle the ideas of Molly Kelly, the opponent of premarital sex (9–10)? To what degree do Eisner's ideas differ from Kelly's?

Questions for Argument

1. Eisner indicates that some characteristics of teenagers make either condom use or chastity unlikely options: teens forget to take out the garbage; they believe they're infallible; they aren't likely to "exercise ultimate restraint" (11–12). Do you think she's being fair to teenagers or are these stereotypes of teenage behavior?
2. The author worries that today's sex-ed programs may deliver a mixed message, "confusing and potentially dangerous" (7) or that they "deliver a potent dose of hypocrisy" (11). Do you agree that such programs may confuse teenagers rather than help them?

Writing Assignments

Informal

1. Eisner compares her lack of sex ed in youth to the thoroughness of the education her child is receiving about sex (1–4). Write a journal entry in which you describe how your sex education was similar to or differed from Eisner's and her child's.
2. What other factors besides the availability of condoms might be causing the dramatic downward shift in teen motherhood among all schools, both public and private? Write an informal paper in which you suggest other factors that could be producing this downward trend.

Formal

3. Teen pregnancy has been labeled one of "our most serious social problems" by President Bill Clinton (7). Brainstorm with your class to identify the negative effects on teens, their families, their futures, and their communities that make teen pregnancy such a problem. Then brainstorm to generate ways in which society might, instead of campaigning to prevent teens from pregnancy, resolve those factors that make pregnancy such a disaster for all concerned. Write an essay in which you argue either (a) that it is not the teen pregnancy that is the problem but society's attitude about it or (b) that teen pregnancies just point out ways in which our society in general is hostile to motherhood or (c) that teens need to be educated not only about sex but about the realities of how motherhood affects whole families and communities.
4. **Dialogue.** Eisner writes that "not only are the messages about sex more pervasive than when I was young, the consequences of sex are far more serious" (8). She lists HIV/AIDS and sexually transmitted diseases as ways in which "indiscriminate sex can mean death." Would Molly Kelly, the advocate of chastity, agree that disease is a more serious consequence than the "emotional havoc and moral decline" she says results from premarital sex (10)? Join with one or two other people in your class to write a dialogue between Kelly and Eisner or between a college student and Kelly on the issue of what young people should be taught about sex today. Have your dialogue disputants begin with ideas specifically stated in the essay and then extend their views as the dialogue develops.

5. **Primary-Research Opportunity.** Eisner wonders whether the availability of condoms in the school health center encourages students to have sex or encourages condom use in those who are sexually active. She turns to the statistical evidence, but, because it encompasses all city schools, it isn't definitive. As the author indicates, another way to find out how teens would think about sex (and act) if condoms were easily available is to ask them. Work with a group of other class members, and, using as your respondent base the lower classes of your college, design a questionnaire to survey older teenagers about the condom-versus-chastity issue. (Refer to Chapter 5 for information about survey research.) Then administer your survey and tabulate responses. On the basis of what you find out, write an essay in which you support or criticize the distribution of condoms in high school clinics.

■ ■ ■

It's Called Poor Health for a Reason

RICHARD A. SHWEDER

Richard A. Shweder is a cultural anthropologist at the University of Chicago. He wrote this article for the *New York Times*, where it appeared in 1997. (Copyright 1997 by the New York Times. Reprinted by permission.)

From a cerebro-vascular, genito-urinary, gastro-intestinal, psycho-therapeutic or mortuary point of view, the rich and famous have never had it so good. Yes, their children are more prone to acne and allergies. Nevertheless, during the last half of the 20th century, people in the developed world with an elevated social status have been producing health, well-being and longevity at a faster rate than those with lower social standing. 1

Physical and mental health run parallel to social rank. In England, commoners die sooner than aristocrats. In the military, sergeants have more heart attacks than generals. Blue-collar workers—and not only those working in mines, construction sites and chemical plants—have more respiratory infections and hacking coughs than white-collar workers. Office clerks are more anxious and depressed than office managers. Lower-middle-class Americans are more mortal, morbid, symptomatic and disabled than upper-middle-class Americans. With each little step down on the educational, occupational and income ladders comes an increased risk of headaches, varicose veins, hypertension, sleepless nights, emotional distress, heart disease, schizophrenia and an early visit to the grave. 2

The funny thing is, no one knows why. 3

Of course, people who are socially well placed have not always been spared the ravages of disease. Mythic images of wounded elites come to mind: gout-endamaged royalty, wan and hysterical Victorian ladies, ascetic malnourished Brahman widows, Mandarins eating vitamin-deficient polished rice and bearing beriberi. In the 1920's and 30's, coronary heart disease was apparently a mark of social distinction among men in England. In the 1940's and 50's, the polio virus crippled those at the top in the United States. And even today there are a few afflictions, like breast cancer and malignant melanomas, that seem to prevail among citizens of high station. 4

5   On the whole, though, the upper-crust neuroses and illnesses have all but disappeared from Europe and the United States. During the last 50 years, Western men and women of higher status have lived longer and have been healthier and saner than the people they outclass.

6   The study of "social inequalities in health" is today one of the hottest areas in epidemiology, medical sociology and health psychology. Only last December, the John D. and Catherine T. MacArthur Foundation established a research network on socioeconomic status and health, under the direction of Nancy Adler, a psychologist at the University of California, San Francisco.

7   Much of the excitement dates from the 1980 publication of the "Black Report," when Sir Douglas Black (a former president of the Royal College of Physicians) and his medical, social science and public policy associates showed the statistical association between illness and social class in England and Wales. The Conservative Government detested the Black Report, viewing it as a trespass of social medicine into politics, an ideological tract produced by welfare-state advocates longing to redistribute wealth and level the social class system. Liberal egalitarians, just as predictably, took the study as proof that social hierarchy is a public health problem.

8   Politics aside, no one knows precisely why people with high status are more healthy and less crazy.

9   It is not primarily because they have better access to health care. Socioeconomic differences exist for diseases that are not amenable to treatment. In fact, since the advent of the British National Health Service in 1948, the gap in health between occupational statuses in England has widened. (Perhaps this confirms the dismal economic principle that publicly financed institutions—hospitals, schools, highways and courts—always benefit the well-to-do most.)

10   The health gap cannot be blamed mostly on hazardous work or living conditions, either. Social status differences in health persist even when members of different social classes are exposed to similar levels of pollutants and carcinogens in their environment.

11   Nor is poverty itself the prime reason. Consider, for example, the famous "Whitehall Studies," an investigation of the tidy, hierarchically graded world of relatively well-off white-collar British civil servants, conducted by the epidemiologist Michael Marmot and his public health colleagues at University College, London.

12   The Whitehall study showed that with each tiny descent in civil service rank, from senior executive officer down to executive officer, comes more angina, more diabetes and more rough cough with phlegm. In this securely employed population, the mortality gap between senior administrators and clerical workers is even greater than the health divide in the general population. Moreover, as comparisons between richer and poorer countries in Europe have shown time and again, greater national wealth does not readily translate into greater national health. A 45-year-old Greek male can expect to live longer than his English peer.

13   The health gap cannot be blamed primarily on life style differences, either. It's true that clean living (no smoking, alcohol or fatty foods and lots of exercise) is a high-status religious activity (though professional women probably drink more liquor than working-class women). Nevertheless, it turns out that most of the social inequality in coronary heart disease remains even after such life-style differences are taken into account.

14   Could the health gap exist because unhealthy people are downwardly mobile or because healthy women marry up? Those things do happen. Some people rise in status because

they are vigorous and others are "selected" for demotion because they are disabled or out of their minds. But social migration isn't enough of a stampede to explain all the health effects.

Neo-conservatives believe that both health and high social rank are jointly produced   15
and justly earned by hard-working, intelligent people who avoid reckless risks, educate themselves and take a long view of life. And liberal-minded egalitarians believe that health is a common good that ought to be provided and regulated by the government (just like highways, schools, courts and national defense). But neither side has explained how the health divide is actually produced.

Perhaps it is karma. Perhaps it is in the genes. Perhaps it is all of the reasons above. Per-   16
haps it is a statistical artifact. Perhaps the safest thing one can say is that the socioeconomic health gradient is a "multiple complex synergistic non-linear incremental cumulative threshold-bound lag effect." Social scientists like to talk like that when they think they are looking at something important but don't really know what is going on.

Questions for Inquiry

1. What is Shweder's claim? Is it explicit or implied? Is it a claim of fact, causation, values, policy, or mixed?
2. What exceptions are there to the generalization that the upper classes are healthier than the lower? Why does Shweder discuss these exceptions?
3. What are the political objections to the research findings of the Black Report?
4. What possible reasons does Shweder suggest for the health differentials between the rich and the poor? What evidence refutes each reason?

Questions for Argument

1. Which argument about the cause of upper-class healthiness makes the most sense to you? What do you think of the evidence refuting this factor as a cause?
2. In his last paragraph, Shweder jokingly suggests that social scientists would provide a polysyllabic but meaningless statement about the paralleling of health and status to cover up their inability to explain it. Do you think that the epidemiologists, medical sociologists, and health psychologists mentioned in paragraph 6 have embarrassed themselves by failing to pin down causes for this phenomenon? Do you think this failure shows the limits of science in understanding complex human issues?

Writing Assignments

Informal

1. "A 45-year-old Greek male can expect to live longer than his English peer," Shweder notes, because "greater national wealth does not readily translate into greater national health" (12). Write a journal entry in which you imagine the life-style factors that might make a Greek live longer than an Englishman.
2. Have you noticed "social inequalities in health" (6) among people you know? Write an informal paper in which you examine the poor or excellent health of someone you know. Compare the life and work of this person to the factors Shweder discusses as possible causes of poor or good health.

Formal

3. One possible cause of class differences in health is that poor health makes people "downwardly mobile" (14). Find out more about the concept of "upward mobility" and free-write to generate examples of this concept of movement between social classes and income levels drawn from people you know. Then write an essay in which you define the factors, health-related or otherwise, that you think lead people to be either upwardly or downwardly mobile. Use examples to support your choice of factors.

4. **Dialogue.** Shweder indicates that political beliefs affect how people evaluate the fact of health differences between people of different classes and incomes (15). (You may wish to do some research to find out about the beliefs of neoconservatives and liberals.)

5. **Argumentation.** Select one or two of the possible reasons for the health-income correlation discovered by the Black Report and the "Whitehall Studies" and imagine that this reason or reasons were proved true. What should society do as a result? Should there be social programs to ensure that more people are healthy? Assuming that certain causes of upper-class health have been discovered, write a paper in which you describe potential policies that might help the lower classes improve their health. Then argue for or against establishing these policies.

■ ■ ■

Chapter 9

The Logic of Argument

■ Read the following statement, then respond as indicated below:

> The quarrel is no friend of logic, and frequently represents argument at its worst.
>
> —Douglas N. Walton, *Informal Logic: A Handbook for Critical Argumentation*

Writer's Journal

What is the difference between an argument and a quarrel? Or do you consider them the same thing? What role does logic play in a typical quarrel? Write your interpretation of Walton's commentary about logic and argument. Do you consider yourself a friend of logic? Or is logic a friend of yours? Use specific incidents to flesh out your response to this quotation. Strive for an entry of at least 150 words.

Most people accept that clear thinking and good arguing have something to do with logic, and most people also agree that logic—or being logical—is hard. We tend to build our arguments instinctively and hope the logic is there. It is, in fact, quite difficult to actively use logic in constructing an argument. British logician Stephen Toulmin even wrote that logic's "primary business is a retrospective, justificatory one," in helping us to critique an argument and make sure that its conclusions are sound (6). And, in a broad sense, appealing to *logos,* or reason, involves many aspects of an argument—the development of evidence, a tone of reasonableness, and so on. But the appeal to reason also means being logical.

Classical logic divides reasoning into two types: reasoning from the general to the particular (deduction) and reasoning from the particular to the general (induction). Formal logic is studied as a branch of philosophy, and throughout the twentieth century logicians have struggled to relate the categories of formal logic to the way people think in ordinary life. British logician Alec Fisher writes, "There is no doubt that traditional formal logic contains many ideas and insights which are useful if one is to understand and evaluate arguments. On the other hand, it is clearly difficult to *apply* it to *real* arguments—to arguments of the kind one finds for example in newspapers, magazines, and learned journals" (140). This difficulty may result from the complexity of real-life arguments. As Douglas Walton notes, "real arguments are often macrostructures made of many smaller arguments, or subarguments" (108). In addition, the emphasis in classical logic on achieving the correct pattern or "form" of reasoning prevents formal logic from fitting day-to-day discourse.

Toulmin's revision of logic, which you learned about in Chapter 6, is specifically intended as a description of how we operate when we reason in real life. Rather than being "mathematical" or formal, Toulmin logic displays the process of making claims and supporting them in relation to the assumptions of those to whom the argument is directed. Toulmin likened everyday reasoning to courtroom justice. "Logic (we may say) is generalised jurisprudence. Arguments can be compared with law-suits, and the claims we make and argue for in extralegal contexts with claims made in the courts, while the cases we present in making good each kind of claim can be compared with each other" (7).

Toulmin believed that "the traditional way of setting out arguments—in the form of two premises followed by a conclusion—may be misleading" (113). In particular, he felt that formal logic oversimplifies what transpires in an argument (111, 141–145) and that arguments must be understood within the context of an attempt to persuade a particular audience, not in isolation (180–181). For Toulmin, the logic of argument should be viewed in the context or in the discourse community of the law and legal argumentation rather than in the context of mathematics.

The traditional way of understanding reasoning still dominates discussion of logic in the civic discourse community, however. So it is still necessary to come to terms with the basic elements of formal logic, especially because most critiques of reasoning in our culture tend to be expressed in its terms.

■ TWO TYPES OF REASONING: INDUCTION AND DEDUCTION

To critique the logic of an argument, you need, first of all, to establish the mode of reasoning the author is using. In classical logic, there are two complementary types of reasoning, inductive and deductive. Most real-life arguments mix the two, although one or the other often predominates.

Deduction is reasoning from a generalization to a particular situation. It proposes a rule held to be universally true of a class or category of individuals, situations, or events, and applies it to a specific instance. For example, if cold water removes fruit-based stains, and you've just dropped a forkful of cherry pie on your shirt, you can reasonably deduce that a dash to the bathroom to douse the spot with cold water will rescue your shirt. Whatever will remove fruit stains, in other words, will remove cherry pie because the cherry is classified as a fruit. Deduction relies heavily on classification and definition. The Declaration of Independence (a reading selection at the end of this chapter) uses deductive argument.

Here are some tip-offs that an argument is deductive:

- use of definitions
- establishment of categories or classifications
- lack of examples
- chains of reasoning, with one conclusion leading to another

Induction is reasoning from the particular to the general. It involves examining the evidence of a situation—the facts, data, experiences, observations, and so forth—and forming a general statement or conclusion that should apply to all similar situations. The scientific method, in which scientists gather evidence and generate a scientific principle or rule, is a form of inductive reasoning, one that is highly privileged—that is, honored—in our discourse community. Induction is essentially a comparative mode of reasoning: what is true of one instance or item is held to be true of other similar instances or items. Induction results in an inference—that is, a leap of interpretation or generalization. Inference is a crucial factor in the construction of knowledge.

Here are some tip-offs that an argument is inductive:

- specific cases and examples—names, dates, places, and so on
- statistics and other numerical presentations of facts
- comparisons and analogies
- use of experts and authorities to vouch for conclusions drawn from evidence
- personal experiences
- examination of causes and effects or results

■ *Activity 1*

Identifying Induction and Deduction, p. 368

Inquiring into the Logic of Argument

When a text seems extreme in tone or viewpoint, a reader might suspect the logic. But sometimes writing that uses a moderate, rational tone and presents an informed content may also incorporate unsound logic. It's a good idea to step back and get a perspective on the logic of any argument, perhaps especially those that strike you as convincing.

The first step in analyzing an argument is to determine whether deductive or inductive reasoning predominates or if the argument is a mixture. Inductive logic can be easy to spot; any sustained presentation of facts, statistics, or other specifics is usually part of an inductive phase of an argument. Then, think about the assumptions you have to make in order to credit the argument. What values are assumed by the argument? And are these values ones that seem acceptable?

Take, for example, the editorial "NATO Rearms the World," from *In These Times* (a reading selection at the end of this chapter). Certainly the tone is reasonable and the opening perspective seems probing and responsible. A quick overview reveals that three paragraphs present factual evidence: 2, where there is a historical rundown of invasions of Eastern Europe; 3, where public opinion polls are cited; and 7, where budgetary matters are confronted. These are the inductive discussions in the editorial.

The remaining paragraphs analyze the issue of NATO expansion using deductive thinking. Paragraph 4 presents the argument made by NATO leaders for expansion, and the following paragraph directly refutes it, challenging its main assumption by citing what "we have learned . . . over the past 50 years." Then paragraphs 7 and 8 provide additional deductive arguments against the expansion. Paragraph 7 analyzes finances, but a close look shows that the figures are not supported and seem to be broad estimates; the quality of the evidence in this inductive part of the editorial needs to be examined carefully.

Numerous assumptions underlie the editorial's position. The first paragraph reveals some basic assumptions underlying the critique of NATO: that "the Cold War is barely a memory" and that "there is no military threat to any of NATO's members" ("such a threat is almost unimaginable"). (A full analysis of the logic in "NATO Rearms the World" is presented later in this chapter.)

How Deduction Supports Argument: Syllogisms

Deduction provides a structure of reasoning, a framework or architecture, a scaffold on which to lay out a particular argument. This scaffold is called a **syllogism**, a three-part series of statements that assure a logical conclusion. The three parts are the major premise, the minor premise, and the conclusion. The **major premise** is the general rule, assertion, or definition that is the basis of the reasoning. Here are some examples of major premises:

> All skaters fall sometimes.
>
> All those infected with HIV will die prematurely.
>
> Under the "three-strikes law," anyone convicted of a third felony will spend at least twenty-five years in prison.

Notice that each of these statements asserts something to be true of a class or group of people: skaters, those infected with HIV, those with three felonies. We may agree or not that the premise is true; its truth will affect whether we accept the argument, but the validity or soundness of the argument depends not on whether it is true but on whether it adheres to the correct deductive structure.

The **minor premise** of a syllogism asserts that an individual is a member of the group described in the major premise. Here are some examples:

> Lucy is a skater.
>
> Rianne has HIV.
>
> Harrison was convicted of felonies three times.

When the major and minor premise are considered together, a **conclusion** appears. This conclusion is considered logically valid. Here are the conclusions of the three pairs of major and minor premises used as examples above:

All skaters fall sometimes.
Lucy is a skater.
Therefore, Lucy sometimes falls.

All those infected with HIV will die prematurely.
Rianne has HIV.
Therefore, Rianne will die prematurely.

Under the "three-strikes law," anyone convicted of a third felony will spend at least twenty-five years in prison.
Harrison was convicted of felonies three times.
Therefore, Harrison will spend at least twenty-five years in prison.

In each case, the conclusion is considered valid because the argument follows correct syllogism form.

To understand how syllogisms create validity, it is important to comprehend the way syllogisms classify. Diagraming a syllogism helps to show how the classification process operates. Figures 9.1, 9.2, and 9.3 diagram the syllogisms discussed above. In other words, what is asserted of the group named in the major premise applies to the individual(s) named in the minor premise *only* if the minor-premise individual(s) is a member of the group in the major premise.

Implied and Shortened Syllogisms: Syllogisms in Actual Discourse

Rarely do actual syllogisms appear in argumentative discourse. Instead, the line of reasoning is expressed informally, and the reader or listener must pull out the deductive sequences. This can be sticky because frequently writers omit some parts of the syllogism, implying them or assuming they are understood. Usually, if the writer can correctly tune in to the discourse community that is the intended audience, some ideas

FIGURE 9.1   Diagram of Syllogism 1

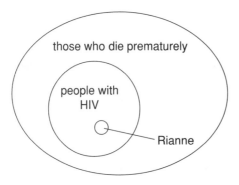

FIGURE 9.2   Diagram of Syllogism 2

FIGURE 9.3   Diagram of Syllogism 3

can be assumed. For example, a writer might discuss Rianne's experiences as a victim of HIV:

> For two years after learning she had HIV, Rianne had few effects. She went to work at the day-care center, cared for her children, and dated different boyfriends. When she suddenly lost weight and developed cancerous lesions on her ovaries, she suffered an intense depression. After her death a year and a half later, her children were parentless and were placed in foster homes. This happened because her half-sister and her ex-husband's parents fought over who should have custody. Clearly, Rianne should have dealt with the care of her children before her death. She needed to write a will and formally arrange

guardianship for them. That's why counseling of HIV sufferers must include advice about wills, guardianship, and so on.

Here, the fact that all HIV sufferers will die prematurely is left understood, creating what is called an *enthymeme,* a syllogism in which one premise is implied. Other syllogisms with understood premises are embedded in the paragraph:

> Children of deceased parents need a home and care. [understood]
> Rianne's children have a deceased parent.
> Therefore, Rianne's children need a home and care.

> People who are dying should write wills. [understood]
> HIV sufferers are dying.
> Therefore, HIV sufferers should write wills.

> Parents who are dying should arrange guardianship of their young children. [understood]
> Some parents are dying from HIV.
> Therefore, parents who are dying from HIV should arrange guardianship of their young children.

In the previous examples, premises are also assumed. This argument,

> Lucy should have known better than to skate without any protective gear. She deserved to break her wrist.

contains several embedded syllogisms:

> Skaters should realize that skating can be dangerous. [understood]
> Lucy is a skater.
> Therefore, Lucy should realize that skating can be dangerous.

> Skaters who don't wear protective gear are likely to break a bone.
> Lucy is a skater who doesn't wear protective gear.
> Therefore, Lucy is likely to break a bone.

■ *Activity 2*

Recognizing Syllogisms in Text, p. 368

How Syllogisms Can Go Wrong

If the audience to which a syllogism is directed does not accept the premises as true, then the syllogism will not be true for that audience. This is so no matter how correct the syllogism is in structure—that is, no matter how valid it is. For example, someone might not agree with the premise "all those with HIV will die prematurely" because of recent breakthroughs in treatment. This person might wish to modify the premise to "many people with HIV will die prematurely."

Sometimes, what appears to be logical reasoning is actually a faulty or illusory syllogism leading to an invalid conclusion. This illusion of a syllogism can occur when the minor premise asserts something other than membership in the class or group cited in the major premise. Sometimes both the major and the minor premise are statements we recognize as true, but if the relationship between the premises is not formally correct, then no valid conclusion can be asserted. For example:

> All those infected with HIV will die prematurely.
> Brice is dying prematurely.
> Therefore, Brice has HIV.

Here, the major premise is true, and the minor premise is true. But the minor premise does not assert that Brice is a member of the group of people who have HIV. In fact, it may be true that Brice suffers from a fatal kidney ailment, a condition unrelated to any HIV infection. Likewise, the following syllogisms are invalid:

> Under the "three-strikes law," anyone convicted of a third felony will spend at least twenty-five years in prison.
> Burton is serving a thirty-year prison sentence.
> Therefore, Burton was convicted of three felonies.

■ *Activity 3*

Recognizing Valid and
Invalid Syllogisms,
p. 369

> All skaters fall sometimes.
> Joanne fell and broke her wrist.
> Therefore, Joanne is a skater.

Conditional Arguments

Another form of deductive argument takes the form of an "if . . . then . . . " statement. This is known as a **conditional** or **hypothetical** argument. This type of argument focuses on possibilities and their fulfillment rather than on what is.

You may know that in grammar a conditional sentence is one that sets up a possibility using the conjunction *if* and then completes the sentence with a statement of the result that would occur, using or implying the word *then*. For example:

> If parents forbid scary TV shows, [then] children will have fewer nightmares.

> If more people imitated Mother Teresa instead of Madonna, [then] the world would be a better place.

> If more expansion teams are created, [then] more people will become fans of major league baseball.

The two halves of the conditional statement form the two premises. The possible action is called the **antecedent,** and the dependent result is called the **consequent.** Set up as a logical argument, conditionals follow this pattern:

> A]   Antecedent
> therefore B]   Consequent

> A]   If parents forbid scary TV shows
> therefore B]   children will have fewer nightmares.

> A] If more people imitated Mother Teresa instead of Madonna
> therefore B] the world would be a better place.

> A] If more expansion teams are created
> therefore B] more people will become fans of major league baseball.

Validity

As with any deductive argument, whether you accept the truth of the premises determines whether you believe the argument. Independent of the truth of the premises, however, conditional arguments are either valid or invalid, depending on the pattern formed by the premises. Consider the first conditional statement:

> A] If parents forbid scary TV shows
> therefore B] children will have fewer nightmares.

There are two ways this argument can be seen as valid: (1) if the first premise is positive or "affirmed" or (2) if the second premise is negated or "denied."

In the first case, the conditional argument becomes valid when the antecedent is affirmed:

> A] Parents do forbid scary TV shows.

As a result, the consequent is true:

> therefore B] Children have fewer nightmares.

This argument takes the form:

> If A occurs, then B.
> A occurs.
> Therefore, B.

In the second case, if the result of the conditional is shown to have not occurred or is denied, the consequent is denied also:

> Not B] Children do not have fewer nightmares.
> Therefore, not A] Parents have not forbidden scary TV shows.

This argument takes the form:

> If A, then B.
> Not B.
> Therefore, not A.

Failed Validity

A conditional argument is invalid (1) when the antecedent is shown not to have occurred or (2) when the result of the possible action has occurred, suggesting that perhaps something other than the condition of the argument may have produced the result.

In the first case, if the antecedent has not occurred (is denied), then the conditional is invalid:

> Not A]   Parents do not forbid scary TV shows.

As a result, the conclusion is invalid:

> Therefore Not B]   Children do not have fewer nightmares. [Children continue to have nightmares.]

This conditional argument is invalid because children may continue to have nightmares as a result of other factors—witnessing a car crash, perhaps, or being told scary stories by older siblings. Arguments of the form:

> If A, then B.
> Not A.
> Therefore not B.

are always invalid because even when A is denied, other circumstances can cause B to come about.

In the second type of invalidity, the result is shown to have occurred, but this does not mean that the action was the cause of the result. Something else may have brought the result about. In our example, the result is:

> B]   Children are having fewer nightmares.

The invalid conclusion is:

> Therefore A]   Parents have forbidden scary TV shows.

This is clearly invalid because there could have been many other causes for the children not having nightmares. This invalid argument takes the form:

> If A, then B.
> B.
> Therefore A.

Improper Wording

The statements in the conditional argument must be related as action and result of the action; sometimes in English it is possible to state a conditional in reverse. For example, the conditional argument discussed above can be stated another way:

> If parents are interested in preventing nightmares in children, they will forbid scary TV shows.

In this version, the result of possible action (the prevention of nightmares) is couched in the *if* clause, and the action itself is expressed in the second clause. If you try to analyze the conditional this way, you will get all mixed up. Instead, you need to recognize the inversion of action and result, and revise the statement's language so that the argument focuses on the action and result and not on the psychological condition of being "interested" in a result.

Induction

Most people find induction fairly easy to understand, possibly because it does not have to conform to a preformatted structure like the syllogism. Rather than following a tripartite form, induction admits any amount of information into a line of reasoning. Its formula is simple:

evidence 1 + evidence 2 + evidence n = conclusion

Induction is essentially fact finding followed by data analysis. And it's not just for logicians. We use induction on a daily or even hourly basis as we discover and understand the world around us. All these are examples of inductive reasoning:

- a poll showing that the governor of your state is extremely unpopular with both younger and older voters
- an experiment showing that seedlings grew faster with a certain fertilizer than without it
- a tenant deciding not to rent again from realtor X after receiving poor responses to maintenance calls during her lease year
- a parent deciding not to send her ten-year-old to sleepaway camp after she learns her young niece felt lonely and miserable during summer camp

The amount of evidence deemed necessary for a particular conclusion is relative; it depends on who is being convinced, how much they know about the situation already, whether similar conclusions have been reached before, or whether the conclusion is unusual and therefore difficult to support. It will take less evidence to convince your father that your old car needs replacement than that your car is a space alien about to depart for home or even that only a brand-new car will be reliable enough for your needs.

In life, we often require slight evidence before jumping to a conclusion, partly because we generalize from other situations we've been in and partly because we like to make quick sense of our experiences. Few of us can tolerate holding a wait-and-see attitude for long. We like certainty. But the academic discourse community requires stricter research and larger amounts of data before reaching a conclusion. However, all inductive research is partial, in that no one can ever collect and analyze all the possible instances of a particular phenomenon. The researcher has to stop somewhere and draw a conclusion. Inductive conclusions, thus, are based on incomplete evidence and require an **inductive leap** from the limited number of pieces of evidence to the general statement of the conclusion. An inductive leap is similar to what we mean by the term **inference**: our best guess based on our prior experience and current assessment of a situation.

The **scientific method** is an inductive activity. It requires collecting individual examples of a situation, comparing them to find similarities or repetitions, and generating a conclusion about those similarities. A scientist roaming the banks of the Amazon might conclude, after collecting a certain number of a newly identified frog species, that all members of the species are yellowy-green with raised brown spots. The "certain number" necessary to form this conclusion is a matter of judgment. Examining hundreds of frogs might be ideal. But it's likely that the individual scientist will settle for a smaller number, say a few dozen or even a few (if the frogs are sufficiently rare), as the basis for a conclusion.

Induction is always at the mercy of practicality. How much research can humanly be done in the time available or how many individual bits of data can be assessed vary depending on the situation and the type of research being conducted. And the frog-counting scientist would always recognize that there was more to find out about this newly discovered frog. Another researcher might come along, examine additional members of the species, and discover that the frogs in this species did occasionally sport bright red spots as well as brown.

■ USING LOGIC TO EVALUATE AN ARGUMENT

The editorial "NATO Rearms the World" (at the end of this chapter) criticizes U.S. and NATO policy for pursuing expansion when none is needed—in fact, when expansion may create problems in Europe. The editorial mixes inductive and deductive reasoning, with deductive predominating. Several syllogistic and conditional arguments are developed, beginning in the first paragraph.

In fact, not only does this paragraph set up a syllogism fundamental to the argument, but it also implies that the expansion of NATO and the desire of three Eastern European nations to join it is illogical in the face of certain facts: the Cold War is "barely a memory" and there is no military threat—in fact, "such a threat is almost unimaginable." It makes this point through an implied syllogism and rhetorical questions that translate as criticisms.

The minor premise of the implied syllogistic argument is "protecting NATO members from military threat is not necessary today." Behind this lies an implied major premise: "NATO's purpose is protecting members from military threat." Set in syllogistic form, the reasoning looks like this:

Protecting members from military threat is NATO's purpose.
Present-day Europe does not need protection from military threat.
Therefore]   Present-day Europe does not need NATO.

No support is offered for the first premise; the reader is assumed to agree to it. The support offered for the minor premise is general. The common knowledge that the Cold War is over is invoked, and military threat is labeled "almost unimaginable." Probably, most mainstream readers would agree to this premise despite its weak support. It is a valid syllogism most would probably accept as true, lending strength to the implication that NATO's expansion is illogical.

After this strong opening, the editorial intertwines deductive reasoning and empirical evidence in a contradictory way. A syllogism concluding that Eastern Europeans feel endangered as a result of history is backed up with a historical sketch revealing numerous invasions of that region:

Nations that have histories of being invaded and overrun want protection. (implied)

Poland, Hungary, and the Czech Republic are nations that have histories of being invaded and overrun. (supported with historical sketches)

Therefore]   Poland, Hungary, and the Czech Republic want protection.

In paragraph 3, the editorial states it clearly: these countries "still fear Russia." The last sentence of the paragraph, however, provides evidence that undermines this idea; statistics indicate that only Poland's people are strongly in favor of membership in NATO: "only 47 percent of Hungarians and 40 percent of Czechs do." Although these statistics place these Eastern European citizens on the same antiexpansion side as the editorial, a fairly convincing case for the NATO position has been conveyed as well. At this point, a reader who is looking closely at the argument may be stymied; either the people of these nations fear invasion and support NATO membership, or they don't.

In paragraph 4, the editorial turns to the major issue of the argument, the question of whether expanding NATO will create stability in Europe. Western leaders reason that it will, but the editorial refutes the pro-NATO stance by proposing opposite arguments starting in paragraph 5. The reasoning on both sides is logically sound: the editorial maintains that its premise, that fifty years of experience show that expansion of military might results in destabilization, is more true than the premise of the Western leaders, that NATO is a stabilizing force.

The editorial also supplies other arguments against the expansion of the alliance in paragraphs 6–8. In paragraph 6, the proexpansion argument is labeled as rhetoric, and the "undermining" facts are provided in paragraph 7. According to the editorial, if they join NATO, the three Eastern European nations will have to pay huge amounts to upgrade their military power; the editorial cites State Department estimates of $13 billion and projects a series of negative consequences: that the Czech Republic, Hungary, and Poland will have to cut crucial domestic spending to pay for military upgrades; that established members will foot at least half the military hardware bill of new members; and that U.S. taxpayers will have to pay for the rearming of Eastern Europe. Evidence for these arguments is lacking, except in the case of Poland.

Paragraph 8 then alleges that the underlying motive for expansion is to benefit providers of military hardware, mostly U.S. suppliers. No evidence is offered for this point, only the implied reasoning:

Selling arms to NATO countries must benefit someone.
Arms dealers will sell arms to NATO countries.
Therefore]   Arms dealers will benefit.

The final paragraph sums up the editorial and presents the main argument couched in conditional form. This conditional is flawed, however, in a way that shows the major problem with the overall argument. The conditional as stated in the text is reversed, with the *if* clause containing the result, and the second clause containing the action:

If the Clinton administration was truly interested in stabilizing Europe and the rest of the world, it would move toward a dissolution of NATO.

The argument in appropriate conditional argument form looks like this:

A]   If the Clinton administration moved toward dissolution of NATO
Therefore B]   it would promote stabilizing Europe and the rest of the world.

The administration worked to enlarge NATO, not dissolve it, so the first clause of this conditional is denied:

Not A]   If the Clinton administration did not move toward dissolution of NATO

And, the editorial would have us believe that as a result of this, Europe and the world will be destabilized:

Therefore not B]   it would prevent stabilizing Europe and the rest of the world.

A conditional argument of this form—"not A; therefore not B,"—is not valid. This means that even if the editorial has demonstrated that enlarging NATO would destabilize Europe, the opposite cannot be held to be automatically true. Eastern Europe will not necessarily become stable if NATO is not expanded. Likewise, the other implied conditionals in the last paragraph, that ending the "proliferation of international armaments" and allowing the nations "to develop [economically] in their own way" are invalid.

Examining the editorial's logic shows that throughout the text premises resting on unproven assumptions dominate the reasoning; in addition, a contradiction exists between the deductive argument that Eastern Europe's people are afraid and wish protection and the evidence of lukewarm attitudes detected in polls. Finally, the conclusion drawn from the analysis overstates the case for dissolving NATO on the mistaken premise that if expansion has negative effects, dissolution would create positive ones.

Using a Toulmin Approach

Below, one of the editorial's main arguments is diagrammed according to Toulmin's argumentation structure:

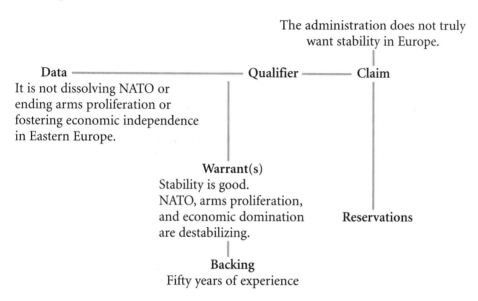

Laying out the editorial's main argument in Toulminian form reveals its weaknesses. There is no qualification. The data are limited. The warrants are fairly easy to discern, but only one, that international stability is a plus, is likely to be universally agreed to. Finally, the backing for the warrants is vague: no details of how the policies cited in the warrant are destabilizing are provided.

Toulmin logic reveals that the editorial's argument is not moderated by qualifiers and is based on general assumptions about what policies create what outcomes. The context for the argument provided by the editorial is not adequate to support it. Toulmin himself noted that "language . . . consists, not of timeless propositions, but of utterances dependent in all sorts of ways on the context or occasion on which they are uttered" (180). The editorial treats certain foreign-policy possibilities as if they are "timeless propositions."

◼ LOGICAL FALLACIES

A logical fallacy (or just a fallacy) is a statement that seems logical but actually is not. It's a case of superficial logic that falls apart when examined. Numerous patterns of thought can create this deceptive logic, and they have been identified and labeled. The fallacies described in this section are only some of the more common ones.

Fallacies occur in people's arguments because they seem so logical. Arguers who use fallacies usually are not aware that their reasoning is fallacious. They believe they are being logical and are in a sense fooled by their own fallacies. Occasionally, however, unscrupulous position holders will knowingly include fallacious arguments because they think their audience will not recognize the illogic. Often, when people need to cling to a belief or idea because it allows them to boost their ego, maintain order and familiarity in their lives, or avoid facing reality, fallacies result. But, as Professor Ray Perkins, Jr., writes, "We are, all of us, in our discourse with our fellows, obliged to avoid—or at least [to] try to avoid—fallacious reasoning. Fallacious reasoning is a kind of counterfeit, and like bad money, it should be identified and rejected whenever encountered" (xiv).

When writing is illogical, there are several ways of showing its illogic. When writing is fallacious, often a number of fallacies seem to occur in the same spot. Fallacies overlap and intertwine. When asked to tease out the fallacies from a piece of illogical writing, students often locate more of them than the instructor because recognizing fallacies depends on interpretation. Although one person might see the statement "everyone who favors capital punishment must favor abortion on demand" as a "bandwagon" appeal, another might label the statement a false dilemma, requiring an all-ornothing commitment to execution and abortion. When propagandists for a cause attempt to draw in the public, they may resort to the use of fallacies, in some cases deliberately. In particular, some of the fallacies overlap with the techniques of propaganda, as will be discussed in Chapter 10.

The two reading selections by Ray Perkins, Jr., at the end of this chapter discuss common fallacies.

Non Sequitur

Meaning "it does not follow," non sequitur describes an argument in which the reasons do not produce the conclusion. There's more than an inductive leap; there's a chasm between the evidence and the conclusion. "The Japanese make excellently engineered cars. Veronica will love her new Subaru." Here, the evidence, that a particular country's cars are well made, does not support the conclusion because a person's "love" for a car is not rational but emotional and does not have to have anything to do with the car's excellence. A person, after all, might love a jalopy because he earned the money for it himself or because it reminds him of enjoyable times.

Red Herring and Straw Man

These fallacies involve distracting the reader away from the true issue and substituting another. A red herring was used to make hunting dogs lose the scent of a hunted animal; likewise, a red herring in an argument moves the reader's attention toward a stronger, "stinkier" issue than the one under debate. A straw man is a distortion of the opponent's position that is easy to demolish and that distracts attention from the main concern.

Begging the Question

Begging the question means leaving the question begging for an answer; in other words, the issue at hand is skirted over and remains in need of explanation. Circular reasoning is one type of question begging. The proponent of the flat tax who advocates it because "everyone is taxed the same" is not adding anything to support his view; he's merely restating it. Likewise, definitional statements beg the question when proof is required: saying that "the city should arrest deadbeat landlords for not paying their gas, water, electric, and property-tax bills" is merely saying that "the city should arrest deadbeat landlords for being deadbeats." Perhaps they should be arrested, but their "deadbeat" status should be proved first.

False Dilemma

Also known as the either/or fallacy, false dilemma occurs when it is insisted that one or another of two alternatives must be chosen. Often such a binary choice denies the reality—that there may be many other positions besides the two, usually extreme ones offered. For example, saying society has a choice between locking up juveniles who commit serious crimes or being overrun by wild young criminals is to present a false dilemma.

Fallacies of False Causation

A number of logical fallacies have to do with distortions of the cause-effect relationship.

Post Hoc

The most well known causal fallacy is *post hoc*. Part of the Latin phrase *post hoc, ergo propter hoc* (meaning "after this, therefore because of this"), a *post hoc* fallacy is one in which sequence in time is held to be proof of causation. When an event follows another, causation is often inferred. For example, after a new policing style was introduced in New York City, crime rates fell, and officials touted "community policing" as a success. Many other changes, however, also occurred in the city at that time: the unemployment rate fell; awareness campaigns about "black-on-black" crime were mounted; the Brady gun-control bill went into effect; the penal code regarding treatment of juveniles and repeat offenders underwent modification; the percentage of young males in the population began to decline after decades of increase; and so on. Particularly telling were similar decreases in crime in cities that had not introduced the new policing method. In order to substantiate the cause-effect relation between community policing and lowered crime rates, in-depth research would be needed.

False Prediction

Similar to *post hoc* is false prediction, in which a result, either positive or negative, is predicted for a particular event or change without any substantiating evidence that would indicate the effect would be a necessary result of the change. For example, arguing against stricter emissions standards for cars because the increased fees charged would result in many more people driving with fake inspection stickers is to argue in a void. Only if proof is offered, such as evidence that drivers in other states with high inspection costs sought illegal stickers, is the argument worth something. Anyone can make predictions about anything.

Slippery Slope

Also known as the domino theory, this fallacy predicts that once a small change is made, effects will snowball until drastic effects occur. Young people are familiar with this fallacy because it is committed all the time by parents and teachers. "No, I can't let you stay out 'til 1:00 tonight because then you'll want to stay out 'til 2:00 next week, and before you know it, you'll be drinking and driving, doing drugs. . . ." "No, I can't let you do work for extra credit because then I'll have to let everybody do extra-credit work, and then students will want to do extra extra credit, and it'll never end." In actuality, anyone in charge of rules can make a considered decision to allow an exception: "I understand you wrote this paper under the stress of your mother's serious illness, and so in this unusual circumstance I will let you write another paper as extra credit."

Another arena in which slippery-slope fallacies abound is in public debates over social policies. Some insist legalizing marijuana for medical use is a step down the slippery slope to abolition of all restrictions on drugs. Others argue that permitting the assisted suicide of a terminally ill person is the beginning of a slide into mandated euthanasia of the elderly and of hopeless patients of all ages.

Sweeping or Hasty Generalization

This fallacy means exactly what it sounds like: pronouncing as fact an impression based on one or few examples. Ethnic and other forms of stereotyping are often a result of such generalizations. "I had to have my car towed once, and I can tell you that tow-truck drivers are rude, slow, and sarcastic when they know you need their services."

Ad Hominem (Name Calling)

This fallacy refers to arguing "against the person" rather than against the person's ideas. Labeling an opponent is a quick way to tempt your audience to be prejudiced against the person's views: "free spending," "bleeding heart," "rightist," "hard-shelled," and other categorizations can obstruct a reader's clear view of someone's ideas. Another type of personal attack occurs when a person's character or behavior becomes the issue instead of his or her argument. Examples of hypocrisy, infidelity, debt, and other personal failings are often invoked to disqualify people's arguments; for example, a mayor accused of abusing his spouse may be an effective administrator but lose favor in the public's eye because of the accusation. Readers need to decide for themselves a standard for measuring the extent to which a person's character or actions should be held to affect the validity of his or her opinions or ability to govern.

Ad Populum

Arguing "to the people" is the fallacy of invoking popular opinion rather than proving a point. In this fallacy, the writer or speaker champions common values such as honesty, family, efficiency, tradition in order to gain support for an issue. A writer might remind the audience, "If it ain't broke, don't fix it," and thus appeal to the value of avoiding needless effort and change as a way of promoting the status quo and opposing a proposal. Such an appeal avoids analyzing or evaluating the specific proposed policy.

Bandwagon

"Everybody's doing it, so should you" is a type of pressure brought to bear against holdouts and independent thinkers. Much advertising operates on this idea: what everybody drinks, wears, or washes with is obviously the best product. Appeals to opinion polls and other evidence of popularity are false ways of supporting an opinion. For example, citing a statistic that 85 percent of Americans identified personal safety as an important political issue in a recent poll means only that worrying about crime is popular; it does not prove that crime is a serious threat in our society.

False Analogy

In this fallacy a comparison of divergent items is used for proof. Although comparisons of unlike things often serve as lucid illustrations or explanations, analogies should be used only rarely to support an idea or interpretation. For an analogy to have weight as support, the things compared must be alike in significant ways. It might be apt, for example, to compare the situation of the Soviet Union in Afghanistan with the situation of the United States in Vietnam in order to prove a point about Soviet foreign policy—that is, if the similarity of the two historical situations can be defended. However, arguing that eighteen-year-olds should be trusted to drink legally because we trust them with fighting wars and voting is to compare activities with little in common; responsible use of alcohol requires social maturity, while soldiering and voting involve other abilities: willingness to follow orders and physical strength and endurance, on the one hand, and political judgment, on the other.

Appeal to (False) Authority

This fallacy occurs when support for an argument is enlisted by referring to an agreeing expert, celebrity, or other notable person. If the person cited is truly an expert, using him or her as an authority is acceptable. But often people "famous for being famous" are cited as authoritative support, especially in advertising and politics. For example, if baseball player Mike Schmidt were to endorse a sports or fitness-related item, he might be an acceptable authority. But in a commercial for pickup trucks, he is simply a famous guy some people would like to emulate, by purchasing a vehicle he supposedly drives.

■ *Activity 4*

Recognizing Fallacies, p. 369

◼ WRITING ABOUT OPPOSING VIEWS

There are two ways in which you might be called on to write about views other than your own. You might be asked to write a critique of an essay or article. Or, in developing your own argument on an issue, you might wish to discuss flaws in the reasoning of those who disagree with your position. Below, you will find a discussion of how to write a paper critiquing an argument. How to use refutation in an argument of your own is discussed in Chapters 7 and 8.

Typically, right after students learn about fallacies, they see them everywhere, just as people often imagine they have contracted the new disease they just heard about on the news. It's good to be alert to problems in logic, but try to avoid seeing illogic everywhere. As Toulmin wrote, "Statements are made in particular situations, and the interpretation to be put upon them is bound up with their relation to these situations. . . . The ways in which statements and utterances require to be criticized and assessed reflect this fact" (180). The context determines which assumptions will be accepted and the extent to which the reasoning in an argument needs to be spelled out.

Critiquing versus Attacking

An article that you critique should be treated respectfully, no matter how little you agree with its ideas or how bitterly you oppose its position. There are several reasons for this. A fair and reasoned critique reflects on you, the writer. A slash-and-burn attack on the article may cause readers to turn against you, whether or not they agree with the point of view expressed in the article you critique. Aggressive negativity may distract your readers from the points you are making. Finally, your analysis will be more acceptable to readers, of whichever position, if you show restraint in your wording and fairness in how you write about another's ideas. After all, there is likely some truth in some of the things said in the article. It's against the odds that any writer would be 100 percent totally wrong. You need to make sure that you recognize the strengths of an article you are critiquing as well as point out the flaws.

Guidelines for Writing a Critique

Here are the steps you need to take to produce a critique.

1. Read the article.

2. Free-write about your reactions to the ideas. Note how intense a reaction the piece produces in you. Do you feel your values or core ideas are violated or confirmed by the essay? What sections of the essay or particular passages or wording causes emotional reactions on your part?

3. Re-read for understanding and analyze the essay. Seek its claim, and note whether and where the claim is explicitly stated. Try to break the argument down into stages or sections, and strive to identify and number the reasons and evidence presented in support of the claim. Decide what type of logic is used, and sort out evidence

from deduction. As you go, make annotations in the margins, on sticky notes, or on a piece of paper. Make sure to note where the writer moves into a conclusion stage and whether suggestions, solutions, or changes are proposed.

4. Identify places where you feel the writer's ideas are flawed. Make notes about these problems, keeping track of the paragraph in which they appear. Here is a summary of some of the ways we've discussed arguments can go awry:

- evidence problems—too little evidence, inappropriate kinds of evidence (such as personal evidence where objective evidence is necessary), irrelevant evidence
- problematic assumptions—assumptions behind the claim or behind the choice of evidence that are not universally accepted or that need support; crucial definitions that are not universally agreed on
- oversimplified position or overgeneralized claim—a qualification or limitation of claim is necessary
- faulty deductions from acceptable premises—minor premise doesn't assert a particular membership in the category of the major premise
- presence of logical fallacies
- statistics that seem suspect or need substantiation
- lack of documentation for ideas and information supposedly from outside sources

5. Organize and evaluate your criticisms.

- Group them, so that similar types of problems are together. For example, if you discover a red-herring fallacy in paragraph 2, a causation fallacy in paragraph 5, and two sweeping generalizations in paragraphs 9 and 10, you would note that these fallacies form a serious problem in the essay. Then you might note that both the fifth paragraph and paragraphs 7–9 contain questionable assumptions. You might also note that four of five references to statistics are attributed to responsible sources, and that the only unattributed statistic is fairly minor.
- Sort your criticisms into types and decide which are major, which are quite important, and which are less so.
- Select the most important criticisms for discussion, given the length of the critique you are going to write. If the flaws are not numerous, you might decide to discuss them all. But most likely you will choose to present the major problems and not bother with those that are minor.

6. Plan an organization for your critique by sketching a rough outline. Arrange your clusters of criticisms in some order. To do this you need to decide whether to discuss the text paragraph by paragraph or to discuss the problems one after the other. Going through the text from start to finish can be tedious; usually, discussing the types of problems is more workable. You need to arrange these types in some coherent pattern from minor to major. Or if each type of problem is associated with a particular stage of the author's reasoning, you might discuss a problem that predominates early in the essay, then move onto one that occurs mainly in the middle of the development, and finish with a flaw that mars the conclusion of the author's reasoning.

7. Draft the substance of your critique. It often works best to jump right into the meat of your ideas; leave writing an introduction for later. Remember:

- Be specific about what you are criticizing. Identify the specific problematic statement by paraphrase or quotation.
- Be clear about the problem. If there is a logical fallacy, explain what makes the sentence or passage fallacious. If there is an unwarranted assumption, make the assumption explicit and tell why it is not acceptable.

8. Draft the introduction. Make sure you identify the title and author of the text you are critiquing. Then present a brief, accurate summary of the author's ideas. Make sure you use neutral, fair language. Then introduce a thesis for your critique that indicates the flaws you find in the essay.

9. Write a conclusion. Sum up your findings about the strengths and weaknesses of the essay. If it suits your analysis, propose a more acceptable, reasonable, or supportable claim than the one promoted by the author.

10. Get feedback on your critique and revise in response. The best reviewers of your work will be people who are familiar with the text you've discussed or who are also currently thinking about argumentation's strengths and flaws.

11. Proofread.

STUDENT ASSIGNMENT

Eric Malloy, "A Critique of Nicholas von Hoffman's Pro-Abortion Stance"

Eric Malloy wrote the following paper in response to an article by Nicholas von Hoffman (a reading selection at the end of this chapter):

Nicholas von Hoffman's argument that supporting abortion is a "pro-life" opinion is made aggressively and with an exaggerated tone. Exaggeration applies to von Hoffman's claims as well. He gets carried away by his enthusiasm and commits several logical fallacies.

Von Hoffman sets up a series of false-dilemma fallacies. His example of his mother telling him that he is alive because she didn't believe in abortion is a valid either-or situation. A person is either alive or dead. But other oppositions are much less valid. In paragraph 9, he suggests our choice is to become a victim of crime or see that unwanted babies are aborted: "To save ourselves from being murdered in our beds and raped on the streets, we should do everything possible to encourage pregnant women . . . to get rid of the thing before it turns into a monster."

He presents another either-or opposition when he says that those who believe in capital punishment must believe in abortion on demand; to be consistent, a person has to be for both or neither. Then he states another false either-or, that "it is far, far better to abort an unwanted child than to let it grow up into a homicidal monster." His "bumper sticker" presents this false dilemma in another way: "The fetus you save will grow up to mug you." His presentation of the types of men who support abortion rights is a false dilemma; they are divided up among "male feminists" and "unwilling father(s)" who don't want to pay child support.

Von Hoffman also creates false analogies. In stating that a fetus is "a nonsentient life form" and not a baby, he compares it to "the snail darter and the spotted owl." Most people would say that comparing an embryonic form of life to a full-grown animal of another species isn't a good analogy. Also, our society went to great measures to preserve these two particular life forms, but he's suggesting that abortion is not any worse than "dispatching" them. To make his point, it might be better to compare the fetus with a life form most people don't value, like ants or flies.

Also, von Hoffman brings in issues that are not tied to abortion. In paragraph 6, he says that our society's streets are "blue with gunsmoke" and that the anti-abortionists' stance compensates for the children killed in crimes. Through this image, he suggests that the anti-abortion stance is sentimental and not good sense, but this argument is a red herring. It's an interesting idea but doesn't add to his point.

The whole argument rests upon a sweeping generalization from some criminal cases, in which the crimes have allegedly resulted from cruel treatment done to the accused as a child. In paragraphs 11 and 12, von Hoffman cites "murder case after murder case," but actually discusses only one.

This hasty generalization is a false prediction that underlies the whole argument, that unwanted children will become criminals as adults. It's *post hoc* reasoning to assume that because child abuse occurred, the adult became violent. Abuse may have occurred, but to attribute total causation to the abuse is not valid. There may have been other factors.

The largest problem with von Hoffman's article is not the fallacies. It is the illogical deduction which he has made from his basic premise. He seems to be making this syllogism:

Murderers are abused as children.
Unwanted children are abused.
Therefore, unwanted children become murderers.

But this isn't valid because the minor premise says that unwanted children are in the class of abused children. For the syllogism to be valid, they would have to fall into the category of "murderers." So the premise of the entire article is illogical.

Eric organized his critique according to the types of logical problems he found: various fallacies located in specific statements of the text, fallacies underlying the entire argument, and a faulty syllogism in the main argument. In revising, Eric worked to improve transitions. He altered his claim statement so it pointed to the syllogism problem as well as fallacies. Some of his classmates felt he needed to round off his essay with a concluding summary, but Eric decided that being blunt about this author's failings was more suitable.

Activities

1   Identifying Induction and Deduction

Examine the following statements and decide whether the logic used is inductive or deductive.

1. If recovery from a mental illness is defined as the ability to choose appropriate life roles and responsibilities and to maintain them, with or without therapeutic assistance, then most sufferers can achieve recovery.

2. In a study of three hundred problem drinkers, it was discovered that problem drinking was more often correlated to the motive the person had for drinking than to the style or situation in which the drinking was done.

3. Patterns of assignments and reporting by women journalists were tracked in five major city newspapers over a period of several months. The result was clear: all the papers had female journalists; most of them covered features or human-interest stories; few were given opportunities to cover significant national, political, or international news. The print press is still, in the late 1990s, dominated by male reporters.

4. A woman was eliminated from the jury pool because of her attitudes toward the media and the defendant. She said she never watched TV because "everything you see on TV news is garbage," and she indicated total unfamiliarity with the murder. After hearing some of the broad details of the case, she exclaimed, "It's just as I say. Killers make the news because they're disgusting perverts. I don't want anything to do with him!" pointing to the defendant. The defense then asked to have her removed from the juror list.

5. Today, all financial markets are linked. If the Asian economy is in trouble, it's likely that eventually Americans will feel it. If the Japanese stock market drops, then there will probably be some selling on Wall Street.

2   Recognizing Syllogisms in Text

For the following passages, determine the syllogism(s) that underlie the reasoning.

1. Allure Dress Shops, Inc., chose Perker-Mayron Co. as its new ad agency. Having relied on direct mail for its advertising over the last decade, Allure is inexperienced when it comes to promoting itself in the marketplace. According to Hally Stephens, director of marketing, the company needs to learn more about its typ-

ical customer in order to design a campaign to draw "new customers of the buy-ing not the 'just browsing'" type.

2. "We sell about one-third of our exports to Asia, and if the Asian financial diffi-culties worsen, then the value of Asian currencies goes down; they don't have money to buy exports any more, their exports to our country and to others be-come much cheaper, and, more important, they lower the overall rate of economic growth in the world, which would hurt Americans," Clinton said. "That is the most likely negative consequence."

3. The Food and Drug Administration has approved sibutramine as a diet drug; the agency believes it is safe when administered by a physician. The drug is intended for patients more than 30 percent above correct weight, those who are genuinely obese. Critics say it causes high blood pressure, a serious problem because many obese people already have high blood pressure.

3 Recognizing Valid and Invalid Syllogisms

Examine the passages below to pull out the pattern of deductive logic. (Some syllo-gisms are implied.) Then determine whether the logic is sound or faulty.

1. Charles and Maggie Lepler have donated nearly a million dollars to the new cul-tural center. Mrs. Lepler is a great-granddaughter of the packing and shipping magnate, Hiram Hillsbough. As usual, the big donors come from wealthy old families.

2. Old Soviet nuclear submarines are rusting in Russian harbors. Years of deteriora-tion could create leaks of radioactivity. Russia lacks the funds to disassemble these ships safely, resulting in a potential environmental hazard.

3. The next generation of computers is likely to be faster than ever, but eventually the ceiling in computing speed will be reached.

4 Recognizing Fallacies

Read the following passages to determine what fallacy or fallacies are coming into play.

1. Anyone who is against animal research would totally disagree with using animals for the benefit of humankind. But what if an animal-rights activist has a child who is seriously ill? What if a drug has been developed to cure the disease but has not been tested to ascertain whether it is if truly safe? I bet this activist, if he or she truly loves the child, would support testing the drug on animals if it would save the child's life.

2. Pornography relates to the physical violence against women and children. In Mis-sissippi, the banning of pornographic books correlates with the reduction of sex crimes by 20 percent. Citizens are entitled to protect themselves from that which threatens their welfare as free people. If we do not start defending ourselves against pornography, we will eventually lose our morality and our treasured social order.

3. "Handguns annually murder at least 1,500 Americans," writes Nan Deska in her ar-ticle "Why Handguns Must Be Outlawed" (23). What she doesn't understand is that handguns are not killing people. People aiming and pulling the trigger are to blame.

4. Most of the politicians who are trying to get handguns and shotguns banned are the same ones who have the extensive alarm systems and who do not need guns for protection from burglars. They're so filthy rich they can protect themselves in other ways.

5. Do we disapprove of injustice in our country? If so, why is the abuse of animals in medical research tolerated? By allowing acts of cruelty toward animals, we are at the same time supporting unmerciful acts against them.

6. Another problem exists in the proposal to pay campus athletes who play on major college teams. If you pay one athlete, you must pay them all: the swimmers, the tennis players, the track team, the women's field-hockey team, and so on. Then, members of other campus activities would want pay also. The marching band, the cheerleaders, the debate team might demand rights equal to those of the salaried athletes. This could get expensive.

7. There are laws against illegal vending, and police can confiscate merchandise if it's being sold without a license. But, like most criminals, these vendors are back on the street the next day.

8. The people who are trying to remove sexist language from the Bible are missing the entire point of the Bible. Maybe these individuals who are trying to rewrite scripture to portray God as neutral ought to first determine whether they themselves are truly Christians.

9. If we are willing to take a life for a life, then should we not rape a rapist?

Assignment

Choose one of the following essays from this text and write an analysis of its logic; include any critiques you have of its development. Or choose an editorial or opinion piece from a periodical and write to evaluate the logic of its argument.

Myriam Miedzian, "How We Can Tune Out Children from Television Violence" (Chapter 4).
Editorial "Kids and Guns" (Chapter 5)
William D. Ehrhart, "In a War, All Should Suffer" (Chapter 6)
Ed Carson, "Pay Organ Donors to Increase the Supply" (Chapter 7)
David Cole, "Five Myths about Immigration" (Chapter 8)
David Walsh, "Liberty Calls Us to a Higher Purpose" (Chapter 10)

■ **WORKS CITED**

Fisher, Alec. *The Logic of Real Arguments.* New York: Cambridge, 1988.
Perkins, Ray, Jr. *Logic and Mr. Limbaugh: A Dittohead's Guide to Fallacious Reasoning.* Chicago: Open Court, 1995.
Toulmin, Stephen. *The Uses of Argument.* New York: Cambridge, 1958.
Walton, Douglas N. *Informal Logic: A Handbook for Critical Argumentation.* New York: Cambridge, 1989.

Readings

The Declaration of Independence

THOMAS JEFFERSON

In Congress, July 4, 1776
The unanimous declaration of the thirteen
United States of America

When in the course of human events, it becomes necessary for one people to dissolve the political bands which have connected them with another, and to assume among the powers of the earth, the separate and equal station to which the Laws of Nature and of Nature's God entitle them, a decent respect to the opinions of mankind requires that they should declare the causes which impel them to the separation.   1

We hold these truths to be self-evident, that all men are created equal, that they are endowed by their Creator with certain unalienable rights, that among these are life, liberty and the pursuit of happiness. That to secure these rights, governments are instituted among men, deriving their just powers from the consent of the governed. That whenever any form of government becomes destructive of these ends, it is the right of the people to alter or to abolish it, and to institute new government, laying its foundation on such principles and organizing its powers in such form, as to them shall seem most likely to effect their safety and happiness. Prudence, indeed, will dictate that governments long established should not be changed for light and transient causes; and accordingly all experience hath shown, that mankind are more disposed to suffer, while evils are sufferable, than to right themselves by abolishing the forms to which they are accustomed. But when a long train of abuses and usurpations, pursuing invariably the same object evinces a design to reduce them under absolute despotism, it is their right, it is their duty, to throw off such government, and to provide new guards for their future security. Such has been the patient sufferance of these Colonies; and such is now the necessity which constrains them to alter their former systems of government. The history of the present King of Great Britain is a history of repeated injuries and usurpations, all having in direct object the establishment of an absolute tyranny over these States. To prove this, let facts be submitted to a candid world.   2

He has refused his assent to laws, the most wholesome and necessary for the public good.   3

He has forbidden his Governors to pass laws of immediate and pressing importance, unless suspended in their operation till his assent should be obtained; and when so suspended, he has utterly neglected to attend to them.   4

He has refused to pass other laws for the accommodation of large districts of people, unless those people would relinquish the right of representation in the Legislature, a right inestimable to them and formidable to tyrants only.   5

He has called together legislative bodies at places unusual, uncomfortable, and distant from the depository of their public records, for the sole purpose of fatiguing them into compliance with his measures.   6

He has dissolved representative houses repeatedly, for opposing with manly firmness his invasions on the rights of the people.   7

8   He has refused for a long time, after such dissolutions, to cause others to be elected; whereby the legislative powers, incapable of annihilation, have returned to the people at large for their exercise; the State remaining in the meantime exposed to all the dangers of invasion from without and convulsions within.

9   He has endeavoured to prevent the population of these States; for that purpose obstructing the laws of naturalization of foreigners; refusing to pass others to encourage their migration hither, and raising the conditions of new appropriations of lands.

10   He has obstructed the administration of justice, by refusing his assent to laws for establishing judiciary powers.

11   He has made judges dependent on his will alone, for the tenure of their offices, and the amount and payment of their salaries.

12   He has erected a multitude of new offices, and sent hither swarms of officers to harass our people, and eat out their substance.

13   He has kept among us, in times of peace, standing armies without the consent of our legislatures.

14   He has affected to render the military independent of and superior to the civil power.

15   He has combined with others to subject us to a jurisdiction foreign to our constitution, and unacknowledged by our laws; giving his assent to their acts of pretended legislation:

16   For quartering large bodies of armed troops among us:

17   For protecting them, by a mock trial, from punishment for any murders which they should commit on the inhabitants of these States:

18   For cutting off our trade with all parts of the world:

19   For imposing taxes on us without our consent:

20   For depriving us, in many cases, of the benefits of trial by jury:

21   For transporting us beyond seas to be tried for pretended offences:

22   For abolishing the free system of English laws in a neighbouring Province, establishing therein an arbitrary government, and enlarging its boundaries so as to render it at once an example and fit instrument for introducing the same absolute rule into these Colonies:

23   For taking away our Charters, abolishing our most valuable laws, and altering fundamentally the forms of our governments:

24   For suspending our own Legislatures, and declaring themselves invested with power to legislate for us in all cases whatsoever.

25   He has abdicated government here, by declaring us out of his protection and waging war against us.

26   He has plundered our seas, ravaged our coasts, burnt our towns, and destroyed the lives of our people.

27   He is at this time transporting large armies of foreign mercenaries to complete the works of death, desolation and tyranny, already begun with circumstances of cruelty and perfidy scarcely paralleled in the most barbarous ages, and totally unworthy the head of a civilized nation.

28   He has constrained our fellow citizens taken captive on the high seas to bear arms against their country, to become the executioners of their friends and brethren, or to fall themselves by their hands.

29   He has excited domestic insurrections amongst us, and has endeavoured to bring on the inhabitants of our frontiers, the merciless Indian savages, whose known rule of warfare, is an undistinguished destruction of all ages, sexes, and conditions.

30   In every stage of these oppressions we have petitioned for redress in the most humble terms: our repeated petitions have been answered only by repeated injury. A prince whose

character is thus marked by every act which may define a tyrant is unfit to be the ruler of a free people.

Nor have we been wanting in attention to our British brethren. We have warned them from time to time of attempts by their legislature to extend an unwarrantable jurisdiction over us. We have reminded them of the circumstances of our emigration and settlement here. We have appealed to their native justice and magnanimity, and we have conjured them by the ties of our common kindred to disavow these usurpations, which would inevitably interrupt our connections and correspondence. They too have been deaf to the voice of justice and of consanguinity. We must, therefore, acquiesce in the necessity, which denounces our separation, and hold them, as we hold the rest of mankind, enemies in war, in peace friends.   31

We, therefore, the Representatives of the United States of America, in General Congress assembled, appealing to the Supreme Judge of the world for the rectitude of our intentions, do, in the name, and by the authority of the good people of these Colonies, solemnly publish and declare, That these United Colonies are, and of right ought to be Free and Independent States; that they are absolved from all allegiance to the British Crown, and that all political connection between them and the State of Great Britain, is and ought to be totally dissolved; and that as Free and Independent States, they have full power to levy war, conclude peace, contract alliances, establish commerce, and to do all other acts and things which Independent States may of right do. And for the support of this declaration, with a firm reliance on the protection of Divine Providence, we mutually pledge to each other our lives, our fortunes, and our sacred honor.   32

Questions for Inquiry

1. What is the claim in the Declaration? Is this document an example of deductive or inductive reasoning? Why?
2. In Toulminian terms, what is Jefferson doing when he states that "we hold these truths to be self-evident" (2)? Were these truths, in fact, self-evident to the king of England?
3. Identify the place in paragraph 2 and elsewhere in the Declaration where Jefferson moves from the general truths to the particular. What evidence is offered to back up the application of the "truths" to the case of the colonies?

Questions for Argument

1. According to the Declaration, what is the purpose of government? What other purposes for government can you imagine? Do you think our government has shifted its purpose since Jefferson's time?
2. Obviously we know now that the Declaration of Independence began a war—that it was, in a sense, a declaration of war or of willingness to go to war. In reading the charges against Great Britain, do you agree that it was time to separate and risk war? Or should there have been more work toward a peaceful solution (or peaceful dissolution)?

Writing Assignments

Informal

1. In your journal, write your reactions to re-reading the Declaration of Independence. Do you find its eighteenth-century style intrusive? Or does it lend majesty to the ideas? What is the document's overall effect on you?

Formal

2. **Deductive Argument.** The Declaration does not advocate rebellion lightly; it contains some cautions about changing governments: that "prudence" dictates that temporary problems should not inspire changes in "governments long established" and that people are naturally reluctant to begin "abolishing the forms to which they are accustomed" (2). Brainstorm with others to identify situations—perhaps personal, perhaps educational or organizational—in which a "rebellion" occurred. It may have been high school students walking out of classes to protest an administrative decision or members of a club refusing to contribute time toward a project of which few approved; or it may be a time when one individual protested parental power. Then choose one such situation and work with a group to generate a "declaration" of protest and resistance using Jefferson's document as a model for the argument. Your declaration may not end in "independence" but instead argue for some other resolution as appropriate.

3. **Research Opportunity.** Use the library or Internet to identify declarations of rights or of independence patterned after the Declaration of Independence. Choose one and read it to discover points of comparison and difference with the Declaration of Independence, particularly in how the argument is developed. Then write a paper in which you discuss the significance and influence of the U.S. Declaration on other groups suffering oppression.

■ ■ ■

Sex and Drugs: Just Say "No No"

RAY PERKINS, JR.

Ray Perkins, Jr., teaches philosophy at Plymouth State College in New Hampshire and has authored a book on the Soviet-American arms race. His book *Logic and Mr. Limbaugh*, from which these selections are taken, was published in 1995. (Copyright 1995 by Open Court Publishing Company, a division of Carus Publishing Company. Reprinted by permission.)

1   In our first example, Rush [Limbaugh] attempts to refute a sex education advocate on the basis of an analogy that omits some relevant differences between sex and drugs.

> Chancellor Joseph Fernandez vigorously fought the idea [of teaching abstinence in the sex education program], saying it would do great damage to their existing program! . . . This is tantamount to opposing a drug education program which instructs students not to use drugs because it would not be useful.
>
> (*The Way Things Ought to Be*, pp. 132–133)

2   The main reasoning here is an ARGUMENT BY ANALOGY, and it is based on the alleged similarity of sex education and drug education when it comes to abstinence. Rush implies (but doesn't actually say) that because opposition to abstinence in the case of drugs would be ab-

surd, it is equally absurd in the case of Fernandez's sex education program. We may represent the reasoning as:

(1) A sex education program is like a drug education program (as regards the role of abstinence).
     It would be absurd to oppose abstinence from drugs on the grounds that it would be not be useful.
     ↓Fernandez's position (that teaching abstinence in sex ed would not be useful) is absurd.

What we have here is a FALLACY OF FAULTY ANALOGY. We should recall that ARGUMENT by ANALOGY is not fallacious *per se*, provided that the things being compared are not unlike in relevant ways. When we look at Rush's analogy, we can see some important differences between drug education and sex education. Some of the main differences include the facts that: 1. one can, with proper sex education, avoid (or dramatically increase one's chances of avoiding) the bad consequences of sex (disease, unwanted pregnancy) without abstaining from sex, whereas one cannot (or not very easily) avoid the bad consequences of drugs (addiction, jail) without abstaining from drug use; 2. drugs are illegal, sex is not; 3. human interest in sex, but not in drugs, is rooted in a biological drive, an instinct. For these reasons, at least, Rush's analogy is weak.

Flying Condoms

In this example, Rush turns his logical guns on the condom.

> The worst of all of this is the lie that condoms really protect against AIDS. The condom failure rate can be as high as 20 percent. Would you get on a plane—or put your children on a plane—if one in five passengers would be killed on the flight?
>
> (*The Way Things Ought to Be*, p. 134)

This bit of reasoning is relatively simple. Rush is apparently trying to convince his audience that it is a "lie" that condoms really protect. This seems to be the main conclusion. And toward establishing that conclusion he argues that using a condom (or recommending its use to our children) is like flying on an airplane (or having our children fly on one) that has a 20 percent chance of crashing—obviously an irresponsible risk. The heart of the reasoning depends on an analogy between flying on a plane with a 20 percent chance of crashing and having sex using a condom with a 20 percent chance of failing. Here's the essential reasoning:

(1) Condom failure rate can be as high as 20 percent.
     Using a condom with a 20 percent failure rate is like flying with a 20 percent chance of a fatal plane crash (both risk death).
     No responsible person would fly with a 20 percent chance of fatally crashing. (Unexpressed *premise*)
     ↓No responsible person would use condoms to prevent AIDS. (Implied)
     ↓The claim that condoms protect against AIDS is a lie.

This is an especially instructive example because it illustrates the three general kinds of FALLACIES in one relatively simple piece of reasoning (INVALIDITY, UNWARRANTED PREMISES, OMITTED EVIDENCE).

4   First, even if no responsible person would use condoms to prevent AIDS, the second conclusion does not follow. A *lie* ordinarily is a false statement *made with the intention to deceive.* But even if the claim about condom protection is false, nothing Rush says even begins to establish that it has been made with the intention to deceive. Hence, his reasoning, as an ARGUMENT for the second CONCLUSION in (1), is a NON SEQUITUR (and therefore INVALID); the CONCLUSION does not follow from the PREMISE. (And notice that if Rush intends to support the assertion that the claim is merely false, rather than a lie, his own evidence that condoms do not "fail" at least 80 percent of the time surely suffices to establish the truth of the statement that "condoms really protect against AIDS," though admittedly it's not perfect protection.)

5   Second, his condom failure rate, as a general statistic, is suspect, even if it "can be as high as" he says. The phrase "can be as high as" is a weasel phrase which has little relevance in this argument. No doubt somewhere there is a batch of condoms all of which are defective and which therefore prove the claim that the failure rate "can be as high as" 100 percent. Obviously, this won't do as a statistic about condoms generally.

6   According to *Consumer Reports* (March 1989), of 40 brands tested, 32 had a failure rate of 1.5 percent or less; 6 had a failure rate of 4 percent or less; and only 2 brands had a failure rate of more than 10 percent. I conclude, therefore, that Rush's figure of 20 percent, as a general statistic about condom failure, makes his argument a fallacy of UNWARRANTED PREMISE.

7   (A further difficulty here has to do with the definition of "condom failure." If we extend the idea of condom failure to include failure due to human error, that is, to misuse, then the failure rate, though harder to measure, would no doubt be closer to 20 percent (though one would expect it to decline with increased sex education and perhaps also with instruction in less risky sexual activity . . . calling Dr. Elders). But sources I have seen indicate that even by that definition, 20 percent is too high as an average figure.)

8   Finally, we should notice that the second PREMISE in (1) makes a FAULTY COMPARISON which fails to mention an important difference between the danger from condom failure and that from plane crashes. An airplane crash is tantamount to death; a condom failure is not. This makes the reasoning a FALLACY OF OMITTED EVIDENCE.

9   We can fully agree with Rush that it would be irresponsibly risky to fly with a 20 percent chance of crashing. He is obviously comparing being killed in a plane crash to dying of AIDS. The trouble is, even if we use the 20 percent condom failure rate that Rush claims, the chance of dying of AIDS if one uses a condom for sex is very much smaller than 20 percent.

10   That probability is the product of the probabilities of the component conditions involved in the behavior in question. Specifically, it would be: a) the chance of condom failure multiplied by b) the chance that your partner is infected with the virus; multiplied by c) the chance that you will contract the virus from an infected partner if unprotected.

11   The percentage of the population with AIDS or HIV varies from group to group, of course. Among the teenage population it is rising, but is almost certainly less than 5 percent. Let's say 10 percent to be safe.

12   Experts differ in their estimates of the sexual transmissibility of the virus, though it is known to be more easily transmitted from men to women than vice versa. Most estimates of the chance of transmission (from men to women) by ordinary vaginal intercourse are in the range of 1 in 100 to 1 in 500 per sex act.

13   I will use the more conservative estimates (Rush would want it that way). In this context, that means the most gloomy estimates. Let's assume the worst. I will accept Rush's condom failure rate, exaggerated though it is.

To find the probability of dying from AIDS because of one act of sex using a condom, we have to multiply 20 percent (the condom failure rate) by 10 percent (the chance that your partner has HIV), and then multiply again by 1 percent (the chance that you will get the virus from an infected partner). 14

Since some readers may not be used to multiplying percentages, let's convert these to fractions. Twenty percent means one-fifth. Ten percent means one-tenth. One percent or "one in a hundred" means one-hundredth. So: 15

$$\frac{1}{5} \times \frac{1}{10} \times \frac{1}{100} = \frac{1}{5,000}$$

The answer is one-five-thousandth (or 0.02 percent). This is *one thousand times smaller* than the 20 percent (or one in five) death rate claimed by Rush. 16

Using a condom cuts your risk of death from AIDS to one-fifth of what it would be without the condom. In other words, on average, without a condom, you would have to have vaginal intercourse one thousand times, in order to catch the lethal HIV, whereas with a condom, you would have to have vaginal intercourse five thousand times. 17

Now let's get real, my dear dittoheads. Suppose that a condom fails, not once in five times, but once in a hundred times. Then your chance of catching HIV from one act of ordinary vaginal intercourse, with a properly used condom, is one in a hundred thousand (0.001 percent). On average, a person would need to have intercourse with a condom a hundred thousand times to die of AIDS. This is probably not very different from your chance of being struck by lightning while on your way to church. 18

Questions for Inquiry

1. What fundamental rule about analogies does Rush Limbaugh neglect in "Just Say 'No No' " and "Flying Condoms"?
2. In both these selections, would you say Perkins's argument is a deductive or inductive one? What does Perkins gain by quoting Limbaugh's reasoning before analyzing it and then rewriting the logic?
3. In "Flying Condoms," Perkins discusses several fallacies. Which does he refute deductively? Which inductively?

Questions for Argument

1. To what extent would you say the problems in Limbaugh's reasoning stem from his choice of words or his selection of a particular comparison. Do you feel you get his point and see the rationality of some of his ideas even though they are stated in a fallacious way? If you read Limbaugh "cooperatively," as discussed in Chapter 2, can you ignore the fallacies and make "good" sense of his ideas? Or would you say that his points are irreversibly damaged by the way he couches them?
2. Perkins himself ends "Flying Condoms" with an analogy. Is this a fair use of analogy? Or has Perkins committed a fallacy of his own?

Writing Assignments

Informal

1. In these samples of his writing, Limbaugh makes much use of overstatement and oversimplification. In your journal, write about a time when you or someone you know

overstated the case in an attempt to get attention or achieve a goal. Decide whether you believe exaggeration can sometimes be an effective strategy in human affairs.

Formal

2. Perkins concludes "Just Say 'No No'" with a statement of how different drugs and sex are. In addition to differences in legality, he says that (1) drugs' negative consequences cannot be avoided no matter how educated you are about them, and (2) "human interest in sex, but not in drugs, is rooted in . . . an instinct." There are some who would argue, however, that many people have used drugs, certain drugs at least, for years or decades without any noticeable addiction or brain damage and, if they are lucky, without arrest and jail. Others have pointed out that the drives for pleasure and escape into fantasy are also strong and universal in humans and that they represent psychological instincts if not biological ones. Discuss these positions with class members and then generate an argument in which you either defend or refute one of these two differences. Use specific examples from research or personal experience to support your claim.

3. **Research Opportunity.** Use the Internet or the library to locate additional examples of Limbaugh's reasoning (or you may wish to listen to his radio show and take notes about his ideas). Target one paragraph that seems particularly illogical and write an essay in which you expose the fallacies and lack of sound logic in the passage. Set your essay up as Perkins did, with a blocked quotation at the start and with brief, blocked outlines of Limbaugh's essential logic.

■ ■ ■

NATO Rearms the World

JIM WEINSTEIN

Jim Weinstein is editor of *In These Times,* a monthly magazine of current affairs. This piece was published in the magazine in July 1997 as an unsigned editorial. (Reprinted by permission of the author.)

1   The expansion of NATO, agreed upon at a summit meeting in Madrid on June 8, comes at a time when the Cold War is barely a memory and when there is no military threat to any of NATO's members—indeed, when such a threat is almost unimaginable. Why, then, are the existing 16 member nations eagerly pursuing expansion, and why are Eastern European countries clamoring to get in?

2   The second question is easier to answer than the first. The three countries invited to join NATO at the Madrid meeting—Poland, the Czech Republic and Hungary—all have histories of fighting off incursions from the East. Poland, in particular, has been the victim of Russian, and later Soviet, expansion. From the 16th century, when Catherine the Great took much of what is now Ukraine from Poland-Lithuania, to the Soviet absorption of much of eastern Poland during and after World War II, Poles have been victimized by Russia. So, in more recent times, have the Hungarians. The Soviets annexed Hungary's trans-Carpathian territories after World War II and suppressed the country's democratic revolution in 1956. The Czechs had their own democratic revolution crushed by Soviet troops in 1968.

The people of these countries, especially Poland, still fear Russia, while for their leaders, NATO membership promises a massive infusion of modern military technology as well as integration into the highly developed European economy. Even so, only in Poland does a large majority of the population support joining NATO. According to recent opinion polls, 88 percent of Poles favor joining the alliance. By contrast, only 47 percent of Hungarians and 40 percent of Czechs do.

Western leaders say that enlarging NATO to include the nations of Eastern Europe will promote "stability" and reinforce the commitment to open markets—and to the demands made by the World Bank and IMF for financial "responsibility," meaning Western-style austerity.

But if we have learned anything over the past 50 years, it is that larger and more heavily armed military forces serve only to destabilize regions. And the bottom line of NATO expansion is a vast expansion of militarization throughout Eastern Europe since NATO requires member countries to buy Western weapons and equipment.

Aside from the threat to stability that larger and better equipped armies present in themselves, there are two other aspects of NATO expansion that undermine all the rhetoric about how this move will foster the protection of democracy.

First, there is the huge cost. The Poles, Czechs and Hungarians will have to put pressing social needs aside and come up with part of the hundreds of billions of dollars that it will cost to replace the obsolete Warsaw Pact equipment they now use. The State Department estimates that the new nations' share of the total cost will be a mere $13 billion over the next 12 years. This figure is a gross underestimation designed to sell NATO expansion to the U.S. Senate, which must approve the new members. Even an outlay of $13 billion, however, would impose a terrible burden on the three new invited members. To give an idea, Poland, which has the strongest economy and highest growth rate of the three, was recently forced to cut military equipment purchases in half because it couldn't afford them. In any event, current NATO members, especially the United States, will end up paying at least half the cost of the modernization. That means, of course, that the American people will pay to rearm these three countries, and eventually most of Eastern Europe, if NATO expansion continues.

And who will benefit from this massive rearmament effort? Who will receive the lucrative contracts and cost overruns for all these modern guns, tanks and aircraft? You guessed it: the giant military suppliers, mostly American, whose welfare the Clinton administration and Congress have assiduously protected and enhanced.

If the Clinton administration was truly interested in stabilizing Europe and the rest of the world, it would move toward a dissolution, not an enlargement, of NATO. It would end the proliferation of international armaments. And it would allow the newly independent nations of Eastern Europe to develop in their own way, rather than imposing on them "market reforms" designed only to benefit corporate America.

Questions for Inquiry and Argument

1. What is the editorial's claim? Is it explicit or implied?
2. Does Eastern Europe's need for protection or the Western nations' desire to sell arms more strongly motivate the expansion of NATO, according to Weinstein? What evidence does he offer that this is so?

3. Weinstein cites historical evidence about the vulnerability of the Eastern European nations to attack. Do you find this historical evidence effective and convincing? Would you expect people in these countries to want protection? Does the argument that large arms caches destabilize regions (made in paragraph 5) effectively counter their fear of invasion?

Writing Assignments

Informal

1. Most of us are immersed in our personal lives and goals, and we give rather minimal attention to international affairs unless a war breaks out. We don't feel much connection to the international civic discourse community. In your journal, write about the international news that does tend to interest you or about why you usually ignore international goings-on.

Formal

2. **Research Opportunity.** The editorial concludes that world stability results from ending the growth of arms stockpiles around the world, not from supporting it (9). Do you agree that the United States should promote disarmament around the world? Find out more about the concept of international disarmament through research in the library or on the Internet. Then write an informed essay in which you focus on one type of disarmament (nuclear, for example, or land mines) or on one argument for or against disarmament itself and argue for a particular international policy regarding arms proliferation.

■ ■ ■

Understand That Pro-Abortion Is Pro-Life and Vice Versa

NICHOLAS VON HOFFMAN

Nicholas von Hoffman has been a commentator and staff writer for the
New York Observer. This article appeared in the *Philadelphia Inquirer* on
July 10, 1992. (Reprinted by permission of the author.)

1   The abortion question entered my life early. When I was seven or eight, my father sat on a jury hearing the case of a back-alley abortionist who had killed one of his patients. A gruesome coat-hanger and rusty-nail job. My father talked about the case, and the details stained my memory forever.

2   My mother also had decided opinions on the question. On those days when I was being a particularly obnoxious child, she would wiggle-waggle her index finger in front of my nose and tell me, "Just remember, young man, the only reason you're here is that I didn't believe in abortion." She died without having formally renounced her opposition to the practice, although her son's behavior gave her reason enough to reassess her stance.

If mother had snuffed me in my protoplasmic state, I wouldn't have known the differ- 3
ence, but her belief in my right to live allowed me to grow up to human consciousness and
mischief, for which I am grateful. Nevertheless, my escape from early eradication didn't
make an anti-abortionist out of me.

It did convince me, though, that the anti-abortionists are right when they insist abor- 4
tion kills. The right-to-choose people try to squirm out of facing what they are doing—
extirpating a most primitive form of human life. Preferring to speak of privacy, choice, they
don't like to use that word abortion, because its use reminds us that abortion is killing, although to call it baby killing is a propagandistic exaggeration.

If mother had offed me, the me in question would have been a nonsentient life form of 5
the sort this society dispatches all the time. Consider the fate of the snail darter and the spotted owl.

It is fitting that in a society whose streets are blue with gunsmoke, a great cry should 6
be made about embryo squashing, the most innocuous of the many forms of daily death.
Perhaps it's denial or expiation for the murders of post-fetal tots shot down playing in the
mud in front of public housing projects.

The pro-abortion people, in their self-evident embarrassment at owning up to what 7
abortion is, are inept at presenting their case. They have tied their rhetorical hands behind
their backs and reduced the scope of their cause to a brand of personalism. The argument
in favor of abortion has been whittled down by its proponents into a "woman's issue." What
this wrestling match is all about, they tell us, is a woman's right to her body, etc., etc.

Which is fine and good and unexceptional, but that's only part of what the abortion 8
struggle is about. This is not just a women's issue, something of no concern to men unless they're one of those contemporary, sensitive, fellow-traveling male feminists or an
old-fashioned, unwilling father who wants her to have an abortion so he won't be socked
with child support.

Free, cheap abortion is a policy of social defense. To save ourselves from being murdered 9
in our beds and raped on the streets, we should do everything possible to encourage pregnant women, who don't want the baby and will not take care of it, to get rid of the thing before it turns into a monster. Put it another way, everyone who favors capital punishment
must favor abortion on demand. It is far, far better to abort an unwanted child than to let it
grow up into a homicidal monster.

Let's say what we think, spit out what we only whisper and hope that we can stiffen the 10
mettle of the squeamish with bumper stickers proclaiming: *Caution!* THE FETUS YOU SAVE
WILL GROW UP TO MUG YOU!

During the long process that led to the state of California putting Robert Harris in the 11
gas chamber, it was claimed that child abuse had turned him into a murderer. In murder
case after murder case, the plea is made to spare the killer because a hellacious childhood of
neglect and sadism turned the little tyke into a brute and a sociopath.

Again and again, murderers are described by civil liberties lawyers as men who had a 12
mother able to bear children physiologically but unable and unwilling to raise them. Choirs
of experts tell us that three-quarters or more of violent crimes can be traced to cruelties the
criminals suffered during their earliest years.

The anti-abortionists call themselves pro-life. Better they should call themselves pro- 13
murder, since many of the fetuses they save will grow up to become Uzi-wielding maniacs
spraying bullets down the streets of Los Angeles or Philadelphia or wherever.

14   There will be a sufficiency of fine, healthy, taxpaying, contributing citizens even with abortion legal and easily available. Let's not make it even tougher on ourselves,

15   At their demonstrations, the anti-abortionists parade around with pictures of dead and dismembered fetuses. The pro-abortionists should meet these displays with some of their own—pictures of the victims of the unaborted—murder victims, rape victims, mutilation victims, pictures to remind us that the fight for abortion is but part of the larger struggle for safe homes and safe streets.

Questions for Inquiry and Argument

1. What is von Hoffman's claim? Is it explicit or is it implied?
2. How would you describe the tone of this essay? Why do you think von Hoffman chose this tone? What does it say about the relationship he wishes to establish with his audience?
3. Von Hoffman indicates that unwanted children are a menace to society because they grow up to be criminals. What should society's role be in relation to families in which children may be neglected or abused? To what extent should society interfere in families?

Writing Assignments

Informal

1. In your journal, write about your feelings about abortion as a personal issue and as an action that is currently regulated by laws.

Formal

2. Von Hoffman says abortion has "been whittled down . . . into a 'woman's issue' " (7). Is it? Should women determine whether an abortion is appropriate? Who else should have a say in the decision? Is abortion, as the author believes, a societal concern because of the effects it, or its absence, has on our communities? After a class discussion of this issue, develop an argument that delineates who are and are not the "stakeholders" in an abortion decision, what is the relative size of their "stakes," and who should have input into making that decision.

■ ■ ■

Chapter 10

Examining Style
in Argument

■ Read the following selection carefully, then respond as indicated below.

> In our time it is broadly true that political writing is bad writing. . . .
> Political language has to consist largely of euphemism, question-
> begging and sheer cloudy vagueness. . . . All issues are political issues,
> and politics itself is a mass of lies, evasions, folly, hatred and schizo-
> phrenia. . . . Political language . . . is designed to make lies sound
> truthful and murder respectable, and to give an appearance of solidity
> to pure wind.
>
> —George Orwell, "Politics and the English Language"

Writer's Journal

Why might "political writing" be "bad writing"? Do you agree or disagree with the flaws Orwell ascribes to politics? Respond in a journal
entry of about 150 words.

In the academic discourse community, arguments are expected to proceed
through appeals to reason, not to emotion, and to a lesser extent the civic discourse
community also values rational, evidenced writing. But language inevitably affects our
emotions in some way—that is, some appeal to *pathos* is inevitable. And since all writers of argument strive for effective and convincing language, all arguments are **rhetorical** in that they employ language and structure to encourage readers to accept the ideas
argued. Temple University Professor of Rhetoric and Communications Herbert Simons
notes, "There is no escape from rhetoric: no escape from informal argument, or from
figures and tropes, or from the . . . appeals to good sense that mark the discourse of the
civic arena" (23). Even language that is scientific makes use of rhetoric—its serious
tone, objective style, use of hard facts, and dispassionate logic are rhetorical strategies
of major importance in the academic discourse community. For most argumentative

writing, in fact, rhetoric—the use of language to connect with and influence a reader—is fundamental in creating dialogue with the audience.

Argumentation focused on emotional appeals shades into **persuasion**. Persuasion differs from argumentation in that its goal is convincing the audience to change beliefs or behavior (often by any means possible), while argumentation provides space for investigation into various interpretations. Later in this chapter some powerful persuasive techniques will be discussed.

■ LANGUAGE AND PURPOSE IN ARGUMENT

Awareness of a particular readership or audience helps a writer choose a presentation strategy and style. An author writing for an audience of like-minded people might write to reinforce a point of view or urge action rather than to convince. When an audience seems apathetic or uninformed, the writer's purpose may be to demonstrate the significance of an issue or to argue reasonably for a particular view of the subject. When the writer confronts an audience that is resistant, the purpose may be toned down to opening their minds to new views of the topic; or it may be angled toward showing that there is a flaw in their viewpoint or toward providing extreme amounts of contrary evidence to unsettle their opinion. In other words, writers modify their purpose in relation to the readership and strive for a style that assists this purpose.

A writer's style can tap powerful feelings and foster strong involvement by readers in a particular viewpoint. In the best cases, emotionally powerful writing assists a strong rational argument; other times, writers may substitute an appeal to emotions for the appeal to reason. In the civic and academic discourse communities, using a neutral tone, emphasizing evidence, and including authoritative quotations creates a convincing argument. The use of a serious or academic style is, in itself, persuasive. In other words, "neutral" is a style with its own persuasive effectiveness, and it is every bit as much a style as sarcastic, superior, and angry are styles.

■ WORD CHOICE

Words are the smallest building blocks of an argument, and writers give careful attention to them because they powerfully affect how ideas are perceived. Often, readers pay most attention to paragraphs and sections as they search to construct an interpretation of a text. It can be easy to glide over individual words and images with a view to the larger meaning. But word choice can exert a powerful almost magnetic force on the reader, pulling the reader's responses in the direction of the author's viewpoint. Thus, readers need to be sensitive to language at the level of words and phrases. Admittedly, attending to word choice requires readers to slow down, examine small bits of text, and exert the counterpressure of analysis to the emotional pull of style. In choosing words for their effect, writers work with connotations as well as denotations, use euphemisms that suit their purpose, strive for an appropriate level of abstraction, control figurative meanings, and monitor the diction level.

Denotations and Connotations

The denotation of a word is its meaning, or referent, as we all understand it. People usually think of the denotation as the "dictionary" definition. But, in addition to this base meaning, words also have connotations—that is, echoes of feelings and associations. Some of these connotations are shared by most users of the word, but connotations can also be local or even private. For example, consider the nexus of meanings surrounding the word *storm.* Denotatively, this is a simple word meaning weather involving a great deal of wind and rain or snow. Yet on hearing this word many have an emotional reaction, often negative: perhaps dread, annoyance, or fear. Probably few people have a positive reaction to this term, except for those who have private associations with storms that might cause them to feel excitement, joy, or perhaps even peace when they hear or read the word.

Connotations range away from neutral toward the extremes of positive or negative. Some words are fairly neutral; some are slightly colored with feeling; others convey strong emotion, either positive or negative. Examining pairs or groups of words with the same or almost the same denotative meaning reveals how powerful the connotations of a word can be. Synonyms mean the same thing denotatively but often have different connotations. Consider these words: *employer, supervisor, foreman, manager, boss, the man.* These words may all refer to the same person, but they differ in connotation. A writer who uses "boss" rather than "employer" might be writing to criticize or demean or to convey roughness. "Manager" might give an image of neutrality and efficiency. As a reader or writer, you need to recognize the positive or negative effect of word choice and be aware that word choice stacks the cards for or against a position through connotations.

Here's another example: the sun might be described as shining, blazing, or peeking. Each term means the sun is lighting the earth, but beyond this basic meaning each word conveys a different feeling. Under the blazing sun, you are likely to be uncomfortable, overheated, wary of burning, and in need of sunglasses. When the sun is peeking, you might reach for a light sweater and even carry an umbrella. And when the sun is shining, your mood might be upbeat and all will seem right with the world. This example shows that connotations attach to all sorts of words, not just to nouns but to adjectives, verbs, adverbs, and clusters of words as well.

■ *Activity 1*
Connotations and
Denotations, p. 405

Euphemisms

Euphemisms are terms that disguise or weaken a meaning. They substitute for a term that may have unpleasant connotations. Euphemisms may be abstractions that direct attention away from unpleasant details (see the following section, Level of Abstraction), or they may be equivalent terms with more positive associations. Sometimes euphemisms are figurative—that is, they invoke a picture image (see the later section, Figurative Language). For example, we say "rest room," "bathroom," "powder room," or "ladies' (or men's) room" so we don't have to ask for the "toilet." Euphemisms tend to lose their effect over time—the word "toilet" was originally a euphemism conveying a place for grooming, or being "at one's toilette." Many euphemisms are harmless and are in common and constant use: "passed away" for "died," "go to the bathroom" for excretion, and so on. But sometimes euphemisms can be used to steer our reactions.

The *Quarterly Journal of Doublespeak* collects examples of "doublespeak," or euphemisms that disguise information and thereby attempt to manipulate the public's feelings and ideas about events and policies. Its editor points out many examples: "preventative detention" for holding people without a conviction (Lutz 100); "downsizing" and "employee repositioning" for firing people at will (118–119); and "passenger facility charge" for airport tax (155). He writes, "Doublespeak turns lies told by politicians into 'strategic misrepresentation,' 'reality augmentation,' or 'terminological inexactitudes,' and turns ordinary sewage sludge into 'regulated organic nutrients' that do not stink but 'exceed the odor threshold' " (4).

Writers sometimes enlist euphemisms, and their opposites, disphemisms, which put a negative spin on ideas, to sway readers. The abortion debate, for example, has produced euphemisms—calling supporters of legal abortion "pro-choice"—and disphemisms—calling abortion "murder." The procedure of aborting a severely deformed fetus is termed "intact dilation and extraction" by the medical discourse community; this is doublespeak and conceals the nature of the procedure. But the term used in Congress and by abortion opponents, "partial-birth abortion," is clearly disphemistic and designed to create discomfort with the procedure.

■ *Activity 2*

Euphemisms, p. 406

Level of Abstraction

Another quality that affects a reader's response to words is the level of abstraction—that is, how specific or general words are. General terms encompass a broad range of references. Specific or concrete terms refer only to a few things or to one thing. For example, "mammal" is a general word encompassing all warm-blooded, fur-covered animals. The extremely specific term "Tabasco" is the name of an individual cat who lives with the author. In between range a series of terms varying in specificity: red tabby, domestic short-hair cat, feline, carnivore, and so on.

Level of abstraction is often represented as a ladder standing on solid ground and reaching up into the clouds. On the bottom of the ladder is the most specific name for an individual being or thing: Tabasco, Mrs. Grady's hen, Hank's copy of *Interview with the Vampire,* and so on. On the rung above is the next most specific way of referring to that same item: red tabby, Buff Cochin breed of chicken, paperback edition of *Interview with the Vampire.* One rung above contains the next most specific term: domestic feline, barnyard chickens, and Anne Rice novels. At the top of each ladder is the most abstract or general term: mammal, bird, communication medium. The ladder can have as many rungs as different terms exist for an entity. With the analogy of the abstraction ladder, writers who use general or abstract terms can truly be said to speak with their "head in the clouds."

Consciously choosing a level of abstraction is important. If you are speaking inclusively, broadly, or theoretically, general terms may be called for. However, sometimes abstractions let writers evade specific support or analysis of down-to-earth situations. The language we use to speak about our values, after all, is usually abstract: honesty, privacy, reliability. In addition, many abstractions, particularly those pertaining to values and mental states, have strong connotations: consider the emotional echoes resonating from such terms as love, hope, corruption, truth, deceit.

Writers who use language from lower down on the ladder of abstraction are usually speaking about experience, empirical research, behavior, and pragmatics. Concrete language also conveys emotions; if a writer describes a storm with the rather general verb "arriving," not much feeling is conveyed. But if the writer chooses a specific verb, such as "raging," "blasting," or "scouring," a reader may have stronger feelings. Including facts, statistics, descriptions, and other types of evidence in an argument is often a sign that the writer is writing concretely and recognizes the need of most readers for down-to-earth support and applications.

■ *Activity 3*
Ladder of Abstraction, p. 406

Figurative Language

Another technique for introducing emotional echoes is figurative language—that is, language that makes use of imagery and metaphor.

Simile

Sometimes writers make overt comparisons between two usually unrelated things. Using "like" or "as," such a comparison is called a simile:

> The independent candidate for governor whines like a power saw, slashing wildly at every economic policy of his opponents.

> Dressed in their newly mandated school uniforms, the children looked like flat, identical paper dolls.

In both these examples the presence of the simile creates a feeling; in the first, a reader will probably dislike the independent candidate; coming across the second, a reader is likely to feel sorry for the children and to regret the uniforms.

Metaphor

Often imagery and figurative language are introduced without direct comparison using "like." Instead, the imagery just slips in as details or description. Such imagery may form metaphors—that is, implied comparisons between things not usually considered to be alike. These comparisons can be made by using adjectives and adverbs or through the use of colorful verbs:

> Most Americans are too isolated in their suburban cocoons to care about helping the urban poor. Typical suburbanites live in neighborhoods padded by green turf and pillowy bushes, work in slick company castles breathing carefully purified air, and drive landscaped, high-walled roadways that tunnel past urban devastation.

Here, descriptive adjectives form implied comparisons of the suburbs to a cocoon, neighborhoods to rooms full of carpets and pillows, and workplaces to castles. The verb *tunnel* makes highways seem like isolated tubes through the city. And additional nonmetaphoric images—"carefully purified air" and "landscaped, high-walled roadways"—add to the effect that suburbanites are separated from the real hardships many people encounter.

In the following passage, Jesse Jackson uses a set of metaphors based on music to express his doubts about President Clinton:

> Alas, no one now speaks for the working people. . . . President Clinton often hits the right notes but sings a conservative tune. Instead of a program that works for working people, all the candidates ratchet up their populist rhetoric to mask their conservative status quo policies. But it's hard to sing one song and dance to another—soon enough people begin to understand that something is out of rhythm.
>
> —"Republicans Go from Bold to Brazen in '96"

■ *Activity 4*
Simile and Metaphor, p. 406

Jackson counterpoints this "music" with the lack of real programs to alter the "conservative status quo" and ends with an image of musical confusion. (Jackson also mixes metaphors here by introducing the image of ratcheting up, or increasing, populist rhetoric.)

Clichés

Some writers design new comparisons and invent fresh images, but often the figurative language of public discourse is composed of stock images and clichés. These timeworn comparisons, used frequently and commonly in our larger discourse community, evoke standard responses in readers. In the example about suburbia, the word *cocoon,* used to suggest self-indulgent isolation, is a cliché. Likewise, Jackson relies on a stock image of a public figure singing a tune, but he enlivens this image and gives it new life by extending it further.

■ *Activity 5*
Exploring Clichés, p. 406

A writer who makes much use of clichés is counting on readers to react automatically to language triggers rather than to read and think analytically. The tactic of using clichés may thus say a great deal about a writer's goals and about audience expectations.

Diction Level

The level of diction refers to whether the language used is formal, standard, or informal. In the academic and civic discourse communities, writers usually choose language ranging from formal to standard in "register," or level, but sometimes writers do use informal language to create a particular effect.

Formal Diction

Formal language is reserved for formal occasions and situations. It often uses abstractions, multisyllabic words, and avoids contractions. Sentences are sometimes long and make use of special structural techniques, such as parallelism, repetition, and balance, to create emotional power. This level of diction often impresses, and its use of abstractions means that the writer may be attempting to marshal the reader's emotions in a particular way. Marian Wright Edelman uses formal diction in her book *The Measure of Our Success:*

> All our children are growing up today in an ethically polluted nation where instant sex without responsibility, instant gratification without effort, instant solutions without sacrifices, getting rather than giving, and hoarding rather than sharing are the too-frequent signals of our mass media, business, and political life.

Standard Diction

Standard or middle-range diction is the level of language used in everyday public life—that is, in businesses and stores, on the radio, and in schools. Commonly understood words are used, and contractions are acceptable; sentence length is moderate, with sentence structure loose and uncontrived. This book uses standard diction.

Informal Diction

Informal language uses colloquial terms and is casual and, often, not very precise. Day-to-day informal language occurs all around us and is more often spoken than written. Many of us use informal language frequently, with friends, "off-stage" at our jobs—that is, out of the view of the public or our boss—and at home. Writers sometimes use informal language to establish a bond with readers or to make use of the connotative power of informal vocabulary. "Cop," for example, is informal and creates a negative image that a writer critical of police behavior might want to convey.

In a jocular article about legislating a national speed limit in the Senate, Donald Kaul uses the informal tone to underscore his criticism:

> But the Senate didn't stop there, no sir. You would think that with the terrible imbalance in the budget and the coming crises in Social Security . . . the Senators wouldn't have time to be traffic cops, too, but you'd be wrong.
>
> —"Helmet On, Helmet Off"

Slang

Slang is a version of informal language, one which is difficult to define because in large part it is the impact of slang on listeners or readers that is "the ultimate identifying characteristic of true slang" (Dumas and Lighter qtd. in Eble 12). Slang's purpose is to identify the user as belonging to a particular social set, in-group, clique, generation, or other socially demarked group. In content, slang is "ever changing," "innovative," and "ephemeral" and is easily recognizable to speakers of a language even though the particular words within a body of slang are constantly changing (Eble 11–13).

Sometimes slang terms become part of mainstream informal language, but they are still considered slang—that is, casual and less acceptable than standard talk. For example, "yo" is no longer a slangy greeting typical of South Philadelphia; it has entered our national vocabulary. It is, however, still considered slang. Connie Eble, in her study of campus slang, *Slang and Sociability,* notes that "bones," meaning dice, has been in use since the age of Chaucer (about 1400) but the term is still considered slangy (16).

The term "ripoffs," however, has shifted from being slang to being a mainstream, albeit informal, word. Few today would blink if a presidential candidate spoke of "corporate ripoffs," but in the 1960s, when this term was new, the public might have been shocked to hear a public figure utter this word.

Another dimension of slang use is that many standard words, such as "hurl," "pitch," "heave," and "toss," can be used in a slangy way to convey a meaning quite different from the standard denotation.

■ *Activity 6*
Slang, p. 407

■ *Activity 7*
Diction, p. 407

When readers encounter slang, they should recognize it as part of a writer's strategy. Authors who use slang may be trying to link themselves with a particular group of readers, display their down-to-earth side, or make use of the connotations, often humorous, of slang terms. As Eble writes, "The raison d'etre of slang is its power to evoke connotations based on human associations" (52).

■ POINT OF VIEW

Point of view refers to whether the argument is couched in the first, second, or third person. Although choosing a pronoun may seem like a simple and mindless grammatical decision, in actuality it can create effects that greatly influence a reader's reaction.

First Person

A writer may choose to write personally using "I" or to change into the first person at some stage of an argument. Using "I" often creates a sense of intimacy, of privileged information, of frankness or openness. Writers who describe their own personal experiences or feelings must use "I," but many writers on other subjects find the first person appealing precisely because because it gets away from the impersonal approach usually used in texts about ideas.

Charles Krauthammer, in a commentary about euthanasia in Holland and the United States (a reading selection at the end of Chapter 4), drops into the first person for one paragraph of his argument:

> I'm not even talking here about the thousand cases a year of Dutch patients put to death by their doctors without their consent. I'm talking here about Dutch doctors helping the suicide of people not terminally ill, not chronically ill, not ill at all, but like our lady of Assen, merely bereft.

The first person jolts the reader and provides impact; Krauthammer's personal indignation lights up the page.

Using the first person plural, "we," can also have a powerful effect by uniting the writer and reader or creating a unified community of opinion. Krauthammer concludes his article with a powerful change to the first person plural:

> In modern society, suicide is no longer punished, but it is still discouraged. . . . We are now being asked to become a society where, when the tormented soul on the ledge asks for our help, we oblige him with a push.

Third Person

To create a neutral tone and to establish a sense of objectivity, writers use the third person, plural or singular. This point of view causes the personality and stance of the writer to recede from view and presents the subject for analysis or examination. Most of the Krauthammer article is in the third person:

> In Holland, physician-assisted suicide is for all practical purposes legal, but Dr. Chabot was tried anyway because this woman wasn't terminally ill. She wasn't even ill. In fact, she wasn't even psychiatrically ill.

Second Person

A different effect results when the writer chooses the second person, "you." In speaking directly to a reader, the writer draws the reader within the frame of the text, putting the reader in place, on the scene, in the action. Here's an excerpt from an article by consumer advocate Ralph Nader exposing how supermarkets sell shelf space to food manufacturers, a system that drives up food prices. Nader uses the second person effectively in this excerpt to let you try on the roles of food producers so you can feel the injustice of a system that favors established manufacturers:

> If you are a big and rich manufacturer of food, drink and other supermarket items, you can pay for the space. . . . But if you are a small company trying to sell to retail outlets—even if you have a top quality and competitively priced product—it is hard to come up with money for this form of payola.
>
> —"Grocery Shelf Fees Ultimately Cost Consumers"

A few paragraphs later, Nader uses the second person again, to place the reader in the position of a consumer, who also suffers from this system of "payola":

> You are directly paying for [the shelf fees] in higher prices and indirectly paying the price of a squeeze play on up-and-coming small companies that could give you better value.

And, near the end, Nader suggests that the reader take action, again using the second person:

> Next time you come upon a supermarket manager while you are shopping, ask him or her what dollar amount of slotting fees are being paid in the store. After all, you're paying for them.

Sometimes writers use the implied second person, the imperative, to draw the reader into the action. Here is Evelina Giobbe dramatically casting her reader as a consumer of pornography. (Giobbe's article appears at the end of this chapter.)

> Drop in another coin and watch. . . . Reach in your pants for just one more quarter. . . . Or walk back to the magazine section. . . . Pick up a later edition.

The pronoun "one" is also second person, and you can use it when you want your tone to be more formal:

■ *Activity 8*
Point of View, p. 407

If one were to be abroad for years, even a decade, the changes in U.S. life-style would be more apparent.

■ SENTENCE STYLE

As much as word choice or point of view, sentence style can influence a reader's response to a text. Such devices as questions and imperatives, two sentence styles easy to notice, relate the subject to the reader; other sentence techniques create emphasis and sometimes drama, whipping up a reader's emotions. Here are some sentence types to be aware of when you are analyzing a text or writing an argument of your own.

Questions

Questions create involvement and sometimes suspense. Writers' use of questions falls into three categories: the rhetorical or reader-answerable question; the writer-answerable question; and the genuine exploratory question.

Writers often use questions the reader can answer; these **rhetorical questions** lead the reader along a line of reasoning. The reader mentally moves from question to answer, feeling smart and in sync with the writer. For example, when Thomas Geoghegan asks his readers, "How many Op-Ed articles in favor of [job] training have we all read?" he assumes they will think "many." He is setting the groundwork for his ideas about how our society can go beyond mere training.

Aside from these rhetorical, self-answering, or reader-answerable questions, writers sometimes ask writer-answerable questions, which they alone can answer. In doing this, they focus the reader's attention on an issue and dramatize their own opinion. Here is Krauthammer again, using questions and his answers to great effect:

> Why is this [the Dutch trial of Dr. Chabot] important for Americans? Because last week the U.S. Supreme Court was asked to decide whether physician-assisted suicide should be legal in America. . . . Once you start by allowing euthanasia for the terminally ill, what evidence is there that abuses will follow?
> The answer, in a word, is Holland.

Nader uses a writer-answerable question to open his article about grocery-store practices:

> Ever wonder how some name products in your supermarket seem to have a large amount of shelf space compared to other well known brands?

The rest of the piece is devoted to explaining the phenomenon of slotting fees.

When writers distill their ideas into such focusing questions and answers, they are creating drama and emphasis for their response. Such questions intrigue a reader and can also enliven a less-than-electric subject like grocery-store stock policies.

Finally, sometimes writers use questions as genuine points of inquiry. They may have a partial answer, or they may want to suggest a line of questioning and inquiry that has been overlooked or needs follow-up. Some of the questions in Krauthammer's article seem rhetorical and self-answering, but they are posed ironically—that is, Krauthammer doesn't agree with the answers they elicit—and ultimately stand as inquiry questions that the Supreme Court and Americans will have to answer. He conveys his opinion through the ironic tone, to be sure, but the drama and power of the questions remain:

> By what logical principle should the relief of death be granted only the terminally ill? After all, the terminally ill face only a brief period of suffering. The chronically ill, or the healthy but bereft—they face a lifetime of agony. Why deny them the relief of a humane exit? . . .
>
> But on what logical ground can this autonomy [to choose a time to die] be reserved only for the terminally ill?

Questions can thus serve many purposes in an argument. However, sometimes writers fall into posing questions when they should be providing reasons and explaining evidence. Questions, especially rhetorical ones, can be used to cover up weaknesses in an argument. When you notice strings of questions in an argument or in your own writing, it's a good idea to slow down and make sure that the questions don't disguise a lack of solid reasoning or support.

See the selected reading by David Walsh at the end of this chapter for examples of the use of questions.

Imperatives

Imperatives are sentences that direct the reader to some kind of activity. These are the "you understood" sentences we were taught about in grade school. Imperatives can draw the reader into an idea and help make a transition to a new supporting point. The previously cited passage by Giobbe uses the imperative. "Drop in another coin and watch. . . . Reach in your pants for just one more quarter." This evocative style, almost hypnotic in its intensity, places the consumers—that is, the readers—at the hard-hearted core of the porn industry.

■ SENTENCE LENGTH AND PATTERN

In addition to sentence style, writers can use sentence length and pattern to create emphasis and special effects. Most English sentences are of medium length, about ten to fourteen words. Consciously using shorter or longer sentences or sentences that are highly structured can help a writer add drama or intensify emotion.

Length

Short sentences piled on can create humorous, dramatic, or other effects. In developing definitions of simple and complex addictions, Frank Reissman and David

Carroll use sentences that imitate the concepts. In writing about "simple addiction," they include several short simple sentences:

> Take sugar. Some people eat large amounts of sugar-based foods every day, yet never develop an addiction. The sweets carry no charged symbolic value. The taste alone is the attraction. Such people have a simple addiction.

Following their definition of complex addiction, they write a paragraph composed of one long sentence full of examples and possibilities:

> In complex addiction, people not only derive taste pleasure from sugar but cathect to it as well, finding in a candy bar or bowl of ice cream a deep psychological comfort, a sense of security or self-reward that developed in childhood.
>
> —"A New View of Addiction: Simple and Complex"

Pattern

In addition to length, the pattern of a sentence can also influence the mood, tone, or effect of a piece of writing. Most English sentences use "natural order"—that is, the subject precedes the verb, and this pair of terms is usually located near the beginning of the sentence. By noticing unusual sentence patterns, readers can assess their impact. Sentence patterns directly affect the pace and directness of the text's meaning: whether that meaning is released quickly or slowly, directly or with interruptions.

Writers can play with sentence pattern in a number of ways. They can, for example, delay the subject and predicate by using many introductory phrases. This type of indirectness can build suspense and heighten feeling:

> Throughout the history of this project, from its inception through the planning stages to the completion of blueprints and specifications, on to the groundbreaking and actual construction of our magnificent new concert hall, the oversight committee members have worked tirelessly to make sure our city got the best public architecture and acoustics in the tri-state region. Let's give them a hand!

Or writers can use an inverted sentence structure, in which the predicate precedes the subject, again adding drama:

> After and only after this investigation will I agree to sign a contract with this company.

Writers can also create a sense of importance by using balanced or parallel phrases or sentences. William Lutz uses parallelism to great effect in his article "Words and the World" (a selected reading at the end of this chapter):

> The flag is not the country; the uniform is not the person; the crucifix, the Star of David, or the Crescent is not the religion; . . . the medal is not the courage; the college degree is not the skill or knowledge.

Another technique to create emphasis and elegance is to write sentences that do not reveal their full meaning until near the end. This type of sentence, the periodic, withholds its meaning, creating suspense. Here is columnist Robert Reno writing about the average voter's support for Republicans in the 1994 congressional elections:

> That huge numbers of voters depressed by declining real incomes, increasing job insecurity and widening income disparities should be turning to the party that favors lighter taxation of the rich and preferential tax treatment of capital gains, which is the traditional friend of those now making the huge profits, is one of the weird anomalies of this political year.
>
> —"The Sad, Weird Anomalies of This Political Year"

In this sentence, the reader first encounters the economically struggling yet Republican-voting public and only at the end finds out Reno's judgment about them. Compare Reno's version of the sentence with the following rewrite into a loose structure:

> It is one of the weird anomalies of this political year that huge numbers of voters, depressed by declining real incomes, increasing job insecurity, and widening income disparities, turned to the party that favors lighter taxation of the rich and preferential tax treatment of capital gains and which is the traditional friend of those now making the huge profits.

You might find this rewrite somewhat easier to read because it gets to its point more quickly than Reno's version. But it lacks the drama and impact of the original. It speaks of an irony, while Reno's version enacts the strain and irony in its convoluted structure.

Interrupted Sentences and Fragments

These two almost illegal-seeming techniques are indeed part of a writer's arsenal for introducing sentence variety and personality into a text. By using a dash or dashes, a writer may interrupt a sentence or change its direction. This might be done for any of a number of reasons. Interruptions can create a sense of spontaneity:

> At some point in the next century, our nation—our self-congratulatory, fun-loving, hale and hearty general public—is going to wake up from its self-satisfied dream into a nightmare of shortages: water, oil, clean air, and even sunlight.

Or interruption may be a way of introducing complexity:

> To withstand the competition of the many newly industrializing countries, our nation must see to it that our richest resource, our people—all our people, not just the top echelons, but our technicians, our agricultural, transport, and maintenance workers, our clerks and customer-relations staffs—achieve their potential and are offered suitable, stable, and gratifying work.

Or it might indicate a shift to specifics:

> Despite years of complaint and protest, today's educators earn little more—about 4 percent more adjusted for inflation—than they did ten years ago.

> The courses that now attract you—art history, modern poetry, Chinese culture—may not lead to a career but will enrich your life forever.

Fragments—when used intentionally and with flair—can also add impact. A fragment may convey surprise, sarcasm, or another strong emotion:

> One little card, like a credit card. That's all. Your entire medical history, genetic make-up, and brain biochemistry, coded and imprinted on one card. You'll carry it with you everywhere, and if you get sick or injured, medical personnel will know exactly how to treat you. That will be health care at the end of the twenty-first century.

> The plane was held up for an hour because one of the first-class passengers had lost something. An earring. That's right. We were late to the inauguration because of an earring. Not even a diamond earring either. Just plain gold, "with sentimental value."

■ *Activity 9*

Sentence Style,
Length, and Pattern,
p. 408

■ TONE

By tone, we mean the writer's attitude toward the topic and the reader. All the stylistic devices discussed in this chapter affect tone and can be consciously manipulated to create specific effects. Most formal and academic argumentation strives for a neutral tone, one that avoids appeals to emotions and that focuses on objective reasoning and evidence. This neutrality in itself, however, creates a sense of seriousness and fairness in tone.

In the civic discourse community, a broad range of tones occurs in writing designed to argue and persuade. While some writers concentrate on convincing readers through reasoning, many others—politicians, political observers, champions of causes, and advertisers—wish to persuade their audiences any way that works, and emotionality of tone certainly "works" for many readers and listeners.

Tone is closely related to diction level but is not exactly the same thing. We may speak of a formal, informal, or conversational tone but really mean the level of diction. Tone as "attitude" refers to whether a writer approves or disapproves of specific ideas, whether the expressed views involve positive or negative emotions, whether the discussion is serious, ominous, mocking, or humorous. There are as many tones as there are emotions.

A writer may exhibit bitterness, as Geoghegan does in this comment about the futility of job programs without available, decent-paying jobs:

> Hardly anyone is really against job training. . . . Let the workers train and train, like an army without rifles.

In these sentences, Giobbe's tone is ominous:

> I am a woman whose youth is frozen in time, frame by frame, in the technological recycling bin of prostitution: I am a woman who has been used in pornography.

Writing may also convey positive tones, such as encouragement, certainty, or celebration. Here's Cynthia Tucker writing about the 1996 Olympics:

> Somewhere along the way, I had lost all faith in the merits of athletic competition. . . . These Centennial Olympic Games have renewed my faith. From the Opening Ceremonies to medal rounds of gymnastics and swimming and Greco-Roman wrestling, athletes have shown us something about courage and character. . . . There is still an Olympic ideal—still a joy in excellence for its own sake, still a valor that fights on in the face of adversity.
>
> —"Olympic Heroism Gives Us Something to Cheer About"

Sarcasm, exaggeration, and irony are common approaches to arguments that involve critiquing or refuting an opposing viewpoint. In this passage, economist Walter Williams rejects common reasons for the upsurge of crime:

> Why have crime, hoodlumism and wanton property destruction risen? Depending on the "expert," you'll get psycho-socio-babble like: poverty, Vietnam, Reagan, the times, and other assorted nonsense.
>
> —"Bring Back That Old Dodge City Justice"

By putting the word *expert* in quotation marks and using such derogatory terms as "psycho-socio-babble" and "nonsense," Williams clues us in to his critical view of these and similar reasons. And Indian essayist Taslima Nasrin uses irony in writing about the situation of women in her homeland:

> Six hefty cattle from India are certainly more attractive, more productive and more valuable than an undersized Bangladeshi girl. I think they are rather getting cheated taking a girl in exchange.
>
> —"Women and Cattle"

When you encounter irony, mockery, or satire (as in the selected reading by Ed Anger at the end of this chapter), you need to slow down and make sure you understand the point the author is making. Although perhaps blatant and exaggerated, articles employing humor convey their opinions indirectly, by negating or blitzing opposing views with ridicule. As reader, you need to establish the humor's background line of reasoning and evaluate its critique for reasonableness.

Direct Statements of Attitude

Sometimes writers directly tell their readers what attitude to hold toward their subject or use a format that in itself conveys a strong message about the content.

William Lutz, author of "Words and the World," uses a direct style: "we must always re-member that the symbol and what it stands for are not the same thing."

Certain types of adverbs and transitional devices can steer a reader's response. Ad-verbs are terms, usually ending in *ly*, that suggest an attitude or judgment. Used as tran-sitional devices, such adverbs as "unfortunately," "hopefully," or "justifiably" can sway the reader's response.

Here is an example from Kurt Mack, writing an opinion piece in *Newsweek* about the verdict in the O. J. Simpson criminal trial:

> Sadly, the cheering hordes of black sympathizers have confused power with justice. . . .
> This "eye for an eye—payback is a bitch" sentiment will certainly come back to haunt us.
> —"O. J. Is Not a Black Hero"

The word *sadly* expresses Mack's attitude, but it also subtly tells the reader how to feel. Later in the passage, Mack uses the adverb *certainly* to assert a prediction for which he offers no proof. Sometimes, writers use expressions of certainty to lead the reader along to agreement even if there is no or weak corroborative evidence or solid reasoning to back up the point.

Repetition

Writers often use repetition of words, synonyms, sentence style, or sentence pat-tern to create emphasis and to heighten the impact of their ideas. Awareness of such repetition can help you trace the way a writer creates momentum and power. In her argument for a larger national investment in our children, Marian Wright Edelman uses repetition to great effect. She repeats phrases and reuses sentence patterns to build emphasis:

> All our children are growing up today in an ethically polluted nation where instant sex without responsibility, instant gratification without effort, instant solutions without sac-rifices . . . are the too-frequent signals. . . .
> All our children are threatened by pesticides and toxic wastes and chemicals pol-luting the air, water and earth. . . .
> All our children are affected by the absence of enough heroines and heroes in pub-lic and daily life. . . .
> All our children are affected by escalating violence.

Here is an example from Lutz:

> We must fight to reassert the primacy of the responsible use of language by everyone, from individual citizen to political leader. We must fight to make the responsible use of language the norm, the requirement, for the conduct of public affairs. We must fight to make the language of public discourse illuminate not obscure, lead not mislead, include not exclude, build not destroy. We can restore language to its proper role in public dis-course. We not only can, we must.

Format

The format in which ideas are presented can also influence a reader's reactions. A format that puts structure in the foreground, such as the use of headings, numbered lists or sections, and so forth, conveys a sense of objectivity and even scientific precision. The use of strong transitional devices to direct the reader through the text, such as enumeration of points, also conveys precision, linearity, use of the scientific method, or objectivity. And if a writer avoids transitions but juxtaposes points bluntly, this technique also affects the tone and the reader's response.

■ ARGUING VERSUS PERSUADING

The difference between argument and persuasion is sometimes a question of degree, of the balance between reasoned presentation of evidence and language strategies that ring the reader's emotional bells. Most writers do use persuasion instinctively because they believe in their viewpoint. Some critics maintain that all argument is persuasion, because the arguer aims to convert the reader, and that all arguers employ subtle techniques of word choice, organization, and selection.

However much that may be so, there still is quite a difference between producing a well-investigated, logical argument (an argument with its roots in *logos*) and deploying material designed to play on the reader's needs and perhaps even subvert a reasoned response (*pathos*). Most would advise the careful use of material that appeals to *pathos* or *ethos* in support of well-evidenced arguments.

Propaganda

Persuasion at its most extreme shades into propaganda. Although many of us associate propaganda with foreign dictatorships and oppressive regimes of bygone eras, in actuality propaganda is alive and well in our civic life today. Everyday advertising uses many propaganda techniques, and the tactics of pressure groups and extremists—political, religious, and issue-oriented—also derive from propaganda.

An official definition of propaganda comes from the Institute for Propaganda Analysis, an agency chartered to come to terms with fascist and communist propaganda during World War II; propaganda is "an expression of opinion or action by individuals or groups deliberately designed to influence opinions or actions of other individuals to predetermined ends" (qtd. in Merrill and Dennis 166). In their dictionary of "isms," Alan and Theresa von Altendorf write that "propagandism" is "the practice of promoting an idea, principle, or political entity through the deliberate creation and spread of information favoring the cause in question and often disparaging the opponent. In general," they conclude, "the term connotes the tactic of spreading lies" (245).

Propaganda is goal-oriented rather than inquiry-oriented; it strategizes to achieve noticeable, active change in beliefs and behavior. The desired action may be to buy a certain product, adopt a certain life-style, vote a particular way, contribute money to a specific organization, or become an active leaflet-dispensing, letter-writing supporter of a cause.

Modern people are engulfed in propaganda. Public messages have "become increasingly devoid of content and more and more become synthetic substitutes for genuine expressions of experience," wrote Israel Gerver and Joseph Bensman as long ago as 1954 (67–68). Pessimistically, they concluded, "the 'real' world is a public relations world, that is, one of claims and counterclaims by different types of experts and different organizations. Only a few are able to confront this public relations world with their limited experience. . . . [The rest] passively accept or compulsively affirm particular authoritative pronouncements on the . . . world about them" (69).

Propaganda makes great use of extreme, emotionally laden language. Seven distinct techniques were identified by the Institute for Propaganda Analysis and are presented in the article "How to Detect Propaganda," a reading selection at the end of this chapter. In a study of Nazi propaganda during the Second World War, Leonard Doob quotes Nazi propaganda director Joseph Goebbels's guidelines for successful propaganda. These include the use of "distinctive phrases or slogans" that play on "responses that the audience previously possesses" and that are "easily learned" and "utilized again and again . . . in appropriate situations" (209). In addition, Doob shows that, for Goebbels, whether a statement was believable or not determined whether a public communication would be truthful or deceptive.

Propaganda is a tool of ideology, of fixed belief systems that barricade themselves against inquiry. Ideology is discussed in Chapter 11.

■ CHOOSING A STYLE

The style you choose for a particular statement depends on many variables. Your audience will be a prime consideration: To what style will the readers be most receptive? But audience is not the only factor; if it were, all writing for the same audience would use a similar style. A writer's particular opinion on a topic and even his or her personal slant on life can affect the way writing turns out. Your style will reflect how impassioned, frustrated, embittered, or otherwise emotional you are about the issue as well as how much information you have.

Addressing similar mainstream audiences on the same unpopular claim in favor of drug legalization, three professional writers nevertheless chose different styles. In 1990, *Rolling Stone* editor Jann Wenner wrote a piece for the *New York Times* advocating the end of the war on drugs. His introduction establishes the style he chose:

> Despite decades of interdiction and enforcement efforts that have cost billions of dollars, there are more drugs and more blood on the streets than ever before. Our courts and prisons are crowded beyond capacity, corruption is rampant at home and governments abroad are under siege.

Words like *interdiction* and *enforcement efforts,* the long sentences, and the impersonal tone convey a rational approach, one the *Times* reader would endorse. Wenner's urgency on the issue comes through, however, in the direct declarative statements that form the second sentence and in some of the wording: the repetition of "more" and the use of "blood on the streets" to stand for "drug-related violent crime." As the editor of a youth-oriented magazine, Wenner may have felt a straightforward and sophisticated style would gain him credibility with *Times* readers.

Writing in the *New Republic*, Glenn Loury begins his essay against drug prohibition by subtly setting up the reader as expert. He invokes what "everyone knows," and then fills in details in a highly information-oriented piece:

> As everyone knows, America's eternal war on drugs has inflicted collateral damage of immense proportions on black males. Over the last decade, the prison population has exploded with mostly young, non-white, inner-city males caught in the drug trade. In 1992 alone, two-thirds of those admitted to state prisons for drug offenses were black. And the number of black males held in prisons, as a proportion of the adult population, nearly doubled from 3.5 percent in 1985 to 6.7 percent in 1994. (The corresponding number for whites in 1994 was only 0.9 percent.)

The phrase *collateral damage* is both technical wartime jargon and a negative image that elaborates on the "drug-war" metaphor. The words *exploded* and *caught* convey shadings of negative emotion, but the overall emphasis is on data and facts. Loury may have realized that drawing unpopular conclusions (that, as he says elsewhere in the article, "our drug policy is now too punitive") from current common knowledge about drug arrests requires solid grounding in information, especially with a conservative-leaning readership.

Finally, we have Barbara Ehrenreich taking a quite different approach in addressing the readers of *Time* magazine about illegal drugs. Known as a satirist, Ehrenreich begins mock-ominously:

> An evil grips America, a life-sapping, drug-related habit. It beclouds reason and corrodes the spirit. It undermines authority and nourishes a low-minded culture of winks and smirks. It's the habit of drug prohibition, and it's quietly siphoning off the resources that might be better used for drug treatment or prevention.

Ehrenreich comically portrays drug prohibition as itself an addiction with many nasty side effects. She uses repetition and parallelism, two techniques of formal oratory ("It beclouds reason and corrodes. . . . It undermines authority and nourishes. . . . It's the habit"), to add to the exaggerated style. Throughout, she uses humor and cleverness to delight readers and perhaps soften them to her view:

> Marijuana prohibition establishes a minimum baseline level of cultural dishonesty that we can never rise above: the President "didn't inhale," heh heh. It's O.K. to drink till you puke, but you mustn't ever smoke the vile weed, heh heh.

But she also provides information and uses analysis:

> Drugs can kill, of course. But drug prohibition kills too. In Washington, an estimated 80% of homicides are drug-related, meaning drug-prohibition related. It's gunshot wounds that fill our urban emergency rooms, not ODs and bad trips.

As these examples show, in choosing a style, many factors come into play: strategy about the audience, to be sure, but also depth of knowledge, individual intensity about the claim, and even personality.

■ WRITING AN ANALYTIC PAPER ABOUT STYLE

If you are reading an argument with an essay about style in mind, then you will pay special attention to the language. Your first endeavor, as always, will be to make sure you comprehend the argument. If you err in understanding, then your comments about style might be off-base. When you annotate, you might want to keep your notations about the ideas in one margin, and notations about style and language in the other. Or you might want to use different color ink. If your text is on-screen, you might want to use different fonts for different types of comments. Then you will probably wish to go beyond annotation to make notes about or lists of features of the writer's style.

Your paper about style should have a main idea. After examining the language of the text, you should make a judgment about how the author uses the elements of style to make the most effective statement about the evidence. Your paper will argue this judgment, using quotations from the article as evidence for your view.

■ *Guidelines for Writing an Analytic Paper about Style*

- Begin by identifying the piece you're analyzing.

- Choose a few stylistic techniques to discuss. These should be the main techniques you perceive the writer to be using in the paper. For example, an author might make great use of highly connotative language, long and loose sentences full of descriptions, and abrupt changes in topic. These three techniques might be the three you focus on in your analysis.

- Don't discuss infrequently used techniques. For example, make little or no mention of techniques the author uses only once or twice, such as questions, the imperative voice, or metaphor.

- Plan to discuss each of the techniques in turn. Most of the time, you should use your own points about the writer's techniques to structure the paper. Within each point about technique that you are making, it's a good idea to discuss examples in the order in which they appear in the source essay.

- Arrange your points in logical order. Often, this will be in emphatic order—that is, moving from least important to most important. To determine your emphatic order, you need to decide which factors make a technique "important." You may decide that the technique used the most is the most important, for example, or you may decide that the technique that creates the strongest reaction is the most important. Or, if the points seem equal, sequence your discussion to cover, first, techniques pertaining to the wording, and then those that affect the sentence style. Or use some other logical pattern.

- For each technique that you discuss, include examples from the text by quoting words, phrases, and sentences that reveal the writer's techniques. Sometimes, instead of quoting, specify particular sections or sentences that demonstrate the techniques you are discussing. You can do this by singling out particular sentences: "In the first sentence of every paragraph, the author uses the imperative to . . ." or "The third and fourth sentence of paragraph 4 show this balanced eloquence . . ." or "Throughout the fourth paragraph the author uses exaggerated descriptions to add humor to her portrayal of . . ."

- Don't clog your analysis with quotations. A few for each point you make will do; just be sure to choose significant examples.

- Go beyond just pointing out the main stylistic techniques. Explain the effect these techniques are likely to produce and how or why these effects help the author achieve his or her purpose.

STUDENT ASSIGNMENT

Josh K. Zeller, "Persuasive about Persuasion"

Josh Zeller analyzed an article about persuasion to identify the techniques that made it so powerful a critique of advertising.

ASSIGNMENT: Choose an article or opinion piece that you find strongly appealing. Examine it to identify the techniques the writer uses to enlist your enthusiasm and encourage your agreement. Using specific references to the language of the argument, discuss the effectiveness of the writer's style.

Here is his essay:

Jean Kilbourne's "Deadly Persuasion" is itself very persuasive that alcohol advertising sets a trap for young consumers that is literally "deadly." She clearly considers her subject to be of crucial importance and writes in a style that is very human as well as extremely direct. She also makes her argument convincing through the numerous examples that she analyzes and the statistics that back up her points.

Kilbourne shows that she is writing in the reader's interest by referring to "you" and using "we" frequently, especially in the introduction. She describes the effects of alcohol advertising as it pertains to "you": "Alcohol is magic, a magic carpet that can take you away. It can make you successful, sophisticated, sexy. Without it, your life would be dull, mediocre and ordinary," she writes in paragraph 2. She also uses "you" in stating some of the myths that the advertising industry has created. Myth #2 reads, "You Can't Survive without Drinking." And Myth #3 is "Alcohol Is a Magic Potion That Can Transform You."

The author uses "we" to link herself with the consumers of advertising, the general public, which she wishes to alert about the craftiness of alcohol advertising. "We are surrounded by the message that alcohol is fun. . . . We get this message many times a day. We get it from the ads and . . . we get from the media" (4). In her conclusion, she uses "we" to encourage us to present a unified front in combating the negative force of alcohol advertising. "We can investigate. . . . We can consider. . . . We can insist. . . . We can raise the taxes. . . . We can become more aware . . . and work to teach."

Another powerful technique Kilbourne uses is to present strong short statements and to put them in parallel. She begins her essay with simple sentences which parallel each other by using alcohol advertising slogans as the subjects. Other short direct sentences abound: "It can make you successful, sophisticated, sexy." "Everyone wants to believe in happy endings." "We get this message many times a day." There are far too many simple sentences to list them all.

Other parallel statements that are strongly emphatic occur in paragraphs 5 and 22: "Alcohol is related to parties, good times, celebrations and fun, but it is also related to murder, suicide, unemployment and child abuse." Later, she writes, "Alcohol lies at the center of these ads, just as it is at the center of the alcoholic's life." And the final paragraph uses sentences with parallel openings starting with "we" to emphasize the actions that a reader can take about the alcohol advertising problem.

The most persuasive things about Kilbourne's article are the specific ads she uses as examples and the shocking statistics she provides. Right from the start we get images of alcohol ads, in paragraph 1 and then again in the paragraphs discussing the myths. We are reminded of "the joy of six" campaign, the "less filling" chant of lite beer, the holiday slogans of "pour a party" and "holidays were made for Michelob," and the many lovely scenes presented as typical of drinking: "yachts at sunset," "your special island," "your mountain hideaway." Kilbourne also mentions the cute alcohol ads directed at children, Spuds Mackenzie the most prominent.

Her statistics about the realities of alcohol abuse and the profits of advertising are particularly attention-getting. Her first statistic, that 10% of all deaths, but especially suicides and homicides, are alcohol related is shocking. Her statement that responsible drinking by adults would practically put the liquor industry out of business is revealing. And, her statistics showing that alcohol is far a more dangerous killer than any of the illegal drugs points to the pain and suffering caused by the media advertising of alcohol.

Combining statistics, examples, and a direct strong tone, Kilbourne writes an unforgiving attack on alcohol advertising, without ever losing her image as a responsible, informed, and pro-audience writer.

Activities

1 Connotations and Denotations

A. What connotative differences do you find among the following sets of terms:

> employee, worker, laborer, workingman/workingwoman, associate, partner, staff, crew, gang, team
> motive, impulse, cause, incentive
> government, ruler, administration
> associate, colleague, friend, confidant, supporter, hanger-on, crony, buddy, side-kick, companion
> disclaim, lie, misrepresent, evade, fabricate, deceive, commit perjury (perjure oneself), fib, put up a front

B. Working in a group or as a class, list as many synonyms as you can for each of the following words, and then arrange them in order from most negative to most positive.

> end   fake   flaws
> free   success

C. For each of the italicized words in the sentences below, brainstorm several synonyms with different connotations. Discuss how the change of one word affects the emotional impact of the sentences.

1. I celebrate the *demise* of the network news.
2. The truly *educated* get all the news they need from the Internet.
3. There, in current-events news groups, *people* write about their beliefs in a truly *passionate* way.
4. The news is not just *dusty* words read by a *bored* and *highly experienced* anchor.
5. *Unfortunately,* the Internet might soon be taken over by *powerful* forces in the business world.
6. The business world sees the Net as just another *collection* of *consumers.*

2   Euphemisms

In a group or individually, brainstorm as many euphemisms as you can for the following terms:

> a smell
> a car crash
> to lie
> to get lost
> to lose a job
> to fail a test

3   Ladder of Abstraction

Place each of these terms on a ladder of abstraction, and then generate at least six more steps to the ladder:

> the pop star Jewel
> the Washington Monument
> architecture
> a sibling or cousin of yours
> the Space Mountain ride at Disney World
> a river
> Winnie-the-Pooh

4   Simile and Metaphor

Brainstorm alone or with others to use similes and metaphors to describe each of the following. Make sure your imagery depicts a specific thing, time, or place.

> a ninety-eight-degree day at the beach
> a city street at dawn
> your first taste of something wonderful
> a silly toy
> a dull party or gathering
> an offensive (but not famous) person

5   Exploring Clichés

Brainstorm alone or with others to generate a list of clichés; you may find the following list of types helpful in getting started:

> weather clichés
> emotion clichés
> vehicular or travel clichés
> nature clichés
> clichés for describing people
> education clichés

6 Slang

A. Brainstorm with classmates to create a list of current slang of a particular sort—for example, campus slang, current high school slang, Gen X slang, or some other sort. Each group should read its list to the class. Can you identify themes within the connotations and associations evoked by the various slang terms?

B. Rewrite the following paragraph using the slang of a particular group (such as one of those listed in 6A).

College officials today have many concerns about the personal lives of students on their campuses, but they have generally avoided acting *in loco parentis* since the campus uprisings of the 1960s. In other words, administrators have taken the position that college students are adults and should not be overly restricted by curfews, sign-in procedures, and so forth. Yet, at the same time, officials are legally obligated to make sure that their campuses are safe and that laws are not broken. This means somehow monitoring use of the campus by nonstudents and keeping student behavior within bounds. It often seems like an impossible task to those who deal with student life day by day.

7 Diction

Identify the level of diction in the following passages and discuss the specific elements of language that contribute to the diction.

[A] Babies are born with a number of obvious genetic traits, like brown or blue eyes, black or red hair, dark or light skin. But parents take note: infants also enter this world equipped with a genetically determined number of taste buds embedded into the tips of their tiny tongues. Some have a few hundred or so buds, while others are endowed with tens of thousands of receptors for sweet, sour, salty or bitter foods.

From birth to old age, this inborn characteristic helps determine what foods people crave or leave on their plates, scientist say.

—Sandra Blakeslee, "Chocolate Lover or Broccoli Hater?"

[B] All the world's megacities are different from one another. Only Sao Paulo, Beijing, and Mexico City are not seaports. All megacities are economic centers, but New York and Tokyo are far wealthier than Sao Paulo, which is better off than Buenos Aires, Argentina. Sao Paulo cannot match the squalor of Calcutta, India, but it comes close, and while it is better built than Jakarta, Indonesia; Cairo, Egypt; and Manila, Philippines; it has none of the civic nobility of Paris or even Los Angeles.

—David Harris, "Sao Paulo, Megacity"

8 Point of View

Examine the following brief excerpts. Determine the point of view taken in each passage and describe the effect this choice is likely to have on a reader.

[A] As we approach this mine-laden social-psychological terrain, among the questions we should be asking is, What does it mean to be an African American at the end of the Twentieth century? In the same breath we should ask, what does it mean to be an American?

These questions are at the heart of the unresolved tension in discussions about cultural pluralism: balancing what is perceived to be universal with ethnic particularism.

—Itabari Njrei, "Sushi and Grits"

[B] In America, with all the constriction that its swirling racial consciousness implies, claiming is a kind of freedom. Every ethnic group suffers its crisis as members of a fresh generation reject the claim as the last generation understood it, although, to the new generation, the claim is not rejected but transformed. The word that describes the process is assimilation.

—Stephen L. Carter, "The Black Table, the Empty Seat, and the Tie"

[C] But there were definitely times I was made to feel I wasn't black enough and wished somehow that I could get a handle on being so, being properly black. I felt this way, even though, when I want to, I can use my father's dialect, as well as a number of others, that are considered to be more or less black. . . . When I spoke in my own ideolect, I lacked authority. When I borrowed my father's I felt like an impostor, and still lacked authority.

—Reginald McKnight, "Confessions of a Wannabe Negro"

[D] Go to college. Study. Get high grades. Get an internship. Show your stuff. Make an impression. Graduate. Get hired. Pass Go and collect a great salary at age twenty-three. A large number of high schoolers think this will be their life script. Boy, are they wrong!

[E] To be a professional is to be spared the worst ravages of racism, but the many small daily slights that are the price of living here add to a miasma of racial exclusion. It is almost a cliché that if you're black you can't get a taxi in a major city, and it isn't quite true—but it isn't quite false, either. Even in a business suit, it can be difficult; if one is dressed more casually, it can prove impossible.

—Stephen L. Carter, "The Black Table, the Empty Seat, and the Tie"

[F] Let me set the stage. Take one young, eager black American journalist—that was me. One aging actress/singer/star—that was Josephine Baker. And one luminary of black letters: James Baldwin. I was twenty-two, a London-based correspondent for *Time* magazine, and I felt like a mortal invited to dine at his personal Mount Olympus.

—Henry Louis Gates, Jr., "The Welcome Table"

9   Sentence Style, Length, and Pattern

Examine the following passages and discuss the impact that the authors' decisions relating to sentence style, length, and pattern have on you, the reader.

[A] The [standard testing] abolitionist's use of rhetoric is most noticeable in attempts to capture the moral high ground through emotional appeal. On first glance, what right-thinking person would not want "schools with high standards," an "attitude of excellence," "genuine accountability," more "quality than quantity," "authentic evaluation," or "empowerment for teachers"?

But what does this jargon really mean? Are any of these phrases meant for any purpose except to make us feel bad about evaluation and to make us feel good about poorly defined alternatives? I don't think so. In fact, all the moaning and glooming about current practice suggests a new moniker around which the abolitionists can rally: "genuine assessment."

—Gregory J. Cizek and Ramsay Selden, "Nonstandard Tests Should Not Be Eliminated from Schools"

[B]   To my utter astonishment, the extensive research I conducted for this book brought me to one inescapable and irrefutable conclusion: I had been wrong. The statistics and anecdotes I gathered forced me to scuttle my well-prepared plans. I had to face the fact that writing a "morally neutral" book showing divorce to be just another option—a life choice no better or worse than staying married—would be irreparably damaging to the audience I wanted to help.

—Diane Medved, *The Case against Divorce*

[C]   This is what a neuron looks like, surrounded by a thicket of tiny tendrils that serve as communications channels. Now multiply that neuron 100 billion times. Crammed into the skull of every human individual are as many neurons as there are stars in the Milky Way.

—J. Madeline Nash, "The Frontier Within"

[D]   Now is the first chance on a new basis with new technologies to create a civilization of unprecedented openness and pluralism. A civilization of the polycentric mind. A civilization that leaves behind forever the ethnocentric, tribal mentality. The mentality of destruction.

Los Angeles is a premonition of this new civilization.

—Ryzard Kapuscinski, "America as Collage"

Assignment

Locate an article that you find appealing because of its striking style. You may wish to look in the opinion pages of newspapers or magazines or you may wish to choose an essay from this text. Examine the essay to identify the techniques the writer uses to enlist your enthusiasm and encourage your agreement. Using specific references to the language of the argument, discuss the effectiveness of the writer's style.

■ WORKS CITED

Eble, Connie. *Slang and Sociability: In-Group Language among College Students.* Chapel Hill: U North Carolina, 1996.

Doob, Leonard W. "Goebbels' Principles of Propaganda." In *Propaganda.* Ed. Robert Jacknall. New York: NYU, 1995. 190–215.

Ehrenreich, Barbara. "Kicking the Big One." *Time* 28 Feb. 1994: 70.

Gerver, Israel and Joseph Bensman. "Towards a Sociology of Expertness" [1954]. In *Propaganda.* Ed. Robert Jacknall. New York: NYU, 1995. 54–73.

Loury, Glenn C. "Getting a Fix." *New Republic* 30 June 1997: 25.

Lutz, William. *The New Doublespeak.* New York: HarperCollins, 1996.

Merrill, John C., and Everette E. Dennis. *Media Debates: Issues in Mass Communication.* White Plains: Longman, 1996.

Simons, Herbert W. "Preface." *The Rhetorical Turn.* Chicago: U of Chicago P, 1990.

von Altendorf, Alan, and Theresa von Altendorf. *Isms: A Compendium of Concepts, Doctrines, Traits, and Beliefs from Ableism to Zygodactylism.* Memphis: Mustang 1993.

Wenner, Jann. "Drug War: A New Vietnam?" *New York Times* 23 June 1990: 26.

Readings

How to Detect Propaganda

INSTITUTE FOR PROPAGANDA ANALYSIS

> This article originally appeared in the monthly newsletter of the Institute
> for Propaganda Analysis, an agency in existence between 1937 and
> 1945, which was founded to study propaganda and public opinion. The
> article was reprinted in *Propaganda,* edited by Robert Jacknall. (Copyright
> 1995 by New York University Press. Reprinted by permission.)

1   We are fooled by propaganda chiefly because we don't recognize it when we see it. It
may be fun to be fooled but, as the cigarette ads used to say, it is more fun to know. We can
more easily recognize propaganda when we see it if we are familiar with the seven common
propaganda devices. These are:

1. The name-calling device.
2. The glittering-generalities device.
3. The transfer device.
4. The testimonial device.
5. The plain-folks device.
6. The card-stacking device.
7. The band-wagon device.

2   Why are we fooled by these devices? Because they appeal to our emotions rather than
to our reason. They make us believe and do something we would not believe or do if we
thought about it calmly, dispassionately. In examining these devices, note that they work
most effectively at those times when we are too lazy to think for ourselves; also, they tie into
emotions that sway us to be "for" or "against" nations, races, religions, ideals, economic and
political policies and practices, and so on through automobiles, cigarettes, radios, toothpastes, presidents, and wars. With our emotions stirred, it may be fun to be fooled by these
propaganda devices, but it is more fun and infinitely more in our own interests to know how
they work.

Name Calling

3   "Name calling" is a device to make us form a judgment without examining the evidence upon which it should be based. Here the propagandist appeals to our hate and fear. He
does this by giving "bad names" to those individuals, groups, nations, races, policies, practices, beliefs, and ideals that he would have us condemn and reject. For centuries the name
"heretic" was bad. Thousands were oppressed, tortured, or put to death as heretics. Anybody who dissented from popular or group belief or practice was in danger of being called
a heretic. In the light of today's knowledge, some heresies were bad and some were good.

Many of the pioneers of modern science were called heretics; witness the cases of Copernicus, Galileo, Bruno. Today's bad names include: fascist, demagogue, dictator, red, financial oligarchy, communist, muck-raker, alien, outside agitator, economic royalist, utopian, rabble-rouser, trouble-maker, Tory, constitution wrecker.

"Al" Smith called Roosevelt a communist by implication when he said in his Liberty   4
League speech, "There can be only one capital, Washington or Moscow." When Smith was running for the presidency many called him a tool of the pope, saying in effect, "We must choose between Washington and Rome." That implied that Smith, if elected president, would take his orders from the pope. Recently Justice Hugo Black has been associated with a bad name—Ku Klux Klan. In these cases some propagandists have tried to make us form judgments without examining essential evidence and implications. "Al Smith is a Catholic. He must never be president." "Roosevelt is a red. Defeat his program." "Hugo Black is or was a Klansman. Take him out of the Supreme Court."

Use of bad names without presentation of their essential meaning, without all their   5
pertinent implications, comprises perhaps the most common of all propaganda devices. Those who want to maintain the status quo apply bad names to those who would change it. For example, the Hearst press applies bad names to communists and socialists. Those who want to change the status quo apply bad names to those who would maintain it. For example, the *Daily Worker* and the *American Guardian* apply bad names to conservative Republicans and Democrats.

Glittering Generalities

"Glittering generalities" is a device by which the propagandist identifies his program   6
with virtue by use of "virtue words." Here he appeals to our emotions of love, generosity, and brotherhood. He uses words such as truth, freedom, honor, liberty, social justice, public service, the right to work, loyalty, progress, democracy, the American way, constitution defender. These words suggest shining ideals. All persons of good will believe in these ideals. Hence the propagandist, by identifying his individual group, nation, race, policy, practice, or belief with such ideals, seeks to win us to his cause. As name-calling is a device to make us form a judgment to reject and condemn, without examining the evidence, glittering generalities is a device to make us accept and approve, without examining the evidence.

For example, use of the phrases "the right to work" and "social justice" may be a de-   7
vice to make us accept programs for meeting the labor–capital problem which, if we examined them critically, we would not accept at all.

In the name-calling and glittering-generalities devices, words are used to stir up our   8
emotions and to befog our thinking. In one device "bad words" are used to make us mad; in the other "good words" are used to make us glad.

The propagandist is most effective in the use of these devices when his words make   9
us create devils to fight or gods to adore. By his use of the bad words, we personify as a "devil" some nation, race, group, individual, policy, practice, or ideal; we are made fighting mad to destroy it. By use of good words, we personify as a god-like idol some nation, race, group and so on. Words that are bad to some are good to others, or may be made so. Thus, to some the New Deal is "a prophecy of social salvation" while to others it is "an omen of social disaster."

From consideration of names, "bad" and "good," we pass to institutions and symbols,   10
also "bad" and "good." We see these in the next device.

Transfer

11   "Transfer" is a device by which the propagandist carries over the authority, sanction, and prestige of something we respect and revere to something he would have us accept. For example, most of us respect and revere our church and our nation. If the propagandist succeeds in getting church or nation to approve a campaign on behalf of some program, he thereby transfers its authority, sanction, and prestige to that program. Thus we may accept something that otherwise we might reject.

12   In the transfer device symbols are constantly used. The cross represents the Christian Church. The flag represents the nation. Cartoons such as Uncle Sam represent a consensus of public opinion. Those symbols stir emotions. At their very sight, with the speed of light, is aroused the whole complex of feelings we have with respect to church or nation. A cartoonist, by having Uncle Sam disapprove a budget for unemployment relief, would have us feel that the whole United States disapproves relief costs. By drawing an Uncle Sam who approves the same budget, the cartoonist would have us feel that the American people approve it. Thus, the transfer device is used both for and against causes and ideas.

Testimonial

13   The "testimonial" is a device to make us accept anything from a patent medicine or a cigarette to a program of national policy. In this device the propagandist makes use of testimonials. "When I feel tired, I smoke a Camel and get the grandest 'lift.'" "We believe the John Lewis plan of labor organization is splendid; C. I. O. should be supported." This device works in reverse also; counter-testimonials may be employed. Seldom are these used against commercial products such as patent medicines and cigarettes, but they are constantly employed in social, economic, and political issues. "We believe that the John Lewis plan of labor organization is bad; C. I. O. should not be supported."

Plain Folks

14   "Plain folks" is a device used by politicians, labor leaders, business men, and even by ministers and educators to win our confidence by appearing to be people just like ourselves—"just plain folks among the neighbors." In election years especially candidates show their devotion to little children and the common, homey things of life. They have front-porch campaigns. For the newspaper men they raid the kitchen cupboard, finding there some of the good wife's apple pie. They go to country picnics; they attend service at the old frame church; they pitch hay and go fishing; they show their belief in home and mother. In short, they would win our votes by showing that they're just as ordinary as the rest of us—"just plain folks,"—and, therefore, wise and good. Business men are often "plain folks" with the factory hands. Even distillers use the device. "It's our family's whiskey, neighbor; and neighbor, it's your price."

Card-Stacking

15   "Card stacking" is a device in which the propagandist employs all the arts of deception to win our support for himself, his group, nation, race, policy, practice, belief or ideal. He stacks the cards against the truth. He uses under-emphasis and over-emphasis to dodge is-

sues and evade facts. He resorts to lies, censorship, and distortion. He omits facts. He offers false testimony. He creates a smoke-screen of clamor by raising a new issue when he wants an embarrassing matter forgotten. He draws a red herring across the trail to confuse and divert those in quest of facts he does not want revealed. He makes the unreal appear real and the real appear unreal. He lets half-truth masquerade as truth. By the card-stacking device, a mediocre candidate, through the "build-up," is made to appear an intellectual titan; an ordinary prize fighter a probable world champion; a worthless patent medicine a beneficent cure. By means of this device propagandists would convince us that a ruthless war of aggression is a crusade for righteousness. Some member nations of the Non-Intervention Committee send their troops to intervene in Spain. Card-stacking employs sham, hypocrisy, effrontery.

The Band Wagon

The "band wagon" is a device to make us follow the crowd, to accept the propagandist's program en masse. Here his theme is: "Everybody's doing it." His techniques range from those of medicine show to dramatic spectacle. He hires a hall, fills a great stadium, marches a million men in parade. He employs symbols, colors, music, movement, all the dramatic arts. He appeals to the desire, common to most of us, to "follow the crowd." Because he wants us to follow the crowd in masses, he directs his appeal to groups held together by common ties of nationality, religion, race, environment, sex, vocation. Thus propagandists campaigning for or against a program will appeal to us as Catholics, Protestants, or Jews: as members of the Nordic race or as Negroes; as farmers or as school teachers; as housewives or as miners. All the artifices of flattery are used to harness the fears and hatreds, prejudices and biases, convictions and ideals common to the group; thus emotion is made to push and pull the group on to the band wagon. In newspaper articles and in the spoken word this device is also found. "Don't throw your vote away. Vote for our candidate. He's sure to win." Nearly every candidate wins in every election—before the votes are in.   16

Propaganda and Emotion

Observe that in all these devices our emotion is the stuff with which propagandists work. Without it they are helpless; with it, harnessing it to their purposes, they can make us glow with pride or burn with hatred, they can make us zealots in behalf of the program they espouse. Propaganda as generally understood is expression of opinion or action by individuals or groups with reference to predetermined ends. Without the appeal to our emotion— to our fears and to our courage, to our selfishness and unselfishness, to our loves and to our hates—propagandists would influence few opinions and few actions.   17

To say this is not to condemn emotion, an essential part of life, or to assert that all predetermined ends of propagandists are "bad." What we mean is that the intelligent citizen does not want propagandists to utilize his emotions, even to the attainment of "good" ends, without knowing what is going on. He does not want to be "used" in the attainment of ends he may later consider "bad." He does not want to be gullible. He does not want to be fooled. He does not want to be duped, even in a "good" cause. He wants to know the facts and among these is included the fact of the utilization of his emotions.   18

Keeping in mind the seven common propaganda devices, turn to today's newspapers and almost immediately you can spot examples of them all. At election time or during any   19 campaign, "plain folks" and "band wagon" are common. "Card-stacking" is hardest to detect because it is adroitly executed or because we lack the information necessary to nail the lie. A little practice with the daily newspapers in detecting these propaganda devices soon enables us to detect them elsewhere—in radio, newsreel, books, magazines, and in expressions of labor unions, business groups, churches, schools, political parties.

Questions for Inquiry

1. What is the claim of the article? Is it explicit or implied? What type of claim is it?
2. What is the goal of the article? How does this goal influence the style of the writing?
3. Why, according to the article, are propagandists "helpless" to influence us without our emotions (17)? What about their goal forces them to appeal to readers subversively rather than rationally?

Questions for Argument

1. The authors of the article state that an intelligent citizen "does not want to be fooled, . . . does not want to be duped, even in a 'good' cause" (18). Do you agree? Or do you see "intelligent" (relatively) citizens eager to be led along by advertising and political sloganeering? Do you think the U.S. population is or wants to be "intelligent" about propaganda?
2. Propaganda is used to "sway us to be 'for' or 'against' nations, races, religions, ideals, economic and political policies and practices, and so on through automobiles, cigarettes, radios, toothpastes, presidents, and wars" (2). Are there any areas of life on which propagandists should not "sell the public" or matters of belief and conscience that should be avoided as inappropriate? Or do you think it's fine for all issues and products to be fair game for propagandistic promotion?

Writing Assignments

Informal

1. When we are influenced by "good words," we "personify" someone or something as "a god-like idol," and when we are influenced by "bad words," we "personify" someone or something as a "devil" (9). Write a journal entry about a time when you "idolized" or "demonized" someone or something. To what extent were you affected by emotionally laden generalities?

Formal

2. **Collaboration.** "Turn to today's newspapers and almost immediately you can spot examples of . . . all [seven propaganda devices]," the Institute wrote in 1937. On your own or with a group, gather some news coverage of a recent political campaign, vociferous congressional debate over a bill's passage or a nominee's confirmation, or criticism of government policy by a labor union, business group, church, political party, private foundation, think tank, or special-interest group. Examine the statements issued by the opposing sides in the dispute to identify whether there was an attempt to sway public opinion using propaganda techniques. Then, alone or with your group, write an essay in which you argue that propaganda techniques are being used by one

or both sides of the campaign or dispute. Use specific examples of the various propaganda techniques to support your claim.

3. **Primary Research.** On your own or with a partner, investigate the use of propaganda techniques in advertising. You may wish to specialize in ads for a certain type of product, such as for automobiles or for beer, or in ads that appear at a certain time, such as during football games or soap operas, or in a certain medium, such as in a particular fashion magazine or on a music video or comedy channel. Search for patterns in the use of propaganda techniques and identify examples of the techniques that appear frequently. Then write a report in which you present your findings about the propaganda content of the advertising you studied. Use specific examples to support each point, and in a final section argue that the use of the propaganda techniques is or is not a subject of concern.

■ ■ ■

Words and the World

WILLIAM LUTZ

William Lutz, an attorney and professor of English at Rutgers University, has served as editor of the *Quarterly Journal of Doublespeak* since the 1970s and is the author of several books about language. This excerpt is from *The New Doublespeak*. (Copyright 1996 by HarperCollins Publishers. Reprinted by permission.)

Toward the end of the movie *The Wizard of Oz*, Dorothy watches as the Wizard gives the Scarecrow a college degree, which makes him smart, then gives the Cowardly Lion a medal for courage, which gives him courage, and finally gives the Tin Man a watch in the shape of a heart, which gives him the capability to experience emotions.   1

Of course, we know that's not the way things work. A medal is only a symbol of courage; it's not the quality itself, nor even an act of courage. A heart is only a symbol of emotion; it's not the emotion itself, nor is it the ability to experience the emotion. A college degree is only a symbol of learning, not the learning itself. And many people with college degrees are not very smart, or even very educated.   2

We must always remember that the symbol and what it stands for are not the same thing. The flag is not the country; the uniform is not the person; the crucifix, the Star of David, or the Crescent is not the religion; the actor is not the character portrayed; the medal is not the courage; the college degree is not the skill or knowledge.   3

The Word Is Not the Thing

Another way of saying that the symbol and what it stands for are not the same thing is *the word is not the thing*. The word "hamburger" is not the hamburger. Eating the paper on which the word "hamburger" is printed won't do much to alleviate your hunger. And you certainly won't get rich by writing the word "money" on pieces of paper. The word "sewage" doesn't smell, "boom" doesn't sound loud, and the word "mucus" isn't disgusting.   4

5   When we confuse words with the things they represent, we engage in a process called *reification*, which simply means that we treat something we have created verbally as if it had real substance. We make something out of nothing. When this happens, words become traps, as Werner Heisenberg observed, where "the concepts initially formed by abstraction from particular situations . . . acquire a life of their own."[1]

6   The verb "to be" is the principal way we engage in reification. Since this verb accounts for about one-third of all the verbs that occur in normal discourse, we have a tendency to engage constantly in reification. In fact, we do it so often that we rarely notice we're doing it, and notice even less what this process is doing to us and to our attempts to communicate with one another.

7   It's not unusual to run across something like the following comment:

> Don't call them "guerrillas" or "revolutionaries" or "freedom fighters." Those who use car bombs to kill innocent civilians in the name of freedom for the Palestinian people are "terrorists" and "murderers," and that's what we should call them.

8   What our commentator seems to be saying is that someone who kills another, whether intentionally or unintentionally, by exploding a car bomb might be called a "guerrilla" or a "freedom fighter," but the *real* name for such a person is murderer. Our commentator suggests that our discussions would be a lot clearer if we would just use the real names, the right words, for things instead of allowing false and inaccurate words to be pinned on things.

9   This, of course, is the error of believing that there is a "real" name for something, that the name is inherent in the thing itself. It's very much like the practice of some societies in which you keep your "real" name secret because anyone who knows your "real" name has power over you. (The fairy tale of Rumpelstiltskin is an illustration of this belief in the power of names.) While we dismiss such a belief as "primitive," we may well believe what our commentator above believes: that the "real" name for someone who kills civilians is "murderer." What that person *is* is one thing; what a person *is called* is quite another matter.

10   In 1992, the U.S. Department of Justice investigated serious environmental crimes at the Rocky Flats, Colorado, nuclear weapons plant. The grand jury investigating the crimes, and many other officials, believed the government should have pursued criminal charges against the officers of the Rockwell International Corporation, the company that operated the plant under contract with the federal government. But the government settled the charges against Rockwell for a record $18.5 million fine and no criminal prosecutions. Deputy Assistant Attorney General Barry Hartman, head of the Justice Department's Natural Resources Division, explained why no criminal charges were pressed:"Environmental crimes are not like organized crime or drugs. There you have bad people doing bad things. With environmental crimes, you have decent people doing bad things."[2]

11   Again, we have to remember that people are neither decent nor bad. People may do things that we label decent or bad, but it is the action and not the person who is bad. When we call someone a bad person, we really mean this is a person who does what we call bad things. That is, a person isn't bad or decent until we label him, and we base our label on the person's actions.

12   Mr. Hartman thinks that people have a "real" name, that there are bad people and decent people, and he can tell them apart. For Mr. Hartman, the people running the Rocky Flats plant are "good" people, and such people don't commit criminal acts. Therefore, anything they did couldn't be criminal because "good" people don't commit criminal acts.

1. [Werner] Heisenberg, *Physics and Philosophy,* p. 262. [New York: Harper, 1958: 58]
2. *New York Times,* 1 November 1993, p. A18.

I would argue that the executives running the Rocky Flats plant are neither bad nor decent people, but they are people who, according to a grand jury, did bad things: They committed environmental crimes. But Mr. Hartman knows that some people are "decent," even if they commit crimes. I do not mean to make too strong a comparison, but it reminds me of the accounts of how the people running the concentration camps in Germany were such cultured people, listening to opera at night, reading Goethe, and playing with their children. Were they "decent" people too? For Mr. Hartman, bad people sell drugs; decent people commit environmental crimes. Which really has to make you wonder what other things "decent" people do.   13

Words and the World

There is a difference between the "world" and the words we use to talk about that world. On the one hand, there is the world, which consists of things, processes, and events. On the other hand, there are the names we create for these things, processes, and events. The two are quite separate and distinct and in no way connected, except as we choose to connect them. Yet we keep forgetting this basic fact about language and symbols, and because we keep forgetting, we get ourselves into all kinds of trouble and end up saying some pretty stupid things.   14

Naming things or pinning labels on them—that is, using symbols—is an act of the human mind, and a very creative act. But it is just that: a creative act that has nothing to do with the "real" name of anything. Any name we choose to use comes from *us*, not from the thing itself or from nature. We forget this principle at our peril.   15

Our commentator can call a person who sets off car bombs whatever he wants; that is his privilege. If he wants to call that person a "terrorist" and a "murderer" he certainly can. But that doesn't make those who set off the car bomb either "terrorists" or "murderers." What our commentator is really saying is that this is what he *thinks* such a person should be called. In his political framework and from his political point of view, these are the appropriate labels we should use.   16

So too with Mr. Hartman of the Justice Department. He can call the executives who committed environmental crimes whatever he wants. But unlike our commentator, whose words have no effect on the lives of the people he labels, when Mr. Hartman decides to use a label, we might say that some criminals escape prosecution.   17

Others may not agree with our commentator. I am sure that some people, including not a few high officials in a number of governments, would use such words as "freedom fighters," "soldiers," "heroes of the revolution," "defenders of the people," and any number of others. While it is true that the words you use to describe such people depends on your point of view, it is also true that people who set off car bombs don't have a "real" name any more than anyone else. Consider the following paragraph in place of the one previously cited: 18

> Don't call them "military personnel" or "our brave boys" or "air crews." Those who use laser-guided bombs to kill innocent civilians in the name of freedom for the American people are terrorists and murderers, and that's what we should call them.

You might object to my version because U.S. Air Force personnel who do their duty aren't murderers. To which I would point out that U.S. Air Force bomber crews aren't anything until someone pins a name on them. And the name that gets pinned on them will depend on the point of view of the name pinner. Whatever name is used will tell us more about the person who has chosen the name than about the thing being named. The use of "terrorist" and "murderer" tells us about the political viewpoint of our commentator and little about the people who set off the car bomb.   19

20   Finally, you might note the phrase "innocent civilians." What, you might ask, is a civilian, and what makes a civilian innocent? During World War II, the Korean War, the Vietnam War, and every war since then, "innocent civilians" have been killed, many quite deliberately, as in the massive bombing of cities in England, Germany, Japan, and many other countries. Were such bombing attacks acts of "terror" and "murder"? Or were they an unfortunate but unavoidable consequence of a strategic bombing campaign to reduce the enemy's ability to wage war? Or were they instances of "incontinent ordnance"?

The Three Umpires

21   The problems of confusing words and things is illustrated in the story of the three umpire who are describing what they do. The first umpire says, "There are balls, and there are strikes, and I call them as they are." The second umpire says, "There are balls, and there are strikes, and I call them as I see them." The third umpire says, "There are balls, and there are strikes, but they're nothing until I call them."

22   The first umpire confuses the word and the thing by assuming that "balls" and "strikes" exist and his job is to identify which is which. This umpire assumes that the label he uses identifies the reality. The second umpire realizes that the word is not the thing and that whatever word he uses is simply his perception of reality. However, the third umpire illustrates the social power of treating words as things. Those who put labels on things exercise great power, for the consequences of labels are significant and far-reaching. After all, are those who planted the car bomb "terrorists" and "murderers" or "guerrillas" and "freedom fighters"?

23   Naming things is a human act, it is not an act of nature. We are the ones who through language create things out of the phenomena around us. Yet we forget that we control this process and let the process control us. We act as if the very things we have created are beyond our control. Indeed, we act as if there's nothing we can do about it. The world we create with words is not the same as the world in which we live. We confuse the two at our peril.

24   The Cowardly Lion has no more courage after receiving his medal than before, the Tin Man is as emotionless after receiving his heart as before, and the Scarecrow is as ignorant after receiving his college degree as he was before the degree was conferred by the Wizard. The word is not the thing. The menu is not the meal.

Notes

1. [Werner] Heisenberg, *Physics and Philosophy*, p. 262. [New York: Harper, 1958.]
2. *New York Times*, 1 November 1993, p. A18.

Questions for Inquiry

1. What is Lutz's claim? Is it explicit or implied? What type of claim is it?
2. What techniques of point of view and style does Lutz use to make his discussion of abstract semantics accessible to general readers?
3. According to Lutz, what impact does the verb *to be* have on our habits of applying labels to things and people (6)?

Questions for Argument

1. In paragraph 20, Lutz asks a string of questions about wartime bombings of civilians. How would you label such acts? From what point of view would such acts be called "unfortunate" consequences of a campaign to limit an opponent's offensive ability or

"incontinent ordinance"? Do you agree that any label put on such bombings—even the label "tragedy"—represents a point of view and not a "truth"?

Writing Assignments

Informal

1. Re-read Lutz's anecdote of the three umpires (21–22), and then brainstorm with a group to list other situations in which items, actions, or people are categorized or evaluated. Invent three statements paralleling the mottos of the three umps. For example, three movie raters might utter variations on "There's G, there's PG, there's R, and there's NC-17, and I label them as they are." Or three CD-shop owners might give variations of "There's rock, and there's country, and there's country rock, and I display them as they are." See how many variations your group can devise, and then compare them to those of the other groups in your class.

Formal

2. **Argumentation.** In paragraph 12, Lutz describes Mr. Hartman somewhat mockingly: Hartman knows "there are bad people and decent people, and he can tell them apart." Lutz would say, rather, that there are bad and decent acts, and the same people commit both. Do some research about a person who has been in the news recently for committing a "bad" or "decent" (or some other labeled) act. Then write a paper in which you argue that there is more to this person than the label(s) being applied. Use information from your research into the person's life and achievements to back your argument and tie your essay into the problems resulting from the labeling of people and actions.

3. **Collaboration.** Lutz writes that "the name that gets pinned on [anyone] will depend on the point of view of the name pinner" (19). For instance, a person labeled a complainer by the boss may think of herself as assertive. The self-labeled "aggressive driver" may be labeled "a dangerous fool" by a highway patrol officer. Brainstorm with others to identify sets of labels that could be applied to the same person or the same action, depending on one's point of view. Then individually or as a group generate an essay in which you explain the "name pinner" maxim above and support it with specific examples.

■ ■ ■

The Bargain Basement in the Marketplace of Ideas

EVELINA GIOBBE

Evelina Giobbe directs a nonprofit organization of ex-prostitutes who have escaped prostitution; she lectures widely on pornography and the sex industry. This excerpt is from *The Price We Pay: The Case against Racist Speech, Hate Propaganda, and Pornography,* edited by L. J. Lederer and R. Delgado. (Copyright 1994 by Evelina Giobbe. Reprinted by permission of Hill and Wang, a division of Farrar, Straus & Giroux, Inc.)

1   In intellectual discourse, the "marketplace of ideas" is a figure of speech that we use to frame discussions about where, how, and with whom we have discussions. It is a metaphorical place and time where the democratic exchange of ideas occurs. But for many women, women like myself in particular, the marketplace of ideas is a very concrete space where we are walled into a compound built on the illusion of a slippery slope; where brick upon brick is mortared together with the specious rhetoric of free expression and the door is bolted shut with the First Amendment.

2   In the bargain basement of the marketplace of ideas, men's fantasies are projected onto the blank screens of women's lives.

3   In the bargain basement of the marketplace of ideas, women's experiences are captured in camcorders, frozen on reels of thirty-five-millimeter film, trapped in the tangle of yards and yards and yards of video tape.

4   In the bargain basement of the marketplace of ideas, human beings are transformed into pictures and words, sealed in the plastic shrink wrap of the Constitution, and carried away in unmarked graves of plain brown paper wrappings.

5   I live in the bargain basement of the marketplace of ideas. A red tag special, tossed on the sale rack, picked up and picked over by countless sweaty palms, the pages of my life thumbed through by anonymous hands and sticky fingers. I am a woman whose youth is frozen in time, frame by frame, in the technological recycling bin of prostitution: I am a woman who has been used in pornography.

6   If you peruse the racks of this very real marketplace, you will find me sandwiched somewhere between my sisters in the video section, among such titles as *Abused Runaway*, *Teen Street Slut*, and *Call Girl*. You can buy us; rent us; or, if you don't want to take us home, you can stroll over to the peep show booth, drop a quarter in the coin box, and watch us caught in an endless pornographic loop of sexual humiliation and abuse. With a pocketful of change you can see us bend, twist, turn, and spread our legs for your pleasure. Drop in another coin and watch us lie with any manner of man or beast, and if there is no living thing within reach, any common household object will do. Another coin and you can hear us beg for more. Reach in your pants for just one more quarter, quickly though, before the metal curtain snaps shut on the object of your desire, a tortured smile captured in a freeze frame, dead eyes staring out at you.

7   Or walk back to the magazine section and you can see me as a child, painted and dressed in a garish pornographic parody of a woman. Pick up a later edition, and you can see the woman I'd become, genitals shaved and exposed, hair in pigtails, a grotesque parody of the nymph child. One of a thousand pseudo-Lolitas whose market appeal declined before her twenty-first birthday.

8   [Because I was] raised in a brothel by pimps and johns, pornography is my family photo album. If you lay the pictures end to end you can track the destruction of a human being, the death of a woman, and her reconstruction and resurrection as a whore: desired, despised, discarded.

9   I've been out of the sex industry for about two decades. I've survived the prostitution; outlived a good many of the johns. But the pornography that was made of me still exists. Somewhere some pimp masquerading as a publisher is packing up a shipment of magazines, while some other pimp, somewhere else, masquerading as a film distributor, is filling a truck with pornographic video cassettes. Waiting for these deliveries on the other end is some sticky-fingered john, with a pocketful of quarters, waiting to buy yet another piece of my

youth, in the bargain basement of the marketplace of ideas. I want them to stop. I want us to stop them.

Questions for Inquiry

1. What is Giobbe's claim? Is it explicit or implied? What type of claim is it?
2. Examine the opening paragraph of the essay, from its beginning with the open-air metaphor of the "marketplace of ideas" to the imagery in its last sentence. What scene does this imagery call up? How is it related to the image of the marketplace?
3. Identify places in the essay where Giobbe makes use of repetition. What is the effect of this style on the reader? How does it affect your receptivity to her ideas?

Questions for Argument

1. The author includes an important U.S. civic value in the negative prison imagery of the first paragraph: walling bricks are mortared with "the specious rhetoric of free expression" and "the door is bolted shut with the First Amendment." What is the purpose of these images? After reading her essay, do you agree that free expression and the First Amendment are the culprits in creating the prison of pornography? Or is the problem located in some other aspect of our society?
2. Giobbe's essay is marked by extreme frankness about her life and about the contents and use of pornography. Do you agree that she had to write in such an exposing way to make her point with maximum effectiveness? Or do you think that she has violated her own privacy in writing about this social problem in such a personal way?

Writing Assignments

Informal

1. In your journal, write your reactions to Giobbe's life as she depicts it in her essay.

Formal

2. Publishers of pornographic magazines are, Giobbe indicates, really "pimps" masquerading as businesspeople; the same is true for film distributors: they are "pimps" in disguise (9). Look up the meaning of the word *pimp*, and then brainstorm to generate material for an essay in which you agree or disagree that this metaphor is an accurate one to use for those who distribute or sell pornography.
3. **Research Opportunity.** As Giobbe implies in paragraph 1, pornography is often defended as a matter of free speech, but her essay depicts it as a "marketplace," a "bargain basement," a business operated by "pimps." Use the library and the Internet to research the business side of pornography. For example, how many and what types of people profit from the sale or rental of pornography? How much profit does this industry make each year? Then, on the basis of your research, decide whether the pornography issue is one of free speech or free trade, and write an essay in which you argue for your conclusion about the legitimacy of the pornography business.

■ ■ ■

Fry Death Row Creeps in Electric Bleachers!

ED ANGER

Ed Anger writes a regular column for the *Weekly World News*, a tabloid newspaper. This excerpt is from *Let's Pave the Stupid Rainforests*. (Copyright 1996 by Weekly World News. Used by permission of Broadway Books, a division of Bantam Doubleday Dell Publishing Group.)

1   I'm madder than a tomcat with his tail in a light socket over this latest bleeding-heart campaign to outlaw capital punishment.

2   If our Founding Fathers didn't believe we should fry killers and rapists like pieces of bacon, they wouldn't have mentioned the electric chair in the Declaration of Independence, for crying out loud!

3   But if the whining, sniveling liberals want to stop these weekly executions of human cockroaches, then I've got a wonderful solution.

4   Let's kill 'em all once a year in electric bleachers!

5   You heard me right, folks. We could hot-wire portable bleachers like you see at Little League baseball games and zap up to 500 sex fiends, murderers, and crooked congressmen at the same time. Just file 'em into these cheap seats at gunpoint, tell 'em to have a seat, and hit the juice.

6   The thing would light up like a backyard bug zapper, by gum. It'll sound like about 10,000 hamburger patties sizzling on the grill!

7   And let's face it. The prissy, squealing liberals would only have to scream about capital punishment once a year instead of every damn day!

8   Legend has it that our late, great President Abe Lincoln ordered the first double electrocution in a crudely wired porch swing.

9

**Ed Anger
Electric Bleacher
Poll**

10   ❏ **YES:** I agree with Ed Anger that we should fry 500 killers and rapists at a time in electrified bleachers. It would save taxpayers money and clean out our prisons fast.

11   ❏ **NO:** Electric bleachers would be cruel. These poor criminals deserve a second chance and should be let go to enjoy life.

Check one box and send to:
ELECTRIC BLEACHER POLL
c/o Weekly World News
600 S. East Coast Avenue, Lantana, Fla. 33462

The device was effective if not efficient—it took nearly six hours on high before the two men accused of raping a young schoolmarm finally died.

"The meat just fell off the bones when they were pulled out of the electric swing," said one eyewitness in a diary discovered some 20 years after the execution in 1883.

Our best Death Row statistics say there are over 800 of these human scum currently awaiting their one-way trip to Hell—if you get my drift. And their room and board is costing hardworking American taxpayers nearly 34.7 million dollars a year! So my electric bleachers idea is sounding better all the time—right, folks?

Questions for Inquiry

1. This article is satire and operates on two levels: the obvious, surface level and a subterranean level of mockery. What is the claim of the surface level of the article? Is it stated or implied? What ideas would you say Anger is mocking?
2. Consider the opening image of the essay. Why might Anger have chosen this particular metaphor to open the essay?
3. Examine the story of Abe Lincoln inventing the multiple execution (8–10). What purpose do these details ostensibly serve in the development of Anger's argument? What role do they play in the satiric level of the essay?

Questions for Argument

1. Anger bases his argument for the most effective capital punishment device on its advantages over individual executions. What are these advantages? Do you agree that the issue of capital punishment boils down to what method is "advantageous"? Do you think the writer agrees?
2. Obviously, the name "Ed Anger" is not the author's real name. Would you consider "Ed Anger" to be a pseudonym or is it a role the author is playing? Does this name tell you anything about the purposes of his satire? Do you think the author is "copping out" by not using his real name?

Writing Assignments

Informal

1. On a gut level, did you find yourself agreeing somewhat with Anger's ranting? In a journal entry, identify which of his comments hit home for you and then consider the frustrations or experiences of yours that might have made you receptive to these ideas.

Formal

2. Humor often risks or even courts offense. Do you find yourself offended by this essay? Write a paper in which you either critique or defend the use of disgusting imagery, coarse slang, name calling, and deliberate misinformation as techniques to create humor and characterize a type of person.
3. In this opinion piece, the voice advocating mass executions seems filled with both anger and glee. Obviously, the issues of crime and punishment affect us all emotionally. To what extent, in your view, should the quite valid emotions of anger and righteousness—or pity and hopefulness on the other side—determine our opinions about how to solve society's problems? What role should practicality, such as the cost or difficulty of a solution, have on policy? Write an essay in which you define the extent to which emotions, pragmatism, or some other standard should determine the decisions we make to resolve our country's problems. You may wish to choose a controversial issue, such as capital punishment, and use it as an example or focus for your analysis.

■ ■ ■

Liberty Calls Us to a Higher Purpose

DAVID WALSH

David Walsh is professor of politics at the Catholic University of America
and the author of *After Ideology*. This selection appeared on July 4, 1997,
in the *Philadelphia Inquirer*. (Reprinted by permission of the author.)

1   The Fourth of July seems like the simplest holiday of all. It celebrates American independence. It is the day when America became a nation by throwing off the constraints of British rule.

2   What could be more self-evident than the Declaration of Independence? Nothing, except that the purpose of independence was nowhere clearly defined. It is merely assumed as an unlimited good without further explanation as to why it is so. Above all it is the brevity of the Declaration's articulation of purpose as "life, liberty and the pursuit of happiness" that causes our problems. The very lack of definition seems to mock the celebration itself.

3   Could it be that there is no more to the Declaration than hollow rhetoric? That the much vaunted freedom we celebrate is no more than the maximization of opportunities for self-indulgence? Is America really defined by the parameters of the advertising, entertainment and leisure industries? Has the goal of all that heroic struggle been to serve no higher end than the easy pampered lifestyle we are daily exhorted to pursue? Has freedom really come down to the narcissistic self-absorption of the consumer society? Is this what all the blood and toil of centuries has brought forth?

4   Then we remember the most recent American casualties in the ongoing struggle for freedom. The 19 killed and the scores injured in the Saudi truck bomb explosion remind us of the seriousness of the issue. They are not posted to the desert as part of a summer camp adventure. Nor were they there merely to protect our access to cheap oil. They did not die to preserve our freedom to drive! Theirs was a sacrifice on behalf of freedom in the full sense of the word.

5   They embody for us today the meaning of the American revolution. That is, that it is only freedom in the service of what is noble and good that is worthy of the name.

6   The other freedom, for self-indulgence, self-absorption and escape, is merely a shadow of the real thing. Freedom, if it is to mean anything, must be anchored in a moral order beyond ourselves. It does not mean the freedom to choose our own values, however selfish, superficial and irresponsible they may be. In the most important sense, freedom is the means by which we give ourselves in service to others and become in the process better than we were. Freedom is the road to moral growth.

7   It is the absence of any sense of the purpose of freedom that deprives our celebration of anything worth celebrating. The Fourth has become a microcosm of our predicament as a society. In contrast to the celebration of public holidays in the past, we have now eliminated most of the more solemn components. Thinking that enjoyment would be enhanced by accentuating the lighter side, we have become incapable of finding any deeper sources of satisfaction in the whole event. As with so many other occasions, having fun becomes hard work. We find ourselves exhausted by a joyless pursuit of joy.

8   The irony is that we no longer have as much fun because we no longer have as much seriousness. Lightening up does not mean that life becomes one long party. It is that party-

ing becomes one long job from which we get no relief. This is why the endless levity of public celebrations is so oppressive. It is a strain to have to be so happy all the time. What, after all, can be more oppressive than to be forced to have a good time? Enjoyment, like freedom, turns out not to be something completely under our control. They both work best when they are allowed to follow an order beyond our command.

This is why the celebration of the Fourth must include more than the freedom from re-   9
straints. Liberty that is merely license is not liberty at all. It turns out to be merely the liberty to wear ourselves out in the pursuit of ever-less satisfaction. In its full sense, liberty is defined as the freedom to serve what is good independent of our personal likes and dislikes. Only a liberty that draws us toward our full human stature is worthy of the name.

Questions for Inquiry

1. What is Walsh's claim? Is it explicit or implied? What type of claim is it?
2. What meaning do you make out of the string of questions that make up the third paragraph? Why might Walsh have decided to make this point through questions instead of through a direct statement?
3. What evidence does Walsh offer for his view that Americans have the wrong idea of liberty and are wearing themselves out "in the pursuit of ever-less satisfaction" (9)? What is his means of convincing his audience?

Questions for Argument

1. Walsh seems to critique the Declaration of Independence because it did not define "independence" or "life, liberty and the pursuit of happiness." (The Declaration of Independence appears at the end of Chapter 9.) Do you agree that this document was too vague? Should it have spelled out what Americans should aspire to do with their freedoms?
2. What is the connection between "freedom" and "what is noble and good" (5–6)? Do you think the author proves that this definition of freedom is the only real definition and that other meanings are "a shadow of the real thing"?

Writing Assignments

Informal

1. Re-read Walsh's essay to locate what for you is its most inspiring—or its most insipid—idea. Then write a paper in which you expand on this idea to show either its validity or its emptiness. You may want to bring in personal experience or events and examples from our common civic discourse community. Or you may wish to use analysis or discussion to develop your response.

Formal

2. **Argumentation.** The author contrasts the freedom "for self-indulgence" with the freedom to "give ourselves in service to others" (6). Do you accept that there are two

opposite definitions of freedom? Or can you think of other ways freedom can be defined? Brainstorm with others to generate as many possible definitions and uses of freedom as possible. Then write an essay in which you defend one of these definitions as the best one.

3. **Dialogue.** Walsh asserts that Americans have become "exhausted by a joyless pursuit of joy" (7). Do you find evidence around you that your peers or those in other generations have worn themselves out in a futile search for joy? Work with one or two partners to dramatize a debate between Walsh and a "joyful, successful seeker of joy" or between Walsh and a citizen whose goal in life has been neither "self-indulgence" nor "service to others." Let the debate evolve until one side convincingly evokes concessions from the other.

■ ■ ■

Chapter 11

Evaluating Sources

The World of Ideas in the Civic Discourse Community

■ Consider the following passage and respond as indicated below:

> America has been enriched from the beginning by two great political traditions: conservatism and liberalism. It is the creative tension and competition between these two traditions that is the genius of American politics. The danger is not from either of these mainstream, competing traditions, but from intolerant, extremist ideologues.
>
> —George McGovern, "McGovern Retorts"

Writer's Journal

How well acquainted are you with these "two great political traditions"? Do you associate your own ideas with either conservativism or liberalism? Write about your political point of view and then consider what McGovern might mean by stating that the "creative tension and competition" between these perspectives is the "genius" of our system. Strive for an entry of at least 150 words.

The world of media sources is natural to us, a part of the landscape of our modern lives. Few of us have even spent a week or weekend or even a day without media. We wake to music or news, drive to tapes or talk radio, scan newspapers, or view CNN before or during dinner . . . we may even watch our favorite sitcom or comedy show while doing our assigned reading. The natural environment of modern people is composed as much of the media as of nature.

Residing in this landscape, we cannot help but have ideas, attitudes, and mind-sets leach into our thoughts, nourishing us, perhaps, with information and exposure to worlds we would never otherwise experience—or, on the contrary, distracting us from the truly important, hypnotizing us, transforming our minds without our realizing it.

Whether you take the optimistic or pessimistic view of media's pervasiveness, it's crucial to understand the many sources in our civic discourse community that have input to our thought processes. In addition, as a student actively searching for information, you need to evaluate sources consciously and effectively in order to determine their reliability. Your decision about using a source should result from an informed evaluation. Because students still overwhelmingly use books, journals, and magazines for research, the discussion that follows concentrates on understanding and evaluating print media, particularly periodicals (whether accessed in a library or online). A second major resource for students is the Internet, particularly the World Wide Web, and so a discussion of evaluating web sites is included here. You need to be aware of two dimensions of sources in evaluating them: the **level** of audience they are intended for and the **positioning** of the source in regard to political, social, and cultural themes.

■   EVALUATING SOURCES FOR LEVEL

Classification of Sources

In general, books and periodicals can be classified according to the intended readership—that is, as **popular, exploitive, serious,** or **scholarly.** As in any classification system, these categories work in the main, but there are many exceptions that seem to fit more than one category or that fall midway between categories. This discussion focuses on periodicals, but books and electronic media can also be classified this way. For practice in evaluating the intended audience for a speech, read the selection by Leon Botstein at the end of this chapter.

Popular

The book and magazine sources that you are most likely familiar with are those that are directed at the widest audience, the mainstream general public. These popular sources are intended for the "populace," and many of their characteristics are explicable in light of this appeal.

Popular periodicals are designed to meet the public's need for information on a wide range of subjects but are also designed to please. They use inventive design, color, and photography and are instantly recognizable as a result. They contain numerous ads and are commercial in that they make their profit through the sale of advertising space rather than through the purchase price. The reading level of such popular magazines is quite easy, usually at a middle-school level in vocabulary and style. Because a wide readership is desired, the content of popular periodicals ranges over many topics without going into much depth on any. Some popular publications are *Time, Newsweek, Sports Illustrated, U.S. News and World Report,* and *Vanity Fair.* Most newspapers also fall into this category in terms of their readership, reading level, content, and commercialism.

The writers for popular periodicals are journalists trained in writing and research; many are generalists—that is, they are able to write about just about any topic—while some specialize in a particular field, perhaps national affairs, women's issues, or sports.

Information found in such publications varies in reliability; the major newsmagazines do have solid reputations for checking information and requiring rigor of on-site reporters. Only informal references to the sources of information are supplied. Some material in popular periodicals is generated by the editorial staff; such articles may be unsigned.

Popular books are called "trade" books—that is, books designed to be marketed by booksellers, those in the "book trade." Bestsellers, "how-to" and self-help books, and autobiographies penned by celebrities and others in public life are all examples of popular books.

Popular sources are frequently used by high school students doing research, and so most college students are familiar with such publications and how to locate and use them as sources. However, most college research requires students to go beyond the popular level.

Lightweight or Exploitive

Lightweight or exploitive publications are designed to appeal to the public's emotional side and only minimally to the reader's rationality. Lightweight publications such as *People* and *Us* appeal to people's curiosity about the famous and the infamous; *Glamour* and *Cosmopolitan* vie for readers by appealing to their vanity; *Good Housekeeping, Gourmet, Mechanics Illustrated,* and *Field and Stream* appeal to people's lighter interests and hobbies. Further down the scale are the publications that exploit people's superstitions and emotions: *National Enquirer, Penthouse,* and so on.

All such periodicals are heavy on visuals and light on text, which is written in the simplest style. There are multitudes of ads—in women's fashion magazines, ads consume more pages than do the actual articles, or "editorial copy." Material in exploitive periodicals is often generated in-house without benefit of research and is unsigned. At some publications, everything is written in-house: "readers' letters" are faked, for example. At other exploitive publications, writers are liberally supplied with cash with which to bribe informants.

Complicating this category are the publications that fit in some ways and not others. *Playboy* contains much material that is exploitive of the readers' sexual interests; this same magazine, however, has often published attention-getting interviews with important public figures, including President Jimmy Carter while he was in office, and other "redeeming" prose. Nevertheless, it is generally understood that most readers are not buying *Playboy* for intellectual stimulation.

Publications in this category are not acceptable for college research. Even when serious topics are discussed, the sources of the information are rarely indicated, and the use of paid informants and other nonstandard journalistic practices render suspect all material in such journals.

Serious

Serious periodicals are designed to appeal mainly to the reader's need for information and rational discussion of current issues and cultural pursuits. Such publications usually focus narrowly on a subject; while *Time, Newsweek,* and *U.S. News,* for example, attempt to cover the main news, including political, cultural, media, and sports news, serious journals, such as the *Nation, New Republic, Harper's,* and *Atlantic Monthly,* pick and choose among political and cultural events and issues to discuss.

The level of writing in serious publications is higher than in popular ones, perhaps high school level. Writers are journalists who specialize and who may have degrees in a field such as political science, biology, or literature; sources of information or ideas are supplied to the reader through informal references. Some newspapers, among them the *New York Times* (NYT), the *Wall Street Journal* (WSJ), and the *Washington Post,* provide serious journalism. Most other newspapers contain much that is popular or even exploitive in appealing to emotions—human-interest stories, recipes, comics, advice to the lovelorn, and so forth—as well. The NYT and WSJ are unique in refusing to provide comics; the WSJ also refuses to use photography in its editorial and reportorial material (though advertisements contain photos).

Some serious magazines look very much like commercial ones; the *New Yorker, Harper's,* and the *Atlantic* have lots of advertisements and glossy paper. The amount of text, however, greatly exceeds photography and design elements in these periodicals; feature pieces are often quite lengthy. Other serious periodicals, such as the *Nation* and the *New Republic,* use cheap paper stock, have small ads for intellectual products like books and magazines, and can be recognized as serious just by appearance. Serious publications can be good sources for college research, unless you are doing specialized research in a discipline.

Scholarly

Scholarly journals are designed for professors, researchers, and specialists in academic fields. These journals appeal purely to the reader's need to know current research and theory in an academic field, and most are instantly recognizable as scholarly: they usually use minimal visual appeal in their presentation and are often sized and bound like paperback books. While most people throw out their general-interest magazines after a few weeks, scholars keep their journals for future reference, and so the booklike appearance serves this need for a shelvable, durable resource.

Scholarly journals are produced in academic departments at universities and colleges or at academic-style research organizations. They are supported by their subscriptions and, occasionally, contributions from the host institution. Most scholarly journals focus fairly narrowly on a discipline or a subspeciality in a discipline. In addition, articles are narrowly focused and cover a topic in depth; scholarly articles may run twenty-five or even fifty pages. Authors are, with few exceptions, academics with Ph.D.'s in their fields, and the writing is complex, ruminative, and laden with the terminology of the academic discourse community it emanates from.

Scholarly journals contain few visuals, except in fields in which visuals are significant, such as art, theater, and some sciences, and there is usually no commercial advertising, only some ads for related journals and scholarly books. Few scholarly periodicals are available on newsstands, and, in the main, the general public is oblivious to their existence. Town, county, and high school libraries rarely receive scholarly journals, and so college and university libraries are the main resource for searching for information at this level. Scholarly material is a good source for college research papers, as long as you are immersed deeply enough in the discipline to be able to understand and interpret the sources appropriately.

Mixed

Sometimes periodicals possess qualities of more than one category. As mentioned above, some primarily exploitive publications occasionally carry material of serious interest. Likewise, some periodicals considered to be lightweight because of their focus on pop music or youth culture—*Rolling Stone* and *Spin* magazine are two examples—do often include serious, in-depth political journalism and social commentary. The *Village Voice* (which looks like a newspaper but which is generally considered to be a magazine with a national audience), with its frank, in-depth, and hip approach to sexual subjects, is considered exploitive by some, yet its reviews of the arts and its political reporting and commentary are sophisticated and serious. Sometimes publications shift between types; many would claim that the *New Yorker* has of late become less serious as its new editors aim for a wider readership.

Evaluating Periodicals for Level

When you are examining a periodical to determine its type, you should:

1. Notice its physical format. Is it glossy and commercial in appearance? Is it full of photos and creative layouts? Are there lots of ads? Or is it minimally designed, with inexpensive paper stock and few visuals? Is it magazine-sized or book-sized?
2. Determine the intended audience. What does the reading level seem to be? Are the articles short, mid-length, or very long? Do they take a broad or general approach to the topics, or are they narrowly focused or specialized?
3. Evaluate the writers in the periodical. Look for writer biographies. Are the writers staff members, syndicated or national figures, or freelancers? Are they general journalists, specialists in a type of reporting, or experts in the subject at issue?

Evaluating Books for Level

Books can be evaluated for audience appeal, educational and reading level, author's credentials, specialization of topic, and so forth, just like periodicals. College libraries do some sifting for you, and their collections emphasize serious and scholarly books, with a smattering of popular ones. Often you need to look closely at the title page and the contents of a book to determine level. These days, serious and scholarly books, as well as popular and lightweight ones, are published in paperback; sometimes there is a size difference. *Pocketbook* paperbacks are smaller (about 4 × 7 inches) and use cheaper paper; this format is used mostly for lightweight and popular books. *Quality* paperback format is larger (about 5 × 8 inches), uses thicker paper and a better binding, and is used for some popular books and for serious and scholarly paperbacks. Here are some guidelines for evaluating books:

Lightweight or exploitive books typically have covers with an enticing picture or drawing and are in pocketbook format. Authors' names sometimes sound made up ("Desiree Dundon" or something equally pompous, sexy, or mysterious). Little or no biographical information about authors is provided. The reading level is simple.

Popular books have appealing covers that sometimes include banner lines with flashy quotations from positive reviews. The size may be pocketbook or quality. The author is a generalist (has written on many subjects) or has some professional (not academic) experience in the book's subject. The reading level is easy; the topic may be fairly broad. There are no indexes, notes, reference lists, or lists of additional readings.

Serious books may have a neutral, decorative cover and quality formats. The writing style is more difficult than for popular books; the topic may be narrow. The author is a specialist in the subject and possibly has academic credentials. There will be an index, and possibly notes or a reference list. The publisher can be a nationally known one, a small publisher specializing in a field, or, sometimes, a scholarly or university press.

Scholarly books have minimally decorated covers, possibly with only type. They usually have a quality format, sometimes with economy paper. The author is an academic researching in the field; the topic is specialized, and ease of reading will depend on knowledge of the field. An index, notes, a reference list, appendices, and other scholarly apparatus will be present. The publisher will often be a university press or a scholarly publisher focusing on books in one discipline, and rarely a trade publishing house.

Mixed books span these categories. In particular, serious or even scholarly books that appeal to a widespread educated public may be marketed heavily and take on some of the trappings of popular books: colorful covers, reviewer blurbs across the front, and so on. The content of the book is the ultimate criterion, even if heavy marketing has presented the book as exciting, significant, or timely. *A Brief History of Time* by Stephen Hawking, *You Just Don't Understand* by Deborah Tannen, and *The Language Instinct* by Stephen Pincker are all serious-to-scholarly books that have been mass-marketed.

Evaluating Nonprint Media for Level

Television and even radio journalism have formats that parallel those of print media and can be evaluated the same way. There are many serious, popular, and lightweight topical and news shows, as well as real-time or tape-delayed coverage of current and political events and speeches. You can differentiate them by examining such factors as the following:

- appeal to emotions, intelligence, or both
- intended audience and educational level
- length of story segments (longer and in-depth indicates more serious)
- types of experts used (average people, workers, government or corporate spokespeople, academic experts)

Serious news coverage appears in magazine shows such as *20/20* and *60 Minutes;* discussion and interview shows such as *Meet the Press* and *Washington Week in Review;* in-depth news shows such as those on public television (*The News Hour with Jim*

Lehrer) and the National Public Radio news such as *All Things Considered*. Popular coverage of news issues occurs on network and local news shows and specials; lightweight or exploitive coverage can be seen in "tabloid" shows such as *Hard Copy*.

Those channels supported by advertising, especially the broadcast networks, have proven to be susceptible to market forces. In particular, the competition for viewers has sometimes led to sensationalizing, distortion, and contrived video footage. Satirist Al Franken comments, "I think the Information Superhighway should more accurately be called the Infotainment Superhighway. And . . . all of us who work in the media should be called 'infotainers.' Dan Rather is an infotainer. Maybe more info than tainer. Connie Chung is about half info, half tainer. Her husband more tainer than info. Rush Limbaugh is a disinfotainer" (206). And Franken concedes a fear that more of us viewers "are driving more on the tainment lanes than the info lanes" (207).

■ *Activity 1*
Evaluating Periodicals for Level, p. 447

■ *Activity 2*
Evaluating Electronic Media for Level, p. 447

■ EVALUATING SOURCES FOR POSITIONING

Beyond establishing the level of a source, you need to evaluate it to determine whether it has a political or other special affiliation and whether this affiliation affects its treatment of its contents. Views about social policy—what should be done to solve society's ills, how people should live their lives, international political and economic decisions made by our government, and many others—can be based on evidence and clear reasoning or on prejudice, partiality, and unproven beliefs. When researching a topic, it's a good idea to at least consider the possibility that a source's views may result from a preset belief as much as from an evaluation of evidence.

Among the mainstream media, much lip service is paid to objectivity, neutrality, and fairness. Melvin L. DeFleur and Everette E. Dennis, authors of a mass-media textbook, write that, "by world standards, American reporters had long been and still are very objective. For decades, they have tried hard to separate fact and opinion, keeping factual accounts in the news columns and opinions on the editorial page" (400). Although it's good to be aware that bias does occur, you should avoid the other extreme: seeing bias everywhere.

The Continuum of Left to Right

In our civic discourse community, political and societal opinions are discussed according to their place on a continuum, or line, from left to right. The relationship between types of ideas and physical locations derives from the French parliament of the late 1700s, where the parties in favor of the king sat to the right of the hall as viewed by the king, and the parties opposed to him sat on his left. To this day, the terms *left* and *right* hint at their origins in the eighteenth century. To oversimplify somewhat, we can say that on the "right" are conservatives, those who believe that the past ways and traditions are best, that change is likely to be bad, and that the power of authority figures should be limited (a change away from a valuation of centralized power). The Republican Party is considered moderate to conservative by most people. On the "left" are liberals and progressives, those who believe that change is necessary to improve

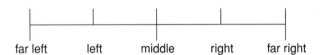

FIGURE 11.1   The Political Continuum

conditions, that progress is good, and that people, as embodied in organizations such as unions and the government, should act in their own behalf (a change away from the valuation of opposition to government power). The Democratic Party is considered moderate to liberal by most people. To the "far left" are leftists, socialists, and communists, and to the "far right," libertarians and fascists. These distinctions can be applied to numerous areas of opinion, not just the political arena. For example, there are liberal religions and conservative ones, and middle-of-the-road ones too. There are also liberal, middle-of-the-road, and conservative economists. The political spectrum is typically represented as a continuum, or range, because parties don't fall into strict categories of liberal or conservative, left or right (see Figure 11.1). For a humorous look at partisanship in our culture, read the selection by Al Franken at the end of this chapter.

Political literacy—an awareness of the ways power is distributed in our society and the ways it is discussed—goes hand in hand with media literacy: the awareness of the context and background of each individual media source. The media reflect the power structure of our culture, in addition to acting as major players in our civic discourse community. You may be aware of the allegiance of a source to a point of view because the writer is obvious about it. Or such allegiance may be obvious to you because you are politically and media literate—that is, you have a sophisticated and complex understanding of what the media are, how they operate, and how points of view are arrayed in our society. If writers are to use information responsibly, they need to understand the conditions under which that information is generated and made available in our shared discourse community.

The Situation of the Media in Society

The mass media are those forms of communication that are one-way and that move from one unified sender to a large number of receivers, the "masses." This type of communication dominates modern life. We seem to have more and more media options every day, such as TV monitors with integrated Internet browsers and direct satellite TV. But the mass media include print as well as the electronic and photographic sources: newspapers, magazines, books, television, radio, CDs, audio tapes, World Wide Web sites, films, and films on video are all mass media.

With these many forms of information and entertainment constantly in our lives, "we have moved from a condition of essential isolation into one of intense and almost unbroken mediation. A finely filamented electronic scrim has slipped between ourselves and the so-called 'outside world,' " writes media critic Sven Birkerts (5). It's hard to "see the role that . . . all electronic communications . . . has assumed in our lives because there is no independent ledge where we might secure our footing" (119). Understanding the situation of the media in our society is important when constructing knowledge from media sources. Many colleges offer entire courses on the mass media; although you may not want to devote three credit hours to a study of our media environment, becoming media literate is important to the functioning of both students and citizens today. Only the briefest sketch of the factors affecting today's media can be given here.

Economic Dimensions

Most mass media make their profits through the sale of advertising and not by purchases or payments from readers, viewers, and other users. Only film and the recording industry are mainly supported by consumers buying tickets or CDs. For commercial media, appealing to an intended audience is important, however, because advertising rates—what *Time* magazine or the producers of *Friends* can charge for an ad or a spot—are based on the number of readers or viewers who will see or hear the ad.

The most prominent mass media in our society are owned and produced by large trans-media corporations, not by individuals. These companies own media in many categories. For example, ABC/CapCities owns newspapers, magazines, book publishers, cable channels, video production companies, more than twenty radio stations, and eight television stations (Straubhaar and LaRose 225). The Paramount Corporation, the Hollywood film and television production company, is now owned by Viacom, which also controls several book publishers (including Allyn & Bacon, the publisher of this textbook), Blockbuster Video stores, and the *Star Trek* shows and movies.

These economic factors make the media vulnerable to influence by their corporate owners and advertisers. As Martin A. Lee and Norman Solomon write in their book *Unreliable Sources: A Guide to Detecting Bias in News Media,* journalism today occurs at "the intersection of Madison Avenue, Wall Street, and Pennsylvania Avenue, . . . a heavily-trafficked zone, where lies and facts cohabitate as convenience and opportunism dictate" (332). Although the journalistic tradition of objectivity is intended to counteract overt influence on the news, in many cases the interests of owners or sponsors have affected content. Numerous articles, for example, have documented the ways the media, especially the print media, have protected the tobacco industry from attack because cigarette advertising has been the lifeblood of many popular periodicals (Lee and Solomon 4–7; Bagdikian 168–173; Tye 257–260).

In addition, the economics of the media assures certain values will be assumed or even actively promoted. These include the ideas that the status quo in the United States today is good, that shopping and buying are valid preoccupations, that physical attractiveness is extremely important, that "fanship"—an interest in sports and a fascination with the lives of celebrities—is normal and a worthwhile use of one's time and energy, and so on. Users of media need to recognize that these sources convey values as well as "infotainment."

Philosophical Dimensions

The media, especially the information segment, have numerous philosophical forces acting on them. Foremost is the conflict between the concept of free speech, guaranteed in the First Amendment of the Constitution, and society's need to restrict content of the media environment. Restriction may be in the form of government regulation, especially of the electronic media, and court decisions about obscenity, violence, subversiveness, and child-inappropriate material. Or attempts at restriction may come from private organizations, religious groups, or other special interests in our society. Attempts to restrict or influence media content are a major area of audience interplay with the media.

The information media in general respond to these competing forces by walking a middle line. Sometimes this strategy has ironic results. Media critic John Leo reports that, in the controversy over 2 Live Crew's so-called obscene rap lyrics, only 11 newspapers out of 108 searched described the content of the lyrics. Most newspaper readers, including those of the *New York Times* and the *Washington Post*, couldn't decide the issue for themselves unless they listened to the album.

Journalistic Factors

By deciding what is news and what is not, the mass media affect what topics will come under public scrutiny. They act as gatekeepers controlling which problems, events, scandals, and so forth the public will hear about. They also function as an agenda-setting influence. If the media decide the national budget is too intricate or too boring to discuss on the nightly news, Americans won't be bothered by what it does and does not pay for. If a woman alleges sexual harassment by a high governmental official, and the media reports this charge more prominently than the outbreak of revolution in Mexico, Americans will be ignorant of a crisis affecting millions of people but well informed about a senator's womanizing.

When the news media attempt to cover all sides of an issue, in the interest of balance and fairness, the "official" view is often given the most play or the most prominent position. This is an unfortunate effect of the admirable journalist's code of objectivity. Whenever a story breaks, reporters call the appropriate spokespersons for their input, and thus end up privileging the views of government and business. They are also likely to turn to professional, lobbying, religious, and membership groups (like the American Medical Association and the American Association of Retired Persons) for input and omit the viewpoint of individuals or outsiders. Since the mid-1970s "outsider" organizations have formed specifically for the purpose of articulating the arguments of environmentalism, consumer interests, and many one-issue causes. Once alerted to the influence of all these types of organizations, people can be cautious about accepting wholesale such input into news coverage.

Journalists also get background from academic experts—professors and university-affiliated researchers, who base their input on their academic studies and who usually have credibility as informed and objective sources. But sometimes the media take comments from experts who are affiliated with research organizations, known as "think tanks," some of which hold strongly to particular political views or value systems. Few people are aware of the significant influence of these organizations on the media.

Early foundations devoted to research, such as the Russell Sage Foundation and the RAND Corporation, earned a reputation for objectivity and ethical management of data, which many people still associate with independent, nongovernment-sponsored research organizations. But today, many think tanks exist mainly to advance partisan perspectives on social, national, and international issues, all the while presenting themselves as neutral and mainstream. In *The Idea Brokers,* James Allen Smith charts the rise of think tanks since the mid-1970s and their powerful effect on public opinion and governmental policy.

These research outfits feed ideas and information to the media and offer their own vehicles—reports, press releases, and even videos—to ease the inclusion of their viewpoints in media stories. The Heritage Foundation, for example, is a conservative propaganda powerhouse that allocates 35 to 40 percent of its budget to public relations (Smith 201). Few citizens understand either the nature or the power of these research organizations because, as liberal gadfly Ben A. Franklin notes, "none [of these think tanks] are familiar newspage names" (1).

Over many decades, there has been debate over whether the personal beliefs of journalists deform the news. In particular, many critics have asserted that the media is overly liberal. But survey research has shown that most journalists are middle-of-the-road or conservative, with editors, who directly control what is published or broadcast, even more conservative than reporters. If anything, such accusations of liberalism have caused journalists to "bend over backwards not to seem at all critical of Republicans," notes media analyst Mark Crispin Miller. Adam Myerson, the editor of *Policy Review,* a journal emanating from the right-leaning Heritage Foundation, conceded in 1988 that "today, op ed pages are dominated by conservatives" (both qtd. in Lee and Solomon 143–145). It's a good idea, thus, to think about the possibility that media sources, especially those in the popular category, are not really neutral.

Understanding Opinion, Partisanship, and Bias

Reading for information and ideas means we read sources that offer opinions, judgments, and points of view. As long as a writer uses evidence responsibly, examines and fairly critiques opposing views, and avoids emotionalism or fallacious reasoning, you can accept the source as a good one to use. In other words, the presence of opinion is not the same as bias.

An **opinion** is the point of view maintained by an author. When it is defended with information and logical analysis, it is considered the assertion or proposition in an argument. It is usually considered appropriate for news coverage and informational articles to reach conclusions about the facts but not to include or argue opinions. Sometimes there is a fine line between interpretation and opinion however.

Partisanship occurs when a writer or publication is overtly associated with or represents a point of view. It can occur when a periodical's editor or, more likely, its publisher strongly espouses a political, religious, or other opinion. The view may then become the "official" perspective of the publication, or it may influence some or all of the contents. In addition, some periodicals are issued by organizations or agencies with a viewpoint or an interest in promoting a special perspective; such periodicals obviously promote that perspective throughout the text. Individual writers may also be partisan, either because of their personal viewpoints or because they are affiliated with or represent a special interest.

■ *Understanding the Print Media*

PAPER OF RECORD   A major newspaper that provides its own coverage (as opposed to relying on wire services) of all important political and governmental events in the region and also regularly publishes a list of legislative activity and the votes of all elected representatives. The *New York Times* is the national and New York region newspaper of record, and the *Washington Post* is the federal and District of Columbia paper of record. The *Boston Globe*, the *Philadelphia Inquirer*, and the *Los Angeles Times* perform this function for their cities and regions. College libraries carry the *New York Times*, the *Washington Post*, the newspaper of record for the particular region, and usually several others from around the country.

TABLOID   A newspaper that appeals to its readership by stressing entertainment and excitement rather than serious news. Numerous pictures, clever or shocking headlines, brief articles, and anonymous authors typify the tabloid. *Tabloid* also refers to the 11 × 15 paper size of such periodicals.

PUBLISHER   The owner of a periodical or book company; the publisher may or may not have a day-to-day say in content.

EDITOR   Controls content, assigns articles (called "stories"), and determines the placement of stories in a publication.

COPY EDITOR   Corrects grammar, rewrites awkward sentences, cuts articles, provides transitions, writes the headlines.

HEADLINES   Titles of articles in periodicals, they are generated by the copy desk, not by the writers.

IN-HOUSE OR STAFF-WRITTEN ARTICLES   Articles written by the publication's full-time employees.

FREELANCE ARTICLES   Articles written by outside writers who are paid by the word, by the "inch," or by the "story."

STRINGERS   Freelance reporters who regularly cover stories for a newspaper or magazine but who are not full-time employees; they may be identified as "correspondents" or have "special to [newspaper name]" beneath their byline.

WIRE SERVICES   News-supplying companies that send out stories by "wire" (electronic hookup) to papers that cannot afford to hire reporters on the scene. Used by small papers to cover national and international stories; such coverage is usually brief and shallow. Examples are the Associated Press and Reuters (British). Some newspaper chains supply national news to member papers.

NEWS COVERAGE   Articles reporting events, problems, political developments, and so forth that have recently happened, written quickly by reporters who go to the scene and do phone and computer research. These articles may be produced by a staff writer, a stringer, or a wire-service reporter.

FEATURE ARTICLE   An in-depth exploration of a topic, usually lengthy, representing days or weeks of research and writing by the author(s). Such an article may be on a news topic, entertainment, life-style, or other subject and may be written in-house or by a freelancer or may be syndicated.

EDITORIAL   An opinion piece written by the editorial staff of a newspaper, magazine, or broadcast news organization. An editorial represents the opinion of the publisher, the editor, or the editorial board. It is located on the designated editorial page and is usually unsigned.

OP-ED PIECE   An opinion piece written by any number of different kinds of writers: an appointed columnist on the periodical's staff, a syndicated columnist, a nonstaffer such as a freelance writer, government official, academic researcher, expert professional, or informed citizen. In newspapers, op-ed pieces are located on the page opposite the editorials.

LETTER TO THE EDITOR   Appearing next to the editorial column, these letters comment on the ideas or events described in particular news stories, features, editorials, or other items in the paper or on current events themselves. These are usually edited for length and printed with the letter writer's express permission. Some papers accept letters by e-mail.

COLUMNIST   A writer who comments regularly on a particular area of the news, such as international, national, economic, social, cultural. May be an in-house staffer or a syndicated writer. Columnists often become known for their special style or point of view. Columns on news topics usually appear on the editorial or op-ed page, but columnists on everything from managing your finances to personal health and fitness appear in the relevant sections of most newspapers.

SYNDICATED WRITER   A columnist based at one newspaper whose columns are distributed by a syndication company for publication in subscribing newspapers or periodicals. Opinion columns, editorial-page cartoons, comic strips, and articles on life-style, entertainment, and other topics are offered through syndication. Ellen Goodman, based at the *Boston Globe*, comments on political and national news of all types. William Safire is a *New York Times* writer whose political columns are widely read around the country.

ANALYSIS   An article that discusses a news issue in depth and offers background information, conclusions, and opinions. Such articles are usually researched and written by a journalist who specializes in the subject and are labeled clearly as analysis.

Magazines well known to have a conservative perspective include the *National Review,* formed expressly by William Buckley to present that viewpoint. The *Wall Street Journal* also sees things from a conservative or establishment perspective in its opinion pieces but is also considered a reliable and responsible source of information. *U.S. News and World Report* is a weekly newsmagazine with a conservative slant. (For an example of an article that appeared in a conservative magazine, see the reading selection by Virginia Postrel at the end of this chapter.)

Liberal publications include two newsmagazines, the *Nation* and the *Progressive,* as well as the *Village Voice.* The rock music magazines, such as *Rolling Stone* and *Spin,* are also liberal. (For an example of an article appearing in a liberal magazine, see the reading selection by Luis Rodriguez at the end of Chapter 6.)

In the mainstream media, *Time* is considered more conservative than *Newsweek,* but most consider both magazines mainstream and reliable. Conservatives consider the *New York Times* to be too liberal, and liberals believe the *New York Times* is in the pockets of the moneyed class, the conservatives. Probably, you will consider the *Times* to be mainstream.

Bias in a source refers to the presence of predetermined opinions that no evidence of any kind will modify. Biased writers ignore information or misrepresent opposing views in order to persuade the reader of their opinions. Often the attempt to spread their ideas is a no-holds-barred one, in which illogic, fallacies, slanted language, and so on play as much a role as solid argument, logic, and evidence. Some partisan writers and publications are biased; others strive to handle information responsibly and to refrain from extreme persuasive techniques.

Knowing whether a writer is a supporter of a particular cause or a member of an advocacy group or is publishing in a journal with a known viewpoint is a first step in judging the reliability of your source.

Bias in Argument

In a certain sense, bias is a flaw in the process of building an argument because it reflects an unwillingness to consider all the evidence. Biased writers fail to search for answers with an open mind. They are willing to distort the facts about the subject under discussion. When a writer is addressing a sympathetic audience—that is, in a partisan publication—cheerleading and reinforcement of preset viewpoints may be a main goal. In overtly aligned media, you may see emotional appeals, highly connotative language, and an emphasis on examples, human-interest stories, and personal testimony.

Distortions such as these are not always easy to spot from the text itself. A researcher needs to dig out the best information by reading sources from different places on the political spectrum. Notice that I don't say, "Seek out 'neutral' sources" because there may not be any. What we call "neutral" is a bias toward the mainstream assumptions that are commonly held in our culture. These include the ideas that extremes are bad and moderation is good, that gradual change is better than revolution, that agreement and consensus are important goals and persuasion is an acceptable practice, that prosperity is good and accumulation is "natural," that capitalism is the best economic

■ *How to Evaluate for Partisanship*

Aside from finding an obvious statement of allegiance to a point of view, how can a reader or listener tell whether an alignment may be influencing a source? Here are some ways to check for partisanship:

Periodicals and Books

Checking for partisanship of a periodical in which an article appears is possible only if you have the entire publication; if you access an article through the Internet, you will obviously not be able to examine the context in which it appeared.

- Examine the frontmatter of a book, the table of contents, the staff box in a periodical, and publication information.

  Look for a statement of affiliation, such as "published by the Society for the Protection of Aardvarks" (not all publications are affiliated however).

  Look for a statement of purpose in a periodical or admission of partisanship in a book preface or introduction.

  Examine the staff list of a periodical to see whether any editors or advisors are well-known partisans of a particular party or point of view.

  Examine titles of articles to see whether they show a tendency toward a point of view, such as criticism or advocacy.

- Skim the contents of a periodical.

  Look at visuals such as cartoons and illustrations for a consistent theme.

  Examine advertisements to see whether any clearly partisan books, organizations, T-shirts are promoted.

Writers

- Read the writer's biography if supplied (located at the start or end of an article or in a contributors' list in the front or back of a periodical).

- Recognize the names of well-known representatives of points of view. For example:

  William Buckley, George Will, and William Safire are on the right.

  Barbara Ehrenreich, Nat Hentoff, Katha Politt, and Alexander Cockburn are on the left.

Electronic Media

Most mainstream electronic media—network or national cable stations— at least strive to be middle-of-the-road. They balance their commentators and

continued

◼ *How to Evaluate for Partisanship (continued)*

coverage by getting all sides or at least the "liberal" and "conservative" sides. Often, however, market considerations—appealing to an audience and not ruffling the feathers of important advertisers—rather than adhering to a preordained viewpoint dominate decision making about content and approach. You will need to evaluate each television or radio source on the basis of internal signs of bias (as discussed below). Sometimes local cable or public stations will present material generated by partisan organizations or will include shows that represent the point of view of the owner. Some channels and radio stations in some markets are owned by partisan organizations, such as religious groups. You need to listen or watch long enough to get a sense of whether the station has a political or propagandist agenda or is strongly influenced by its commercial ties.

World Wide Web Sites

- Find out who or what organization is responsible for producing the site by tracing links to find the home page of the site. Look for statements of purpose, affiliation, and so on.

- If you are in doubt about the objectivity of a web site, use the e-mail address, if supplied, to question the source about its affiliations, its goals, point of view.

system. So even seemingly "neutral" publications may have hidden assumptions and a kind of "party line."

Those holding more extreme points of view, on both the right and the left, accuse the mainstream of being secretly biased toward established viewpoints, especially those of government officials, major religious and professional groups, and corporations. They accuse mainstream audiences of being oblivious and vulnerable to such bias. So, to some extent, bias is in the eye of the beholder.

For another discussion of media bias, see the selected reading by Janine Jackson at the end of this chapter.

What Bias Is Not

Be aware that having a special field of coverage or being narrowly focused doesn't, in itself, mean a publication is biased. The magazine *Art Forum,* for example, contains articles only about the fine arts (painting, drawing, sculpture, and so on). This focus, however, doesn't make the magazine editorially biased. It's just about art. Contemporary art is its field of content. Indeed, quite obviously, the publication is in favor of fine art, but this is hardly a bias. You'd have to be familiar with the "art scene" and the magazines that cover it to know whether *Art Forum* has a bias. And it does—*Art Forum* leans toward the experimental and the avant-garde in art. Conventional painters producing portraits or employing realism (like Andrew Wyeth, for example) are ignored or even derided by this publication. But notice that the "bias" is within the world of art; the bias is not simply its being a periodical about the art scene.

Many periodicals feature some items that are intentionally opinionated. Editorials, letters to the editor, essays on an op-ed or opinion page, articles labeled "analysis," and such are easily identified as vehicles of opinion. The presence of these features does not mean everything in the publication is biased. In an affiliated or overtly partisan publication, however, opinion pieces will be chosen to reflect the official point of view.

Ideology

At its most extreme, bias shades into ideology. Ideology refers to powerful beliefs that dominate the life of a person, group, or even nation. Literary critic Terry Eagleton (borrowing an image from British poet Thom Gunn) writes that "what persuades men and women to mistake each other from time to time for gods or vermin is ideology" (xiii). He continues, "One can understand well enough how human beings may struggle and murder for good material reasons—reasons connected, for instance, with their physical survival. It is much harder to grasp how they may come to do so in the name of something as apparently abstract as ideas. Yet ideas are what men and women live by, and will occasionally die for."

Eagleton connects ideology with oppression; ideology, he says, is what causes people to accept and sometimes even honor powers that deprive them of liberty and even a decent life. As he puts it, "The study of ideology is among other things an inquiry into the ways in which people may come to invest in their own unhappiness" (xiii). Communism and fascism are two of the famous ideologies of our century. Eagleton's point, however, is that any belief system can become ideological when it is held in the face of contradictory realities. Some might say, for example, that a wife who remains with an abusive husband because "divorce is wrong" or because she "loves him" is under the sway of a belief that oppresses her—that is, an ideology.

Internal Signs of Bias

If you have determined that a publication or writer is aligned to a particular viewpoint, you will be extra alert for signs of bias. But a careful reader is suspicious and looks carefully for evidence of bias even when the publication is considered mainstream. Most mainstream periodicals feel compelled, in the interests of fairness, to publish a wide range of viewpoints, and so a reader must rely on signs within an article to determine bias.

The first hint of bias in a source may come through the writer's tone. An emotional or heightened tone and highly connotative language may signal the presence of partiality, bias, and preconceptions. Often, biased writers do not care how they get you to agree, only that you do come around to the offered point of view. So slanted language often signals the bias of the writer.

Sometimes writers who have conscientiously weighed evidence and followed logic are also impassioned about their ideas, and their reasoned argument may still be spiced with colorful language and persuasive imagery. So an emotional tone and imagistic language should be noted as possibly indicating bias, but they are not a sure sign.

An even, objective, low-key, and formal tone may signal careful treatment of the evidence. It is possible, however, for a biased source to use the neutral and objective tone to disguise bias and to play to an audience that expects and respects objective evidence. Many partisan publications that wish to appeal to educated readers use an objective tone and evidential structure while still remaining committed to their cause.

In addition to stylistic clues, signs of bias include:

Failure to discuss opposing views. Biased writers may feel compelled to omit challenges to their perspectives, so a failure to engage in refutation can indicate a lack of objectivity.

Extremely negative treatment of the opposition. The etiquette of argumentation in our culture is to treat opposing ideas with respect even while criticizing them or showing their weaknesses. Mockery, dismissal, and cruelty are signs of a closed mind.

Omission of evidence. Ignoring nonsupportive evidence is a common way of insulating an idea against contradiction. It's difficult for a general reader to know whether something has been left out of an argument. Only reading widely on the topic can give you the background to recognize when some research is being ignored.

Failure to screen out logical fallacies. Biased writers may be so carried away by their commitment to their cause that they fail to examine their own arguments carefully. Or they may not care if their logic is flawed as long as it seems persuasive. (See Chapter 9 for examples of logical fallacies.)

Subtle Forms of Influence or Slanting

■ *Activity 3*

Evaluating Sources for Partisanship and Bias, p. 447

Many media experts caution that mainstream publications known for objective reportage and neutral analysis are still subject to subtle (and sometimes not-so-subtle) influencing. Here are some indications of such slanting:

■ *Activity 4*

Evaluating Newspapers for Bias, p. 447

- use of unnamed sources, usually governmental, or spokespersons from corporations or organizations providing the "official" interpretation of events
- use of quotes or commentary from academic "experts" who are allied with partisan foundations and organizations
- "news" footage supplied by government agencies or corporations

Guidelines for Evaluating World Wide Web Sites

Determine Who Sponsors the Site

The site's sponsor may be obvious: printed in capital letters across the top of the page. If it's not, here are some ways to discover sponsorship. First, click on any links on the page that might lead to higher-level pages, "Home" or "Main" pages, within the site, for these might contain statements of affiliation, sponsorship, purpose, goals, and so on.

Second, inspect the site address (URL) for clues as to the sponsor. Some sites are located on commercial service providers and the URL is not meaningful. But other times, the web-site sponsor is indicated in the host name. For example, consider this URL:

http://www.education.unesco.org/unesco/educprog/lwf/doc/portfolio/opinion8.htm

The phrase *unesco.org* tells you right away that this site emanates from UNESCO (United Nations Educational, Scientific, and Cultural Organization), the U.N. agency that works for human rights and welfare. The term *education* before the host name indicates that the page is from the "education" server within the larger UNESCO site. On the basis of the URL, the site looks like a responsible one.

Third, clip the URL to go to higher pages of the site (if there are no links to Home). To the right of the organization-type tag (.com, .edu), the path will be indicated using slash marks and words or letters. Beginning at the rightmost end of the path, delete chunks and try to go to the site represented by the shortened URL. If there is no such site, cut off more of the path, and so on; in this way, you can work your way up to higher-level pages within the main site.

For example, Scott Heste, the student who wrote the sample research paper in Chapter 13, used a search engine to find "Public Broadcasting Worthy of Support," a page of text lacking any links. Scott then inspected the URL:

http://www.house.gov/boucher/docs/pubtv/htm

He could tell the site emanated from the federal government, from the House of Representatives server. He could identify that "pubtv" represented the page he was looking at. He decided to cut "docs/pubtv/htm" from the path and go to the resulting site: http://www.house.gov/boucher. It turned out that "boucher" was the name of House member Rick Boucher of Virginia. The paper on public television was a position statement that Representative Boucher had placed on the web. Scott decided this was a solid source.

Evaluate the Source Sponsor

- Recognize sites derived from well-known periodicals, institutions, educational organizations, and so forth. Most such sites are as credible (or not) as their parent organizations.
- Research the sponsor if you are unfamiliar with it. Read around in linked sites looking for clues as to the sponsor's agenda, mission, political position, and so forth.
- Use the e-mail address if one is provided to contact the source and inquire about its goals and viewpoints.

Use Internal Evidence to Evaluate the Site

- Examine the layout and graphic design of the site. Is it plain or text oriented? It may emanate from a serious organization—or an individual with few resources. Is it graphically elaborate or commercial-looking? This may indicate institutional or organizational sponsorship. Are there advertisements? This is a sure sign that the site is commercial, from a business, a magazine, or other profit-making organization.

- Determine the purpose of the site. Is it informative, factual? Does it offer help for a problem? Does it support or promote some cause or agenda? Is it a commercial site for a product or service? For example, the NetNoir site announces its mission clearly: the California corporation that sponsors it plans "to be the leading new media company promoting, developing, digitizing, archiving and distributing distinctive Afrocentric programming and commercial applications." The site Revolution announces that it is "a searchable collection of facts, arguments and statistics furthering the libertarian idea of individuals freely collaborating in society" and is the product of one person, named on the site, working privately.

- Look for references to writers, public officials, institutions, organizations, or print or other media that you recognize. Depending on the attitude expressed (endorsement, criticism) about this recognizable person or entity, you may be able to guess the site's political positioning and credibility. For example, the UNESCO site discussed above refers to recognizable entities. The text, "Opinion Article 8: Creating a Learning Revolution," is attributed to Nicholas Negroponte, Mitchel Resnick, and Justine Cassell, listed as affiliated with the MIT Media Lab. Recognizing MIT as a major university, a student would feel secure about using this article. Negroponte himself—the founder of the MIT media lab and *Wired Magazine*—is quite famous as an expert on the Internet, and, knowing his name, a student would also view the site as a solid source. Another site, titled "Nobadaddy versus the Salamander" and containing a page of text and no links, also gives clues about its point of view. The lead quotation, attacking Republican Newt Gingrich, gives a reader a distinct impression of political bias.

- Examine the text for its reading level, internal signs of partisanship, and linguistic competence. A site with spelling errors, for example, is probably the work of one individual, who may be no more responsible about his or her evidence than about the details of language. A site with extreme language tips you off to its alignment with a point of view. In the "Nobadaddy" site mentioned earlier, one paragraph begins, "Monopoly has utterly undermined the very foundations of representative democracy." The ranting style, full of generalities, lacking any examples, suggests close-mindedness and weakens the appeal of the site as a source.

- Examine the text for signs of responsible scholarship. Does the site indicate where its information comes from? Are sources informally or formally documented? Evaluate the sources used—are they serious, by well-known or institutionally affiliated authors? Are they mainstream? esoteric? politically positioned?

Do sources represent a range of viewpoints? Has the author considered a variety of perspectives on the topic? Or is the viewpoint insular?

Helpful Web Sites

You might find helpful the following web sites about media literacy:

FAIR: Fairness & Accuracy in Reporting, Inc.:
   http://www.fair.org
"Media Literacy—What Is It and Why Teach It?" by Media Awareness Network:
   http://cii2.cochran.com/mnet/eng/med/bigpict/what.htm
National Telemedia Council main page:
   http://danenet.wicip.org/ntc/
"Various Resources for Media Criticism":
   http://www.cep.org/resources.html
"Thinking Critically about World Wide Web Resources":
   http://www.library.ucla.edu/libraries/college/instruct/critical/htm

Activities

1   Evaluating Periodicals for Level

Using the library or a bookstore (one well-stocked with periodicals and that allows lengthy browsing), identify one periodical (not discussed in this chapter) that fits each category: lightweight, popular, serious, scholarly. Be prepared to explain why the periodicals fit the categories in which you have placed them.

2   Evaluating Electronic Media for Level

With classmates, brainstorm a list of electronic media shows in current events and political affairs. Divide shows into groups, perhaps by day and time (Sunday morning, dinner time, prime time, and late night, for example) and have a committee of students investigate each group by watching the designated shows, taking notes, and then determining the audience level through discussion. Groups should present their findings to the class orally or in a handout.

3   Evaluating Sources for Partisanship and Bias

Working with the same periodicals as for Activity 1, examine the contents carefully to determine whether the periodical—or writers published in it—exhibits signs of partisanship or bias.

4   Evaluating Newspapers for Bias

Read several days' worth of coverage of one specific news event or incident in three daily newspapers, at least one a paper of record and one your regional or local newspaper. Then fill out the chart (Figure 11.2).

Topic or current event: _____

Names of newspapers   1. _____

2. _____

3. _____

Types of articles read:

_____ news reportage   _____ editorials   _____ op-ed   _____ analysis

Similarities in coverage:

_____

_____

_____

Differences in coverage:

1. _____

2. _____

3. _____

Indications of bias:

1. _____

2. _____

3. _____

Your estimation of the reliability of each source (with reasons):

1. _____

2. _____

3. _____

Value of each paper to a college student researching this topic?

1. _____

2. _____

3. _____

FIGURE 11.2   Newspaper Evaluation Chart

Assignments

1. Informal Writing   Read the following excerpt and then write a substantial journal entry or free writing based on it. Explain what the passage means to you and what questions about it occur to you.

> We hear of "brainwashing," of schemes whereby an "ideology" is imposed upon people. But should we stop at that? Should we not also see the situation the other way around? For was not the "brainwasher" also similarly motivated? Do we simply use words, or do they not use us also? An "ideology" is like a god coming down to earth, where it will inhabit a place pervaded by its presence. An "ideology" is like a spirit taking up its abode in a body: it makes that body hop around in certain ways; and that same body would have hopped around in different ways had a different ideology happened to inhabit it.

—Kenneth Burke, "Definition of Man," *Language as Symbolic Action*

2. Short Formal Writing: Comparing Periodicals' Treatment of a News Topic
In this assignment, you will compare the way three mainstream current-affairs magazines or newspapers approached a topic recently in the news. Work with the periodicals in one of the groups below. With your instructor's assistance, choose a problem, event, or controversy that has been in the news recently. Look up articles on this subject that appeared within the same time period in the journals in your group. Strive for articles of the same type—all news articles, analyses, opinion pieces, or editorials—so that you are not comparing "apples" and "oranges." Read each article carefully, prepare a two- to three-sentence summary, and then write a few sentences in which you describe the tone, attitude, or perspective that the periodical takes toward the subject. Finally, write a short essay of about 250 words in which you compare the treatment of the current-events topic in the three periodicals, and, if possible, come to a conclusion about the presence or lack of political bias in the periodicals.

Magazines

Nation, Newsweek, and *National Review*
Commonweal, Time, and *Commentary*
New Republic, Time, and *U.S. News and World Report*
Washington Monthly, Newsweek, and *In These Times*

Newspapers (choose three)

New York Times
Washington Post
Los Angeles Times
Boston Globe
Chicago Sun Times
Houston Chronicle
Philadelphia Inquirer
Wall Street Journal
USA Today
Christian Science Monitor
a regional or local newspaper

3. Short Formal Report: Evaluating One Periodical in Depth   Choose a periodical with which you are not familiar. (Your instructor may provide a list or may allow you to choose freely.) Examine a few current or recent issues of the periodical and take notes about its type, audience appeal, content focus, goals, level or type, editorial perspective, and any signs of partisanship or bias. Write a short report of about 250 words in which you summarize your findings about the periodical and express your conclusions as to its usefulness as a source for a college student. Attach at least three relevant pieces of the periodical to your report (cover, table of contents, editorials, ads).

4. Formal Report: Exploring a Journal in Your Academic Field   Write a report about a scholarly periodical in the field in which you plan to major or in a field you enjoy. You should examine several issues of the journal, reading or skimming some items in each of its sections. You should also discuss the journal with a faculty member in the appropriate field. Specifically, consider the following:

Origins: Identify the frequency of publication, the publishing institution or organization, subspeciality covered, stated purpose (if any), affiliation of editor(s). Is the journal juried or peer-reviewed? What is the audience for the journal?

Contents: What departments or sections appear regularly? What is the typical length of the main articles? Are the articles analytic, descriptive, theoretical, or data-based? Are there reports of primary research or experimentation?

Format: What style or manner of documenting secondary sources is used?

5. Informal Writing: Understanding Your Own Political Perspectives   In a series of in-depth free writings or journal entries, discuss your current political "bias" or slant. Use the following prompts to get you going.

Describe your main political point of view in terms of beliefs and how it applies to some current news issues. Indicate which political label you'd put on the beliefs you are detailing.

Explain where you came by your ideas about how the world ought to run: from your parents, friends, teachers, or other sources. Have you developed "oppositional" positions in relation to those you were raised with? Have you sought out what seems to you the truest position by examining information and using logical reasoning?

Examine to what extent your political and cultural beliefs interfere with your objectivity in reading about current events. Give examples of times when you were or were not able to remain neutral in the face of other opinions or significant news events.

■   **WORKS CITED**

Bagdikian, Ben. *The Media Monopoly.* 4th ed. Boston: Beacon, 1992. 168–173.

Birkerts, Sven. *Gutenberg Elegies.* New York: Ballantine, 1994.

DeFleur, Melvin L., and Everette E. Dennis. *Understanding Mass Communication: A Liberal Arts Perspective.* 5th ed. Boston: Houghton, 1994.

Eagleton, Terry. *Ideology.* New York: Verso, 1991.

Franken, Al. *Rush Limbaugh Is a Big Fat Idiot and Other Observations.* New York: Island, 1996.

Franklin, Ben A. "Washington's Conservative Think Tanks Influence Government Policy." *Washington Spectator* 15 Apr. 1996:1.

Lee, Martin A., and Norman Solomon. *Unreliable Sources: A Guide to Detecting Bias in News Media.* New York: Stuart, 1991.

Leo, John. "Our Squeamish Press." *U.S. News and World Report* 22 June 1992: 102.

Smith, James Allen. *The Idea Brokers: Think Tanks and the Rise of the New Policy Elite.* New York: Free Press, 1991.

Straubhaar, Joseph, and Robert LaRose. *Communications Media in the Information Society.* Belmont: Wadsworth, 1996.

Tye, Joe. "Buying Silence: Self-Censorship of Smoking and Health in National Newsweeklies." In *Mass Media Issues,* 5th ed. Ed. Denis Mercier. Dubuque, Kendall, 1996. 257–260.

 *Readings*

Loaded Language and Secondary Sources: Economic News Speaks Loudly between the Lines

JANINE JACKSON

Janine Jackson wrote this piece for the July–August 1997 edition of *EXTRA!,* the magazine produced by Fairness and Accuracy in Reporting, Inc. (FAIR). (Copyright 1997 by FAIR. Reprinted by permission.)

1   When the *New York Times* begins a news report on global trade pacts with the assertion, "Free trade means growth. Free trade means growth. Free trade means growth" (12/15/93), it's easy enough to spot the bias. But even economic reporting that doesn't so obviously promote a particular perspective often contains linguistic "cues"—terms and images that, while they seem only to present information, also tell readers what to think about it.

2   Take the May 2 *New York Times* front-page article on the federal budget: A box accompanying the story summarized the status of budget negotiations between the White House and the congressional leadership: "Domestic programs," the paper said, will face "$68 billion in program cuts," while Medicare will have "$115 billion in savings." Medicaid will see "$24 billion in savings," but the military "$85 billion in cuts."

3   What's the difference, exactly, between "savings" and "cuts"? In each case, the *Times* is describing reductions from the level of growth necessary to keep programs at the same level of services. But both President Clinton and Republican leaders prefer not to speak of "cuts" to Medicare or Medicaid, in view of these programs' popularity. Rather than find neutral terms, the *Times,* like many other outlets, simply mimics politicians' spin.

Corporatespeak

4   Similarly, the *Times* adopted corporatespeak in a report (3/28/97) on the practices of for-profit hospital giant Columbia/HCA. The company, the *Times* reports, is under investigation for "a practice known as upcoding, in which hospitals receive larger payments from Medicare by inflating the seriousness of illnesses they treat." Of course, such a practice is

more commonly known as "fraud," a fact that the industry's euphemistic terminology is designed to obscure. Even though the story contained much damning information, the paper's softball language—a chart caption reads, "Columbia bills Medicare aggressively," a subheadline refers to "a propensity for higher fees"—tends to let the company off the hook.

5   To advocates for workers and the poor, being quoted in the mainstream media is an all-too-rare opportunity. But even then a number of factors—how the sources are introduced, the placement of their comments within the story—affect the way their perspective is received and understood.

6   Sometimes labor's point of view gets in, only to be trumped by the reporter's "objective" voice, as in a *Washington Post* report (3/7/97) on the possible privatization of welfare case management. The story does quote labor representatives who register public employee unions' alarm at the idea of profit-driven companies deciding who is or isn't eligible for assistance. Such concerns may have swayed Clinton to slow down privatization plans, but they sounded unconvincing in the *Post*, where they were counterposed with the reporter's claim that "states see privatization as a way to inject efficiency, up-to-the-minute technology and private sector performance into the backwaters of their welfare offices." That government offices are "backwaters" while corporations are models of "performance" is considered a given.

Secondary Sources

7   Even an apparently straightforward Associated Press item (5/3/97) on a dip in the unemployment rate couches tacit commentary. The factual lead—the country's jobless rate dropped below 5 percent in April—is immediately followed by the zealous interpretation of "economist Allen Sinai of Primark Decision Economics," who crows: "It's worker heaven. This myth that the American worker is an unhappy camper went away eight to ten months ago. There are plenty of jobs available."

8   Now, most economists would admit that unemployment rates are incomplete indicators; they don't include people who can find only part-time jobs, or those who have given up searching. And the numbers say nothing of the quality of the jobs available, whether they pay a living wage or even enough to lift a family out of poverty

9   But not until halfway through the AP piece is there any inkling of a more complex scenario: Varying jobless rates for blacks, Latinos, women and teenagers, it seems, suggest that "the 'worker heaven' hasn't been universal." (This acknowledgment illustrates the fact that economic events affect different people differently, a fundamental point so often absent from mainstream economic reporting.)

10   At the article's end is a quote from the Economic Policy Institute's Larry Mishel, who points out that, in an era of skyrocketing corporate profits, even those workers who aren't losing ground are "not getting their share of the growth, either." EPI is described as "a union-funded think tank."

11   Both Mishel and Sinai are economists, with opinions about the meaning of unemployment statistics. But by giving Sinai's perspective at the story's start, and placing Mishel's comment at the end, AP sends readers a message about which of the two is more legitimate. Sinai's idea, that the new data make the U.S. "worker heaven," comes off as the consensus view, while Mishel is cast as the dissenter, the nay-sayer. Coming at the end of the story, Mishel is only permitted to respond to the line already put forward, not to lay out an alternative view.

And then there's that qualifying tag "union-funded": It isn't exactly untrue (although   12
EPI receives only about a quarter of its funds from unions), but if it's relevant, why don't we
learn how Primark Decision Economics gets its funds?

By scrutinizing loaded language and the use of sources, it becomes clear that main-   13
stream economic reporting often constrains debate and marginalizes viewpoints—while appearing to present "just the facts."

Questions for Inquiry and Argument

1. What is Jackson's claim? Is it explicit or implied? What type of claim is it?
2. What are some examples of "linguistic cues" that indicate subtle bias in major newspapers?
3. How, according to Jackson, can "objectivity" of tone create bias?

Writing Assignments

Informal

1. Jackson comments that the *New York Times* "mimics politicians' spin" or angle on economic news instead of rewording the idea neutrally (3). Does it surprise you that a
   major newspaper would slant news toward the government view? Do you think there's
   a plot? Or does the "mimicking" result from carelessness? Or something in between?
   Write an informal paper expressing your impressions of why the "news" comes out the
   way it does.
2. Is there such a thing as "objectivity," to your mind? The examples of slanting that Jackson provides are not only subtle but require some depth of knowledge about economics and current affairs to decipher. Is it possible that what seems like "objectivity" is
   usually slanted? Write a journal entry about whether there is "objectivity" in the news.

■ ■ ■

Affirmative Action:
The Case for the Mushball Middle

AL FRANKEN

Al Franken has worked as a comedian, notably on *Saturday Night Live,*
and has written several books, including *Rush Limbaugh Is a Big Fat Idiot
and Other Observations* (1996), from which this article is taken. (Copyright 1996 by Al Franken, Inc. Used by permission of Delacorte Press, a
division of Bantam Doubleday Dell Publishing Group, Inc.)

Jonathan Alter of *Newsweek* recently made the compelling argument that debate on af-   1
firmative action has become so polarized that there is no room for those of us in "the mushy
middle."

That's right. I said "us." I consider myself a moderate.   2

3   See. I hope it's clear to you by now that this book is a *satire* about the breakdown in the civility of public discourse. I'm making fun of meanness in public debate by being mean myself. It's called "irony." Perhaps you've heard of it?

4   And I know that I've been a little harsh about a few public figures. That's what I'm supposed to do as a satirist. But I want you to know that I admire everyone I'll be making fun of in the book. Except Pat Robertson. He's a lunatic.

5   And I really don't like Limbaugh. And Pat Buchanan, let's face it, is a racist. Ralph Reed, I have no use for. And Gingrich just plain scares me.

6   You know what I dislike most about these guys? They're always so certain. They're always 100 percent sure of what they're saying. Even if it's wrong. It must be a great feeling for a guy like Rush Limbaugh. To be able to sit there and say, "There are more Indians alive today than when Columbus landed," and really believe it.

7   This is why I like being a Democrat. When we see a complicated, seemingly intractable problem, we have the only really genuine, authentic human reaction you can have: we're confused.

8   Fortunately, I believe that "confused" is a majority position in this country.

9   I am not talking about stupid, uninformed confusion. I'm talking about intelligent, over-informed confusion. The kind you get from watching *MacNeil/Lehrer,* C-SPAN, and *Nightline,* listening to three experts from the Cato Institute, four from the Heritage Foundation, two each from the Urban Institute and the Progressive Policy Institute, then reading eleven different newspaper accounts that cite six different polls and four studies. And after all that, you *still* don't know what to think about grazing fees on federal lands.

10   Affirmative action is an issue that stirs more passion than grazing fees. And it has certainly been hotly debated. On the one hand, those in favor of it believe affirmative action is essential in overcoming the inherently racist nature of our society. I definitely agree with that.

11   On the other hand, those opposed say that for America to be truly color-blind we must eliminate group entitlements which set one race against another. That also makes sense.

12   There are horror stories on both sides. You've heard them; you're sick of them. So am I. And it gets even more confusing when the strongest opponents of affirmative action are among its biggest beneficiaries.

13   Justice Clarence Thomas, for instance, was admitted to Yale Law School under a 1971 affirmative action plan whose goal was 10 percent minority students in the entering class.

14   In remarks to his EEOC staff in 1983, Thomas said that affirmative action laws were the best thing that ever happened to him: "But for them, God only knows where I would be today. These laws and their proper application are all that stand between the first seventeen years of my life and the second seventeen years."

15   Something must have happened to Thomas in his third seventeen years, because the guy really did a 180. 1 don't know what it was. Maybe a high-tech lynching.

16   In his concurring opinion in the affirmative action case of *Adarand Constructors v. Pena:*

There can be no doubt that racial paternalism and its unintended consequences can be as poisonous and pernicious as any other form of discrimination.

17   A mean person could interpret the change of heart to reflect an "I've got mine" attitude. I'll leave that to a mean African American person.

18   One mean person who won't say it is Rush Limbaugh. In *The Way Things Ought to Be,* Limbaugh describes Thomas as "a man who has escaped the bonds of poverty by methods other than those prescribed by these civil rights organizations." Not true, but at this point,

who's counting? Anyway, Thomas returned the favor two years later, performing the ceremony at Limbaugh's third wedding. I can't think of anything more romantic for a blushing bride than having Clarence Thomas perform your nuptials.

Of course, the first President to apply affirmative action to the Supreme Court was   19
Ronald Reagan, who pledged to appoint a woman during the '80 campaign. When he nominated Sandra Day O'Connor, George Will was not happy:

> Reagan dug about as deep as any President ever has into the state judiciary for a nominee. But, then, his sexual criterion excluded about 95% of the law school graduates in the relevant age group.

Will seems to be applying a mathematical formula: that it was nineteen times more   20
likely that a man would be the most qualified nominee. Forgetting that the women admitted to law school at the time were probably twenty times more qualified than the men, Will doesn't seem to understand or accept the value of diversity. Now, I don't know if the fact that Sandra Day O'Connor has two ovaries inherently makes her better able to interpret the law as it affects women. Actually, I'm not sure she has two ovaries. I'll ask my research assistant, Geoff, to look it up. (Sometimes my writing gets ahead of the research.)

While we're waiting for Geoff, I'd like to speak to an affirmative action program which,   21
as a Harvard graduate, I do like. And that is affirmative action for the children of Ivy League grads. Here's how it works. All applicants to Harvard, say, have to meet certain minimum requirements: SAT scores, G.P.A., and (a new one) lack of murder convictions.*

The applicants who meet those requirements are thrown into a pool from which the   22
next year's freshman class is chosen. At this point, they start looking at special abilities. Does the orchestra need an oboe? Does the Sanskrit department need a kid who is actually willing to study Sanskrit? Is there a point guard with 1200 on his SAT's who's not good enough to be recruited by Duke or Georgetown?

And: Is the kid a legacy? That is, the child of an alumnus? If so, the kid is in. There are   23
all kinds of good reasons for this. Well, one really. Fund-raising. But as it stands, it's an affirmative action program for one of the most privileged groups in the country: the sons and daughters of people like me.

Now we're told that one of the "poisonous and pernicious" "unintended conse-   24
quences" of affirmative action is that it taints the real accomplishments of qualified blacks who have earned their place at the table. I'm sure that's true. But I think that's just further evidence of the racism in our culture. All the time I was at Harvard, I never heard a Lowell or a Cabot remark, "I dare say, I despise this godawful legacy policy. It makes me so suspect in the eyes of my classmates."

A small digression. This is an absolutely true story. The first guy I met at Harvard was   25
a legacy. I had flown in from Minneapolis, taken a taxi directly to Harvard Yard, and, lugging my duffel bag and electric Smith Corona, found my freshman dorm. In the entryway was a young man my age, but somehow older. Khakis, polo shirt, tortoiseshell glasses. He extended his hand in a friendly yet proper manner and said, "William Sutherland Strong. I'm from northern New Jersey, but my family moved from Massachusetts."

"When?" I asked.   26

"In the late eighteenth century."   27

---

*Last spring Harvard had to rescind its acceptance of Gina Grant after the college learned she had murdered her abusive mother. Though she had served her time in juvenile prison, Harvard felt that there were other equally deserving applicants on the waiting list who had murdered neither of their parents.

28   It took a beat to sink in. I said, "Al Franken. I'm from Minneapolis. But my family moved from Kraków in the early twentieth century."

29   I returned to Harvard in 1992 to speak to a standing-room-only crowd at the JFK School of Government. The week before, the speaker had been the editor of the only opposition newspaper in El Salvador, and only six people showed up. I think that was because he had never worked with John Belushi.

30   Except for the Eddie Murphy years, *Saturday Night Live* has always had a reputation as a white male bastion, and during the Q&A period I was taken to task for it. "Why doesn't the show hire more women and people of color?" At the time we had two very talented African American performers, Ellen Cleghorne and Tim Meadows, and I pointed out that another cast member, Rob Schneider, is half Filipino. Was that of any help?

31   No. And after I gave what I felt was a sufficiently exhaustive and responsive answer, the questioner pressed further. Finally, as a joke, I said, "Well, another reason, of course, is that minorities just aren't funny." Everyone, including the relentless questioner, laughed.

32   The next day *The Harvard Crimson* reported that "Mr. Franken said . . . 'minorities just aren't funny.'" No mention of the good-natured irony or the warm wave of laughter.

33   So, having had someone imply (wrongly) that I'm a racist, and having myself accused (rightly) Pat Buchanan of the same, I think I have some perspective on both sides of this prickly issue.

34   That's why I was happy when Bill Clinton, the hero of the Mushball Middle and our greatest post-war president, decided to study affirmative action. And when he came down firmly on the "mend it, don't end it" side, it helped me make up my mind. That's what leadership is all about.

35   Geoff just came back with the research. Both of Justice O'Connor's ovaries are intact.

36   By the way, Geoff is black.

37   No, he isn't. He's a white guy from Harvard. But wouldn't it have been a great ending to this if he was?

38   But he's gay!

39   No, he isn't.

Questions for Inquiry

1. What is Franken's claim? Is it explicit or implied? Is he serious about this claim? Or is it ironic?
2. According to Franken, what are the good points about being a "mushball," a moderate, and a Democrat?
3. What is the difference, according to Franken, between stupid confusion and intelligent confusion? Why does he use "grazing fees on federal lands" as his example of a topic to be intelligently confused about (9)?
4. What makes affirmative action confusing, according to the author? Despite this confusion, what kind of affirmative action does he say he approves of? Do you feel any irony in his discussion of legacies at Harvard?

Questions for Argument

1. Franken takes potshots and personal swipes at various public figures in this piece (notably Clarence Thomas and Rush Limbaugh). He excuses this as "being mean" himself

in order to "mak[e] fun of meanness in public debate" (3). Does this justification work for you? Or do you think he's being too personal? Is it satire, or is it just mean?

2. The author got himself in trouble at a speaking engagement at Harvard when he ended a discussion on the lack of minorities on *Saturday Night Live* with a joke that "minorities just aren't funny" (31–33). Do you think he deserved to be criticized for being racist?

Writing Assignments

Informal

1. Select one passage in the essay that you find funny, and study it to determine what about it makes you laugh. Then write an informal paper explaining the technique that Franken uses to create humor in this passage.

Formal

2. **Argumentation.** Think about Franken's distinction between "stupid confusion" and "intelligent confusion." Brainstorm with a group of other students to think of examples of each type—ideally, parallel sets of examples about the same subject. Then, with your group or individually, write an essay in which you defend or refute Franken's statement that "intelligent confusion" is a "majority position in this country" (8–9).

3. **Research Opportunity.** Affirmative action has been controversial since its inception. Use library or Internet research to establish its current status; has it withstood the numerous attacks leveled at it? Has it been "mended"? Are people more or less distressed by it now than previously? Then write a paper in which you assess the prospects for affirmative action. Will it survive?

■ ■ ■

TV or Not TV?

VIRGINIA POSTREL

Virginia Postrel is editor of *Reason* magazine, a conservative-to-libertarian bimonthly. This editorial appeared there in August–September 1993. (Copyright 1997 by the Reason Foundation. Reprinted by permission.)

Americans are worried about violent crime. That's a major reason Republican Richard Riordan is now mayor of Los Angeles, an overwhelmingly Democratic city. Riordan promises to make the city safer by putting 3,000 more cops on the street and beefing up citizen patrols. 1

On Capitol Hill, they have a different approach to fighting crime. Their answer is censorship. 2

In late May and early June, the Senate Judiciary Committee's Constitution Subcommittee held two rounds of hearings on television violence. The legislative agenda was diffuse, but the message was emphatic. Said Sen. Howard Metzenbaum (D-Ohio): "The television industry ought to recognize one thing and not forget it. They don't own the airwaves. They have a franchise, and what Congress giveth, Congress can taketh away." 3

4   And, in a litany of double-talk, we heard:

- From Sen. Paul Simon (D-Ill.), the committee's chair, "We face ultimately a choice between censorship and voluntary, responsible conduct."
- From Sen. Herb Kohl (D-Ohio), "We do not want to impose unnecessary rules and regulations and even perhaps violate the Constitution. . . .The question is, What are these people prepared to do by themselves? What kinds of regulations are they willing to accept, self-imposed, so that government doesn't have to step in?"
- And from Sen. Carol Moseley Braun (D-Ill.): "The senators here seated today would not—would be the first to object to—the use of censorship as a solution to television violence. However, the fact remains that a television license is a privilege, and along with that privilege comes responsibility. The TV and motion picture industries cannot dodge these responsibilities by hiding behind the First Amendment."

5   In other words, censor yourselves, or we'll jerk your licenses. Metzenbaum put it bluntly: "If we can't stop it any other way, then maybe we'll find a way to take back some of those TV franchises in the hands of the networks and local stations. You have until December 1 to do something."

6   Television violence is a centrist issue; although the lead censors are liberal Democrats, they have allies across the political spectrum. And no wonder. The typical intellectual thinks TV is made up of, in Meg Greenfield's words, "the vivid, colorful sight of exploding heads and strung-out guts and guys endlessly careering around shooting other guys as a matter of mindless, pointless habit. Most of this stuff has long since abandoned any pretense to what the Supreme Court once called, in the context of an obscenity ruling, 'redeeming social value.' "

7   That is a statement by someone who does not watch television. Outside the occasional vampire movie or rerun of *Raiders of the Lost Ark*, exploding heads are truly a rarity on TV, and if Greenfield has really seen "strung-out guts," she must have been watching *Lifetime* broadcasts meant for physicians.

8   Unlike Greenfield, I watch a lot of TV, including a range of police dramas: the respectable prime-time *Law & Order*, the trashy late-night *Silk Stalkings*, and the juvenile family-hour *Time Trax*. These shows never show gore. They always emphasize the tragedy of violence, particularly violent death. They feature highly moral protagonists. They are shot full of "redeeming social value." Indeed, for a conscious meditation on the role of a moral man in an immoral world, it is hard to top Stephen Cannell's *Wiseguy* series.

9   The social scientists and their politician friends remove dramatic violence from its moral and imaginative context. They treat heroes the same as villains and cartoon cats and mice the same as real-life murderers. A recent survey finds the educational, politically correct *Young Indiana Jones Chronicles* the most violent—and, by implication, most dangerous— prime-time network show.

10   I do not pretend to be an expert on the social-science literature on television violence. But from reading often-cited studies, I have noticed a few trends. The clinical experiments almost all depend on creating highly artificial situations, are rarely truly double-blind, and observe only small changes in behavior.

11   The statistical studies leave out obvious variables, such as family size, the degree of parental attention, and family religious observance.

12   Studies are rarely duplicated; clinicians seem to redesign experiments from scratch, while statisticians rarely look at the same data twice. Survey articles include suspicious phrases such as "the association between adult criminal violence and childhood exposure to

television violence *approached* statistical significance." (Emphasis added.) In other words, the relation wasn't meaningful. One cannot help suspecting researchers of bias.

The most interesting epidemiological study—which has turned up everywhere from *JAMA* to *The Public Interest*—is by Brandon S. Centerwall, a psychiatrist affiliated with the University of Washington. Centerwall testified before Simon's committee and is among the most prominent voices declaring that "children's exposure to television and television violence should become part of the public-health agenda."   13

Unfortunately, Centerwall's study proves nothing about television violence. It does not even examine the issue.   14

Rather, Centerwall compares homicide rates among whites in the United States and Canada before and after the introduction of television to the rate in South Africa, where television wasn't available until 1975. From 1945 to '74, he finds that the white homicide rate jumped 93 percent in the United States and 92 percent in Canada but fell by 7 percent in South Africa. From 1975 to '87, however, the white homicide rate in South Africa increased by 130 percent. Centerwall's conclusion: Children raised watching television start killing each other when they become adults.   15

There are problems with Centerwall's study. Aside from looking at the existence of capital punishment, for instance, he evinces very little interest in the very different criminal-justice systems in the three countries and how they changed over time.   16

But the main problem is that Centerwall's study proves too much. It doesn't prove that violence on television causes harm. It proves that television itself causes harm.   17

Assuming his conclusion is correct, violent shows may have nothing to do with the shift. Television might disrupt family life in important ways, encouraging parents to pay less attention to kids or interrupting family conversations. It might undermine legal and parental authority. It might shorten attention spans and encourage instant gratification. Banning *Wiseguy* reruns or *America's Most Wanted* wouldn't affect any of these dynamics.   18

And even Centerwall sees the effect as a one-time shift in the distribution of aggression within the population. This means modifying television content isn't likely to make a difference. And it means that television causes harm only by affecting the small number of people who are particularly prone to violence.   19

That's enough for the censors. They are quite willing to sacrifice the freedom of the many to the willful violence of the few, to ban powerful works of art because some people commit evil acts. That way you don't have to make moral judgments. You can simply blame television for crime.   20

Questions for Inquiry

1. What is Postrel's claim? Is it explicit or implied? What type of claim is it?
2. The beginning of the editorial emphasizes the actual wording of the congressional debate on TV violence. Why might Postrel have provided quotations from four senators and a *Newsweek* columnist (Greenfield)? What kind of response can she count on from her expected readership?
3. Why does Postrel defend television and television violence?

Questions for Argument

1. Postrel dismisses most research on television violence as artificial and insignificant (10–12). The much-talked-about research by Centerwall she refutes as "prov[ing] too

much": that "television itself causes harm" (17). Where do you stand in relation to this research and this topic?

2. Do you consider Postrel's treatment of the opposition acceptable or is it tactlessly harsh? Consider these comments: "In other words, [the senators are saying] censor yourselves, or we'll jerk your licenses" (5). "That's enough for the censors. They are quite willing to sacrifice the freedom of the many to the willful violence of the few. . . . That way you don't have to make moral judgments. You can simply blame television for crime" (20).

Writing Assignments

Informal

1. Meg Greenfield, whom Postrel quotes in paragraph 6, mentions "redeeming social value," the famous Supreme Court standard for whether something was obscene. What, in your view, would make extreme film or television violence have "redeeming social value"? Write an informal paper in which you define this term for yourself and provide examples of what would and would not be acceptable violence.

Formal

2. **Primary Research/Collaboration.** Work with a group to study some of the shows that Postrel appreciates (8) and some other shows that contain violence as well. You might assign individuals or a team to view particular shows or types of shows. Then meet to discuss and compile your reactions. Decide whether, as a group, you see Postrel's point or whether you find the violence in these shows potentially harmful. Then write an essay, either as a group or individually, in which you support or refute Postrel's views about television violence.

3. Does Postrel's point of view seem contrary to conservative "ideology"? Would you expect a conservative to be pro-censorship? Research the conservative and libertarian positions on censorship of media violence to determine whether Postrel's view is "in line" or is maverick. Then write an essay in which you discuss the spectrum of viewpoints about media violence that exists on the right.

■ ■ ■

Educating in a Pessimistic Age

LEON BOTSTEIN

Leon Botstein is president of Bard College. This essay is adapted from a lecture he delivered at the 92nd Street Y in New York City in 1993. It was published in *Harper's* in August 1993. (Reprinted by permission of the author.)

1   Since the mid-1970s there has been a great deal of public discussion about the declining quality of American education. The argument is pretty simple: once upon a time the American school system worked, but something happened along the way. Conservatives

argue that the decline began sometime in the 1960s and was the result of rebellion on American campuses and the triumph of a kind of softheaded liberalism that crept into the general culture, including the training of teachers. But whatever the cause, by the mid-1970s there was general agreement that something was quite wrong with the functioning of the American school system and the standards of American education. Today, after twelve years of nostalgia with respect to American education, one would hope that serious consideration will be given to change.

It doesn't make sense to argue that we should fix American education by re-creating a past that never existed. Since at least the 1930s, American college educators have been complaining bitterly about the quality of American schooling, about the fact that kids coming out of high school really couldn't do college work. We should also keep in mind that the students they were complaining about were a more elite group than students today; it wasn't until the 1940s that 50 percent of the young people in America were graduating from high school.

Although people worry today about the decline in SAT scores, we should really be impressed by how *little* SAT scores have declined, given the growing percentage of the population that takes the test. I would argue that if one had anticipated the massive democratization of the school system that took place in the 1960s and 1970s, one would have predicted a much more radical decline in the scores. So it doesn't help to re-enact an imaginary past; rather, one has to find the proper standards against which to judge the present.

The circumstances in which education takes place have become very, very difficult. Whether kids go to Head Start or elementary school or to high school or college, they are being educated in a context in which the adult community believes the future will be worse than the present. This may seem irrelevant, but it isn't. Diminishing expectations about the quality of life are inherently related to the ideas of progress upon which our educational system is based. For better or worse, my parents, and the world around me when I was a child, believed that the future would be better than the past. Nowadays every child picks up an inherent pessimism in the adult community: Once upon a time the city was clean, the subway cost a dime, there was no crime, everything was civilized, everything worked. Now it doesn't. And there is absolutely no expectation that it's going to get better.

It is impossible to educate in a climate of cultural pessimism, impossible to cultivate serious motivation. Education demands allegiance to the most archaic conception of time. We tell children that if they get through twelve years—maybe more—of school, they'll see the rewards some twenty years down the line. The amount of delayed gratification inherent in education made sense when the society thought in terms of generational time. But kids now grow up in a world in which people change their jobs every few years and their relationships every few months; they assess their success in the workplace and in the economy by the day, if not by the minute. Children are left with no sense of permanence, and thus no understanding of why they should make a long-term investment in their own education.

The founders of this nation, Jefferson particularly, believed that education was a key to progress, that one could appeal to the rational faculties of people and create a better world rapidly through social improvement. Our belief in education reflected the hopefulness of America.

It's significant that this shared optimism should have begun to come apart just as access to American education became widespread. It was all right as a theory when most Americans never finished high school, but in the postwar period, when Americans in large *(margin notes: - Compare & contrast / - logic (stats))*

numbers had access not only to high school but to college, people began to worry about whether the system could work. The "education crisis" began. Though the symptoms of the "crisis" were usually expressed in terms of SAT scores and reading levels, elitist fears—on the Left as well as the Right—were in fact at its root. On the Right, the "decline of standards" was decried by those who were made uncomfortable by the prospect of the democratization of education. But such people could be found on the Left as well, where "politically correct"—yet patronizing—attacks on core curricula and "Eurocentrism" cloaked a perverse and equally corrosive form of elitism.

(margin notes: subclaim / Inquiry)

8   The real challenge America puts forward is whether one can reconcile equity and excellence, whether a society can have a truly democratic educational system and still educate its brightest children properly. But before we give up on this challenge, as the conservative administrations of the last twelve years essentially did, we've got to remember that we've never really *had* a democratic educational system. This experiment was not even possible until the late 1960s, when the racial, social, and economic obstacles to democratic education began to fall; as soon as the experiment began, as the difficulties of the project became apparent, people started abandoning ship, declaring its failure. The task has been grotesquely underestimated; the nation has never made the investment that democratic education required.

(margin notes: logic / some emotion)

9   How do we go about changing the system? First of all, I would simplify the curriculum and focus on a few very basic things: a command of language, reading and writing, mathematical reasoning. Science and mathematics, as opposed to the humanities, should be at the center of the curriculum from the beginning. I take this radical position because what is taught in the humanities—in reading and writing and history—has become so politicized that science is the last common ground we have. It's also the easiest curiosity to sustain; every child wants to know how the world works. College is too late to develop a curiosity in science and mathematics; it can only be done early in life.

(margin notes: Inquiry / offers a solution / logic & credibility / a lot of opinion)

10   I would eliminate the American high school, because it is not fixable in its current design. High school is a nineteenth-century structure that has run its course: it is no longer congruent with the rapid development and autonomy of adolescents, their physical maturation, and the independence that society now permits them. I would divide schooling into five or six years of elementary school and then middle school. At the end of what is now the sophomore year of high school, students would feed into the community college system, which works very well by comparison, doing what high schools should be doing.

(margin notes: Sub-Solution / Support / logically appeals)

11   I think we also have to face the fact that we must make teaching a desirable profession. In order to do so, we have to raise teachers' salaries. But more importantly, we have to change the working conditions in our public schools. Why do good people go to private schools to teach, even though salaries are considerably lower than at public schools? Because in public schools the teaching profession is bureaucratized, teachers are not treated as professionals, there is enormous regulation, the conditions of work are horendous, there is no professional community. The administration and organization of schools need a radical overhaul.

(margin notes: Sub solution / Support / Inquiry / logic/emotion)

12   Particularly now that the disenfranchised part of our population has some reasonable expectation of access to the educational system, our entire society depends on it more than ever before. We have to struggle with our own sense of pessimism as adults and create an environment that is much more about hope.

(margin notes: sub- claim/solution)

13   I want to close with this notion of hope. One of the ugliest changes in grammar that have taken place during the twentieth century is the use of the word "hopefully." As you

know, "hopefully" is an adverb and is properly used only to modify a verb. Nowadays, however, it is used in common parlance as a surrogate for the words "I hope." Why has that usage become acceptable to our ears? Because it fits absolutely with a cultural shift, a tendency to displace responsibility. Saying "Hopefully, the school system will be better," is very different from saying "I hope the school system will be better." Because if you say "I hope," the next question is, What are you going to do about it? *emotion (gets a reaction)*

Inquiry logic

Our politicians have to understand that education is not just another special-interest budget item that adds to the national debt. Education is of primary importance. The Clinton Administration has chosen instead to focus on health-care reform. But the question we must ask is, Health care for what? Do I want to live longer and more healthfully in a totalitarian society where there's no free speech because no one thinks and therefore no one has a dissenting opinion? Where intolerance is so rampant that we take any dissenting opinion as a reason to hate the other person? Where language doesn't communicate anymore? Where there is no shared knowledge, no shared experience, no shared discourse, and therefore no democracy? I prefer to skip the immunization.

14

Sub claim

Inquiry based on Logic

emotion (his own)

15

Education must be at the center of the future of America. The sooner this administration comes up with a serious national education policy, the better off we all will be. We must stop our crushing our children with our own ill-earned pessimism. We must learn again to hope.

Final claim

Questions for Inquiry

1. What is Botstein's claim? Is it explicit or implied? What type of claim is it?
2. How has a shift in our sense of time played into a change in educational ambition (5)?
3. What type of audience and readership do you think Botstein expected for his analysis of education today? What indicators in the text create this impression?
4. Why did the perception of educational crisis begin when "large numbers had access . . . to college" (7), when we had just begun to have a "democratic educational system" (8)? Why does Botstein label concerns about the weakness of education today as "elitist" (7)?

Questions for Argument

1. Do you agree that this is an era of "cultural pessimism" (5)? Are people less motivated now than previously, in your opinion? And is this because their expectations are depressed? Or are there other reasons why young people are less motivated to achieve?
2. The author says that education should concentrate on the basics, with science and mathematics at the heart of the curriculum rather than the humanities (9). Do you agree that education should become more science-oriented right from the start?

Writing Assignments

Informal

1. Hope is tied to the way we think about time, Botstein suggests, and to our sense that progress is possible (5–6). Do you agree that we live in a hopeless era, when a lack of permanence sends the signal that trying hard or "mak[ing] a long-term investment" is

just not worth it? Write a journal entry about whether you see hope or hopelessness among your peers.

Formal

2. **Argumentation.** Botstein says he would eliminate high school because it is outdated (10). Instead, he would send students directly to community college after tenth grade and presumably from there to work or to the junior year of a four-year college. Discuss this option with other students and with faculty or administrators on your campus. Then write a paper in which you argue that starting junior college at sixteen and getting an A. A. degree at eighteen is an exciting innovation or a preposterous idea.

3. Is education a more important governmental priority than health care, as Botstein argues in paragraph 14? Examine his reasons and then write a position paper in which you support additional federal funding for either reform of health care or reform of education. Support your position with analysis and with information, acquired through research if necessary.

■ ■ ■

Part III

The Formal Research Paper

Chapter 12

Extended Inquiry and In-Depth Research

Research skills can serve you well throughout life, not just in college. Researching is part of being an informed citizen, but, even more, research can be your anchor in lots of life situations—when a relative becomes seriously ill or when you need to choose a school for your child, you may go online to ransack the web for everything on multiple sclerosis or head to the library to brief yourself on Montessori philosophy and home schooling's pluses and minuses.

The research-paper assignment is an opportunity to deepen your research abilities. It also provides a structured period of investigation into a subject that intrigues you and a chance to formally synthesize your findings. Writing this paper can lay the groundwork for the papers you will do throughout college and in your major. The papers required by the various academic disciplines are variations on a theme. Learning how to do the argumentative research paper well will serve you in all courses, although you may never do exactly the same type of paper again.

■ UNDERSTAND THE REQUIREMENTS

In any course in which a research assignment is given, you must make sure you clearly understand the professor's requirements as well as those of the academic discipline. Most instructors take care to provide explicit information on an assignment's length, extent, and type; you should ask for more instructions if you are uncertain about the process for completing an assignment or about the required final form.

You may find it helpful to fill out a chart of research project requirements such as the one included on the next page.

The paper discussed in this chapter is an argumentative research paper—that is, a paper on a narrowed topic that expresses and supports a viewpoint about the topic. This assignment calls for combining your preparation in inquiry with your understanding of argumentation. Within these limits, some of the requirements will be established by your instructor—for example, length, appropriateness of primary research, citation type, tone, and style.

■ *Research-Paper Requirements*

Date due: _____   Length (in typed pages): _____

Topic: assigned _____   chosen from approved list _____
                  self-determined _____   self-determined
                                                and approved _____

Type: broad coverage of issue _____   focused, in-depth _____

Report:
organized results of research, no viewpoint expressed _____
balanced report on views on two or all sides of issue _____

Claim-oriented paper: research leads to support of a
                            viewpoint _____

Sources: primary _____   secondary _____

                  type(s): _____   type(s): _____
                  (interview, observation)   (general, serious, scholarly,
                                                or mix; recent, historical, or
                                                mix)

                  number: _____   number: _____

Citations: formal _____   informal _____
                  number: _____   style to use (APA, MLA): _____

Audience: instructor _____   classmates _____   other _____
                  academic _____   general _____

Tone and Style: objective/neutral _____   personal _____

Presentation:
straight-through essay style _____   sectioned (headings and
                                           subheadings) _____

required sections _____

Additional required items (outline, note cards):

■ OVERVIEW OF THE RESEARCH PROCESS

Writing a research paper is similar in many ways to writing any serious piece designed for an audience. The process is generally the same, and each writer flows though it in his or her own way, customizing it to the particular assignment, personal circumstances, and individual work style.

Here's an overview of the process as applied to the argumentative research paper:

Preparation
      Discovering your topic
      Doing background or preliminary research
      Forming a preliminary claim or research question
      Developing a preliminary outline
Planning the Research
      Writing a research proposal
      Creating a working bibliography
Locating Sources and Taking Notes
Writing
      Generating a draft outline plus Works Cited page
      Writing the first draft
      Revising to form the final draft
      Editing
      Preparing the final manuscript

■ DISCOVERING YOUR TOPIC

When you are given a research assignment, your topic may be spelled out for you, you may be able to choose from a list of acceptable topics, or you may have free rein. Students sometimes complain when a topic is assigned, but they should instead be grateful; much of the preliminary labor of determining whether a topic is workable has been done for them. If the choice is yours, your first move should be to make sure you understand any specified limits on the topic. Those mentioned below may not be the same as your instructor's.

You may already know exactly what you would like to write about. Perhaps an issue has come your way while reading in the textbook for this or another class, or some civic debate has caught your interest. But if you draw a blank, then some of the techniques listed here may help you. If you are unsure, don't just grab the first topic you see; aim for a rough list of five to ten possibilities, and then choose the one that seems to work the best.

Survey your landscape. Look through this text and others you have for courses that held your interest. Jot down topic possibilities. Read the newspaper, watch or listen to broadcast news or public-affairs shows; talk to your friends and listen to what others are discussing in the cafeteria or in the hallways.

Choosing an Appropriate Topic

When you are exploring to locate a topic for an argumentative research paper, keep in mind the following guidelines. Your topic will be workable if it meets these criteria:

1. It is relevant or controversial.
2. It is academically researchable.

   - It must be approachable in an academic way.
   - It must be focused or narrowed.
   - It must be amenable to rational investigation.
   - Recent research must be available on it.
   - It must mesh with your college library's collection.

3. It suits you.

   - You are interested in it.
   - It is new to you as a research topic.
   - You can be open-minded about it.

4. It fits the assignment.

The Topic Is Relevant or Controversial

For an argumentative research paper, you should seek a topic on which there is a variety of opinion. "Controversial" does not mean that the topic must be on the television news every night or that it causes your relatives or neighbors to foam at the mouth. The topic may, in fact, be currently debated—for example, school vouchers or welfare or international trade policies. Or it may be a quietly persistent social issue, such as housing discrimination, high school dropouts, or the effect of divorce on children. It should be a topic on which many positions are possible and a topic of concern to the civil discourse community.

The Topic Is Academically Researchable

Your topic should lend itself to research in a college-level library. This means it must possess a number of characteristics.

First, *the topic must be approachable in an academic way.* If it is, you will be able to identify a body of written opinion, investigation, and analysis about it in your college library. General and scholarly works on subjects related to the academic disciplines and the professions constitute the bulk of college-library holdings. Such libraries do not hold much material on nonscholarly subjects. For example, there may be few books on the how-tos of parenting in a college library, while your town or county library at home may contain a dozen or more. However, a parenting-related topic such as corporal punishment would be researchable in a college library. The difference is that the academic topic is a focus for investigation by researchers and analysis by scholars.

In choosing a topic, determine which academic disciplines would concern themselves with the issue. There may be more than one; a paper on corporal punishment, for example, might pull from psychology, education, law and justice, and sociology. Although your paper for this course is not going to be an in-depth academic treatment of your subject, it should include both serious general-interest treatments and academic perspectives.

Second, *the topic must be focused or narrowed.* Sometimes, whether a subject is researchable in an academic library depends on how focused it is. Academic topics are usually narrower than general-interest versions: corporal punishment is a narrow topic compared with parenting. A student might further narrow corporal punishment to educational issues or legal issues. Working with a narrow topic also makes managing your time and the project easier because you are not "solving the world's problems."

Narrowing your topic can occur at any time in the planning stages of your research paper and, frankly, sometimes during the research stage as well. The more you can narrow the topic at the start, the better off you are.

Third, *the topic must be amenable to rational investigation.* Because the academic discourse community emphasizes reason and analysis, subjects that go beyond these bounds will not be reflected in a college library's holdings. So you should avoid topics pertaining to "new-age" or occult issues, such as astrology, unidentified flying objects (UFOs), or extrasensory perception (ESP). Although these topics are fascinating to many, academics do not research them; they are covered only in general and popular periodicals and books. If the government does study UFOs, the research is classified, making most of what has been written purely speculative. ESP has been studied by psychologists and discounted.

Topics considered trivial in academe should also be avoided. The retro trend in women's fashions may strike you as intriguing, but most college libraries have little on this subject. Other topics not much covered in academic libraries include rock and movie stars, automobiles, sports, and gardening.

Also, beware of topics for which there is only one source. Certain concepts invented or investigated by one writer have been discounted in the main by academe; as a result the only source is the originator of the idea. For example, subliminal seduction, a theory about how advertising works, was developed by Wilson Bryan Key, who has written many books about it. But little other work on the subject exists. Another example is the Harvard professor and psychologist who specializes in treating people who claim to have been abducted by aliens. John Mack maintains in his published work that these folks are not deluded. Aside from his work, however, there is no other academic material on this subject, and a student researching alien abduction in a college library would come up dry.

Fourth, *recent research must be available on the topic.* Because your paper is going to be about a controversy of interest to the civic discourse community, you will need to make sure that the subject has been covered recently in appropriate sources. Recent usually means within the last ten or so years, although on some topics pivotal research may have been done as long ago as twenty or more years. In order to speak to the issue today, however, you need to include current sources. If a topic is not currently being researched and discussed, then it is probably not a good topic for your argumentative research paper.

If your topic is extremely current, however, there may not be any academic research on it at all. New medical procedures or treatments and recent political events, such as a terrorist bombing or current election campaign, may be extensively covered in newspapers and newsmagazines, but you will not be able to locate books and scholarly studies about it. Academic work takes several years to produce and publish, and on a topic that is too current you will find a paucity of material.

Fifth, *the topic must mesh with your college library's collection.* The size and nature of your institution are likely to affect what books and periodicals the library has; no library can have everything. Knowing what departments exist on your campus and what graduate programs are offered can help you determine what holdings your library may have. A college with a large communication department, for example, may have an extensive collection covering advertising, film, the other media, and popular culture. You may find it difficult to research an advertising or radio topic at a school that lacks such a department. A college with a graduate school of education should have deep holdings in this area.

The Topic Suits You

You will be investing several weeks' time in your topic. Thus, your topic should have the following characteristics.

First, it should interest you sufficiently to hold your attention for a few weeks. You may have unanswered questions on the topic, for example.

Second, it should be new to you as a research topic. You may have done an excellent job on a paper in high school, and you may still be interested in the topic. But you should still pick a fresh subject for a college research paper. The paper requirements won't be the same as they were in high school, and you won't get mixed up if you are working on a new topic. And trying to "retrofit" an old paper for new requirements will probably to lead to disaster. If your instructor requires you to proceed step-by-step in your research, you will have to falsify some steps by creating note cards and so on— and faking research is obviously unethical.

Third, you can be open-minded about it. Being overly involved in the outcome of an argument can blind a person to the strength of opposing arguments or evidence. Therefore, you should avoid topics that you feel emotional about or that touch on your deepest-held beliefs. If a member of your family has been the victim of a violent crime, your ability to write fairly about the treatment of convicted criminals may be blunted. If you already hold an extreme position or have a passionate commitment to one view of an issue, you probably should pick some other topic for your paper.

The Topic Fits the Assignment

For this research paper, you want to pick a topic that is not too specialized or discipline-based. You may wish to choose a topic related to your major, but you need to make sure researching it does not require advanced knowledge. And you should avoid topics that are controversial only within the academic discourse community. For example, what happened to the dinosaurs and how old the universe is are controversies within the fields of paleontology and astrophysics. Although many nonacademics are aware of and are interested in these controversies, their resolution has no policy consequences. Opinions on these topics, no matter how well supported, will not affect our civic discourse community.

■ *Activity 1*

Evaluating Research-Paper Topics, p. 496

Inventorying the Topic

Once you have decided on a topic that you think is workable, you should pause for an inventory of what you have "in stock" on this issue. Working on notebook or scrap paper, ask yourself questions like these:

> What do I already know about this issue? What part of this is knowledge, and what is assumptions?
> What sources do I already know of (such as readings in this book or material in a textbook from another course)?
> What definitions should be clarified? What confusions of language may occur?
> Do I understand the background or history of this issue?
> Do I understand the technical processes of or developments within this issue?
> Which of my values come into play when I work on this topic?
> Can I be objective on this topic? Do I already have a preferred position on this issue?
> What is my audience likely to know or assume about the topic?
> What values is my audience likely to bring to the topic?

Working within Your Discourse Community

Your preliminary work on your topic should also include some conversation. Your instructor may provide time for small-group meetings in class in which you present your topic, your focus of research, and your discoveries in your preliminary inquiry. Your group can serve as a sounding board and as a source of fresh ideas or leads. They may be able to help you if you get stuck: they may know the names of bibliographies in a field or where a certain resource is located in your library or what headings to try in your search.

Collecting Viewpoints

Just as you inventoried your own preresearch understanding of your topic, you should spend a few minutes creating a rough list of all the opinions and points of view you can think of. Then start talking to people about the issue. Find out how much they know and what their views are. Your instructor may allow class time to explore the opinion range of your peers on your topic. (You will probably discover that most people are only mildly informed about it.) Collecting viewpoints on your topic puts at your disposal the conventional and commonplace thinking on the issue.

◼ CHECKING OUT THE TOPIC: PRELIMINARY RESEARCH

Preliminary research has many potential benefits. And it can occur in various places in each individual's research process. Here are some of the reasons to do preliminary research:

- to discover a topic
- to narrow a topic
- to discover whether a topic is researchable

- to preview the topic and understand its context or history
- to discover the headings under which your topic is listed in the library
- to determine which academic fields provide research on your topic
- to determine the extent of your library's holdings in this field or related fields

Preliminary research can take from two to six hours spread over one to three days during the first week of research. Your goal will be to get an overview of the subject and determine whether college-level research is possible on the subject.

If you still need to narrow your subject, your preliminary reading should help you get a feel for the broad subject and the issues within it and help you on your way toward a narrow focus. If you have landed on a narrowed topic, your preliminary reading should help you situate the issue within its larger subject. Preliminary reading will also show you what academic discipline or disciplines can provide you with information on your topic.

An early goal in your research will be to formulate a **preliminary claim** about your topic; your preliminary research can also steer you toward the first glimmerings of a claim.

Preliminary research involves several activities:

1. Check out your topic in the reference room of your library. (See Chapter 5 for how to use the reference room.) Using encyclopedias and other reference works, find out some general information on your subject.
2. Do a quick check of bibliographic resources to discover the headings your subject is classified under. You also need to determine whether general bibliographic sources show entries on the subject and which academic fields offer material on it.
3. Discover whether your library has a reasonable stock of books and periodicals in your area of research.

In order not to be overwhelmed by the wealth of information in reference sources, you should read reference works intelligently, in the light of your goal. You might skim through elaborate historical or technical information if you are seeking to limit your topic; or you may zoom in on only specific sections of the source article.

Taking Notes in Preliminary Research

You should go to the library equipped to take some notes when you do your preliminary research. Record any general or background information you need to keep straight in your mind and not entrust to your memory. You might come across technical or official definitions, for example, which you would take down as quotations, or you might discover statistics or technical or process descriptions that could be summarized or paraphrased.

If you are still in the process of narrowing a topic, you need to gain a sense of the possibilities, so you might jot down or chart the branches of issues within a topic. You might also need to know what the "live" questions are about your topic.

You should bring 3 × 5 cards to record bibliography information about your reference sources. You want to know what you looked at, especially if for some reason you need to backtrack. Also, many reference works list sources consulted or important sources on the topic at the end of each article. You will want to record these as possible sources for your own paper. (Later in this chapter you'll find the specifics of what you should put on your bibliography cards.)

Preliminary research should also include a check of bibliographies in order to determine:

- whether research exists on your topic
- whether your topic is appropriately limited
- the headings under which you should look for your topic
- the academic fields in which your topic is researched

You should look in general bibliographic sources, in print or online, and also in specialized bibliographies to determine which academic disciplines produce research on your topic.

Handling Reference Sources in Your Final Paper

Reference sources you use for background reading will be just that, background. Include a reference source on your Works Cited list only if you explicitly use it in your paper—for example, by quoting a definition or summarizing some facts or figures from it. Bibliographies you consult are truly background. As essential as they are, you should never list bibliographies on your Works Cited page.

■ CHOOSING A LINE OF INQUIRY

Your preliminary research should have helped you focus on a particular issue or aspect of your topic. To further guide your in-depth research, it's a good idea to have in mind a line of inquiry. In the form of a **preliminary claim** or a **focusing question,** a line of inquiry defines what you need to know to write an argument about your narrowed topic. It gives you a direction or thread to follow in confronting available material.

Preliminary Claim

A **preliminary claim** is just what it sounds like, a claim or assertion that represents your early thinking about your narrowed topic. It is a stepping-stone to an arguable claim.

People arrive at their preliminary claim at different points in their research. Because the civic discourse community fills our heads with ideas, it's quite possible that you will start with a preformed notion about your topic. But your preliminary claim should not be just an off-the-top-of-your-head opinion about your topic. It should be informed by inquiry discussions with others and by your preliminary research.

Sometimes, your preliminary claim will come to you during your preliminary reading or while you put together your working bibliography.

It's optimal to have a preliminary claim as you launch your main research. Here are examples of workable preliminary claims:

The medical use of currently illegal drugs should be permitted.

Convicted murderers and sex offenders should never be paroled.

Resist settling on a preliminary claim until you have narrowed your topic. Working with a preliminary claim in a broad subject area can prevent you from narrowing your subject and tie you to researching too broadly. Here are some examples of preliminary claims that are overly broad:

Drugs should be legalized.

Parole should be eliminated from our criminal justice system.

Mainstreaming of the handicapped does not work and should be avoided.

Having a preliminary claim does not mean you will advocate for it during your research. Rather, your claim is a product of your early thinking on your topic, and it will be tested against additional evidence during your research. Your preliminary claim is like a hypothesis, which in the sciences is an explanation that is to be tested through experimentation. Although you probably won't be able to set up an experiment to test your preliminary claim, you will be evaluating it over and over again as you collect information

Focusing Question

Rather than work with a preliminary claim about what is true about your topic, you may prefer to use a **focusing question** to help you establish a line of inquiry. Focusing questions are useful when you have a claim but are not sure it is valid. You can easily turn such an uncertain claim into a focusing question:

Would legalizing medical use of prohibited drugs such as marijuana cause an increase in overall illegal drug use?

In what situations is mainstreaming a handicapped person successful and not successful? What limitations should be established on mainstreaming those with handicaps?

Is the label *learning disabled* applied too frequently to children whose failure to learn has other explanations?

During your research, your question should turn into a preliminary and then a final claim.

Brainstorming for a Preliminary Claim or Focusing Question

If a preliminary claim or focusing question does not form in your mind, you may have to search actively for one. Here are some techniques to try to develop a preliminary claim or question:

- Look back over the material you developed in inventorying your topic (as described above).
- Look back over the notes you have taken in your preliminary research. You may want to use a highlighter to single out issues that seem open to debate or call for additional evidence.
- Try bouncing your possibilities off classmates or friends to prompt a line of inquiry.

In connection with any of these techniques, you can brainstorm or free-write to get your ideas down on paper.

■ *Activity 2*

Evaluating Preliminary Claims and Focusing Questions, p. 497

Getting Perspective on Your Line of Inquiry

Whether you are working with a preliminary claim or a focusing question, you should step back and examine it to determine which type of claim you are working toward. Will your claim argue for a fact, value, or recommended policy? Will establishing a definition or clarifying a causal relationship be a facet of your argument? You should keep the type of argument you are building in mind as you collect material in your research.

Developing a Preliminary Outline

Once you have your preliminary claim or focusing question, you may be able to develop a rough outline of what your paper will look like. Such an outline will be speculative, but it may help guide your research.

A preliminary outline results from studying your preliminary claim or question and spinning off from it the points you would need to support in order to draw your audience to your position. Although your final draft may not follow this outline, having one early in the research process can give direction to your investigation.

■ WRITING A RESEARCH PROPOSAL

Both research proposals and research progress reports (discussed later in this chapter) communicate the researcher's intentions and progress to a "higher authority"—a grant-giving organization, perhaps, or a supervisor, employer, publisher, or, in the case of students, an instructor. Not all research requires a proposal; many academics perform research on their own initiative, individually, without proposals or progress reports;

likewise, students are only occasionally required to prepare proposals for assigned papers. Research proposals are common, however, when researchers apply for grants and in industry and the corporate world.

The ultimate shape of a research proposal depends on the stated requirements of its intended audience. The format for a formal proposal discussed here is typical, but your instructor may set other requirements. Some instructors require an informal rather than formal proposal, and guidelines for this type of proposal are also included here.

In an academic setting, the research proposal is usually written after some preliminary research has helped establish a line of inquiry and potential sources—that is, after you've gotten the "lay of the land" of your research territory. Whether the proposal is formal or informal, its purpose is to explain the focus of your research and to justify the topic as a subject of inquiry. Proposals should be concise, so summary will serve you well in conveying what material you have gleaned from your preliminary research.

The Formal Research Proposal

In a formal proposal, you should strive for a neutral tone, similar to that of the final paper. Underneath this objective surface, however, your proposal will argue the fitness of your topic and approach for a research project.

Formal proposals are usually structured with headings and sectioning rather than straight text. Here are possible sections for such a proposal:

Definition or Background of the Topic
Statement of the Preliminary Claim or Research Question
Research Plan
Preliminary or Working Bibliography (if required)

Definition or Background of the Topic

In this section, you should briefly describe the problem or controversy, indicate its context, and establish the boundaries of your investigation. The reader should understand why your topic needs study after reading this section. You might convey this by:

- pointing out the causes or development of the problem
- indicating negative or problematic effects of the situation
- providing statistics or facts showing the extent of the problem
- describing the concern of officials, researchers, or members of the public about the situation

Your preliminary research may not enable you to cover all these topics, nor is it necessary to do so. For example, if your research effort were going to establish causes, your proposal would mainly define the need to know these causes.

This section should also establish the boundaries of your investigation. In other words, the topic you describe should be narrowed as much as possible.

Statement of the Preliminary Claim or Research Question

In this section you should describe the particular line of inquiry you will pursue. You should explicitly state your preliminary claim or raise the question that animates your research. If possible, identify your claim as to type. When your proposal is directed to a college instructor, it is usually acceptable and even helpful to mention any uncertainties about your line of research. (But be aware that in a proposal directed to a grant sponsor or workplace supervisor, a tone of assurance and the omission of potential drawbacks may be more appropriate.)

Research Plan

You should briefly summarize the extent of your research to this point; for a research paper, this will be preliminary research in reference works, newspapers, and serious magazines. Then you should explain your plans for in-depth research: the type of sources you expect to find useful, information you know you need to find, and any concerns you have about the research. If you have developed a preliminary outline, you might discuss how it will guide your research. Also, if a separate working bibliography is not required, then you should describe the status of your bibliographic research in this section.

Preliminary or Working Bibliography

If a working bibliography is required, you should list all the sources you have identified as potentially useful. (You do not need to have examined them at this point.) You should use the standard bibliographic format that will apply to your paper, either MLA or APA style.

The Informal Research Proposal

An informal proposal is a personal statement of your interest in and early investigation of a topic. Usually the first person is acceptable, and the tone is expressive. Often, a narrative or loosely topical organization is sufficient. The informal proposal may touch on any of the following points, not necessarily in any particular order:

Topic
- the reasons you are interested in it
- concerns you have about its suitability for an argumentative paper
- any choices about direction or approach you may have to make
- ways the topic could be narrowed
- an indication of the type of claim you expect to make

Preliminary Research
- what you have read and what you were looking for
- what you found out that helps you narrow the topic, select an approach, or refine your questions
- the types and availability of sources for research on this topic

Goals

- the preliminary stages you still need to accomplish: additional preliminary research, further narrowing of topic, and identification of sources for the working bibliography
- where you will start in your in-depth research, what you will be looking for, and any other ideas you have about your investigation

In response to the assignment to write an informal research proposal, Jenny Russo discussed how she narrowed her focus to a problem in mental health.

STUDENT ASSIGNMENT

Jenny Russo, "Proposal for a Paper on Mental Health Care"

In my intro to psych textbook, there's a chapter on abnormal psychology, which fascinates me. There I learned that multiple personality disorder is a real psychological problem, not just something you see in movies.

I spent several hours in the library and online looking up multiple personality disorder and found there's not a lot on it in general reference works. There was also little in general periodical indexes, and *Psychological Abstracts* listed very technical articles. But after checking the library book database, I spent a fascinating afternoon reading around in about six books. And I concluded that any claim I could make about this topic would be very technical. I couldn't locate a controversy in the larger discourse community about this disease.

But in one book, the author kept describing his failure to find someone to treat "multiples" because of problems with the health care system. Long waiting lists for appropriate doctors, uncooperative insurance companies, the inability to pay, and the patients' inconsistent commitment to treatment all got in the way. I was shocked that treatment for such a deep psychological problem would be hard to set up. I decided I wanted to research how mental problems are handled in our health care system.

I decided to talk to my psych prof about whether this was an arguable issue, and she said absolutely. She suggested I talk to Prof. Armsted, who treats patients and who might help me get a handle on the issues. That appointment is set for Thursday. I plan to go to the library tomorrow to look up mental health care.

I expect my claim will be something like, "Our health care system needs to be improved to make it easier for people to get mental health treatment." My paper will probably focus on causes of why getting mental health treatment is difficult and suggest remedies.

■ PLANNING THE RESEARCH

Once you have an approved topic and have completed your preliminary inquiry, it is time to plan your research. You should have a preliminary claim or focusing question at this point.

Some instructors will set up a schedule for your research and will check your progress periodically. If your instructor does not do this, you should do it for yourself. You (or your instructor) will need to establish specific due dates for the landmarks of your research:

- complete a preliminary bibliography
- do in-depth research
- formulate a defensible claim
- plan the paper
- write a rough draft
- revise and edit the draft and prepare a final version
- polish the final manuscript

For example, if your instructor has set your final paper due date six weeks away, and you've used a few days in your preliminary research, set up a specific date by which you want to have half your research done, and quantify this for yourself. If you are required to use fifteen sources, you might set yourself the goal of finding and taking notes from ten relevant sources within three weeks. This leaves you time to finish your research, write and revise, and prepare the final manuscript.

Having the Research Mentality

Researchers must be focused and goal-directed in order to be efficient in their work. This is why having a preliminary claim or focusing question is helpful. At the same time, researchers must be objective and ready to harvest relevant information and ideas without prejudice so as to give all evidence its appropriate weight in the inquiry process.

These two qualities may seem somewhat at odds with each other, but they really are not. Having a focus is a matter of being sensible, of limiting your task to what you have time for. It does not mean you will search only for information that supports your preliminary claim or that you will allow your personal values to slant your choice of evidence. Rather, an open mind toward evidence and a willingness to confront disparate information are important values in the academic discourse community. You need to strive for an objective and neutral view toward the sources you read, at least at the start.

Doing research well also means being prepared. You need to bring the right equipment or your time can be wasted. Library research requires not just some blank pages in the back of a notebook but a particular array of materials:

index cards (3 × 5) for bibliographic notes
note cards (4 × 6) for content notes
paper clips, rubber bands, ministapler

change for copy machines
pens, highlighters, stick-on notes

Even when you've completed your preliminary bibliography, you should always have some blank 3 × 5 cards with you. You will probably add to your bibliography as you do your research because sources lead to other sources.

Establishing a Working Bibliography

Your **working bibliography** of potential sources should be considerably larger—even three times larger—than the number of sources you are required to use. You may discover that some titles are unavailable and others are unhelpful. In constructing your working bibliography, you should strive for a variety of types of sources, ranging from books to periodicals to nonprint and online sources, and ranging from the scholarly to the serious, from the academic to the general interest.

When you examine sources, you will discard some as poorly evidenced, blatantly biased, or unsuitable in some other way. (See Chapter 11 for evaluation of sources.) As your research progresses, you will begin to discover sources that merely repeat information or arguments you have already encountered. In addition, some sources will not be available in your library for any number of reasons. Developing a working or preliminary bibliography helps you maneuver around all these possibilities by giving you lots of titles to examine. (See Chapter 4 for how to use bibliographic resources.)

Choosing Sources to Record

In selecting potential readings, you should skim the titles of bibliographic listings seeking those that seem related to your narrow topic. You need to look through all possibilities, not just the first few listings. If timeliness of your sources is a consideration, look at dates as well.

Using Index Cards or Not

There is no standard way of recording bibliographic information. Many people make out an index card for each potential source; others, particularly in this age of database print-outs, find putting a working bibliography on cards tedious. Your instructor should guide you in this regard.

There are reasons to use cards, even though it may seem that a page of notebook paper would do as well. When you have your working bibliography on cards, you can arrange them as you like. You can separate out the cards of sources that your library holds. You can put current periodicals, online-accessible periodicals, bound journals, and book sources in separate piles representing areas of the library you need to work in. You can leave behind the cards of sources you've already looked at. Finally, you can alphabetize the cards of sources you do use and read from them one at a time as you construct your Works Cited page.

If you use your own jotted lists, all you need is sufficient information to locate the source: author, title, and call number for a book; author, title, periodical name, date or volume (number) and year, and page range for a journal article. Then, when you do use a source, you should immediately fill out a bibliography card with the correct information.

Filling Out Bibliography Cards

On the cards, you should enter complete bibliographic information, plus any information necessary to find the source in your library (call number or location). You should put the information on the card in the format of the Works Cited style you are going to use in the paper. In both MLA and APA styles (see Chapter 13 for extended descriptions of these styles), Works Cited format includes the author's name, the title, and publication information. The format for periodicals is slightly different than that for books, and you should heed the difference so that you collect the correct information.

Here is what is needed for *books* in MLA format:

name(s) of author(s) (or editor of a compilation)
title and subtitle (if any), separated by a colon
indication of edition beyond the first, such as *3rd ed.*
name of translator or editor (if any), preceded by *Trans.* or *Ed.*
city or town of publication
publisher
year of publication
page numbers (add after note taking for sections read)

If the source is an *article within a book,* then you need to record the article's author and title (placed in quotation marks) before the author or editor of the book:

name(s) of author(s)
title of article or selection (in quotation marks)
editor of book plus the abbreviation *Ed.*
title of book and subtitle (if any), separated by a colon
indication of edition beyond the first
city or town of publication
publisher
year of publication
page range on which article appears

For *periodicals,* you need to record the following information:

Scholarly Journals	Magazines	Newspapers
author's name	author's name	author's name
article title (in quotation marks)	article title (in quotation marks)	article title (in quotation marks)
title of periodical (underlined)	title of periodical (underlined)	title of periodical (underlined)
volume number (and issue number, if needed)	date (day, month, year)	date (day, month, year)
	pages	edition (if there is more than one)
year		pages
pages		

For scholarly journals, volume number is sufficient if the journal is paged continuously. If each issue starts on page 1, then issue number is needed.

When you use the source, recheck the accuracy of the information on your bibliography card. Be sure all information is in the correct form:

- Name(s) of author(s) should be spelled correctly, with initials (if any). Authors should be listed in the same order as in the article or book.
- The title and subtitle should have a colon between them even if no colon appears in the article or book.
- The publisher's brief name should be used (without "Co.," "Inc.," or other tag).

MLA style is shown in Figures 12.1 and 12.2. APA reference style is quite different in arrangement from MLA, but it contains the same information (see Figures 12.3 and 12.4). However, in APA, authors' names are always listed with just last names and initials for the first and middle (if any) names: "Montcrier, D. F." not "Montcrier, Dolores Fried." This is true for editors and translators as well. For APA citations of periodicals, you need only volume and issue number, even for magazines, rather than date. For newspapers, as in MLA, take down the date. Exact details of the Works Cited format are provided in Chapter 13.

Using Electronic Databases as Your Bibliographic Resource

Information you discover through electronic databases, either online or installed, should be recorded on bibliography cards, just like information from print bibliographies.

Sometimes library electronic databases allow you to print out a list of sources, making it easy to avoid using cards. The only problem then is that you have to carry

> *Rapping, Elayne. The Looking Glass World of Nonfiction TV. Boston: Southend, 1987.*
>
>
> *PN*
> *1992.6*
> *R37*

FIGURE 12.1   Bibliography Card for Book, MLA Format

Keller, William W., and Louis W. Pauly.
   "Globalization at Bay." *Current History*
   Nov. 1997: 370+.

                              Current Periodicals

FIGURE 12.2   Bibliography Card for Magazine, MLA Format

Rapping, E. (1987). *The looking glass
world of nonfiction TV*. Boston: Southend.

                              PN
                              1992.6
                              R37

FIGURE 12.3   Bibliography Card for Book, APA Format

around a stack of papers with your annotations about what to look for, what you've found and used, and so on. So, many instructors will recommend that, even if you have a print-out, you should sort through and place promising titles on cards.

If an electronic bibliographic source allows you to save a list to your own disk, then you can later reformat source information on your computer, using margins and spacing to replicate the shape of 3 × 5 cards. You can then print, cut the paper to card size, and shuffle the paper cards in with your other 3 × 5 cards.

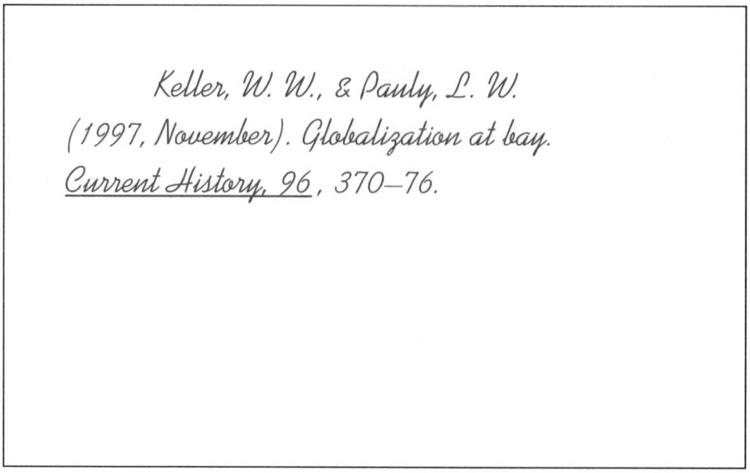

> *Keller, W. W., & Pauly, L. W.
> (1997, November). Globalization at bay.
> <u>Current History, 96</u>, 370–76.*

FIGURE 12.4 Bibliography Card for Magazine, APA Format

■ LOCATING SOURCES AND TAKING NOTES

On each bib card, you should note your attempt to locate the source—its location in your library or the reason for your failure to find it (not held in your library or not on the shelf). Revisit the stacks after a few days to see whether a book has been returned. Some libraries provide a print-out of checked-out or reassigned works, allowing you to locate a book that has been put on reserve or that is in a graduate student's carrel, a field-specific reading room, or another location. If there is no such list, you may still be able to find a book by doing a bit of legwork. A source frequently mentioned in your reading may be a standard one in the field, so you should check for it at the reserve desk and in any special reading rooms for the discipline.

If you can't locate a significant source in your library, you may want to request it through interlibrary loan. Or you may want to visit another college or a city library to use the book there—but call ahead first. If you are searching for a journal article that is unavailable in your library, you may be able to access it electronically. (See Chapter 4 for information about online periodical sources.)

Preparing to Take Notes

After you have completed your preliminary bibliography, you are ready to take notes. Sort through your bib cards in order to make your library work efficient. You might start by dividing the cards according to type and location of source: book sources (located in stacks); periodical sources in microfiche room; current periodicals; government documents; and so forth. If you are seeking several articles in the same journal—for example, three pieces that appeared in the *New York Times*—group those cards and do your research in the *Times* on one trip.

Once you've sorted your cards, you may still have some rather large piles. Go through and prioritize the sources. You might want to locate the serious journals and newspapers first, to give yourself an overview of the topic, and then move to the scholarly sources. Or you might want to look at the books first.

Taking Notes on Cards

The time-honored way of doing research is to use index cards. The researcher chooses chunks or bits of information in the source and enters them on cards, usually 4 × 6 cards, which have enough space for a complex idea but not so much that you can run on. The purpose of using cards is to liberate the information you collect from its context. Once information is on cards, you can place it with other information about the same idea or aspect of your topic. The note becomes a building block in the construction of your argument, rather than part of the flow of your source's ideas.

This defense of note cards is necessary because these days there are other ways of capturing information: photocopying and downloading. Both these options give you your own copy of a source to have at home. Admittedly, many academic researchers make lots of photocopies and print-outs. But many of them also take notes on cards from these copies. In this section on note taking, both the note-card system and some other options are discussed; your instructor will indicate which system is required in your course.

Format

Each note card has four pieces of information on it. There is a heading, consisting of two elements, and then the note plus the page number in the source. All these elements should be on the front of the card; avoid using the back because one purpose of cards is to "chunk" the information into small enough bits so that the contents can be seen at a glance. If your notes keep running over to the back, probably you are not chunking enough. If you must run over, it's probably best to take a second card, label it as continued from the first, and clip them together.

The *heading* should indicate the source from which you are taking the note. The *author's last name* is sufficient in most cases to identify a source because you have full bibliographic information on a 3 × 5 card. Because your bib card starts with the author's name, using the author's name as the note-card heading makes sense. Don't use a phrase from the title as your heading. Some instructors, particularly in the lower grades, teach you to number your bibliography cards and use the number on your note card. But numbers are easily confused, more so than names, and so an author's-name system works better if you have many sources. Also, using a name is appropriate to the academic discourse community, in which attribution of ideas and information to the author is necessary.

The second item in your card heading is a *key term* telling you what the note is about. Often, you'll take the note first, and then write the key term on the top line afterward. As you accumulate notes, the key terms for various aspects of your topic will start to become routine, and assigning key terms will become easier. It's important not to omit the key term because without it you have to read the card to tell what it is about.

In the outlining and writing stages of your paper, you will appreciate not having to read all your note cards each time you pick them up to determine what ideas they cover.

Angling Notes

Taking notes to develop an argument is different from taking notes on a chapter in a textbook. Your goal in that case is completeness. When you review those notes for the exam, you want them to include everything important in the text. But when taking notes on a narrowed topic, you have a specific agenda: to only record information that pertains to your topic. Your notes will thus be angled toward your preliminary claim or focusing question.

You don't want to waste time taking notes that you are not going to need. But you also don't want to have to backtrack to a source because you didn't take enough notes. Your background reading and preliminary outline should help you gauge what notes you need. Inevitably, however, you will have notes that don't make it into the final paper. And that is acceptable; there's no rule that says every note card must be represented in the final argument. If your instructor collects or checks note cards at the end of the paper project, he or she will expect you to have cards left over, perhaps 30 percent more than you use. That's just part of the process.

■ *Activity 3*

Selecting Angled Notes, p. 497

Types

The notes you take on your cards will be in the form of a summary, a paraphrase, a quotation, or a clearly marked mixture of these. Before writing on each card, you will need to decide which type of note to take, use utmost care in rephrasing and quoting, and mark your note cards appropriately.

When you look at your cards later, or your instructor does, the assumption will be that any words in quotation marks are accurate, exact quotes, and anything not in quotation marks is your own wording of a source idea. Your note taking should reflect these assumptions. Sometimes it is hard to remember to paraphrase fully, but doing so is important. Anyone turning to the source that you have paraphrased or summarized should not find the same words and phrases. If, in fact, key words and phrases or the sentence style have migrated into your text from the source, you will be charged with, at the least, sloppy research methods, and, at the worst, plagiarism.

Using Quotation, Summary, and Paraphrase

Quotations are a way of ensuring that you have got the source's ideas down correctly. You should choose to take down word-for-word what a source says in the following circumstances:

- The source's idea is complex or subtle.
- The source's idea or information is surprising, shocking, or new.
- The source presents information or ideas in an eloquent or memorable style.

Researchers sometimes take down introductory, thematic, and conclusion statements as quotations to make sure there is no mistake about what the writer means. Especially if the source makes complex or subtle points, you should use quotations so that you don't change the meaning in your paraphrase. And statements that are surprising, shocking, or highly emotional should be quoted, so that when you look over your notes later you don't wonder whether you somehow paraphrased the idea incorrectly.

When you quote from a source, you are borrowing the style of the writer as well as the ideas or information. Sometimes people choose to quote because the source says it so much better than they could.

Taking down a quotation gives you some flexibility when you are writing your paper. When you have a quotation on a note card, you can always summarize or paraphrase later. And doing so later may give you the time you need to write a truly representative paraphrase.

When you do use quotation, make sure you put quotation marks on the card, so that the note is instantly recognizable as a quotation when you look at it later. (See Chapter 3 for reminders about choosing and using quotations.) Figure 12.5 is a sample quotation note card.

Summary comes in handy when a source goes into too much detail or is too technical for your purposes. Summary also is appropriate when you are reading a source that, in the main, repeats information or ideas you have already encountered and recorded. You might just summarize the source on a card and indicate on the bottom that it corroborates an earlier source. You might summarize a whole article, a section of an article, or a few paragraphs. Figure 12.6 is a sample summary note card.

Paraphrase is appropriate when you wish to record information in some detail or when you want to represent an idea fully but don't need or want to quote. It allows you to collect material from chosen sections of a text. You might paraphrase a sentence, a paragraph, or a short section of a source. Figure 12.7 is a sample paraphrase note card.

Many times, researchers write *mixed* notes, in which they use both quotation and paraphrase or summary. If you are paraphrasing but run into a phrase or key term that

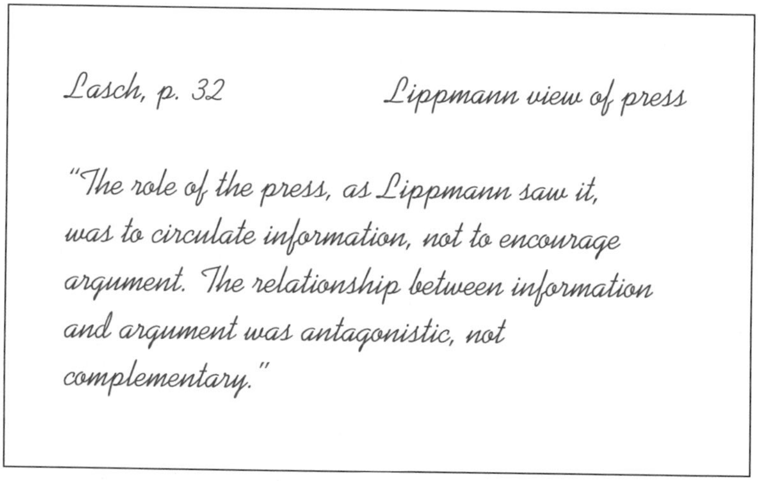

Lasch, p. 32 *Lippmann view of press*

"The role of the press, as Lippmann saw it, was to circulate information, not to encourage argument. The relationship between information and argument was antagonistic, not complementary."

FIGURE 12.5 Quotation Note

Lasch, p. 32 *Professionalism in Journalism*

Walter Lippmann laid groundwork for this, based on concept of objective reporting. The public, he felt, wasn't sophisticated enough to participate in debate on issues, and should be given information instead. Information would reveal the best course of action so debate wouldn't be needed.

FIGURE 12.6 Summary Note

Lasch, p. 32 *Professionalism in Politics*

During Progressive era the philosophy was to run government smoothly and efficiently, with experts making decisions instead of the public. This during time of T. Roosevelt, Woodrow Wilson, William Jennings Bryan.

FIGURE 12.7 Paraphrase Note

resists rewording, you might just take it down word for word, being careful to put quotation marks where they belong. Figure 12.8 is a sample mixed note card.

Sentence Notes, Jotted Notes, and List Notes

The sample notes in Figures 12.5 through 12.8 are all in full-sentence format, but you may find it convenient to break away from correct sentences in your note taking. In fact, note taking is a fragment writer's heaven. Researchers often jot down phrases and clauses instead of full sentences, and there is nothing wrong with this, as long as you continue to be careful about paraphrasing correctly and dropping quotation marks

Lasch, p. 32   *Advertising and Objectivity*

Objectivity or "a responsible press, as opposed to a partisan or opinionated one" drew broad-minded readers best. "Avoidance of controversy" became the rule in the responsible press.

FIGURE 12.8   Mixed Note

around any exact wording. If your paraphrases and summaries are not in full sentences, you'll have to do some rewriting when placing such notes in your final paper, but frankly, notes don't usually fit right in without rewriting anyway. Figure 12.9 is a sample jotted note card.

Listing can also be a quick note-taking method. Especially if you are dealing with numerical data, using a list can be appropriate. Be careful not to add anything that is not in the source, such as enumeration. If your source does number the items in your list, indicate this on your note card. Figure 12.10 is a sample of a paraphrased list.

Lasch, p. 32   *Advertising and Objectivity*

Objectivity = "responsible press, as opposed to a partisan or opinionated one"
— Drew broad-minded readers best
— "Avoidance of controversy" same as responsibility

FIGURE 12.9   The Mixed Note in Jotted Form

Lasch, p. 32   *Information as Fraud*

Lasch's idea:
Information disconnected from debate is
—— not relevant
—— slanted
—— derived from promotion efforts
    for sales/polit. races/ social issues
It sells w/o any real debate

FIGURE 12.10   Paraphrased List Note

Notes of Your Own Ideas and Comments

Note taking is both an external process of filling up cards and an internal process of increasing your understanding and knowledge about your topic. As you learn more, you will start to have your own ideas and form your own judgments about your topic. It's a good idea to take down these fleeting ideas on note cards. If you add a comment of your own to a note card, make certain you indicate the comment is yours, not the source's. The standard way of indicating that an idea comes from the self is to use square brackets around it: [ ]. Even then, you should also circle or box your comment and write "me" or "mine" next to it so later you know it's your idea. And you can devote whole cards to your own ideas or questions. Figure 12.11 is a sample comment note card.

■ *Activity 4*

Taking Notes, p. 497

About Lasch & news "information" today

Me → There's no proof in his article for idea that
a lot of news today comes from press releases
& official agencies and is reprinted mindlessly
(paragr. 19)—Can I find some backing on this
point?

FIGURE 12.11   Comment Note

The Process of Note Taking

At the Start

Note taking can be tedious, and we want to get it over with. The temptation is to turn to the article or chapter and plunge directly into taking notes. It's best, however, to pause a minute and scan the source quickly to evaluate it. (See Chapter 11 for information on evaluating sources.)

If you are not familiar with a periodical, you should try to get a sense of its type, purpose, and partisanship, if any. Skim through an article or chapter to ascertain its overall contents and point of view. You might even want to write a note giving your evaluation of the source or indicating any notable features of it that strike you.

Before you begin, mentally identify the sections of the source from which you want to take notes. Then, get out a pile of blank cards and start your jotting and paraphrasing.

Midway through Your Research

Pause and sort your cards. Pile them up and read each pile. Ask yourself how what you have learned thus far affects your preliminary claim or answers your focusing question. Does your claim hold up? Under the pressure of evidence, do you need to modify it? Has your research modified your question? Are you ready to convert your question to a claim? Are you finding too much research? Is it possible your topic still needs narrowing, and your claim or question needs refocusing?

Don't wait until the end of your research to take stock because then there may not be enough time to change your focus if necessary. Here are some situations that might require revising your claim or refocusing your question:

- An overabundance of research indicating your topic is not limited enough. You need to zoom in and follow a narrower avenue of research.
- Sources immersed in a debate about values when you'd rather work on an evidence-oriented issue. For example, you might find the research you've done on euthanasia heavily philosophical. Within it, however, you might be attracted to a stream of psychological research into the state of mind of terminally ill patients. Now is the time to narrow your focus to a claim about the effect of psychological counseling and the use of medications on terminally ill patients' attitude toward dying.
- An overly technical trend in the research, leaving you feeling swamped by jargon and data charts as well as bored and confused. Your topic may have been too narrow, and you may need to broaden it. For example, an inquiry into whether elderly and terminally ill patients should be given psychometric drug treatment to lift their moods might take you into a pharmacological nightmare. You might do well to broaden your topic to include the effectiveness of all psychological treatment of near-death patients.

Change or modify your topic now, before you are totally entrenched in a stream of research that will commit you to writing a shallow paper on a huge subject or to making judgments about issues too sophisticated for your level of knowledge. If you do dramatically shift, narrow, or enlarge your claim at the midpoint of your research, do tell your instructor so there's no big surprise on the day the paper is due.

Approaching the End of Your Research

Take stock again. Check on how your claim is holding up. Ask yourself what additional research needs to be done. What holes or gaps are there in the evidence?

Photocopying and Downloading

Photocopies are a fact of life, and many, if not most, researchers use them. As French philosopher Michel Foucault is reported to have said of copying, "It's so

---

■ *Writing a Progress Report*

Progress reports are not usually required in the academic discourse community but are common in professional settings, both for projects and for research. Their purpose is to let an overseer know of the forward movement—or lack thereof—toward a predetermined goal. In professional settings, a progress report often emphasizes whether the project is on time and on budget. A progress report for an assigned academic research paper is usually focused on your research accomplishments. If you write the progress report midway or most of the way through the period of time allotted for research, it might include the following:

- A summary of the research accomplished
    major sources read
    aspects of the topic that have been researched
    whether relevant differing views have been researched

- A summary of major findings (should be brief so as to not distract from the focus on progress)
- A brief discussion of problems or areas of uncertainty
- An indication of any changes in direction of your research
- A statement of revisions to your claim or question, plus a rationale for the change
- An indication of what research remains to be done
    sources or type of sources that need to be obtained
    issues or subtopics that remain to be studied

A progress report written later in the process might include organization plans, whether an approach to opposing positions has been determined, and so on.

tempting . . . so easy. . . . But it takes away the need to really read. . . . And above all it destroys the charm of the text, which becomes almost lifeless when you no longer have the printed page before your eyes and in your hands" (qtd. in Macy 455). All too often, researchers carry home packs of unread copies, texts that, as Foucault realized, become "almost lifeless," a blur of verbiage on page after page of identical copy paper.

The positive side is that owning a copy of major or important sources gives you security: if you are in doubt about a paraphrase or a transcribed quote, you can check the original. So, these days, researchers carry not only cards and pens to the library but also loose change or dollar bills. You should also have a pocketful of paper clips or a ministapler so your photocopies don't turn into a disheveled heap of paper lettuce.

Take Notes Even When Photocopying

Why take notes if you can own a copy of the source? There are many reasons. You truly read the text when you take notes; you assimilate ideas and information more thoroughly. Also, you do the work of paraphrasing and summarizing along the way, rather than as you are writing your paper. And notes "liberate" the source's ideas from their context, so they can be moved more easily into your own structure of argument. Later, in the organizing stage, you can physically lay out your paper by piling related cards together. So the recommendation from most instructors is to take notes on cards whether you have a copy of the source or not.

Annotating Photocopies Instead of Taking Notes

If you do decide to work with the photocopy alone, here are some guidelines:

- Skim each source in the library. Evaluate its usefulness to you in terms of content, type, and editorial perspective. Don't copy everything in sight. Be selective; save your quarters for material that you can really use, material that sheds light on your inquiry.
- Read and absorb the contents of each photocopy within a day. Not reading your sources subverts one of the important processes you must undergo to write a successfully researched argument: the mental process of learning in-depth, enlarging your view of your topic, and working through all the possible opinions. In addition, you won't know where you stand in your research process. When you do finally read your material, you may realize you do not have as much usable research as you thought. Or you may learn of additional important sources or a related line of inquiry but not have enough time left to explore them.
- Mark each photocopy with identifying information—the author's name at the minimum—right away. Make sure you have all bibliographic information accurately written on your bibliography card. Many researchers put all bibliographic information on the photocopy as well because it may go into their files for future reference.

- If the article is an important source, number the paragraphs in the margin. This way, as you construct your outline, you will be able to refer easily and accurately to specific parts of your copied article.
- Annotate the article to highlight the portions that pertain to your argument. Bracket, highlight, or circle important paragraphs, and write a key term in the margin; this key term should be the one you would use at the top of your note card were you going to write one. Then make margin notes that convey your analysis of the article. Write in questions and comments. If you spot a well-said point, you might put giant quotation marks around it or "Q" in the margin to indicate a pithy quotation for your final paper. Put "?" next to any points you find debatable, and so on. If you have a lot of comments, you might want to put them on stick-on notes or on cards keyed to the article.

Downloading articles presents other issues. If you print out, you should treat your downloaded version as any other copy and proceed as recommended above. But many researchers don't print out. They keep their research in the computer. This is handy for inserting quotations because you can just copy and paste them from your downloaded document to your paper in progress. But this ease can also lead to problems, and has, for professionals as well as for students.

Ruth Shalit, a young writer for the magazine *New Republic,* was found to have plagiarized. After unacknowledged, word-for-word material from another writer was discovered in one of her articles, close investigation of her other writing revealed two other instances of plagiarism. Here's her explanation of how this happened, told to an interviewer from *American Journalism Review:* "The mistake came from having somebody else's words on my screen. From downloading Nexis searches as text files and then putting them onto my screen and later conflating them with my own notes. That is always a bad idea. I'm printing out all of my Nexis searches so somebody else's words are not up on my computer screen and I'm not toggling back and forth" (Shepard 36).

So be warned. If a professional journalist has trouble managing text stored electronically, you should be extra careful. Print out, mark up, write paraphrases and summaries carefully, and copy and paste from other writers' documents to your own with extreme care.

Activities

1 Evaluating Research-Paper Topics

Examine the topics below. Determine which would make acceptable topics for an argumentative research paper and which would not. Are there modifications you could make to those that would not be acceptable to make them workable?

Cameras in courtrooms
Paraparazzi chasing celebrities
Destructive influence of computers on family life

No-fault divorce
Nutritional value of organically grown foods
Life on other planets
Privacy invasion by the press
Viability of NASA
Lost continent of Atlantis
Kennedy-family marital problems
Disney cartoons as art

2   Evaluating Preliminary Claims and Focusing Questions

Examine the following preliminary claims and focusing questions to determine, first, what type of claim is involved and, then, whether the claim would be workable or helpful in guiding your research.

1. Nonnative plants and animals present a long-term danger to our environment.
2. Details of our past lives are accessible to us if only we learn the necessary techniques.
3. Is it a good or bad thing that voters now are told every detail of candidates' and officials' private lives and personal failings?
4. Do "Just Say No" campaigns help young people resist drugs and alcohol?
5. Spiritual channeling is a mysterious but valid way to learn about the past and the future.
6. What dangers are there for children who are allowed to see R-rated movies?
7. People should live with the physical appearance they are born with instead of using plastic surgery to affect their looks.
8. Howard Stern is a hero of the younger generation because of his frankness about race, sex, and other touchy issues.
9. The fad for designer-logo clothing is a decadent sign of consumerism.
10. Despite all the publicity about it over the years, date rape is still a serious problem on campuses and among young working people.
11. Do food stamps improve the nutrition of poor people, especially poor children?
12. Gun education should be mandatory for young people so that gun ownership can remain legal and become safer.

3   Selecting Angled Notes

Assume you are working on a paper on the topic "causes of criminal activity by youths." Read the essay "Education to Learn and Not for Money" by R. Richard Banks (at the end of Chapter 7), and identify by paragraph number the places where you would take notes.

4   Taking Notes

A. Assume you are working on a paper on the topic "youth gang activity" and that your preliminary claim is "youths join gangs out of boredom and in response to peer pressure." Read "Turning Youth Gangs Around" by Luis Rodriguez (at the end of Chapter 6) and take relevant notes on 4 × 6 cards. Make sure you take notes that will help you to probe your topic and develop or refine your preliminary claim. Your notes should make use of summary, paraphrase, and quotation, and include some mixed and jotted notes. Bring your cards to class so you can compare your notes with those of others.

B. For the same paper, take relevant notes from Banks's "Education to Learn and Not for Money" (at the end of Chapter 7). Take notes in a variety of formats, as above, and bring your cards to class for comparison with those of other class members.

■ **WORKS CITED**

Macy, David. *The Lives of Michel Foucault.* New York: Random, 1993.
Shepard, Alicia C. "Interview with Ruth Shalit." *American Journalism Review* (Dec. 1995):34+.

Chapter 13

Writing the Research Paper

On one level, the research process is a series of tasks you perform in a certain basic order, and, indeed, there is a lot of sheer work that must be organized and completed satisfactorily for a research paper to get written. But the research process that matters is the one that happens in your head. You begin with some knowledge and ideas about your topic. You make them public as you brainstorm and consult with others. Your original concept begins to shift and enlarge as you encounter new ideas and information in print sources. You are forced to rework your assumptions, rephrase your main ideas, and maybe even modify or change your point of view. This happens all the while you are taking notes. The inner process is the one that matters, the process that makes writing the research paper possible.

■ PREPARING TO WRITE

Before you pick up your several pounds' worth of inky index cards or scribbled-on printouts and start to transform them into some semblance of a ten-page paper, you should pause and devote some time to conscious planning.

Refocusing Your Preliminary Claim or Answering Your Research Question

Throughout your preliminary research and your note taking, your preliminary claim or inquiry question has been hanging about in your mind. Halfway through your research, you paused to evaluate it. If you have been working with a preliminary claim, it may have become more specific, deepened, shifted, or even reversed itself. For example, a student seeking to support the right of private military colleges to exclude women decided after completing his research that such schools should gradually go co-ed. Sometimes, students feel less sure of of their claim at the end of their research. You may discover that the more you learn, the more complexity you see. With your instructor's permission, you might choose to present a middle view or write a paper that reveals unresolved issues. One student who examined the evidence for marijuana as a gateway drug decided that so many factors intervene in hard-core drug addiction that no easy statement could be made about marijuana's role.

If you started with a research question, you have probably narrowed it and have considered various answers. A working claim may have formed in your mind during your note taking. For example, a student who began with the question "Are nuclear power plants a safe way of producing electricity?" concluded, "Mishaps and accidents at nuclear power plants have caused inconvenience, injury, and death to workers and citizens, indicating that this form of power is too dangerous and should be phased out."

So, at the end of your research, you may be sure of your direction. If so, you are ready for the next stage. If not, read through your cards, and begin to group them in some sensible way, perhaps according to viewpoints or subtopics. Once they are organized, ask yourself some questions: Is there a segment of the argument on which you could focus in depth? Is there a subissue on which you have collected a lot of information and that has emerged as a focused line of inquiry in its own right? Rather than argue a position on the broad issue of euthanasia, for example, can you move toward a position on some narrower aspect, such as laws on assisted suicide? Focus on one aspect that has inspired a strong conviction in you. Make sure you write down your focused claim for reference, rather than just keeping it in your head.

Planning Your Approach or Strategy

Once you have settled on a final claim, you need to choose an overall strategy for your paper. Chapters 7 and 8 discussed possible strategies for developing arguments about controversial topics. You might use standard or classical argumentation format—that is, a direct presentation of evidence plus a refutation of contrary positions. Or, with your instructor's permission, you might emphasize the middle ground or write an inquiry-focused paper that stresses the complexity of and ongoing questions within an issue. Consider the roles that definition, comparison, cause-effect, and other analytic modes might have in your development of your ideas. Think about what an emphatic organization of your points would look like. The more aware you are of the strategies you are using, the better you are able to employ them.

Organizing Your Material

Sort through your piles of cards or your annotated photocopies, this time seeking the reasons and evidence you need to support your assertion. You will probably create "subpiles" of evidence, plus piles for different views or contrary evidence to be confronted in your paper's refutation section.

Then you can make an ordered list of the cards' key terms to provide a rough outline. Sometimes, if you have a lot of cards, arranging them in order on a large surface can help you visualize your paper's structure. Whichever way you choose, you will probably have some cards left over; some material will just not fit in.

If you are working with photocopies or printouts of downloaded material, you should make out a card or slip for each bit of research you want to use. The cards may include the full paraphrase, summary, or quotation or just a note to yourself indicating the needed paragraph or section of each source. Some researchers cut up the photocopies and tape the bits they want to use on cards. Cards or slips representing material in copied sources can be sorted and piled with the rest of your notes.

The overall structure for any document in our discourse community consists of three parts: introduction, middle, and conclusion. When you plan your paper, the middle—the development of your argument—is of major concern. Often, writers begin with the middle—they jump directly into plotting out their argument, realizing it is difficult to plan an introduction to something (the argument) that does not yet exist. Sometimes, however, during research you may discover a powerful quotation or a definitive statement of the opposing view that can serve as a strong entrée for your paper.

Writing an Outline

Following your physical layout of cards, write the working outline. Your outline is your map of where you are going to go and when, to be used as you pour out your rough draft. This outline should be detailed enough to specify which piece or bit of evidence goes where, but it will most likely be informal—that is, it will probably use indentation to indicate levels of discussion, rather than numbers and letters. Here is a process to use to create your working outline. (For a discussion of outlining, see Chapter 2.)

Begin by writing your claim at the top of your page. Pull out the preliminary outline you sketched for yourself midway through your research. Perhaps some parts of it will work in your finished argument.

It's a good idea to write the general level of an outline first. Construct the whole main-point level of the paper before going back through to indicate subpoints. This is helpful to you psychologically as well because on your first cycle of outlining you will have plotted the whole paper in general terms.

Then go back through and note explanations, definitions, and other discussion necessary to develop each main point. Specify which item from your notes goes where by referring to the author's last name and page number, or by numbering or coding your note cards (or photocopy annotations). Continue this way for each main assertion.

You may also use mapping to generate a plan for your paper. Write your claim in the center of the page, and use lines and bubbles to indicate the segments of your argument. Or you may devise your own visual guide to the paper you are writing. It may be a branching tree or a chart of some kind. Be sure your outline or map is as detailed as necessary for you to keep on track when you start to write.

Look back over your outline or map to make sure you have identified where every significant piece of information will go in your argument. Then overview the development to note your use of definition, cause-effect, comparison, refutation, and so forth. Such awareness of your strategies can help you keep on track as you develop your argument.

Quite often, writers deviate from the outline as they draft the paper. This may happen to you. The nature of the writing process forces you to think deeply about your topic, causing you to shift and realign your ideas somewhat. Hence, if you are required to submit a **formal outline,** you should probably complete it after you write the paper, so that you have finalized where each point goes.

Organizing the Sample Student Research Paper

Scott Heste's paper on whether the Public Broadcasting System (PBS) should continue to be funded by the federal government appears later in this chapter. In researching this topic, Scott quickly realized that much of his paper would consist of criticisms that have been made of PBS and his evaluation or response to these criticisms. Also during his research he became convinced that PBS made an important contribution to Americans' lives. This would be his thesis.

When he was through researching, his organization plan was almost completed. He had made some notes along the way about the points he would make and in what order. In the main part of his paper, he would first deal with criticisms about the content of PBS—that it was elitist, liberal, pornographic, obsolete—by refuting them. Then he would cover the main area of criticism, the issue of cost and taxpayer funding, and evaluate the reforms that have been suggested. This organization would follow the emphatic organization principle—that the most important issue would be discussed last. Within this organization, Scott would refute each point as he discussed it, using point-by-point refutation.

His general plan of the body of his paper looked like this:

Criticisms of PBS and refutations
    Criticism of content 1 + refutation
    Criticism of content 2 + refutation
    Criticism of content 3 + refutation
    etc. to the most important
    Criticism of cost + refutation
Suggested reforms
    Suggested reform 1 + evaluation
    Suggested reform 2 + evaluation
    Suggested reform 3 (most important) + evaluation

He looked at his lists of criticisms and reforms and numbered them in order of importance.

Once he had planned the main organization of the paper, Scott turned to his introduction. He realized that in addition to focusing on the problem and presenting his thesis that PBS should survive, he needed to provide some background. The origins of PBS and, in particular, the unique purposes it was designed to serve needed to be explained, he felt, because his defense showed how well PBS fulfilled its original goals. A section of background information would follow the introduction, he decided.

Scott also wanted to present the positive case for PBS by explaining how valuable it was to various groups of people: adults, children, and local stations. This material could follow his discussion of criticisms, or it could come first. Scott decided to put a section about the value of PBS early in the paper, between the background section and the discussion and refutation of criticisms. This placement, he felt, would give the reader a strong positive view before reading about the negatives suggested by critics. His broad plan now looked like this:

Introduction
Background
Value of PBS
Criticisms and refutations
Suggested reforms

Then he decided his wrap-up would restate the value of the public network, and he added "Conclusion" at the bottom of his general outline.

■ WRITING THE ROUGH DRAFT

Write your draft with your outline spread out nearby and your notes and annotations handy. If you used a computer to generate your outline, you should print the outline to use as a reference next to you as you write.

Writing a document as complex as a research paper takes time and energy. Block out a few hours for yourself in a place where you know you will not be interrupted or tempted to distract yourself. If you write by hand, this may be in the library; if you need a computer, you may prefer to go to a computer lab on campus to get away from the distractions of your dorm or apartment.

There is no set way to produce a long document. Some people prefer to write in sections, completing each one fully with all paraphrases and quotations included before going on to the next. Others blitz through the entire text, writing quickly and roughly, using numbered or coded references indicating where evidence, quotations, and other references are to go. Such writers must then cycle back over each section, working in source material and improving the clarity and flow. They must also make sure that nothing has been omitted.

Writing on a Computer

If you are word processing, you can write with your outline on-screen; if you choose to do this, work from a copy of your outline and not from the original file. One technique is to use a split screen to put your outline at the top and the text you are generating at the bottom. In some programs, this means writing the draft in the same file as the outline, and displaying different parts of the same file in the two halves of the screen.

Or you may want to write the draft within a copy of the outline itself. Start with a copy of the outline on your screen, double-spaced, and begin writing. The development of each point should be generated right under that point in the outline. At the end of this process, you have a paper that has the outline interspersed with your writing, and you need to go back and delete the outline fragments.

If you downloaded your research, then you already have in your computer any quotations you wish to use. You may open the relevant file and use "copy" and "paste" to move a quotation between the source and your paper. Make sure that you clearly mark the insert as a quotation so that you don't inadvertently treat the material as your own writing.

Special Issues in Writing Research Papers

Balancing Your Writing and Source Inclusions

You should think of the research paper as your argument for a point of view, not as a display of your research. Material from sources (paraphrased, summarized, or quoted) should be included when relevant, and not otherwise. Your paper should develop your ideas, with source material used as aids in the creation of your argument. You might think of your paper as a building you are constructing from your blueprints and with your beams, nails, and plaster. Your sources come into play as bricks mixed in with your own in the building's final stage.

Transitions

Effective handling of transitions is especially important in a research paper. You must carefully guide your reader from point to point, from main points to evidence, and from your writing to paraphrased, summarized, or quoted sources and back again. In particular, you must make sure your reader understands the relevance of the sources you include.

The first step in an effective transition to the use of a source is to provide a proper **attribution.** (See Chapter 3 for suggestions for writing attributions.) Remember that a lead-in attribution is especially crucial when you are dealing with paraphrases and summaries because there are no formal markers—no quotation marks—to signal that a passage is a paraphrase or summary and not your own ideas.

In addition to giving an attribution, you should also provide **context** for the quotation, paraphrase, or summary. The material from the source should not just be dropped into your paper. Instead, you should interpret the material, letting your readers know what point you wish them to take from the source. You might want to indicate your agreement with the source, point out its reinforcement or support of your idea, or emphasize one element of it.

In incorporating sources, you should be especially careful to avoid the "patchwork" effect. This occurs when quotation follows quotation without any discussion or explanation of the ideas. The paper then seems to be, not your best thinking on the topic, but a patched-together quilt of sources.

Here are a few paragraphs from a patchwork-style research paper:

In *Texas* v. *Johnson*, Supreme Court Justice Rehnquist stated, "Flag burning is the equivalent of an inarticulate grunt or roar, that, it seems fair to say, is most likely to be indulged in not to express a particular idea, but to antagonize others" (190).

An opposing view is expressed by James J. Kilpatrick of the *Washington Post:* "We will probably see more flag burnings, but they will pass, and if the press will ignore such odious demonstrations, their point will be lost. Meanwhile, our most cherished idea—the ideal of freedom—will be maintained" (57–58).

William P. Barr, Assistant Attorney General, stated that "society has a legitimate interest in the flag as a symbol. The flag inspires emotional attachment to the values for which it stands. The flag rallies the spirit of this nation. If we permit the desecration of this unique symbol, these important societal interests will be injured" (231).

Can you tell which position on flag burning seems most valid to the writer of this paper? The patchwork treatment of sources here prevents any interpretation from coming through. Here is a revision of the passage with interpretative transitions inserted (in italics):

Some experts believe that flag burning is not really "speech," but a trivial utterance, and hence not worth discussing in relation to the right of free speech. In *Texas* v. *Johnson,* Supreme Court Justice Rehnquist stated, "Flag burning is the equivalent of an inarticulate grunt or roar, that, it seems fair to say, is most likely to be indulged in not to express a particular idea, but to antagonize others" (190).

Others find flag burning a repulsive trend, but one that will fade and that therefore does not require criminalization by legislation or a constitutional amendment. For example, James J. Kilpatrick of the *Washington Post* writes, "We will probably see more flag burnings, but they will pass, and if the press will ignore such odious demonstrations, their point will be lost. Meanwhile, our most cherished idea—the ideal of freedom—will be maintained" (57–58). *In this view, freedom of speech, even when the speech is "odious," is a higher value than protecting the flag.*

However, the Assistant Attorney General under George Bush has pointed out that the flag of the United States is not just any piece of cloth. Destroying it can represent the destruction of, or at least extreme disrespect to, all the freedoms it represents. As William P. Barr puts it, "Society has a legitimate interest in the flag as a symbol. The flag inspires emotional attachment to the values for which it stands. The flag rallies the spirit of this nation. If we permit the desecration of this unique symbol, these important societal interests will be injured" (231).

When there is context for these quotations, a reader can see that the writer is using the quotations to build toward a position.

■ *Activity 1*

Providing Context for Quotations, p. 542

Style

Research papers are typically written an objective style—that is, in the third person and with a neutral tone. The writer still advocates for a point of view, but in a tone that conveys fairness. For your own credibility as a writer, you need to use your control of tone and style to engender your reader's trust. (See Chapter 10 for discussion of credibility and style.)

Your instructor may permit or even require that you break away from an objective style to include personal experiences, primary-research results, or a personal perspective on the issue. But most instructors will expect you to stick to the objective style.

■ *Activity 2*

Identifying and
Correcting Tone
Problems in Research
Papers, p. 543

Academic Honesty

In learning summary, paraphrase, and quotation skills, you were advised to take care not to confuse source wording with your own because keeping the boundaries of texts clear is crucial to our system of borrowing from sources and giving credit. Whether intentional or not, errors in paraphrase, attribution, or citation are regarded as **plagiarism**, albeit inadvertent plagiarism.

Students seem to have the most problems with accurate and responsible use of sources in research papers. Perhaps this is a result of the sheer size of the research project; it's easy to slip up when one is managing ten or twenty sources instead of three or four. (Also, unfortunately, the research-paper assignment is a standard one in college, more standard than many of the other assignments in this course. As a result, prewritten papers exist, tempting the harried student to take a dishonest shortcut: buying or borrowing someone else's paper.)

To avoid plagiarizing, the following types of information must be documented:

Exact quotations. Material imported from a source must be documented, and the quotation must be exact.

Paraphrases of source ideas or information that is not "common knowledge." Information such as important dates, historical and geographical facts, generally accepted evaluations, well-known quotations, and so forth need not be documented. These include such statements as:

> On July 4th, 1776, the Declaration of Independence was read in the courtyard at Fifth and Market Streets in Philadelphia.
>
> Shakespeare is the greatest English dramatist.
>
> Patrick Henry said, "Give me liberty or give me death!"

Once you are involved in an academic discipline, you may find that some facts, events, and statements do not require documentation because they are common knowledge in the field. All other information and ideas that are not your own must be documented.

Statistics, numerical data, graphs, and so on. There is usually no way to paraphrase a statistic or other quantitative data. Nevertheless, you do not need to put quotations around statistics unless they are embedded in phrasing borrowed from a source. Such borrowed data do, however, require documentation:

STUDENT SENTENCE

By 1990, one to one and a half million Americans had fallen victim to HIV infection, and from 250,000 to 750,000 people would acquire AIDS over the next ten years even if a cure had been found in 1990 (Roach and Fraser 348).

SOURCE SENTENCE

Between 1 and 1.5 million Americans are now carrying the AIDS virus; therefore, if the spread of the virus stopped today, it is estimated that 250,000 to 750,000 would still be struck with the full-blown disease within ten years.

—Patricia Roach and Winifred Fraser, "Teaching about AIDS"

All the following are considered plagiarism:

1. Failing to replace key words and phrases in a paraphrase of a source, even when the source is cited.
2. Failing to use your own style—that is, sentence type, word choice, tone, and overall organization—in a paraphrase of a source, even when the source is cited.
3. Including exact wording from a source in your paper, either carelessly or deliberately, without quotation, even when the source is cited.
4. Representing someone else's work as your own—handing in as yours a paper authored by someone else. Submitting borrowed, purchased, or downloaded papers is the height of dishonesty. It is also dishonest to purchase or download "research material" when the paper you hand in is supposed to be based on your own research in secondary sources. All these replacements for your own academic work violate the accepted code of honor in the academic discourse community.

■ *Activity 3*
For Discussion: A Case of Plagiarism, p. 543

■ *Activity 4*
Identifying and Correcting Plagiarism, p. 544

■ *Activity 5*
Identifying Style Differences Due to Plagiarism, p. 545

■ *Activity 6*
Faulty Use of Sources, p. 545

■ DOCUMENTING YOUR SOURCES

In formal research papers, documentation is required. Throughout this book, formal documentation has been supplied for quotations and paraphrases appearing in the chapters' discussion. The documentation style used here is the Modern Language Association (MLA) research-paper format. If you've been noticing this documentation, you may have already gleaned some idea of how it works. (APA style will be explained later in this chapter.)

MLA research-paper style makes use of parenthetic documentation rather than footnotes. This change, put into effect in 1984, streamlines documentation for both the writer and reader of research papers. After each quotation, paraphrase, or summary, brief information keyed to the Works Cited page (the list of sources used in the paper) appears in parentheses. Research-paper documentation thus consists of two pieces: the parenthetic note and the Works Cited page.

Steps in Adding Documentation to a Paper

If you can, draft your Works Cited page before you begin writing your paper. Then, whenever you are going to refer to a source, you can put in the correct parenthetic reference for it. Because the writing process itself causes shifts in thinking and development, a draft Works Cited page is only provisional. You should go over it carefully at the end of the writing process to make sure you have not omitted sources or included extra ones.

If you are word processing, you also have the option of writing the Works Cited entry right in the text after you make your reference to the source. Then, at the end, you comb through the draft and cut-and-paste the citations to the Works Cited page. Or you may use a split screen to write the Works Cited entry for each source you refer to as you write the paper.

Some people find it easier to generate the Works Cited page after the first full draft. Your references in the draft must be clear and accurate so that you can draw up a correct Works Cited page.

In completing the documentation for your paper, all the busywork of accurately filling out bibliography cards will now show its worth. You can type up your list from the cards. While doing this, refer to the proper format for each type of source in the list below.

In the revision stage, carefully match parenthetic references to your Works Cited list to make sure both are accurate.

Other Types of Notes: Footnotes or Endnotes

Because MLA documentation of research papers is now accomplished parenthetically, footnotes and endnotes have an entirely different use: to provide information or explanations that would be digressive if placed in the main body of the paper. This specialized information or explanation may be about a point you are making or about a source. For example, you can use such a note to discuss some complications of the issue or to provide additional evidence. Or you may indicate that other sources agree with your point or discuss them. You can also provide your readers with bibliographic information for further investigation of a point.

■ PARENTHETIC NOTES IN MLA FORMAT

The basic parenthetic note form consists of:

opening parenthesis
the author's last name
the page number(s) for the quotation, paraphrase, or summary
closing parenthesis
numbers stand alone, with no punctuation or abbreviation for "page"

This format is logical: knowing the author's last name, you can find full information about the source on the Works Cited page, which is alphabetized according to the authors' last names. Given the page number, you can turn to the source and locate the passage referred to in the research paper.

Here is a typical parenthetic note and the listing on the Works Cited page that it refers to:

> One writer about consciousness puts it this way, "We have a memory of a memory" (Sarup 38).

> Sarup, Madan. *Identity, Culture and the Postmodern World*. Athens: U of
> Georgia P, 1996.

Exceptions to this form are many. In some circumstances you use less information than in the typical note, and in many circumstances you need to supply more than in the typical note.

Parenthetic Note without Author's Name

If you refer to the source's name in your lead-in to the borrowed material, you should not put it in the parenthetic note. All that is required is the page number:

> Madan Sarup puts it this way, "We have a memory of a memory" (38).

Parenthetic Note with Organizational Author or No Author

If your source is generated by an organization or corporation, its Works Cited entry will use that entity as its first item instead of an author. If there is no author for the source, then the Works Cited entry will begin with the title. The parenthetic note for both these entries will contain the item that is presented first in the Works Cited entry.

If the author is an organization, use the entire entity in the parenthetic note:

> Many in the neighborhoods were disturbed by how few of their
> recommendations were included in city policy (Coalition on Graffiti 3).

Or you may write the name of the entity into your text:

> Many in the neighborhoods were disturbed by how few of the
> recommendations spelled out in the Coalition on Graffiti report were included
> in city policy (3).

> Coalition on Graffiti. *Recommendations for a Policy for Apprehending and
> Treating "Writers."* New York: Broadside, 1989.

If there is no author, you should use the title as the identifying entity in the parenthetic note. It is acceptable to shorten the title to the first one or two meaningful words if it is lengthy.

> The meeting between the mayor and the parade representatives failed to occur ("Parade Meeting" B2).

> "Parade Meeting Called Off; Rancor Takes Over." *Akron Beacon Journal* 23 Oct. 1995: B 2+.

> Some feel that world peace would be promoted if NATO were dissolved, but instead the U.S. pushes for its expansion ("NATO").

> "NATO Rearms the World." Editorial. *In These Times* 28 July 1997: 2.

Parenthetic Note without Page Number

If your source is unpaged or if it is fully contained on one page, then you do not need the page number in the parenthetic note. The Works Cited page will list the one page. Many newspaper or magazine articles appear on one page. Also, page numbers are irrelevant for downloaded documents and nonprint sources such as television broadcasts.

> Illegal in thirty-nine states, hazing still causes injury and death to naive students who will do anything, apparently, to belong ("Greek").

> "Greek Tragedies." *US News and World Report* 29 Apr. 1996: 26. Online. CompuServe. Ref. #A18227147; file name greek02.txt. 26 July 1997.

Quotation, Summary, or Paraphrase with No Parenthetic Citation

If you use an in-text attribution for a source that is on one page or has no pagination, then you do not need a parenthetic note at all.

> Robert Waddell describes research showing that drinking excessively damages the likelihood of high school students' attending college.

> Waddell, Robert. "Alcohol's Effect on Learning." *New York Times Education Life* 1 Aug. 1993: 6.

Parenthetic Citation with Paragraph Number

If your source has paragraph numbers rather than pagination, as sometimes is the case for downloaded sources, use the paragraph number(s) preceded by the abbreviation *par.* (Do not assign paragraph numbers to a document that does not have them.) Here is an example and the Works Cited reference for it.

As Myriam Miedzian points out, "Boys are at a much higher risk of growing up to be violent than girls are" (par. 4).

Miedzian, Myriam. "Breaking the Cycle." *Sesame Street Parents* July-Aug.
1994: 13t. The Parenting Project. Online. Internet. Available:
http://www.131.91.80.182/meyerowitz/parentingproject/article.htm. 18
Aug. 1997.

More Than One Author

In many situations the parenthetic citation will include more information than just an author's last name and page number.

If your source has more than one author, you should use both or all last names in your parenthetic note. Use the same order of last names as that on the title page or in the byline.

Philosophers made the assumption that women's minds were the same as
men's (Solomon and Higgins 287).

Solomon, Robert C., and Kathleen M. Higgins. *A Short History of Philosophy.*
New York: Oxford UP, 1996.

If your source has more than three authors, use only the first author's last name and the Latin phrase *et al.,* which translates as "and the others." The Works Cited listing will also use et al. Here is a parenthetic citation and Works Cited listing for the book *Negotiation* by Roy J. Lewicki, Joseph A. Litterer, John W. Minton, and David M. Saunders:

In negotiation, perceived power is more important than actual power (Lewicki
et al. 296).

Lewicki, Roy J., et al. *Negotiation.* 2nd ed. Boston: Irwin, 1994.

Two or More Sources by the Same Author

If you use two or more works by the same author, indicate in your parenthetic note which of the two you are currently referring to. In this situation, you place the first few words of the title after the author's name. You should not reproduce the entire title, just enough so the reader can clearly tell which item on the Works Cited page is meant. Here is a parenthetic reference to a writer who appears twice on the Works Cited list:

Postmodernism is controversial because it opposes mainstream modernistic
ways of looking at history and culture (Sarup, *Introductory* 144).

Sarup, Madan. *Identity, Culture and the Postmodern World.* Athens: U of
Georgia P, 1996.

---. *An Introductory Guide to Post-Structuralism and Postmodernism.* Athens: U
of Georgia P, 1989.

Two Sources

Two sources that supplied the same information can be cited together in one note. Just put a semicolon between the two:

> Men and women have such distinct ways of interpreting language that they may take completely different meanings from the same conversation (Hourigan 107; Tannen 13).

> Hourigan, Maureen M. *Literacy as Social Exchange*. Albany: State U of New York P, 1994.

> Tannen, Deborah. *You Just Don't Understand: Women and Men in Conversation*. New York: Morrow, 1990.

Source within a Source

Quoting or paraphrasing a source cited within another source is permissible as long as you indicate in your parenthetic reference that this is what you are doing. Use the abbreviation *qtd. in* before the source author's last name. If you do not mention the name of the original source in your text, then you should provide the name in your parenthetic reference:

■ *Activity 7*
Inserting Citations in a Passage, p. 545

■ *Activity 8*
Writing Correct Parenthetic Citations from Bibliographic Information, p. 546

> In the words of one critic of education, today's teachers must "have the courage to take risks, to look into the future, and to imagine a world that could be opposed to simply what is" (Giroux qtd. in Hourigan 127).

> Henry Giroux advises us that teachers must "have the courage to take risks, to look into the future, and to imagine a world that could be opposed to simply what is" (qtd. in Hourigan 127).

■ THE WORKS CITED PAGE (MLA FORMAT)

The Works Cited list allows your readers, if they choose, to locate sources, read in depth on your topic, or check your use of source material. Truly, readers engaged in research and intrigued by a subject are always looking for more material and find Works Cited lists useful. You may have used a source's list of Works Cited to identify additional reading on your topic. And the Works Cited list has a second important purpose. It's a shorthand indicator of the conversation with writers and experts that the author has engaged in.

Contents

Only works that you refer to in your paper are recorded on your documentation list. You should not include works you read for background or on which you may have taken notes but that were not referred to in your final paper. The Works Cited list is for sources actually cited, not just consulted.

Formats

The most complete set of guidelines for the Works Cited page is provided in the *MLA Handbook for Writers of Research Papers* (Gibaldi). Most college-level handbooks of grammar and style also contain extensive guidelines for citing each type of source. Included here are formats for books, periodicals, electronic sources, and non-print sources.

You don't have to memorize the various formats; instead, you need to keep your book open as you prepare your Works Cited list and make sure you've found the correct format for each source. Each major element—such as author, title, and publication—is punctuated with a period.

Author and title information for books, periodicals, and sources retrieved electronically are handled similarly. But publication information is handled differently for the various types of works.

Overview of Format for Book Citations

Author

Items included on the Works Cited page are listed alphabetically by the last name of the author or of the first listed author if there is more than one. The name is reversed, last name first, but in other respects authors' names should appear the same as on the title page of the book or article, with first names and initials, if any, and in the same order if there is more than one author. Do not include titles, such as Rev., Dr., Sir, as part of the name or degrees, such as Ph.D. or L. D. Do include Jr. or a numeral that identifies a particular individual among family members with the same name. A period follows the author of a work.

Title

The title provided in the Works Cited listing should be complete, including the subtitle if any. Title and subtitle are separated by a colon, even though there may not be one on the title page. The title should be underlined (in typewriting) or italicized (in word processing) and written in lower case with initial capitals for all major words. A period follows the title of a work unless the title itself ends in punctuation, such as a question mark or exclamation mark.

Publication Information

The publication information includes the place of publication and the publisher's name, plus the year of publication. Place is identified by city only. The publisher's name should be shortened by dropping such terms as "Co." and "Inc." The place of publication and publisher are separated by a colon. The year of publication follows the publisher, with a comma in between.

Citation Formats for Books

One Author

Pearson, Carol S. *The Hero Within*. San Francisco: Harper, 1989.

Two Books by the Same Author

Giroux, Henry A. *Border Crossings*. New York: Routledge, 1995.

---. *Disturbing Pleasures*. New York: Routledge, 1994.

Two or Three Authors

Kreisman, Jerold J., and Hal Straus. *I Hate You: Don't Leave Me: Understanding the Borderline Personality*. New York: Avon, 1989.

Breaker, Tyson, Roberta E. Freeman, and Jenni Kaufman. *Lost in Plain Sight: Urban Teens in Crisis*. New York: Marker, 1992.

Four or More Authors

Lewicki, Roy J., et al. *Negotiation*. Boston: Irwin, 1994.

Corporate or Institutional Author

The entity that produced the work is treated as the author even if the same entity is also the publisher.

American College Health Association. *Eating Disorders: What Everyone Should Know*. Baltimore: American College Health Association, 1995.

Edited Work

Sometimes, author, title, and publisher are not sufficient to identify the source, and you should be careful to note additional details.

If you are using the whole of a book that has been edited rather than authored (indicated by the phrase *edited by* on the title page), you should clearly indicate this by placing *ed.* after the person's name (or names, if more than one person has edited the book):

Waugh, Patricia, ed. *Postmodernism: A Reader*. New York: Arnold, 1992.

Selection in an Anthology

If you are using only a part of an anthology or book of readings, you should first identify the author and full title of the selection (placed in quotation marks) and then the title of the book. The editor's name (in natural order), preceded by *Ed.*, comes next. The page range is given last.

Ong, Walter J. "Literacy and Orality in Our Times." *Composition and Literature: Bridging the Gap*. Ed. Winifred Bryan Horner. Chicago: U of Chicago P, 1983. 126–40.

Article in a Reference Work

If a reference work is well known, you need only cite the title, edition number, and publication year:

Newman, Cathy. "Australia and New Zealand." *National Geographic Atlas of the World.* 6th ed. 1992.

If, however, a reference work is less familiar, you should provide full author, editor, and publication information.

Roberts, Andrew Michael. "Multiculturalism and 'The New Internationalism.' " *The Bloomsbury Guide to English Literature.* Ed. Marion Wynne-Davis. London: Bloomsbury, 1995. 310–12.

Introduction, Preface, Foreword, or Afterword

Without underlining, using quotation marks, or italicizing, place the name of the book part you are citing after the author's name. Capitalize the part and follow with a period. Then provide the title of the work. If the author of the part you are citing is different from the author of the whole work, provide the work's author after the title, using the word *By.* The page range of the part cited should conclude the entry.

Mappen, Mark. Preface. *Murder and Spies, Lovers and Lies: Settling the Great Controversies of American History.* New York: Avon, 1996. xi–xii.

Derek Owens. Introduction. *The Essay: Theory and Pedagogy for an Active Form.* By Paul Heilker. Urbana: NCTE, 1996. xi–xvii.

Translation

If the work is translated from a foreign language, both the author's name and the translator's name must be provided. The author's name is the first entry. The translator's name is provided after the title, in natural order, preceded by the abbreviation *Trans.*

Jabés, Edmond. *The Book of Margins.* Trans. Rosemarie Waldrop. Chicago: U of Chicago P, 1993.

Revised Edition

If the work you are using is a revised or later edition of the book, you must indicate this. A new edition of a book contains altered material and is completely reset. The pagination will be different, so it is important for a reader to be able to identify the edition you used (ideally, you will use the most recent edition). A book is a first edition unless the title page includes a phrase indicating it is later or revised: "second edition." To indicate a particular edition, place the edition number and the abbreviation *ed.* after the title:

Davis, Richard. *The Press and American Politics: The New Mediator.* 2nd ed. Upper Saddle River: Prentice, 1996.

Book in a Series

When a book is one in a series of related works, indicate this before the publication information by providing the series name and number, without any marking. When the word *series* appears as part of the name, abbreviate it as *Ser.*

> Johnson, Donald W., Roger T. Johnson, and Karl A. Smith. *Cooperative
>   Learning: Increasing Faculty Productivity.* ASHE-ERIC Higher Education
>   Rpt. 4. Washington: George Washington UP, 1991.

Government Publication

Usually anonymous, government publications are considered to be authored by the government office named as responsible. The government should be named first, and then the division, office, or other agency. Abbreviations should be used if they are recognizable: *Cong.* for Congress, *Sen.* for Senate, and so on.

> United States. Cong. Sen.

> United States. Cong. Office of the Special Prosecutor.

> United States. Bureau of the Census. *U.S. Population Estimates, by Age, Sex,
>   Race and Origin, 1980 to 1991.* Washington: Dept. of Commerce, 1993.

The publisher for a federal government publication is often "Washington: GPO," and the year. (GPO stands for Government Printing Office.) For documents issued by states, cities, other local governments, or international governments, use the publication information located on the title or copyright page.

To cite the standard reference work of congressional proceedings, the *Congressional Record,* use an abbreviation for the title and then provide just the date and page numbers of the material you are citing:

> *Cong. Rec.* date: pages.

Order of Information

The bold-faced items in this list are necessary for a book citation. The other elements should be included as appropriate to the source.

> **author**
> title of chapter, article, or part of book, if relevant
> **title of whole work**
> editor or translator, if any
> edition number, if any
> volume number if multivolume work
> series name and number if book is one in a series
> **publication place, publisher name, publication year**
> page numbers if only a section, chapter, or article was read

Overview of Format for Citation of Articles in Periodicals

Author

The author of a periodical article is entered the same way as the author of a book, as are multiple authors.

Title of Article

The full title of the article should be placed in quotation marks, which is the official way to mark short pieces such as articles, stories, and such. Follow the article title with a period. Use lowercase with initial capitalization of major words, even if the source presents the title differently. (Many newspapers cast headlines in lowercase except for the first letter of the title.)

Periodical Title and Publication Information

The title of the periodical is actually publication information. The periodical title is underlined (in typewriting) or italicized (in word processing). It is followed by specific information needed to locate the particular issue of the periodical. This information differs depending on the type of periodical: scholarly journals paged separately or paged continuously throughout the year, trade magazines, and newspapers require different formats for identifying specific issues. (See Chapter 11 for an understanding of different types of periodicals.)

Page Numbers

Page numbers are preceded by a colon placed immediately after the information indicating the specific issue of the periodical. Include the page or page range for articles appearing on consecutive pages exactly as the pages are indicated in the periodical. Always follow the page(s) with a period.

79–95.

B-4–B-7.

ix–xvii.

sec. 4: 2–3.

If the article is continued on nonconsecutive pages, write only the first page number and a plus sign:

14+.

C-3+.

sec 2: 11+.

Citation Formats for Periodicals

Scholarly Article in a Separately Paged Journal

The issue in a separately paged journal is indicated by the volume number and issue number separated by a period, followed by the year in parentheses. For example:

102.6 (1998)

This information is in turn followed by the page range of the article. Here is an example:

Ranquin-Esquer, Lynn A., et al. "Autonomy and Relatedness in Marital
    Functioning." *Journal of Marital and Family Therapy.* 23.4 (1997): 75–90.

Scholarly Article in a Continuously Paged Journal

Indicate the volume and year of the article you are citing by writing the volume number and following it with the year in parentheses. The issue is indicated only by identifying the pages of the article.

Fogarty, Robin, and Jay McTighe. "Educating Teachers for Higher Order
    Thinking: The Three-Story Intellect." *Theory into Practice* 32 (1993):
    161–69.

Magazine Article

For magazines published monthly or less frequently, indicate the month(s) or season(s), followed by the year, a colon, and the page numbers. Months other than May, June, and July may be abbreviated. Magazines frequently continue articles on nonconsecutive pages; do not forget to use only a plus sign to show additional nonconsecutive pages.

Hallowell, Edward N. "What I've Learned from A.D.D." *Psychology Today* May-
    June 1997: 41+.

For magazines published weekly or biweekly, write the date, day first, then month and year, followed by a colon and the page(s).

Koehl, Carla. "Get Your Life Together." *Newsweek* 5 Feb. 1996: 9.

Newspaper Article

Omit the article *The* from the start of a newspaper name. If the location is not well known or obvious from the name, place the newspaper's location in square brackets after the name: *Sunbeam* [Salem Co., N.J.]. Write the date starting with the day, then month, then year. You may abbreviate months except for May, June, and July. If the edition is listed, you should indicate it by placing a comma after the date and writing the appropriate abbreviation: *natl. ed., late ed., early ed.,* or whatever. Use a colon to separate the edition and the page numbers.

> Barron, James. "Investigators Seek Clues to Explain Derailment." *New York Times* 5 July 1997, natl. ed.: 25+.

Newspapers are often divided into sections, so be sure to indicate the section if appropriate. Often the section is indicated simply by a letter that is part of the page number: "A3," "C-10," "7B." If the section is indicated separately from the page number, include a reference to the section before the page number.

> "Market's Up as Economy Rolls Along." *Philadelphia Inquirer* 13 Sept. 1997: D1.

> "Ever Earnest and Funny, Ever Relevant to Youth." *New York Times* 7 Sept. 1997, sec. 2: 8+.

Editorial or Letter to the Editor

Indicate that the item is an editorial or letter to the editor by adding the appropriate phrase after the title: *Editorial* or *Letter.*

> "The Harassment of Female Troops." Editorial. *New York Times* 13 Sept. 1997, late ed.: 22.

Format for Citation of Electronic Sources

These days most students acquire some of their sources electronically. Entries for such items must indicate their electronic nature. As one online provider of electronic citation format notes, "At this point standards for citing electronic sources are not fully established by the major style manuals" ("Citing"). Online web sites generated by academics and university departments have cropped up to address the omissions of these style manuals. In particular, the MLA's format makes inclusion of site addresses for online sources merely optional, and it does not mention including identifying file or product numbers for online or CD-ROM sources. The format provided here accords with currently recommended styles.

The formats for electronic sources are based on formats for print sources and use essentially the same pattern: author, title, publication information. The publication part of the entry must take into account the electronic nature of the source. And in the case of the many online sources that are electronic versions of print material, it is important to provide the relevant bibliographic information for both the print and the electronic version.

Stable Database Formats

Examples of stable (or "portable" in the MLA's terminology) databases include reference works on CD-ROM and magazine or newspaper databases offered by libraries.

These are, in many ways, the electronic parallels of print books and magazine articles because they don't change unless a new edition or release is issued, the way a new edition of a book might be released.

Here are some general guidelines for these electronic sources:

- The publication information should identify the medium, such as CD-ROM.
- In works that are republications of print material, the print publisher may be different from the electronic publisher or vendor, and therefore both should be identified. Companies republishing periodicals for electronic library access include Wilson, Information Access, SilverPlatter, and Proquest. If you don't know how to locate the name of the company responsible for the database you are using, ask a librarian for help.
- The date of electronic databases should be indicated, along with the identification number for the file or product, if given.

The basic format for permanent electronic sources includes the following information. On occasion, you will have to omit an item because it is not available.

author of electronic version (if known)
title (italicized or underlined)
medium—for example, CD-ROM
place of publication (if known)
publisher or information supplier
date of release (if known)
file, access, or product number (if given)
date you accessed library-held materials

Examples of citations of CD-ROM sources with no print analogue:

"Desert Storm: The War in the Persian Gulf." CD-ROM. Warner New Media
    14001. 1994.

"Global Warming." *Microsoft Encarta Encyclopedia.* CD-ROM. Funk &
    Wagnall's, 1997.

If there is a preexisting print version of the electronic material, you should put the print bibliographic details first, then follow with the information about the electronic version you used:

Hechler, David. "Abused Children." *New York Times* 25 Oct. 1991, late ed.:
    A33. CD-ROM. Proquest. 3 Mar. 1995.

Online Database Formats

An online electronic source could be an electronic version of a printed publication, or it might be an article in an electronic journal—that is, a periodical that exists only online. Or the source might be information that appears online on an organizational or personal web page or an online information service. Occasionally researchers use information posted on a real-time exchange or bulletin board or obtained through e-mail contact; these should also be cited.

Citation of information gathered through both Internet sources and commercial online providers such as America on Line (AOL) should follow these guidelines:

- Provide the path or electronic address for accessing the database.
- Indicate the date on which you access the data because online data are fluid and may change.

The basic format for an online source includes the following information. On occasion, you will have to omit an item because it is not available.

author of electronic version (if known)
title (italicized or underlined)
online medium—for example, Internet, AOL
available protocol—for example, HTTP, e-mail, gopher
site, path, or file address
access date

Examples of citations of online sources with no print analogue:

David, Derek. "The Myth of the Glorious '50s." Online. Internet. Available: http://www.pobox.com/slt/editorial.html. 7 July 1997.

Boyer, Lydie. "5 Points against Legalized Gambling: An Address to the Sutter County Board of Supervisors." 20 Feb. 1996. Online. Internet. Available: http://www.syix.com/dakin/boyer.htm. 22 Nov. 1996.

You should write up gopher sites or FTP (file transfer protcol) sources similarly.

If the source parallels a print version, you should place the print bibliographic information first, even though you may lack some details, such as page range:

Associated Press. "Warner Seeks Study of Gambling." *Virginian-Pilot* 31 Oct. 1995: A2. Online. Internet. Available: http://scholar3.1.b.vt.edu/VA-news/VA-Pilot/issues/ 1995/vp951031/ 95103310327.html. 22 Nov. 1996.

Simon, Paul. "The Explosive Growth of Gambling in the United States." United States. 104th Cong. Sen. *Cong. Rec.* 31 July 1995. Online. Internet. Available: http://www.syix.com/dakin/the_expl.htm. 22 Nov. 1996.

Format for Citation of Nonprint Sources

Your sources may also include television, radio, film, audiotape or CD, videotape, personal letter, e-mail message, public computer posting, an interview you conduct, and so on. Full details about all the possibilities are provided by the *MLA Handbook*. Here are documentation forms for some of the common nonprint sources.

Television or Radio Program

Include the title of the show (in quotation marks) and the name of the program (in italics or underlined), followed by the title of the series, if any. Name the network on which the show appeared, and provide the call letters and city of the local station.

"Mars: The Red Planet." *Discovery.* PBS. WHYY-TV, Philadelphia. 2 July 1997.

You may include other material, such as performer, director, narrator, and so forth by placing it between the title of the program and the name of the network.

"Snowden on Ice." Prod. Gary Smith. Perf. Ekaterina Gordeeva, Kurt Browning, and Scott Hamilton. WKYW, Philadelphia. 28 Nov. 1997.

Film or Video

The citation for these items begins with the title, italicized or underlined, the director, the distributor, and the year issued. Other details may be added between the title and director or after the director's name.

The Commitments. Dir. Alan Parker. Twentieth Century Fox, 1991.

Audio CD, Audiotape, or Record

Begin with the name of the significant person, usually a singer, orchestra, band leader, or other performer. If you are citing a particular song or composition on the record, put it next, in quotation marks. Follow with the title of the recording, underlined, and the company and year, if known. Recordings are assumed to be audio CD unless you write *LP,* for vinyl record, or *audiocassette* for cassette tape.

Carreras, José. *Passion.* Erato, 1996.

Kirk, Roland. *Jazz Masters 27.* Prod. Creed Taylor and Jack Tracy. Audiocassette. Polygram, 1994.

If the recording is an audio version of a printed text, begin with the author of the printed work.

Personal Letter, E-Mail, or Public Electronic Posting

Personal letters and e-mail messages are cited by the writer's name, the identification of the text as a letter or e-mail, and the date.

Herrison, Ronnie. Letter to the author. 31 Aug. 1996.

Major, Erisha. E-mail to the author. 7 Nov. 1997.

You may provide e-mail addresses in your citation:

Major, Erisha (major@voxcoll.com). "Cases of Hanta Virus in Southwest." E-mail to Jared Slefe (slefe@raben.edu). 7 Nov. 1997.

Information located in online bulletin boards or Usenet news groups should be cited. Use the writer's name and title or subject of the document, followed by posting date. Then identify the item as an *Online posting*, followed by the name of the location where the posting was found, the name of the network, the path, and the date of access.

Siegel, Allan. "Forum Inactivity." 17 Mar. 1995. Online posting. Media-Forum. Internet. Available: http://www.medianation.org/media-forum/d950301 msg00079.html. 29 Nov. 1997.

Interview

A printed or recorded interview is handled as a publication or television or radio item. For a personal interview that you conduct, provide the person's name, the type of interview (*Personal interview, Telephone interview*), and the date.

Barrow, Sean. Personal interview. 28 Mar. 1997.

Lecture or Speech

Provide the speaker's name, the title of the presentation (if any), the meeting and sponsoring organization (if any), the location, and the date.

Grishaw, Hal, and Adrienne Parkens. "Resonance and Resistance in Conversion." Forum: Meaning and Structure of Conversion. Society for the Scientific Study of Religion Conference. Chicago. 24 Feb. 1998.

■ *Activity 9*
Preparing Works
Cited Entries, p. 547

■ APA CITATION

As in MLA citation style, smooth reference to sources in APA (American Psychological Association) format means using clear attributions in the text as often as possible. The minimum information necessary for a reference is the author's last name and the date of the item. If both must be included in the parentheses, there is a comma between them. The parenthetic citations are keyed to the list of sources, called References (not Works Cited). Here are some examples:

In Hammelburg's discussion of a 1955 play about Anne Frank, the author discusses the recent attempts to discover the historical girl who wrote the diary (1997).

The revival of the 1955 Broadway play about Anne Frank is based on an attempt to include new information about the historical girl who wrote the diary (Hammelburg, 1997).

These citations refer to this References list entry:

Hammelburg, B. (1977, November 30). A fresh look at "Anne Frank" in search of the historical one. *New York Times*, sec. 2, pp. 1, 4, 12.

Here are examples of references to an online source:

Electronic technologies now offer a way to expand and fundamentally alter the learning of children across the globe, according to Negroponte, Resnick, and Cassell (1997).

Electronic technologies now offer a way to expand and fundamentally alter the learning of children across the globe (Negroponte, Resnick, & Cassell, 1997).

These citations refer to this References page listing:

Negroponte, N., Resnick, M., & Cassell, J. (1997). Creating a learning revolution. *Learning World Forum*. UNESCO. [Online]. Available: http://www.education.unesco.org/unesco/ educprog/lwf/doc/portfolio/opinions8.html.

Overview of Format for References Entries

The authority for APA citation format is the *Publication Manual of the American Psychological Association*. Most college-level handbooks of grammar and style also contain descriptions of APA formats. Included here are formats for the main types of books, periodicals, electronic sources, and nonprint sources.

APA citation format agrees with MLA format in that only works used in the research and preparation of the paper are listed, and the list is double-spaced. And, as in MLA style, the APA citations list is alphabetized according to authors' last names. The APA requires that only material accessible to the reader be listed—meaning that e-mail messages, personal letters, and such are not formally documented.

There are several differences between MLA and APA style. In APA style, authors' names are always reduced to last name plus initials. They are followed by the publication date in parentheses. The place of publication, unless a major U.S. city or international capital, is expressed as city and state. Many references use *p.* or *pp.* before the pages, but not all.

The order of items in a References entry is:

author's name (last, plus initials)
date of publication (in parentheses, year first, then month and day if applicable)

article title, if relevant (no markings, no capitalization except first letter of title)

title (underlined and with only the first letter capitalized) or periodical title (initial capital for all important words)

place of publication (city, with state if necessary for clarity, for books only)

short version of publisher's name

page numbers, if relevant (with *p.* or *pp.,* for books only)

Citation Formats for Books

One Author

The standard reference is as follows:

Readings, B. (1996). *The university in ruins.* Cambridge, MA: Harvard
    University Press.

For two books by the same author, arrange by date with the earliest first.

Toulmin, S. (1958). *The uses of argument.* New York: Cambridge University
    Press.
Toulmin, S. (1990). *Cosmopolis: The hidden agenda of modernity.* Chicago:
    University of Chicago Press.

More Than One Author

List all authors in order as on the title page; use an ampersand (&) rather than the word *and.*

Rubin, R. B., Rubin, A. M., & Piele, L. J. (1996). *Communication research:
    Strategies and sources* (4th ed.). Belmont, CA: Wadsworth.

Group Author

If the author is a corporation or organization that is also the publisher, use the word *author* in place of the publisher.

American College Health Association. (1995). *Eating disorders: What everyone
    should know.* Baltimore: Author.

Additional Elements: Edited Works,
Later Editions, and Translations

Heffron, J. (Ed.). (1994). *The best writing on writing.* Cincinnati: Story Press.

Bagdikian, B. H. (1996). *The media monopoly* (5th ed.). Boston: Beacon Press.

Derrida, J. (1978). *Writing and difference.* (A. Bass, Trans.). Chicago: University
    of Chicago Press.

Selection in an Anthology

Hebdige, D. (1991). What is "soul"? In A. M. Olson, C. Parr, & D. Parr (Eds.), *Video icons and values* (pp. 121–134). Albany: State University of New York Press.

Citation Formats for Periodicals

Titles of articles are not marked in any way, and only the first word is capitalized. Journal articles do not use *p.* or *pp.*

Scholarly Article in a Journal Paginated through the Year

Olson, G. A. (1997). Paulo Freire in context. *JAC: A Journal of Composition Theory, 17,* 322–324.

Scholarly Article in a Journal Paginated by Issue

Liester, M. (1998) Toward a new definition of hallucination. *American Journal of Orthopsychiatry, 68 (2),* 305–310.

Magazine Article

Put the date of the issue after the year. After the title, include the volume number and then the page range. If pages are discontinuous, list them all.

Fine, D. M. (1997, September–October). Grassroots medicine. *American Prospect, 34,* 51–56.

Newspaper Article

Massing, M. (1997, December 6). Heroin and red herrings. *New York Times,* p. A10.

Poll looks at innermost feelings about life's end. (1997, December 6). *New York Times,* p. A8.

If a newspaper article appears on discontinuous pages, list all pages in the citation: pp. 5, 17.

Citation Formats for Electronic Sources

CD-ROM or Other Electronic Datafile or Database

The APA *Manual* does not give an example of a common academic resource for the on-disk retrieval of newspaper or other periodical articles. On the basis of the description of the elements to include in a citation for "Other Electronic Media," the citation for a newspaper article on Proquest would look like this:

> Schwartz, J. (1995, December 8). FDA approves first in new family of AIDS drugs [CD-ROM]. *Washington Post,* p. A3. Proquest: The Washington Post Ondisc. Access no. 95690949.

Online Sources

The APA *Manual* does not cover World Wide Web sources but on analogy to its example of how to cite FTP sources, a source found on the web would be cited as follows:

> Resnick, M. (1996, July). Distributed constructionism. *Proceedings of the International Conference for the Advancement of Computing in Education.* [Online]. Available: http://www.media.mit.edu/groups/et/Papers/mres/ Distrib-Construc.html.

Citation Formats for Nonprint Sources

Film or Video

Wenders, W., & Taplin, J. (Producers), & Wenders, W. (Director). (1997). *Until the end of the world* [Film]. Trans Pacific Films.

Audio CD, Audiotape, or Record

Dylan, B. (1997). Dirt road blues. On *Time out of mind* [CD]. New York: Columbia.

■ PREPARING A FORMAL OUTLINE

Some instructors require you to include a formal outline with your final paper. Writers often deviate from their plans as set out in their first outlines, so prepare your formal outline on the basis of your paper draft. Your working outline can be helpful.

A formal outline uses indentation but also enumeration to indicate the relationships among points. (See Chapter 2 for details about creating an outline.)

To write your formal outline, begin by reading through your paper to locate the main ideas, and write them in as points I, II, III, and so on. Once you have the basic plan of the paper, go through each section and fill in subpoints, sub-subpoints, and so on, completing the outline of each section before going on. Consult your instructor to determine how detailed the outline should be.

A caution: writing a detailed formal outline takes time. Make sure you leave yourself enough time to do the job adequately. Especially avoid skimping on the later sections of the outline.

Working on a word processor can give you the option of using a split screen; you can scroll through the paper in one half and write your outline in the other.

■ REVISING AND EDITING THE DRAFT

Revise for Organization and Logic

Writing a formal outline benefits you as a writer; it forces you to go through your paper scouting out its logic. You may find yourself doing some quick rearranging of the paper as you do the outline. If you discover that a point doesn't work well in a particular place, you can move it. If you do not have to write a formal outline, you might still use outlining as a way to check your organization, especially if you know you deviated from the working outline as you wrote the paper.

Revise for Style and Language

The typical research paper is formal in tone and style. This means writing in the third person, using standard vocabulary and sentence style, and adopting a neutral tone. During the revision stage, you should be on the lookout for any deviations in style and tone. See Chapter 10 for a full discussion of style.

Edit for Correctness

Many writers check grammar and usage as they revise, but it's a good idea to make one more pass over the paper specifically to seek out any errors in grammar. You might try reading the paper sentence by sentence, beginning at the end. This can interrupt the flow of content enough for you to concentrate on each sentence's grammar.

If your computer has a usage or grammar checker, you might use it at this point. If you are not experienced with the program, however, you may find it complicates your attempt to edit by identifying some correct items as incorrect. Also, if you are word processing, it is a good idea to use your spell checker at the end of your editing cycle, when you are through making changes.

■ PREPARING THE FINAL MANUSCRIPT

Use Correct Manuscript Format

Once you are satisfied with the language and substance of your paper, you should format it correctly. These guidelines for the appropriate format are based on those of the MLA.

Paper: 8½ × 11 inches
    Typing: standard weight paper (not onion skin)
    Word processing: standard paper
Page Format
    Margins (top, bottom, and sides): 1 inch
    Paragraph indent: five spaces (typing) or a half inch (word processing)
    Double-spaced throughout

Type Style
  Readable (nonscript) font
  Size: ten or twelve picas
Title Page (optional in MLA)
  MLA indicates that a research paper does not require a title page. Some instructors do require one; here is a generally acceptable format:
  Center and double-space all elements
  Begin first element about one-third of the way down the page
  Elements
    Title in upper- and lower-case letters, plain text (no underline, quotation marks, or other typographic markings)
    Your name
    Professor's name (example: Professor Jonathan Rothkow)
    Course title in plain text (no quotation marks)
      (example: College Writing 5503) plus meeting time if required (MW 12:30).
    Date of submission in inverted form (3 June 1998)
First Page without a Title Page
  Heading: one inch below top paper edge
  On left margin, double-space these elements:
    Your name
    Professor's name (example: Professor Patricia Rilles)
    Course title in plain text (no quotation marks) (example: College Writing 5503)
    Date of submission in inverted form (11 Dec. 1998)
  Title centered, one double-space below heading, in plain text
  Text one double-space below title
Heading for Text Pages
  Place a half inch below top paper edge and a half inch above text
  Flush with right margin on one line put your last name, a space, then page number in Arabic numerals
  Do not use "P." or "page" before page number
  Place heading in upper right-hand corner of each page
Blocked Quotations:
  Indent: ten spaces (typing) or one inch (word processing)
  If quotation begins a paragraph, indent first line three spaces or a quarter inch
  Double-space throughout
Works Cited Page
  Begin on a new page
  Use heading as above
  Center title of page, in plain text: Works Cited
  Place title one inch below top edge of page, and double-space above first item
  Begin each entry flush with left margin
  Indent runover lines five spaces or a half inch
  Use double-spacing throughout

Proofread and Check Accuracy

Re-read your paper carefully one more time before handing it in. Look for typos or word errors. Reading backward is a proofreader's trick that can help you isolate each word and sentence so that you don't flow over errors.

If you are word processing, remember that a spell checker can tell you only that a word is incorrectly spelled. If a word is inadvertently repeated or omitted, your spell checker will not report this. And if you have used the improper form of the word for the context or have used a homophone (for example, "they're" instead of "there"), your checker will not catch it.

Any statistical data or charts of information that you have included in your paper should be cross-checked one last time with the source during the proofreading stage. Also be sure to check the form and the accuracy of the information on the Works Cited page. Because of the amount of data, this is an easy place to make mistakes.

If you find an error, reprint or retype the page. If this is not possible, correct errors by hand, neatly, in ink. Draw one line through the error and write the correct letter or word(s) above the line of type, not below or in the margin. You may use a caret to indicate the place where the inserted items go. If there are many errors on a page, do make every effort to retype or reprint it.

■ STUDENT RESEARCH PAPER

Scott Heste's instructor required that a phrase outline be submitted with the research paper. Following are Scott's outline, sample title page, and research paper.

←1"→ Outline: Should Public Broadcasting Survive?

title one double-space above outline

←1"→ I.   Introduction

   A. PBS for the concerned and intelligent

outline double-spaced throughout

   B. PBS now under attack

   C. Thesis: PBS should be defended ——————————— thesis clearly indicated

II.   Background (history) ————

   A. Began 1967 ————————————————————— necessary background provided early

   B. Purposes

      1. reflect diversity of America

      2. be forum for controversy

      3. vehicle for groups to be heard

III.   Value of public broadcasting ——————————————— positives of topic provided

   A. To adults

      1. in-depth news

      2. how-to shows

      3. coverage of controversy and culture

   B. To member stations and communities

      1. news broadcasts to low-income housing in Evansville, IN

      2. Alaska's remote regions receive news through PBS

      3. New Jersey network delivers telecourses to 10,000 adults

      4. schools use it for information

      5. sets standards: closed captions, satellites, descriptive video   ←1"→

   C. To children

      1. preschool educational programs

      2. lack of interruptions for commercials

      3. avoidance of consumerism

IV.   Content criticisms of PBS ———————————————— criticisms discussed

   A. PBS elitism

      1. in coverage of high culture (opera, classical music, etc).

      2. Refutation ———————————————————— refutation of points clearly indicated

         a. opera viewers are middle income

         b. research shows all Americans watch during week

B. PBS liberal bias

    1. shown in coverage of gays, protests of religions

refutation   2. Refutation: mission is to cover controversy; groups needing voice

    3. content analysis studies do show liberal trend in opinion

    4. Refutation: findings depend on definition of liberal and which shows examined

C. PBS pornographic

    1. coverage of gays and censorship called porn by some groups

    2. Refutation: few consider such fairly rare shows as porn

    3. conservative attacks cause rejection of shows

    4. public television should reflect all sides, not just mainstream

E. Attacks from liberals

    1. PBS is becoming bland, fearful

    2. news show is all white males: "McNeil-Lehrer Report"

    3. too many business shows: "Wall Street Week," "McLaughlin Group"

F. Public views PBS as fair

    1. poll: (82%) agreed PBS is balanced

    2. funding should be increased

V. Criticism of cost of PBS to taxpayers

    A. Refutation: cost is low (16% of PBS budget from federal funds)

    B. Critics say federal funding so low PBS won't miss it if ended

VI. Reforms

    A. Privatization

        1. all stations would have to include education, culture, controversy

        2. would rival other commercial stations for ad money

    B. Other reforms

        1. PBS should get some merchandise revenue

        2. Commercial stations pay fee to support PBS

VII. Conclusion

    A. Public values PBS

    B. Only public broadcasting can be democratic forum

Should Public Broadcasting Survive?

by

Scott Heste

Composition I, Sec. 32

Prof. Eliza Boster

19 Dec. 1997

title page is
optional

begin about ⅓ of
way down page

everything
centered

title with first
letters capped

title has no
additional
markings

double-space items
in title page

Scott Heste

Prof. Eliza Boster

Composition I, Sec. 32

19 Dec. 1997

center title
no special markings

Should Public Broadcasting Survive?

in-text attribution

biographical tag

"PBS was meant to address the American people in their capacity as ←1"→ citizens and students (rather than in their capacity as buyers of life insurance)," Lewis Lapham, the editor of <u>Harper's,</u> wrote in 1993 (314).

parenthetic
citation of source
with titles on
Works Cited list

There is still a need for television that treats its audience as intelligent and concerned, and the only provider for this need is the Corporation for Public Broadcasting, the partially government-funded organization that was set up in 1967 to distribute funds to PBS (Aufderheide, "Will" 20). But now this service is under attack by people who wish to pull its support.

claim

Examination of the criticisms, however, shows that PBS can and should be defended. Its place in broadcasting is unique.

background
paragraph

parenthetic
citation for
material quoted
within a source

The age of public television was started in 1967, after the <u>Carnegie Commission Report on Public Television: A Program for Action</u> set out goals for noncommercial television. Public television was to "help us to see ←1"→ America in all its diversity" and would "serve as a forum for controversy and debate" and "provide a voice for groups that may otherwise be unheard" (qtd. in Sanders and Siegel). With these goals in mind, public broadcasting has built a network of stations throughout the country.

use of specific
examples as
support

What would we lose if public broadcasting is eliminated? Both adults and children would lose out. The programming on PBS provides people with in-depth coverage of news, such as the "News with Jim Lehrer" and "Frontline." Many helpful shows appear as well, such as "This Old House," and there are many shows covering controversial, cultural, and ethnically oriented issues that are not found on commercial broadcasts, on either cable or the big networks. Commercial broadcasters cannot afford controversy, because advertisers do not want to be associated with anything other than "standard" or "mainstream" ideas. Public stations can tailor shows to fill the gaps in commercial broadcasting, focusing on material that is too "serious," too "artsy," or too narrow in appeal. After

Heste   2

all, not everyone enjoys watching the shootouts on "N.Y.P.D. Blue" or finding out who is sleeping with whom on the latest soap. Some would rather be entertained by "Mystery" or learn something on "Nova" or be enthralled by the photography on any number of nature oriented shows.

Not only does PBS provide cultural and educational programming on television, but it also provides important services to the member stations. In Evansville, Indiana, public televisions are installed in low-income housing in order to provide local news coverage (Hentoff). Also, Alaska's rural population receives much of its information from PBS, including news and educational information (Mills 1598). On the New Jersey Network, a PBS station, 10,000 adults earn college credits by telecourses run daily ("NJN").

By cutting off funding for PBS, the country would lose not only television programs but also these helpful and necessary services not provided by other organizations. One writer concludes that public stations

> contribute to public life in quiet ways. For instance public
> television stations serve 90 percent of the nation's schools and
> may become the schools' only hope for being part of an
> "information superhighway." Public broadcasting's technical
> experiments—with satellites, closed-captioning for the hearing
> impaired, descriptive video for the sight-impaired, among
> others—have set standards for the field. (Aufderheide, "Will" 21)

And, of course, the most important PBS shows are for children. Every day, children learn about counting, the alphabet, spelling, social skills, and many other useful abilities on the old favorites of PBS: "Sesame Street" and "Mr. Roger's Neighborhood" and newer shows like "Barney and Friends" and "Shining Time Station." These shows are nonviolent and are not interrupted constantly by commercials. They provide positive role models and don't turn children into needy consumers. Research has linked "Sesame Street," aimed at preschool children, with improved vocabulary and early reading skills (Huston, Watkins, and Kunkel 425).

So why would anyone attack such a positive institution? Attacks come on several fronts. Some accuse PBS of being "elitist" because it

Margin annotations:

transitional sentence

parenthetic citation for source found on one page

parenthetic citation giving author and page

parenthetic citation for source with no author and on one page

← 1" →

blocked quotation

summary of cited source

parenthetic citation for source with three authors

dealing with the opposition begins here

no parenthetic
citation necessary
for source all on
one page with name
given in text

ellipses to show
words omitted

refutation of first
opposing point

second opposing
point

partial quotation

in-text attribution
of source with two
authors

analysis of
opposing view

partial quotation

no page number
necessary for
source on one page

includes classical music, opera, and intellectual discussions among its
offerings. Yet according to Nat Hentoff, most of the people who tune into
the opera earn less than $40,000 a year. Other research shows that

> Public TV reaches about 2 percent of television households in
> prime time, but a third of the public watches it sometime during
> the week. . . . Both [public television and radio] skew toward the
> well educated (although vast numbers of children watching
> "Sesame Street" rebalance the demographics for television).
> Both appeal, overall, to a profile that looks very like America.
> (Aufderheide, "Will" 21)

A second criticism is that PBS is biased toward the liberal. If so, it may
be because it was chartered to serve all the people with a voice and was to
foster debate and controversy as indicated earlier. Shows such as "Tongues
Untied," about black gay men and the indignities they suffer in their communities, and "Stop the Church," about AIDS activists protesting Catholic
policies, have been attacked for their bias—but this seems to imply that PBS
should not give certain groups a voice or report about unpopular protests.

In one study by the Center for Media and Public Affairs, 225
programs were analyzed for content, resulting in the finding that "the
balance of opinion tilted consistently in a liberal direction." However, this
judgment rests on the definition of "liberal." As Randy Sukow and Joe
Flint report in Broadcasting magazine, the study found that shows on race
relations discussed discrimination "as a condition of American society"
without anyone giving an opposing view that it is not; this lack of an
opposing view was considered "liberal" bias. Another tendency noted by
the Center was that documentaries on religion implied religions should
promote social change without any dissenting opinions being offered.
These are very subtle indicators of bias and not anything that could be
called blatant or extreme politicalization. One official at PBS also
disqualified the study because it was selective in what it analyzed for
content, ignoring "nearly 90 percent of the programming distributed by
PBS" in the study period (Sukow and Flint).

Heste   4

Another critic, Don Wildmon of the American Family Association, which defends family values, has attacked public programming for being pornographic. "Tales of the City," a show about gays, and "Tongues Untied" are two of his targets. He also derailed the distribution of a documentary film on censorship, "Damned in the USA" (Bennett 183). However much these shows disagreed with Wildmon's stance on family values, the label "pornographic" seems obviously extreme. In addition, such complaints only touch on a small portion of PBS programming. As an editorial in the Washington Post put it: "The frequent complaints of liberal political bias are unfair when leveled as a general blanket charge against a system as large and diverse in both nature and audience as this one" ("Public Broadcasting").

additional opposing view

in-text attribution for editorial with no author

Even though these attacks on PBS for its liberalism seem strained, they have had an effect. Many shows have been rejected as a result. These include such shows as "The Panama Deception," about the media blackout during the invasion of Panama, "Deadly Deception," about General Electric's problems with nuclear waste disposal, "Manufacturing Consent," about media and corporation critic Noam Chomsky, and "Rights and Wrongs," a civil rights documentary by Charlayne Hunter-Gault. With PBS dropping shows with a hint of controversy, critics from the other side started labeling PBS "the animal channel," "blandly grand," and "coffee table TV" (Bennett 178; Aufderheide, "Funny"). Public television should be for the public, which includes all types of people. Those who would restrict it are really saying that people who aren't totally mainstream shouldn't be represented and should be ignored as an audience.

success of opposing view, negative consequences

specific examples of negative consequences

parenthetic citation with two sources cited for same ideas

In fact, the more liberal group Fairness and Accuracy in Reporting has criticized the "McNeil-Lehrer Report" (now "NewsHour with Jim Lehrer") for constantly using white men in official positions as experts. It has also called PBS biased toward the conservative because it offers shows appealing to the upper-class business elite: "Wall Street Week," "The McLaughlin Group," and so on (Aufderheide, "Funny").

opposing views from a different side

In spite of these critiques from all sides of the spectrum, the public finds PBS acceptable and fair in its coverage of public affairs. A recent poll

refutation of opposing views

Heste   5

conducted by PBS found that 82 percent of respondents agreed to the
statement that "PBS is reasonably balanced in the content of its
programming—neither too conservative nor too liberal" (Edwards C6).
"Nearly half of all Americans—Republicans and Democrats alike—think
federal funding for public television should be increased this year, and an
additional 35 percent think it should be maintained at its current level,"
reports Ellen Edwards of the <u>Washington Post</u> (C1).

Very little of the criticism of PBS focuses on its spending. This is
because public broadcasting is a great deal for the American public. There
is all this outcry and yet the portion of CPB's budget that is supplied by
federal money is just 16 percent (Aufderheide, "Will" 20). As Russell
Saddler, a journalist and professor of communication at Southern Oregon
State College, puts it, "Congress spends about as much on military bands
as it spends on public broadcasting. . . . It can't be the money."

Some, in fact, state that since the government funding portion of
public broadcasting's budget is so low, PBS will do fine without any
taxpayer money. As one commentator who writes an Internet column,
"The Right Side," put it: "It's obvious that zero funding would not kill it,
but only force it to tighten its belt. PBS will simply have to survive on 86
percent of what it once received" (Doane).

Under this plan, the CPB will become completely private. But
privatization could have several consequences. Would "Barney and
Friends," "Mr. Rogers," and "Shining Time Station" be interrupted by a
thousand commercials for gimmicky toys as are the shows on Nickelodeon,
the cable kids' channel? Would the soft, nurturing tone typical of these
public shows give way to the satire and cynicism of cable cartoons for
children, like "Doug" and the "Rugrats"? Remember the well known facts
that both "Barney" and "Sesame Street" were offered to and were refused
by commercial stations before PBS took them on. There is much on PBS
that would not fly on commercial broadcasting.

In a recent speech, the president of PBS, Ervin Duggin, pointed out
several hidden effects of privatizing PBS. Without PBS to be the focus of

---

Margin annotations:

use of statistical
information

introduction to
new point about
cost of PBS

no page number
for online source

explanatory
attribution to
online source

opposing view of
future

refutation: student
analysis of effects
of privatization

Heste   6

government mandates for educationality and seriousness in broadcasting, — paraphrase of
— source ideas
all stations would come under pressure from Congress and the FCC

regarding appropriate content. Also, PBS would become a commercial

network, one that would be a competitor for advertising dollars now

gathered by the networks and cable stations. Privatized public stations   source adds to
student's refutation
which failed to support themselves would be sold to commercial owners

and become another competitor. This would "increas[e] the number of   use of square
— brackets in a
for-profit commercial licensees and dilut[e] the value of incumbent   quotation

commercial broadcasters." Advertising would be cheaper at newly

privatized public stations, and such stations would complete for the

audiences of the commercial stations ("Commercial TV").

    One proposal for reform would require commercial stations, who now   proposal for
reform
receive their license to use a broadcast channel for free, to pay a fee which

would be funneled to support public broadcasting. If the commercial sta-

tions can be convinced to support PBS instead of hoping for its demise, the

public will be better served. There is some support in the media community.

The president of Fox endorsed the continued existence of public broadcast-

ing at a TV industry convention and drew enthusiastic applause. Chicago's   support for reform

Mayor Richard Daley has also come out for the support of public TV by com-

mercial broadcasters, pointing out that they pay their anchors millions.

"Reasonable assessments" on commercial broadcast licenses could be used

to set up a trust fund to back the CBP long term (Sanders and Siegel).

    Americans clearly value the quality programming and the

noncommercial environment on PBS. Legislators and commercial

broadcasters must be made to see this and provide some base of support

for public broadcasting. As Sanders and Siegel persuasively write, "What   two authors
— named in lead-in
is at stake in the current debate is not merely the value and cost of public   attribution

broadcasting, but rather it is the substance and quality of our democratic

institutions; our commitment to an open, unfettered exchange of ideas;

and an expansive cultural arena." They continue, "The simple truth is that   conclusion with
strong assertive
no commercial service, no matter how widely available, will ever fulfill the   quotation

goals outlined in public broadcasting's mission."

Heste   7

Works Cited

article downloaded from commercial online service

two articles by same author

article from scholarly journal

article with no author

article from online magazine site

article on Internet gopher site

newspaper article

source with three authors

article in anthology

edition of book

unsigned editorial

Aufderheide, Pat. "A Funny Thing Is Happening to TV's Public Forum."
        Columbia Journalism Review Nov.–Dec. 1991: 60–64. Online.
        CompuServe. Database Plus. Ref. #A11730856. 18 Nov. 1997.

---. "Will Public Broadcasting Survive?" The Progressive Mar. 1995: 19–21.

Bennett, James R. "The Public Broadcasting Service: Censorship, Self-
        Censorship, and the Struggle for Independence." Journal of Popular
        Film and Television Winter 1997: 177–85.

"Commercial TV Will Be Hurt If Federal Funds Are Cut." PBS Online 11
        Apr. 1995. Available: http://www.pbs.org/insidepbs/news/
        irtsrelease.htm. 28 Nov. 1997.

Doane, Travis. "Zero Funding for PBS Adds Up." Editorial. The Right Side.
        Available gopher://gopher.runet.edu70/00/News9620
        Letters%20%26%Campus%20Publications/TARTAN/Tartan962001. 28
        Nov. 1997.

Edwards, Ellen. "PBS Support Widespread, Poll Says. Both Parties'
        Members Found to Back Funding." Washington Post 17 Jan. 1995:
        C1+.

Hentoff, Nat. "For Elitists Only?" Washington Post 21 Jan. 1995: A15.

Huston, Althea C., Bruce Watkins, and Dale Kunkel. "Public Policy and
        Children's Television." American Psychologist Feb. 1989: 424–33.

Lapham, Lewis H. "Adieu, Big Bird: On the Terminal Irrelevance of Public
        Television." Taking Sides: Clashing Views on Controversial Issues in
        Mass Media and Society. Ed. Alison Alexander and Jarice Hanson.
        3rd ed. Guilford: Dushkin, 1995. 308–15.

Mills, Mike. "Senate Tunes Out Critics, Boosts Public T. V., Radio."
        Congressional Quarterly: Weekly Reports 6 June 1992: 1598–99."

NJN and Its Service to the State." New York Times. 7 Aug. 1994;
        sec. 13NJ: 7. Online. Proquest. 11 Nov. 1997.

"Public Broadcasting, Public Funds." Editorial. Washington Post 19 Jan.
        1995: A24.

Heste   8

Saddler, Russell. "Rupert Murdoch, the Congress, and Public Broadcasting ——— online Internet
    (fwd)." 3 Mar. 1995. Online posting. Media-Forum. Internet. Available: posting
    http://medianation.org/media-forum/d950301/msg00014.html. 26 Nov.
    1997.

Sanders, Scott, and Allan Siegel. "Public Broadcasting: Why is Congress ——— online source with
    Breaking a Contract with America?" 1 Mar. 1995. Online posting.   two authors
    Media-Forum. Internet. Available: http://www.medianation.org/
    media-forum/d950301/msg00001.html. 28 Nov. 1997.

Sukow, Randy, and Joe Flint. "CPB Opponents Hoist Indecency in Funding
    Debate." <u>Broadcasting</u> 9 May 1992: 36.

Activities

1 Providing Context for Quotations

In the following passages from student research papers, quotations are patched together with brief attributions but no other commentary. Rewrite the passages as instructed.

A. Provide interpretative transitions between the four quotations in this passage, breaking it up into two or more paragraphs as you think necessary. The student's goal in this passage was to provide support for a pro-gun stance.

> The Second Amendment to the Constitution states, "A well-regulated militia being necessary to the security of a free state, the right of the people to keep and bear arms shall not be infringed." According to Rich Gardiner, assistant general counsel to the National Rifle Association (NRA), "the right to keep and bear arms guarantees the right of citizens to own guns, such as pistols and revolvers, for self-defense" (342). According to Phoebe Carthy, "The net effect of New York's stiff gun control laws has put disarmed citizens at the mercy of criminals armed with illegal, unregistered and untraceable guns. Or turned otherwise law abiding citizens into lawbreakers because they now own guns illegally out of desperation for their own protection and safety from runaway crime" (13). Gardiner continues, "People who want to commit crimes will get the tools they need. Chicago has a handgun ban, but . . . there are so many of them out there that one of the greatest dangers in the city's crime-ridden sections is that a gun will fall on your head from a building as you walk on the street" (346).

B. Provide interpretative transitions between the five quotations in this passage, breaking it up into two or more paragraphs as you think necessary. The student's goal in this passage was to show support for a program to educate students about hazing's illegality.

> An Oklahoma fraternity declares that "hazing is a tradition that builds pledge unity and provides a means for members to learn the value of membership" (Winston 43). But nationwide, according to Thomas Meyer, "campus officials say hazing is a particularly difficult problem to fight because of its clandestine nature. Normally the victims undergo the rituals voluntarily, and they are always sworn to secrecy" (Meyer 35). Christopher Shea notes, "Hazing is now banned by all national Greek organizations . . . and is a crime in thirty-eight states" (38). Frank Weber of the Texas Interfraternity Council states, "I don't think there is a good legal solution to the problem. . . . Changes are going to come about because the guys are seeing what they are doing is not right. There are laws, and they don't make a difference" (quoted in Meyer 36). As William

Raspberry asks, "What sort of hypocrite will beat you black and blue and when you have 'crossed over' put his arm around you and call you 'brother'?" (18).

2 Identifying and Correcting Tone Problems in Research Papers

Examine the following passages to determine the suitability of their tone and style. Revise any wording that could be more effective.

[A] To myself and many others, it has become apparent that the present "due process" justice system is not adequately performing up to its potential and something has to be done to reestablish law and order. If this means sentencing a couple of cold-blooded murderers to the electric chair, you won't find any of these supporters or me sympathetic in the least bit. The tides for the death penalty seem to be turning in recent years as more innocent people's lives are claimed by the misfits in our society.

[B] If there is any doubt, how can we proceed and kill the person? Ronnie Dunkins only had hope of being at peace with God. Even when the straps of the electric chair were buckled, he did not confess. He had to face his maker, but he did not reveal his guilt. So the cruel high-voltage electricity snapped through his body, singeing his nerves, tormenting him for the seconds or minutes before he went to his rest. And we will never know if he was innocent as he claimed because he is now dead and buried. Capital punishment clouds over the issue of possible innocence until we the people of the United States could be guilty of murder.

[C] Officials claim there is not enough money to build new prisons so that overcrowding and early release programs can be eliminated. Yet they can afford to give high-priced luxury items to deviants who are supposed to be in punishment for their crimes against society. Prisoners having weight rooms and big screen televisions makes many citizens, including yours truly, violently angry. Prison systems should be spending more of their time and effort and our money on expansion and on security.

3 For Discussion: A Case of Plagiarism

In the *Council Chronicle*, a publication of the National Council of Teachers of English, a possible case of plagiarism was described. Some unattributed passages in a scholarly article, "Putting on the Game Face: The Staging of Emotions in Professional Hockey," by Charles Gallmeier, were similar to material in an article published five years earlier, "The Staging of Emotion: A Dramaturgical Analysis," by Louis Zurcher, on emotions displayed by football players. Compare these passages from the articles:

[A] The diffuse emotions that have been worked up before the warm-up were being linked with physical effort, and more important, with specific action. The coach had, in the structured settings of the team meeting and warm-up drills, cued the players to focus their psyched-up state on physical acts that might provide victory over the opposing team. It was now appropriate to be more emotionally flamboyant, so long as the feelings were physically purposive.

—Charles Gallmeier, in the *Sociology of Sport Journal,* Dec. 1987.

[B]   The diffuse emotions which had been "worked" before the warm-up were being linked with physical effort, and more importantly, with specific action. The coaches had, in the structured setting of the warm-up drill, cued the players to focus their "psyched up" state on physical acts which might provide victory over the opponent team. It was now appropriate to be more emotionally flamboyant, so long as the feelings were physically purposive.

—Louis Zurcher, in *Symbolic Interaction,* 5.2, 1982

Would you say Gallmeier was guilty of poor use of sources, sloppy research methods, or outright plagiarism? Gallmeier himself said he failed to clearly demarcate his source's wording from his own thoughts in note taking. He pointed out that he did cite Zurcher in other places in his article. Is he less guilty because he did not intend (he says) to plagiarize?

4   Identifying and Correcting Plagiarism

Compare the student writing to the source material and underline any phrasing you believe is too close to the original. Then rewrite the student passages to eliminate plagiarism.

STUDENT PARAGRAPH

There are those who feel that AIDS should be taught as any other disease. This would be providing students with more scientific information which will place an emphasis on more responsible behavior for self-protection as well as the protection of others (Roach and Fraser 348).

SOURCE PARAGRAPH

Instead, most prefer to approach the teaching of AIDS as one would approach the teaching of other communicable diseases, by providing students with the most objective, scientific information available and by placing emphasis on responsible behavior for self-protection as well as the protection of others.

—Patricia Roach and Winifred Fraser, "Teaching about AIDS"

STUDENT SENTENCE

Turner, Miller, and Moss note that people think that an epidemic is simply a disease that affects a large number of people, but there have been debates over how large the affected population needs to be for a health epidemic (372).

SOURCE SENTENCE

Epidemic is loosely used in everyday talk. For most people, it means a disease that affects a large number of people; thus, debates can arise over how large the affected population must be for a health problem to be called an epidemic.

—Charles F. Turner, Heather G. Miller, and Lincoln E. Moss, *AIDS: Sexual Behavior and Intravenous Drug Use*

5 Identifying Style Differences Due to Plagiarism

On the basis of style alone, can you recognize any plagiarized phrases in the following student paragraph? If the student had placed a citation after this material, would it still be plagiarism, in your view?

> In an effort to educate employees about AIDS, the Georgia Textile Manufacturers Association (GTMA) has made a videotape for the employees to watch with information on AIDS. GTMA is determined to put education foremost in the campaign to defeat the AIDS crisis. This is definitely the right idea. It would be great if everyone educated their employees. The textile industry should be commended for their efforts and interest.

6 Faulty Use of Sources

Compare the student's paragraph with the original. What problems have occurred in this student's use of the source?

STUDENT PASSAGE

> Pesticides are harmful to humans and unborn children. "They have become familiar parts of our life," said Christopher Milne, manager of the pesticide project for the New Jersey Department of Health (qtd. in Leduc 22). The people didn't realize what was sprayed was chemicals.

SOURCE PASSAGE

Pesticides . . . have come to symbolize better living through chemistry. They have become familiar parts of our life, and, says Christopher Milne, who manages the pesticide project for the New Jersey Department of Health, familiarity breeds contempt.

   "It seems like people almost didn't realize that what was sprayed was chemicals," said Milne.

   —Daniel LeDuc, "Clouds of Suspicion," *Philadelphia Inquirer Magazine,* 21 Oct. 1990

7 Inserting Citations in a Passage

The following passage has been deliberately generated to include many more citations than any typical two paragraphs of a research paper so that you can practice writing citations. Insert correctly written parenthetic citations in the passage on the basis of the Works Cited list that follows.

> "The idea of biotherapies has been around for decades, though the first were crude" (item 5). The first enzyme, making DNA production in a test tube possible, was isolated in 1958. The basics of the genetic code were established by scientists in the 1960s (p. 11 of item 1). The actual genetic revolution began in the 1970s, when scientists began to manipulate genes to produce human versions of such materials as insulin (p. 10 of item 6). In the 1980s the pharmaceutical industry was greatly expanded by the introduction of the first

genetically engineered product, human growth hormone (p. 135 of item 2). Because there are over 4,000 genetic diseases, genetic engineering could become a major influence on the health of future humans (item 5). The year 2000 could see the "insertion of a synthetic normal gene into cells to replace the defective gene that causes hemophilia" (item 8). In addition, genetic therapy is now being used to treat nonhereditary diseases such as cancer (page 209 of item 3).

But problems about whether it is proper to alter the very basis of human life began to crop up. Specifically, in germ-line genetic therapy, the improved "genes would be passed on to future generations," thereby altering heredity and the life of every human born into that family in all future generations (pages 355 through 360 of item 7). The ethical questions are less for somatic-cell gene therapy because only the individual receiving the therapy is altered. According to James M. Gustafson, a medical ethicist, the one ethical question pertaining to somatic therapy is, "Do the potential benefits to the patient outweigh the potential risks?" (item 4).

[A]   Burck, Kathy L., and James W. Larrick. *Gene Therapy: Application of Molecular Biology.* New York: Elsevier Science, 1991.

[B]   Friedman, Theodore. *Molecular Genetic Medicine.* Vol. 1. San Diego: Academic, 1991.

[C]   "Gene Therapy Approved for Lung Cancer." *Science News* 26 Sept. 1992: 207+.

[D]   Herman, Robin. "Cancer Vaccine Trial Gets Green Light at NIH." *Washington Post* 8 Oct. 1992: 6.

[E]   Thompson, Larry. "Gene Technique Could Shape Future Generations." *Washington Post* 25 Sept. 1990: A28.

[F]   ---. "Patient, Heal Thyself, Are Words of the '90s." *Washington Post* 30 Jan. 1990: WH10.

[G]   Weatherall, D. J. *The New Genetics and Clinical Practice.* 3rd ed. New York: Oxford UP, 1991.

[H]   World Health Organization. "Cure for Hemophilia Is Seen by Year 2000." *New York Times* 24 Mar. 1994: B11.

8   **Writing Correct Parenthetic Citations from Bibliographic Information**

Write parenthetic citations as indicated on the basis of the Works Cited list that follows.

1. Page 45 in the work by Polanyi and Prosch.
2. Page 161 in John Schultz's published article.

3. Page 4 in John Schultz's unpublished manuscript.
4. Pages 231–35 in Barbara Smith's article
5. Pages xii–xx in Frank Smith's book.
6. Page 5 in Van Keer's article.

> Polanyi, Michael, and Harry Prosch. *Meaning.* Chicago: U of Chicago P, 1975.
>
> Schultz, John. "Story Workshop from Start to Finish." *Research on Composing.* Ed. Charles Cooper and Lee Odell. Urbana: NCTE, 1978. 151–87.
>
> ---. "The Teacher's Manual for *Writing from Start to Finish.*" Unpublished manuscript, 1980.
>
> Smith, Barbara Herrnstein. "Narrative Versions, Narrative Theories." *Critical Inquiry* 7 (1980): 213–36.
>
> Smith, Frank. *Essays into Literacy.* Portsmouth: Heinemann, 1983.
>
> Van Keer, John Rayner. "Process Isn't Everything." *Frontlines* 14 June 1996: 5.

9 Preparing Works Cited Entries

In your major field or field of your choice, locate one item of each type listed below and write a correct MLA Works Cited entry for each.

> Book with two authors
> Book with four authors
> Print version of a general magazine article
> Article in a scholarly journal, paged any way
> Newspaper article
> Online version of an article from a print periodical
> Article or information with no available print analogue (parallel version) derived from an institutional, organizational, or similar web site
> Periodical article from an online electronic magazine
> Message from an online chat room, bulletin board, news group, or archive
> Nonprint source, such as radio, television, film, video, lecture, or speech

■ WORKS CITED

"Citing Electronic Sources—MLA." 5 Mar. 1997. Online. Available: http://www.middlebury.edu/~lib/citing. mla/html. 5 June 1997.

Gibaldi, Joseph. *MLA Handbook for Writers of Research Papers.* 4th ed. New York: Modern Language Association, 1995.

Publication Manual of the American Psychological Association. 4th ed. Washington: American Psychological Association, 1994.

Credits

Anderson, Elijah. "The Reasons for Affirmative Action Still Stand." From *Philadelphia Inquirer*, Apr. 27, 1995.

Anger, Ed. "Fry Death Row Creeps in Electric Bleachers!" From *Let's Pave the Stupid Rainforests*. Copyright 1996 by Weekly World News. Used by permission of Broadway Books, a division of Bantam Doubleday Dell Publishing Group.

Banks, R. Richard. "Education to Learn and Not for Money." From *Philadelphia Inquirer*, 1990. Reprinted by permission of the author.

Bennett, Alysia. "It's Not All Heroes and Demons." From *Washington Post*, Apr. 19, 1997. Copyright 1997 the Washington Post. Reprinted by permission.

Blakeslee, Sandra. "Chocolate Lover or Broccoli Hater?" From *New York Times*, Nov. 27, 1997.

Botstein, Leon. "Educating in a Pessimistic Age." From *Harper's*, Aug. 1993. Reprinted by permission of the author.

Broder, David S. "The Evidence Is Coming In: Dan Quayle Was Right." Copyright 1997 by the Washington Post Writers Group. Reprinted by permission.

Budhos, Marina. "Black Man, Jewish Soul." From *Nation*, Apr. 22, 1996.

Burke, Kenneth. *Language as Symbolic Action*. Berkeley: University of California Press, 1966.

Carson, Ed. "Pay Organ Donors to Increase the Supply." From *Philadelphia Inquirer*, 1997. Copyright 1997 by the Reason Foundation. Reprinted by permission.

Carter, Stephen L. "The Black Table, the Empty Seat, and the Tie." From *Lure and Loathing: Essays on Race, Identity, and the Ambivalence of Assimilation*, edited by Gerald Early. New York: Penguin, 1993.

Chaffe, Tom. "America the Violent." From *Philadelphia Inquirer*, Mar. 9, 1997.

Chaskes, Jay. "The First-Year Student as Immigrant." From *Journal of the Freshman Year Experience*. Copyright 1996 by the University of South Carolina. Reprinted by permission.

Cole, David. "Five Myths about Immigration." From *Nation*, Oct. 17, 1994. Copyright 1994 by the Nation. Reprinted by permission.

Dyer, Gwynne. "Picking Right Enemies for Cuba." From *Philadelphia Inquirer*, Aug. 19, 1997.

Edelman, Marian Wright. *The Measure of Our Success*. Boston: Beacon, 1992.

Editorial. "Kids and Guns." From *Philadelphia Inquirer*, July 24, 1993. Copyright 1993 by the Philadelphia Inquirer. Reprinted by permission.

Ehrenreich, Barbara. "Kicking the Big One." From *Time*, Feb. 28, 1994.

Ehrhart, William D. "In War, All Should Suffer." From *Philadelphia Inquirer*, Feb. 10, 1991. Reprinted by permission of the author.

Eisner, Jane R. "Do Condoms in the Classrooms Encourage Sex, or Safe Sex?" From *Philadelphia Inquirer*, Apr. 2, 1995. Copyright 1995 by the Philadelphia Inquirer. Reprinted by permission.

Franken, Al. "Affirmative Action: The Case for the Mushball Middle." From *Rush Limbaugh Is a Big Fat Idiot and Other Observations*. Copyright 1996 by Al Franken, Inc. Reprinted by permission of Delacorte Press, a division of Bantam Doubleday Dell Publishing Company.

Friedman, Thomas L. "My Fellow Immigrants." From *New York Times*, Sept. 10, 1995. Copyright 1995 by the New York Times. Reprinted by permission.

Gilligan, James. *Violence: Reflections on a National Epidemic*. New York: Random House, 1996.

Giobbe, Evelina. "The Bargain Basement in the Marketplace of Ideas." From *The Price We Pay: The Case*

quirer, Aug. 14, 1992. Reprinted by permission of the author.

Moore, Acel. "The Numbers Unveil Myths about Affirmative Action." From *Philadelphia Inquirer,* Aug. 29, 1997.

Morrison, Toni. "Racism and Fascism." From a speech given at Howard University. Excerpts reprinted in *Nation,* May 29, 1995.

Morton, Frank. "Letter." From *Extra!* July–Aug. 1997.

Nader, Ralph. "Grocery Fees Ultimately Cost Consumers." From *Liberal Opinion Week,* Nov. 21, 1994.

Negroponte, Nicholas. *Being Digital.* New York: Vintage, 1995.

O'Brien, Geoffrey. "The Ghost at the Feast." From *New York Times Review of Books,* Feb. 6, 1997.

Orwell, George. *Shooting an Elephant and Other Essays.* New York: Harcourt Brace, 1978.

Perkins, Ray, Jr. "Sex and Drugs: Just Say 'No No' " and "Flying Condoms." From *Logic and Mr. Limbaugh.* Copyright 1995 by Open Court Publishing Company, a division of Carus Publishing Company. Reprinted by permission.

Pharr, Suzanne. "A Match Made in Heaven." From *Progressive,* Aug. 28, 1996. Reprinted by permission of the author.

Postrel, Viriginia. "TV or Not TV?" From *Reason,* Aug.–Sept. 1993. Copyright 1997 by the Reason Foundation. Reprinted by permission.

Reissman, Frank, and Carroll, David. "A New View of Addiction: Simple and Complex." From *Social Policy,* Winter 1996.

Rice, William Craig. "Reply." From *Policy Review,* July–Aug. 1997.

Rodriguez, Luis J. "Turning Youth Gangs Around." From *Nation,* Nov. 21, 1994. Copyright 1994 by the Nation. Reprinted by permission.

Rotberg, Robert. "Clinton Was Right." From *Foreign Policy,* Spring 1996.

Santiago, William. "Puerto Rico: Where Self-Determination, Statehood Don't Mix." From *Philadelphia Inquirer,* Aug. 19, 1997.

Satullo, Chris. "That's No Panacea." From *Philadelphia Inquirer,* Mar. 19, 1996. Copyright 1996 by the Philadelphia Inquirer. Reprinted by permission.

Seaman, Barbara. "Reply." From *Extra!* July–Aug. 1997.

Shanker, Albert. "Are American Schools Too Easy?" Copyright 1993 by the American Federation of Teachers. Reprinted by permission.

Sheehan, Sharon A. "Another Kind of Sex Ed." From *Newsweek,* "My Turn." Copyright 1992 by Newsweek, Inc. All rights reserved. Reprinted by permission.

Shweder, Richard A. "It's Called Poor Health for a Reason." From *New York Times,* March 9, 1997. Copyright 1997 by the New York Times. Reprinted by permission.

Snyder, Jeffrey B. "A Nation of Cowards." From *Public Interest,* Fall 1993.

Stout, David. "Direct Link Found Between Smoking and Lung Cancer." From *New York Times,* Oct. 18, 1996.

Sullivan, Louis W. "Stop Peddling Tobacco to Kids." From *Philadelphia Inquirer,* June 1990. Reprinted by permission of the author.

Travers, Peter. "Tupac in Hollywood." From *Rolling Stone,* Feb. 6, 1997.

Veit, John. "Futures So Bright in White Suburbia." From *Philadelphia Inquirer,* 1993.

Vermeulen, Karla. "Growing Up in the Shadow of AIDS." From *New York Times,* Sept. 30, 1990. Copyright 1990 by the New York Times. Reprinted by permission.

Von Hoffman, Nicholas. "Understand That Pro-Abortion Is Pro-Life and Vice Versa." From *Philadelphia Inquirer,* July 10, 1992. Reprinted by permission of the author.

Walsh, David. "Liberty Calls Us to a Higher Purpose." From *Philadelphia Inquirer,* July 4, 1997. Reprinted by permission of the author.

Weinstein, Jim. "NATO Rearms the World." From *In These Times,* July 1997. Reprinted by permission of the author.

Wenner, Jann S. "Drug War: A New Vietnam." From *New York Times,* June 23, 1990.

Readings by Topic

Television, Journalism, and Other Media

Violence and Crime

Health

Education

Assisted Suicide

Ethics and Values

Index